PHILIP'S

STREET ATLAS
North Essex

Braintree, Chelmsford, Colchester, Ipswich

www.philips-maps.co.uk

First published in 1999 by

Philip's, a division of
Octopus Publishing Group Ltd
www.octopusbooks.co.uk
2-4 Heron Quays, London E14 4JP
An Hachette Livre UK Company

Third edition 2007
Second impression 2010
NESCA

ISBN   978-0-540-09191-1 (spiral)

© Philip's 2007

o|s Ordnance Survey®

This product includes mapping data licensed
from Ordnance Survey® with the permission of
the Controller of Her Majesty's Stationery Office.
© Crown copyright 2007. All rights reserved.
Licence number 100011710.

Data for the speed cameras provided by
PocketGPSWorld.com Ltd.

Ordnance Survey and the OS Symbol are
registered trademarks of Ordnance Survey, the
national mapping agency of Great Britain.

Printed by Toppan, China

Contents

II **List of mobile speed cameras**

III **Key to map symbols**

IV **Key to map pages**

VI **Route planning**

VIII **Administrative and Postcode boundaries**

1 **Street maps** at 3½ inches to 1 mile

222 **Index** of towns, villages, streets, hospitals, industrial estates, railway stations, schools, shopping centres, universities and places of interest

Digital Data

The exceptionally high-quality mapping found in this atlas is available as digital data in TIFF format, which is easily convertible to other bitmapped (raster) image formats.

The index is also available in digital form as a standard database table. It contains all the details found in the printed index together with the National Grid reference for the map square in which each entry is named.

For further information, please contact victoria.dawbarn@philips-maps.co.uk

Mobile speed cameras

The vast majority of speed cameras used on Britain's roads are operated by safety camera partnerships. These comprise local authorities, the police, Her Majesty's Court Service (HMCS) and the Highways Agency.

This table lists the sites where each safety camera partnership may enforce speed limits through the use of mobile cameras or detectors. These are usually set up on the roadside or a bridge spanning the road and operated by a police or civilian enforcement officer. The speed limit at each site (if available) is shown in red type, followed by the approximate location in black type.

Mike Harrington / Alamy

A12
Braintree, Overbridge nr Kelvedon Interchange

A13
- 30 Castle Point, High St (Hadleigh twds London)
- 30 Leigh on Sea, London Rd
  Southend, Bournes Green Chase
  Southend, North Shoebury
  Southend, Southchurch Boulevard

A1016
- 30 Chelmsford, Waterhouse Lane

A1017
- 30 Sible Hedingham, Swan St
- 30 Witham / Braintree, Rickstone Rd

A1023
- 30 Brentwood, Chelmsford Rd
- 30 Brentwood, London Rd
- 30 Brentwood, Shenfield Rd

A1025
- 40 Harlow, Second Avenue
- 40 Harlow, Third Avenue

A1060
Little Hallingbury, Lower Rd

A1090
- 30 Purfleet, London Rd
- 30 Purfleet, Tank Hill Rd

A1124
- 30 Colchester, Lexden Rd

A113
- 30 Epping, High Rd

A1158
- 30 Westcliff on Sea, Southbourne Grove

A1168
- 30 Loughton, Rectory Lane

A1169
- 40 Harlow, Southern Way

A120
Little Bentley, Pellens Corner
Wix, Harwich Rd nr Colchester Rd

A1205
- 40 Harlow, Second Avenue

A121
- 30 Epping, High Rd
- 30 Loughton, Goldings Hill (j/w Monkchester Close)
  Loughton, High Rd
  Waltham Abbey, Farm Hill Rd
  Waltham Abbey, Sewardstine Rd

A126
- 30 Grays, London Rd
- 30 Tilbury, Montreal Rd

A128
Chipping Ongar, High St
- 30 Ingrave/Herongate, Brentwood Rd
- 40 Kelvedon Hatch, Ongar Rd

A129
- 30 Basildon, Crays Hill
  Billericay, Southend Rd
  Rayleigh, London Rd
- 30 Wickford, London Rd
  Wickford, Southend Rd

A130
- 30 Canvey Island, Long Rd
  South Benfleet, Canvey Way

A133
- 30 Elmstead Market, Clacton Rd
  Little Bentley, Colchester Rd

A134
- 40 Great Horkesley, Nayland Rd

A137
- 30 Lawford, Wignall St

B170
Chigwell, Chigwell Rise
Loughton, Roding Lane

B172
Theydon Bois, Coppice Row

B173
Chigwell, Lambourne Rd

B184
- 40 Great Easton, Snow Hill

B186
- 30 South Ockendon, South Rd

B1002
- 30 Ingatestone, High St

B1007
- 30 Billericay, Laindon Rd
- 30 Billericay, Stock Rd
- 40 Chelmsford, Stock Rd

B1008
- 30 Chelmsford, Broomfield Rd

B1013
- 30 Hawkwell, High Rd
- 30 Hawkwell, Main Rd
- 30 Hockley/Hawkwell, Southend Rd
  Rayleigh, High Rd

B1014
- 30 South Benfleet, Benfleet Rd

B1018
- 30 Latchingdon, The St
- 30 Maldon, The Causeway

B1019
- 30 Hatfield Peveral, Maldon Rd
- 30 Witham, Powers Hall End

B1021
Burnham on Crouch, Church Rd

B1022
- 30 Colchester, Maldon Rd
- 30 Heckfordbridge, Maldon Rd
- 30 Maldon, Colchester Rd
- 30 Tiptree Heath, Maldon Rd

B1027
- 30 Clacton-on-Sea, Valley Rd/Old Rd
- 30 St Osyth, Pump Hill
- 40 Wivenhoe, Brightlingsea Rd

B1028
- 30 Wivenhoe, Colchester Rd
- 30 Wivenhoe, The Avenue

B1033
- 30 Kirby Cross, Frinton Rd

B1335
- 40 South Ockendon, Stifford Rd

B1352
Harwich, Main Rd

B1383
- 30 Newport, London Rd
  Stansted Mountfitchet, Cambridge Rd

B1389
- 30 Witham, Colchester Rd
- 30 Witham, Hatfield Rd

B1393
- 30 Epping, Palmers Hill

B1441
- 30 Clacton-on-Sea, London Rd
  Tendring, Clacton Rd

B1442
- 30 Clacton-on-Sea, Thorpe Rd

B1464
- 30 Bowers Gifford, London Rd

UNCLASSIFIED
- 40 Alresford, St Osyth Rd
- 30 Aveley, Purfleet Rd
  Aveley, Romford Rd
- 30 Barstable, Sandon Rd
- 30 Basildon, Ashlyns
  Basildon, Clay Hill Rd
- 40 Basildon, Cranes Farm Rd (j/w Honywood Rd)
- 30 Basildon, Felmores
  Basildon, London Rd, Wickford
- 30 Basildon, Vange Hill Drive
- 30 Basildon, Whitmore Way
- 30 Basildon, Wickford Avenue
- 30 Billericay, Mountnessing Rd
- 30 Bowers Gifford, London Rd
- 30 Braintree, Coldnailhurst Avenue
- 30 Brentwood, Eagle Way (nr j/w Clive Rd twds Warley Rd)
- 30 Brentwood, Eagle Way
- 30 Buckhurst Hill, Buckhurst Way/Albert Rd
- 30 Canvey Island, Dovervelt Rd
- 30 Canvey Island, Link Rd
- 30 Canvey Island, Thorney Bay Rd
  Chadwell St Mary, Brentwood Rd
- 30 Chadwell St Mary, Linford Rd
- 30 Chadwell St Mary, Riverview
- 30 Chelmsford, Baddow Rd
- 30 Chelmsford, Chignall Rd
- 30 Chelmsford, Copperfield Rd
  Chelmsford, Galleywood Rd
- 30 Chelmsford, Longstomps Avenue
- 30 Clacton-on-Sea, St Johns Rd
- 30 Clacton, Kings Parade
- 30 Clacton, Marine Parade East
- 30 Colchester, Abbots Rd
- 30 Colchester, Avon Way
- 30 Colchester, Bromley Rd
  Colchester, Ipswich Rd
- 30 Colchester, Old Heath Rd
- 30 Colchester, Shrub End Rd
- 30 Corringham, Southend Rd
- 30 Corringham, Springhouse Rd
  Danbury, Maldon Rd
- 30 Daws Heath, Daws Heath Rd
- 30 Eastwood, Green Lane j/w Kendal Way
- 30 Eastwood, Western Approaches j/w Rockall
- 30 Grays, Blackshots Lane
- 30 Grays, Lodge Lane
  Grays, London Rd (nr Angel Rd)
  Grays, London Rd (nr Bransons Way)
- 30 Hainault, Fencepiece Rd
- 40 Harlow, Abercrombie Way, twds Southern Way
- 40 Harlow, Howard Way
- 30 Hawkwell, Rectory Rd
- 30 Hockley, High Rd
- 30 Hullbridge, Coventry Hill
- 30 Laindon, Durham Rd
- 30 Laindon, High Rd
- 30 Laindon, Nightingales
- 30 Laindon, Wash Rd
  Langdon Hills, High Rd
- 30 Leigh on Sea, Belton Way East
- 30 Leigh on Sea, Belton Way West
- 30 Leigh on Sea, Blenhelm Chase
- 30 Leigh on Sea, Grand Parade/Cliff Parade
- 30 Leigh on Sea, Hadleigh Rd
- 30 Leigh on Sea, Highlands Boulevard
- 30 Leigh on Sea, Manchester Drive
- 30 Leigh on Sea, Mountdale Gardens
- 30 Leigh on Sea, Western Rd
- 30 Loughton, Alderton Hill
- 30 Loughton, Loughton Way
  Loughton, Valley Hill
- 30 Maldon, Fambridge Rd
- 30 Maldon, Holloway Rd
- 30 Maldon, Mundon Rd
- 30 Pitsea, Rectory Rd
- 30 Prittlewell, Kenilworth Gardens
- 30 Prittlewell, Prittlewell Chase
- 30 Rayleigh, Bull Lane
  Rayleigh, Downhall Rd
- 30 Rayleigh, Trinity Rd, nr Church Rd
- 30 Rochford, Ashingdon Rd
- 30 Rochford, Rectory Rd
  Rush Green, St Osyth Rd
- 30 Shoeburyness, Ness Rd
- 30 South Woodham Ferrers, Hullbridge Rd
- 30 South Woodham Ferrers, Inchbonnie Rd
- 30 Southend on Sea, Lifstan Way
  Southend, Bournemouth Park Rd
- 30 Southend, Hamstel Rd
  Southend on Sea, Bournemouth Park Rd
  Southend, Western Esplanade/Westcliff on Sea
- 30 Springfield, New Bowers Way
- 30 Stanford le Hope, London Rd
- 30 Tendring, Burrs Rd, Clacton
- 30 Tendring, Frinton Rd, Frinton
  Tendring, Harwich Rd, Wix Arch Cottages to Cansey Lane
- 30 Tendring, Osyth Rd, Rush Green
  Theydon Bois, Piercing Hill
- 30 Thorpe Bay, Barnstaple Rd
- 30 Thorpe Bay, Thorpe Hall Avenue
  Waltham Abbey, Paternoster Hill
  Weeley Heath, Clacton Rd
  Weeley Heath, Clacton Rd
- 30 West Thurrock, London Rd
- 30 Westcliff on Sea, Chalkwell Avenue
- 30 Westcliff on Sea, Kings Rd
- 30 Wickford, London Rd
- 30 Wickford, Radwinter Avenue
- 30 Witham, Powers Hall End
- 30 Witham, Rickstones Rd

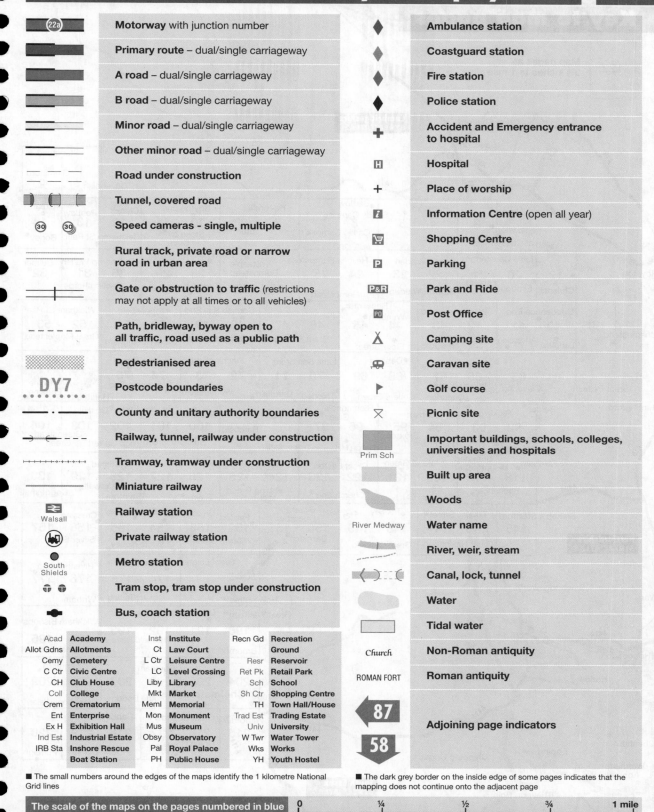

Motorway with junction number		Ambulance station
Primary route – dual/single carriageway		Coastguard station
A road – dual/single carriageway		Fire station
B road – dual/single carriageway		Police station
Minor road – dual/single carriageway		Accident and Emergency entrance to hospital
Other minor road – dual/single carriageway		Hospital
Road under construction		Place of worship
Tunnel, covered road		Information Centre (open all year)
Speed cameras - single, multiple		Shopping Centre
Rural track, private road or narrow road in urban area		Parking
Gate or obstruction to traffic (restrictions may not apply at all times or to all vehicles)		Park and Ride
Path, bridleway, byway open to all traffic, road used as a public path		Post Office
Pedestrianised area		Camping site
Postcode boundaries		Caravan site
County and unitary authority boundaries		Golf course
Railway, tunnel, railway under construction		Picnic site
Tramway, tramway under construction		Important buildings, schools, colleges, universities and hospitals
Miniature railway	Prim Sch	
Railway station		Built up area
Walsall		Woods
Private railway station		Water name
South Shields	River Medway	
Metro station		River, weir, stream
Tram stop, tram stop under construction		Canal, lock, tunnel
Bus, coach station		Water
		Tidal water
	Church	Non-Roman antiquity
	ROMAN FORT	Roman antiquity
	87	
	58	Adjoining page indicators

Acad	Academy	Inst	Institute	Recn Gd	Recreation Ground
Allot Gdns	Allotments	Ct	Law Court		
Cemy	Cemetery	L Ctr	Leisure Centre	Resr	Reservoir
C Ctr	Civic Centre	LC	Level Crossing	Ret Pk	Retail Park
CH	Club House	Liby	Library	Sch	School
Coll	College	Mkt	Market	Sh Ctr	Shopping Centre
Crem	Crematorium	Meml	Memorial	TH	Town Hall/House
Ent	Enterprise	Mon	Monument	Trad Est	Trading Estate
Ex H	Exhibition Hall	Mus	Museum	Univ	University
Ind Est	Industrial Estate	Obsy	Observatory	W Twr	Water Tower
IRB Sta	Inshore Rescue Boat Station	Pal	Royal Palace	Wks	Works
		PH	Public House	YH	Youth Hostel

■ The small numbers around the edges of the maps identify the 1 kilometre National Grid lines

■ The dark grey border on the inside edge of some pages indicates that the mapping does not continue onto the adjacent page

The scale of the maps on the pages numbered in blue is 5.52 cm to 1 km • 3½ inches to 1 mile • 1: 18103

0	¼	½	¾	1 mile

| 0 | 250 m | 500 m | 750 m | 1 kilometre |

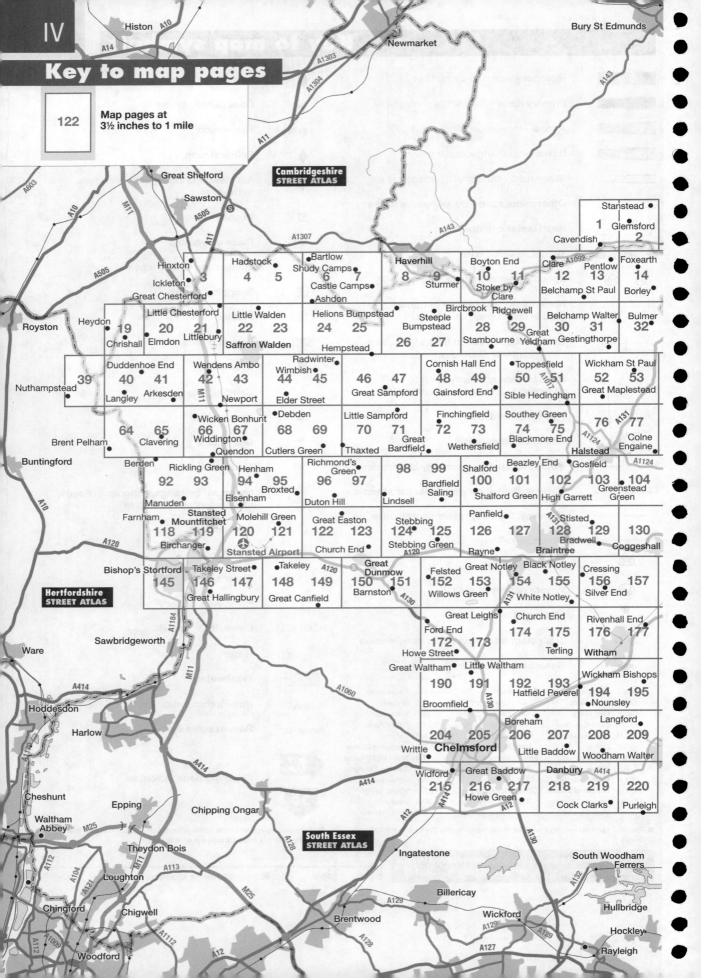

IV

| 122 | Map pages at 3½ inches to 1 mile |

Cambridgeshire STREET ATLAS

Great Shelford

Sawston

Stanstead
1 Glemsford 2
Cavendish

Hinxton
Ickleton
Great Chesterford
Hadstock
4 5 Shudy Camps 6 7
Castle Camps
Ashdon
Haverhill
8 9 Sturmer
Boyton End
10 11 Stoke by Clare
Clare Pentlow
12 13 Belchamp St Paul
Foxearth
14 Borley
3

Heydon
19 Little Chesterford 20 21 Littlebury
Chrishall Elmdon Saffron Walden
Little Walden 22 23 Helions Bumpstead 24 25 Hempstead 26 27
Steeple Bumpstead
Birdbrook Ridgewell
28 29 Great Yeldham Stambourne
Belchamp Walter 30 31 Gestingthorpe
Bulmer 32
Royston

Nuthampstead
39 Duddenhoe End 40 41 Arkesden Langley
Wendens Ambo 42 43 Newport
Radwinter Wimbish 44 45 Elder Street
46 47 Great Sampford
Cornish Hall End 48 49 Gainsford End
Toppesfield 50 51 Sible Hedingham
Wickham St Paul 52 53 Great Maplestead
Brent Pelham 64 65 Clavering Wicken Bonhunt 66 67 Widdington Quendon
Debden 68 69 Cutlers Green Thaxted
Little Sampford 70 71 Great Bardfield
Finchingfield 72 73 Wethersfield
Southey Green 74 75 Blackmore End
76 77 Colne Engaine
Halstead
Buntingford

Berden 92 93 Manuden
Rickling Green Henham 94 95 Broxted Elsenham
Richmond's Green 96 97 Duton Hill
98 99 Lindsell
Shalford 100 101 Shalford Green
Bardfield Saling
Beazley End 102 103 High Garrett
Gosfield 104 Greenstead Green
Farnham Stansted Mountfitchet 118 119 Birchanger
Molehill Green 120 121 Stansted Airport
Great Easton 122 123 Church End
Stebbing 124 125 Stebbing Green
Panfield 126 127 Rayne
Stisted 128 129 Bradwell Braintree
130 Coggeshall
Bishop's Stortford

Hertfordshire STREET ATLAS
145 Takeley Street 146 147 Great Hallingbury
Takeley 148 149 Great Canfield
Great Dunmow 150 151 Barnston
Felsted 152 153 Willows Green
Great Notley Black Notley 154 155 White Notley
Cressing 156 157 Silver End
Sawbridgeworth

Ware
Great Leighs Ford End 172 173 Howe Street
Church End 174 175 Terling
Rivenhall End 176 177 Witham

Hoddesdon
Great Waltham 190 191 Broomfield
Little Waltham 192 193 Hatfield Peverel
Wickham Bishops 194 195 Nounsley

Harlow
204 205 Writtle Chelmsford
Boreham 206 207 Little Baddow
Langford 208 209 Woodham Walter

Cheshunt
Widford 215 Great Baddow 216 217 Howe Green
Danbury 218 219 Cock Clarks 220 Purleigh

Waltham Abbey
Epping Chipping Ongar

Theydon Bois
South Essex STREET ATLAS
Ingatestone
South Woodham Ferrers

Chingford Chigwell
Billericay
Hullbridge

Woodford Brentwood
Wickford
Hockley
Rayleigh

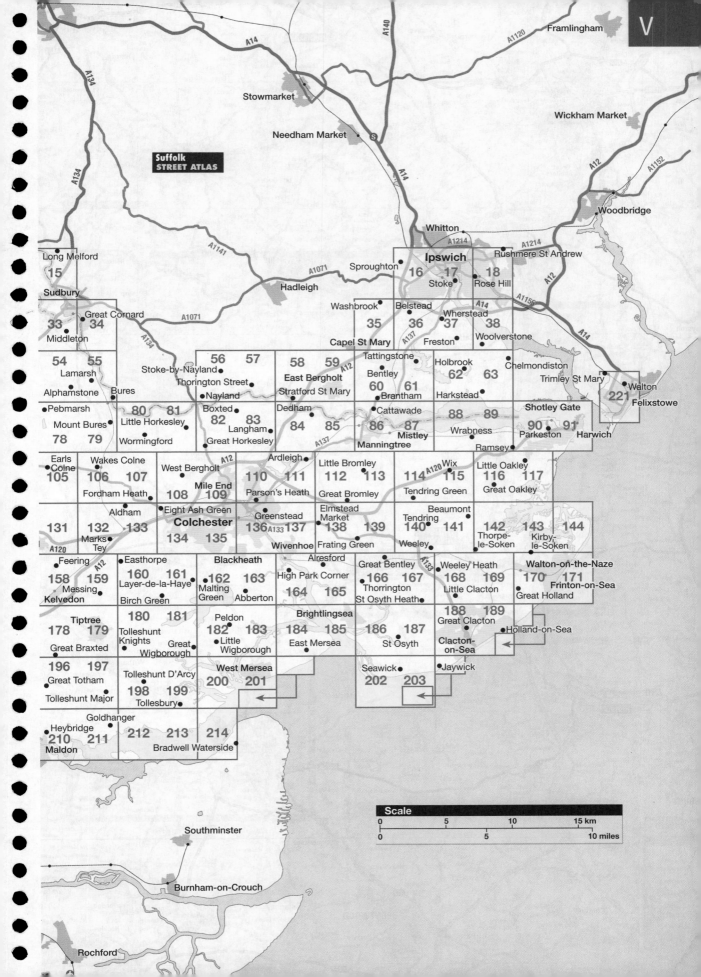

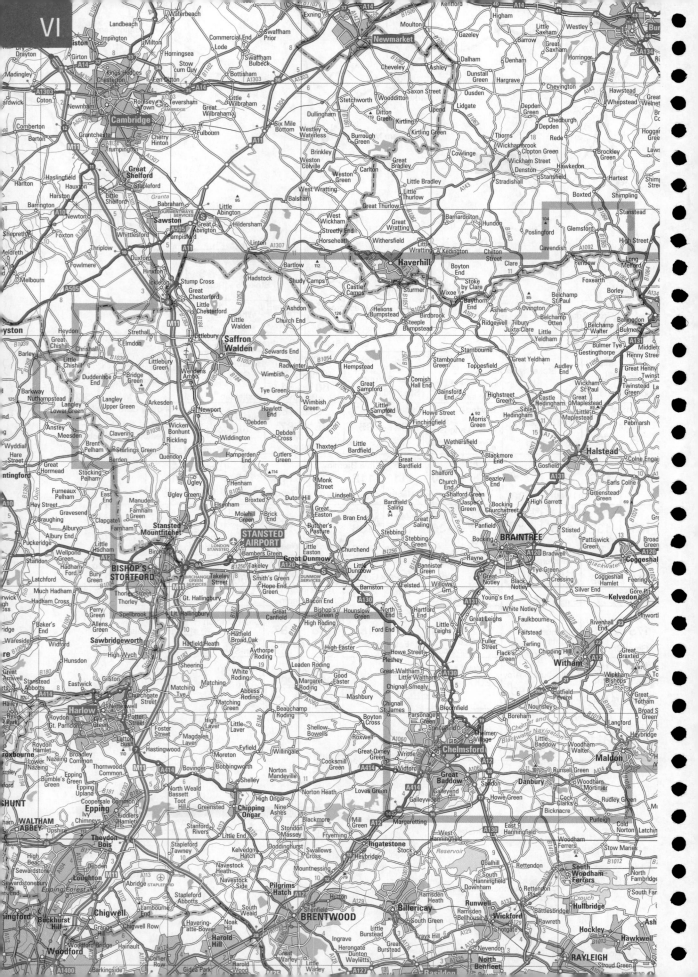

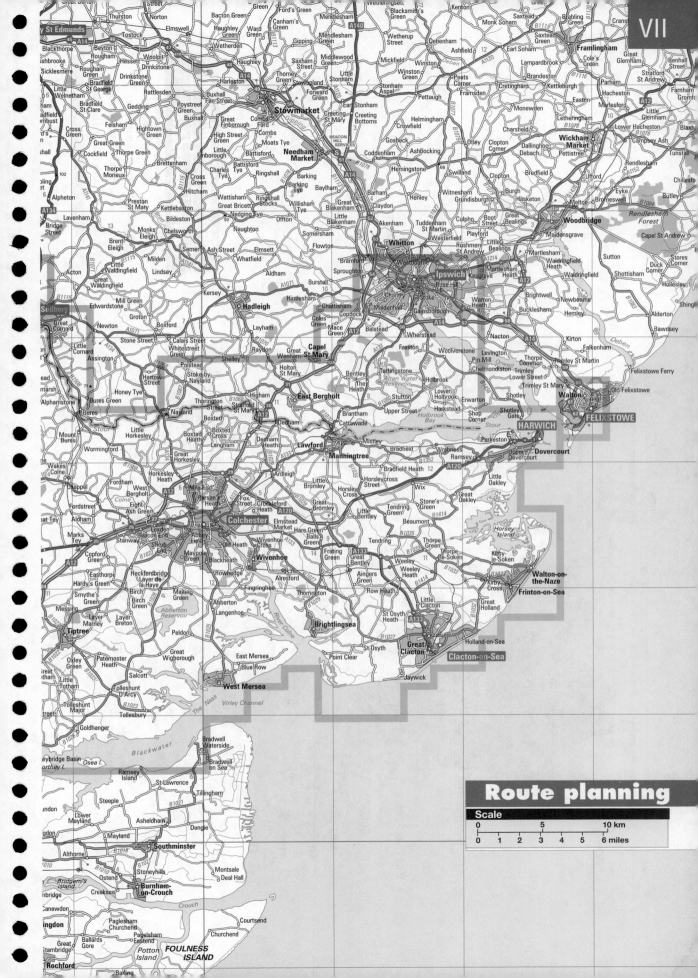

Route planning

Scale

0   5   10 km

0   1   2   3   4   5   6 miles

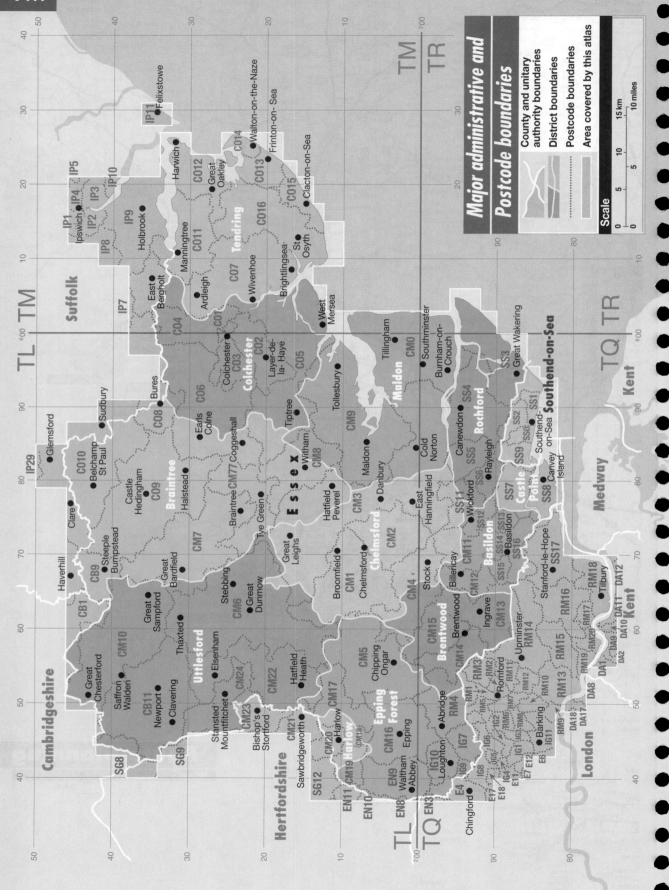

Major administrative and Postcode boundaries

County and unitary authority boundaries
District boundaries
Postcode boundaries
Area covered by this atlas

Scale

0   5   10   15 km
0   5   10 miles

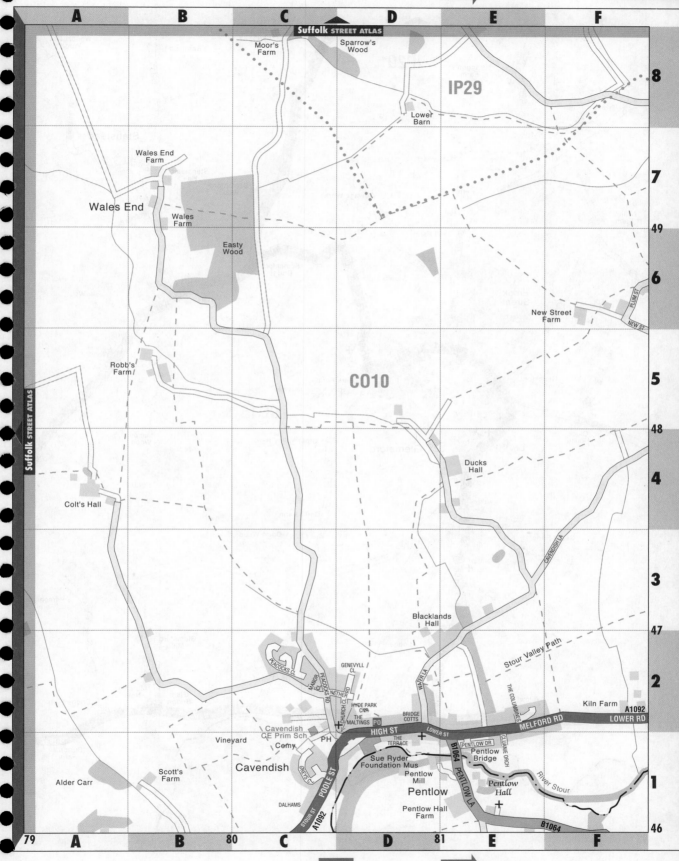

Suffolk STREET ATLAS

IP29

CO10

A B C D E F

8
7
49
6
5
48
4
3
47
2
1
46

Moor's Farm
Sparrow's Wood
Lower Barn
Wales End Farm
Wales End
Wales Farm
Easty Wood
New Street Farm
PLUM ST
NEW ST
Robb's Farm
Colt's Hall
Ducks Hall
CAVENDISH LA
Blacklands Hall
Stour Valley Path
PEACOCKS CL
GENEVYLL CL
WATER LA
THE COLUMBINES
Kiln Farm
A1092
MANOR RD
PEACOCKS RD
NETHER
CHURCH CL
HYDE PARK CNR
BRIDGE COTTS
MELFORD RD
LOWER RD
Cavendish CE Prim Sch
THE MALTINGS
PO
HIGH ST
Vineyard
Cemy
PH
THE TERRACE
Pentlow Dr
B1064
CLUANIE ORCH
Scott's Farm
Cavendish
POOLE ST
STOUR ST
Sue Ryder Foundation Mus
Pentlow Mill
Pentlow Bridge
River Stour
Pentlow Hall
Alder Carr
DALHAMS
A1092
Pentlow
PENTLOW LA
Pentlow Hall Farm
B1064

Suffolk STREET ATLAS

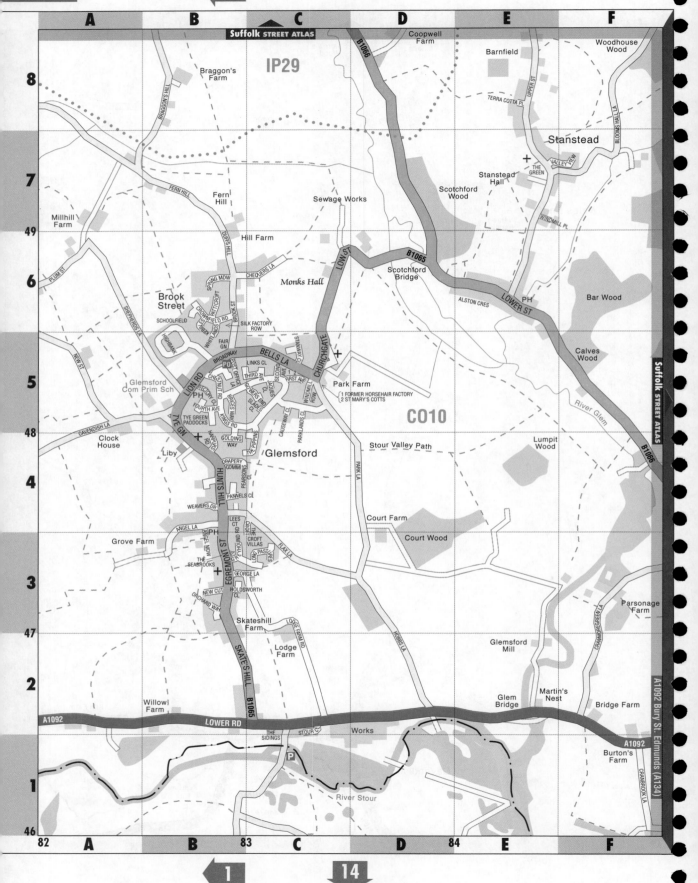

A1301 Cambridge (A1309)

Cambridgeshire STREET ATLAS

A11 Newmarket (A1304)

CB21

Cambridgeshire STREET ATLAS

M11 Cambridge (A1309)

Hinxton

Ford
DUXFORD RD
MILL LA
HUNTS LA
Hall Farm
HINXTON RD
NORTH END RD
HIGH ST
CHURCH GN
Red Lion (PH)
NEW RD
Hinxton Mill
Hinxton Hall
ICKLETON RD

CB22

LC

Cemy
BROOKHAMPTON ST

The Bungalow

Field Farm

Field Farm Cottages

Field Farm Cottages

The Limes

The Barn
PARK FARM

A1301

M11

A11

STUMP CROSS

CB10

PARK RD

Dell's Farm

Sewage Works

B184

B1383

Mill House Farm

BUTCHER'S HILL
MILL LA
CHURCH ST
PO
PH
ABBEY ST

Ickleton

River Cam or Granta

FRIDGE ST

BIRDS CL
SOUTHFIELD
BICK'S PRIORY CL
ICKNIELD
COPLOE RISE
THE STACKYARD

Fairacre

NEWMARKET RD

JACKSON'S SQ
MEADOW RD
JACKSON RD
SPENCER RD
HYLL CL
THE WILLOWS
FOUR ACRES
THE ELMS
ROOKERY RD
STANLEY RD

WALDEN RD

Chesterford House

COW LA

Icknield Way Path

CARMEL ST
EASTGATE
PO
SCHOOL ST
Sch
CARMEL ST
ST JOHNS CL
HIGH ST
SOUTH ST
PILGRIMS CL
ROSE LA
PH
BARTHOLOMEW CL

GRANTA COTTS

CHURCH ST

HAGGERS CL

MANOR LA

M11

COPLOE RD

M11 Cambridge (A1309)

LC

ICKLETON RD

9

WHITEWAYS

MILL VIEW

Smock Hill House

Great Chesterford

LONDON RD

GRANTA CL
A520 SN

GREAT CHESTERFORD CT

Great Chesterford

Manor Farm

Coploe Hill

Rectory Farm

B1383

Highfield House

B184

8 7 45 6 5 44 4 3 43 2 1 42

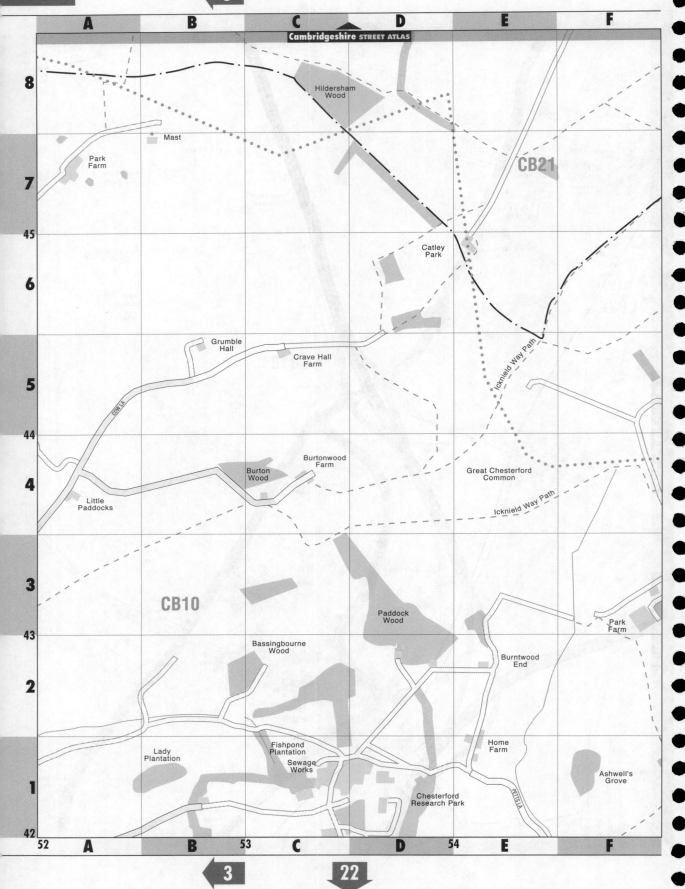

Cambridgeshire STREET ATLAS

8

Hildersham Wood

Mast

Park Farm

CB21

7

45

Catley Park

6

Grumble Hall

Crave Hall Farm

Icknield Way Path

5

44

Burtonwood Farm

Burton Wood

Great Chesterford Common

4

Little Paddocks

Icknield Way Path

COW LA

3

CB10

Paddock Wood

Park Farm

43

Bassingbourne Wood

Burntwood End

2

Lady Plantation

Fishpond Plantation

Sewage Works

Home Farm

Ashwell's Grove

1

Chesterford Research Park

PETTS LA

42

52   A   B   53   C   D   54   E   F

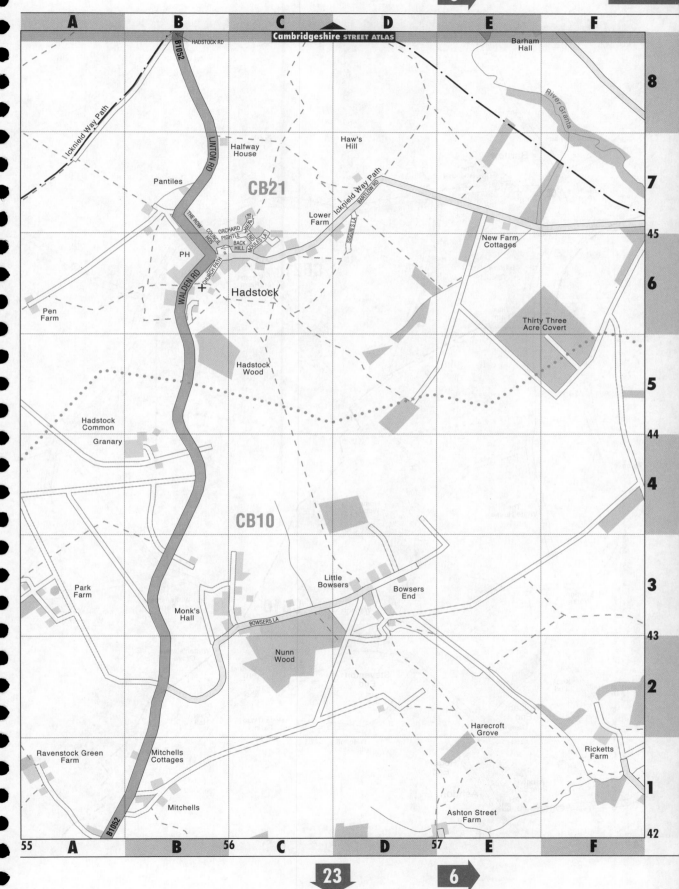

6

Cambridgeshire STREET ATLAS

A B C D E F

8
7
45
6
5
44
4
3
43
2
42
1

55 A B 56 C D 57 E F

Barham Hall

River Granta

Icknield Way Path

Hadstock Rd

B1052

LINTON RD

Halfway House

Pantiles

CB21

Haw's Hill

Icknield Way Path

BARTLOW RD

Lower Farm

SUGIN'S LA

New Farm Cottages

THE ROW

ORCHARD PIGHTLE

COUNCIL HOS

BILL'S END HILL

NOTTLES LA

BACK HILL

PH

WALDEN RD

CHURCH PATH

Hadstock

Pen Farm

Thirty Three Acre Covert

Hadstock Wood

Hadstock Common

Granary

CB10

Park Farm

Monk's Hall

Little Bowsers

Bowsers End

BOWSERS LA

Nunn Wood

Harecroft Grove

Ravenstock Green Farm

Mitchells Cottages

Ricketts Farm

Mitchells

B1052

Ashton Street Farm

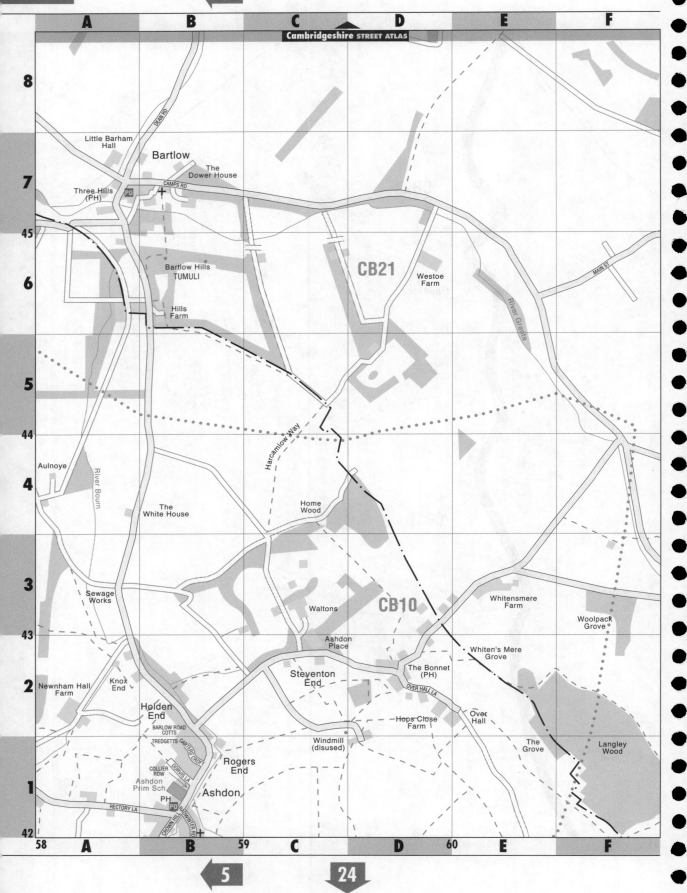

Cambridgeshire STREET ATLAS

A B C D E F

8

Little Barham Hall

Bartlow

The Dower House

7

45

Three Hills (PH)

CAMPS RD

DEAN RD

PO

CB21

Bartlow Hills
TUMULI

Westoe Farm

6

River Granta

Hills Farm

MAIN ST

5

44

Harcamlow Way

Aulnoye

River Bourn

The White House

Home Wood

4

3

Sewage Works

Waltons

CB10

Whitensmere Farm

Woolpack Grove

43

Ashdon Place

Whiten's Mere Grove

2

Newnham Hall Farm

Knox End

Steventon End

The Bonnet (PH)

OVER HALL LA

Over Hall

Holden End

BARLOW ROAD COTTS

CARTERS CROFT

TREDGETTS

Hops Close Farm

The Grove

Langley Wood

COLLIER ROW

DORVIS LA

Rogers End

Windmill (disused)

Ashdon Prim Sch

PH

PO

CROWN HILL

BOWKER RD

Ashdon

1

RECTORY LA

42

58 A B 59 C D 60 E F

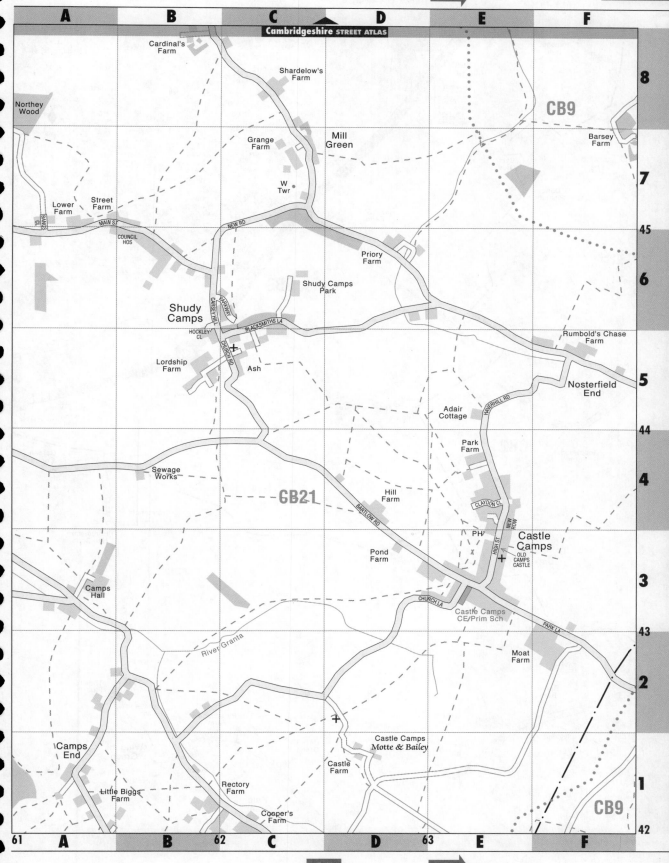

CAMBRIDGESHIRE STREET ATLAS

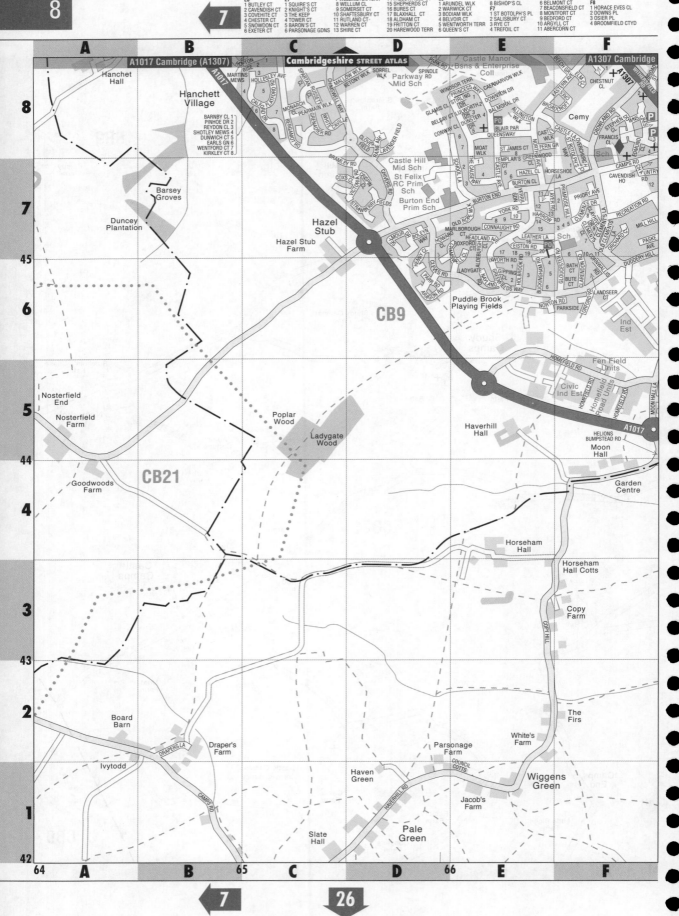

E6
1 BUTLEY CT
2 CAVENDISH CT
3 COVEHITE CT
4 CHESTER CT
5 SNOWDON CT
6 EXETER CT

E7
1 SQUIRE'S CT
2 KNIGHT'S CT
3 THE KEEP
4 TOWER CT
5 BARON'S CT
6 PARSONAGE GDNS

7 WELLINGTON TERR
8 WELLUM CL
9 SOMERSET CT
10 SHAFTESBURY CT
11 RUTLAND CT
12 WARREN CT
13 SHIRE CT

14 FALLOWFIELD CT
15 SHEPHERDS CT
16 BURES CT
17 BLAXHALL CT
18 ALDHAM CT
19 FRITTON CT
20 HAREWOOD TERR

E8
1 ARUNDEL WLK
2 WARWICK CT
3 BODIAM WLK
4 BELVOIR CT
5 WENTWORTH TERR
6 QUEEN'S CT

7 BISHOP'S CT
8 BISHOP'S CL
F7
1 ST BOTOLPH'S PL
2 SALISBURY CT
3 RYE CT
4 TREFOIL CT

5 BEAUFORT CT
6 BELMONT CT
7 BEACONSFIELD CT
8 MONTFORT CT
9 BEDFORD CT
10 ARGYLL CT
11 ABERCORN CT

12 CHAINEY PIECES
F8
1 HORACE EVES CL
2 DOWNS PL
3 OSIER PL
4 BROOMFIELD CTYD

Cambridgeshire STREET ATLAS

A1017 Cambridge (A1307)

A1307 Cambridge

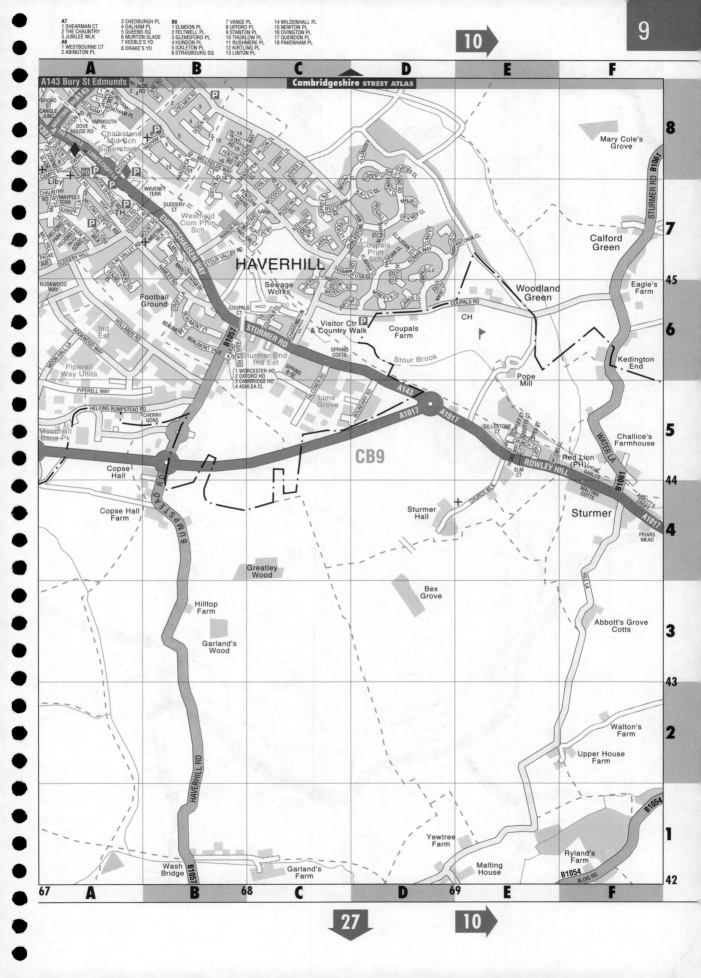

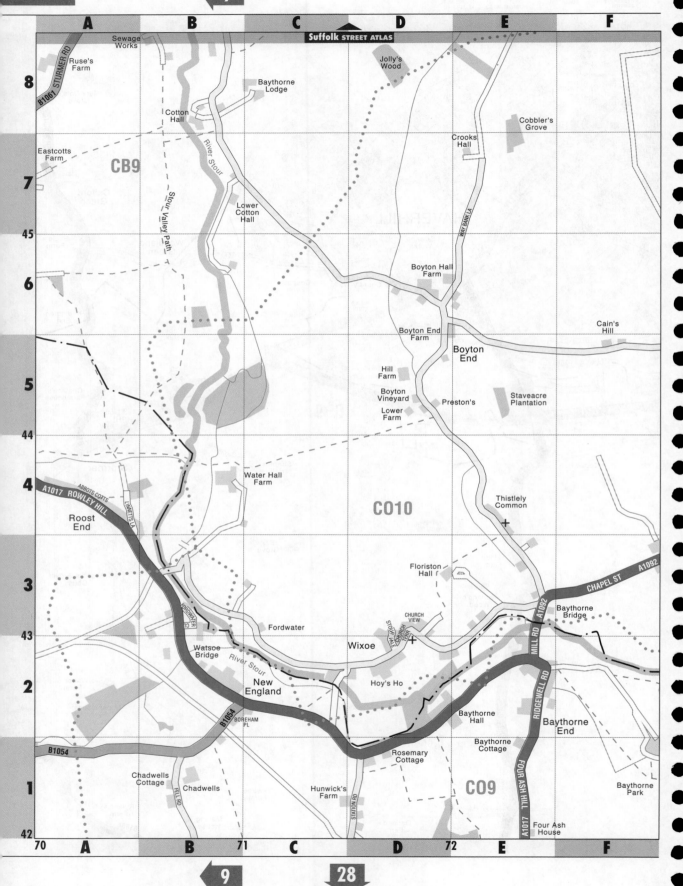

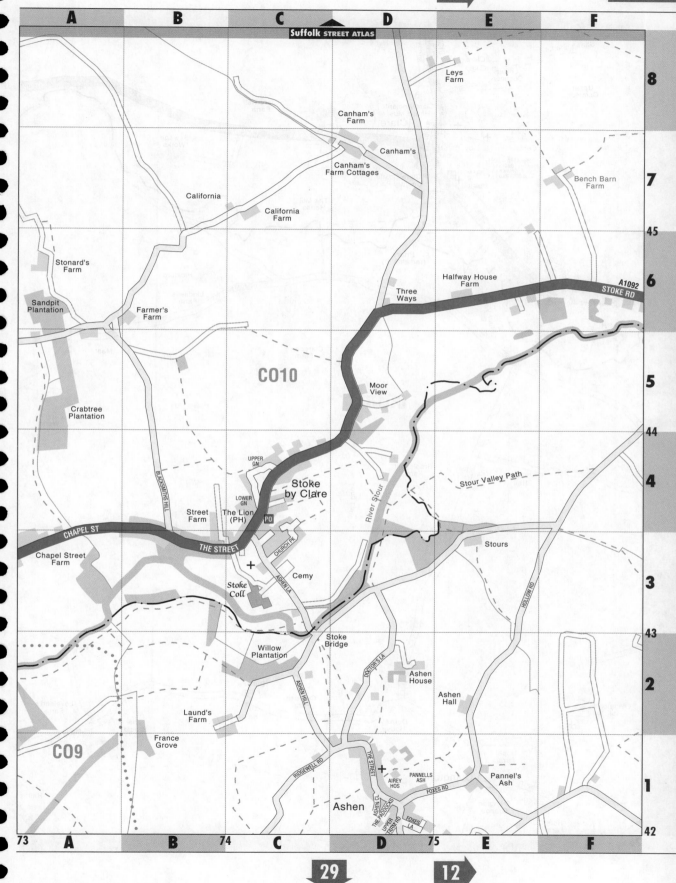

Suffolk STREET ATLAS

A   B   C   D   E   F

8

Leys
Farm

Canham's
Farm

7

Canham's

Canham's
Farm Cottages

Bench Barn
Farm

45

California

California
Farm

Stonard's
Farm

Halfway House
Farm

6

A1092
STOKE RD

Three
Ways

Sandpit
Plantation

Farmer's
Farm

CO10

Moor
View

5

Crabtree
Plantation

44

BLACKSMITHS HILL

UPPER
GN

Stour Valley Path

4

LOWER
GN

Stoke
by Clare

River Stour

Street
Farm

The Lion
(PH)   PO

CHAPEL ST

THE STREET

CHURCH PK

Stours

3

Chapel Street
Farm

Chapel Street
Farm

ASHEN LA

Cemy

HOLLOW RD

Stoke
Coll

43

Stoke
Bridge

Willow
Plantation

ASHEN HILL

DIXTON'S LA

Ashen
House

2

Ashen
Hall

Laund's
Farm

France
Grove

RIDGEWELL RD

THE STREET

PANNELLS
ASH

Pannel's
Ash

1

CO9

AIREY
HOS

FOXES RD

Ashen

THE PADDOCKS

ASHEN CL

UPPER FARM RD

FOXES
LA

42

73   A   B   74   C   D   75   E   F

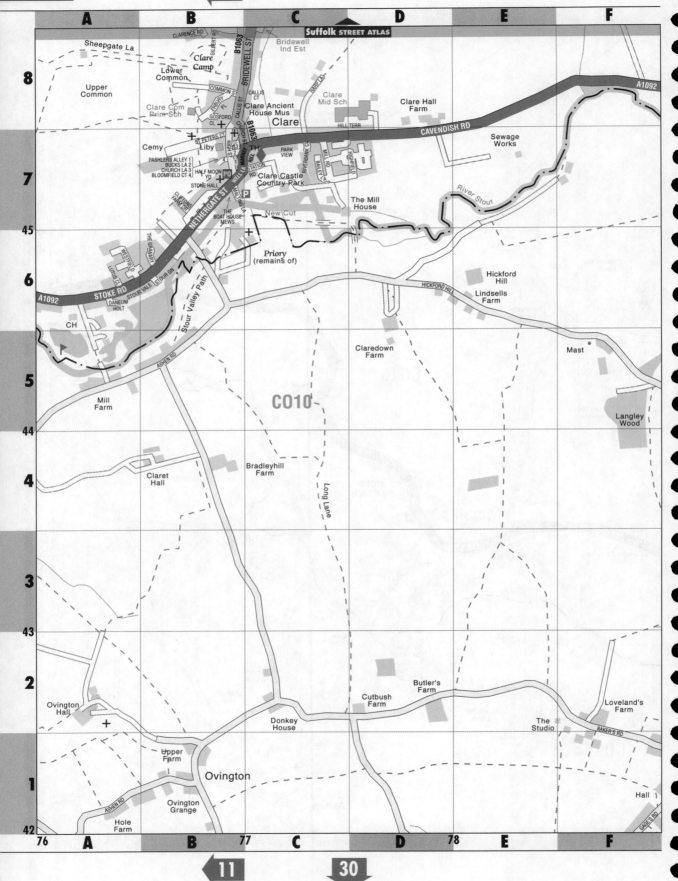

Suffolk STREET ATLAS

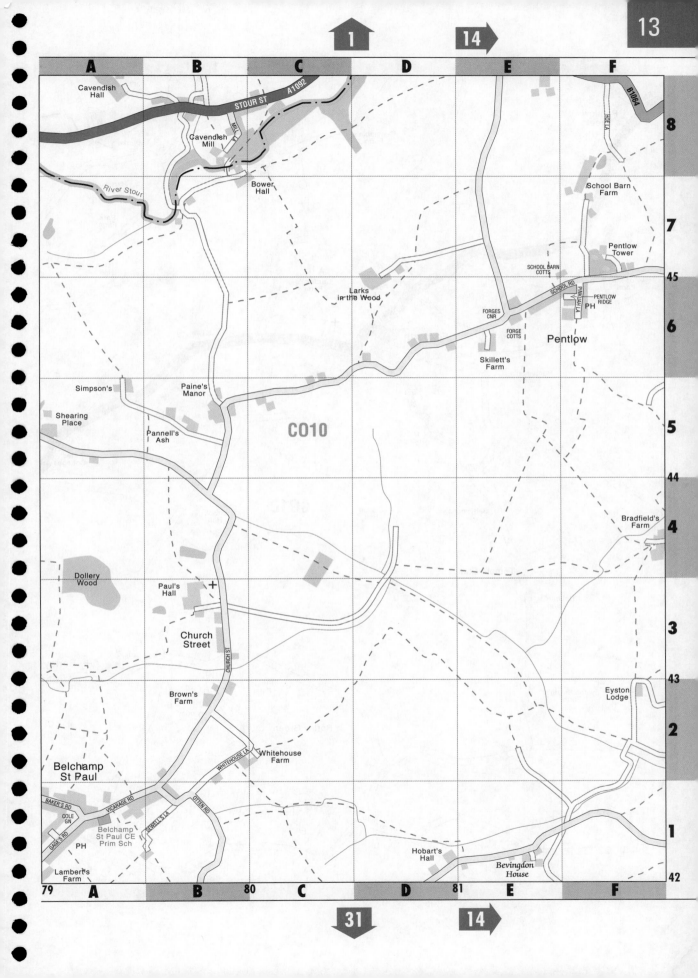

Cavendish Hall

STOUR ST

A1092

Cavendish Mill

Bower Hall

River Stour

B1064

HOE LA

School Barn Farm

Pentlow Tower

SCHOOL BARN COTTS

Larks in the Wood

SCHOOL RD

PINKUAH LA

PENTLOW RIDGE

PH

FORGES CNR

FORGE COTTS

Pentlow

Skillett's Farm

Simpson's

Paine's Manor

Shearing Place

CO10

Pannell's Ash

Dollery Wood

Paul's Hall

Bradfield's Farm

Church Street

CHURCH ST

Eyston Lodge

Brown's Farm

Belchamp St Paul

WHITEHOUSE LA

Whitehouse Farm

BAKER'S RD

VICARAGE RD

COLE GN

SEWELL'S LA

OTTEN RD

GAGE'S RD

PH

Belchamp St Paul CE Prim Sch

Lambert's Farm

Hobart's Hall

Bevingdon House

13
2

| | A | B | C | D | E | F |

B1064
THE STREET
Pentlow
Street

8

Constable's
Farm

Liston
Gardens

Weston
Hall

Works

Hartsbuckle
Farm

PENTLOW HILL

Park
Farm

7

45

Roper's
Farm

Bunting's
Farm

Foxearth
Hall

Cardinal's
Farm

Liston
Hall

THE STREET

6

Foxearth

THE CHASE

SCHOOL ST

Hawk's
Farm

Huntsman's
Farm

The
Plantation

MILL RD

CLAYPITS LA

5

Mill
Cottage

B1064

Red
Cottages

44

Bellybones

Claypit
Hall

CO10

Brook
Hall

4

Temple End

Hubbard's
Farm

3

Borley
Place

Borley

43

HALL RD

Eyston Smyth's
Farm

Purkis
Farm

Borleylodge
Farm

2

Borley Green

Eyston
Hall

1

Bardfield
Bridge

42

| 82 | A | B | 83 | C | D | 84 | E | F |

13
32

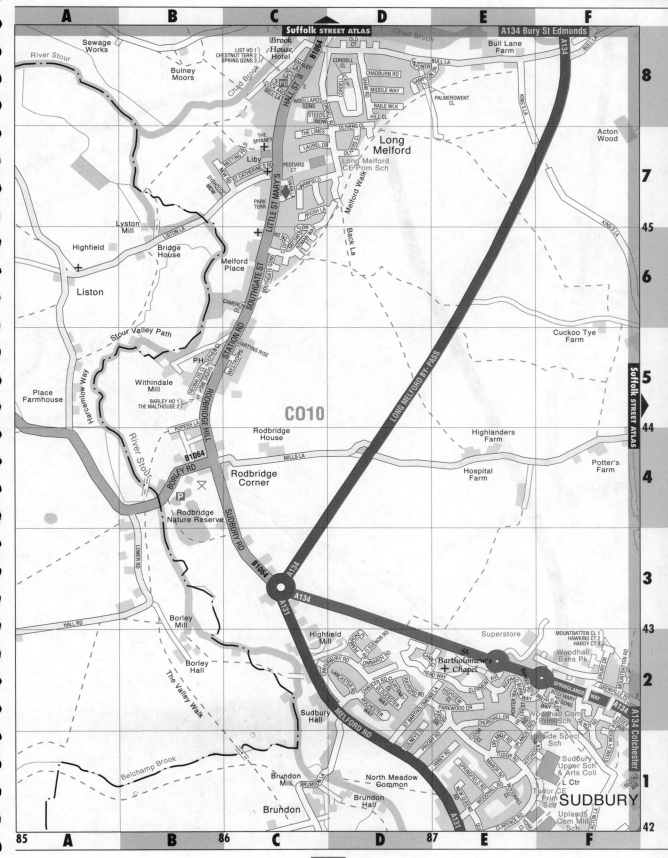

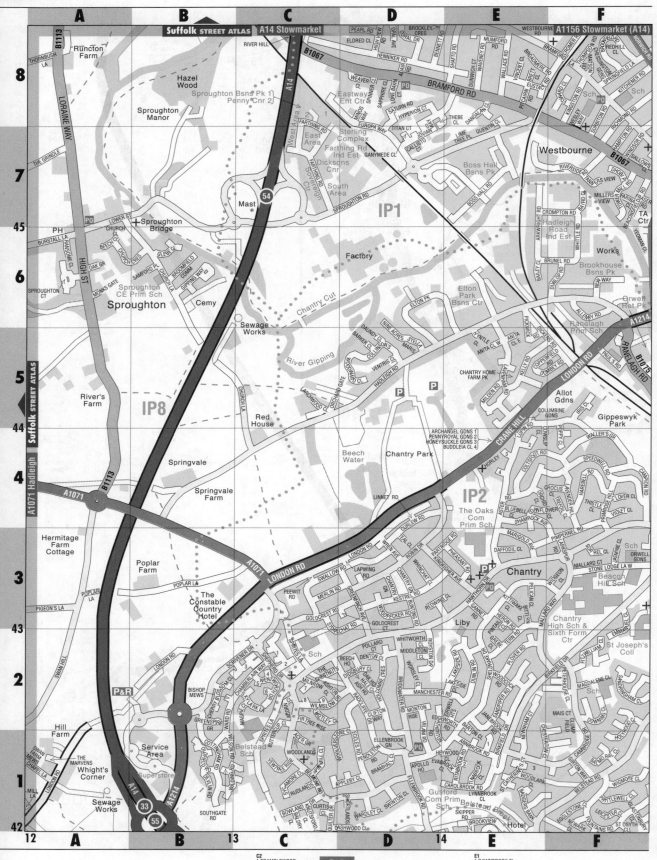

C2
1 BRAMBLEWOOD
2 LABURNUM CL
3 BROAD MEADOW
4 INNES END
5 PEACOCK CL
6 HALFORD CT
7 MERRION CL
8 MATLOCK CL
9 MOTTRAM CL

E1
1 DAWNBROOK CL
2 HILDABROOK CL
3 VINNICOMBE CT

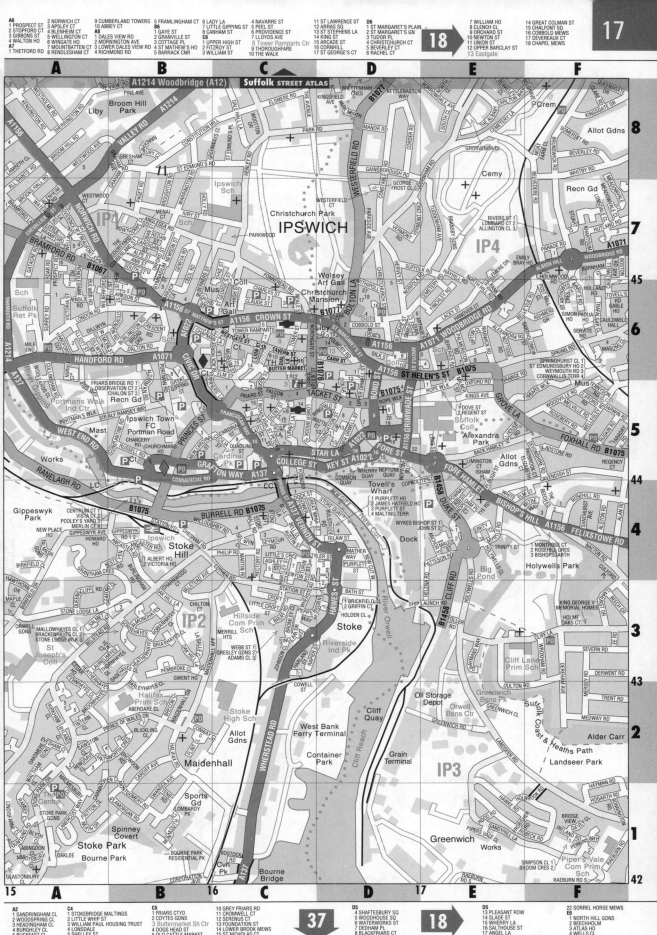

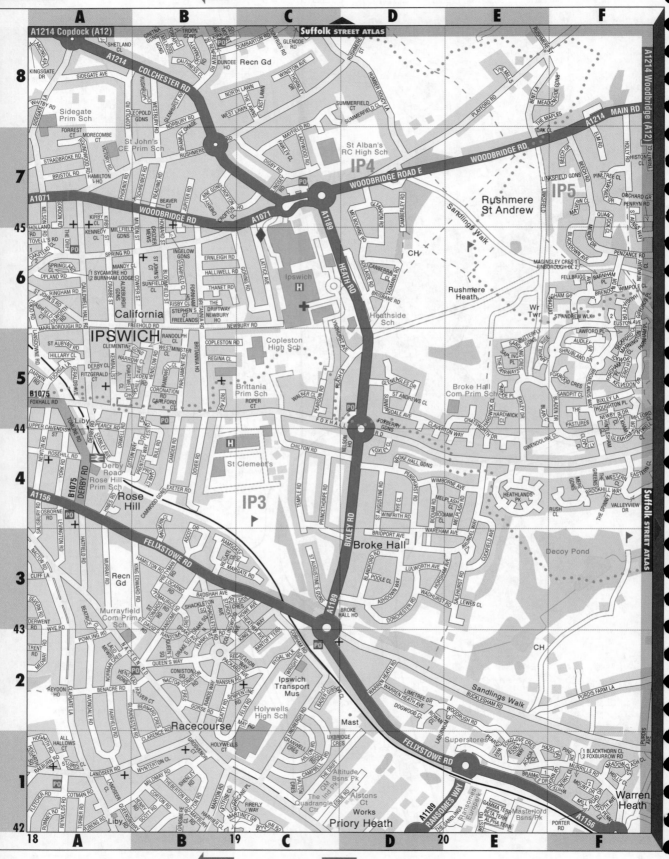

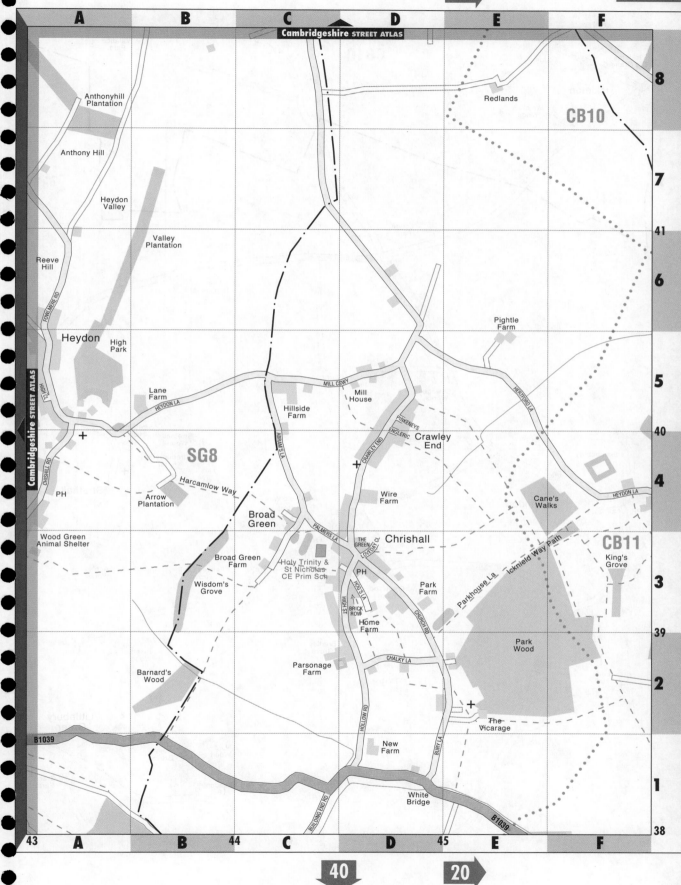

Cambridgeshire STREET ATLAS

CB10

CB11

SG8

Anthonyhill Plantation

Anthony Hill

Heydon Valley

Valley Plantation

Reeve Hill

Heydon

High Park

Lane Farm

Hillside Farm

Mill House

Mill Cswy

Pinkeneys

Engleric

Crawley End

Pightle Farm

Redlands

Harcamlow Way

Arrow Plantation

Broad Green

Wire Farm

Cane's Walks

Heydon La

King's Grove

Wood Green Animal Shelter

PH

Broad Green Farm

Wisdom's Grove

Holy Trinity & St Nicholas CE Prim Sch

PALMERS LA

THE GREEN

LOVEDAY CL

Chrishall

Park Farm

Parkhouse La

Icknield Way Path

PH

HOG'S LA

HIGH ST

BRICK ROW

Home Farm

Park Wood

Barnard's Wood

Parsonage Farm

CHALKY LA

CHURCH RD

HOLLOW RD

BURY LA

New Farm

The Vicarage

B1039

White Bridge

B1039

HEYDON LA

ABRAM'S LA

CRAWLEY END

HERTFORD LA

CHISHILL RD

FOWLMERE RD

TO A505

Cambridgeshire STREET ATLAS

Cambridgeshire STREET ATLAS

CB10

8

Ickleton
Old Grange
GRANGE RD
The Lodge

Ickleton

Welches Wood

7

41

Valance Farm

Argers

Lodge Farm

ROYSTON LA

6

The Poplars

QUICKSET RD

5

Sewage Works

New Jersey Farm

40

Elmdonbury

Strethall Wood

Strethall Hall

Strethall Wood Farm

BURY GDNS
ICKLETON RD
HORSESHOE CL
ELM CT
THE GLEBE

4

HEYDON LA

Elmdon

HOLLOW RD

Icknield Way

Strethall

PH

Church Farm

Free Wood

Felsted Croft Grove

Ann's Wood

FREEWOOD LA

Mill Hill

Freewood Farm

3

39

QUEEN ST

Bradley Grove

Bixett Wood

Lofts Hall

ESSEX HILL

2

CB11

Littlebury Green

Lee Wood

Ash Grove

THOMAS WLK

Elmdon Lee

Green Farm

1

38

46

47

48

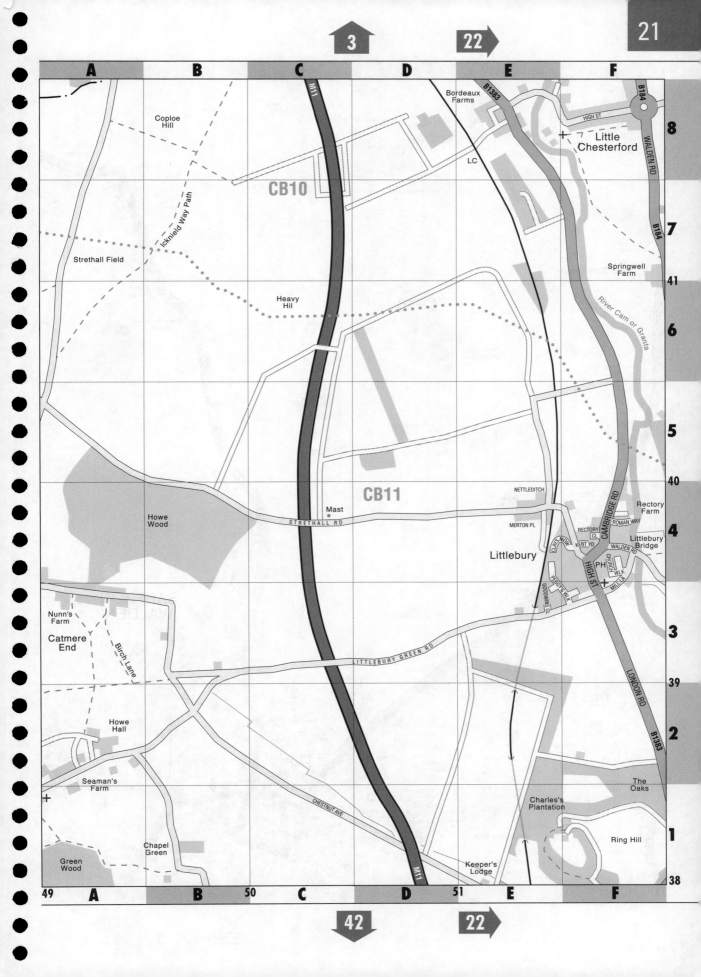

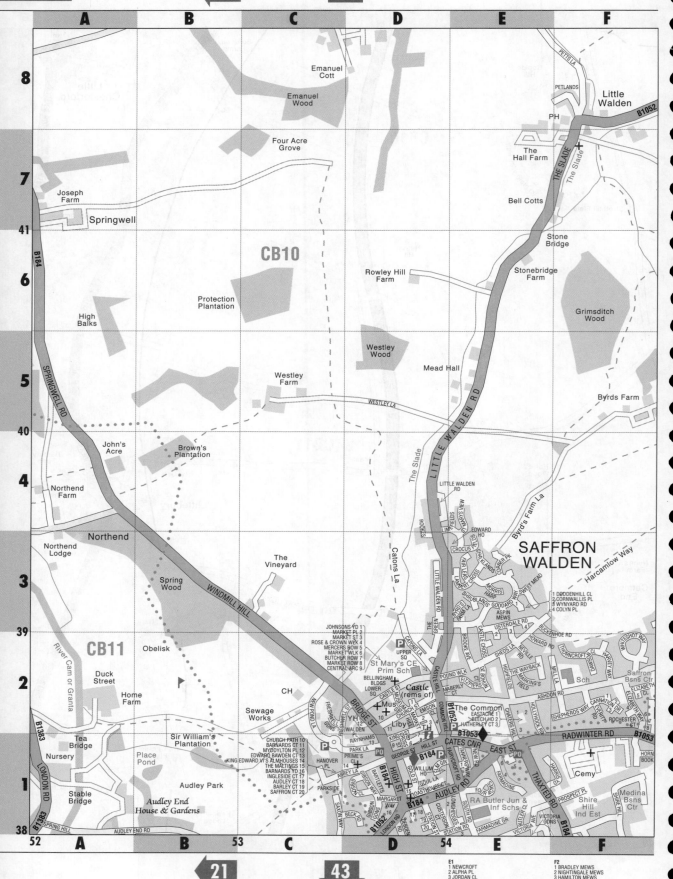

A B C D E F

8

Emanuel Cott

Emanuel Wood

Four Acre Grove

7

Joseph Farm

Springwell

Little Walden

PH

The Hall Farm

The Slade

The Slade

B1052

PETTS LA

PETLANDS

41

B184

Bell Cotts

Stone Bridge

Stonebridge Farm

CB10

6

Protection Plantation

High Balks

Rowley Hill Farm

Grimsditch Wood

Westley Wood

Mead Hall

5

Westley Farm

WESTLEY LA

Byrds Farm

40

John's Acre

Brown's Plantation

4

Northend Farm

LITTLE WALDEN RD

LITTLE WALDEN RD

The Slade

Byrd's Farm La

Harcamlow Way

Northend Lodge

Northend

The Vineyard

SAFFRON WALDEN

1 DODDENHILL CL
2 CORNWALLIS PL
3 WYNYARD RD
4 COLYN PL

3

Spring Wood

WINDMILL HILL

Catons La

USTERDALE RD

BUCKENHOE RD

39

CB11

Obelisk

JOHNSONS YD 1
MARKET PL 2
MARKET ST 3
ROSE & CROWN WLK 4
MERCERS ROW 5
MARKET WLK 6
BUTCHER ROW 7
MARKET ROW 8
CENTRAL ARC 9

RADWINTER RD

B1053

River Cam or Granta

Duck Street

Home Farm

CH

St Mary's CE Prim Sch

The Common

2

Sewage Works

Castle (rems of)

Mus

Liby

The Common
EASTACRE 1
BEECH HO 2
HATHERLEY CT 3

Cemy

HORN BOOK

Tea Bridge

Sir William's Plantation

CHURCH PATH 10
BARNARDS CT 11
MYDDYLTON PL 12
EDWARD BAWDEN CT 13
KING EDWARD VI'S ALMHOUSES 14
THE MALTINGS 15
BARNARDS YD 16
INGLESIDE CT 17
AUDLEY CT 18
BARLEY CT 19
SAFFRON CT 20

EAST ST

B1053

Medina Bsns Ctr

1

Nursery

Place Pond

Audley Park

HANOVER PL

PARKSIDE

HIGH ST

AUDLEY RD

THAXTED RD

B184

RA Butler Jun & Inf Schs

Shire Hill Ind Est

Stable Bridge

B1383

LONDON RD

SPRING HILL

Audley End House & Gardens

AUDLEY END RD

B1052

LONDON RD

38

52 A B 53 C D 54 E F

E1
1 NEWCROFT
2 ALPHA PL
3 JORDAN CL
4 FARMADINE CT
5 JOHN DANE PLAYER CT
6 FARMADINE HO

F2
1 BRADLEY MEWS
2 NIGHTINGALE MEWS
3 HAMILTON MEWS
4 HADLEIGH CT
5 ST JAMES CT
6 LAVENDER FIELD
7 THE SPIKE
8 CAVENDISH CT

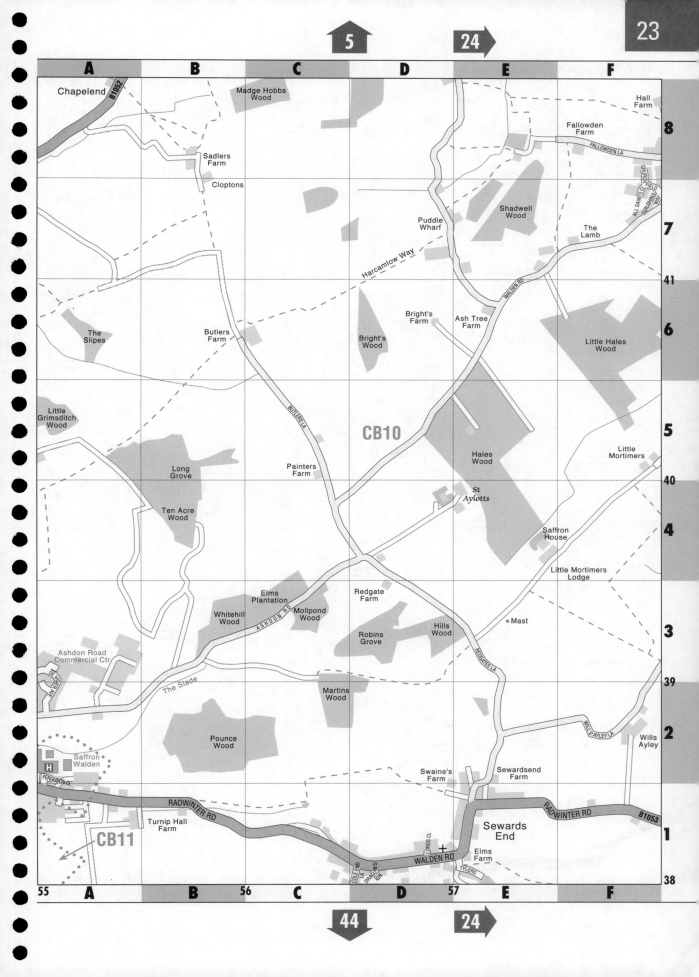

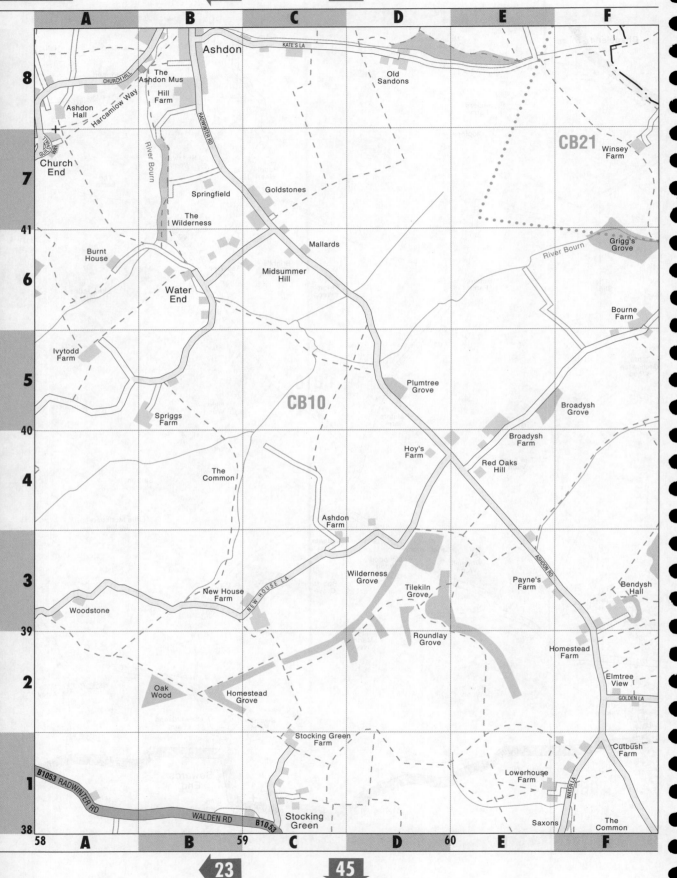

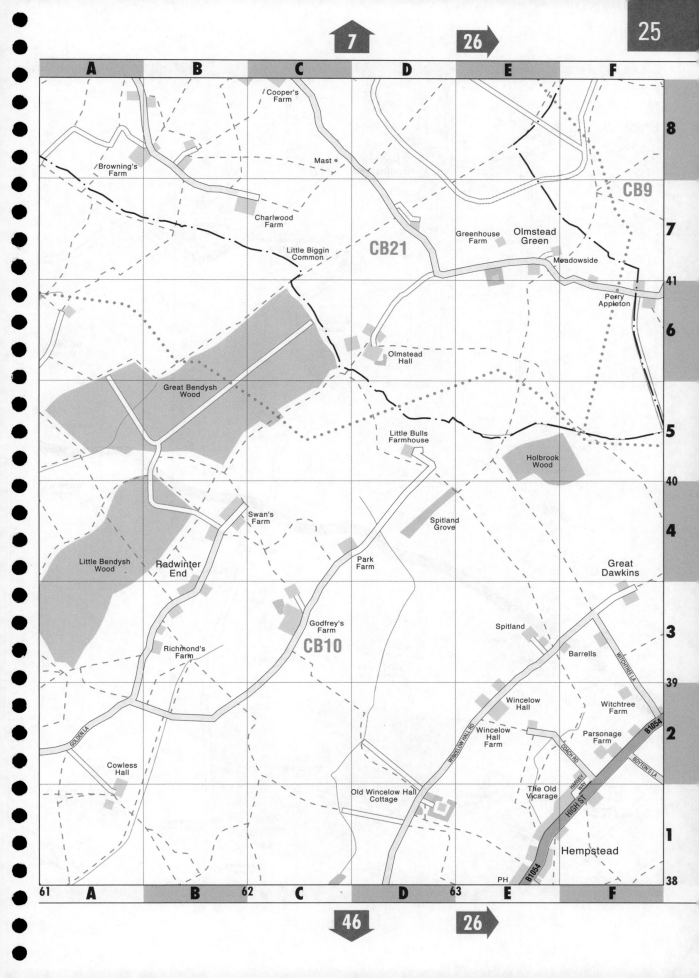

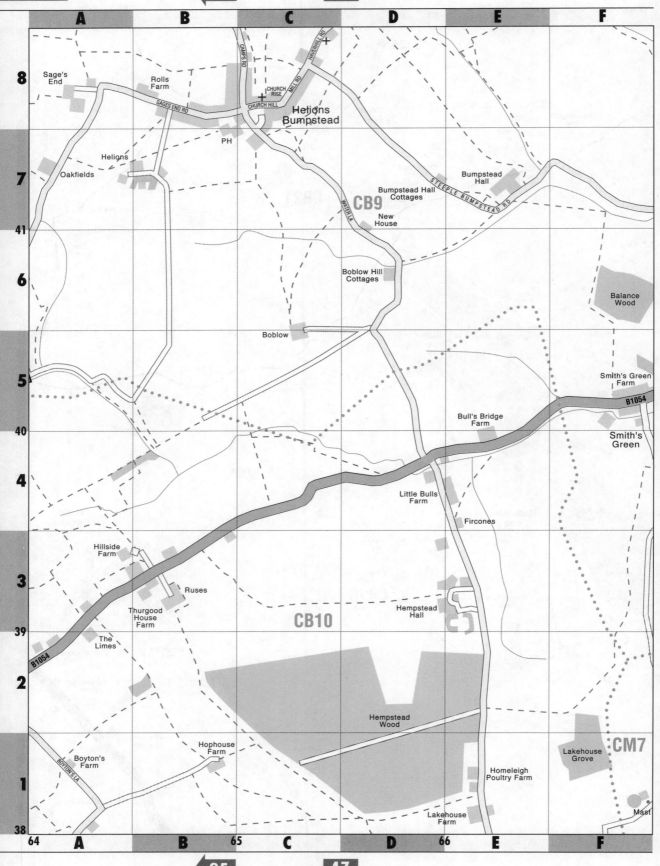

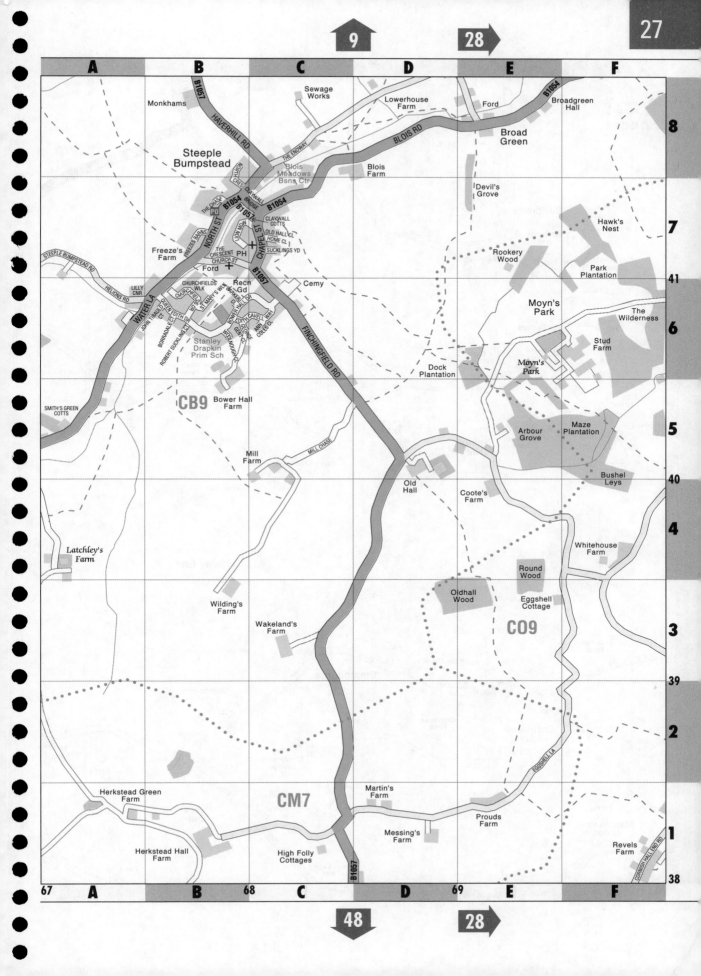

27 10

A B C D E F

8

Moyn's Wood

CB9

Birdbrook

7

Birdbrook Hall

Churchfield Grove

The Plough (PH)

The Street

MOAT FARM

DAW ST

MOAT RD

STATION RD

Whitley House

A1017

FOUR ASH HILL

THE CAUSEWAY

A1017

Causeway Hall

41

6

Paddock Belt

SCHOOLFIELD

The Rectory

Wash Bridge

Carter's Bridge

Wash Farm

5

Stubland's Farm

Highfield Clump

Wash Farm

Finkle Green

Bailey Hill Farm

Bailey Hill

CO9

Woodview

Three Chimneys Farm

Three Chimneys Wood

Essex Hall

STAMBOURNE RD

Pettyfield La

40

4

Park Wood

WESLEY END RD

Wesley End

3

Warren Farm

BIRDBROOK RD

Little Collin's Farm

MILL RD

Hill Farm

Stambourne

CHURCH RD

Stambourne Hall

39

Slough Farm

CHAPEL END WAY

PO

Chapelend Way

Oldhouse Farm

2

CORNISH HALL END RD

Stambourne Grange

DYERS RD

Stambourne Hall

Mill Farm

Greenfield's Farm

1

Moat Hall Farm

Stambourne Green

Dyer's End

FINCHINGFIELD RD

Great Tagley Farm

Elm's Farm

38

70 A B 71 C D 72 E F

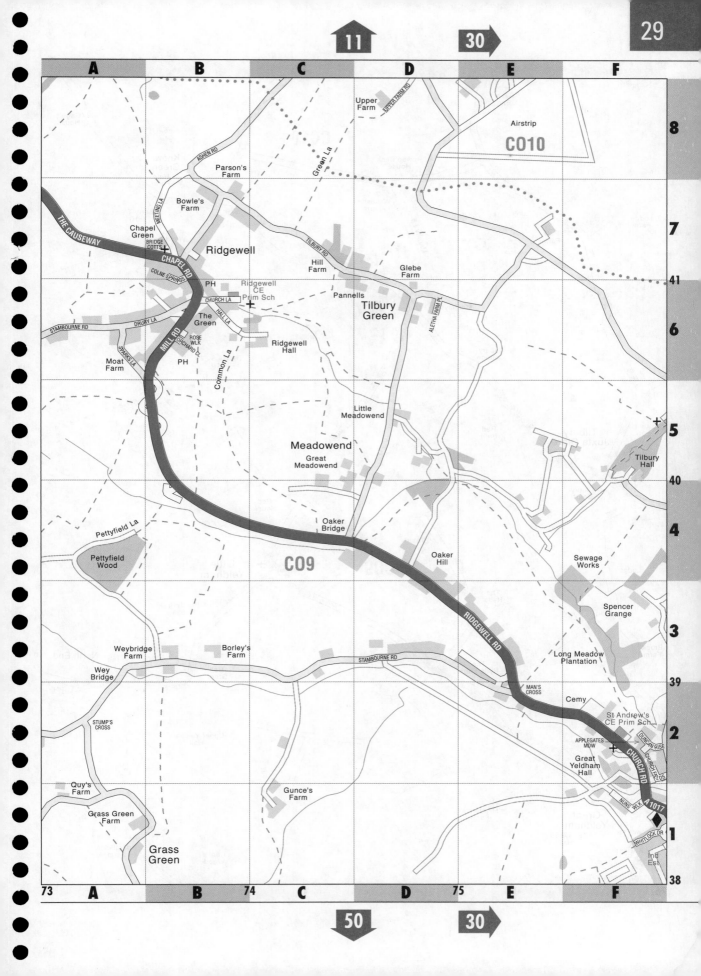

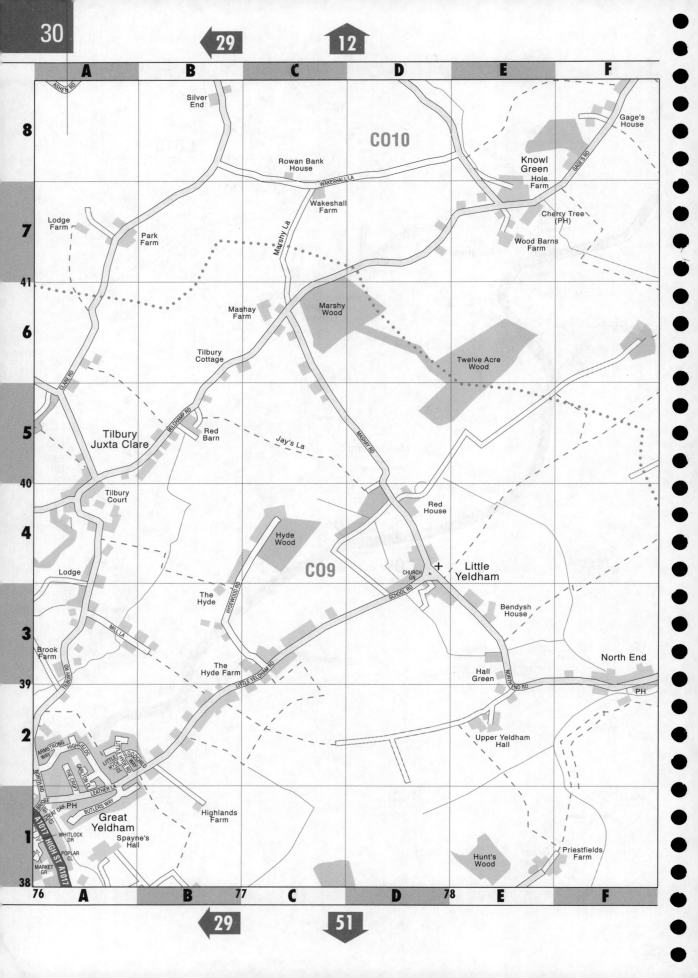

A B C D E F

8

CO10

Silver
End

Gage's
House

Knowl
Green

Rowan Bank
House

Hole
Farm

GAGE'S RD

WAKESHALL LA

Wakeshall
Farm

Cherry Tree
(PH)

7

Lodge
Farm

Park
Farm

Marshy La

Wood Barns
Farm

41

Mashay
Farm

Marshy
Wood

6

Tilbury
Cottage

Twelve Acre
Wood

CLARE RD

BELCHAMP RD

5

Tilbury
Juxta Clare

Red
Barn

Jay's La

MASHAY RD

40

Tilbury
Court

Red
House

4

Lodge

Hyde
Wood

CO9

CHURCH
GN

+

Little
Yeldham

HYDEWOOD RD

The Hyde

SCHOOL RD

Bendysh
House

North End

MILL LA

3

Brook
Farm

The
Hyde Farm

Hall
Green

PH

TILBURY RD

LITTLE YELDHAM RD

NORTH END RD

39

2

ARMSTRONG WAY

HIGHFIELDS

GOODCHILD WAY

LITTLE HYDE RD

Upper Yeldham
Hall

NORTH RD

THE CROFT

CARLTON RD

LEATHER LA

BUTLERS WAY

Highlands
Farm

1

BRIDGE ST

GREAT OAK ST

PH

Great
Yeldham

Spayne's
Hall

Hunt's
Wood

Priestfields
Farm

A1017 HIGH ST A1017

WHITLOCK
DR

POPLAR
CL

MARKET
GR

38

76 A B 77 C D 78 E F

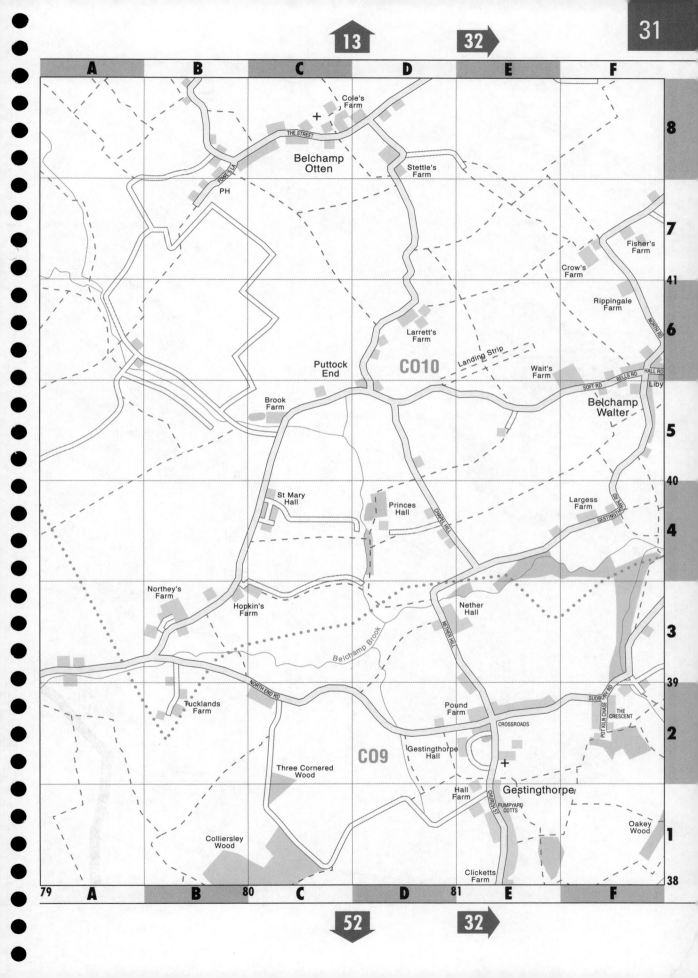

↑ 13

32 →

A   B   C   D   E   F

8

Cole's Farm
+
THE STREET
Belchamp Otten
Stettle's Farm

FOWE'S LA
PH

Fisher's Farm   7

Crow's Farm   41

Rippingale Farm   6

Larrett's Farm

Puttock End   CO10   Landing Strip   Wait's Farm

NORTH RD

SOFT RD   BELLS RD   HALL RD   Liby

Brook Farm   Belchamp Walter

5

St Mary Hall   40

Princes Hall   CHAPEL HILL   Largess Farm   4

GESTINGTHORPE RD

Northey's Farm   OLD RD

Hopkin's Farm   Nether Hall

NETHER HILL   3

Belchamp Brook

NORTH END RD   39

Pound Farm   SUDBURY RD

POT KILN CHASE

THE CRESCENT

CROSSROADS   2

Tucklands Farm   Gestingthorpe Hall

CO9   +   Gestingthorpe

Three Cornered Wood   Hall Farm   PUMPYARD COTTS

CHURCH ST

Oakey Wood   1

Colliersley Wood

Clicketts Farm   38

79   A   B   80   C   D   81   E   F

↓ 52

32 →

A B C D E F

8
7
41
6
5
40
4
3
39
2
1
38

The Rookery

Newbon

Clark's Farm

Smeetham Hall

Heaven Wood

Smeetham Hall Cottages

SMEETHAM HALL LA

SUDBURY RD

Belchamp Brook

HALL RD

Belchamp Hall

Springgate Farm

New Barns

Goldingham Hall

CO10

Grigg's Farm

THE STREET

SWAINS CROFT

ST ANDREW'S RISE

BULMER ST

PO

CHURCH MDW

Bulmer

Blackhouse Farm

SANDY LA

Auberies

Lower Houses

Brakey Hill

CHURCH RD

St Andrew's CE Prim Sch

OLD CHURCH LA

SUDBURY RD

Hill Farm

New Barn

CO9

UPPER HOUSES

Hilltop Farm

Wiggery Wood

Bulmer Tye

PARK LA

A131

OLD CHURCH LA

Jenkins Farm

TYE CNR

PH

BLACKSMITHS LA

Parsonage Wood

Wesborough Hill

Hole Farm

Tyecorner Farm

A131

HEDINGHAM RD

82 A B 83 C D 84 E F

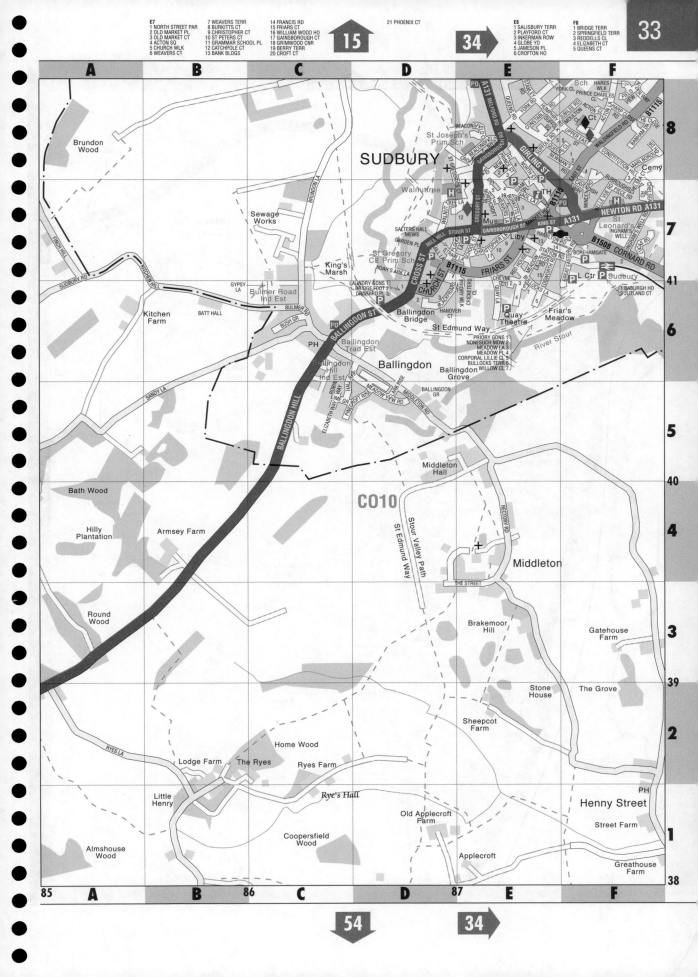

33

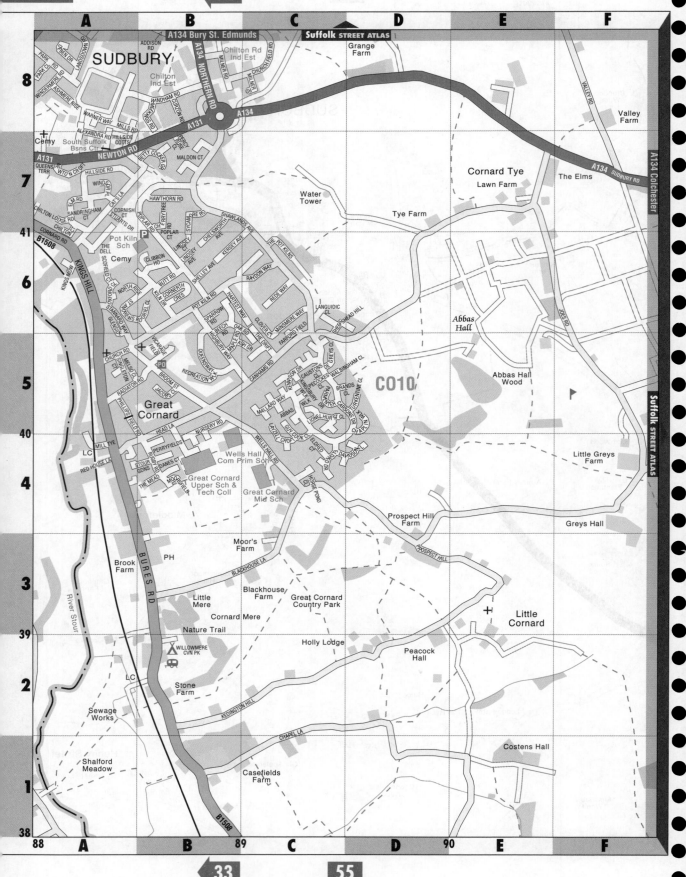

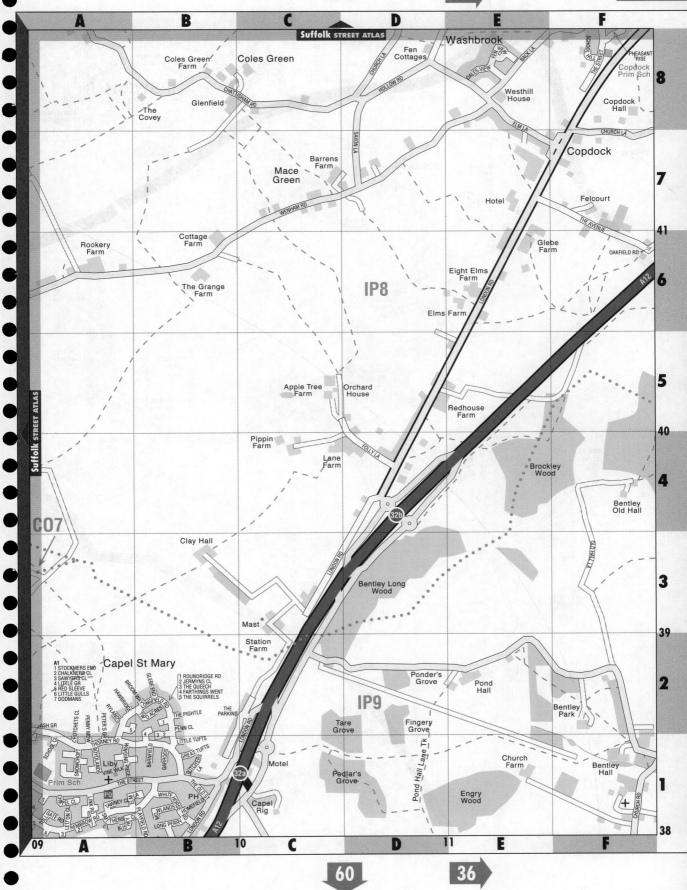

36

Suffolk STREET ATLAS

Suffolk STREET ATLAS

Washbrook

Coles Green Farm

Coles Green

Fen Cottages

The Street

Pheasant Rise

Copdock Prim Sch

8

Dales View

Back La

Fen View

Glenfield

Chattisham Rd

Hollow Rd

Church La

Westhill House

Copdock Hall

The Covey

Elm La

Church La

Copdock

7

Barrens Farm

Saxon La

Hotel

Felcourt

Mace Green

The Avenue

41

Rookery Farm

Wenham Rd

Cottage Farm

Glebe Farm

Oakfield Rd

IP8

Eight Elms Farm

London Rd

A12

6

The Grange Farm

Elms Farm

Apple Tree Farm

Orchard House

Redhouse Farm

5

Brockley Wood

40

Pippin Farm

Lane Farm

Folly La

Bentley Old Hall

4

32b

Clay Hall

Bentley Long Wood

Old Hall La

3

Mast

Station Farm

39

Capel St Mary

A1
1 STOCKMERS END
2 CHALKNERS CL
3 SAWYERS CL
4 LITTLE GR
5 RED SLEEVE
6 LITTLE GULLS
7 DODMANS

1 ROUNDRIDGE RD
2 JERMYNS CL
3 THE QUEECH
4 FARTHINGS WENT
5 THE SQUIRRELS

Ponder's Grove

Pond Hall

Bentley Park

2

Broom Way

Glebe End Rd

Longfield Rd

Longfield Rd

Two Acres Rd

The Pightle

Penn Cl

Little Tufts

Great Tufts

The Parkins

London Rd

IP9

Tare Grove

Fingery Grove

Pond Hall Lane Tk

Bentley Hall

Hambridge

Rylands

Peter's Gr

Penny Mdw

Ash Gr

School Cl

Chotchets Cl

Snowcroft

Dovelands

Thorney Rd

Wining There

Barnfield

Garrods

Butchers La

Key

Liby

Vine Wlk

The Street

Prim Sch

P.O.

Tawney Rd

Chapel Cl

Link Rd

Smithers Cl

White Horse

The Old Ct

Playfield Rd

Homefield

32a

Motel

Capel Rig

Pedlar's Grove

Church Farm

Engry Wood

Bentley Hall

1

Gate Rd

Lefton Cl

Rembrow Rd

Long Perry

Buss Cl

Wlands

London Rd

Church Rd

38

60

36

C07

PH

GROVE HILL 1
SPECKLED WOOD CL 2
MONARCH WAY 3
GROVE WLK 4
GREEN OAK GLADE 5

SWALLOWTAIL CL 6
SKIPPER RD 7
TORTOISESHELL CL 8
FRITILLARY CL 9
GATEKEEPER CL 10
BOATMAN CL 11
MAYFLY CL 12
LACEWING CL 13
SPRINGTAIL RD 14

15 BLACK ARCHES
16 COPPER GR

Copdock Mill
Belstead Rise
Belstead Hall
Belstead
IP8
Mill Poultry Farm
Alder Carr
IPSWICH
IP2
Belstead Bridge
Ashground Plantation
Alder Carr
Spring Wood
Thorington Hall
Blacksmith's Corner
Street Farm
Charity Farm
Spinney Wood
Wherstead Wood
Pannington Hall
Pannington Hall Cottage
Hill Covert
Old Hall Wood
Clubs Heath
Bluegate Farm
Newcome Wood
Bentley Manor
Hubbard's Hall Farm
Tattingstone Trout Farm
Park House
Road Farm
IP9
Holbrook Park
White Horse Cotts
PH
Tattingstone White Horse
Shrub Wood
Lemons Hill

MILL LA
CHURCH LA
OAKFIELD RD
BUCK'S HORNS LA
CHAPEL LA
HOLLY LA
GROVE HILL
BENTLEY LA
THE STREET
A12
A14
A14
A137
VALLEY LA
COXHALL RD
WHITE HORSE HILL
SCHOOL RD
A137

HOLLY BLUE CL
BOBBITS LA

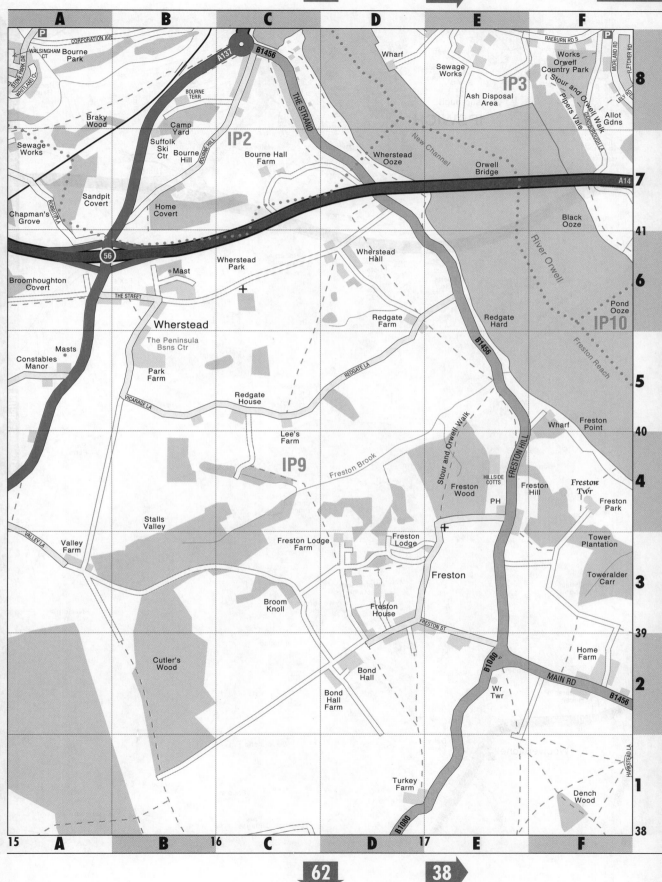

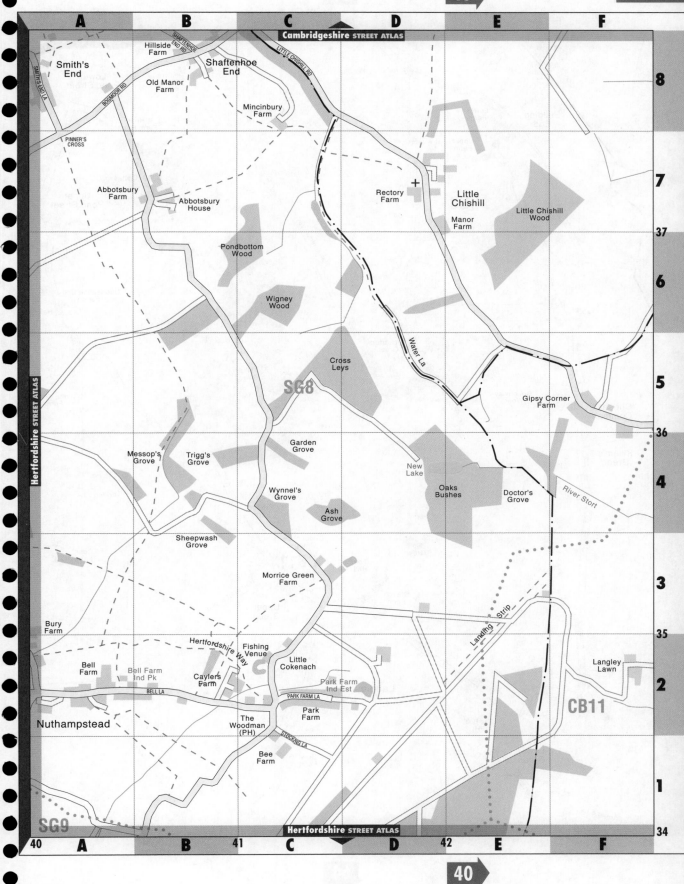

Smith's End
Hillside Farm
Shaftenhoe End
SHAFTENHOE END RD
Old Manor Farm
LITTLE CHISHILL RD
Mincinbury Farm
PINNER'S CROSS
BOGMOOR RD
SMITH'S END LA
Abbotsbury Farm
Abbotsbury House
Rectory Farm
Little Chishill
Manor Farm
Little Chishill Wood
Pondbottom Wood
37
Wigney Wood
6
SG8
Cross Leys
Water La
5
Gipsy Corner Farm
Garden Grove
36
Messop's Grove
Trigg's Grove
New Lake
Oaks Bushes
Doctor's Grove
River Stort
4
Wynnel's Grove
Ash Grove
Sheepwash Grove
Morrice Green Farm
3
Landing Strip
Bury Farm
35
Hertfordshire Way
Fishing Venue
Bell Farm
Bell Farm Ind Pk
Caylers Farm
Little Cokenach
Park Farm Ind Est
Langley Lawn
2
BELL LA
PARK FARM LA
CB11
Nuthampstead
The Woodman (PH)
Park Farm
STOCKING LA
Bee Farm
1
SG9
34

39
19

A **B** **C** **D** **E** **F**

Monkshole
Wood

8

Building End Rd

Building
End

Lower
Farm

Chiswick
Hall

Lower
Pond Street

Hope
Farm House

B1039

B1039

7

Upper
Farm

Building End Rd

Common La

SG8

Mead Bushes
Wood

Upper
Pond Street

School La

37

Harcamlow Way

Wicken Water

6

Duddenhoe End
Farm

Hall

Broomsties

Chrishall
Common

Common La

Pickerton
Green

High
Wood

5

Roughway
Wood

Oldfield
Grove

White Friars
Farm

36

Killem's
Green

4

Lorking's La

Park La

River Stort

Grange
Farm

Duddenhoe
Grange

Cosh
Farm

3

Hall
Grove

The Hall

Church
Farm

The Causeway

CB11

Harcamlow Way

Upper
Green

35

Bull La

Hall

The Kangels

Long
Ley

2

Langley

Highfields

The Bull
(PH)

Lower
Green

Ford

Bury
Farm

1

Waterwick Hill

Roper's La

New
Farm

34

43 **A** **B** **44** **C** **D** **45** **E** **F**

39
64

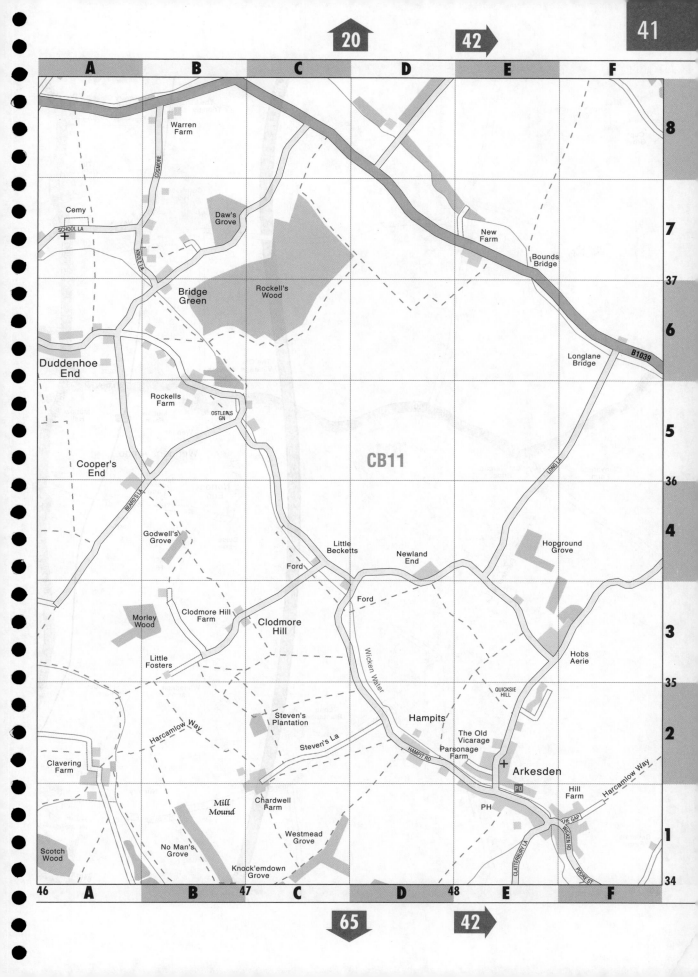

A   B   C   D   E   F

8

Warren
Farm

7

Cemy
SCHOOL LA
COGMORE

Daw's
Grove

New
Farm

37

Bounds
Bridge

Bridge
Green

Rockell's
Wood

6

KNOX LA

Longlane
Bridge

B1039

Duddenhoe
End

Rockells
Farm

OSTLER'S
GN

5

CB11

36

Cooper's
End

BEARD'S LA

LONG LA

4

Godwell's
Grove

Little
Becketts

Newland
End

Hopground
Grove

Ford

Ford

Morley
Wood

Clodmore Hill
Farm

Clodmore
Hill

Hobs
Aerie

35

Little
Fosters

Wicken Water

QUICKSIE
HILL

3

Steven's
Plantation

Hampits

The Old
Vicarage

Harcamlow Way

Steven's La

Parsonage
Farm

Clavering
Farm

HAMPIT RD

Arkesden

Harcamlow Way

2

Mill
Mound

Chardwell
Farm

PO

Hill
Farm

PH

THE GAP

Scotch
Wood

No Man's
Grove

Westmead
Grove

CLATTERBURY LA

WICKEN RD

POORE ST

1

Knock'emdown
Grove

34

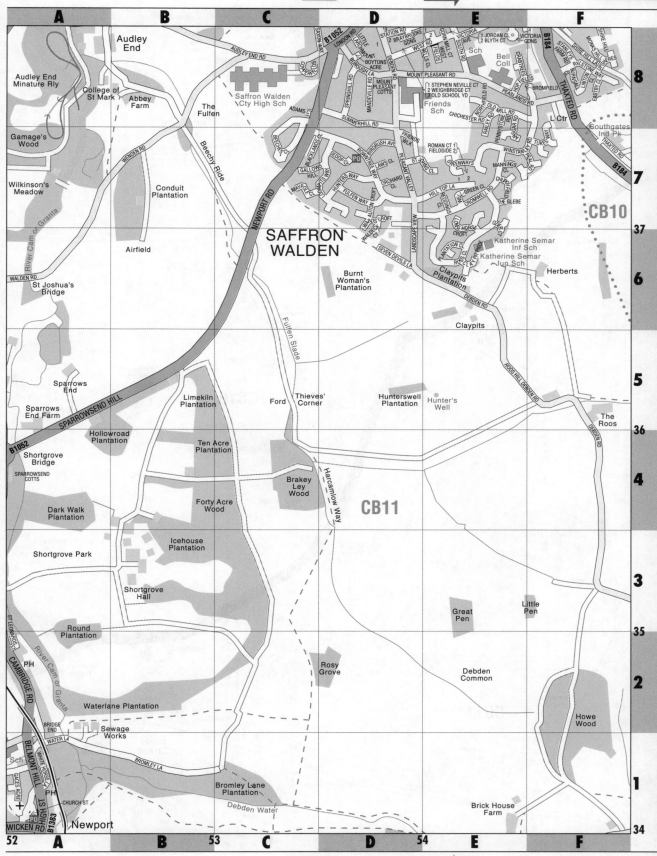

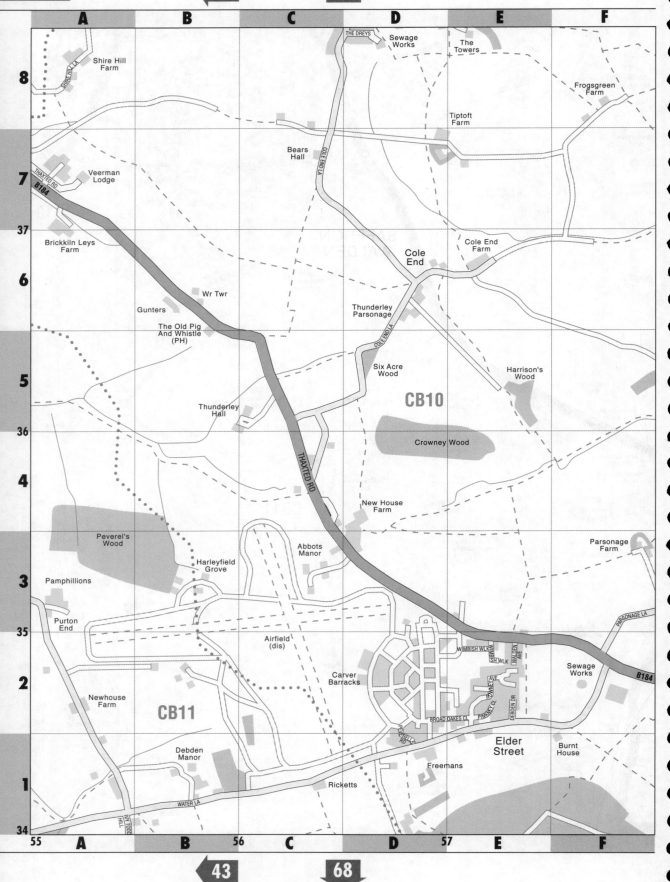

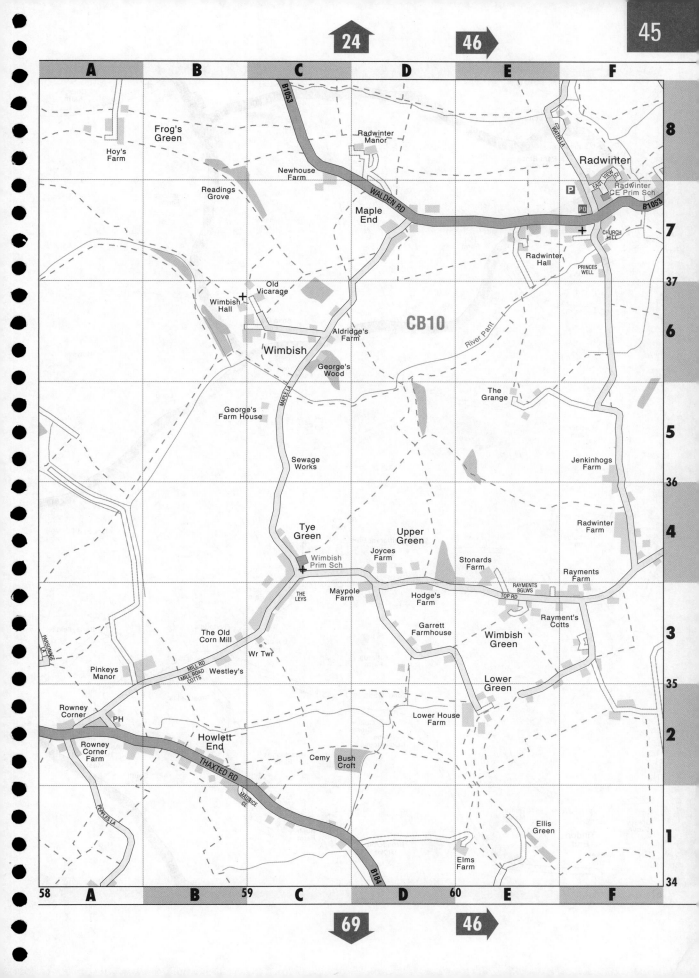

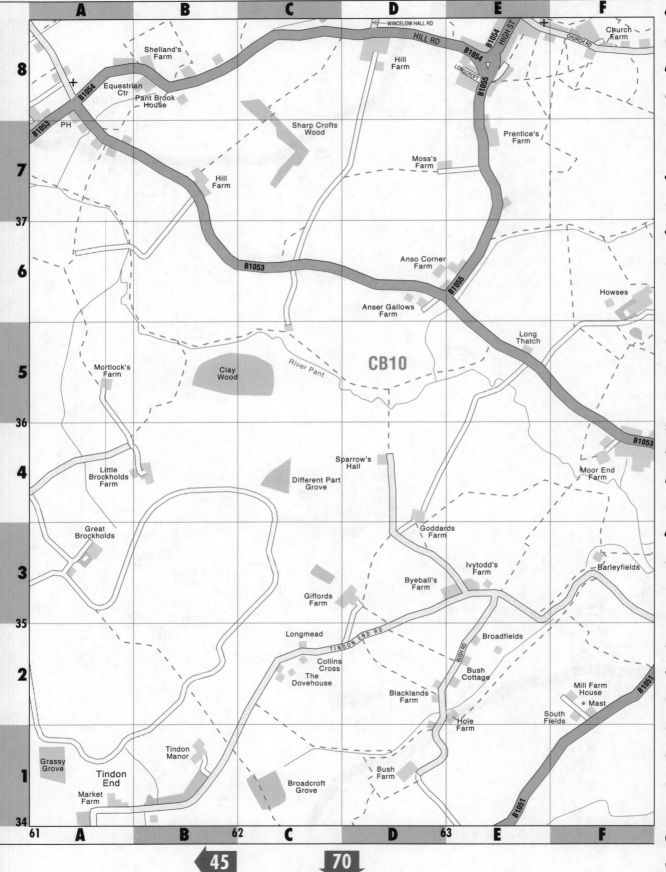

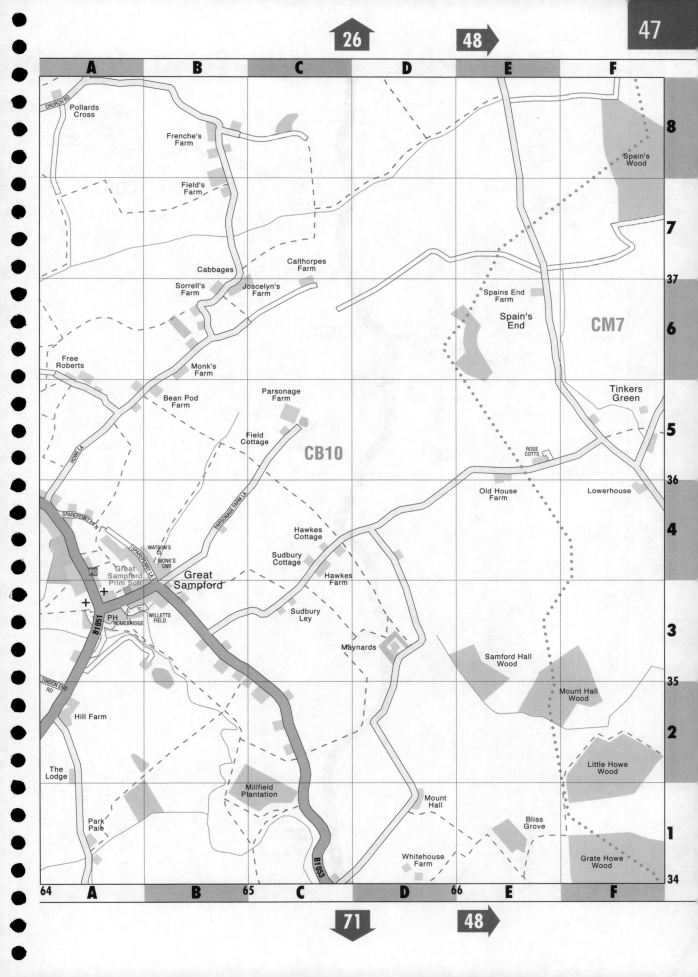

A B C D E F

8

7

37

6

5

36

4

3

35

2

1

34

CO9

Little
Nortons

Old Robin

Great
Nortons

CORNISH HALL END RD

Lopham's
Farm

Rockall's
Farm

Springlette

Sewage
Works

Bushy Grove

Howsey
Wood

Shore
Hall

The Grove

Rivett's Farm

Briar Cottages

White House
Farm

MILLERS
ROW

HEARDS LA

PH

Cornish Hall
End

CM7

Heard's
Farm

Whitleys

HEARDS LA

WHITLEYS
CHASE

Hole Farm

Cornish Hall

Jekyll's Farm

JEKYLLS LA

Unwin's
Farm

New
Cover

Little London

Hobtoe's
Farm

MILL LA

Rook Hall

Yeldhams

Howe
Farm

Obourne's
Farm

Howe
Street

Spainshall
Farm

Spain's
Hall

Bumpstead
Lodge

Tridgate
Ley

B1057

B1057

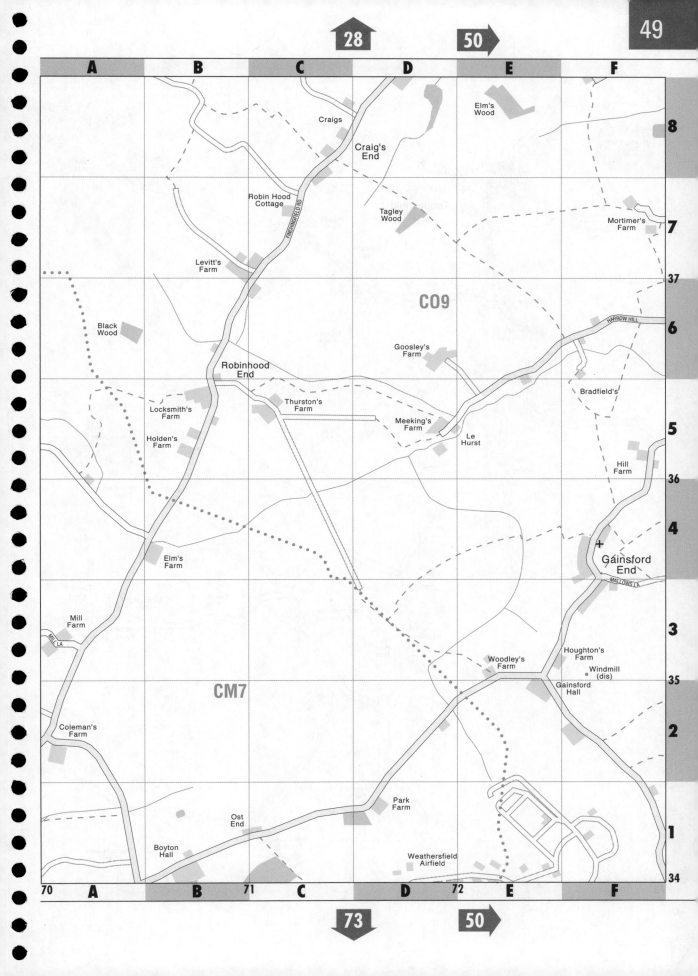

28

50

73

50

A B C D E F

8
7
37
6

CO9

5
36
4

Gainsford
End

3
35
2
1
34

70 A B 71 C D 72 E F

Craigs

Craig's
End

Elm's
Wood

Mortimer's
Farm

FINCHINGFIELD RD

Robin Hood
Cottage

Tagley
Wood

Levitt's
Farm

HARROW HILL

Black
Wood

Goosley's
Farm

Bradfield's

Robinhood
End

Locksmith's
Farm

Thurston's
Farm

Meeking's
Farm

Le
Hurst

Hill
Farm

Holden's
Farm

Elm's
Farm

Mill
Farm

MILL LA

MALLOWS LA

Houghton's
Farm

Woodley's
Farm

Windmill
(dis)

CM7

Gainsford
Hall

Coleman's
Farm

Park
Farm

Ost
End

Boyton
Hall

Weathersfield
Airfield

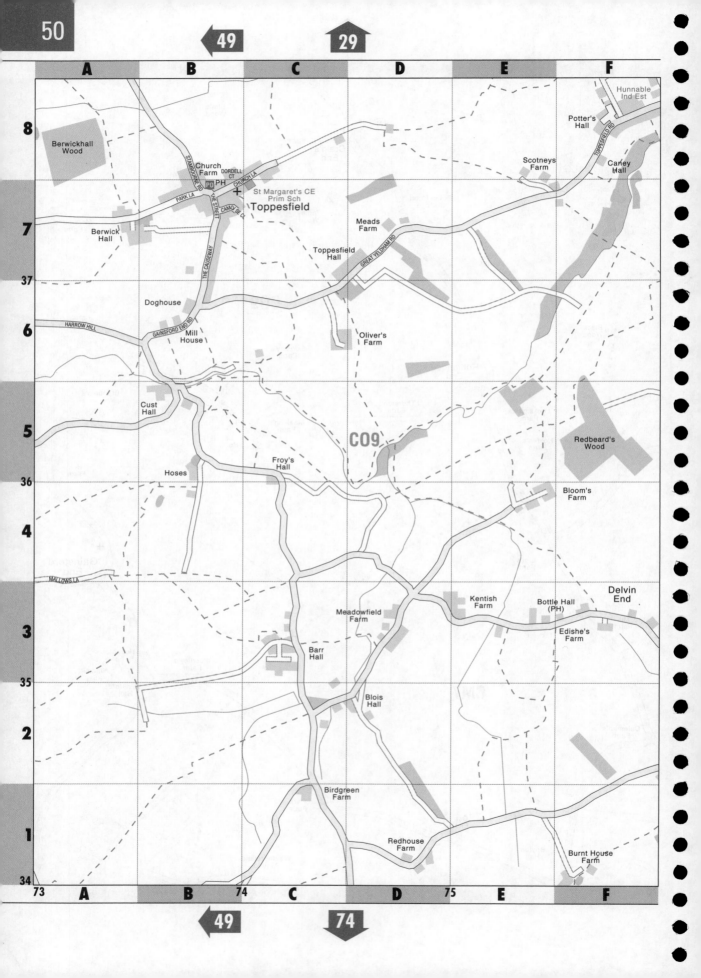

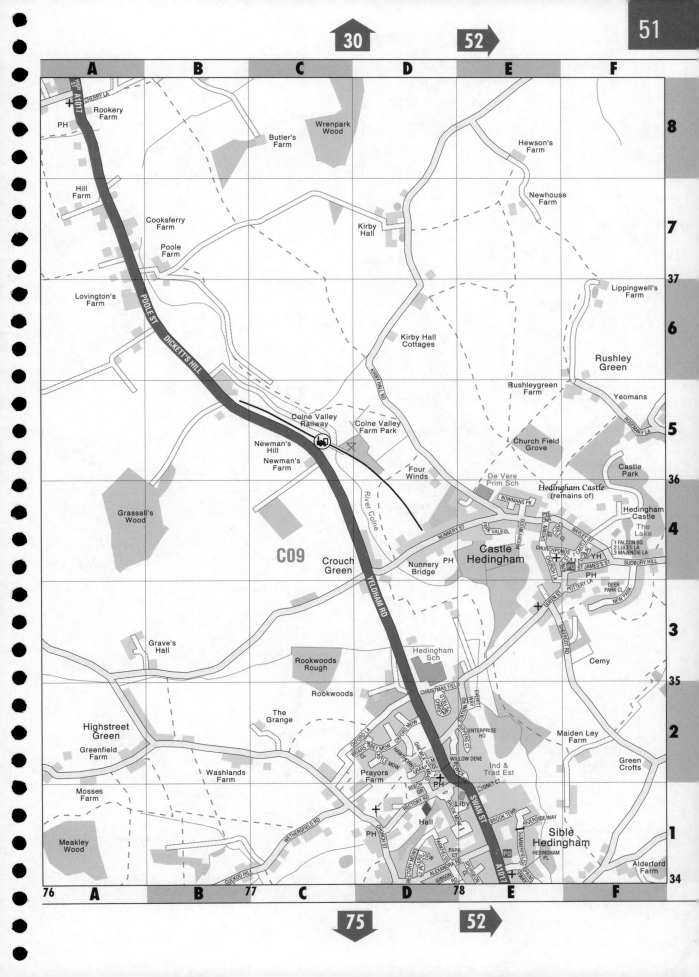

51
31

A B C D E F

8

7

37

6

5

36

4

3

35

2

1

34

79 A B 80 C D 81 E F

51
76

Ridley's Wood

Delvyn's Lane

Delvyn's Farm

Audley End

CHURCH ST

PH

Edeys Farm

Rectory Farm

Parkgate Farm

DELVYN'S LA

Crouch House

Great Lodge Farm

Branwhite's Grove

The Moat

C09

Lawrence's Farm

Pannells Ash Farm

Odewells

Rosemary Farm

ROSEMARY LA

SUDBURY RD

Pantile Cottage

Little Chelmshoe House

Kendallscroft Grove

ST JAMES'S ST

Byham Hall

Little Lodge Farm

New Barn

Chelmshoe House Farm

Monks Lodge Farm

Monks Lodge

MONKS LODGE RD

Hosden's Farm

St Giles CE Prim Sch

ST GILES CL

Link Hills

Hopwell's Farm

STONE COTTS

Great Maplestead

Lucking Street

Luckinghouse Farm

CHURCH ST

Little Lodge Farm

Purls Cottage

Barrett's Hall

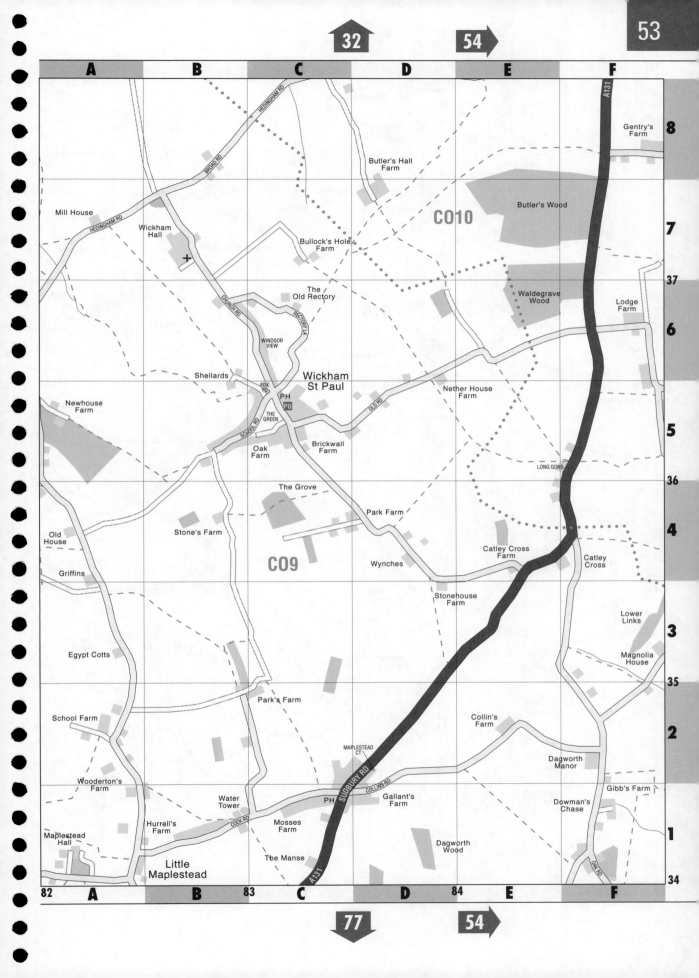

CO10

Gentry's Farm

Butler's Hall Farm

Butler's Wood

Mill House

HEDINGHAM RD

Wickham Hall

BROAD RD

HEDINGHAM RD

Bullock's Hole Farm

Waldegrave Wood

Lodge Farm

CHURCH RD

The Old Rectory

RECTORY LA

WINDSOR VIEW

Shellards

FOX YD

Wickham St Paul

PH
PO

OLD RD

Nether House Farm

Newhouse Farm

SCHOOL RD

THE GREEN

Oak Farm

Brickwall Farm

LONG GDNS

The Grove

Park Farm

Stone's Farm

CO9

Old House

Wynches

Catley Cross Farm

Catley Cross

Griffins

Stonehouse Farm

Lower Links

Egypt Cotts

Magnolia House

Park's Farm

School Farm

Collin's Farm

Dagworth Manor

MAPLESTEAD CT

SUDBURY RD

COLLINS RD

Gibb's Farm

Wooderton's Farm

Water Tower

COCK RD

PH

Gallant's Farm

Dowman's Chase

OAK RD

Hurrell's Farm

Mosses Farm

Dagworth Wood

Maplestead Hall

The Manse

A131

Little Maplestead

8
7
37
6
5
36
4
35
3
2
1
34

A B C D E F

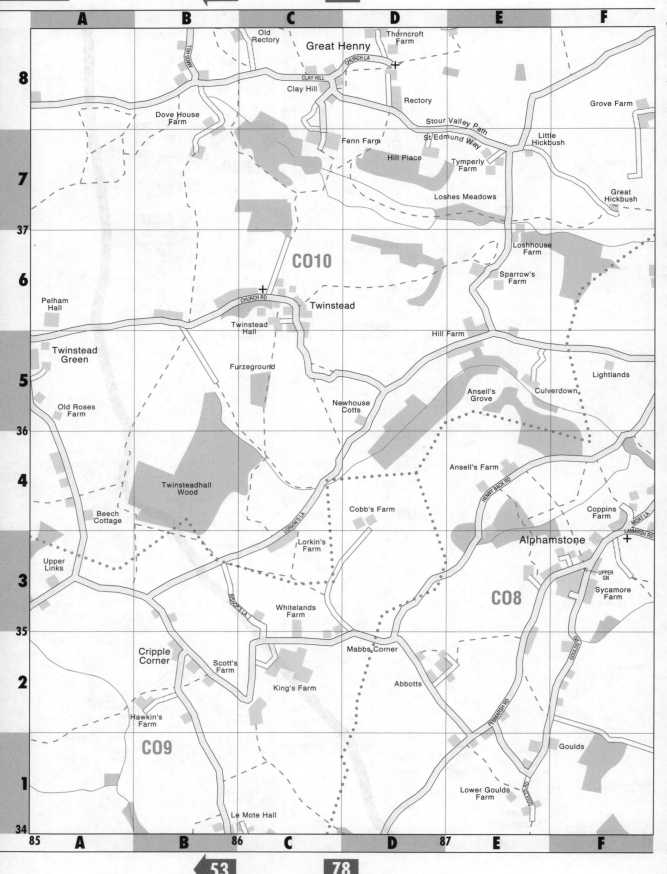

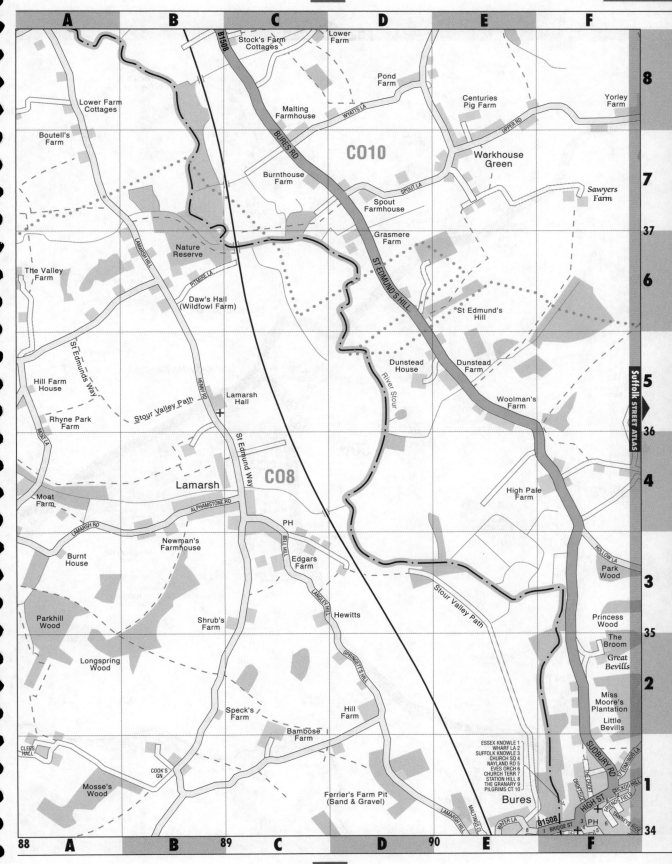

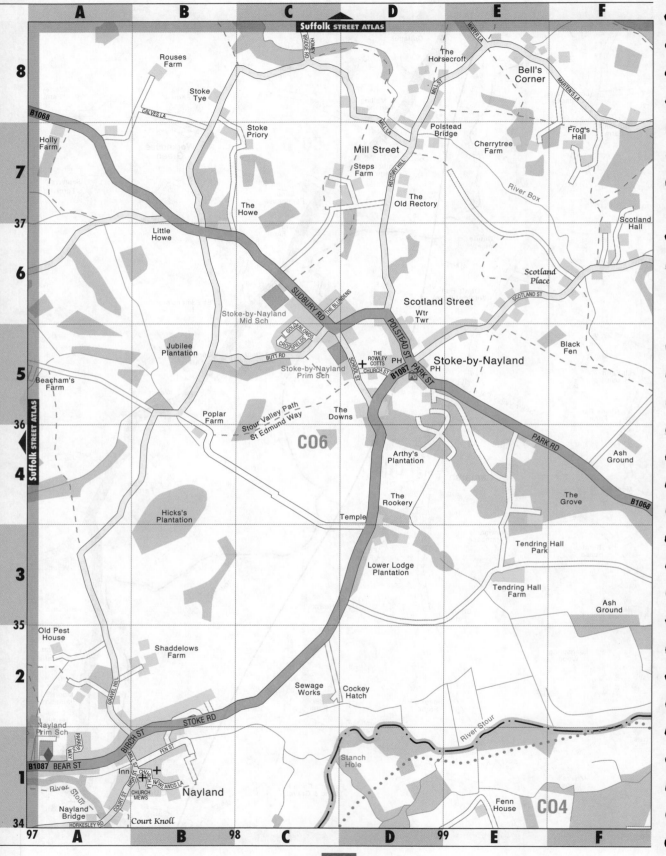

A   B   C   D   E   F

8

7

37

6

5

36

4

3

35

2

1

34

97   A   98   B   C   D   99   E   F

B1068

Holly Farm

Rouses Farm

Stoke Tye

CALVES LA

Stoke Priory

The Howe

Little Howe

Stoke-by-Nayland Mid Sch

SUDBURY RD

THE BLUNDENS

GOLDCROWDS
CROSSFIELDS

BUTT RD

Jubilee Plantation

Beacham's Farm

Poplar Farm

Stour Valley Path
St Edmund Way

Stoke-by-Nayland Prim Sch

SCHOOL ST

THE ROWLEY COTTS

CHURCH ST

B1087

PH

POLSTEAD ST

PARK ST

PO

PH

Stoke-by-Nayland

The Downs

CO6

Arthy's Plantation

The Rookery

PARK RD

The Grove

B1068

Ash Ground

Hicks's Plantation

Temple

Lower Lodge Plantation

Tendring Hall Park

Tendring Hall Farm

Ash Ground

Old Pest House

Shaddelows Farm

GRAVEL HILL

Sewage Works

Cockey Hatch

River Stour

Stanch Hole

BIRCH ST

STOKE RD

FEN ST

Nayland Prim Sch

PARKERS WAY

B1087 BEAR ST

Inn

HIGH ST

COURT ST

CHURCH MEWS

CH LA

NEWLANDS LA

Nayland

River Stour

Nayland Bridge

HORKESLEY RD

Court Knoll

Fenn House

CO4

Suffolk STREET ATLAS

Suffolk STREET ATLAS

HONEY BRIDGE RD

WATER LA

MILL ST

The Horsecroft

Bell's Corner

MARTEN'S LA

Frog's Hall

MILL LA

Polstead Bridge

Cherrytree Farm

River Box

Scotland Hall

Mill Street

RECTORY HILL

Steps Farm

The Old Rectory

Scotland Place

SCOTLAND ST

Scotland Street

Wtr Twr

Black Fen

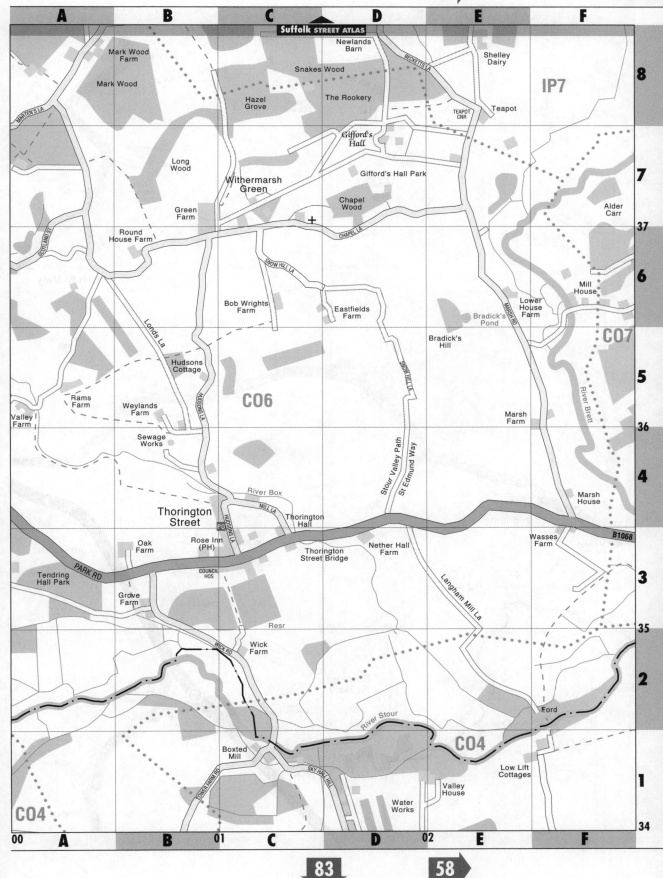

Suffolk STREET ATLAS

IP7

Mark Wood Farm

Mark Wood

Newlands Barn

Snakes Wood

Hazel Grove

The Rookery

Shelley Dairy

BECKETTS LA

TEAPOT CNR

Teapot

Gifford's Hall

Long Wood

Gifford's Hall Park

Withermarsh Green

Green Farm

Chapel Wood

CHAPEL LA

Alder Carr

Round House Farm

SNOW HILL LA

Mill House

CO7

Bob Wrights Farm

Eastfields Farm

Bradick's Pond

Lower House Farm

MASSEY RD

Bradick's Hill

River Brett

Londs La

Hudsons Cottage

CO6

Rams Farm

Weylands Farm

HUDSONS LA

Marsh Farm

Valley Farm

Sewage Works

Marsh House

St Edmund Way

Stour Valley Path

River Box

MILL LA

Thorington Street

Thorington Hall

HUDSONS LA

B1068

Wasses Farm

Oak Farm

Rose Inn (PH)

Thorington Street Bridge

Nether Hall Farm

Langham Mill La

Tendring Hall Park

PARK RD

COUNCIL HOS

Grove Farm

Resr

Ford

WICK RD

Wick Farm

River Stour

CO4

Boxted Mill

LOWER FARM RD

SKY HALL HILL

Water Works

Valley House

Low Lift Cottages

CO4

MARTEN'S LA

SCOTLAND ST

37

8

7

6

5

36

4

35

3

2

34

1

00 A   B   01   C   D   02   E   F

Suffolk STREET ATLAS

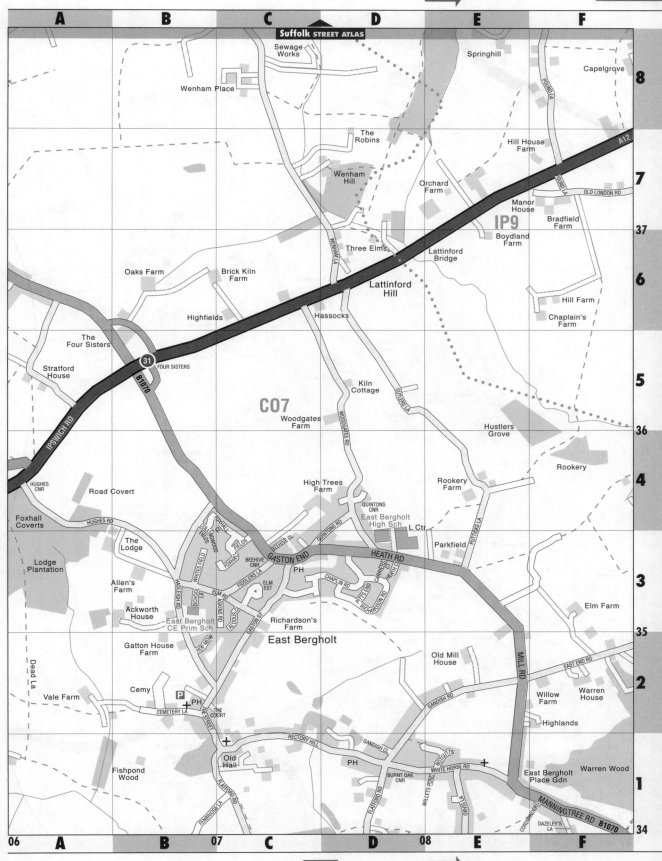

Suffolk STREET ATLAS

A | B | C | D | E | F

8

Sewage Works

Springhill

Capelgrove

Wenham Place

The Robins

Hill House Farm

A12

7

Wenham Hill

Orchard Farm

Manor House

Bradfield Farm

37

IP9

WENHAM LA

Three Elms

Lattinford Bridge

Boydland Farm

6

Oaks Farm

Brick Kiln Farm

Lattinford Hill

Hill Farm

Highfields

Hassocks

Chaplain's Farm

The Four Sisters

Kiln Cottage

Hustlers Grove

5

Stratford House

31 FOUR SISTERS

B1070

CO7

Woodgates Farm

WOODGATES RD

CUTLERS LA

36

Rookery

IPSWICH RD

HUGHES CNR

Road Covert

High Trees Farm

Rookery Farm

4

Foxhall Coverts

HUGHES RD

QUINTONS CNR

East Bergholt High Sch

L Ctr

PUTTOCKS LA

The Lodge

FOXHALL

COLLINGWOOD

FOXHALL FIELDS

BEEHIVE GA.

QUINTONS RD

Parkfield

Lodge Plantation

WHITES FIELD

BEEHIVE CNR

GASTON END

HEATH RD

Allen's Farm

HADLEIGH LA

SCHOOL RD

FIDDLERS LA

ELM EST

PH

CHAPLIN RD

PITTS END

CARRIERS CT

HEATH CT

3

Ackworth House

ELM RD

ALDOUS CL

GASTON ST

RICHARDSON RD

Elm Farm

East Bergholt CE Prim Sch

Richardson's Farm

35

Gatton House Farm

HOP MDW

East Bergholt

Old Mill House

EAST END RD

2

Cemy

P PH

GANDISH RD

Willow Farm

Warren House

Dead La

CEMETERY LA

THE STREET

THE COURT

MILL RD

Highlands

Vale Farm

RECTORY HILL

GANDISH CL

1

Fishpond Wood

Old Hall

PH

BURNT OAK CNR

WHITE HORSE RD

NOTCUTTS

East Bergholt Place Gdn

Warren Wood

FLATFORD RD

FLATFORD RD

WILLETS POND

ORVIS LA

CORDWINDERS

MANNINGTREE RD B1070

DAZELEY'S LA

34

FEMBRIDGE LA

06 | A | B | 07 | C | D | 08 | E | F

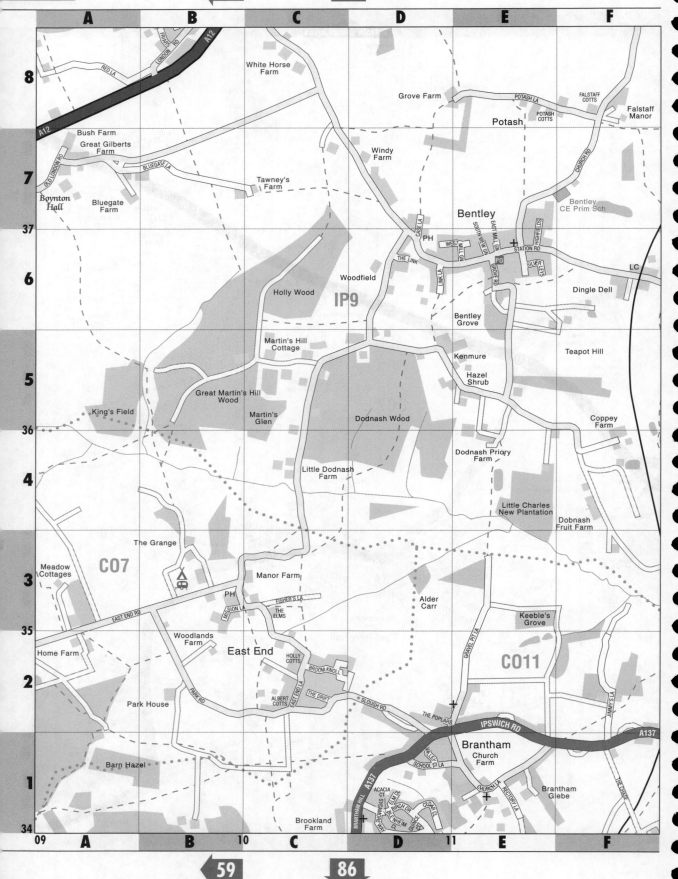

8

7

37

6

5

36

4

3

35

2

1

34

A12
RED LA
FINCHES RD
LONDON RD
White Horse Farm
Grove Farm
POTASH LA
FALSTAFF COTTS
Falstaff Manor
Potash
POTASH COTTS
Bush Farm
Great Gilberts Farm
OLD LONDON RD
BLUEGATE LA
Windy Farm
Bentley
Bentley CE Prim Sch
Boynton Hall
Bluegate Farm
Tawney's Farm
CHURCH RD
CASE LA
EAST MILL GN
PH
SOUTH VIEW GN
WEST MILL GN
GROVE RD
STATION RD
HIGHFIELDS
PO
SILVER LEYS
LC
THE LINK
LINK LA
Woodfield
IP9
Holly Wood
Dingle Dell
Bentley Grove
Martin's Hill Cottage
Kenmure
Teapot Hill
Hazel Shrub
Great Martin's Hill Wood
Martin's Glen
Dodnash Wood
Coppey Farm
King's Field
Little Dodnash Farm
Dodnash Priory Farm
Little Charles New Plantation
Dobnash Fruit Farm
The Grange
CO7
Meadow Cottages
Manor Farm
Alder Carr
Keeble's Grove
PH
FISHER'S LA
MISSION LA
THE ELMS
CO11
EAST END RD
GRAVEL PIT LA
Woodlands Farm
East End
HOLLY COTTS
BROOM KNOLL
PARK RD
Home Farm
ALBERT COTTS
EAST END LA
THE DRIFT
SLOUGH RD
THE POPLARS
IPSWICH RD
A137
Park House
Brantham Church Farm
Barn Hazel
VALLEY RD
SCHOOL LA
CHURCH LA
RECTORY LA
Brantham Glebe
THE CHASE
BRANTHAM HILL
A137
ACACIA CT
SYCAMORE WAY
ELM CL
BIRCH DR
QUINCE
CEDAR CL
NHEIM CL
JIMMY'S LA
Brookland Farm

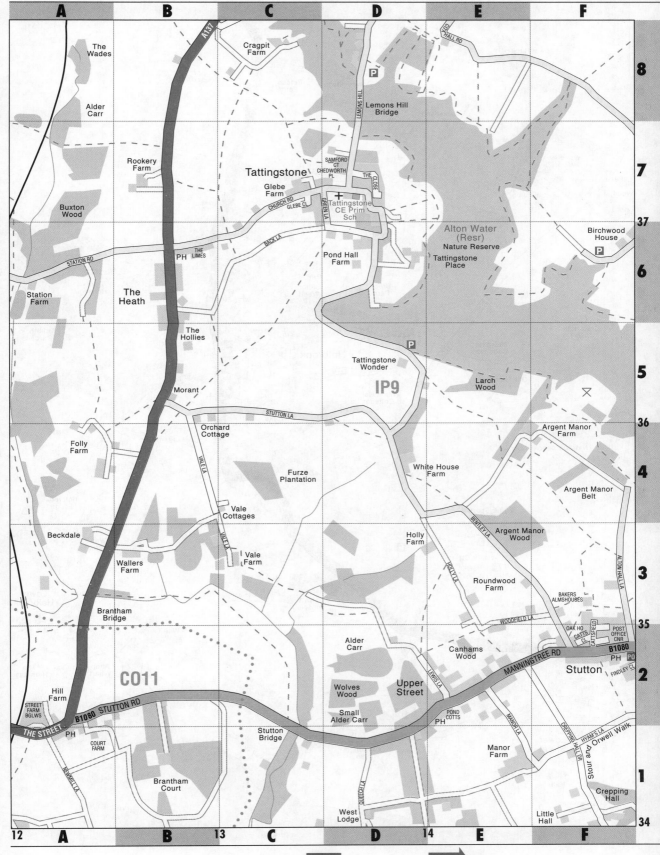

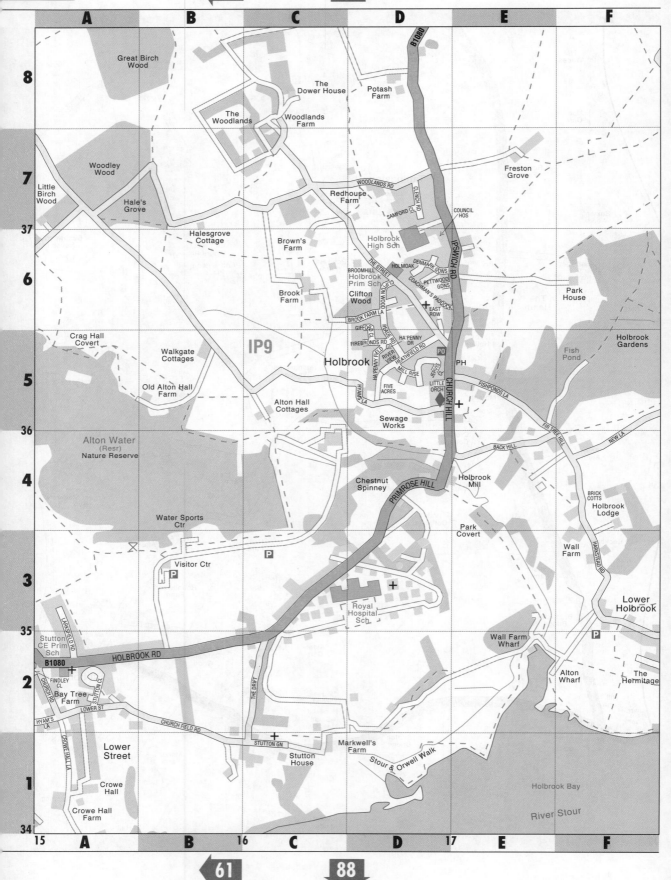

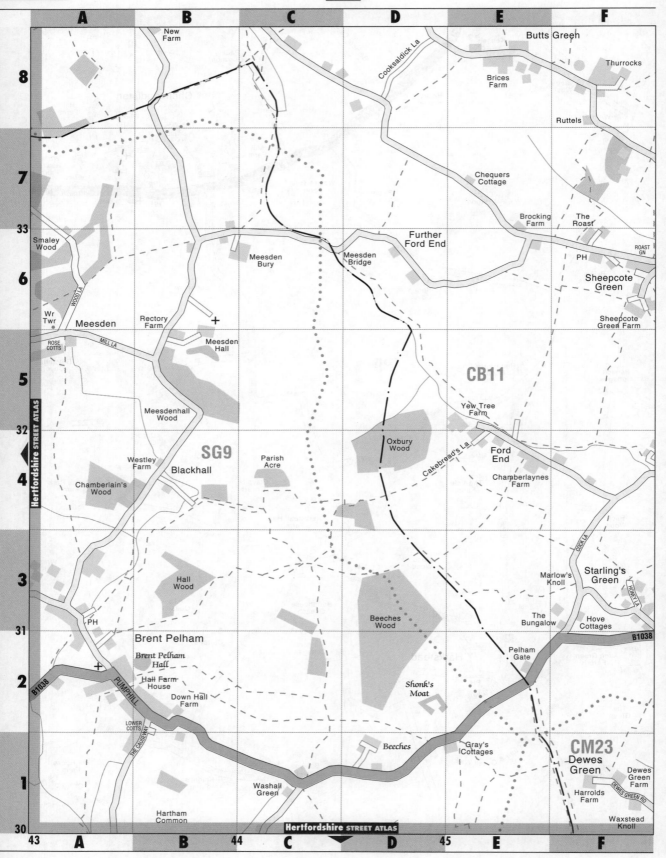

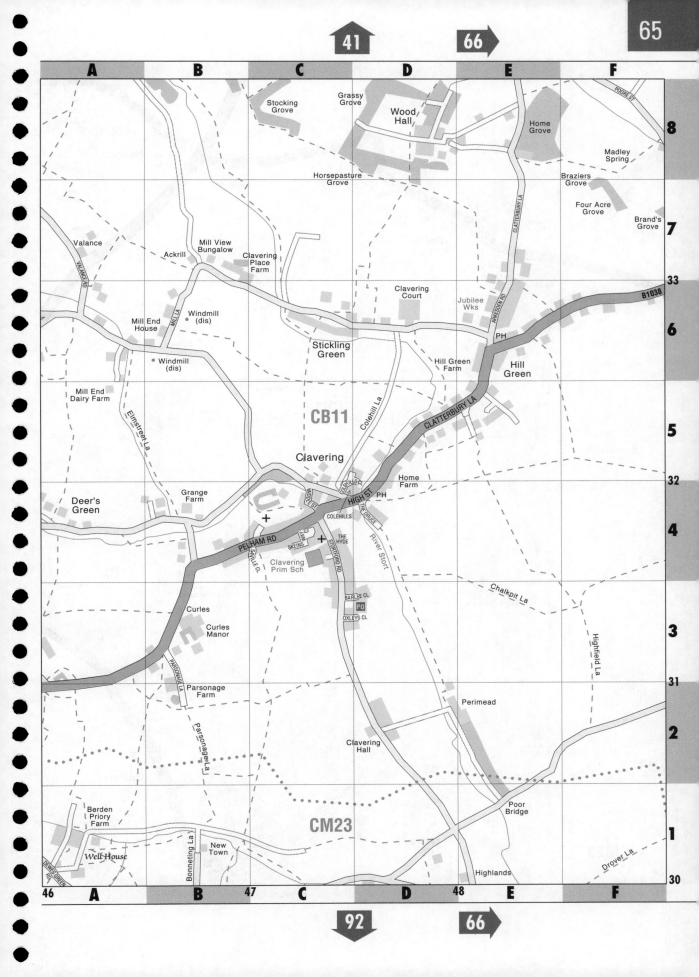

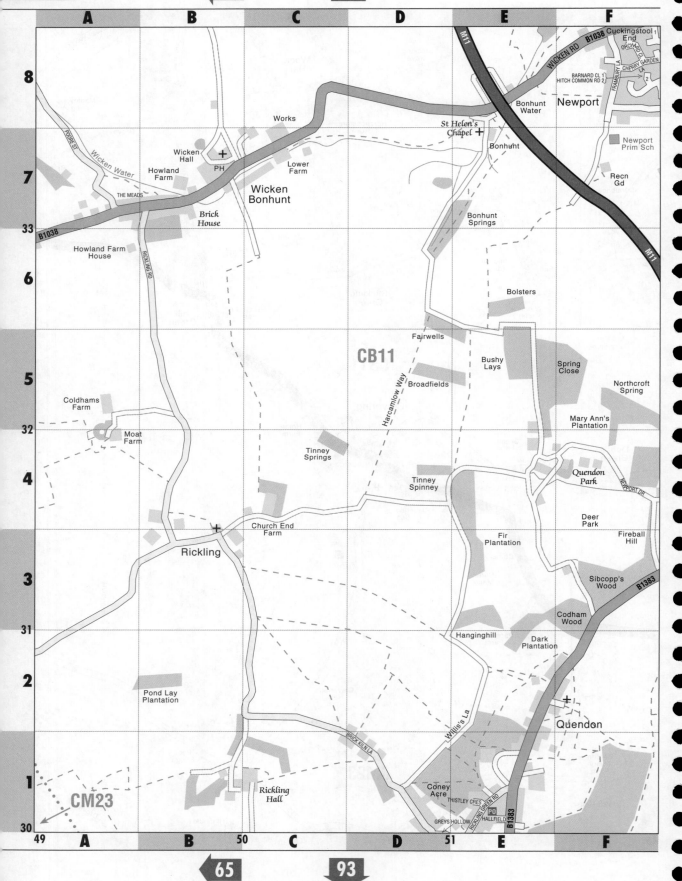

38

65
42

A B C D E F

8

65 B1038 Cuckingstool End
ORCHARD CL
CHERRY GARDEN LA
FRANBURY LA
BARNARD CL 1
HITCH COMMON RD 2
Newport
Newport Prim Sch

Wicken Rd
M11
Bonhunt Water

7

POORE ST
Wicken Water
Howland Farm
Wicken Hall
PH
Works
Lower Farm
St Helen's Chapel
Bonhunt
Recn Gd

THE MEADS
Wicken Bonhunt

33
B1038
Brick House
Bonhunt Springs

Howland Farm House
RICKLING RD

6

Bolsters

CB11
Fairwells
Bushy Lays
Spring Close
Northcroft Spring

5

Coldhams Farm
Harcamlow Way
Broadfields
Mary Ann's Plantation

32
Moat Farm
Tinney Springs
Quendon Park
NEWPORT DR

4
Tinney Spinney
Deer Park
Fireball Hill

Church End Farm
Fir Plantation
Sibcopp's Wood
B1383

Rickling
Codham Wood

3

31
Hanginghill
Dark Plantation

2
Pond Lay Plantation
Willis's La
Quendon

BRICK KILN LA

1
Rickling Hall
Coney Acre
THISTLEY CRES
RICKLING GREEN RD
PO
HALLFIELD
B1383

CM23
GREYS HOLLOW

30
49 A B 50 C D 51 E F

65
93

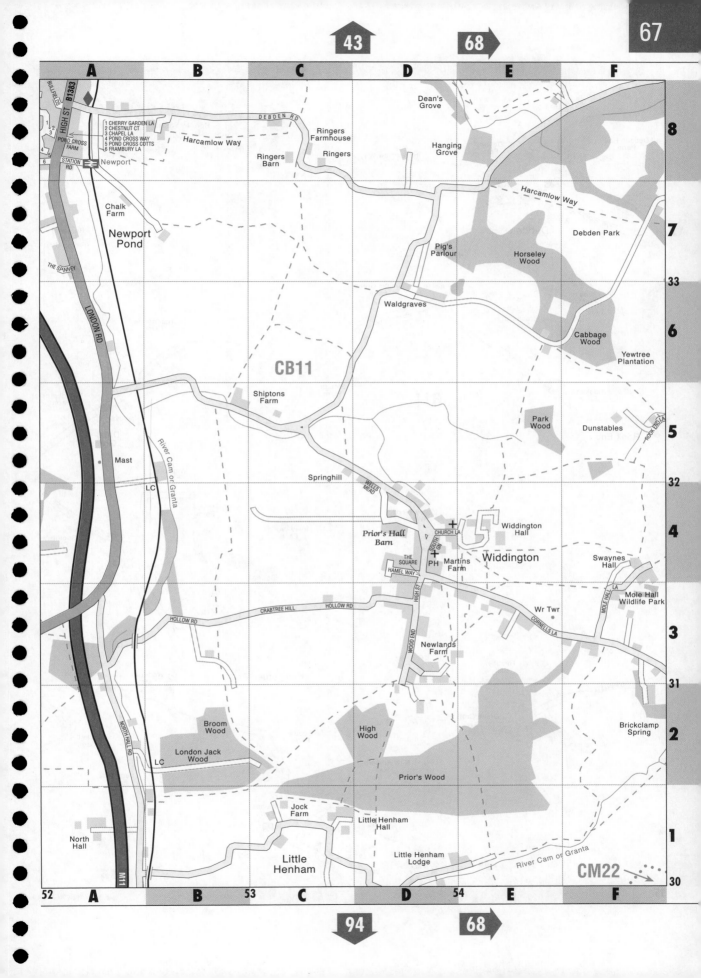

43
68
94
68

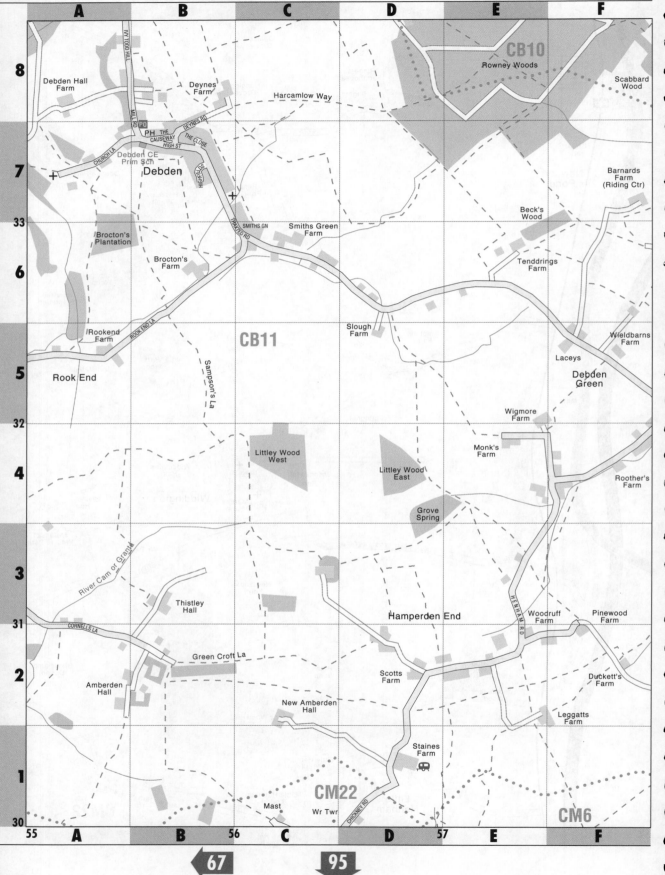

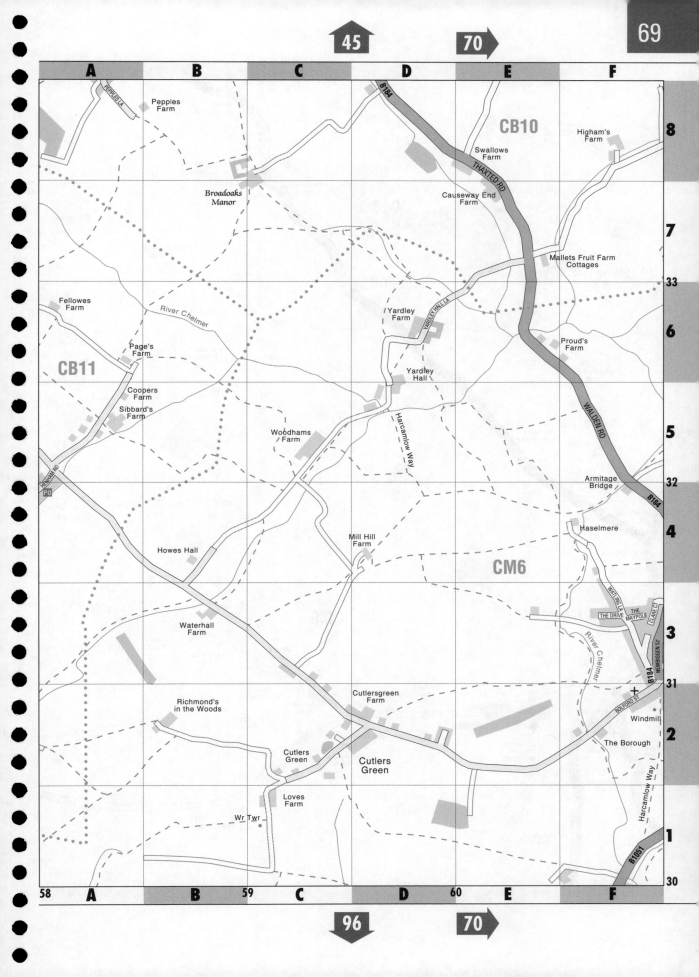

45

70

A B C D E F

B184

CB10

8

Pepples La

Pepples Farm

Higham's Farm

Swallows Farm

Broadoaks Manor

Causeway End Farm

THAXTED RD

7

33

Fellowes Farm

River Chelmer

Yardley Farm

YARDLEY HALL LA

Mallets Fruit Farm Cottages

Proud's Farm

6

CB11

Page's Farm

Yardley Hall

WALDEN RD

Coopers Farm

Harcamlow Way

5

Sibbard's Farm

Woodhams Farm

HEDHAM RD

PO

Armitage Bridge

32

B184

Haselmere

4

Howes Hall

Mill Hill Farm

CM6

WATLING LA

THE DRIVE

THE MAYPOLE

CLARE CT

3

Waterhall Farm

River Chelmer

NEWBIGGEN ST

B184

31

Richmond's in the Woods

Cutlersgreen Farm

BOLFORD ST

Windmill

Cutlers Green

Cutlers Green

The Borough

2

Loves Farm

Harcamlow Way

Wr Twr

1

B1051

58 A B 59 C D 60 E F 30

96

70

69
46

A B C D E F

8

Friar's Farm

CB10

7

Bow Croft Wood

West Wood

Howlett's Farm

Road Farm

Little Clark's Cottage

Tewes Plantation

33

Coppins

Sprigg's Farm

Flemings Farm

6

Tilehall Farm

Great Clark's Farm

Millhall Farm

Goddard's Farm

Terrier's Farm

Golden's Farm

Boyton End

5

Sorrell's Farm House

Highgates

32

Reedscap

B184

B1051

4

WALDEN RD

Hotel

A3
1 VICARAGE MEAD
2 BELL LA
3 VICARAGE MEAD BGLWS

Thaxted

CM6

NEWBIGGAN ST
ROCHELLE CL
CL PH
THE MEAD
WEATHERHEAD CL
WEAV
CL
3

3

VICARAGE LA
WEATHERHEAD LA
HANCHETS DRIVE
NEWSOM RD
BROOK VIEW
COPHALL LA
ORCHARDS

Millars Farm

Hardings Farm

Blunt's Farm

P
THE LEES
31
MARGARET LA

B184

WATLING LA
STONY LA
ST CLEM
GRANGE ST
THE TANYARD

MAGDALEN CL
FIELD
SORHRWS

Hunt's Farm

Freeman's Farm

Bluegate Farm

Black La

FISHMARKET ST
TOWN ST
PO
PH
Thaxted Prim Sch

WAINSFIELD VILLAS

Levetts Farm

BARDFIELD END VILLAS

Liby

MILL END

CLAYPITS VILLAS

Bardfield End Green

BARDFIELD RD

2

Park Farm

PARK ST
STAR MEAD
THE CHASE
THE MALTINGS

Claypitts Farm Buildings

Holly Oak Farm

DUNMOW RD

Totman's Farm

Piggots

North View
The Lodge

1

B1051

Prior's Hall

30

61 A B 62 C D 63 E F

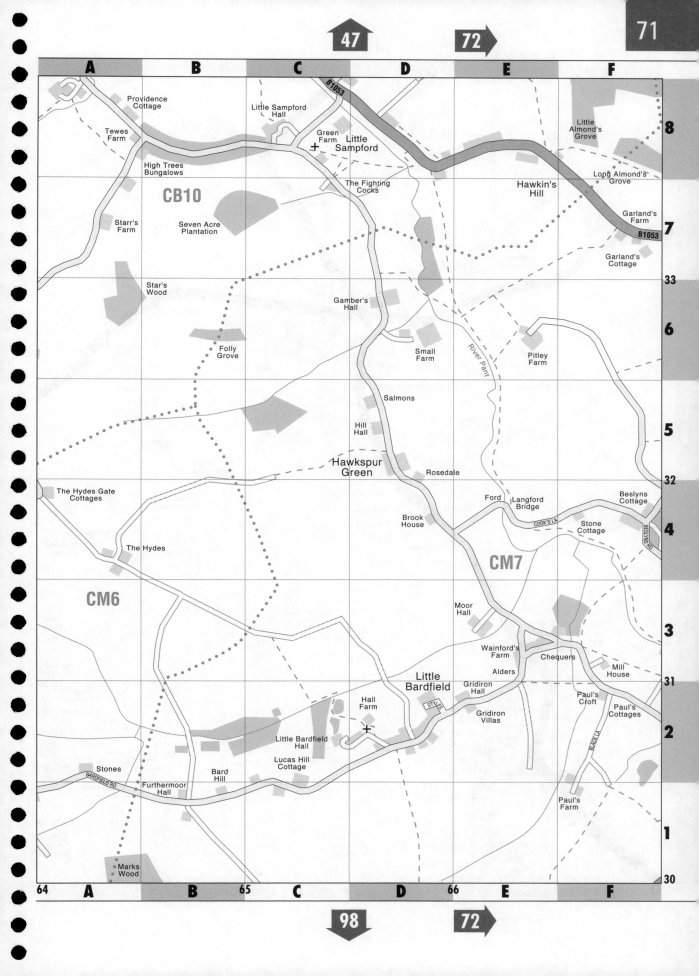

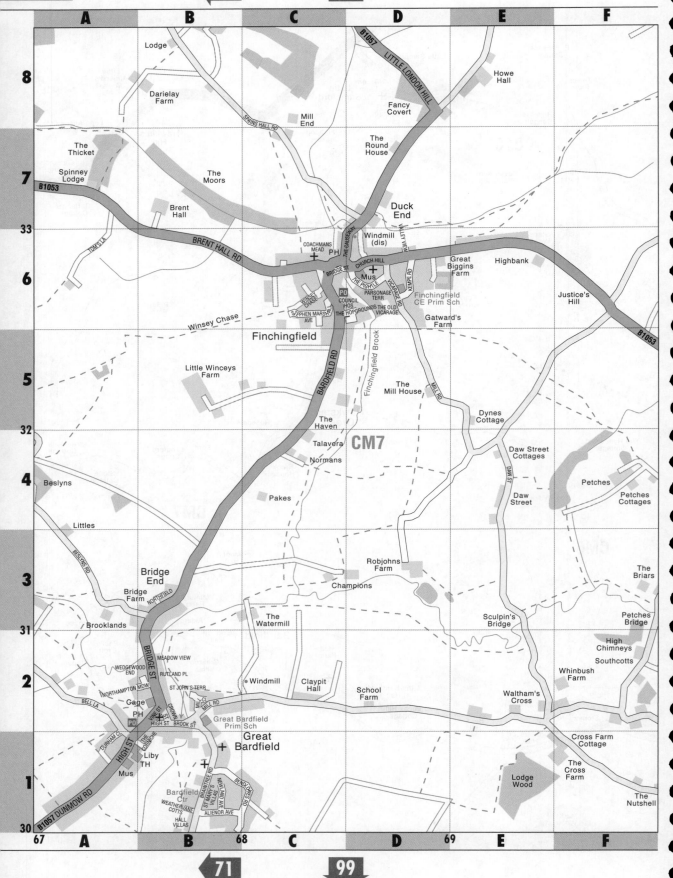

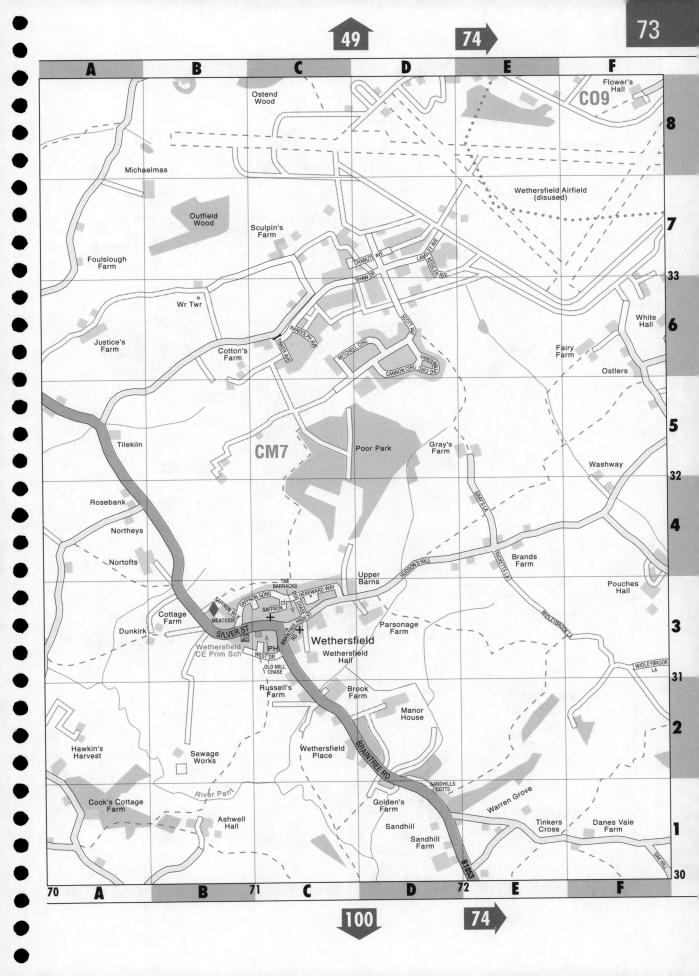

73 50

A B C D E F

8
Wethersfield Airfield
Welcome Slough Farm
Tattersall's Farm
Morris Green
Finch's Farm
Burnt House Farm

7
Deek's Farm
Almshouse Green
Moss Farm
SUGAR LA
Sugar Lane Farm
Barnard's Farm

33

6
Whitehall Farm
Thorley Grove
Upper Wright's Farm
Oak House
Runalong Farm
C09
Runalong Wood

Thorley's Farm
Tredgell's Wood
Cherrytree Farm

5
New Barns
Littley Wood

32

4
Brickkiln Green
CM7

Lower Green
Readings
Patten's Wood
Patten's Farm
Hawks Wood

3
School Green
Lower Green
Lealands
The Readings Spinney

Elms Farm
PH

31
Blackmore End
SYERS FIELD
New Plantation
Baker's Farm

2
Owl's Hall
HYDE LA
SCHOOL RD

Shragg's Wood

1
Hyde Farm
HYDE LA
Summer's Hall
FOUR ASHES
Waver's Farm

Shinborough

30

WIDLEYBROOK LA

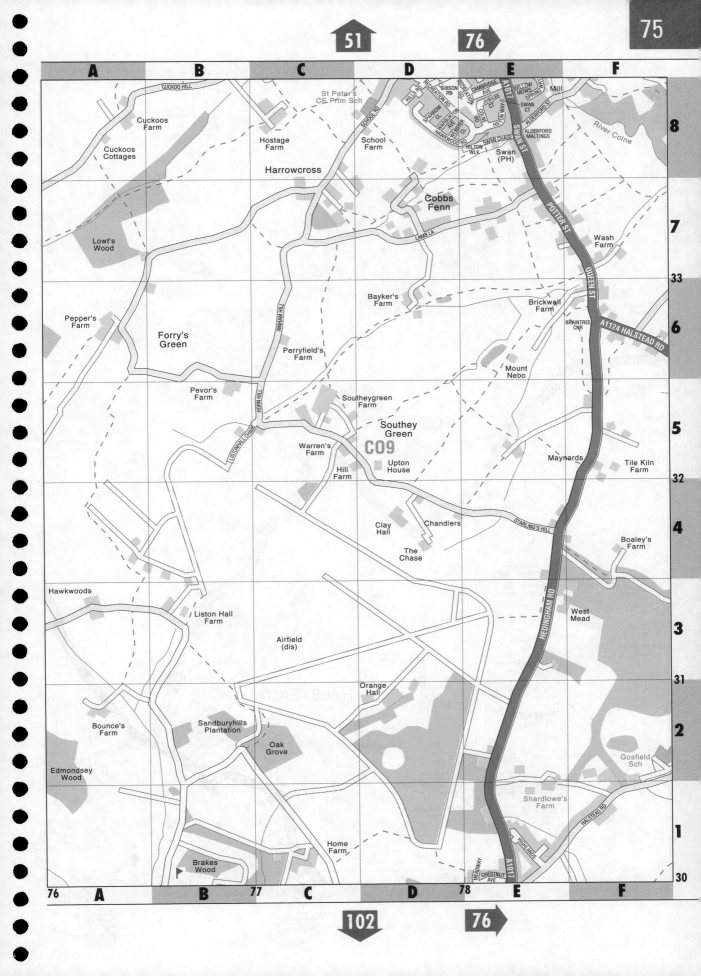

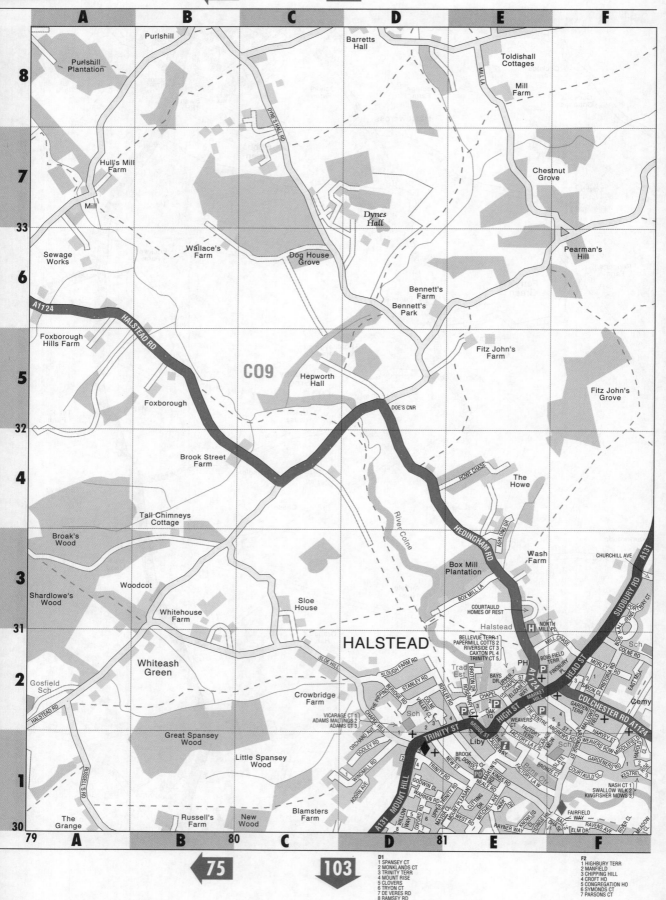

8

7

33

6

5

32

4

3

31

2

1

30

A B C D E F

Purlshill

Purlshill
Plantation

Barretts
Hall

Toldishall
Cottages

Mill
Farm

DYNE'S HALL RD

Hull's Mill
Farm

Chestnut
Grove

Mill

Dynes
Hall

Sewage
Works

Wallace's
Farm

Dog House
Grove

Pearman's
Hill

A1124

Bennett's
Farm

Bennett's
Park

HALSTEAD RD

Foxborough
Hills Farm

CO9

Fitz John's
Farm

Foxborough

Hepworth
Hall

DOE'S CNR

Fitz John's
Grove

Brook Street
Farm

HOWE CHASE

The
Howe

Tall Chimneys
Cottage

Broak's
Wood

River Colne

HEDINGHAM RD

ASHLONG GR

Wash
Farm

CHURCHILL AVE

A131

SUDBURY RD

Shardlowe's
Wood

Woodcot

Box Mill
Plantation

BOX MILL LA

Sch

Whitehouse
Farm

Sloe
House

COURTAULD
HOMES OF REST

Halstead

NORTH
MILL PL

H

HEAD ST

Gosfield
Sch

Whiteash
Green

SLOE HILL

HALSTEAD

SLOUGH FARM RD

Trad
Est

BELLEVUE TERR 1
PAPERMILL COTTS 2
RIVERSIDE CT 3
CAXTON PL 4
TRINITY CT 5

PH

BOIS FIELD
TERR

FINSBURY
PL

MILL CHASE

Sch

COLNE RD

HALSTEAD RD

Crowbridge
Farm

STANLEY RD

BUTLER RD

A1124

HIGH ST

P

COLCHESTER RD A1124

Cemy

VICARAGE CT 1
ADAMS MALTINGS 2
ADAMS CT 3

ORCHARD AVE

Sch

TRINITY ST

Liby

i

Great Spansey
Wood

RUSSELL'S RD

Little Spansey
Wood

MOUNT HILL

A131

Blamsters
Farm

Bens Ct

PO

FACTORY LA

FAIRFIELD
WAY

NASH CT 1
SWALLOW WLK 2
KINGFISHER MDWS 3

The
Grange

Russell's
Farm

New
Wood

79 A 80 B C 81 D E F

D1
1 SPANSEY CT
2 MONKLANDS CT
3 TRINITY TERR
4 MOUNT RISE
5 CLOVERS
6 TRYON CT
7 DE VERES RD
8 RAMSEY RD

F2
1 HIGHBURY TERR
2 MANFIELD
3 CHIPPING HILL
4 CROFT HO
5 CONGREGATION HO
6 SYMONDS CT
7 PARSONS CT

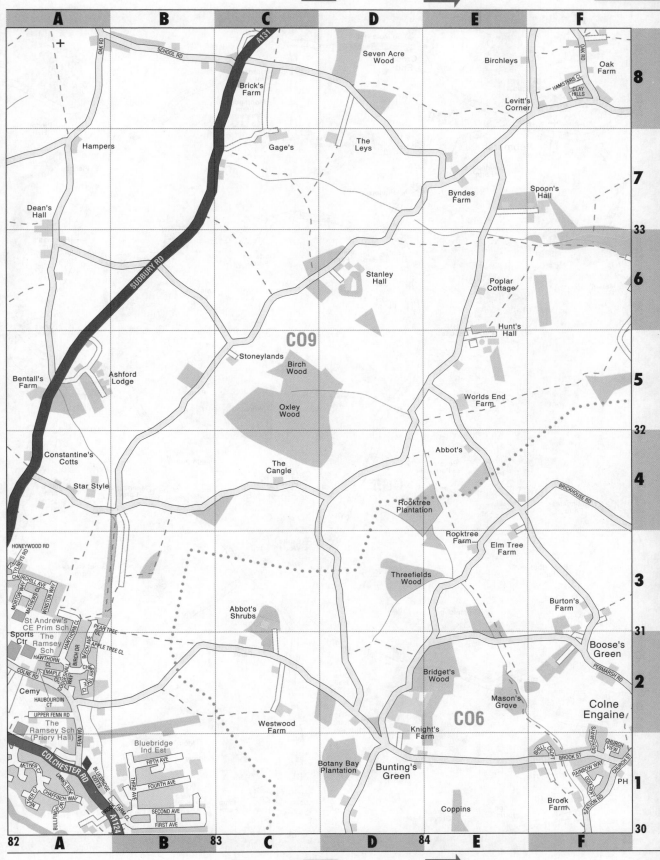

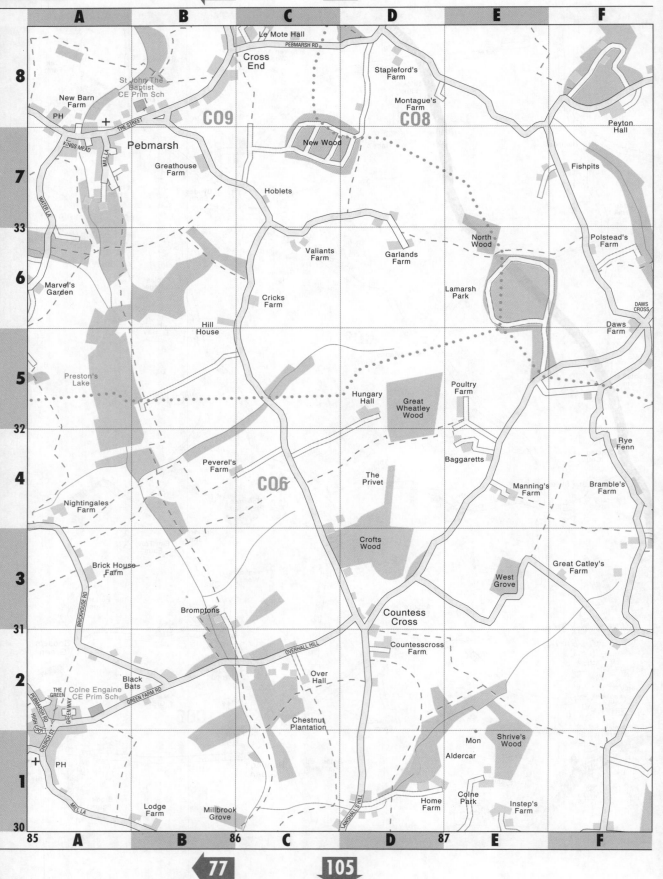

A B C D E F

8

CO9

7

33

6

5

32

4

CO6

3

31

2

1

30

85 **A** 86 **B** **C** 87 **D** **E** **F**

Le Mote Hall
Cross End
PEBMARSH RD
Stapleford's Farm
Montague's Farm
CO8
St John The Baptist CE Prim Sch
New Barn Farm
PH
THE STREET
Pebmarsh
KINGS MEAD
MILL LA
Greathouse Farm
New Wood
Peyton Hall
Fishpits
Hoblets
WATER LA
Valiants Farm
Garlands Farm
North Wood
Polstead's Farm
Marvel's Garden
Cricks Farm
Lamarsh Park
DAWS CROSS
Hill House
Daws Farm
Preston's Lake
Hungary Hall
Great Wheatley Wood
Poultry Farm
Rye Fenn
Peverel's Farm
Baggaretts
The Privet
Manning's Farm
Bramble's Farm
Nightingales Farm
Crofts Wood
Brick House Farm
West Grove
Great Catley's Farm
Bromptons
Countess Cross
OVERHALL HILL
Countesscross Farm
BRICKHOUSE RD
Black Bats
THE GREEN
Colne Engaine CE Prim Sch
GREEN WAY
GREEN FARM RD
Over Hall
PEBMARSH RD
HIGH ST
CHURCH ST
Chestnut Plantation
Mon
Shrive's Wood
Aldercar
PH
MILL LA
Lodge Farm
Millbrook Grove
LAMARSH HILL
Home Farm
Colne Park
Instep's Farm

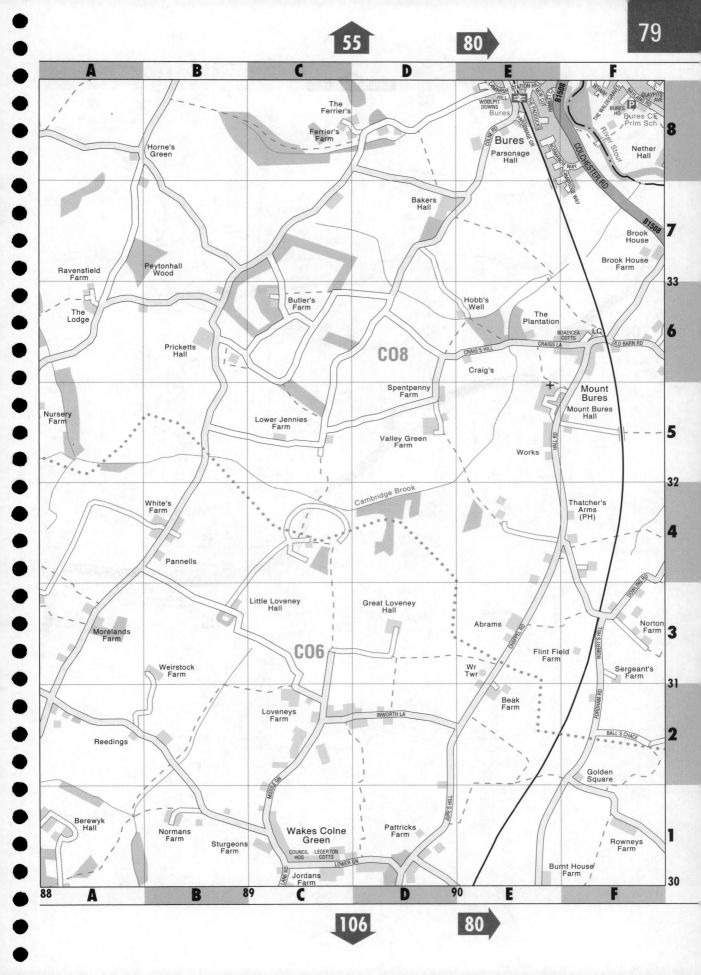

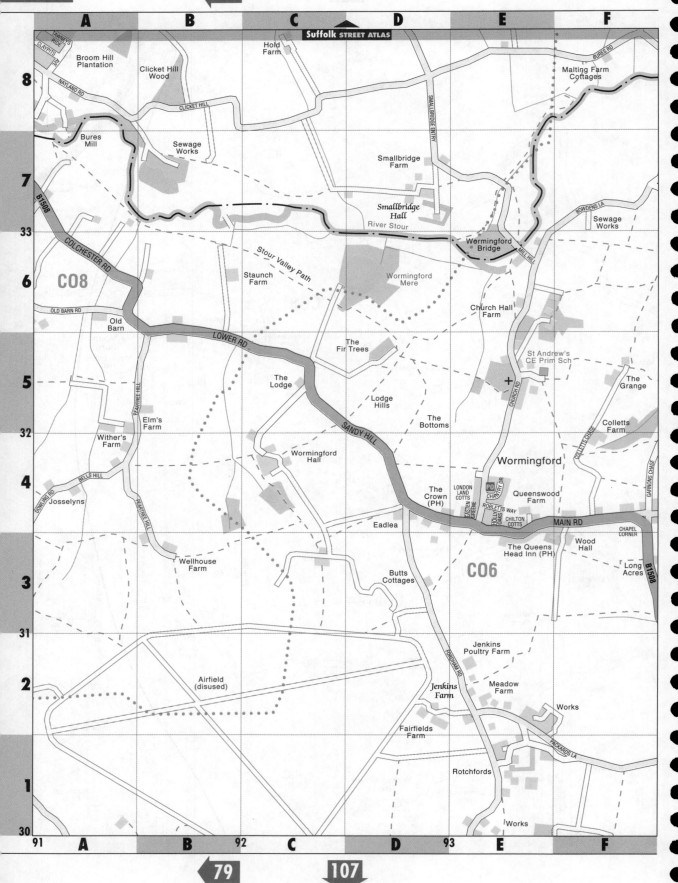

79

Suffolk STREET ATLAS

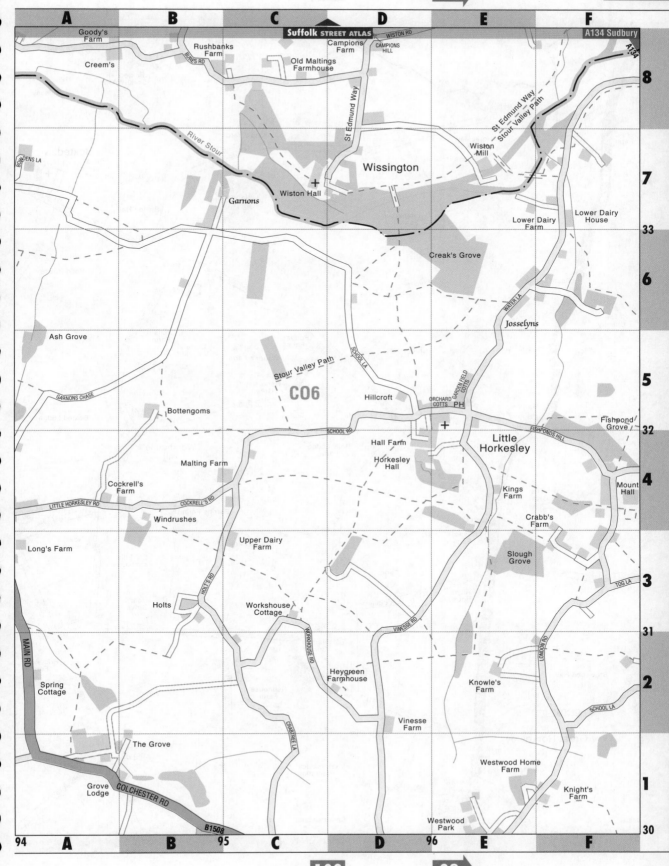

A   B   C   D   E   F

Suffolk STREET ATLAS

Goody's Farm

Creem's

Rushbanks Farm

BURES RD

Old Maltings Farmhouse

Campions Farm

WISTON RD

CAMPIONS HILL

St Edmund Way

A134 Sudbury

A134

St Edmund Way

Stour Valley Path

8

River Stour

BOWDENS LA

Wissington

Wiston Mill

7

Garnons

+ Wiston Hall

Lower Dairy House

33

Lower Dairy Farm

Creak's Grove

6

WATER LA

Josselyns

Ash Grove

Stour Valley Path

SCHOOL LA

5

GARNONS CHASE

CO6

Hillcroft

GARDEN FIELD COTTS

ORCHARD COTTS

PH

Fishpond Grove

32

Bottengoms

SCHOOL RD

Hall Farm

Horkesley Hall

+

Little Horkesley

FISHPONDS HILL

Malting Farm

Kings Farm

Mount Hall

4

Cockrell's Farm

COCKRELL'S RD

Crabb's Farm

LITTLE HORKESLEY RD

Windrushes

Slough Grove

Upper Dairy Farm

Long's Farm

HOLTS RD

TOG LA

3

Holts

Workshouse Cottage

WORKHOUSE RD

VINESSE RD

31

MAIN RD

LONDON RD

Spring Cottage

Heygreen Farmhouse

Knowle's Farm

SCHOOL LA

2

The Grove

CRABTREE LA

Vinesse Farm

Westwood Home Farm

Grove Lodge

COLCHESTER RD

Knight's Farm

1

B1508

Westwood Park

30

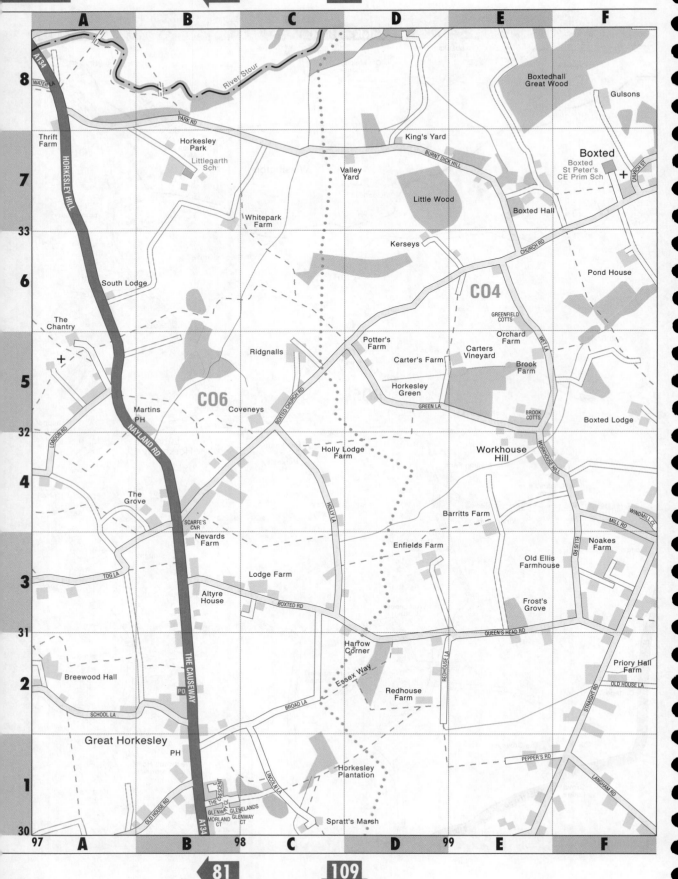

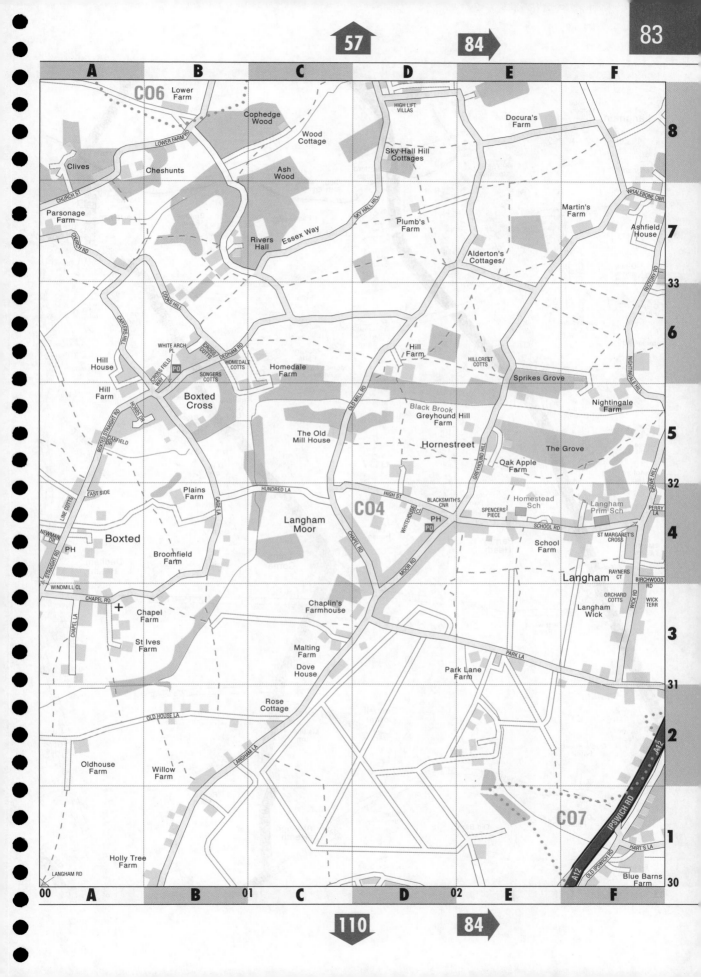

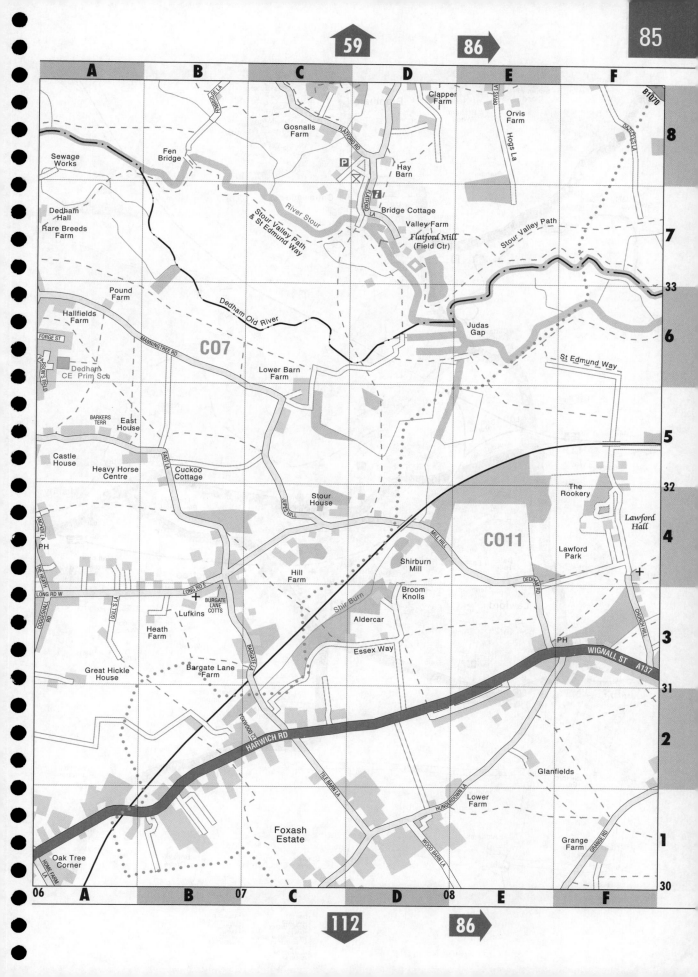

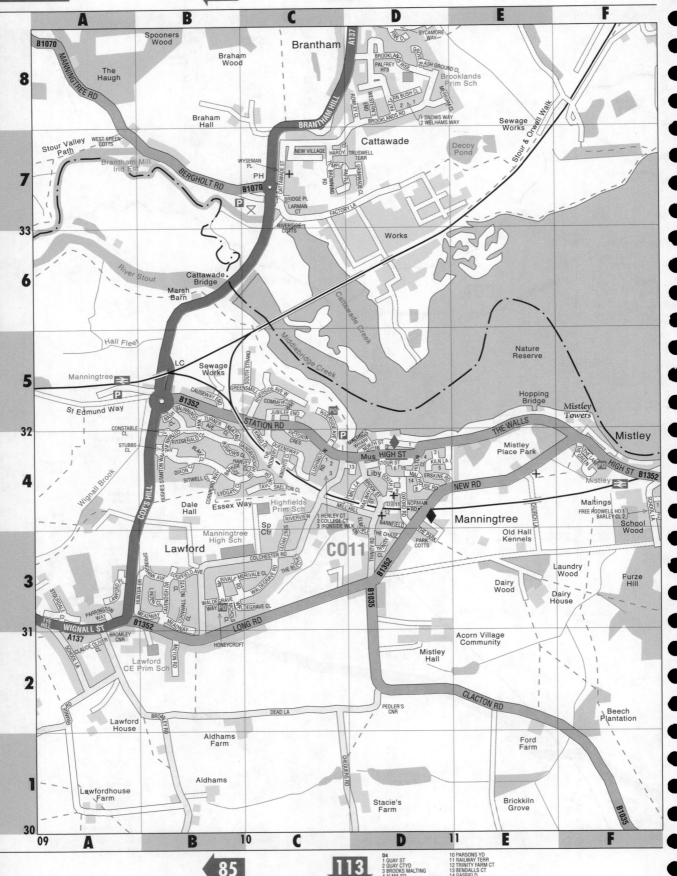

D4
1 QUAY ST
2 QUAY CTYD
3 BROOKS MALTING
4 ALMA SQ
5 THE CENTRAL MAILTINGS
6 ST MICHAELS CT
7 YORK ST
8 FALKLANDS DR
9 REGENT ST
10 PARSONS YD
11 RAILWAY TERR
12 TRINITY FARM CT
13 BENDALLS CT
14 GASFIELD
15 THE OLD LIBRARY
16 COMPASS CT

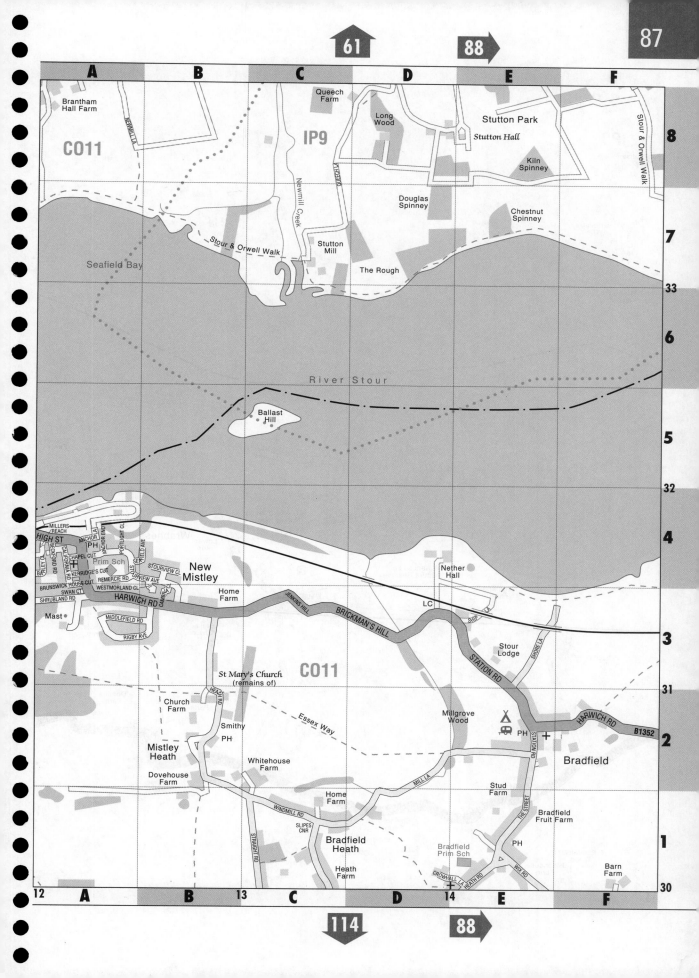

61

88

A B C D E F

Brantham
Hall Farm

NEWMILL LA

CO11

IP9

Queech
Farm

QUEECH LA

Long
Wood

Stutton Park

Stutton Hall

Kiln
Spinney

Stour & Orwell Walk

8

Newmill Creek

Stour & Orwell Walk

Stutton
Mill

Douglas
Spinney

Chestnut
Spinney

7

Seafield Bay

The Rough

33

6

River Stour

Ballast
Hill

5

32

MILLERS
REACH

HIGH ST

BECKFORD RD

CALIFORNIA RD

Ba

CLIFF RD

PH

ANCHOR LA

CHAPEL CUT

KERRIDGE'S CUT

ANCHOR END

Prim Sch

PORTLIGHT CL

SEAFIELD AVE

STOURVIEW CL

New
Mistley

Nether
Hall

4

BRUNSWICK HOUSE CUT

SWAN CT

REMERCIE RD

URVIEW AVE

WESTMORLAND CL

SHRUBLAND RD

HARWICH RD

CAMBRIA CL

Home Farm

JENKINS HILL

BRICKMAN'S HILL

LC

STATION RD

SHIP

SHORE LA

3

Mast

MIDDLEFIELD RD

RIGBY AVE

Stour
Lodge

31

CO11

St Mary's Church
(remains of)

HEATH RD

Church
Farm

Essex Way

Millgrove
Wood

PH

HARWICH RD

B1352

2

Smithy

PH

Stud
Farm

Bradfield

Mistley
Heath

Whitehouse
Farm

Bradfield
Fruit Farm

Dovehouse
Farm

MILL LA

Home
Farm

THE STREET

PH

WINDMILL RD

SLIPES
CNR

Bradfield
Prim Sch

1

STRAIGHT RD

Bradfield
Heath

WIX RD

Barn
Farm

CROWHALL LA

Heath
Farm

HEATH RD

30

12 A B 13 C D 14 E F

114

88

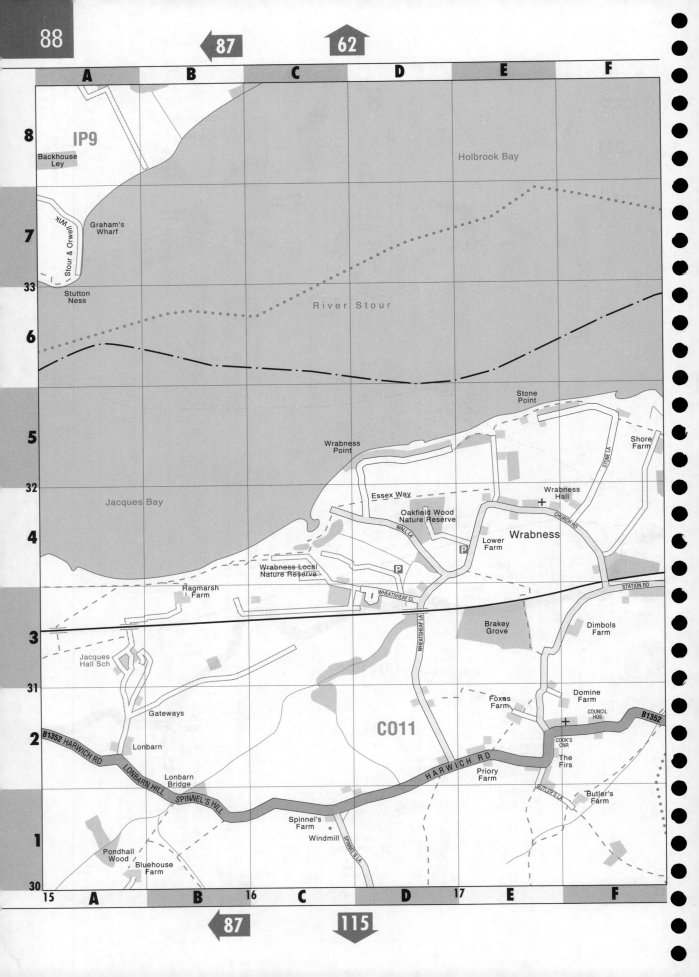

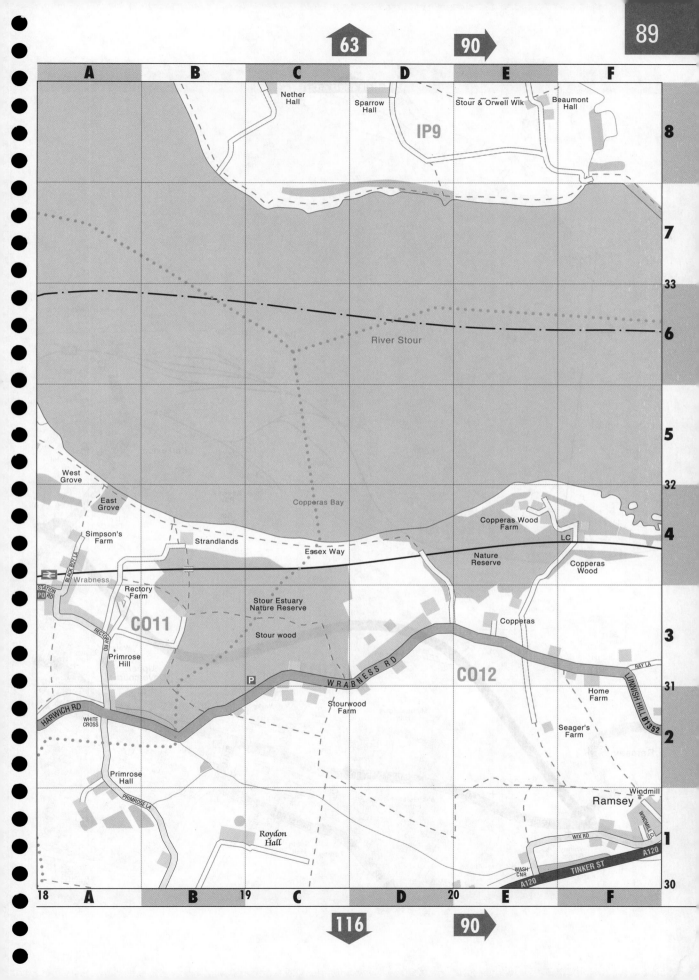

Suffolk STREET ATLAS

Ness Farm

IP9

Waterhouse Creek

Erwarton Bay

8

River Stour

7

Erwarton Ness

33

6

Pier

Parkeston Quay

Harwich International Port

Harwich Parkeston Quay LC

P

EAST DOCK RD

LC

A136

THE ANCHORAGE

WEST DOCK RD

COLLER RD

HAMILTON ST

TYLER ST

PRINCESS ST

GARLAND RD

PARKESTON RD

Refinery

LC

REFINERY RD

RAY LA

FOSTER RD

EDWARD ST

LINA RD

Parkeston

PO

STATION RD

5

Hotel

Harwich Ind Est

EUROPA WAY

A136

32

Ramsey Ray

Ray Farm

Delf Pond

PARKESTONE RDBT

PARKESTON RD

A120

4

Works

Essex Way

Ramsey Creek

CH

SNIDER CT

NORWAY CRES

BRIARDALE AVE

CLARK'S RD

THE HAVEN

POUND FARM DR

DOCKFIELD AVE

FALLOWFIELD

OLD RD

White Cottage

RAY LA

East Newhall

3

Pond Hall Farm

CO12

Works

BLACKSMITH'S LA 1

BELMANS CT 2

TRAFALGAR COTTS

B1352

Sch

31

Upper Dovercourt

Cemy

FITZGERALD COTTS

Michaelstowe Hall

Works

ASH CT

MAIN RD

NORTH SEA VIEW

LOW WAY

HIGH OAKS

CHEVY CT

CLAYTON RD

RAYHAVEN

STOUR CL

VALLEY RD

ROWLAND

UTD FIELD

HOLYROOD

HOWARD

WITCH ELM

LONG MDWS

SALTON WAY

DEANE'S CL

2

B1352

WRABNESS RD

MICHAELSTOWE DR

MICHAELSTOWE CL

Factory

B1414

PO

CHASE CT

CHASE LA

CHASE LANE Prim Sch

DE VERE WAY

GOODLAKE

ARDENNE CL

MINERVA CL

EARLHAMS CL

KILMAINE RD

Ramsey

Michaelstow Farm

RAMSEY RD

RAMSEY RD

BERA RD

DOVE CRES

DEVON WAY

ABBY AVE

WARHAM RD

OLD RD

HAZELVILLE

SWILLAND

BELLE VUE RD

MEADOW

MAUGH CT

THE DALES

GRAVEL HILL WAY

OAK NIGHTINGALE WAY

FRESHFD

KEYNES

1

A120 TINKER ST

BACK PH LA

THE STREET

ORCHARD CL

MAIN RD

REX DRY LA

CHURCH HILL

Essex Way

MILITARY RD

PARADE RD

REGINA

DAVI S LA

MAYES LA

BLVR CL

HEWITT RD

HANK AVE

ARTILLERY DR

OAKLEY RD

BRAMBLE TYE

EARLHAMS MEWS

DENE'S LA

SOUTH ST

BEXLEY

VASS AVE

BULLS

CHAFFINCH

TROS FISHER

MUSGRAVE CL

Whinny Grove

Mill Farm

Two Village CE Prim Sch

BAY VIEW CRES

Terling

South Hall

LOW RD

WHINFIELD AVE

ACORN CL 1
OAKVIEW 2
SHACKLETON CL 3
MUSGRAVE CL 4

B1414

30

21   A   B   22   C   D   23   E   F

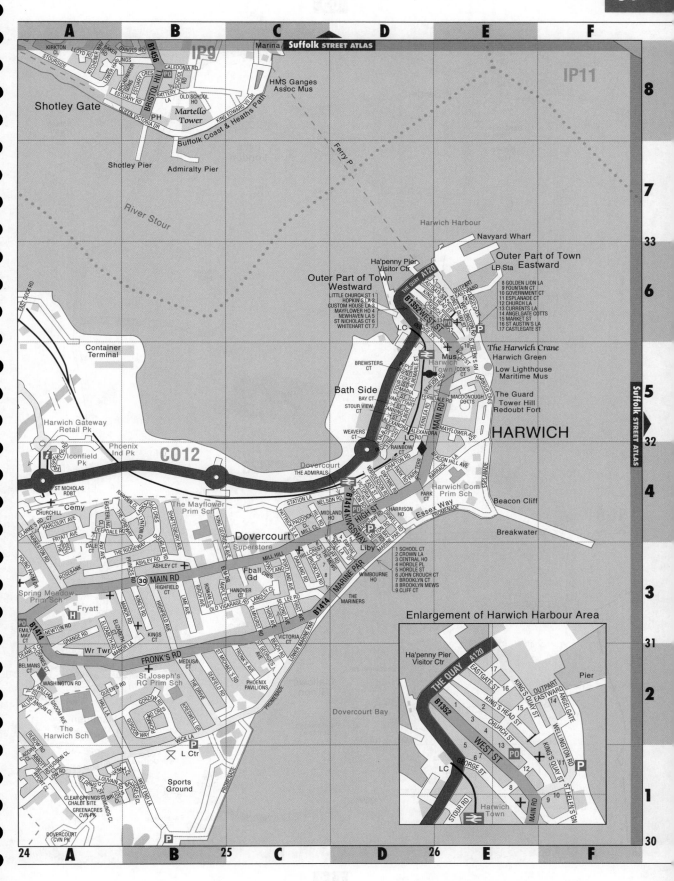

Suffolk STREET ATLAS

IP9

IP11

Shotley Gate

Martello Tower

HMS Ganges Assoc Mus

Shotley Pier

Admiralty Pier

River Stour

Ferry P

Harwich Harbour

Navyard Wharf

Ha'penny Pier Visitor Ctr

LB Sta

Outer Part of Town Eastward

8 GOLDEN LION LA
9 FOUNTAIN CT
10 GOVERNMENT CT
11 ESPLANADE CT
12 CHURCH LA
13 CURRENTS LA
14 ANGELGATE COTTS
15 MARKET ST
16 ST AUSTIN'S LA
17 CASTLEGATE ST

Outer Part of Town Westward

LITTLE CHURCH ST 1
HOPKIN S LA 2
CUSTOM HOUSE LA 3
MAYFLOWER HO 4
NEWHAVEN LA 5
ST NICHOLAS CT 6
WHITEHART CT 7

The Harwich Crane

Harwich Green

Low Lighthouse Maritime Mus

The Guard Tower Hill Redoubt Fort

HARWICH

Container Terminal

Harwich Gateway Retail Pk

Phoenix Ind Pk

CO12

BREWSTERS CT

Bath Side

BAY CT
STOUR VIEW CT

WEAVERS CT

Harwich Town

Dovercourt

THE ADMIRALS

St Nicholas RDBT

Cemy

Churchill

The Mayflower Prim Sch

STATION LA

Dovercourt Superstore

Harwich Com Prim Sch

Beacon Cliff

Breakwater

Essex Way

Spring Meadow Prim Sch

Fryatt

Fball Gd

Liby

1 SCHOOL CT
2 CROWN LA
3 CENTRAL HO
4 HORDLE PL
5 HORDLE ST
6 JOHN CROUCH CT
7 BROOKLYN ST
8 BROOKLYN MEWS
9 CLIFF CT

The Mariners

FRONK'S RD

St Joseph's RC Prim Sch

Phoenix Pavilions

The Harwich Sch

L Ctr

Sports Ground

Dovercourt Bay

Enlargement of Harwich Harbour Area

Ha'penny Pier Visitor Ctr

THE QUAY

A120

EASTGATE ST

KING'S HEAD ST

KING'S QUAY ST

Pier

OUTPART EASTWARD

ANGELGATE

WELLINGTON RD

ST HELEN'S GN

B1352

WEST ST

CHURCH ST

GEORGE ST

STOUR RD

Harwich Town

LC

Suffolk STREET ATLAS

33

8

7

6

5

32

4

31

3

2

1

30

24   25   26

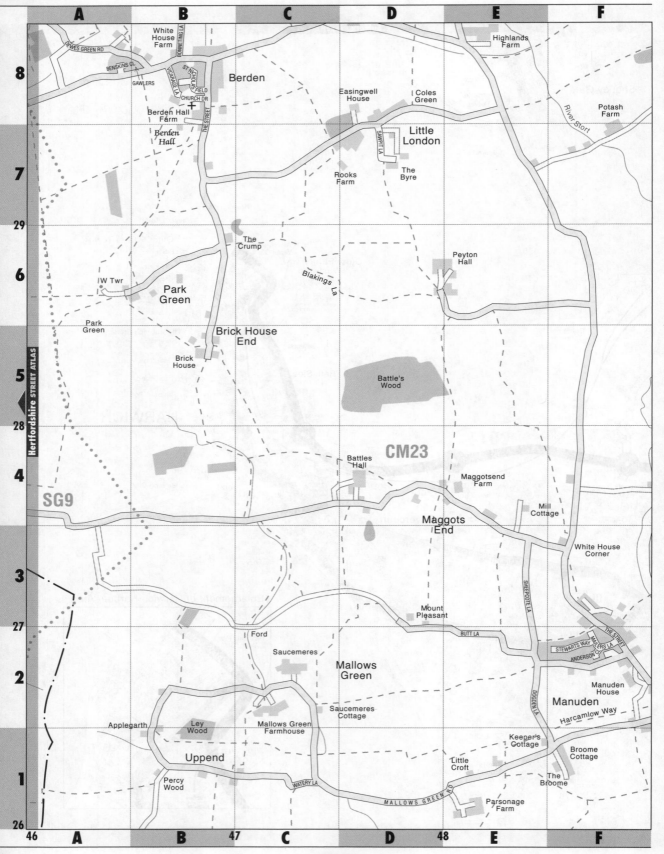

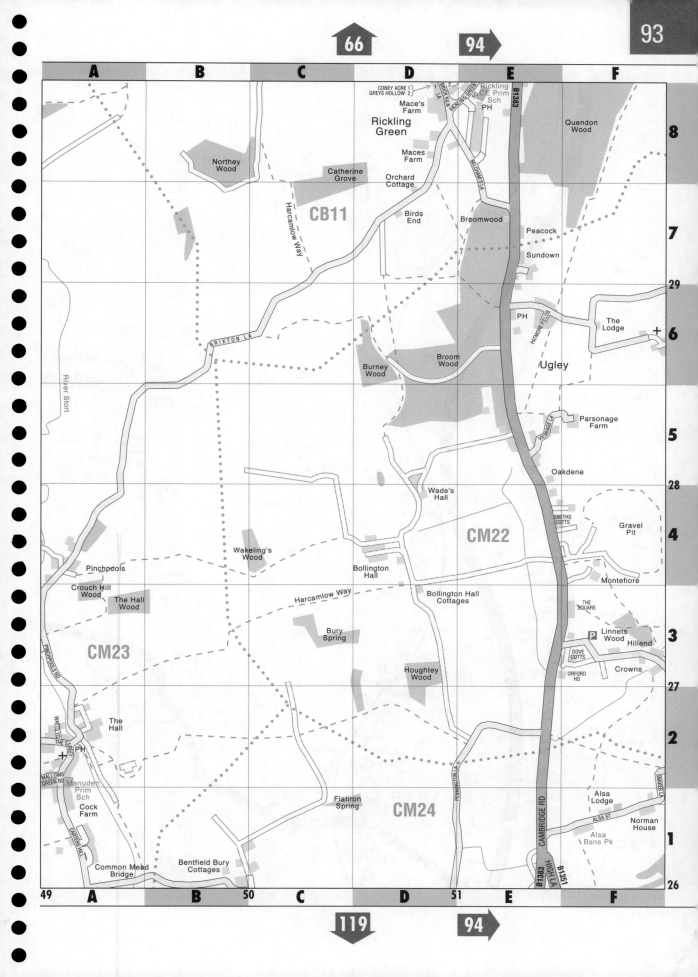

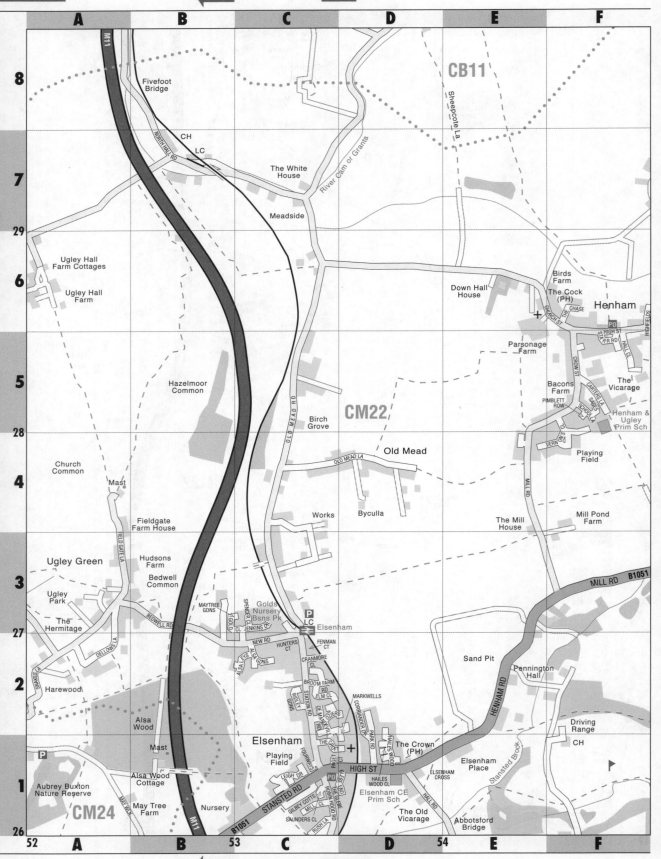

A B C D E F

8

CB11

Fivefoot
Bridge

CH
LC

7

The White
House

Meadside

River Cam or Granta

Sheepcote La

29

Ugley Hall
Farm Cottages

6

Ugley Hall
Farm

Down Hall
House

Birds
Farm

The Cock
(PH)

Henham

PO

Parsonage
Farm

THE CHASE

CHURCH ST

HIGH ST

STA RR RD

HALL CT

HIGHFIELDS

5

Hazelmoor
Common

Bacons
Farm

The
Vicarage

PIMBLETT
ROW

CARTERS LA

SAGES

SCHOOL LA

CROW ST

Church
Common

28

Birch
Grove

CM22

Old Mead

Henham &
Ugley
Prim Sch

VERN S

Playing
Field

OLD MEAD RD

OLD MEAD LA

4

Mast

Works

Byculla

The Mill
House

MILL RD

Mill Pond
Farm

Fieldgate
Farm House

Ugley Green

Hudsons
Farm

FIELD GATE LA

3

Ugley
Park

Bedwell
Common

BEDWELL RD

DELLOWS LA

MAYTREE
GDNS

SPENCER CL

J GOLD

JENKINS DR

Golds
Nursery
Bsns Pk

P
LC

MILL RD   B1051

Elsenham

The
Hermitage

27

NEW RD

ALSA CLS

ALSA GDNS

FENMAN
CT

HUNTERS
CT

CRANMORE
CL

Sand Pit

HENHAM RD

Pennington
Hall

2

SHAKES LA

Harewood

Alsa
Wood

BROOM
RD

FARM

STATION RD

RIDLEY
GDNS

DE MANDEVILLE

ELM CL

SQUIERS

Markwells

CORIANDER DR

HAILES WOOD

PARK RD

The Crown
(PH)

Stansted Brook

Driving
Range

CH

Mast

Elsenham

Playing
Field

THE CROFT CT

PAGET CT

FOURWAYS

LEIGH DR

HIGH ST

PO

STANSTED RD

GILBEY COTTS

FERN WOOD RD

MILL CL

RUSH LA

THE GLEBE

HAILES
WOOD CL

Elsenham CE
Prim Sch

ELSENHAM
CROSS

HALL RD

Elsenham
Place

1

P

Aubrey Buxton
Nature Reserve

CM24

MAY VLK

Alsa Wood
Cottage

May Tree
Farm

M11

B1051

Nursery

SAUNDERS CL

The Old
Vicarage

Abbotsford
Bridge

26

52   A   B   53   C   D   54   E   F

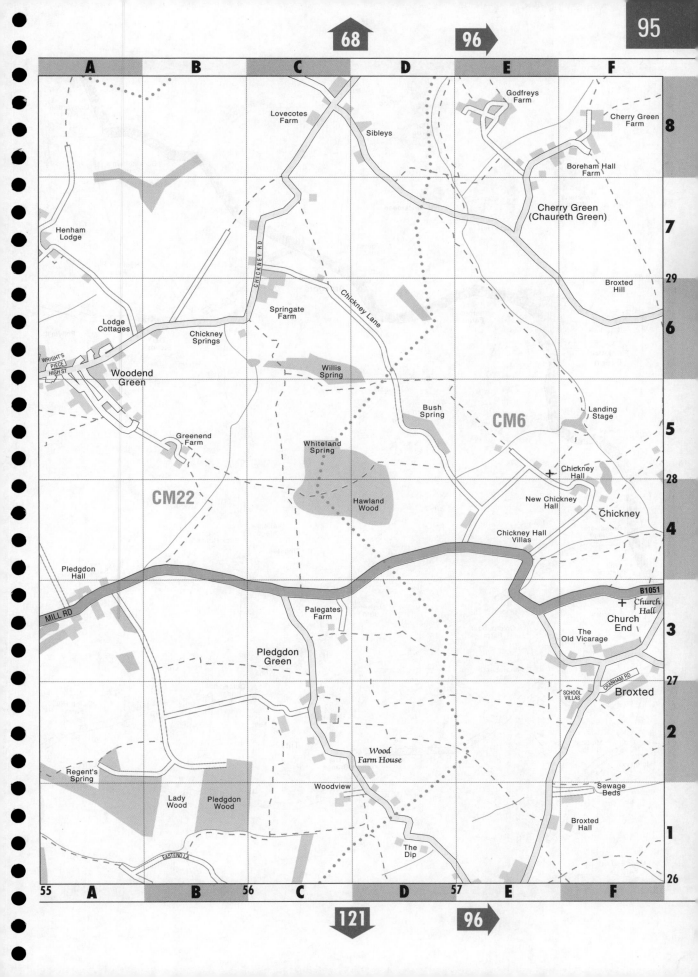

95
69

A B C D E F

8

Brown's Wood

Home Wood

Stan Brook

Hill Farm

Dairygreen Farm

B1051

Buckingham's Farm

Stanbrook

Warrens Wood

Brickmead

7

Horham Hall

Armigers Farm

29

Hart's Grove

Armigers

Hammer Hill Farm

FOLLY MILL LA

Sharpes Farm

6

Suchsted Green

The Stepps

River Chelmer

Follymill

Delfits La

5

Chaureth Hall Farm

CM6

Broadfans Farm

Harcamlow Way

28

Broadwater Bridge

4

Walters Cottage

Brick House Farm

Wolsey's Farm

Hill Pasture

B1051

Tingates

Tilty Hill Farm

3

Coldharbour Farm

Lower Barn

Eseley Wood

Duton Hill

Coldharbour Villas

27

Dutonhill Bridge

Duton Hill Farm

2

Malting Bridge

Home Wood

Mill

PH

The Maltings

Tilty

ABB- VIEW

The Grange

+

1

Moor End Farm

26

95
122

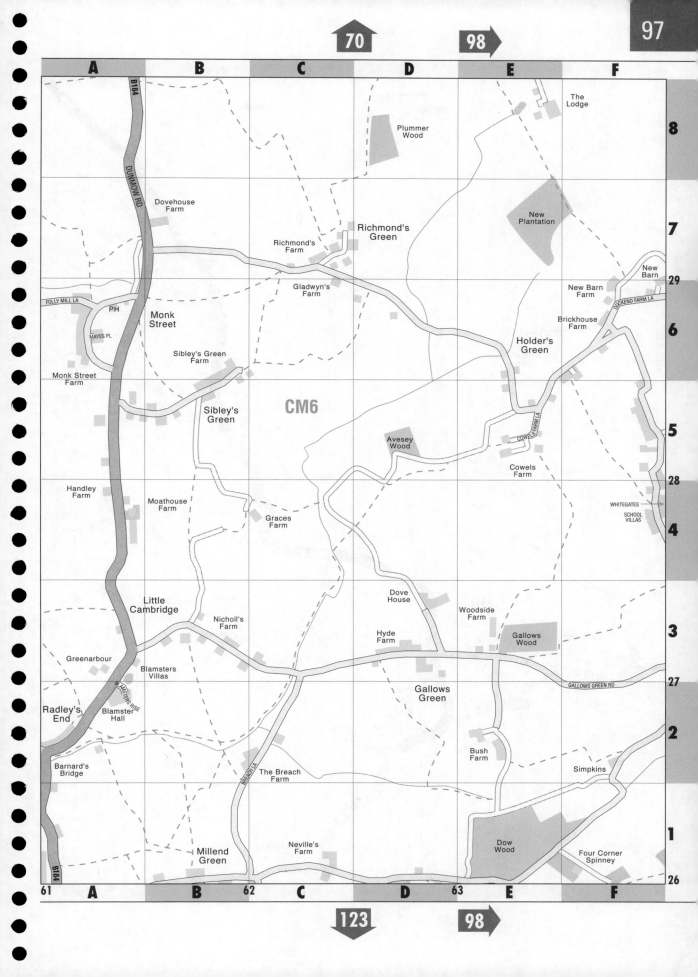

A B C D E F

8
7
29
6
5
28
4
3
27
2
1
26

The Lodge

Plummer
Wood

New
Plantation

New
Barn

B184

DUNMOW RD

Dovehouse
Farm

Richmond's
Green

Richmond's
Farm

Gladwyn's
Farm

New Barn
Farm

Brickhouse
Farm

DUCKEND FARM LA

FOLLY MILL LA

PH

Monk
Street

Holder's
Green

MAYES PL

Sibley's Green
Farm

CM6

Monk Street
Farm

Sibley's
Green

Avesey
Wood

COWELS FARM LA

Cowels
Farm

WHITEGATES

Handley
Farm

Moathouse
Farm

Graces
Farm

SCHOOL
VILLAS

Dove
House

Woodside
Farm

Little
Cambridge

Nicholl's
Farm

Hyde
Farm

Gallows
Wood

Greenarbour

Blamsters
Villas

Gallows
Green

GALLOWS GREEN RD

Radley's
End

BLAMSTERS RISE

Blamster
Hall

Bush
Farm

Simpkins

Barnard's
Bridge

BREACH LA

The Breach
Farm

Dow
Wood

Four Corner
Spinney

Millend
Green

Neville's
Farm

61 A B 62 C D 63 E F

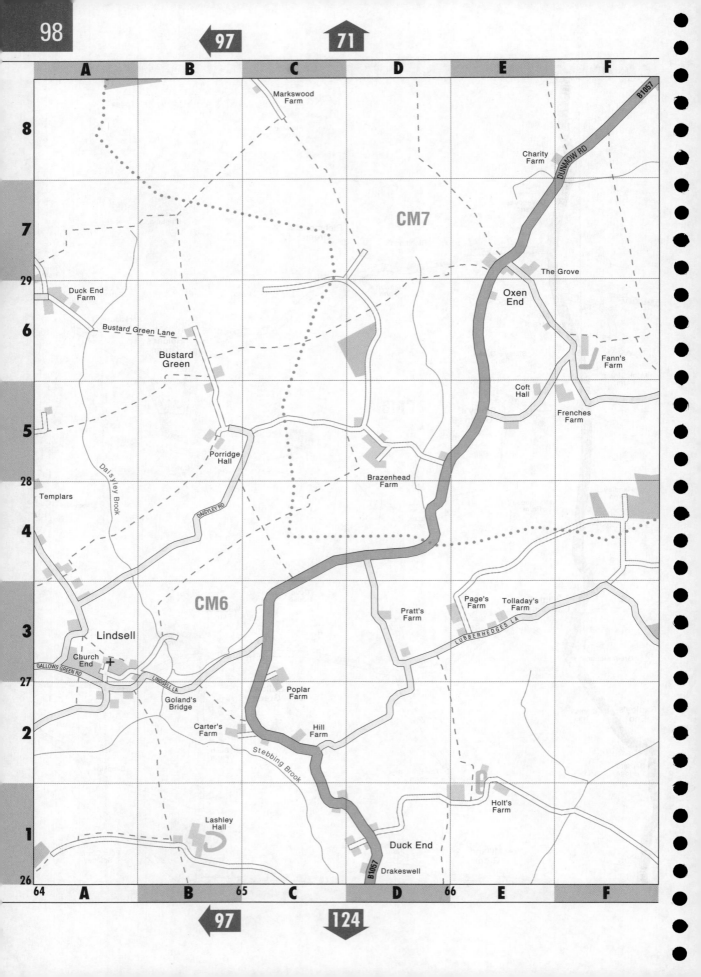

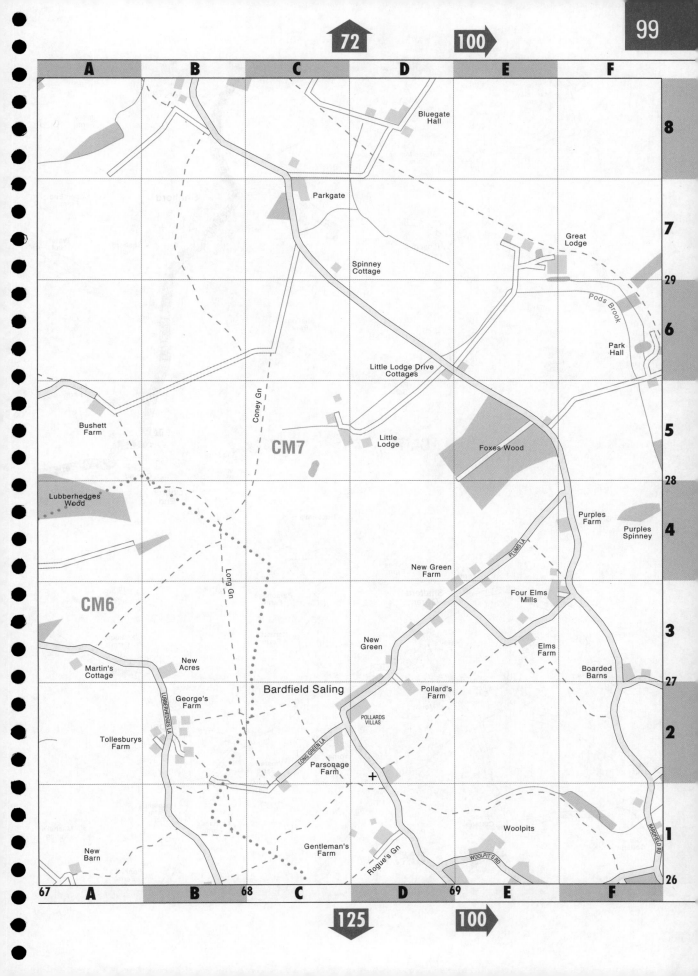

A B C D E F

8
7
29
6
5
28
4
3
27
2
1
26

Bluegate Hall

Parkgate

Great Lodge

Spinney Cottage

Pods Brook

Park Hall

Little Lodge Drive Cottages

Coney Gn

Bushett Farm

CM7

Little Lodge

Foxes Wood

Lubberhedges Wood

Purples Farm

Purples Spinney

Long Gn

CM6

New Green Farm

Four Elms Mills

PLUMS LA

New Green

Elms Farm

Martin's Cottage

New Acres

Boarded Barns

LUBBERHEDGES LA

George's Farm

Bardfield Saling

Pollard's Farm

Tollesburys Farm

POLLARDS VILLAS

LONG GREEN LA

Parsonage Farm

Woolpits

BARDFIELD RD

New Barn

Gentleman's Farm

Rogue's Gn

WOOLPIT'S RD

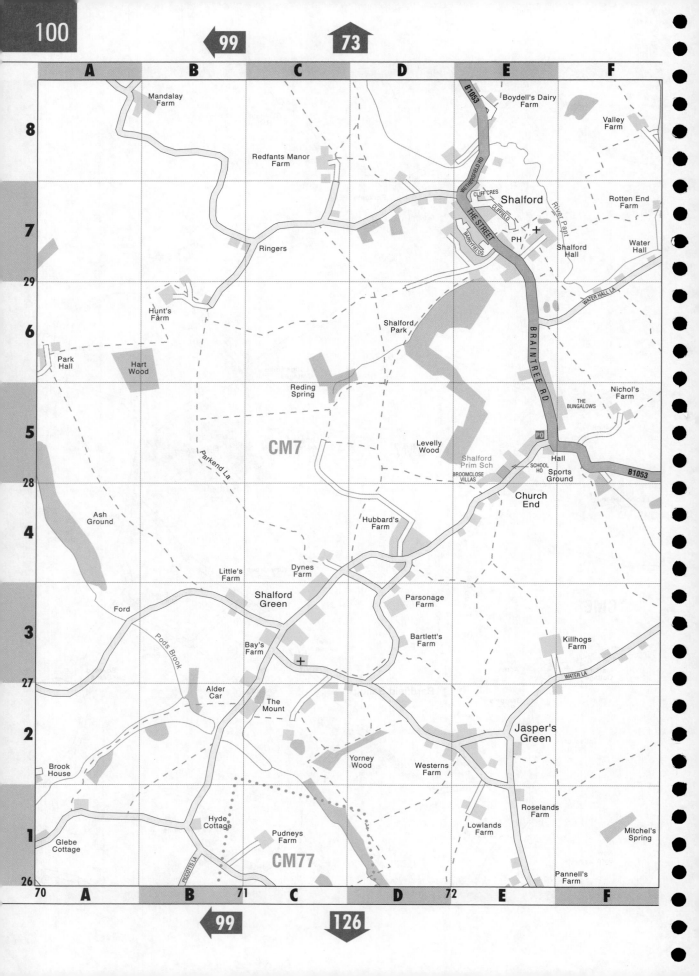

A B C D E F

8 Mandalay Farm
Redfants Manor Farm
Boydell's Dairy Farm
B1053
Valley Farm

7 Ringers
CLIFF CRES
CLIFFIELD
Shalford
THE STREET
BARNFIELDS
PH
River Pant
Shalford Hall
Rotten End Farm
Water Hall
WETHERSFIELD RD

29

6 Hunt's Farm
Shalford Park
BRAINTREE RD
WATER HALL LA

Park Hall
Hart Wood
Reding Spring
THE BUNGALOWS
Nichol's Farm

5 Parkend La
CM7
Levelly Wood
Shalford Prim Sch
SCHOOL HO
PO
Hall Sports Ground
B1053

28 BROOMCLOSE VILLAS
Church End

4 Ash Ground
Hubbard's Farm

Little's Farm
Dynes Farm
Parsonage Farm
Killhogs Farm

3 Ford
Shalford Green
Bartlett's Farm
WATER LA
Pods Brook
Bay's Farm

27 Alder Car
The Mount
Jasper's Green

2 Brook House
Yorney Wood
Westerns Farm
Roselands Farm

1 Glebe Cottage
Hyde Cottage
Pudneys Farm
CM77
Lowlands Farm
Mitchel's Spring
Pannell's Farm

26
70 A B 71 C D 72 E F

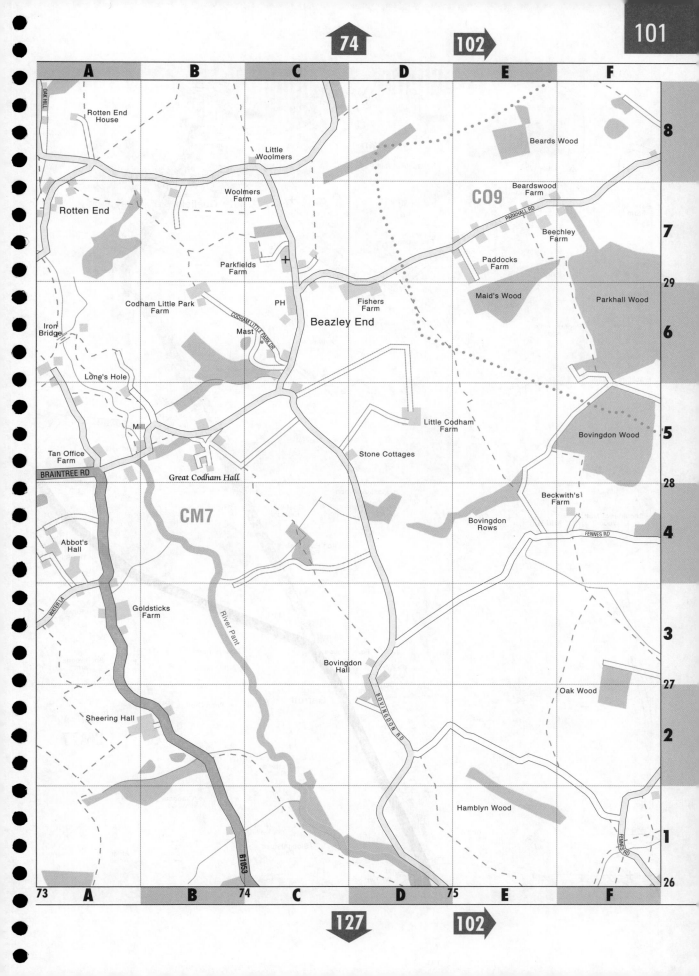

101 75

A   B   C   D   E   F

8

St Margaret's Sch

The Grove

CH

WOODLAND WAY

HALL DR

Gosfield Hall

Gosfield Hall Park

Gosfield Lake

Lake Wood

PARKHALL RD

Parkhall Farm

7

Low Ley Plantation

PH

29

Lake Bridge

CO9

Parkhall Wood

Kemps Wood

6

Pegtantram's Wood

Ayleward's Farm

Blackbird's Wood

Harmas Farm

5

Gosfield Wood

28

Shoulder of Mutton Wood

Mill Hill

Gosfield Eaves

4

Iron Pear Tree Farm

Whiteash Wood

The Slip

Fennes

FENNES RD

Mast

HALSTEAD RD

Rayne Hatch Farm

3

Foley Cotts

Foley House

Boones Farm

Boultwoods Farm

CM7

27

Garrett Farm

High Garrett

Pond Croft

Braintree Wood

2

PH

CM77

A1017 GOSFIELD RD

BRAINTREE RD

NEW RD

PETERFIELD'S LA

Peterfield's Farm

A131

Trotter's Rest

SUNNYFIELDS RD

Clapgate Wood

1

Harriett's Farm

HADLEY CL

ASHPOLE RD

THE VILLES

GROVE ORCH

GROVE FIELD

HIGH GARRETT

Sloughhouse Farm

Alder Wood

26

CHURCH ST

A131

LYONS HALL RD

Wr Twr

76   A   B   77   C   D   78   E   F

Gosfield

THE STREET

A1017

THE FIRS

PARK COTTS

CHEST AVE

MEADWAY

Gosfield Com Prim Sch

CHURCH RD

THE CEDARS

HIGHGATES

NUN'S MOW

THE LIMES

PH

PH

PO

EDMUND

GREENWAYS

GREEN

OX YD

PARK LA

Gosfield Bridge

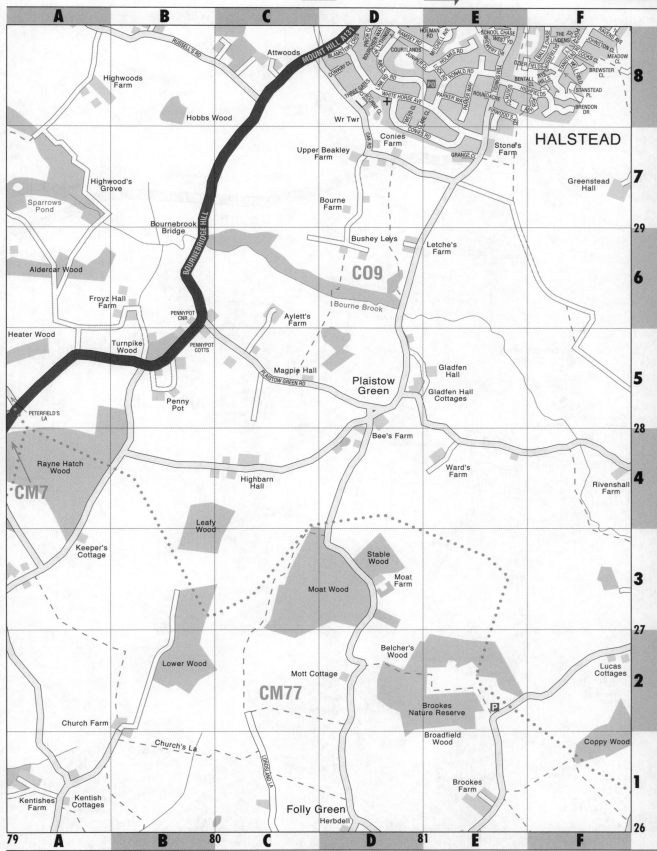

A B C D E F

8

RUSSELL'S RD

Highwoods Farm

Attwoods

MOUNT HILL A131

BLAMSTER'S CRES

PRIOR CL
BOURNBROOK WAY
CONWAY CL
ABLS RD
ISE T THINGS
COURTLANDS
RAMSEY RD
HOLMAN RD
MITCHEL AVE
SCHOOL CHASE
WEST YD
BREWERY DR

Hobbs Wood

THREE GATES
BOURNE CL
WHITE HORSE AVE
JUNIPER CL
RONALD RD
HOLMES RD
MITCHEL AVE

THE LINDENS
STANSTEAD RD
EARL'S CHASE
RAVENS CL
JOHNSTON CL
MEADOW CL

Highwood's Grove

PO
BENTALL CL
HIGHFIELDS
OZIER FIELDS
POPLAR
COOKS CL

TWEED CL
CLARE CL
CONIES RD
PARKER WAY
WALKER WAY
ROUNDACRE
SOUTH RD
FIRWOOD'S RD
RYE HILLS
ASH
BRENDON DR
STANSTEAD PL
BREWSTER CL

Wr Twr

Sparrows Pond

Upper Beakley Farm

OAK RD

Conies Farm

Stone's Farm

HALSTEAD

Bourne Farm

GRANGE CL

7

Greenstead Hall

Aldercar Wood

Bournebrook Bridge

BOURNEBRIDGE HILL

Bushey Leys

Letche's Farm

29

CO9

6

Froyz Hall Farm

PENNYPOT CNR

Aylett's Farm

Bourne Brook

Heater Wood

Turnpike Wood

PENNYPOT COTTS

PLAISTOW GREEN RD

Magpie Hall

Plaistow Green

Gladfen Hall

5

Penny Pot

Gladfen Hall Cottages

PETERFIELD'S LA

Bee's Farm

28

CM7

Rayne Hatch Wood

Ward's Farm

Rivenshall Farm

4

Highbarn Hall

Keeper's Cottage

Leafy Wood

Stable Wood

Moat Farm

3

Moat Wood

27

Lower Wood

Belcher's Wood

Lucas Cottages

Church Farm

Mott Cottage

CM77

P

Broadfield Wood

Coppy Wood

2

Church's La

LORDSLAND LA

Brookes Nature Reserve

Kentishes Farm

Kentish Cottages

Brookes Farm

1

Folly Green

Herbdell

26

79 A 80 B C 81 D E F

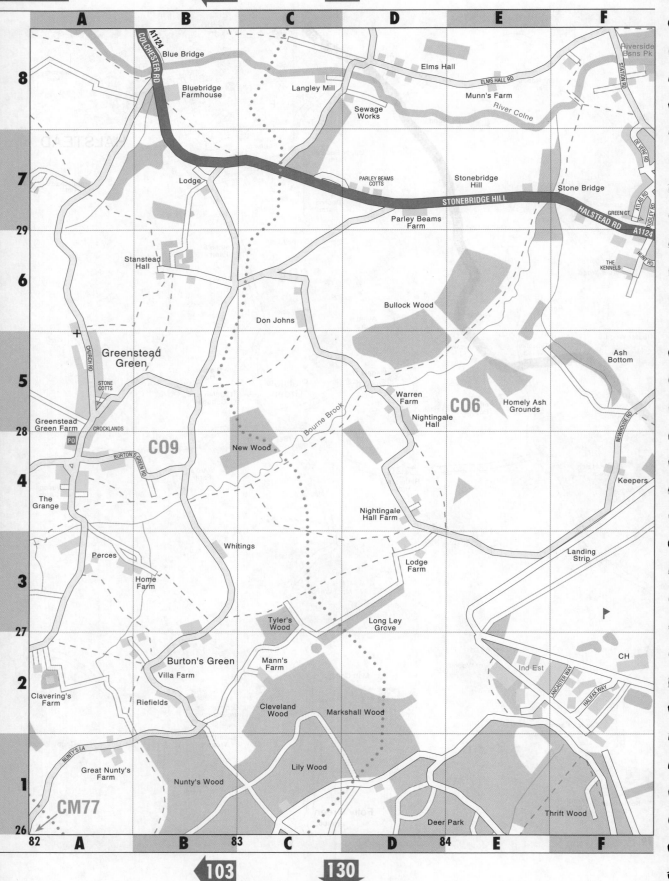

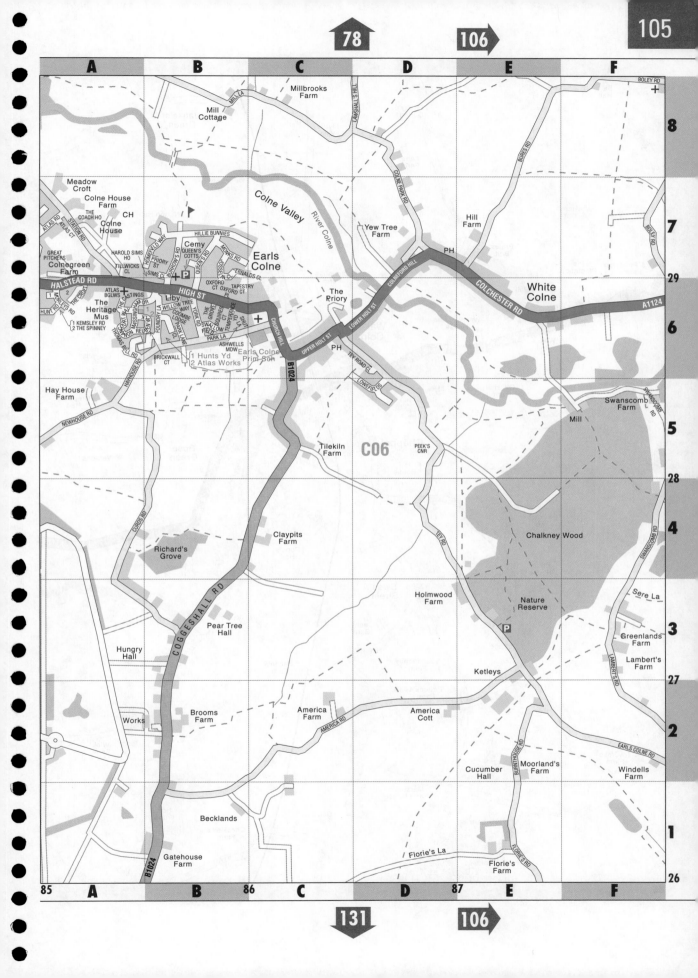

105
79

A B C D E F

8

Bart Hall

Friday's Cottage

Myrtle Villa

Janke's Green

Lane Farm

7

Alder Car

Acorn Wood

Thornfield Wood

Norton Hall Farm

Prales Belt

New Wood

29

Fox & Pheasant Farm

Iris Plantation

Oldhouse Farm

East Anglian Rly Mus

BOLEY RD

A1124

Wakes Hall Farm

Wakes Hall Bsns Ctr

Chappel & Wakes Colne

PONTISBRIGHT COTTS

6

TYBURN HILL

Wakes Colne House

Wakes Colne

The Claypits

Wakes Hall

WAKES ST

NEW COTTS

CHAPPEL CNR

STATION RD

SPRING GARDENS RD

1

Old Hall Farm

Mills

PO

Rose Green Cotts

Crepping Hall

CO6

PH

Chappel CE Prim Sch

5

Chappel

THE STREET

SWAN GR

Allen Cotts

COLCHESTER RD

Rose Green

Vernons

VERNONS RD

28

SWANSCOMB RD

CHAPPEL HILL

Hill House

4

Hickmore Fen

Pope's Hall

POPE'S RD

River Colne

Broom House

A1124

Priory House

OAK RD

PRIORY RD

Oaklands

SWAN ST

Swan Street

Essex Way

3

Croft Cottage

Jenny Barn

BACON'S LA

Bacon's Farm

27

Spendpenny Farm

Pattock's Farm

Woolfney Wood

PATTOCK'S LA

Wick Grove

2

LAMBERT'S RD

Teycross Farm

Wick Farm

Smythers Farm

Mast

Marshalls Farm House

Bett's Farm

Hoe Wood

1

EARLS COLNE RD

CHAPPEL RD

Newbarn

NEWBARN RD

LANGLEYS

LOWER LANGLEY

Great Tey CE Prim Sch

WINDMILLS

Checkley's Farm

MOOR RD

TEY RD

TEY RD

26

FARMFIELD RD

CHISMUND WAY

88 A 89 B C 90 D E F

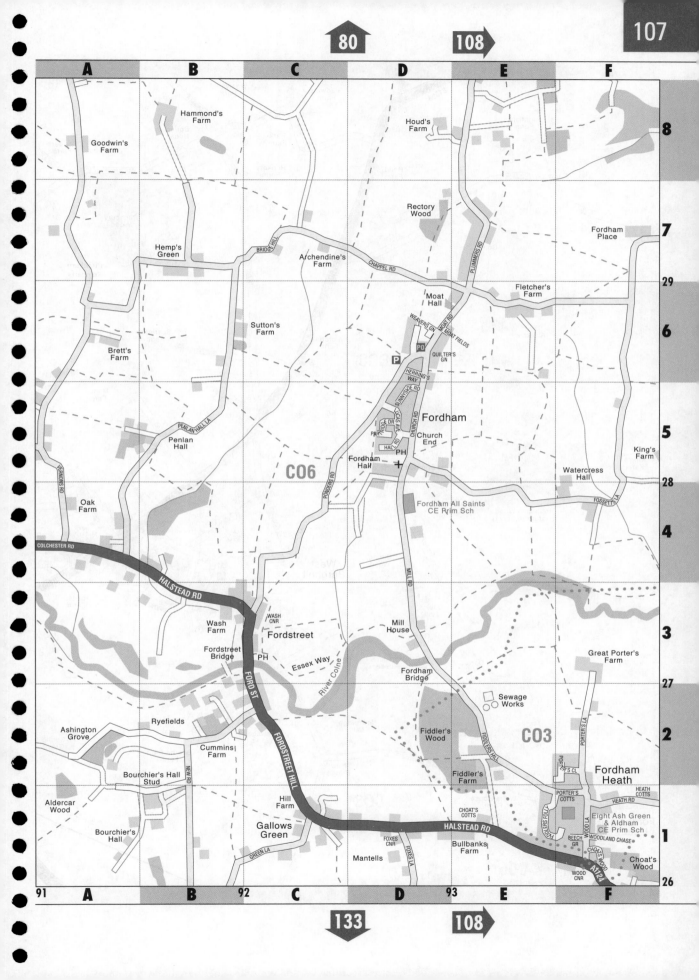

107
81

A B C D E F

8

Highfield Farm

King's Farm

Pond Farm

Gladwins Farm

Westwood Park

Park Farm

Spring House

LONDON RD

Rookery Farm

COACH RD

Ponders Farm

OLD HOUSE RD

B1508
COLCHESTER RD
CRABTREE LA
VINESSE RD

Pitchbury Wood

7

Coney Byes Farm

Kinckhams

MAYLAND RD

BURES RD

29

Pitchbury Ramparts

6

Aldercar

Alcrofts Farm

CO6

Scarlet's Farm

SCARLETTS CHASE

Manor Farm

Stitching Wood

OLD CHURCH LA
HALL ROAD COTTS

PH
WHITE HART LA
THE CRESCENT

MANOR RD

5

King's Farm

West Bergholt Hall

HALL RD

HALL RD

Sports Gd

28

Hillhouse Wood
(Nature Reserve)

CEDAR CT

Sch

COLCHESTER RD

BRADBROOK COTTS
ARMOURY RD
LIGHTWOOD CL
LODGE CT
COOPERS CRES
GARRET CRES
LARKIN WAY
BERKSHIRE LA

4

ESSEX WAY

Spring Wood

West Bergholt

SACKVILLE WAY
FINIMORE CT
ORPEN CL
LEXDEN RD
NEW CHURCH RD
SCHOOL LA
HEATHSIDE
Church CL
PARK CT
ORMONDE CL
ALBANY RD
DANIELLS HO

B1508

3

Poole's Farm

Cook's Hall

Grove Wood

Horsepits House

COOK'S HALL RD

THE AVENUE
QUEEN'S RD
WHITE HOUSE LA
NEWBRIDGE HILL

MILMAFORD DR
DONARD
UPTON CL
MAMFORD CL
CHAPEL RD
PO
ERLE HAVARD RD
SPRING LA
PRIE RD
OAK CL
CHAPEL LA
VALLEY CRES
INGLIS WAY
GRANVILLE CL
GARLING WLK
VALLEY VIEW
THE RETREAT
PH

Hill Ho Farm

27

Cook's Mill

River Colne

Newbridge Mill

Sewage Works

BOURNE RD

Bourne Barn Farm

St Botolph's Brook

Spring Grove

2

ARGENTS LA

New Bridge

CO3

CHITTS HILL

Fordham Heath

HEATH RD
THE BRIDLEWAY
BRICK ST
SPRING LA
PH
SCARLE WAY
HUXTABLES LA
HEATHFIELDS

White House Farm

CO6

A12

1

Choat's Wood

26

94 A 95 B C 96 D E F

107
134

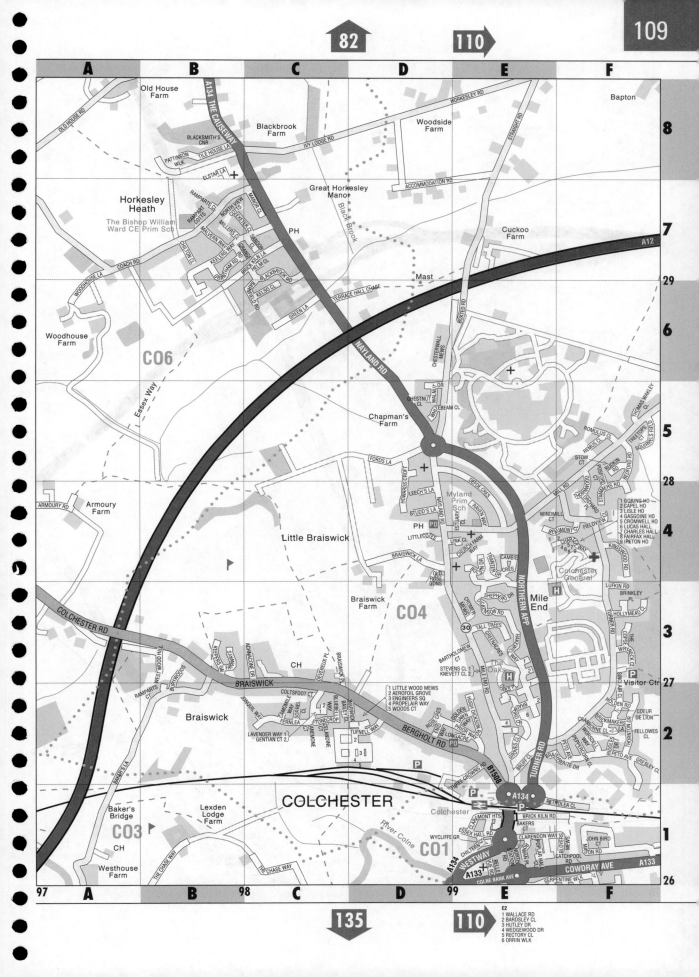

A B C D E F

8

Langham Rd
Runkin's Corner
Langham Lodge
Lodge La
A12
Wick La

Salary Brook
Kiln Wood
Old Ipswich Rd
Turnpike Cl

Whitehouse Farm

7 A12
PH
Crown La N
Hotel
Gatehouse Farm
CO7

29
Cuckoo Farm Bsns Pk
MORTIMER GDNS 1
ROPER CL 2
CHAPMAN PL 3
PARKER RD 4
HALE WAY 5
AUGUSTUS CL 6
THE CRESCENT
A1232
A120
AXIAL WAY

6
COMYNS CL
ARROWSMITH WLK
MILL RD
Kings Ct
FLOOD LA
Colchester Bsns Pk
CAXTON CT
CHARTER CT
STEPHENSON RD
A1232
Plains Farm
Harvey's Farm
OXLEY PARKER DR
Seedbed Ctr
CLOUGH RD
TILFORD WAY
Willow Cl
CROWN GATE
SMEATON CL

5
The Gilberd Sch
HANNINGFIELD WAY
JACK ANDREWS DR
Phoenix Sq
Bullock Wood
Fen Farm
Fox Street
BRINKLEY GROVE RD
A137

28
Brinkley Grove
GRASSMERE
CHINOOK
HALLCROFT CHASE
BULLOCK WOOD CL
GRANCHESTER CT
Heathcote Farm
PH

4
HUNTERS RIDGE
SEA KING CRES
HIGHWOODS APP
CLEVELAND CL
St John's CE Prim Sch
Fox Street
HARWICH RD
FOX ST

PRINCETON MEWS 1
TALLY HO 2
TYNEDALE CT 3
ALDERMAN HOWE LODGE 4
IVOR BROWN CT 5
Sch
Hypermarket
CO4
COTSWOLD CT
ARBOUR WAY
IPSWICH RD
Buildings Farm

3
High Woods
High Woods Country Park
HAREBELL WAY
ALVERTON WAY
GREENWOOD GR
BASCONIA CROFT
ARDEN
GLENTRESS CL
GLENDALE GR
KILDERMORIE
BULLACE CL
KENTMERE
GREEN LA

HILLRIDGE
THISTLEDOWN
THE BRACKENS
St Bartholomew Cl
MYLAND HALL CHASE
ST JOSEPH RD
GILDERON
ST JOHN'S RD
BROAD OAKS PK

27
P
Friar's Grove
Friars Grove Jun & Inf Schs
SILCOCK CL
ST CHRISTOPHER
WILMINGTON RD
ST MARK
ST CLEMENT
ST BERNARD RD
DUNTHORNE RD
Parsons Heath CE Prim Sch
Parson's Heath
THE GLADE
Welshwood Park Rd

2
COLCHESTER
MOUNTAIN ASH CL
ST COLUMB CT
ST LUKE'S CL
ST SAVIOUR CL
ST JUDES
CAMPBELL DR
ST THOMAS CL
VALE CL
Welshwood Park
CO1
PEGASUS WAY
ST BRIDE CT
ST FAITH

1
The Cowdray Ctr
Colne View Ret Pk
HAVERING CL
NORFOLK CRES
SUFFOLK CL
WILSON MARRIAGE RD
Willow Brook Prim Sch
CHAPLIN DR
THURLSTON
Roach Vale Prim Sch
PH
LONGRIDGE
A1232
EDISON GDNS
GORING RD
HARWICH RD
Parson's Heath
A137
BROCKENHURST
HAWTHORN AVE
SALARY CL
MERLIN END

26
COWDRAY AVE
A133
ROMFORD
BAYLEIGH CL
VALENTINES DR

00 A B 01 C D 02 E F

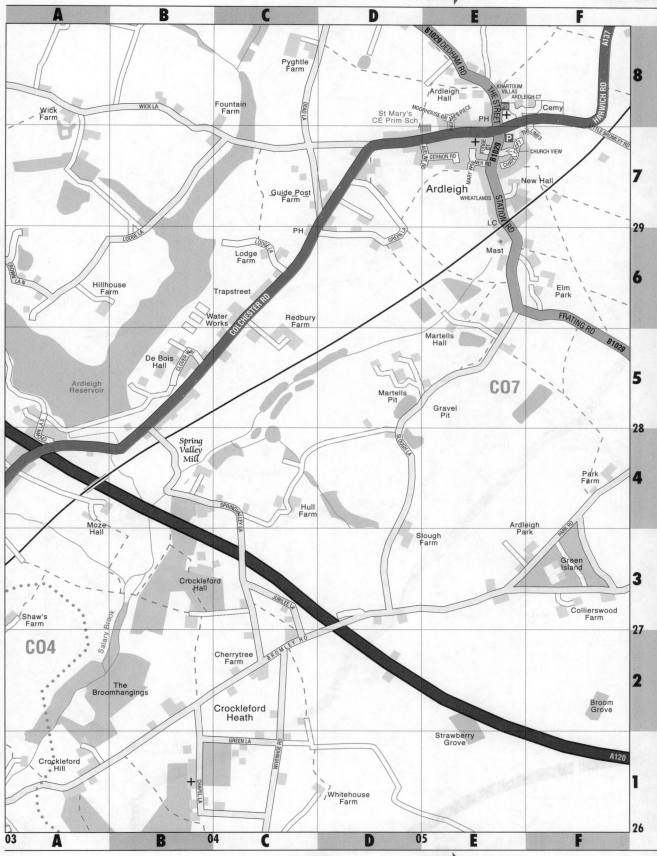

A B C D E F

8
7
29
6
5
28
4
27
2
26

03 A B 04 C D 05 E F

Wick Farm
Pyghtle Farm
Fountain Farm
WICK LA
DEAD LA
B1029 DEDHAM RD
HARWICH RD
A137
Khartoum Villas
ARDLEIGH CT
Ardleigh Hall
THE STREET
St Mary's CE Prim Sch
MOORHOUSE GN
GRAHAM'S PIECE
PH
Cemy
LITTLE BROMLEY RD
AVE WR RD
GERNON RD
B1029
FORGE ST
CHAPEL CROFT
CHURCH VIEW
THE LIMES
Church View
New Hall
Ardleigh
WHEATLANDS
MARY WAY
Guide Post Farm
GREEN LA
PH
STATION RD
LC
29
Hillhouse Farm
LODGE LA
LODGE LA
Lodge Farm
Mast
CROWN LA N
Elm Park
Trapstreet
COLCHESTER RD
Water Works
Redbury Farm
FRATING RD
B1029
Martells Hall
De Bois Hall
CLOVER WAY
Martells Pit
Gravel Pit
CO7
Ardleigh Reservoir
CROWN LA S
Park Farm
Spring Valley Mill
SPRINGVALLEY LA
Hull Farm
SLOUGH LA
Slough Farm
Ardleigh Park
PARK RD
Green Island
Moze Hall
Crockleford Hall
JUBILEE LA
Col/ierswood Farm
Shaw's Farm
SALARY BROOK
27
CO4
BROMLEY RD
Cherrytree Farm
The Broomhangings
Strawberry Grove
Broom Grove
Crockleford Heath
GREEN LA
WIVENHOE RD
CHAPEL LA
Crockleford Hill
Whitehouse Farm
A120

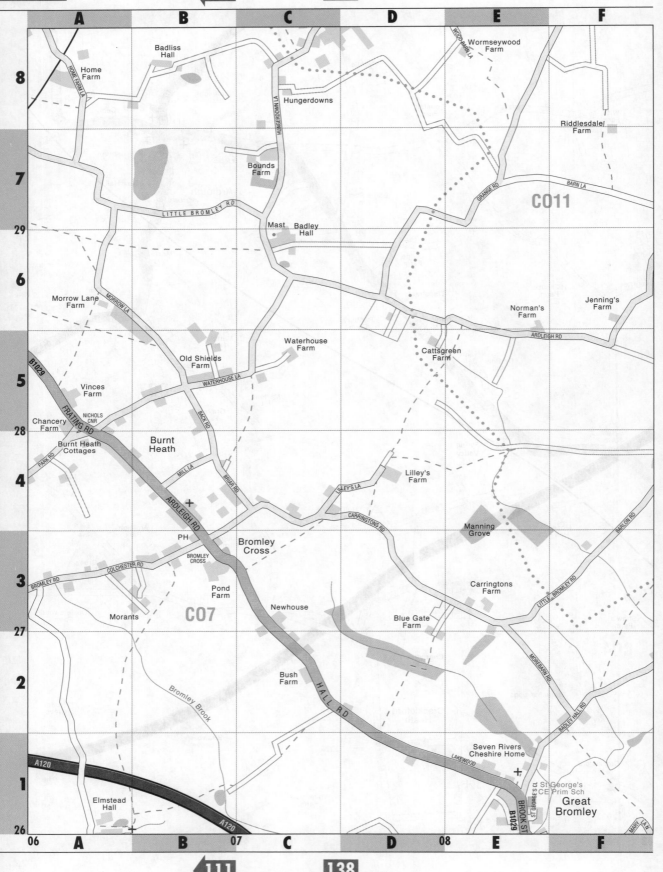

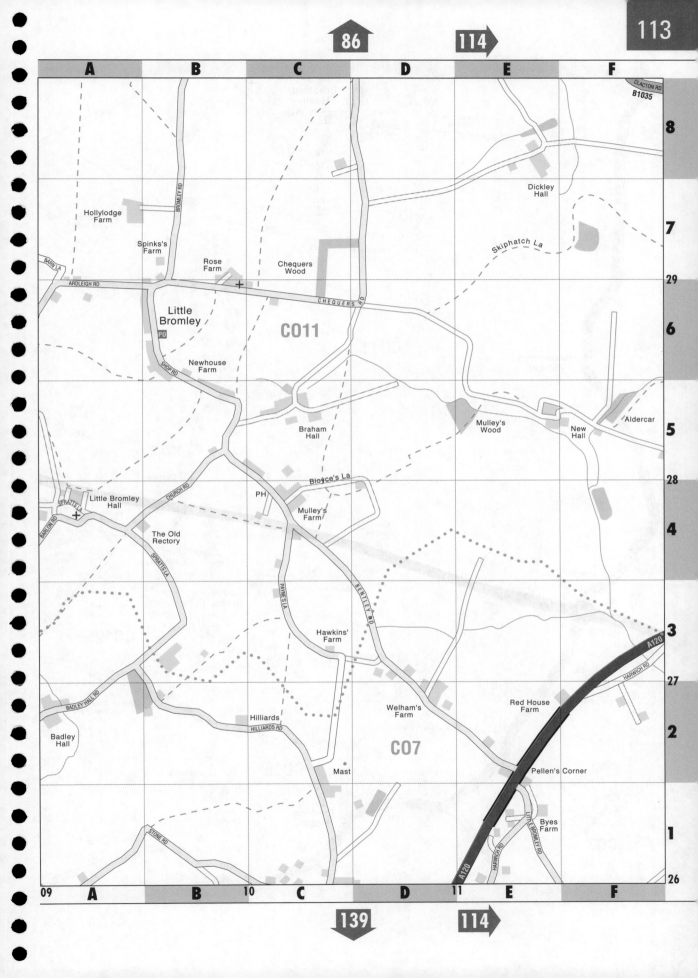

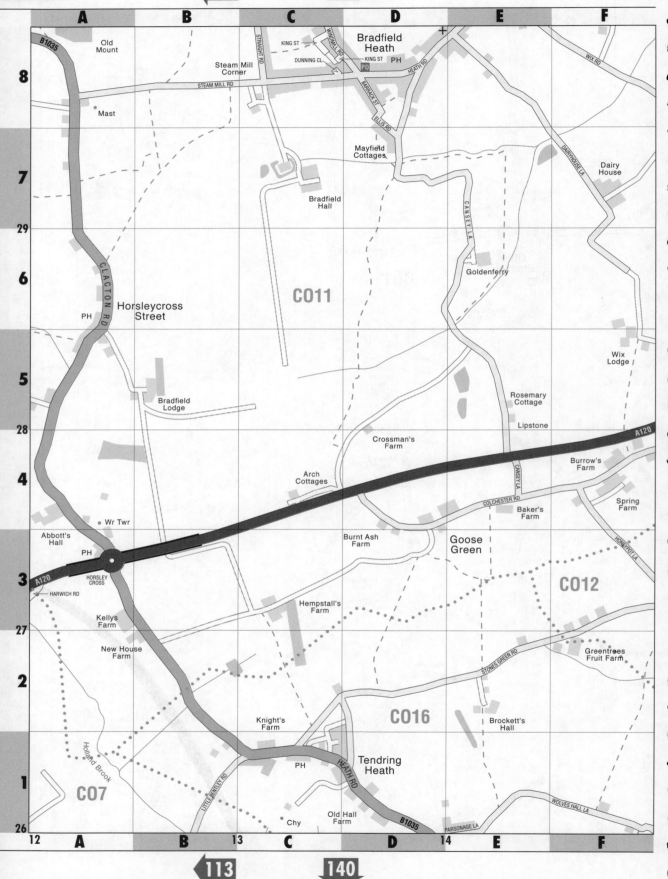

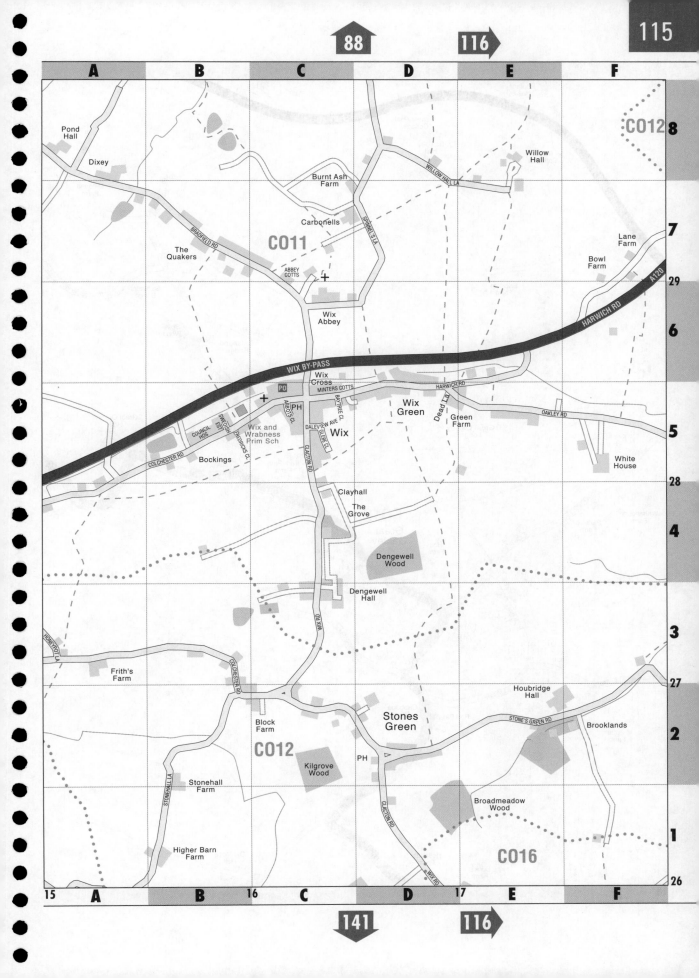

88
116
141
116

CO12

Pond Hall

Dixey

Burnt Ash Farm

Carbonells

CO11

WILLOW HALL LA

Willow Hall

BRADFIELD RD

The Quakers

SPINNEL'S LA

Lane Farm

Bowl Farm

ABBEY COTTS

A120

Wix Abbey

HARWICH RD

29

WIX BY-PASS

Wix Cross

6

MINTERS COTTS

HARWICH RD

PO

Wix Green

OAKLEY RD

PH

BAYTREE CL

Dead La

Green Farm

COUNCIL HOS

SWEDISH EST

FREDRICKS CL

ABBOTS CL

DALEVIEW AVE

GLEBE CL

Wix and Wrabness Prim Sch

Wix

5

CLACTON RD

White House

COLCHESTER RD

Bockings

28

Clayhall

The Grove

4

Dengewell Wood

Dengewell Hall

3

HONEYPOT LA

Frith's Farm

COLCHESTER RD

27

Houbridge Hall

Block Farm

STONE'S GREEN RD

Brooklands

CO12

Stones Green

2

WIX RD

STONEHALL LA

Stonehall Farm

Kilgrove Wood

PH

CLACTON RD

Broadmeadow Wood

1

Higher Barn Farm

WIX RD

CO16

26

15   16   17

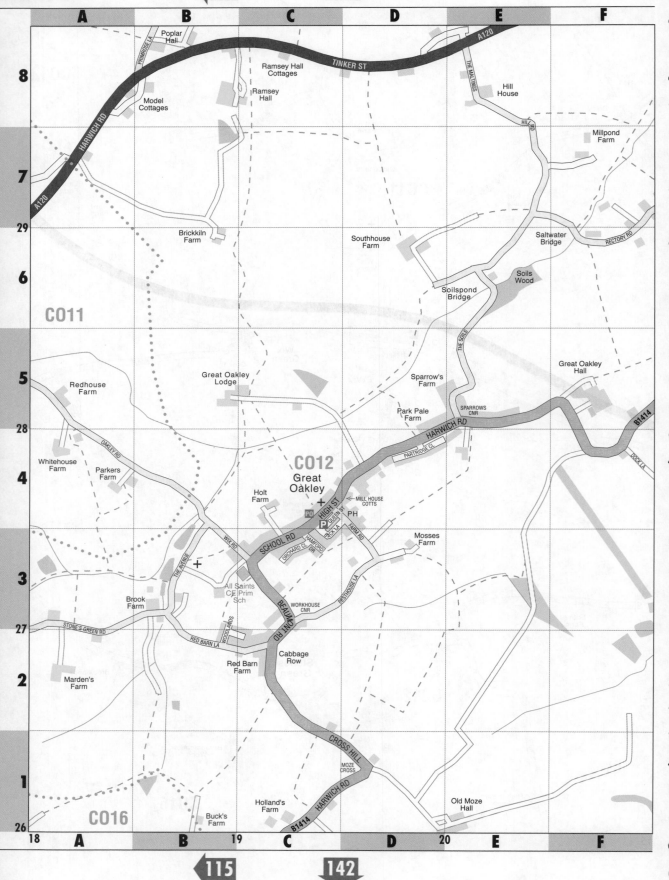

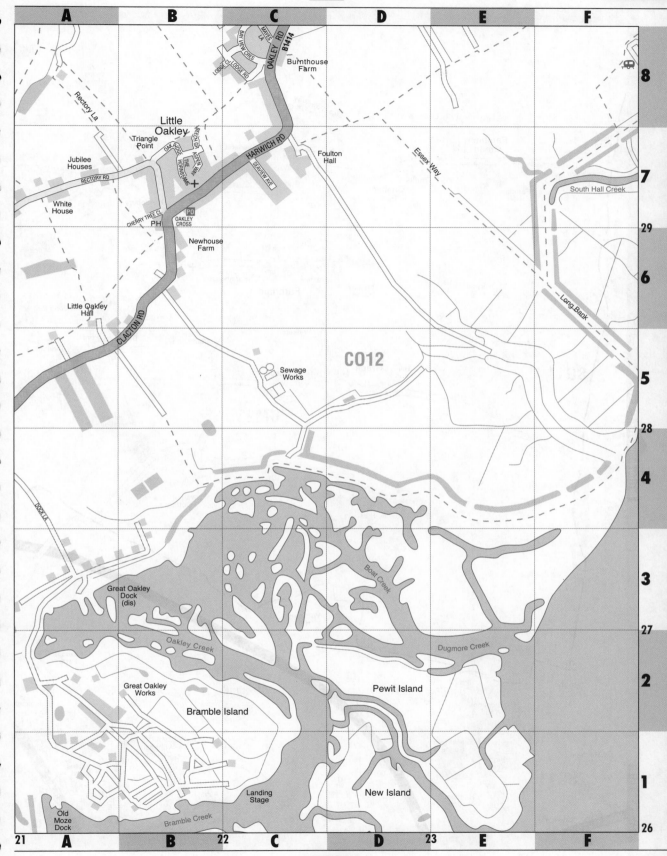

A B C D E F

8

Bay View Cres
Mayes La
Oakley Rd
B1414
Lodge Cl Lodge Rd
Burnthouse Farm

Little Oakley

Rectory La

Beech Gr
Oak Lodge
Aspen Way
The Hornbeams
Seaview Ave
HARWICH RD

Triangle Point

7

Jubilee Houses

RECTORY RD

Foulton Hall

Essex Way

South Hall Creek

White House

Cherry Tree Cl
PH
PO
OAKLEY CROSS

29

Newhouse Farm

6

Little Oakley Hall

CLACTON RD

Long Bank

CO12

5

Sewage Works

28

4

DOCK LA

Boat Creek

Great Oakley Dock (dis)

3

Oakley Creek

27

Dugmore Creek

Great Oakley Works

2

Pewit Island

Bramble Island

1

Landing Stage

New Island

Old Moze Dock

Bramble Creek

26

21 A B 22 C D 23 E F

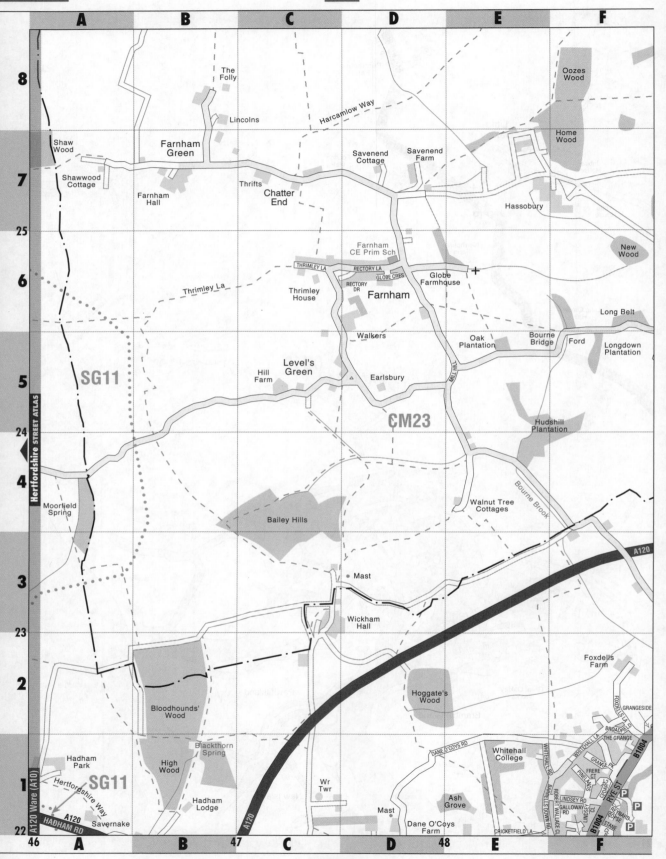

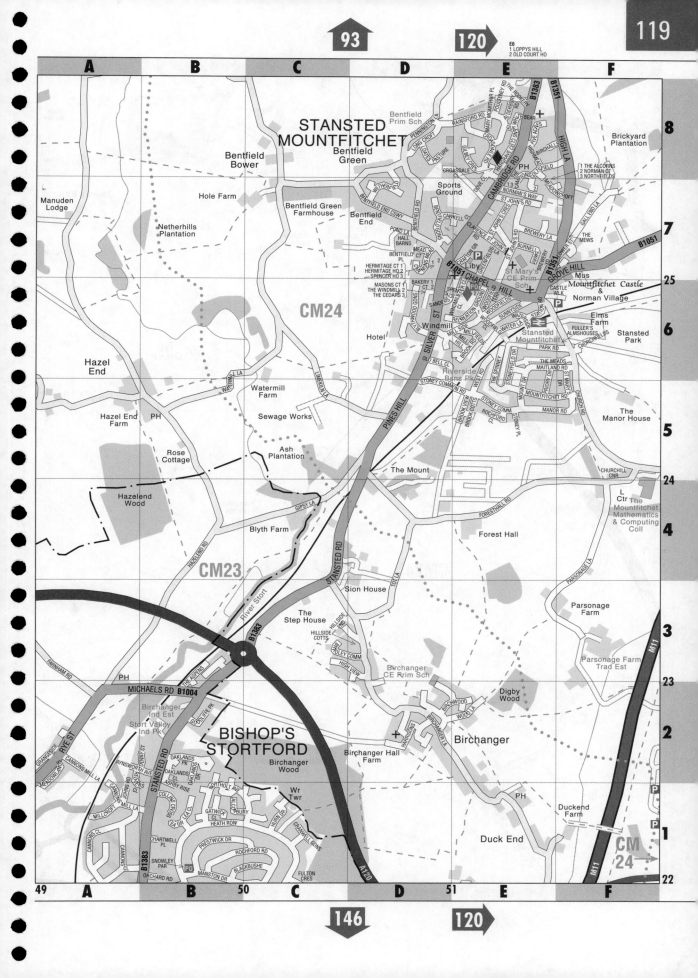

119
94

A B C D E F

8

Maxwick
Stansted Rd
B1051
Old Mill Farm
Elsenham Stud
Hall Rd
Church La
Elsenham Hall
Park Wood

M11
The Down Farm
Mill Wood
Fuller's End
The Bungalow
Gaunt's End

7

B1051
The Lodge
Stansted House
Durrel's Wood
Wilkin's Plantation
Long Plantation
Jubilee Cottage
CM22
Mott's Hall

25

6

Stansted Park
Tye Green Farm
Tye Green

Turners Spring Nature Reserve
The Bourne
Barley Common
Clay Pit Hill
Mast

5

Stansted Hall
Burton Bower
Tall Trees Cvn Pk
Church Rd

24

Old Bury Lodge La
Middleside Cvn Pk
Oak View Cvn Pk
Burton Bury
Burton End
Warman's Farm
Highfields Lodge
Belmer Rd

4

PH
CM24
Control Tower

3

M11
Burylodge Cottages
Bury Lodge La
Sixth Ave
Monks Farm
Pincey Rd

23

Little Bury Lodge Farm
Eleventh Ave
Ninth Ave
Fourth Ave
First Ave
Fifth Ave
Second Ave
Third Ave
Seventh Ave
Works

2

Bury Lodge
P
Roman La
Tenth Ave
Control Tower
London Stansted Airport
Bassingbourn Rd

1

P
P
P
Round Coppice Rd
Hotel
Long Border Rd
Taylors End Rd

22

M11
A120

52 A B 53 C D 54 E F

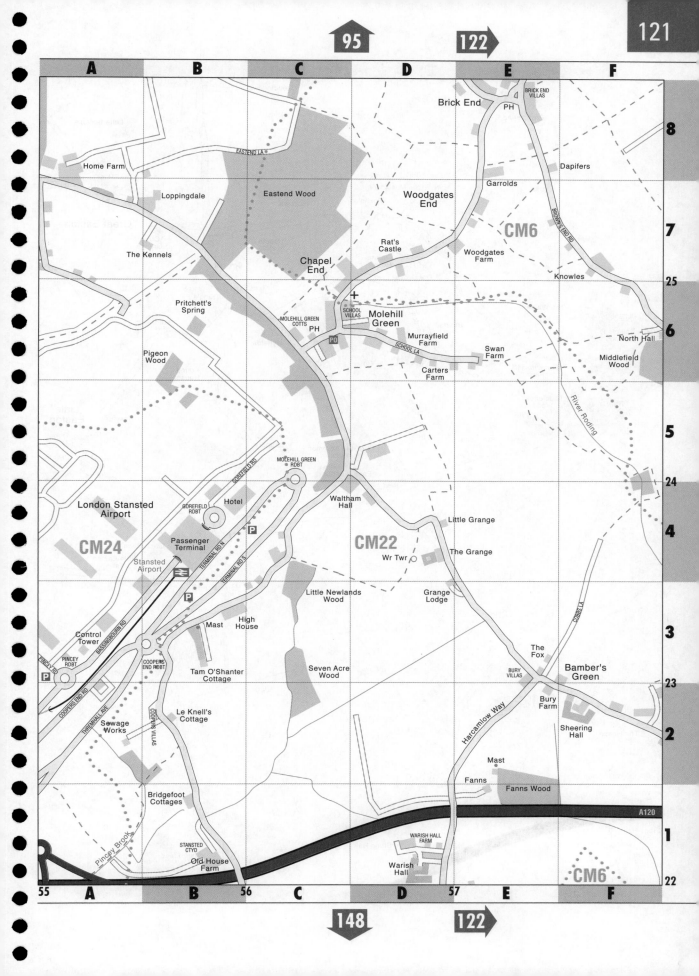

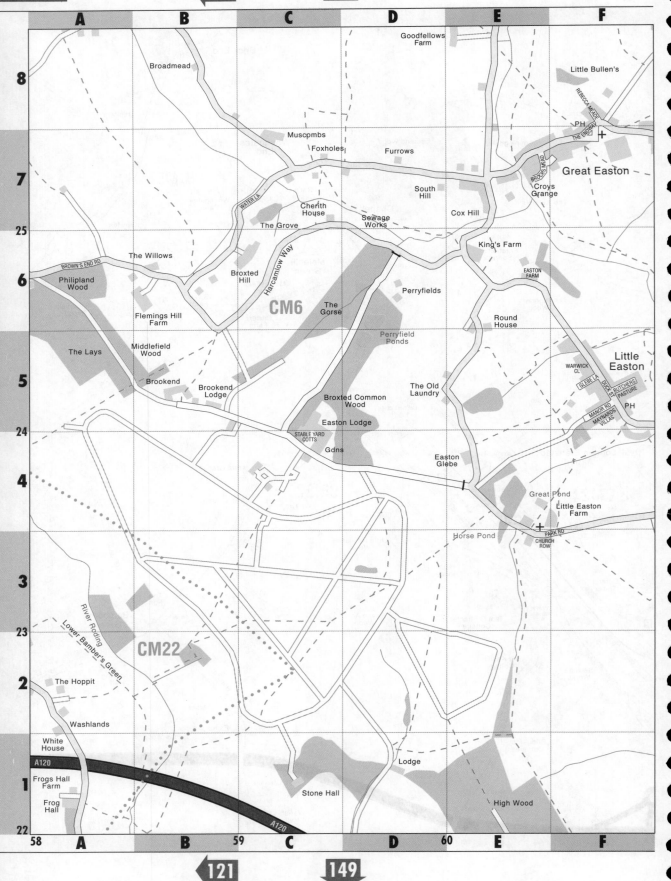

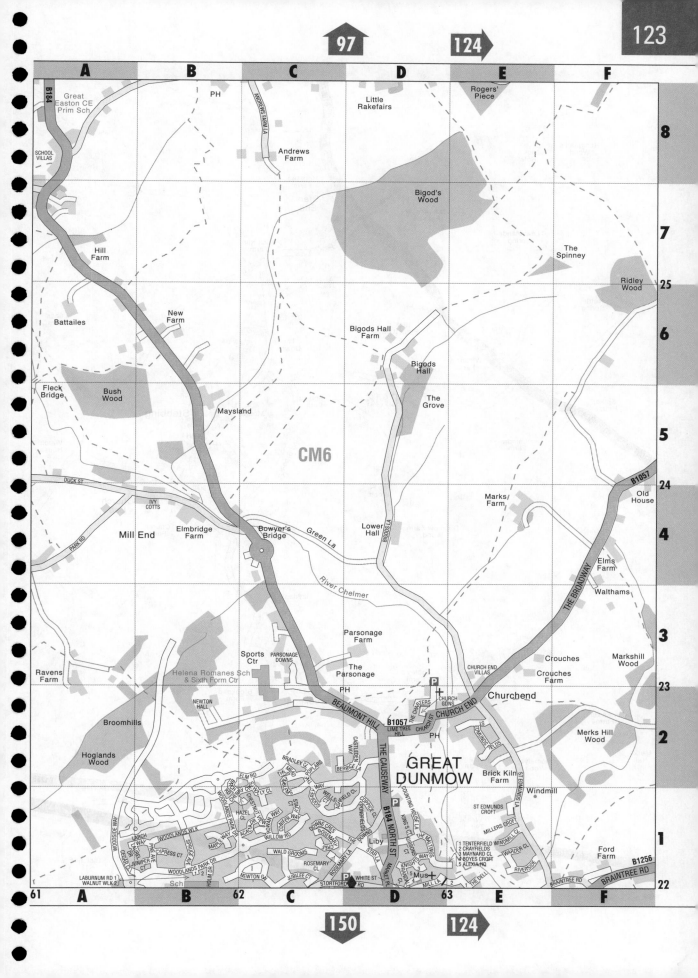

← 123   ↑ 98

A　B　C　D　E　F

8

Hangman's Wood

Nick's Hole

B1057

Hornsea Farm

Bran End

ROSEMARY LA

HORNSEA VILLAS

Tanner's Farm

7

Leaselands Spring

BRAM END FIELDS

PULFORD PL

BRICK KILN LA

Brick Kiln Farm

CLAY LA

25

BROOK FIELDS

Nettle Spring

MARSHALLS PIECE

DOWNS TERR

6

Hick's Plantation

The Downs

POUND GATE

PARK SIDE

GARDEN FIELDS

Lucas Farm

William's Farm

CM6

Stebbing Park

Stebbing Brook

The Mount

Stebbing Prim Sch

Stebbing

WHITEHOUSE RD

Spike House

THE BROADWAY

PO

PH

LIVERY MEWS

PH

Watch House

5

B1057

Dunmow Farm

MILL LA

HIGH ST

MOTTS YD

WAREHOUSE RD

24

WATCH HOUSE RD

The Fir Wood

RUFFELS FIELD

Church End

4

Dunmow Farm Wood

Church Farm

Haydens

3

Tooley's Farm

23

Brookend Farm

Merks Hall Farm

Brookend

Rookwoods

2

Merks Hall

Homelye Wood

Homelye Farm

B1256

A120

1

Wr Twr

HOMELYE CHASE

Throws Farm

BRAMBLE LA

BRAINTREE RD

BRAMBLE LA

Blatches

B1256

A120

22

64　A　B　65　C　D　66　E　F

← 123   ↓ 151

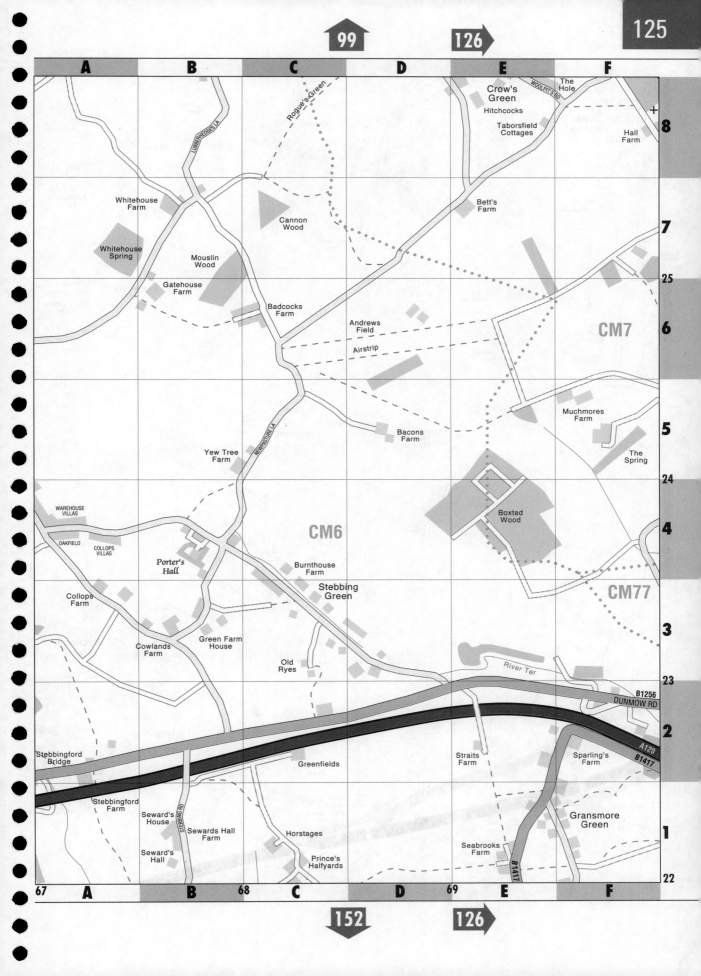

A B C D E F

8

Saling Hall Gardens
Great Saling
GROVE VILLAS
Chapel Hill
Cold Hall Farm
Ivy Hall
KYNASTON RD

PO

7

VICARAGE CL
PH
THE MEWS
Saling Grove
PICCOTTS LA
Piccotts Farm
Mount's Farm
CM7
Kynaston's Farm
HALL RD

25

New Spinney
Lightwaters Farm
Perry Childs Farm

6

CM7
Jubilee Spinney
Park's Farm
Pods Brook

Onchor's Farm

5

Golden Grove
Old Hall

24

Rumley Wood

4

Blackbush Wood
Moor's Farm
Pound Farm
Pound Farmhouse
Gould's Farm

3

Blake House Farm
Craft Ctr
MOORS LA
Moor's Spinney
CM77
SHALFORD RD
Duckend Green

23

PH
Rayne Prim Sch
CAPEL RD
CAPEL
BLYTH'S WAY
LEYSIDE
BRUNWIN RD
SMITHS FIELD
PHILIPS RD

2

B1256
Blake End
B1417
DUNMOW RD
Rayne
Havering's Farm
BAYTREE CT
ELM WLK
BARNARDS ORCH
PHILIPS CL
MAKEMORES CL
A120
B1417
THE STREET
PO
HANCE LA
MEDLEY RD
KIDDER RD
WARNER CL
VAUGH
STATION RD

1

CM6
Broadfield Farm
DUNMOW RD
Hazelmere Farm
B1256
Gatewoods Farm
NEW RD
NEW ROAD TERR
THE RUSKINS
SYMMONS CL
LITTLE PADDOCKS
Fairy Hall
EYRES
SCHOOL RD

22

Graunt Courts
Sorrell's Farm
DRAPERS CHASE
MILL LA
A120
SCHOOL RD

70 A 71 B C 72 D E F

A   B   C   D   E   F

8

7

25

6

5

24

4

3

23

2

1

22

76   A   B   77   C   D   78   E   F

Windmill (dis)
WINDMILL GDNS
MILLERS CL
Round Wood
MONKEN HADLEY
BROAD RD
A131
WILLOUGHBYS LA
Willoughbys Farm
CHURCH W
Dorewards Hall
THE CHASE
B1053
LYONS HALL RD
Bramble Wood
Woolmer Green Farm
THISTLEY GREEN RD
Lyons Hall
Lyonshall Wood
BROAD RD
Thistley Green
Covenbrook Hall
HIGHFIELD CL
THE RIDGE
Highfield Stile Farm
HIGHFIELD STILE RD
Works
Sewage Works
CM7
CM77
B1053
CHURCH LA
CONVENT HILL
Braintree Coll
Mill
CONVENT LA
NURSERY DR
THE CLOISTERS
DOUBLEDAYS GDNS
BRAINTREE
River Blackwater
HEREFORD DR
BOURCHIER AVE
NORTHAMPTON
Jenkin's Farm
KINGS LA
KINGFISHER GATE
VICTORY GDNS 1
TRAFALGAR CT 2
FALKLAND CT 3
MOUNTBATTEN CT 4
ALBEMARLE GDNS
NORRIS
CAVENDISH
RAYLEIGH CL
SHELLEY
BRITPORT DR
STAFFORD
CROWN MDW
PHILLIPS CT
BRADFORD CHASE
RIVER VW
1 GEORGIAN HO
2 LITTLE BRADFORDS
3 THE COURTYARD
Great Bradfords Jun & Inf Schs
BOSCAWEN GDNS
ACH
AVA
AJAX CL
EXETER
ORION WAY
GILBERT GDNS
MOUNTBATTEN GDNS
GUINEA
SOVEREIGN CL
DEERLEAP WAY
DUNOON CL
1 TIDESWELL CL
2 SNOWBERRY CT
BRADFORD ST
BAWN CL
HOLLY WALK
BLACKWATER WAY
VALLEY RD
JULIEN COURT RD
BEAUFORT GDNS
NORTHUMBERLAND CT
ORION WAY
BALMORAL CT
KEYES
RIDINGS
FISHER WAY
BYNG
BEATTY GDNS
NELSON GDNS
STRAFFORD PARK CL
BOWMANS
LINROD CL
NGALL RD
Hatches Farm
BRADFORDS
WARWICK
ESSEX
TRAFALGAR WAY
WELLINGTON CL
EDINBURGH GDNS
DRAKE GDNS
JELLICOE
HARWELL CT
A131
RUTLAND GDNS
NORFOLK GDNS
KENT GDNS
DEVONSHIRE GDNS
CONNAUGHT GDNS
CORNWALL GDNS
YORK GDNS
WHALEY WAY
KINGSMEAD PK
ROCHESTER CL
B1256
COGGESHALL RD
WESTMINSTER
WINDSOR
CUMBERLAND
GLOUCESTER GDNS
DALLWOOD
WAY
Recn Gd
1 ALBERT CT
2 TEMPLETON CT
3 FULLERS CT
ALLEN HO
JOHN RAY ST
TURNPIKE
PORTLAND
CLAY PITS WAY
1 WILD BOAR FIELD
2 DE-MARCI CT
3 BLACK BREAD CL
COURT AULD RD
CROFT CL
MOUNT RD
KEBLE WAY
ALBERT GT
EAST ST
MANOR
BEAUMONT
HOWARD CL
ST MARY'S RD
PO
HAY LAN
WHEATLEY AVE
BARTRAM AVE N
GULLS CROFT
CRABS CROFT
FORE FIELD
TWELVE ACRES
Ind Est
RAILWAY ST
B1256
B1018
CRAIG HO
THE LAURELS
VICTORIA ST
SOUTH ST
TRINOVANTIAN WAY
MANOR ST
TROTTERS FIELD
BADGER GR
BISHOPS AVE
CUNNINGTON RD
THORPE MEWS
BARTRAM AVE S
PEARL DR
RUSTIC
WADERS
LAKES RD
BENFIELD WAY
ENTERPRISE WAY
WITHAM CRINE DR
CHAPEL HILL
STUARTS WAY
BLACKHOUSE WAY
MARKS
WARREN RD
KING BERRIES
A120
Templeborder Wood
B1256
TIMBER YD
ROSE HILL
ROSE AVE
ROSEACRE
Lakes Ind Pk
ANGLIA WAY
Braintree Ind Pk
IRON VIEW
CRESSING RD
Ley Wood
P
STATION APP
Braintree
MILL CT
MILL HILL
Braintree Town FC
THE CHASEWAY
HAYTOR CL
Sch
BRICK KILN WAY
BARN MEAD
BECKERS GREEN RD
TANNERS MDW
DAVIES CT
ANGLE SIDE
MEGS
HUNTER DR
SALCOMBE RD
TAPESTRY WALK
THE LEY
PLAINS FIELD
MIDDLE KING
1 CRESS CROFT
2 PUNDERS FIELD
3 STILEMANS WOOD
4 DEBEN CT
5 STOUR CT
6 FRATING CT
7 GOLDHANGER CT
8 SALCOTT CREEK CT
9 CROUCH CT
10 BOURNE CT
APPLETREE WLK
PEARTREE CL
STRAWBERRY CL
HILLSIDE GDNS
THE RIDGEWAY
LONGACRES
THE LINDENS
SKITTS HILL
MILL PARK DR
BLK RUSH CL
CHERITON RD
RODING CT
LOWER KING
STEPHENSON RD
ORCHARD DR
DRIVERS MEAD
BRISE CL
FREEPORT DR
THEATRE VILLAGE
CANT WAY
THAMES CL
SLOUGH HOUSE CL
BRUNEL RD
WORCESTER
SKITTS HILL IND EST
RUSHMOOR DR
Freeport Designer Outlet
MERSEA FLEET
COLNE WLK
CHELMER RD
MUNDON RD
A120
PH
Cressing Lodge
Lanham Wood
FORD RD
BLACKWOODS
IMPACRES
BRAMLEY
BEADON DR
RUSSET CL
HARRISON
RYE GRASS WAY
RUSHMOOR DR
CHARTER WAY
Freeport
Chapel Hill Bsns & Ret Pk
THE SPINNEY
ROMAN CT
B1018
A120

A2
1 CAMULUS CL
2 GRESLEY DR
3 SIDINGS PL
4 VICTORIA CT
5 GROOMSIDE
6 JACQUARD WAY
7 ALEXANDRA MEWS
8 THE MULBERRIES
9 DAMASK MEWS
10 SOUTHVIEW

B2
1 WINDSOR CT
2 STUART CT
3 TUDOR CT
4 YORK CT
5 LANCASTER CT

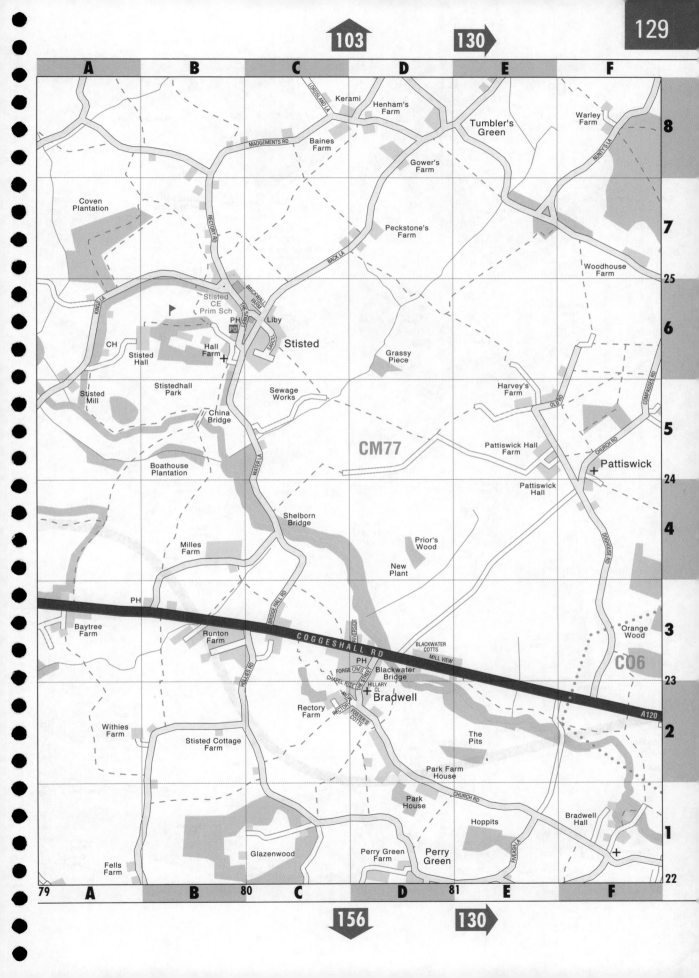

A   B   C   D   E   F

Kerami
Henham's Farm
Tumbler's Green
Warley Farm
8
LORDS AND LA
MADGEMENTS RD
Baines Farm
Gower's Farm
NUNTY'S LA
Coven Plantation
Peckstone's Farm
7
RECTORY RD
BACK LA
Woodhouse Farm
25
Stisted CE Prim Sch
BRICKWALL
THE STREET
Liby
Stisted
PH PO
Harvey's Farm
OLD RD
COMPASSES RD
6
CH
Hall Farm
Grassy Piece
CHURCH RD
Stisted Hall
Stistedhall Park
Sewage Works
Pattiswick Hall Farm
Pattiswick
5
Stisted Mill
China Bridge
CM77
WATER LA
Pattiswick Hall
24
Boathouse Plantation
DOGHOUSE RD
Shelborn Bridge
Prior's Wood
4
Milles Farm
New Plant
Orange Wood
3
PH
Baytree Farm
Runton Farm
COGGESHALL RD
BRIDGE HALL RD
RIVERSIDE
BLACKWATER COTTS
MILL VIEW
CO6
PH
Forge CRES
Blackwater Bridge
23
CHAPEL RISE
THE STREET
HILLARY CL
A120
HOLLIES RD
Bradwell
Withies Farm
Rectory Farm
RECTORY
FOSTER'S COTTS
The Pits
2
Stisted Cottage Farm
Park Farm House
Park House
CHURCH RD
Hoppits
Bradwell Hall
1
Fells Farm
Glazenwood
Perry Green Farm
Perry Green
PYEFASH LA
22
79   A   B   80   C   D   81   E   F

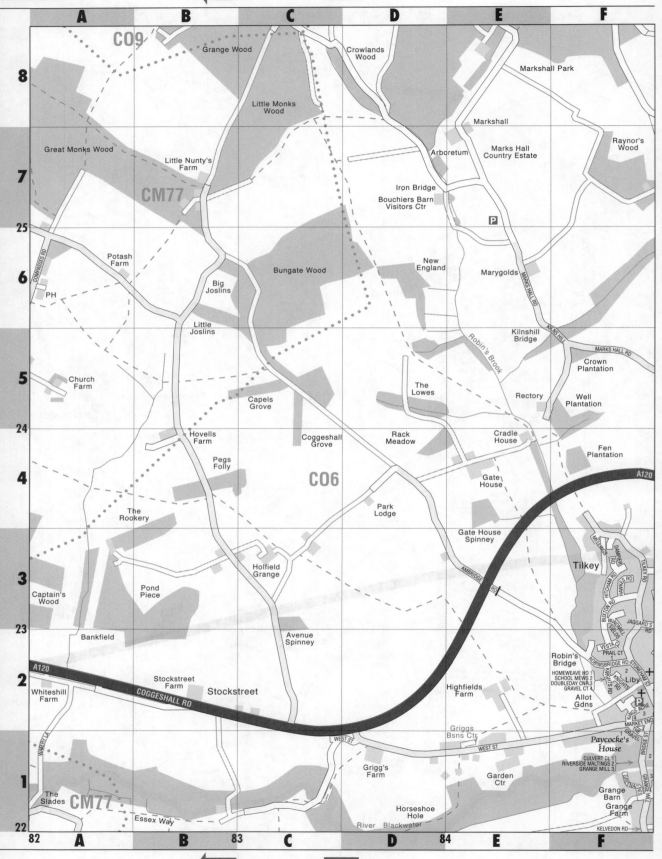

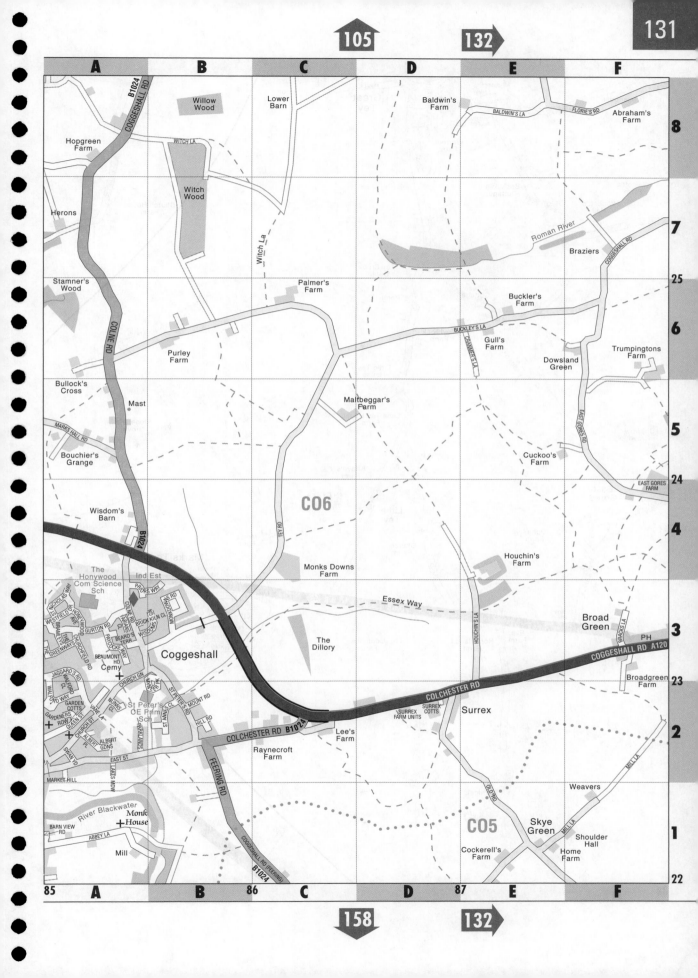

131
106

FLORIE'S RD

Brookhouse

BROOKHOUSE RD

NEWBARN RD

HARVESTERS' WAY

GREENFIELD DR

HOLLAND CRFT

THE STREET

CHAPEL RD

MOOR RD

Great Tey

Moor Farm

WINDMILLS 1
TAMBOUR CL 2

PH

Warrens Farm

NEW COTTS

TEY RD

TEY RD

Hoe Farm

8

Walcott's Farm

Walcott's Hall

COGGESHALL RD

Brick Kiln Cottage

Church House Farm

RECTORY RD

7

25

BROOK RD

Tey Brook Centre

Chase Cottage

Roman River

LC

6

Essex Way

Teybrook Farm

Little Tey House

5

Sparrow Grove

Little Tey House Farm

Stonefield Grove

24

East Gores

EAST GORES RD

Uphall Farm

SALMON'S LA

Knave's Farm

GREAT TEY RD

CO6

Mott's Farm

MOTT'S LA

PH

Marks Tey

4

CHURCH LA

Little Tey

Church Farm

ROXBOROUGH CL

A120

NORBURY RD

ASHBURY RD

MATBURY CL

GODMANS

HAWLMARK END

WEL

PATTEN CL

3

A120

BUXTON COTTS

SALMON'S CNR

Elm Farm

Honeylands Farm

Godbolt's Farm

COGGESHALL RD

40

STONE FIELD

NORMAN

BREE AVE

LEY FIELD

DOMSET

BANK

PROCTOR W

SIDE

JAYS LA

MANDE VILLE RD

KEARN RD

CORNWALLIS RD

JAYS LA

Prim Sch

HOLLYWOOD

DINANTS CRES

LONG GRN

WILSON'S LA

LC

DOBBIES LA

1 KINGSBURY CL
2 STEELE CL

Works

LONDON RD

A12

23

2

ELM LA

LONDON RD

LOGGETTS LA

1

Hornigals

CO5

Wishingwell Farm

A12

22

88 A B 89 C D 90 E F

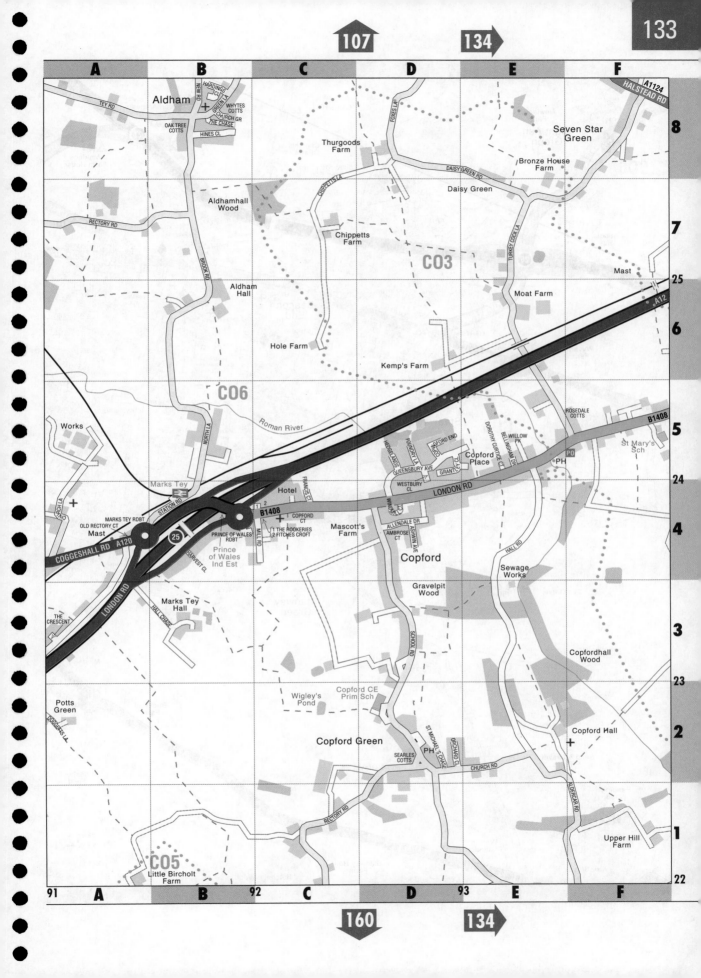

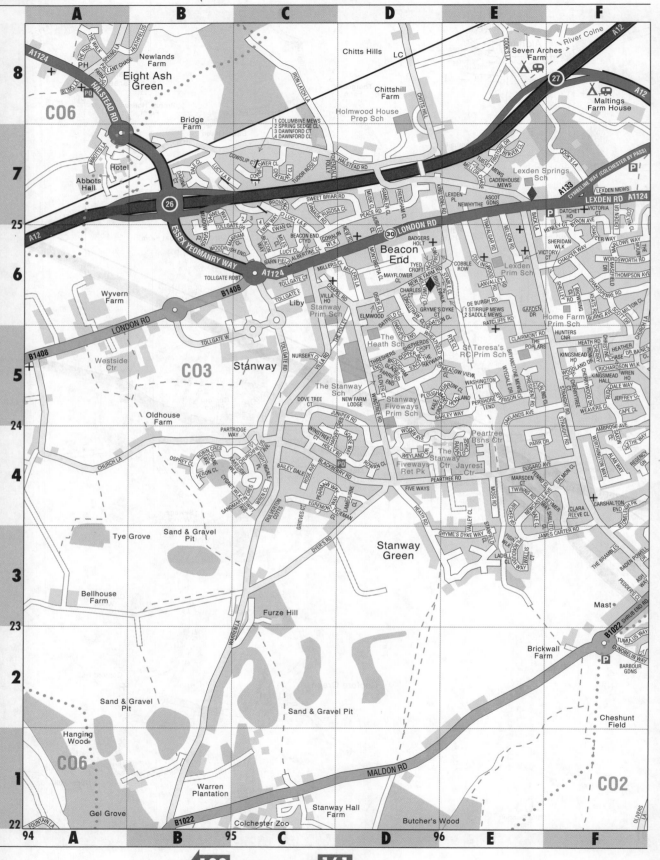

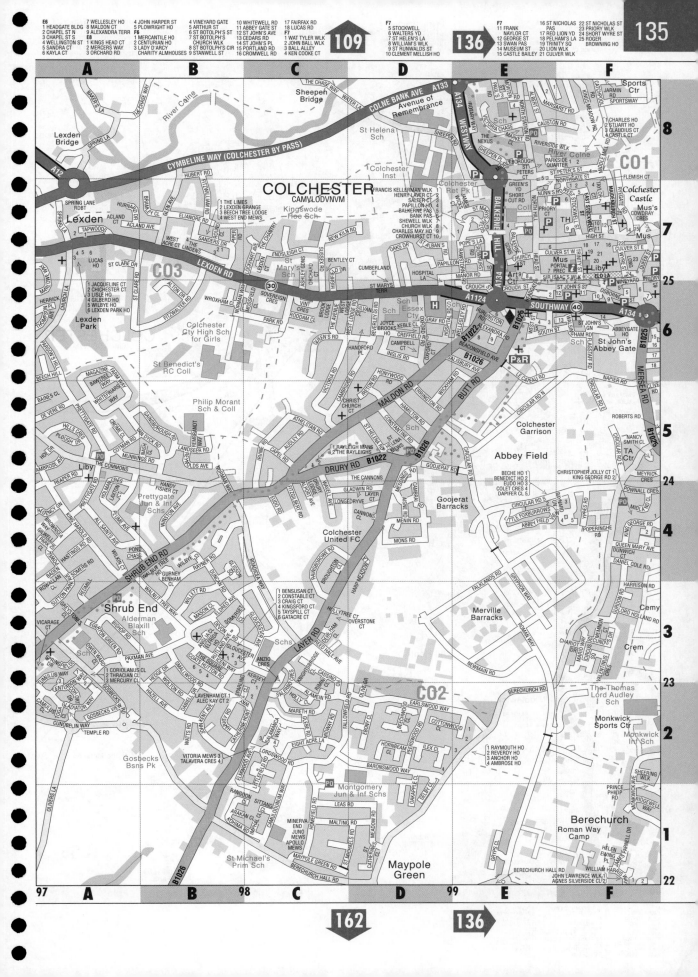

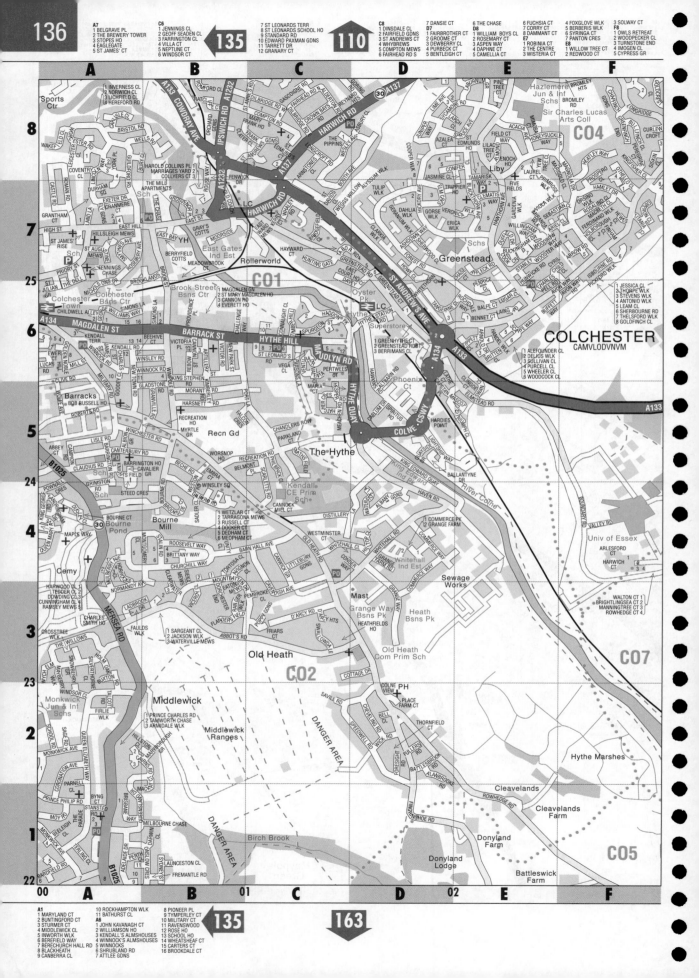

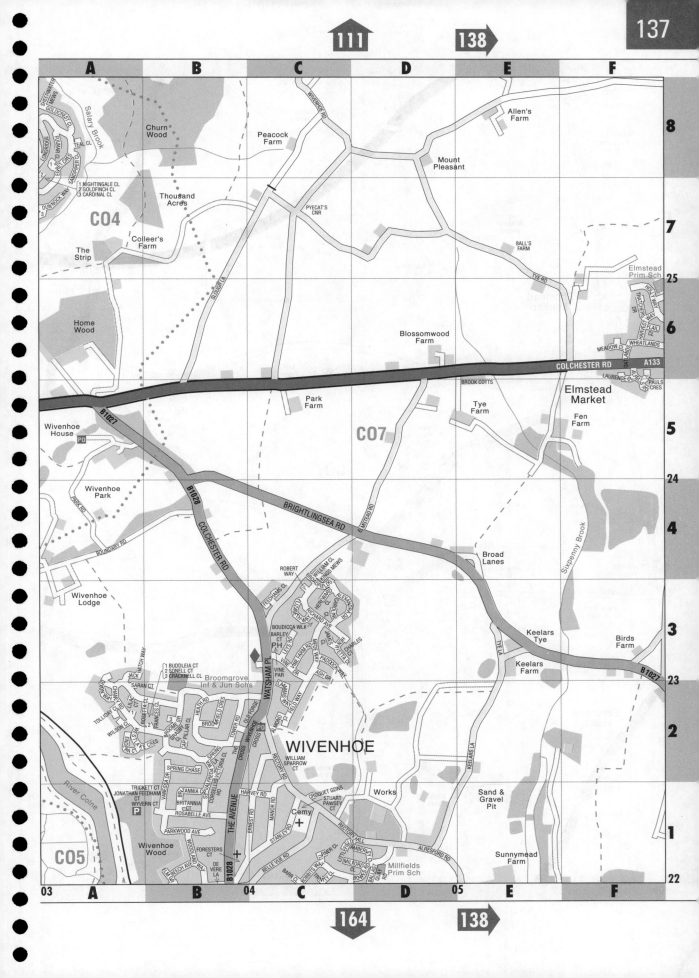

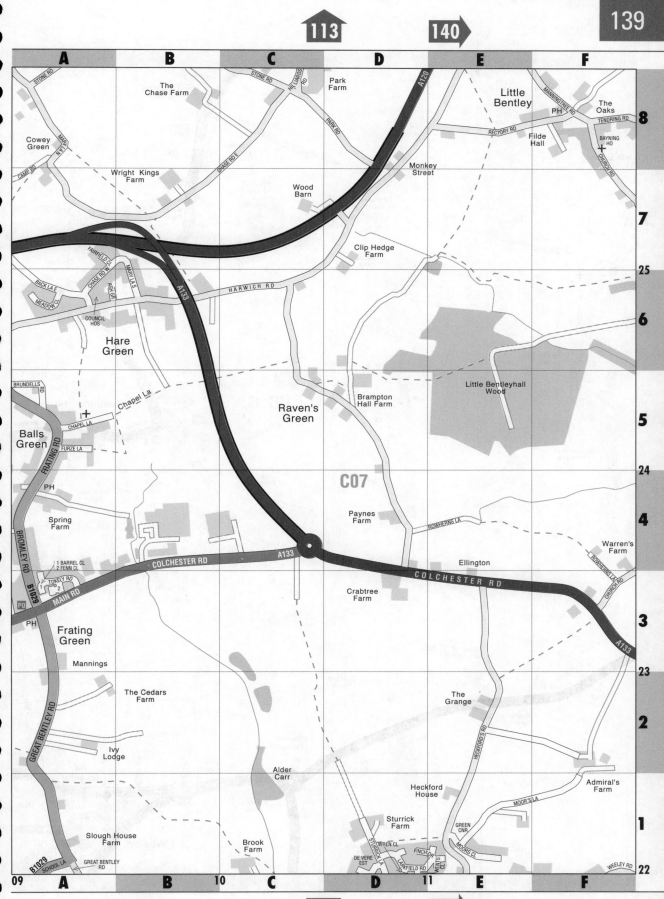

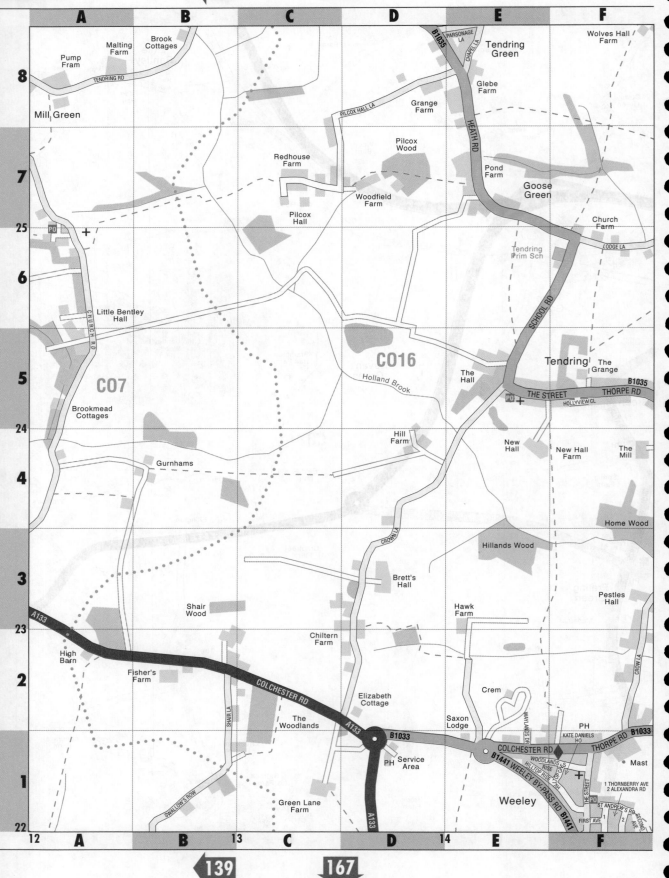

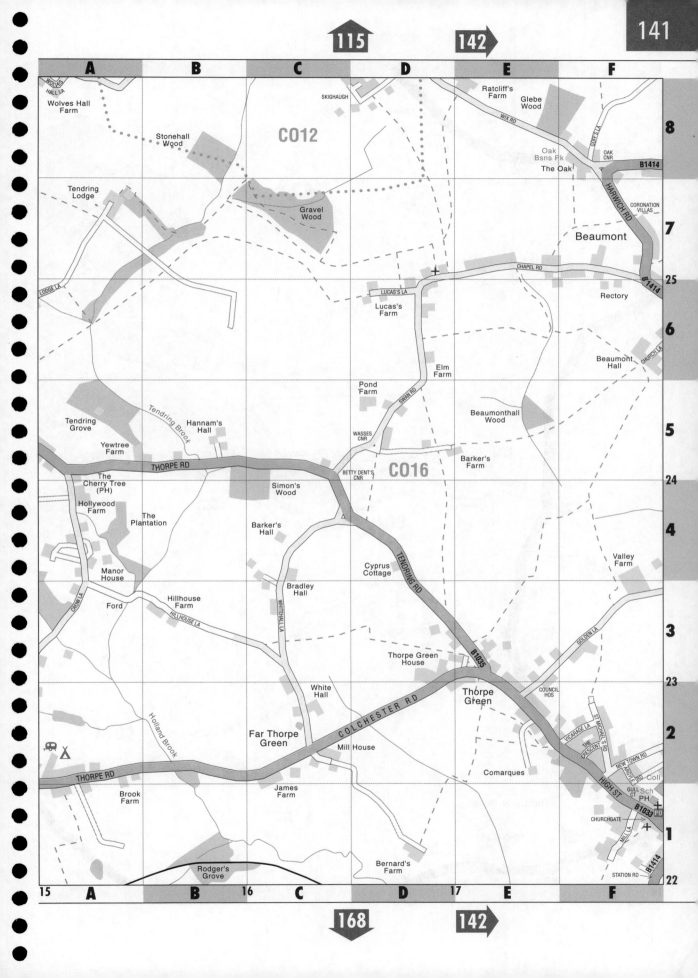

A B C D E F

8

Oldhouse Farm

Glebe Farm

Potland

HARWICH RD

The Horseshoes

New Moze Hall

CO12

Maze Creek

B1414

7

25

Northfield Farm

B1414

HARWICH RD

6

CHURCH LA

THORPE RD

Landermere Creek

LOWER BARN FARM

5

Quay Farm

Quay (dis)

Beaumont Cut

24

QUAY LA

Beaumont Bridge

Beaumont Quay

CO16

White House

GULL COTTS

4

GOLDEN LA

Landermere Hall

Landermere

3

Thorpe Lodge

New Hall

Kentshill Farm

LANDERMERE RD

23

WALTON RD

2

NEW TOWN

PALMERSTON RD

LONSDALE RD

SPENCER RD

KENILWORTH GR

CO13

Dale Hill Farm

ARGYLE

NEW RD

THORPE AVE

ST BOTOLPH CL

THE SPONG

BELDAMS CL

DAMANT'S FARM LA

Coll

Thorpe-le-Soken

ABBEY CRES

OAK CL

ELM FARM CVN PK

BYNG HO

BYNG CL

BYNG CRES

Damont's Farm

Sneating Hall

1

B1414

ABBEY ST

B1033

HALL LA

FRINTON RD

WHITE LODGE CRES

Folly Farm

B1033

B1034

SNEATING HALL LA B1034

B1034

STATION RD

B1414

22

18 A B 19 C D 20 E F

A B C D E F

CO12

8

Hamford Water

7

25

Skipper's
Island

6

Horsey Island

CO14

Ambrose
Point

Nature
Reserve

Honey
Island

Kirby Creek

CO16

Hamford Water
National Nature Reserve

5

Landermere Creek

24

The Wade

4

ISLAND RD.

Causeway

Coles Creek

3

Marsh
House

23

Birch
Hall

Peter's
Point

Refuse
Tip

2

CO13

Kirby
Quay

ISLAND LA.

CO14

1

Sewage
Pumping
Station

MALTING LA.

WALTON RD

THE STREET

PH

Kirby-le-Soken

QUAY LA.

VISTA AVE

PERCIVAL RD

MEADOW VIEW

B1034

22

A B C D E F

8

7

25

6

5

24

4

3

23

2

1

22

Stone Point

Stone Marsh

Stone Creek

Cormorant Creek

The Dardenelles

Standcreek Salts

Salt Fleet

John Weston Nature Reserve

Sewage Works

THE NAZE

Walton Channel

Hedge-end Island

Walton Hall Marshes

CREEK COTTS

The Naze Nature Trail

CO14

Walton Hall

The Naze Tower

The Twizzle

PH

Titchmarsh Marina

COLES LA

NAZE CT
EARLSWOOD LODGE
ELIZABETH CT
LOUISE CL
MAZE CL
OLD HALL A
DINTY POINT

High Tree La

HAMFORD CL

FIRST AVE

SECOND AVE

THIRD AVE

NAZE PARK RD

Mabel Greville Breakwater

D'ARCY HO 1
RIVERS HO 2
SPEN HO
SPENDELLS HO
GREVILLE CL

ROCHFORD HO

FLORENCE RD

Sole Creek

Naze Marine Holiday Pk

TUDOR CL

BEATRICE RD

PERCIVAL RD

CLIFF PAR

Jubilee Beach

WINFIELD TERR

HALL LA

GREEN LA

BARNETT REACH

COASTGUARD COTTS

Walton Maritime Mus

Walton Mere

PENRICE CT 1
EASTCLIFF HO 2
WATERFRONT TERR 3
KINGS REACH 4
HOMELEA 5

EAST TERR

East Terrace Breakwater

CH

Walton Prim Sch

PRINCE'S ESPL

B1034

BRIAN BISHOP CL

COLES LA

MILL LA

Martello Tower

SAVILLE ST

NORTH ST

STANDLEY RD

EAGLE AVE

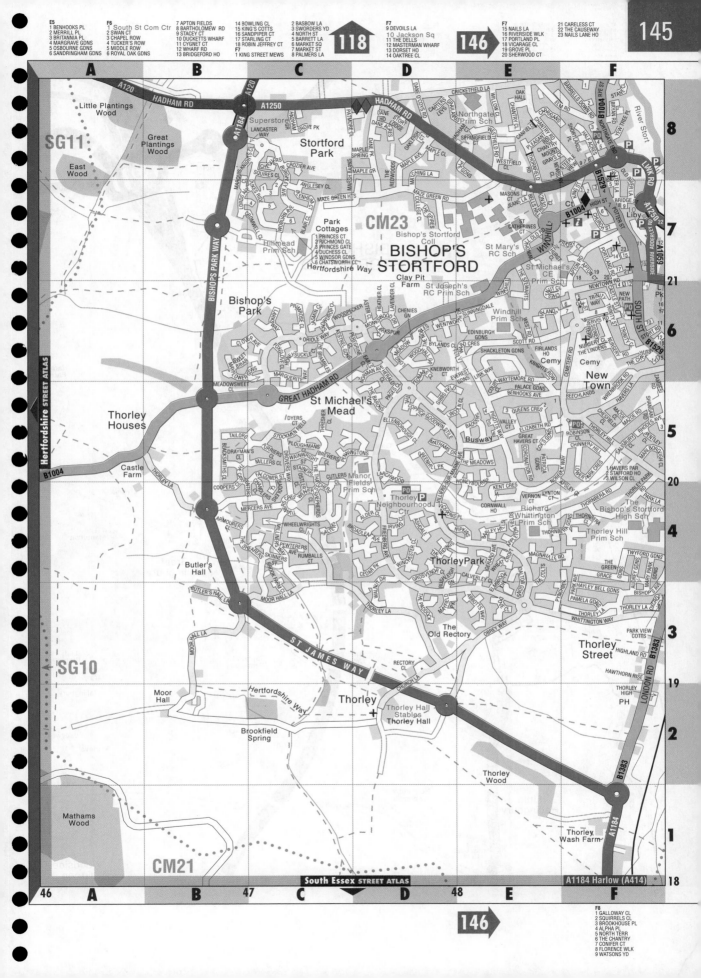

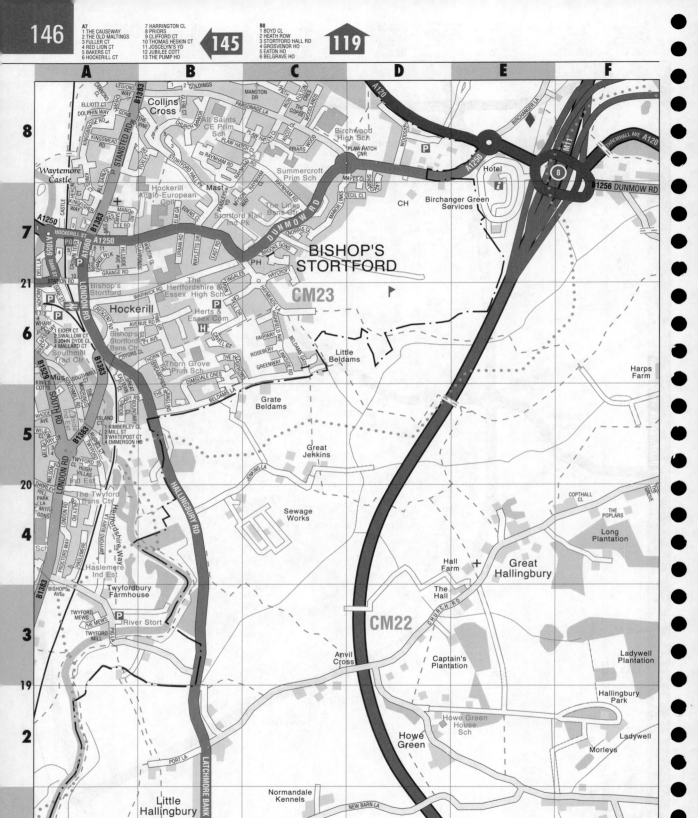

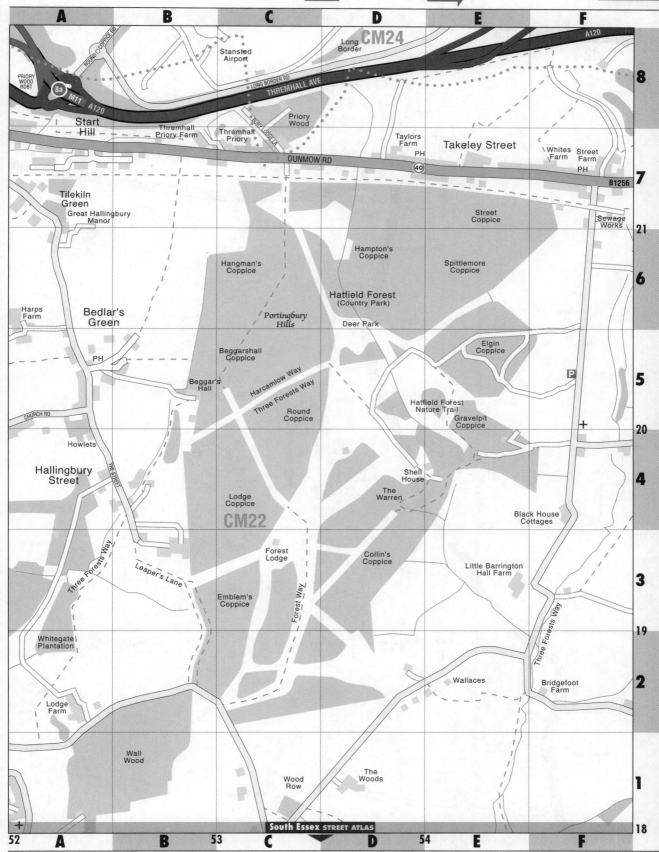

A B C D E F

8

7

21

6

5

20

4

3

19

2

1

18

PRIORY WOOD RDBT

8a M11 A120

Start Hill

ROUND COPPICE RD

Stansted Airport

Long Border

CM24

A120

LONG BORDER RD

THREMHALL AVE

Thremhall Priory Farm

Thremhall Priory

BURY LODGE LA

Priory Wood

DUNMOW RD

40

Taylors Farm PH

Takeley Street

Whites Farm

Street Farm PH

B1256

Tilekiln Green

Great Hallingbury Manor

Street Coppice

Sewage Works

Harps Farm

Bedlar's Green

Hangman's Coppice

Portingbury Hills

Hampton's Coppice

Hatfield Forest (Country Park)

Deer Park

Spittlemore Coppice

PH

Beggarshall Coppice

Beggar's Hall

Harcamlow Way

Three Forests Way

Round Coppice

Elgin Coppice

Hatfield Forest Nature Trail

Gravelpit Coppice

P

CHURCH RD

Howlets

Hallingbury Street

THE STREET

Lodge Coppice

CM22

Shell House

The Warren

Collin's Coppice

Black House Cottages

Little Barrington Hall Farm

Three Forests Way

Leaper's Lane

Forest Lodge

Forest Way

Emblem's Coppice

Whitegate Plantation

Wallaces

Bridgefoot Farm

Three Forests Way

Lodge Farm

Wall Wood

Wood Row

The Woods

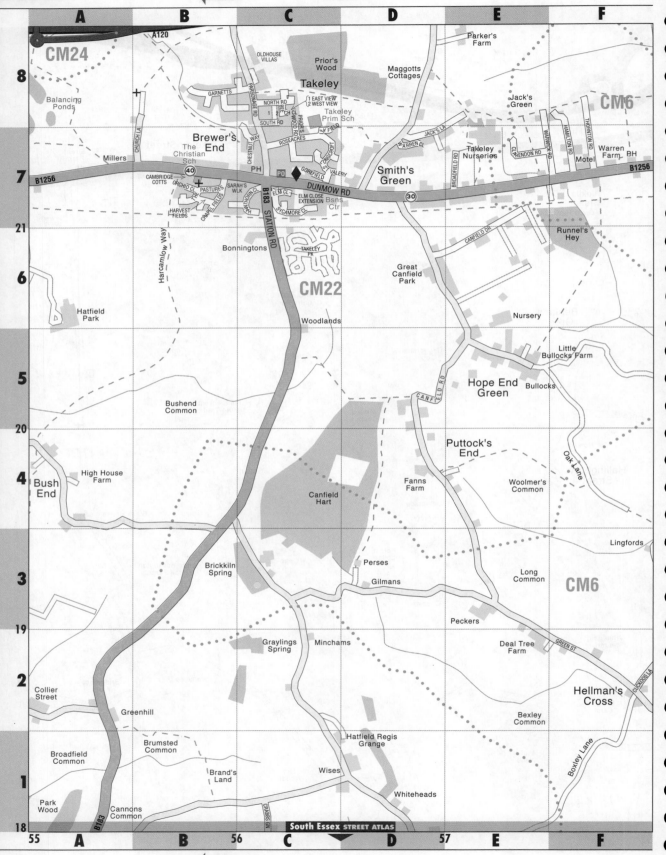

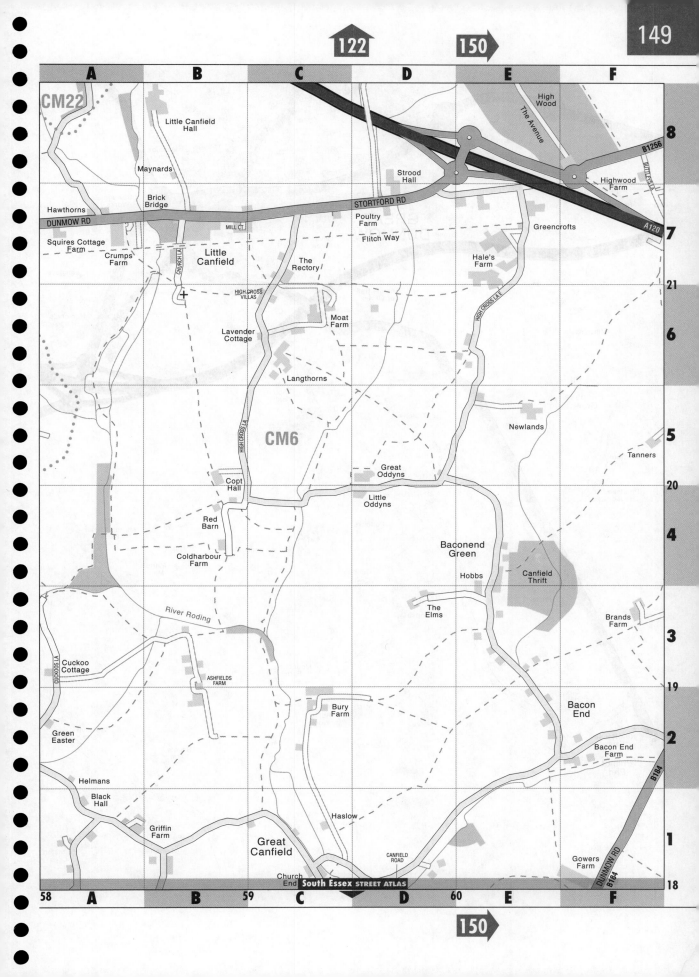

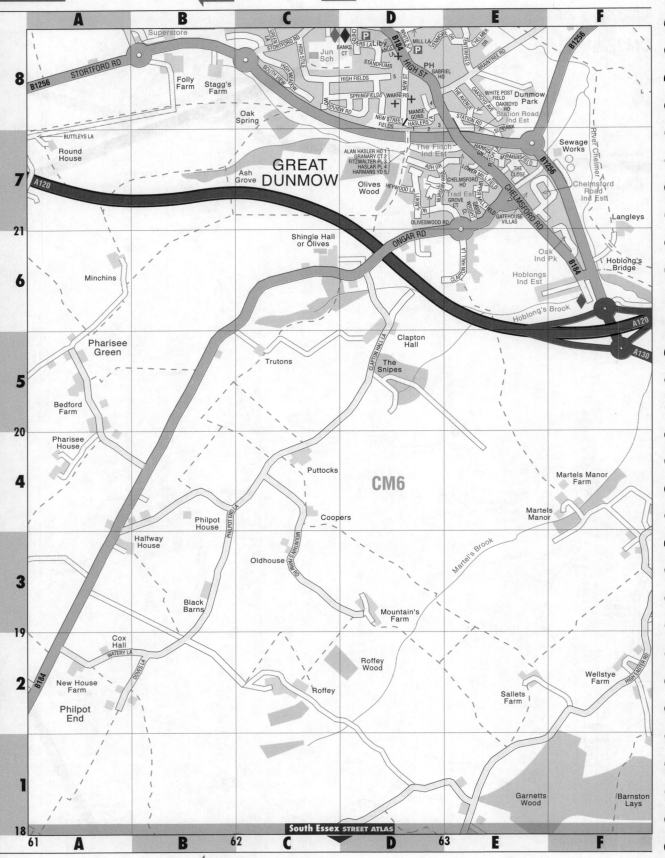

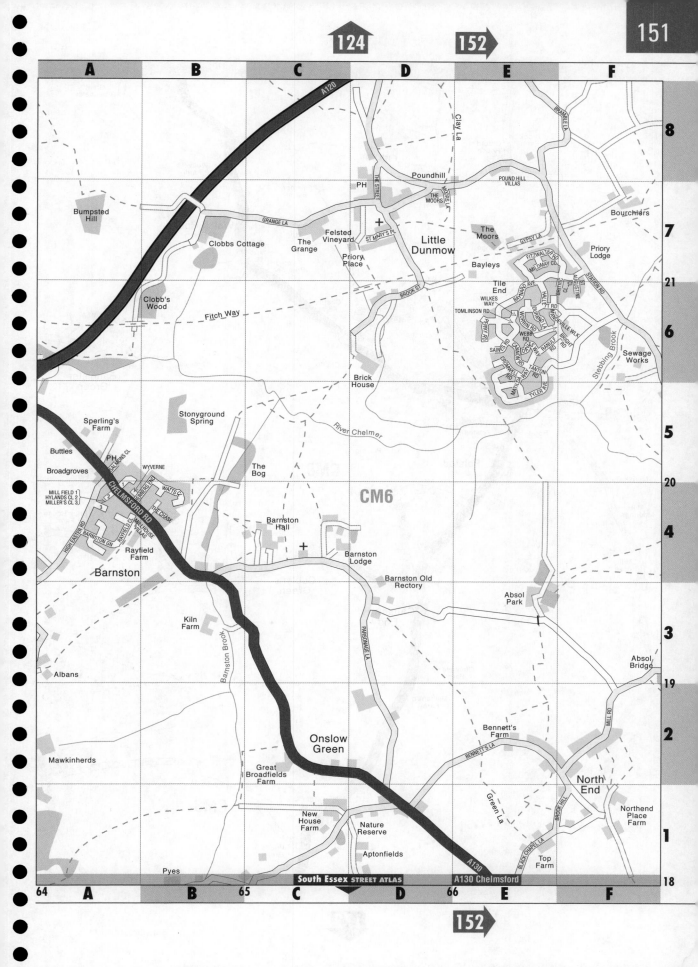

151
125

A B C D E F

8

Stebbing Brook

Brook Farm

Gifford House

Fitch Way

Great Greenfields

7

Miniature Rifle Range

STEBBING RD

Felmoor Farm

Weavers Farm

B1417

Sunnybrook Farm

Watch House Green

WATCH HOUSE VILLAS

21

Wr Twr

CHESTNUT WLK

CHAFFIX CL

PLAYERS CT

GARNETTS LA

CHAFFIX

Chaffix Farm

Felsted Prim Sch

OXNEY VILLAS

RAVENS CRES

BANNISTER GREEN VILLAS

CRESSAGES

STEVENS LA

6

Felsted Sch

ALDERTOW CL

BRAINTREE RD

Chaffix

Oxney's Farm

BURNSTEAD RD

THE CL

PH

Bannister Green

Bury Farm

FELSTED ALMSHOUSES

THE ORCHARD

JOLLYBOYS LA N

5

STATION RD

BURY FIELDS

PO

RICHE CL

GARNETTS VILLAS

GARNETTS BGLWS

Hotel

Felsted Prep Sch

CROMWELL PK

Felsted Pl

Felsted

THE TERRACE

Playing Field

CM6

20

Mariskalls

Mill Moorings

BAKERS LA

Jollyboys

Cleveland's Farm

4

MILL RD

CHELMSFORD RD

JOLLYBOYS LA

BRICKBURN CL

Potash Farm

Cock Green

Brick House Farm

Mill House

LADYSMITH COTTS

CAUSEWAY END RD

Cobler's Green

Pondpark Farm

3

Causeway End

River Chelmer

Glanfield's Farm

19

Millbank's Farm

2

LEEZ LA

The Gate House

CM3

1

B1417

Prior's Green

CAUSEWAY

18

67 A B 68 C D 69 E F

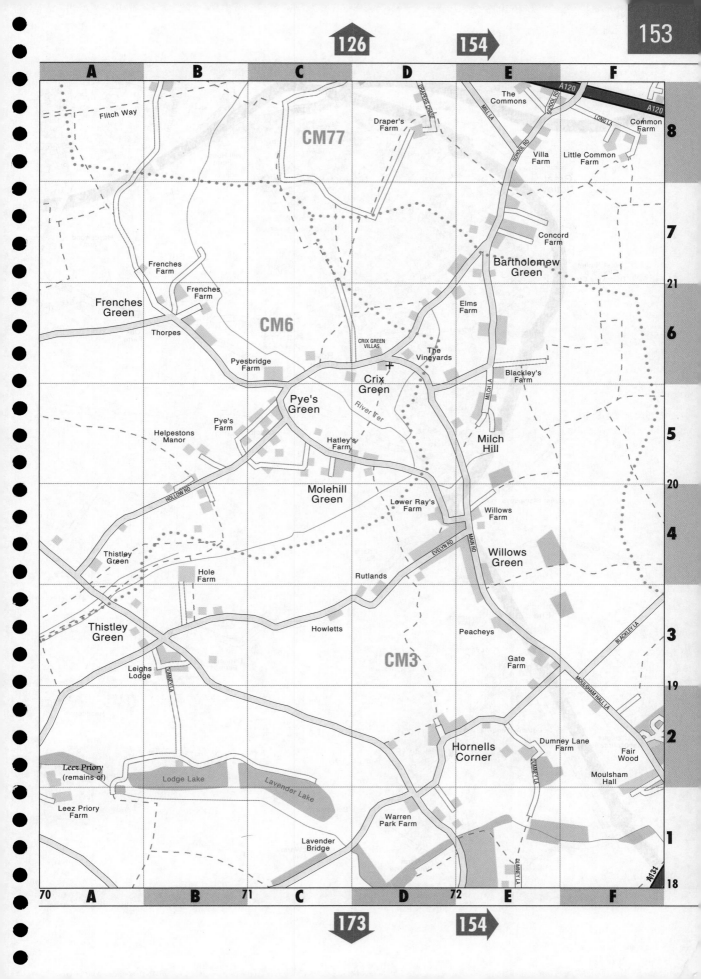

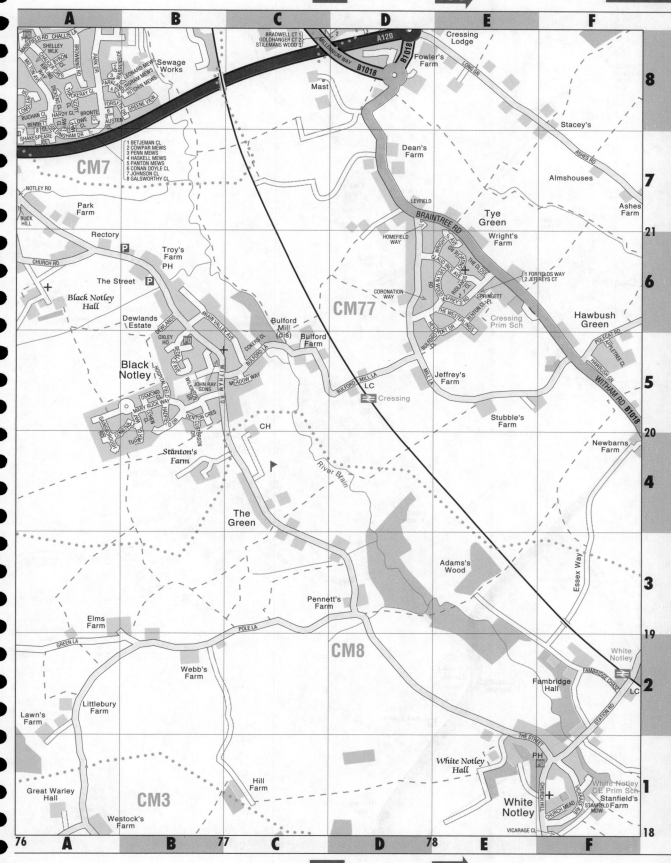

128 156

A B C D E F

CM7

Sewage Works

PO CHALLIS LA
MASEFIELD RD
SHELLEY WLK
BYRON CL
CHALLIS CL
KEBLE WAY
WARRENSIDE
PARK DR
BROWNING RD
LEONARD MEWS
INGRAM MEWS
HITCHIN MEWS
PARK LA
MILTON AVE
DICKENS CL
THACKERAY CL
SCOTT
FORSYTH
GREENE VIEW
LONGS GI
BUCHAN CL
BENNETT
HARDY CL
SWIFT
BRONTE CL
AUSTEN
LOWE CL
SHAKESPEARE
COTTINGHAM DR

1 BETJEMAN CL
2 COWPAR MEWS
3 PENN MEWS
4 HASKELL MEWS
5 PANTON MEWS
6 CONAN DOYLE CL
7 JOHNSON CL
8 GALSWORTHY CL

Mast

BRADWELL CT 1
GOLDHANGER CT 2
STILEMANS WOOD 3

MILLENNIUM WAY
A120
B1018

Cressing Lodge

Fowler's Farm

LONG GN

Stacey's

ASHES RD

Almshouses

Ashes Farm

NOTLEY RD
Park Farm
BUCK HILL
Rectory
CHURCH RD
Troy's Farm PH
The Street
P

Black Notley Hall

Dewlands Estate
DEWLANDS
OXLEY HO
PO
REBE'S AVE
HOSPITAL
BRAIN VALLEY AVE
COKERS CL
BULFORD LA
WITHAM RD
MEADOW WAY

Dean's Farm

LEYFIELD

BRAINTREE RD

Tye Green

Wright's Farm

HOMEFIELD WAY

WRIGHTS AVE
THE CLOSE
CLAUD INCE AVE
JEFFREY'S RD
RIDLANDS
THE WESTERLINGS
BENTON CL
SPRINGETT
PL

CORONATION WAY

CM77

1 FORFIELDS WAY
2 JEFFREYS CT

Cressing Prim Sch

Hawbush Green

POLECAT RD
ASPLETREE CL
HAWBUSH GN

Bulford Mill (dis)
Bulford Farm

Black Notley
JOHN RAY GDNS
MARY RUCK WAY
OSMOND CL
GAINSBOROUGH RD
COSTELLO WAY
COWEN
HADFIELD DR
TURPIN CL
WILKINSON
DENTON CRES
CUSTERSON DR

WITHAM RD B1018

Jeffrey's Farm

BULFORD MILL LA
LC
Cressing
MILL LA

Stubble's Farm

Newbarns Farm

Stanton's Farm

CH

River Brain

The Green

Adams's Wood

Essex Way

CM8

Elms Farm
GREEN LA
POLE LA
Webb's Farm

Pennett's Farm

White Notley
FAMBRIDGE CHASE
LC

Lawn's Farm
Littlebury Farm

Hill Farm

CM3

Great Warley Hall

Westock's Farm

Fambridge Hall

STATION RD

White Notley Hall

THE STREET
PH PO
CHURCH HILL
VICARAGE AVE
White Notley CE Prim Sch
Stanfield's Farm
STANFIELD MDW
White Notley
VICARAGE CL

8 7 21 6 5 20 4 3 19 2 1 18

76 A B 77 C D 78 E F

175 156

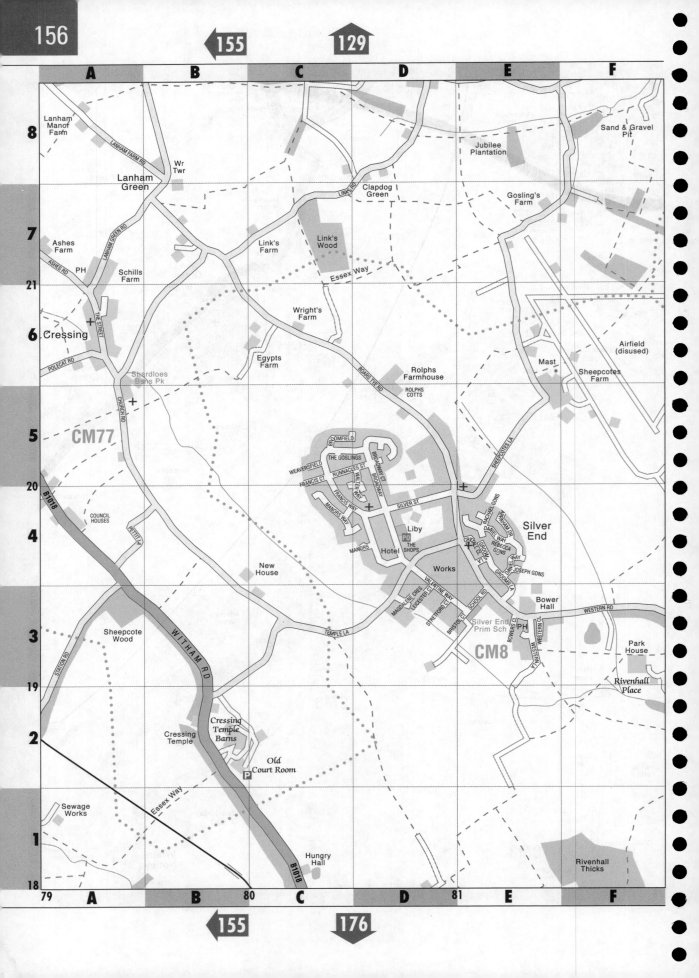

A   B   C   D   E   F

8   Lanham Manor Farm
LANHAM FARM RD
Wr Twr
Lanham Green

Jubilee Plantation
Sand & Gravel Pit

7   Ashes Farm
ASHES RD
PH
LANHAM GREEN RD
Schills Farm
Link's Farm
LINKS RD
Link's Wood
Clapdog Green
Gosling's Farm

21 THE STREET
Essex Way
Wright's Farm

6   Cressing
Egypts Farm
Airfield (disused)
Mast
Sheepcotes Farm

POLECAT RD
Shardloes Bsns Pk
CHURCH RD
Rolphs Farmhouse
BOARS TYE RD
ROLPHS COTTS
SHEEPCOTES LA

5   CM77

BLOOMFIELD
THE GOSLINGS
BROADWAY CT
WEAVERSFIELD
RUNNACLES ST
WALTER WAY
BROADWAY
FRANCIS CT
SILVER ST
RACHEL GDNS
ABRAHAM DR
Silver End

20 B1018
COUNCIL HOUSES
PETTIT
FRANCIS WAY
MANORS WAY
Liby
P.O
THE SHOPS
DANIEL WAY
GROOMS
REBECCA GDNS
DANIEL WAY
JOSEPH GDNS

4   MANORS
Hotel
Works
GROOMS CT
VALENTINE WAY

New House
MAGDALENE CRES
LEICESTER CT
STRETFORD CT
BRISTOL CT
SCHOOL RD
Silver End Prim Sch
PH
BOWERS CL
WESTERN CL
Bower Hall
WESTERN RD

3   WITHAM RD
Sheepcote Wood
STATION RD
TEMPLE LA
CM8
WESTERN A
Park House

19 Rivenhall Place

2   Cressing Temple
Cressing Temple Barns
Old Court Room
P

Essex Way
Sewage Works

1   Hungry Hall
B1018
Rivenhall Thicks

18 79   A   80   B   C   81   D   E   F

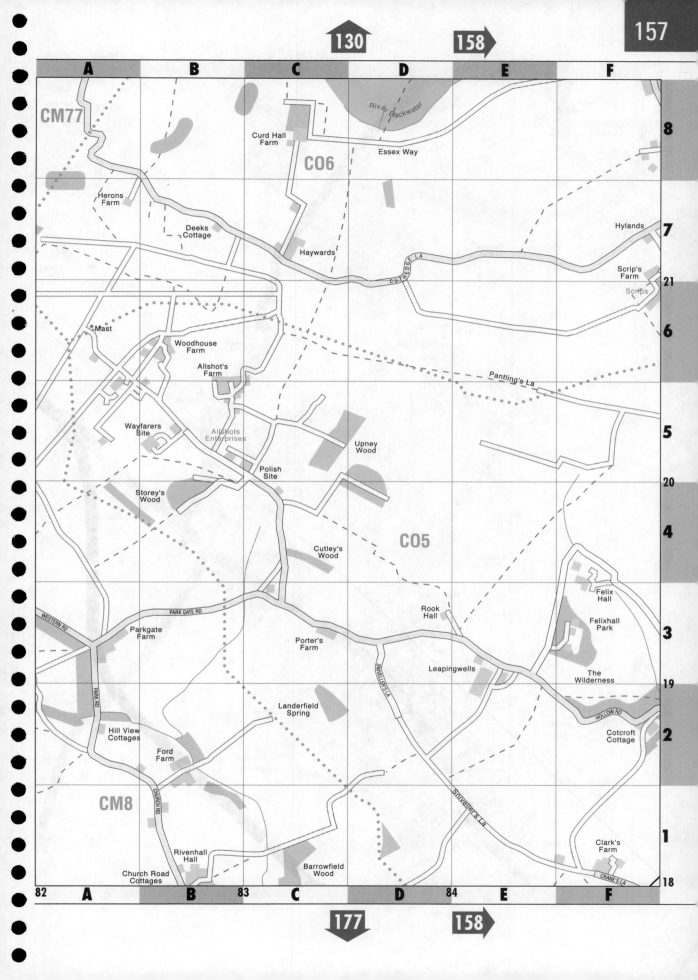

A   B   C   D   E   F

CM77

CO6

8

Curd Hall
Farm

River Blackwater

Essex Way

Herons
Farm

Deeks
Cottage

7

Haywards

Hylands

CUTHEDGE LA

Scrip's
Farm

21

Scrips

Mast

6

Woodhouse
Farm

Allshot's
Farm

Pantling's La

Wayfarers
Site

Allshots
Enterprises

Upney
Wood

5

Polish
Site

Storey's
Wood

20

CO5

4

Cutley's
Wood

Rook
Hall

Felix
Hall

Felixhall
Park

WESTERN RD

Parkgate
Farm

PARK GATE RD

Porter's
Farm

Leapingwells

The
Wilderness

3

PARK RD

SNIVELLER'S LA

19

HOLLOW RD

Hill View
Cottages

Landerfield
Spring

Cotcroft
Cottage

2

Ford
Farm

CM8

CHURCH RD

Sniveller's La

Clark's
Farm

1

Rivenhall
Hall

Church Road
Cottages

Barrowfield
Wood

CRANE'S LA

18

82   A   B   83   C   D   84   E   F

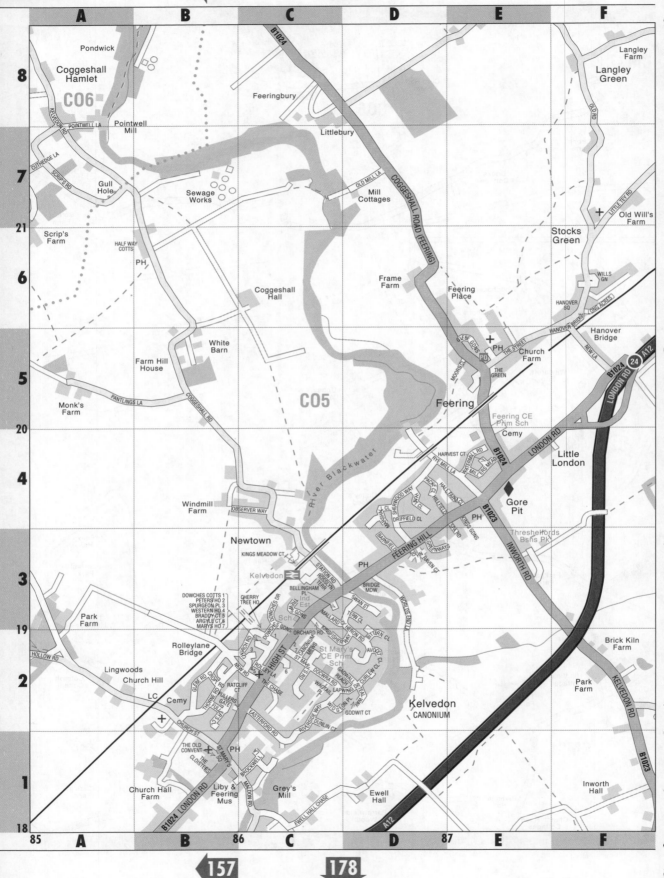

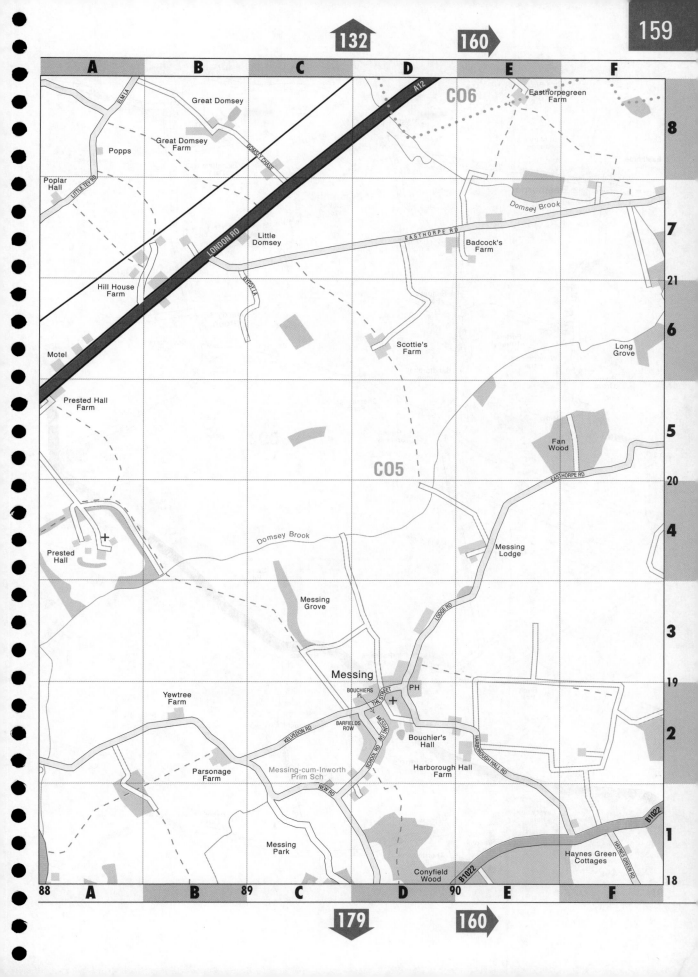

159
133

A B C D E F

8

Little Birch Holt Farm

MULBERRY COTTS

Boarded Barn

CO6

St Mary's Grange

Easthorpe Hall

EASTHORPE RD

Bockingham Hall Farm

PH ONSLOW COTTS Easthorpe

CHURCHWELL AVE

Seller Wood

7

WELL LA

Whitehouse Farm

Potash Wood

21

Hogget's Farm

Hardy's Green

6

Porters Green

Hellens

Beckingham Hall

Winterflood's Farm

Sandfordhall Green

PRIORY COTTS

Round Grove

Shemmings Farm

5

EASTHORPE RD

Cantfield's Farm

Radar Spinney

CO2

Glebe Farm

Greenacres

20

Brake's Farm

Sewage Works

4

BLIND LA

MALDON RD

CAPER LA

Sand Pit

SCHOOL LA

3

Palmer's Farm

ROUNDBUSH CNR

GREENFIELD HSE HILL LA

19

Birch Holt

Roundbush Farm

2

Birch Holt Cottages

CO5

ROUNDBUSH RD

Smythe's Green

Pond Farm

Duke's Farm

WINTER'S RD

WINTER'S HILL

B1022

Layerwood Farm

1

POPLAR COTTS

Layer Wood

Grassreasons Farm

Thorrington's Farm

18

91 A B 92 C D 93 E F

B1022

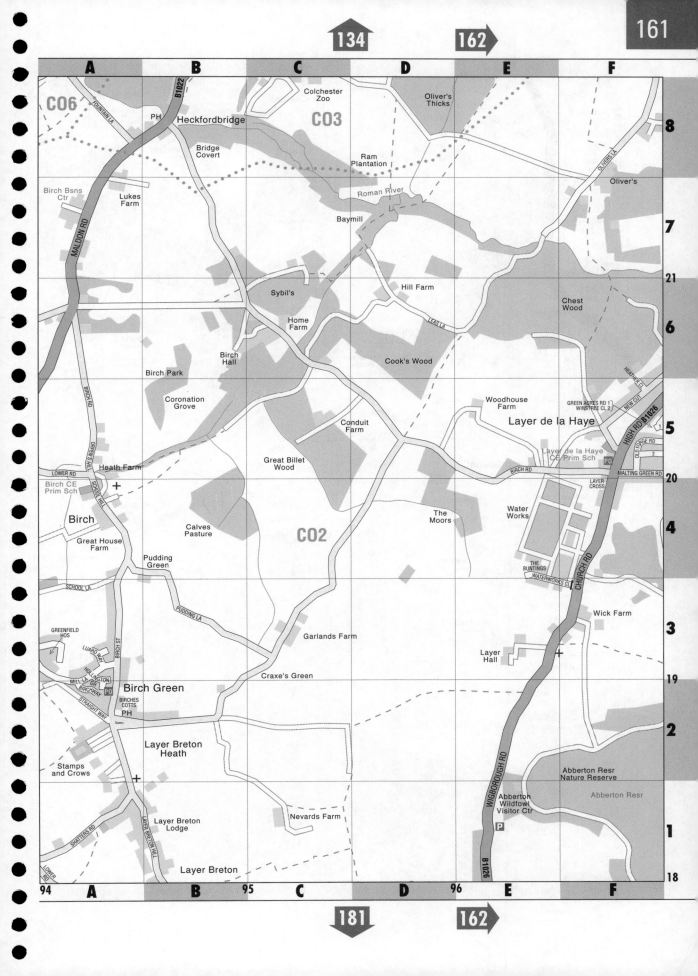

A B C D E F

CO6

PH

Heckfordbridge

Colchester
Zoo

Oliver's
Thicks

8

CO3

Birch Bsns
Ctr

Lukes
Farm

Bridge
Covert

Ram
Plantation

B1022

FOUNTAIN LA

MALDON RD

OLIVERS LA

Oliver's

Roman River

Baymill

7

21

Sybil's

Hill Farm

Chest
Wood

Home
Farm

LEAS LA

6

Birch
Hall

Cook's Wood

HEATHER CL

Birch Park

Coronation
Grove

BIRCH RD

Woodhouse
Farm

GREEN AGRES RD 1
WINSTREE CL 2

NEW CUT

HIGH RD B1026

Layer de la Haye

1

Conduit
Farm

Great Billet
Wood

Layer de la Haye
CE Prim Sch

PO

OLD CYDE RD

2

5

Heath Farm

LOWER RD

Birch CE
Prim Sch

ORPEN S HILL

SCHOOL HILL

BIRCH RD

BIRCH RD

Layer
Cross

MALTING GREEN RD

20

Birch

Calves
Pasture

CO2

The
Moors

Water
Works

4

Great House
Farm

Pudding
Green

SCHOOL LA

PUDDING LA

THE
BUNTINGS

WATERWORKS CL

CHURCH RD

GREENFIELD
HOS

LUARD WAY

BIRCH ST

Garlands Farm

Wick Farm

3

MILL LA

HOLLINGTON
GR

PO

Birch Green

BIRCHWAY

Craxe's Green

Layer
Hall

BIRCHES
COTTS

PH

STRAIGHT WAY

19

Layer Breton
Heath

2

Stamps
and Crows

SHATTERS RD

LAYER BRETON HILL

WIGBOROUGH RD

Abberton Resr
Nature Reserve

Abberton Resr

Layer Breton
Lodge

Nevards Farm

Abberton
Wildfowl
Visitor Ctr

P

1

LOWER
RD

Layer Breton

B1026

18

A B C D E F

94 95 96

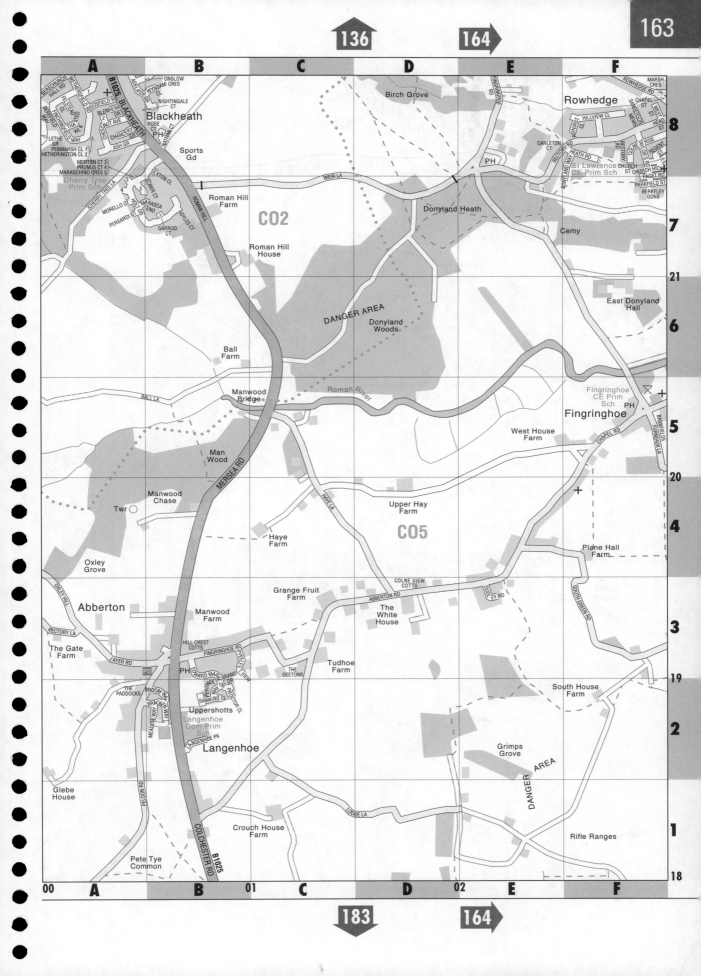

A B C D E F

8

7

21

6

5

20

4

3

19

2

1

18

Blackheath
Rose PH

Sports Gd

ONSLOW CRES
WYNDAM CRES
NIGHTINGALE CT
BLENHEIM DR
ADELAIDE DR
BERECHURCH HALL RD
WETHERSFIELD RD
GOSFIELD RD
B1025 BLACKHEATH
FELSTEAD RD
FINCHINGFIELD WAY
BIRCH THA
ASHGR
CHANCERY GR
NUT AVE
LETHE GR
PEBMARSH CL 1
HETHERINGTON CL 2
MERTON CT 3
PRUNUS CT 4
MARASCHINO CRES 5
Cherry Tree Prim Sch
CHERRY TREE LA
MORELLO CT
PERSARDI CT
KELLY RD
ROBERT CT
MARASCA END
IMPERSCA
SEXTON CL
GARROD CT
BOYLES CT
ROMAN HILL

Roman Hill Farm

Roman Hill House

CO2

Ball Farm

Manwood Bridge

Man Wood

Manwood Chase

Twr

Oxley Grove

Abberton

The Gate Farm

RECTORY LA
LAYER RD
OXLEY HILL

PO
PH
THE PADDOCKS
EDWARD MAR...
HILL CREST COTTS
FINGRINGHOE RD
PYEFLEET VIEW
PETE TREE GR
GRAND
SPRY...
PROCTOR CL
SAWKINS CL
BROOM WAY
MEADOW WAY
BRACKEN WAY
Uppershotts
Langenhoe Com Prim Sch
LANGENHOE PK

THE GEETONS

Manwood Farm

Grange Fruit Farm

Langenhoe

Glebe House

PELDON RD
COLCHESTER RD
B1025

Crouch House Farm

Pete Tye Common

BALL LA

MERSEA RD

HAYE LA

Haye Farm

CO5

Upper Hay Farm

COLNE VIEW COTTS
ABBERTON RD

The White House

Tudhoe Farm

DUDLEY RD

LODGE LA

Birch Grove

WEIR LA

DANGER AREA

Donyland Woods

Roman River

West House Farm

CARLETON CT
HEATH RD
ROWLAND WAY
RECTORY ST
FINGRINGHOE RD

Donyland Heath

PH

Cemy

SOUTH GREEN RD

Plane Hall Farm

South House Farm

DANGER AREA

Grimps Grove

Rifle Ranges

Rowhedge

ROWHEDGE RD
MARSH ST
CHAPEL ST WEST
SANDERSON MEWS
ASHURST
HILLVIEW CL
COLNE TAYLORS CT
HEAD ST
RISE
REGENT ST
CHURCH HILL
PAGET RD
PARKFIELD ST
BERKELEY GDNS
St Lawrence CE Prim Sch

Fingringhoe CE Prim Sch
PH
Fingringhoe

East Donyland Hall

BARNFIELDS
FURNEAUX LA
CHAPEL RD

163
137

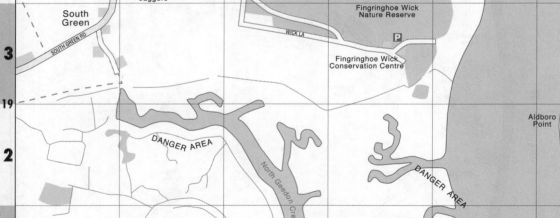

A B C D E F

ELM RD DE VERE LA
CHAPEL RD 1
BLITHE CT 2
BLYTHE LA 3
ALMA ST 4
DENTON'S TERR 5
COLNE TERR 6
ALMSHOUSES 7
BELLE VUE RD 8

DE VERE LA
HIGH ST B1028
Liby
MALTING

REBOW

FRIARS CL
PETWORTH CL

DENHAM
CL

Ballast Quay
Farm

8

1 HEAD ST

TUNNEL
WLK

SUNBEAM
CL

CHAPEL
RD

COLNE CT

DARKHOUSE

Wivenhoe
PH

REGENT ST
The Old
CHURCH ST
School Ho

HIGH ST

MEREDITHS
CL

CARLETON
MEWS

OLD FERRY RD

ALBION ST

STEPHEN
CRADFIELD
CL

2 PAGET RD
3 PARKFIELD ST

IONA WLK
OXTON CL
MARSH
CRES
CHAPEL
ST

REGENT CT

CROWHEDGE
FERRY CT
RD

SPINDRIFT
WAY

ADMIRALS WLK

VALONIA DR

MULBERRY
HARBOUR
WAY

WEST
QUAY

DRY DOCK

THE SHIPYARD

ANCHOR HILL

BLACK BUOY HILL

BATH ST

HAMILTON RD

Station
PH
B1028

CLIFTON TERR

QUEEN'S RD

PHILIP RD

EAST ST

COOK ST

THE FOLLY

WALTER RADCLIFFE WAY

WEST ST JOHN'S

VALLEY RD

NOTTAGE
YD

BALLAST QUAY RD

CASTLEWARD CL

PAGET RD

ANGLESEA RD

NOAK

TIE
MORRIS WAY
SAINT
CLARK'S
CL
LEMON'S

HARDINGS YD 1

THE QUAY

Wivenhoe
Bsns Ctr

Sewage
Works

7

FERRY RD

Sewage
Works

THE
DINGLE

BALLAST QUAY RD

FREE PYEFLEET CL

FREE FROG HALL CL

Ballast Quay
Farm

Marsh
Farm

CO7

21

6

Mill

CHURCH RD

High Park
Corner

BROOK HALL RD

Lower Brickhouse
Farm

CO7

River Colne

Alresford
Grange

Fingringhoe
Hall
Tower

Holmwood
Farm

CO5

Sand Pit

Alresford
Lodge

5

20

4

SOUTH GREEN RD

Jaggers

WICK LA

Fingringhoe Wick
Nature Reserve

P

South
Green

Fingringhoe Wick
Conservation Centre

3

19

DANGER AREA

North Geedon Creek

Aldboro
Point

DANGER AREA

2

Fingringhoe Ranges

Fingringhoe
Marsh

Geedon
Saltings

1

18

03 A B 04 C D 05 E F

165 139

A B C D E F

8

7

21

6

20

5

4

19

3

2

1

18

09 A B 10 C D 11 E F

SCHOOL LA
B1029
STATION RD
Burr's Farm
GREAT BENTLEY RD
Hill House Farm
THORRINGTON RD
DE VERE EST
WREN CL
ROBIN CL
LINNET WY
STURICK LA
CHERRYWOODS
THE PATH
HECKFORD'S RD
Bentley Green
WEELEY RD
LABURNUM
SYCAMORE PL
BIRCH AVE
CEDAR WAY
ELM CL
PINE CL
ROWAN CL
GEOGWYNNS MEWS
THE GREEN
PH
Great Bentley
MILL ON THE GREEN
PO
MORELLA CL
NEW CUT
STATION RD
HALL VIEW RD
Great Bentley Prim Sch
LC
Great Bentley Ind Est
KEEBLE CT
PLOUGH RD
St Mary's Farm
FRATING RD
Lufkins Farm
GREAT BENTLEY RD
FRATING CROSS
LC
Mast
The Talbots
Frating Abbey
FRATING ABBEY FARM RD
Bentley Brook
Lodge Plantation
ST MARY'S RD
COUNCIL HOUSES
WEELEY RD
ST MARY'S RD
PH
AINGERS GREEN RD
Aingers Green
THE PADDOCKS
WOOD GREEN EST
Carpenter's Farm
STATION RD
B1029
Whitehouse Farm
CHURCH RD
ACORN WLK 1
THELMA DR 2
HAZEL CL
CLOVER DR
HEATHLANDS
HONEYSUCKLE WAY
CHAPEL LA
High Barns
Thicket Grove
B1027
Thorrington
ROSEMARY LA
PH
VICTORY CL
CLACTON RD
Glebe Farm
Thorrington Hall
CO7
Thorringtonhall Wood
Saltwater Brook Cottages
Saltwater Bridge
The Lodge
Colles Brook
COLLES BROOK RD
DIAL RD
STRAIGHT RD
SOUTH HEATH RD
Lady Wood
Kellands Farm
HOLLYBUSH HILL
DIAL CNR
MARSH FARM LA
Saltwater Brook
Crocky Grove
Greatmarsh Farm
Cottage Farm
HILL COTTS
CO16
Caravan Site
CH
Hollybush Hill
FLAG HILL
B1027
Dines Farm
FOLKARDS LA
Lowermarsh Farm
Thorrington Creek
DEAD LA

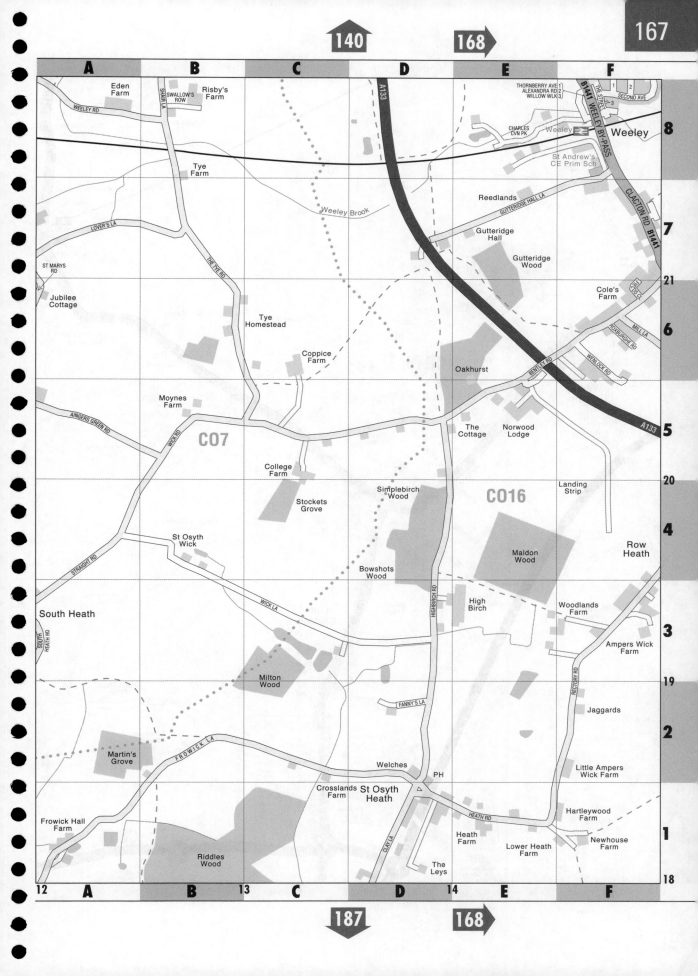

167
141

A B C D E F

LC

Island Grove

Hall Farm

Weeley Lodge

Cradle Bridge (FB)

Holland Brook

B1414

STATION RD

The Grange Farm

Thorpe Maltings

PH

THE MARKET PL.

Thorpe-le-Soken

EDWARD RD

RAILWAY COTTS

Rice Bridge

Church La

Pond Farm

B1441

Weeleyhall Wood

Lower Botany Farm

Woodlands

St Chad's Nurseries

PH

CLACTON RD

MILL LANE CL

WILLOW PK

GREEN LA

MILL LA

Weeley Heath

Edgewood House

CO16

Botany La

Botany Farm

HARWICH RD

Pig Street

EDWARD CL

EDWARD TERR

A133

RECTORY RD

Victoria Rd

Playing Fields

Betts Green Rd

GROVE RD

Crackstakes Farm

KEMPTON PK LA

CONNAUGHT RD

SPRINGFIELD MDWS

GREENGATES MOBILE HOME PK

WEELEY RD

B1414

AMERELLS RD

FEVERILLS RD

Clacton Grove Farm

HALL LA

Honeypot Farm

HONEYPOT LA

BATEMAN'S RD

TALBOT RD

HOMING RD

PLOUGH CNR

THORRINGTON RD

HOMEYPOT LA

LOTTS RD

TALBOT RD

Mast

Ideal Nurseries

Swain's Farm

THE STREET

Little Clacton

Rowheath Farm

Pickers Ditch

DEAD LA

ELM RD

GALLOWAY DR

PH

Street Farm

PH

Reedlands Farm

HOLLAND RD

GREENLAWNS CVN PK

PO

PH

Engaines Prim Sch

FIRS CVN PK

Sunbeam Farm

Swallow Farm

SHELLEY LA

BARRINGTON CL

CLAPGATE DR

PEARTREE WAY

ST OSYTH RD E

ANCHOR CVN CAMP

BERTRAM AVE

ALAN DR

CHRISTOPHER DR

THORPE RD

APPLE LA

Hartley Grove

LONDON RD

SUNNYSIDE WAY

OLD CRES

ST D DR

STONEHALL DR

Village Cl

CENTENARY WAY

CO15

ST OSYTH RD W

ST OSYTH RD

A133

B1442

PROGRESS WAY

B1441

Bovill's Hall

BOVILLS WAY

Superstore

HIGHFIELD HOLIDAY PK

B1442

15 A B 16 C D 17 E F

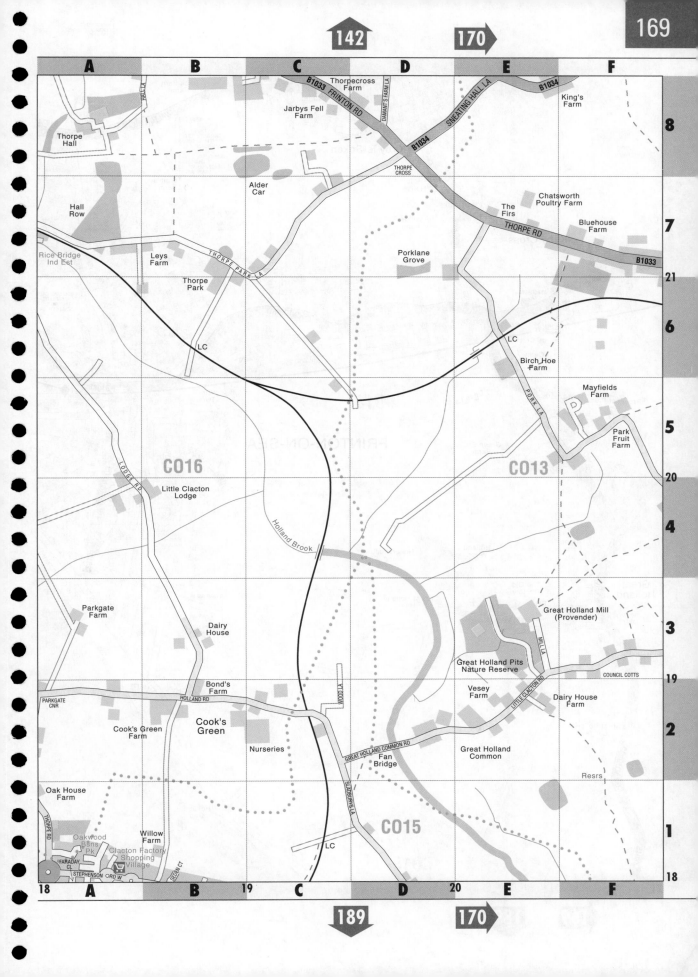

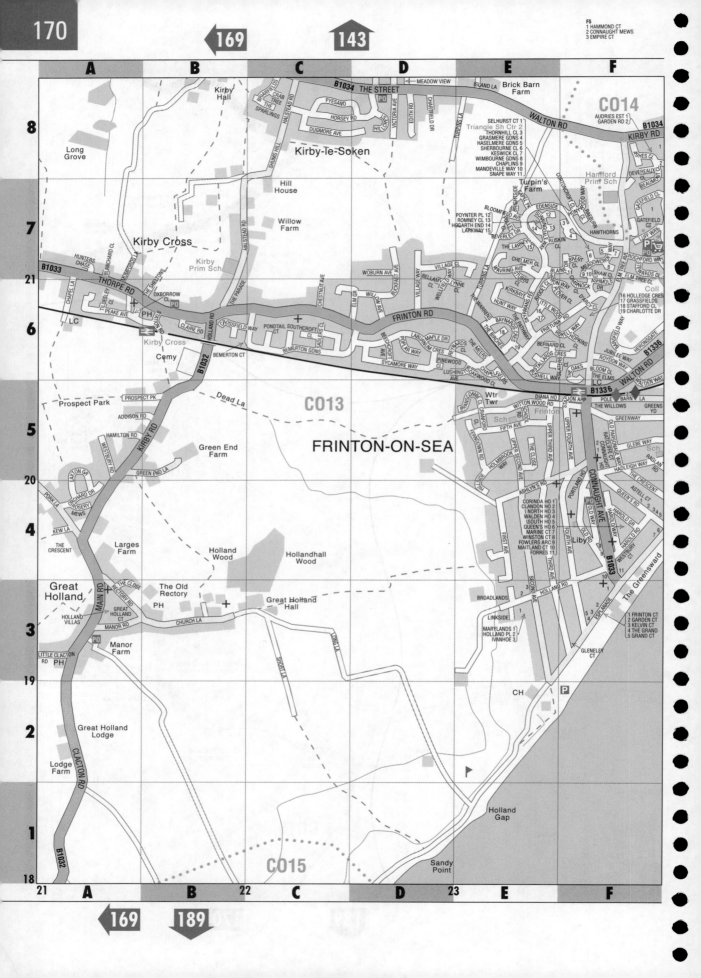

169   143

F5
1 HAMMOND CT
2 CONNAUGHT MEWS
3 EMPIRE CT

A   B   C   D   E   F

CO14

B1034 THE STREET
← MEADOW VIEW
Brick Barn Farm
ISLAND LA
WALTON RD
B1034
KIRBY RD

Long Grove

Kirby Hall

CRAB TREE
THE SPARLINGS
PYESAND
HORSEY RD
DUGMORE AVE
VICTORIA AVE
EDITH RD
CHARTHILL DR
TURPINS LA

AUDRIES EST 1
GARDEN RD 2

Kirby-Te-Soken

SELHURST CT 1
Triangle Sh Ctr 2
THORNHILL CL 3
GRASMERE GDNS 4
HASELMERE GDNS 5
SHERBOURNE CL 6
KESWICK CL 7
WIMBOURNE GDNS 8
CHAPLINS 9
MANDEVILLE WAY 10
SNAPE WAY 11

Hamford Prim Sch

Hill House

Willow Farm

Turpin's Farm

BLOOMFIELD AVE
BRIGHTSIDE
EDENSIDE
DARTONCROFT CL
WOODBURN WAY

POYNTER PL 12
ROMNEY CL 13
HOGARTH END 14
LARKWAY 15

GATEFIELD CT

Kirby Cross

Kirby Prim Sch

HUNTERS CHASE
KOUMBRIDGE
BLANCHARD CL

HALSTEAD RD
SHRUB'S HILL

THE LAWNS
BEVERLEY DR
RUSKIN CL
CHELMER CL
WAVRING AVE
STUBBS
BLAINE
CLANNOCK CL

HOLLEDGE CRES 16
GRASSFIELDS 17
STAFFORD CL 18
CHARLOTTE DR 19

Coll

B1033
THORPE RD
CHAPEL LA
TILBURY CL
PEAKE AVE
OXBORROW CL
THE SHELTONS
CLAIRE RD
HOLLAND RD
CROSSFIELD WAY
THE PARADE

WOBURN AVE
CHESTNUT AVE
VILLAGE WAY
VILLAGE CL
BELLAMY CL
WELLFIELD WAY
LYNNE CL
BLACKFAST LA
ELM GR
WILLOW AVE

FRINTON RD

HUNT WAY
KIRKBAYE
LITTLE WOOD
ANGEL CL
D'ARCY CL
SHAW CL
MEADOWCT
ASHMOLE DR

ROCHFORD WAY
JUBILEE WAY

B1336
WALTON RD

PH
Kirby Cross
Cemy

B1032
BEMERTON CT
PONDTAIL CT
SOUTHCROFT
BEMERTON GDNS
BEECHCROFT
POPLAR WAY
SYCAMORE WAY
MAPLE DR
LABURNUM CRES
REYNARDS
PINEWOOD
OAKWOOD CL
LUSHING
AVE

THE MEERS
BAYNARDS CRES
FRIETUNA
BERNARD CL
CHAPELFIELDS
STALLARDS CRES
SHELL WAY
THE OAKS
ROYDON AVE
HOPKINS CL
BLOOM CL
THE ELMS
LC
WALDEN WAY

Prospect Park

PROSPECT PK
ADDISON RD
HAMILTON RD

DEAD LA

CO13

Wtr Twr

DIANA HO
WITTON WOOD RD
JON APP
POLE BARN LA
THE WILLOWS
GREENS YD
GREENWAY

Green End Farm

KIRBY RD
WESTBURY RD
GREEN END LA

FRINTON-ON-SEA

BRANSCOMBE CL
CRANFORD CL
FIFTH AVE
FERNDOWN RD
HOLMBROOK WAY

Sch
Frinton

OLD PARSONAGE WAY
RATCLIFFE CT
GLEBE WAY
HADLEIGH WAY
ASTELL CT
THE CRESCENT
RAGLAN RD

CLAXTON GR
ORCHARD DR
GROSERY MEWS
PORK LA
KEW LA
THE CRESCENT

ASHLYN'S RD

CORINDA HO 1
CLANDON HO 2
NORTH HO 3
WALDEN HO 4
SOUTH HO 5
QUEEN'S HO 6
MARINE CT 7
WINSTON CT 8
FOWLERS ARC 9
MAITLAND CT 10
FORRES 11

PORTLAND HO
CONNAUGHT AVE
QUEEN'S RD
HAROLD RD
OLD RD
FOURTH AVE
WESTBURY RD
B1033

Liby

Larges Farm

Holland Wood

Hollandhall Wood

THE CLOSE
RECTORY RD
GREAT HOLLAND CT
MANOR RD

The Old Rectory
PH

Great Holland Hall

CHURCH LA

BROADLANDS
LINKSIDE

MARYLANDS 1
HOLLAND PL 2
IVANHOE 3

FRINTON CT 1
GARDEN CT 2
KELVIN CT 3
THE GRAND 4
GRAND CT 5

The Greensward

Great Holland

HOLLAND VILLAS
MAIN RD
LITTLE CLACTON RD
PH
PO
Manor Farm

SHORT LA
LONG LA

GLENELEY CT
ESPLANADE

CH
P

Great Holland Lodge

CLACTON RD
B1032

Holland Gap

Lodge Farm

Sandy Point

CO15

169   189

C8
1 MARINA MEWS
2 VICARAGE LA
3 HAVENCROFT CT
4 STRATFORD PL
5 NEWGATE ST
6 PATERNOSTER ROW
7 NEW PIER ST
8 MARTELLO RD
9 AGAR RD
10 AGAR ROAD APP
11 ST BOTOLPH'S TERR
12 CHURCHVIEW CT
13 CLIFTON CT
14 MARINE BLDGS

A7
1 LITTLE BAKERS
2 LITTLE HARRODS
3 GARDEN RD
4 HOMELANDS CT

WALTON-
ON-THE-NAZE

CO14

CO13

Tendring
Tech Coll

Pedlars
Wood

Albion
Breakwater

New Walton
Pier

Lifeboat
Station

Winchester
Breakwater

1 GREAT EASTERN CT
2 SOUTHCLIFF CT

1 CAMBRIDGE CT
2 FRINTON LODGE

Cemy

Walton-
on-Naze

KIRBY RD
WALTON RD

B1336
B1034

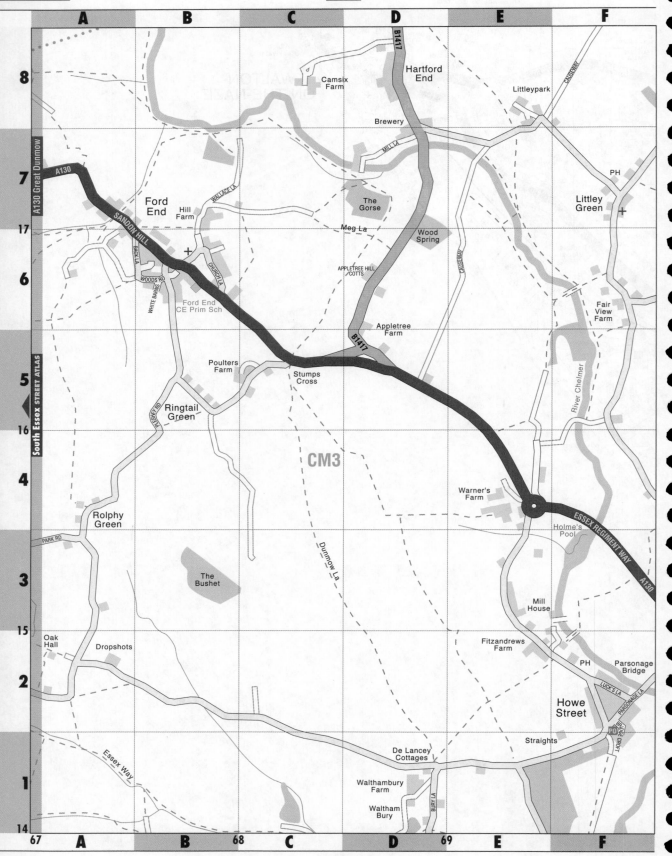

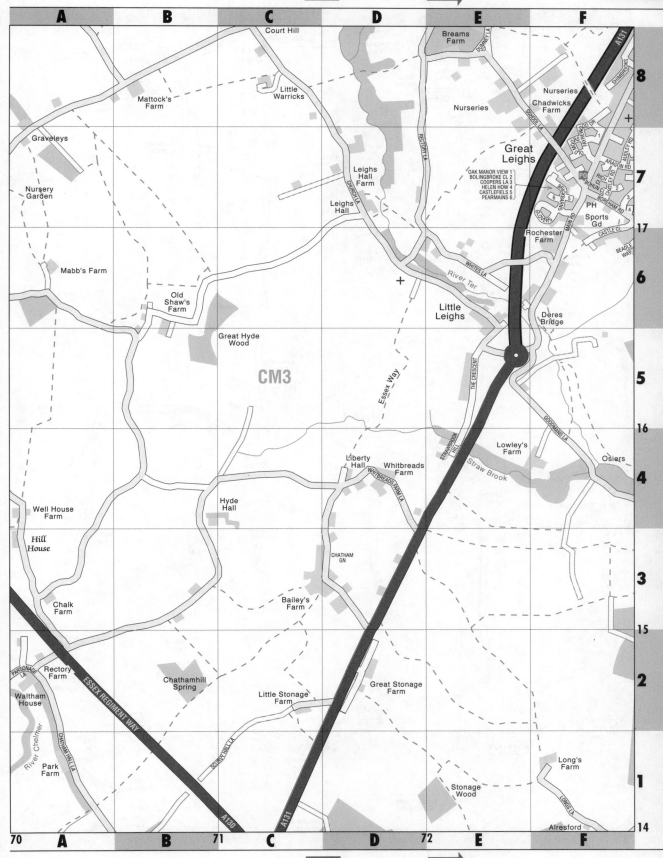

153
174

A B C D E F

8
7
17
6
5
16
4
3
15
2
1
14

Court Hill

Breams
Farm

Little
Warricks

Nurseries

Mattock's
Farm

Nurseries
Chadwicks
Farm

Graveleys

Great
Leighs

Nursery
Garden

Leighs
Hall
Farm

OAK MANOR VIEW 1
BOLINGBROKE CL 2
COOPERS LA 3
HELEN HOW 4
CASTLEFIELS 5
PEARMAINS 6

Leighs
Hall

PO

PH
Sports
Gd

Mabb's Farm

Rochester
Farm

WHITES LA

River Ter

Old
Shaw's
Farm

Deres
Bridge

+

Little
Leighs

Great Hyde
Wood

CM3

Essex Way

Lowley's
Farm

Osiers

Liberty
Hall

Whitbreads
Farm

Straw Brook

Well House
Farm

Hyde
Hall

Hill
House

CHATHAM
GN

Chalk
Farm

Bailey's
Farm

Long's
Farm

Rectory
Farm

Chathamhill
Spring

ESSEX REGIMENT WAY

Waltham
House

Little Stonage
Farm

Great Stonage
Farm

River Chelmer

Park
Farm

Stonage
Wood

Alresford

70 A B 71 C D 72 E F 14

191
174

A130

A131

A131

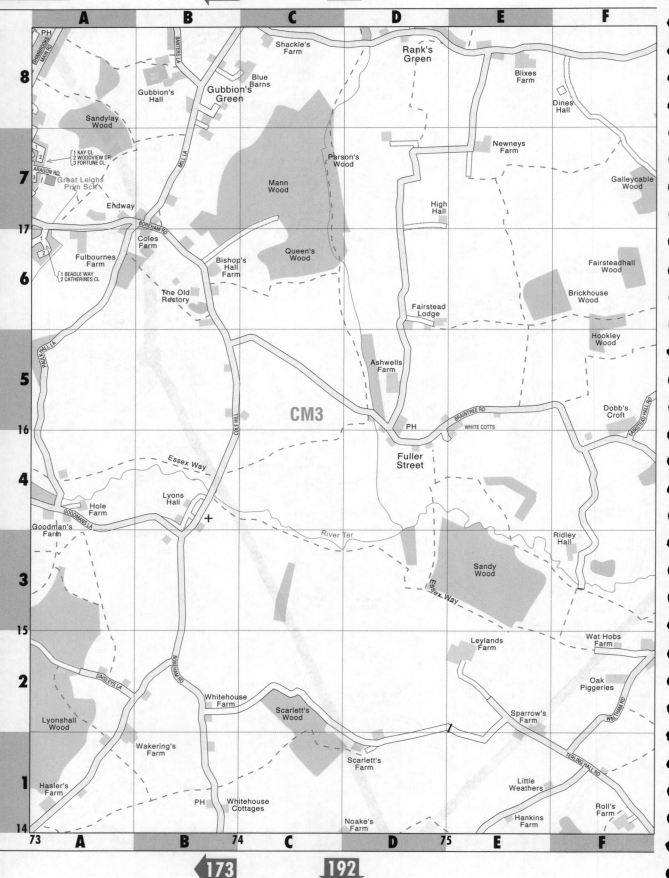

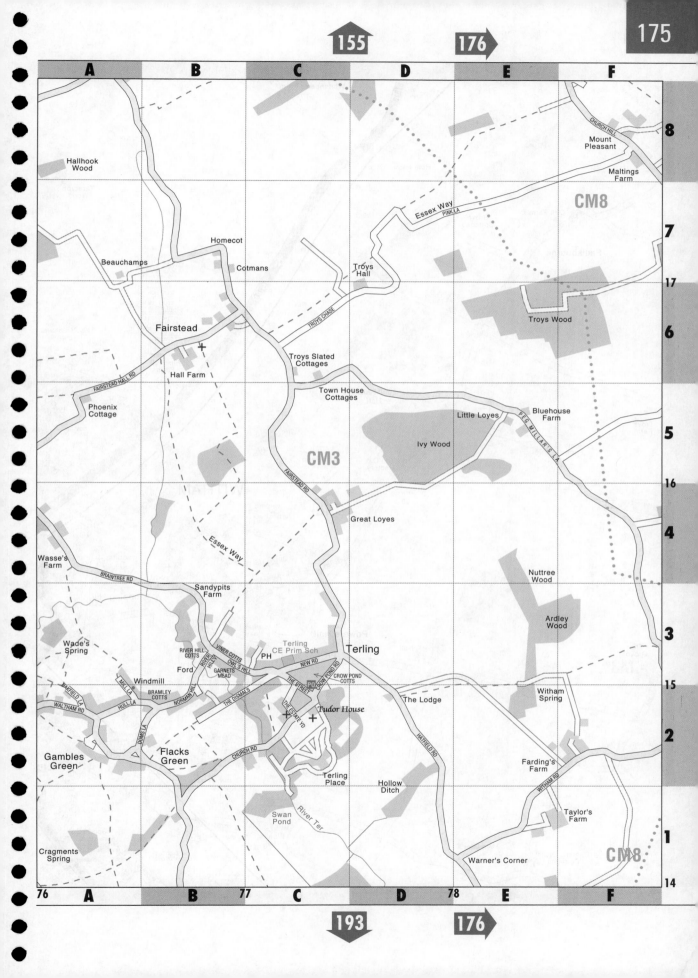

A B C D E F

8

CHURCH HILL

Mount
Pleasant

Hallhook
Wood

Maltings
Farm

CM8

Essex Way
PINK LA

7

Homecot

Beauchamps

Cotmans

Troys
Hall

17

TROYS CHASE

Troys Wood

Fairstead

6

Troys Slated
Cottages

Hall Farm

Town House
Cottages

Little Loyes

Bluehouse
Farm

FAIRSTEAD HALL RD

Phoenix
Cottage

Ivy Wood

PEG MILLAR'S LA

CM3

5

FAIRSTEAD RD

16

Great Loyes

4

Wasse's
Farm

Essex Way

Nuttree
Wood

BRAINTREE RD

Sandypits
Farm

Ardley
Wood

3

Wade's
Spring

RIVER HILL
COTTS

VINER COTTS

OWL'S HILL

Terling
CE Prim Sch

Terling

RIVER HILL

GARNETS
MEAD

PH

NEW RD

CROW POND RD

Ford

Crow Pond
Cotts

Windmill

NORMAN HILL

MILL LA

THE STREET

PO

The Lodge

Witham
Spring

15

BRAMLEY
COTTS

BARFIELD LA

THE DISMALS

THE ESTATE YD

WALTHAM RD

HULL LA

Tudor House

HATFIELD RD

Farding's
Farm

2

DOWNS LA

Flacks
Green

CHURCH RD

Gambles
Green

Terling
Place

Hollow
Ditch

WITHAM RD

Taylor's
Farm

Swan
Pond

River Ter

1

Cragments
Spring

Warner's Corner

CM8

14

76 A B 77 C D 78 E F

175
156

A B C D E F

8 Essex Way
Whiteways
Godfry's Farm

Whitehead's Farm

Hole Farm

Tarecroft Wood

7 Oak Farm
Grove Cottages
CHURCH HILL
Faulkbourne
Hill Farm

17

COURT ONE 1
COURT TWO 2
COURT THREE 3
COURT FOUR 4
COURT FIVE 5
COURT SIX 6
COURT SEVEN 7
COURT EIGHT 8
COURT NINE 9
COURT TEN 10
COURT ELEVEN 11
COURT TWELVE 12
COURT THIRTEEN 13
COURT FOURTEEN 14
COURT FIFTEEN 15
COURT SIXTEEN 16
COURT SEVENTEEN 17
COURT EIGHTEEN 18
COURT NINETEEN 19
COURT TWENTY 20

6

The Rickstones Sch
Southview Sch

CRESSING RD

Elm Hall Farm

CONRAD RD
KEL RD
VIRGIL RD
CAMPBELL RD
SHAW
DOROTHY SAYERS DR
MUNRO RD
HEMINGWAY RD
BRONTE RD
CROSS RD
ELM RISE
SWALLOW
Templars Inf & Jun Schs

5 Troys Farm

Faulkbourne Hall

River Brain

Home Farm

Warren Farm

The Old Rectory

LONGFIELD
UPPER ACRES

16

WITHAM

CM8

LAVENDER CL 1
PRIMROSE PL 2
BUTTERCUP WLK 3
COVERDALE 4

GLEBE CRES
SOUTHCOTE RD
ST NICHOLAS CL

4

HONEYSUCKLE WAY
OXLIP RD
BLACKTHORN RD
LARKSPUR
ORCHID AVE
SNOWDROP CL
BRAMBLE CT
BRAMBLE RD
HAREBELL DR
CAMPION WAY
BLUEBELL CL
THYME MEWS
BENTON RD
CHURCH ST
ROYDS
PENNY
HAVENERS WLK
BRAMSTON GN
BRAMSTON WLK
CHIPPINGS
ST NICHOLAS RD
TEMPLARS CL

BRAINTREE RD

FAULKBOURNE RD
CORNEL CL
BRYONY CL
FLORA RD
SPEEDWELL CL
CALAMINT RD
ROSEBAY CL
FOXGLOVE CL
SAMPHIRE CL

Chipping Hill
CHALKS RD
Sch
WHITE HORSE LA
BELLFIELD RD

3 The Grove
CM3
Resr
Powers Hall

Powers Hall End
PH

MONKS CT
WHITEWAYS CT
SAXON TWR
THE CL
SAXON RD
BARNARDISTON WAY
MONT CHASE
CHIPPING HILL
EARLSMEAD

B1018

15

PEGMILLARS LA

TERLING RD

Powers Hall Inf & Jun Schs
P
PO

EDEN CL
AVON WLK
BRAIN RD
HIGHFIELDS
CROMWELL WAY
ARMOND RD
GIMSON CL
CHELMER RD
TEMPLEMEAD
CROUCH LA
RICHMOND
CROXALL CT

2

WITHAM RD

DANCING DICKS LA

AIRE AVE
DON CT
DART CL
CAM WAY
TAMAR AVE
HAMBLE
SURE DR
FAL
SPA RD
MERSEY RD
TRENT RD

OUSE CHASE
DOUGLAS GR
HELM CT
BRENT CL
CONE CHASE

HUMBER RD
MEDWAY AVE
TEIGN DR
NESS WLK

WHARFE CL 1
AIRE WLK 2
TEES CL 3
DEBEN CL 4
ORWELL WLK 5

PODSBROOK HO 1
GUITHAVON CT 2
REX MOTT CT 3
OLD PARSONAGE CT 4
MILL VALE LO 5

GUITHAVON VALLEY
GUITHAVON RISE
GUITHAVON ST
LOCKRAM LA
NICHOLAS CT

MILLBRIDGE RD
MILL LA
HOLLYBANK
ORCHARDS

Sports Gd

1 Dancing Dicks Cottages
Wheeler's

BLUNTS HALL RD

BLUNT'S HALL DR

Blunt's Hall

STEVENS RD

CUPPERS CL
HIGHFIELDS
SPRING LA
GUITHAVON RD

THE BUNGALOWS 6
NEWLAND CT 7
The John Bramston Sch
Sports Ctr

NEWLAND
TUDOR RD

ST GEORGES CT 3
BARNFIELD PL 4
MOORFIELD CT 5
P

BRIDGE CT
B1389
LUARD WAY

HALCYON CL 1
RICHARDS CL 2

PHILIP RD
SUTOR CL
ALMA RD
TURSTAN RD
EPPING WAY
TUCKER DR

14

79 A 80 B C 81 D E F

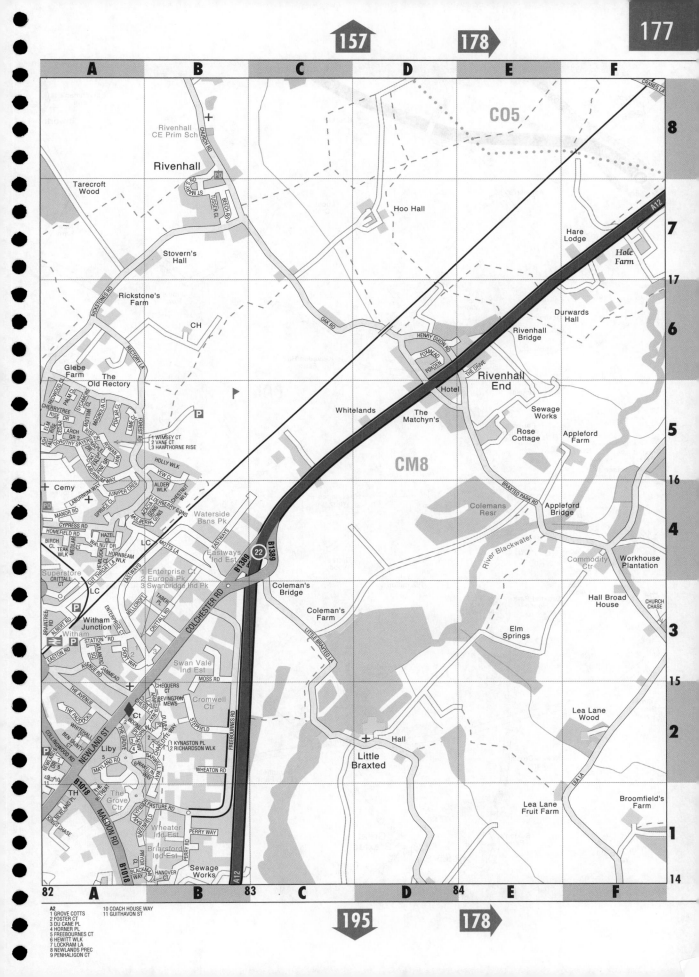

A2
1 GROVE COTTS
2 FOSTER CT
3 DU CANE PL
4 HORNER PL
5 FREEBOURNES CT
6 HEWITT WLK
7 LOCKRAM LA
8 NEWLANDS PREC
9 PENHALIGON CT
10 COACH HOUSE WAY
11 GUITHAVON ST

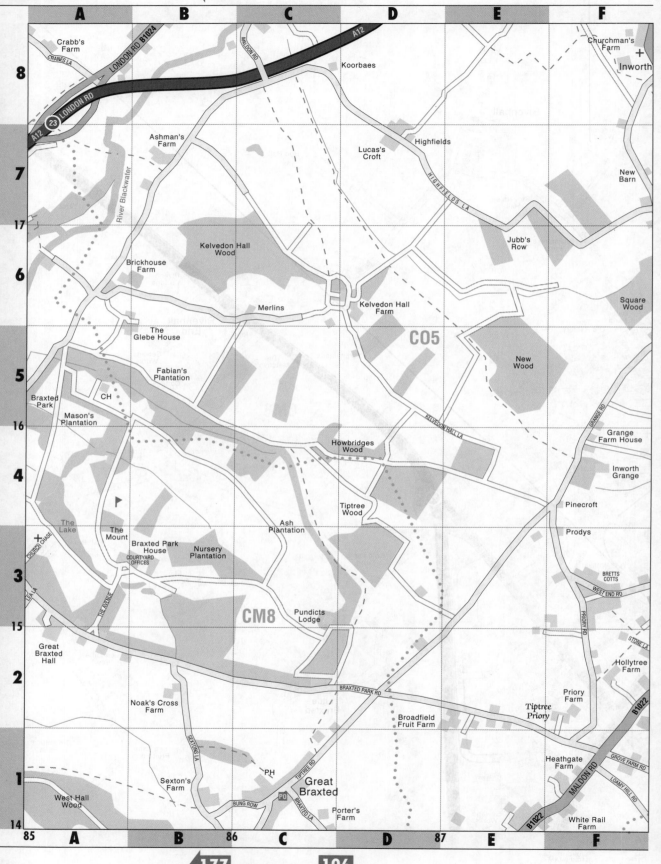

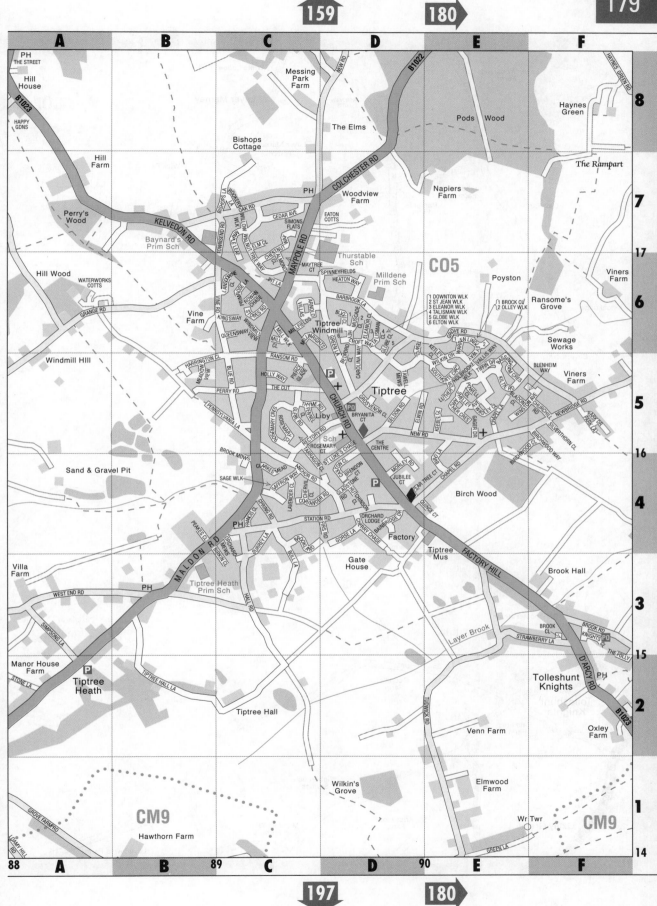

179
160

A B C D E F

8

White Lodge

Layer Woodlands
Farm

WOODVIEW
COTTS

Layer Marney

CO2

HAYNES GREEN RD

STOCKHOUSE RD

Layer Marney
Tower

7

Parkhouse
Farm

Parkgate
Farm

Wick Farm

Oak Farm

Hall Farm

17

NEWBRIDGE RD

CO5

Layer Brook

6

Stockridge
Farm

Silverthorn

Rockingham's
Farm

5

Cadgers Wood

16

Long Wood

4

Park Farm

Beatbush
Wood

CM9

3

Paternoster Heath

PARK LA

15

BROOK RD

HAWTHORN RD

BLACKTHORN WAY

STOCKHOUSE CL

Gobolt's
Farm

Barn Hall Farm

2

ELIZABETH
VILLAS

Tolleshunt
Knights

TOP RD

Palmers
Farm

BARNHALL RD

P

D'ARCY RD

RECTORY RD

Wigborough
Springs

1

B1023

The
Plough Inn
(PH)

BLIND LA

HONEYPOT LA

Krissimon
Farm

Manifold Wick
Farm

OXLEY HILL

Oxley Green

Lovedowns Farm

14

91 A B 92 C D 93 E F

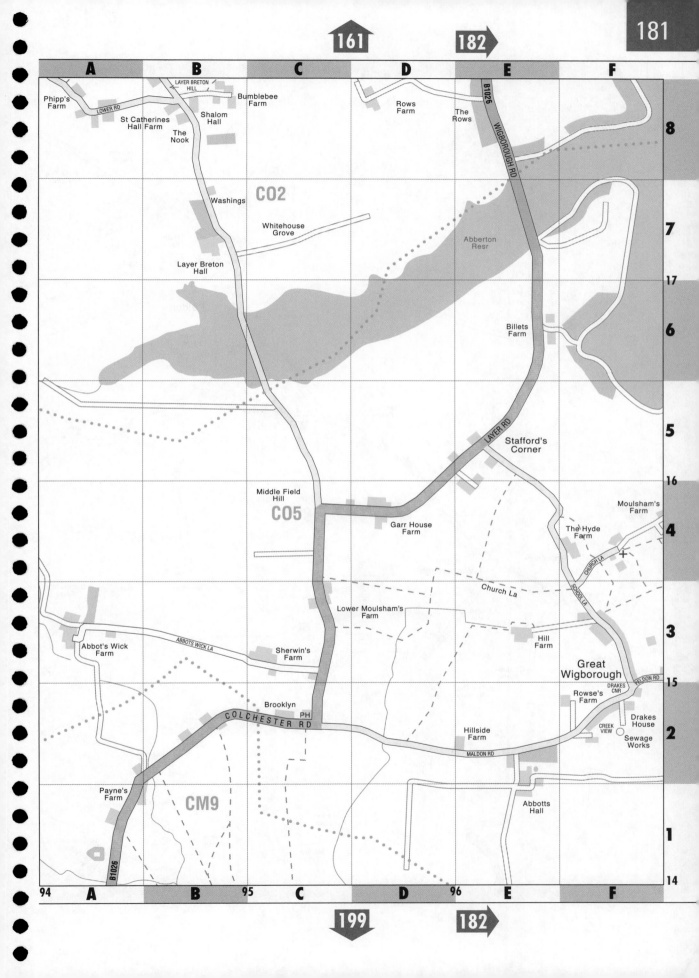

A   B   C   D   E   F

CO2

Abberton Resr

Haxells
Farm

Peldon
Lodge

Pete Tye
Farm

PELDON RD

LODGE LA

Rolls
Farm

MALTING RD

Malting
Farm

Peldon

Peldon
Hall

St Ives
Farm

CHURCH RD

BUTCHER'S
VIEW

ST IVES RD

COUNCIL
HOS

Harvey's
Farm

THE GLEBE

PH

PELDON
CRES

LOWER RD

NEWPOTS CL

MERSEA RD

Kemps
Farm

WIGBOROUGH RD

CO5

NEWPOTS LA

Moulsham's
Farm

Seaborough

Little
Wigborough

Copthall
Grove

Newpots

SAMPSON'S LA

Sampson's
Farm

Kestons
Farm

PELDON RD

Grove
Farm

Chestnuts
Farm

Coopers
Farm

COPT HALL LA

New
Hall

The Old
Rectory

Copt
Hall

Lower
Barn

P

Decoy
Pond

Sampson's
Creek

Nature
Trail

97   A   B   98   C   D   99   E   F

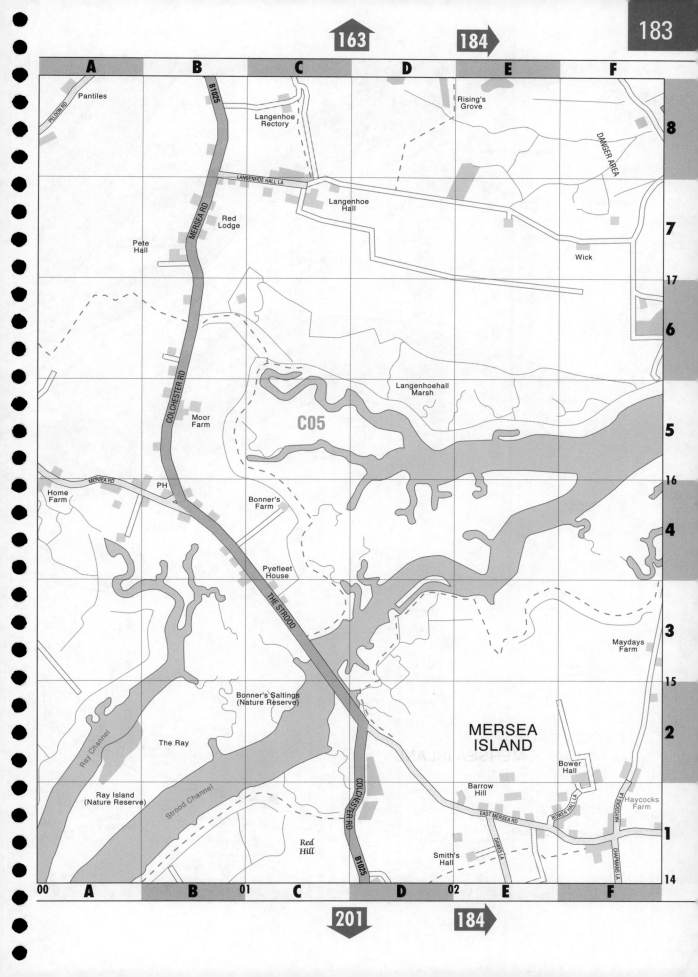

A B C D E F

8

7

17

6

5

16

4

3

15

2

1

14

00 A B 01 C D 02 E F

PELDON RD

Pantiles

B1025

Langenhoe
Rectory

Rising's
Grove

DANGER AREA

LANGENHOE HALL LA

Langenhoe
Hall

MERSEA RD

Red
Lodge

Pete
Hall

Wick

COLCHESTER RD

Moor
Farm

Langenhoehall
Marsh

C05

MERSEA RD

PH

Home
Farm

Bonner's
Farm

Pyefleet
House

THE STROOD

Maydays
Farm

Bonner's Saltings
(Nature Reserve)

Ray Channel

The Ray

MERSEA
ISLAND

Strood Channel

Bower
Hall

Ray Island
(Nature Reserve)

Barrow
Hill

HAYCOCKS LA

Haycocks
Farm

EAST MERSEA RD

BOWER HALL LA

COLCHESTER RD

B1025

Red
Hill

Smith's
Hall

DAWES LA

CHAPMANS LA

183
164

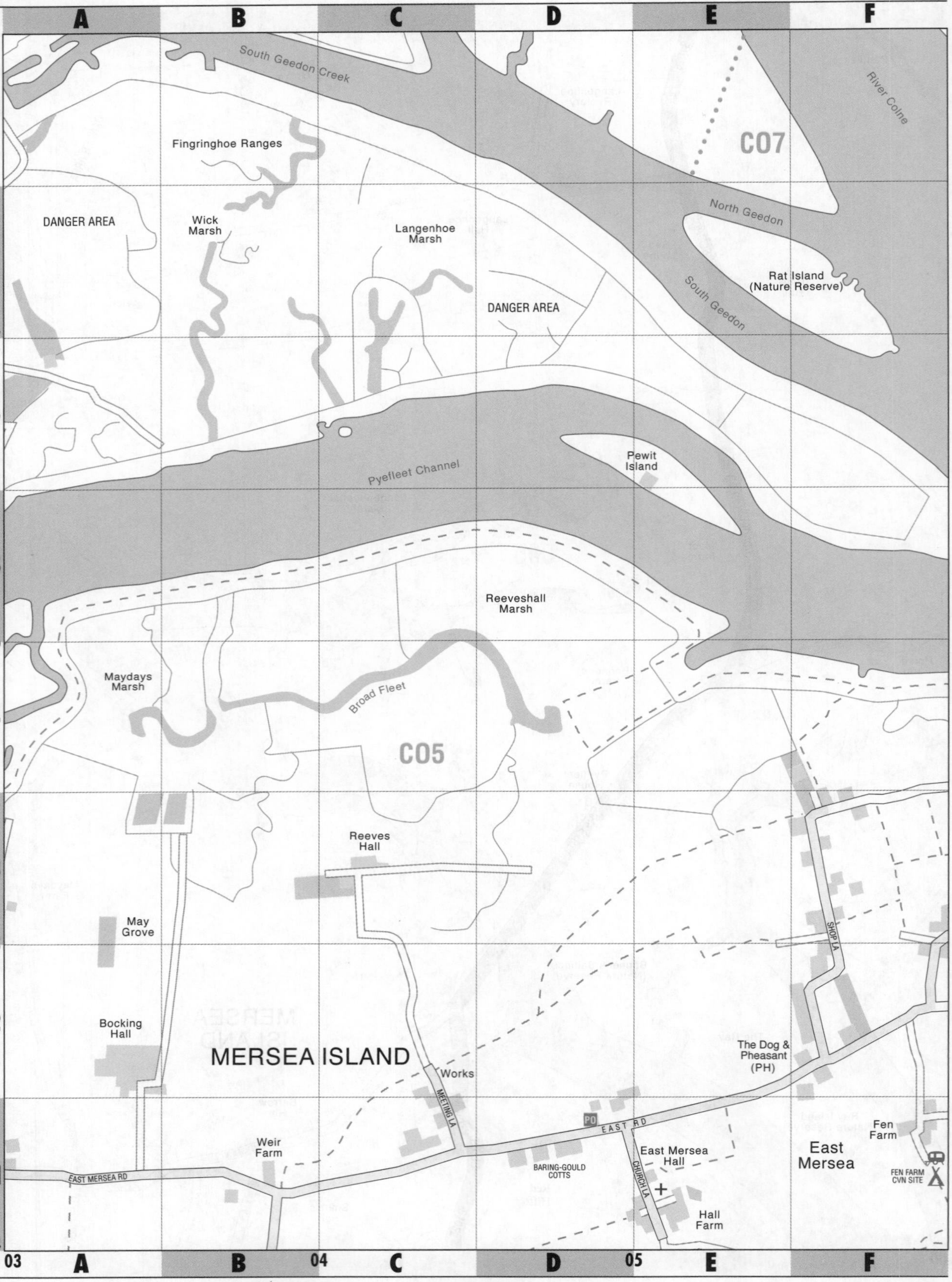

A B C D E F

8

South Geedon Creek

Fingringhoe Ranges

River Colne

CO7

North Geedon

7

DANGER AREA

Wick
Marsh

Langenhoe
Marsh

South Geedon

Rat Island
(Nature Reserve)

17

DANGER AREA

6

Pyefleet Channel

Pewit
Island

5

Reeveshall
Marsh

16

Maydays
Marsh

Broad Fleet

CO5

4

Reeves
Hall

3

May
Grove

15

Bocking
Hall

2

MERSEA ISLAND

Works

The Dog &
Pheasant
(PH)

Fen
Farm

East
Mersea

MEETING LA

PO

EAST RD

East Mersea
Hall

Weir
Farm

BARING-GOULD
COTTS

CHURCH LA

FEN FARM
CVN SITE

1

EAST MERSEA RD

Hall
Farm

14

03 A B 04 C D 05 E F

SHOP LA

185
166

A B C D E F

8

FOLKARDS LA

Marsh Farm House

STONEY LA

BELL GN

RED BARN
BELLFIELD
RED BARN CL/RD

BRIGHTLINGSEA

7

Lower Farm

CO7

BEAUMONT AVE

GRANVILLE WAY

ROBINSON RD

Eastmarsh Point

Wellwick Wharf

Recycling Ctr

FLAG HILL

B1027

COLCHESTER RD

17

STANLEY AVE
HILL HOUSE CT
CHAPEL RD

NELSON CT
HAMILTON CT

FREELANDS

B1027
COLCHESTER RD

ALBERT RD
CHURCH VILLAS
MARGARET CL

KIRKHURST CL
GREENHURST RD
CREEKHURST CL

East End Green

Flag Creek

Kitchen Pond

6

LINK LA
HURST CL
FAIR CL

Kiln Farm

Nun's Wood

Dolphin Pond

BACK WATERSIDE LA
Hurst Green

MILL ST

Engine Pond

5

Brightlingsea Creek

The Folly

Fred's Hard

St Osyth Park

16

Cindery Island

St Osyth Creek

Priory Farm

4

Brightlingsea Creek

CO16

PH

MILL CT
MILL ST

NORTH WALL

Dairy Farm Meadow

GOW LA

GREENLAND GR

Mill Dam Lake

3

COLNE WAY
MERSEA VIEW
NEW WAY
EASTERN SEADOW TERR
ALLEN WAY

Point Clear

ROMAN WAY

ALPHA RD

OAKMEAD RD

Linley Farm

15

LYTON DR
COLNE WAY

POINT CLEAR RD

Pightle Court

2

BEACON WAY
BEACON HTS
DUMONT AVE

LEE WICK LA

WIGBORO WICK LA

1

Sandy Point

BEACH RD

Lee Wick Farm

Wigboro Wick Farm

14

09 A B 10 C D 11 E F

185
202

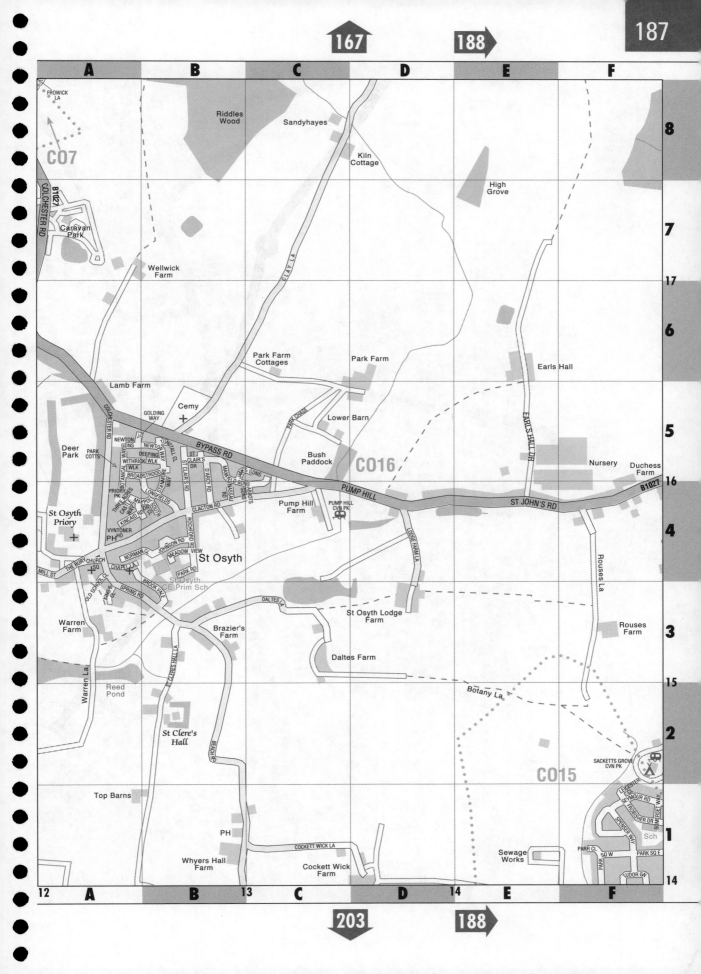

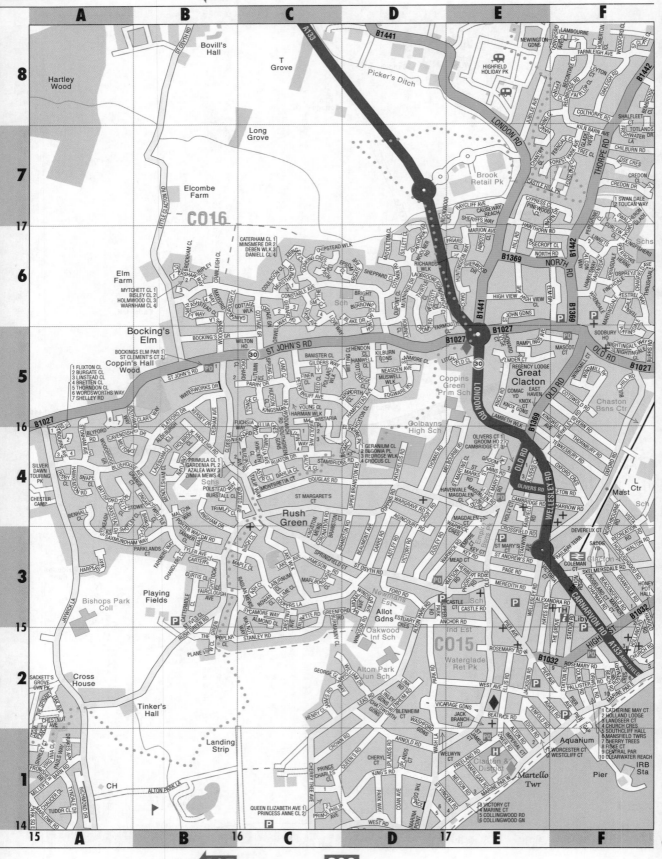

A   B   C   D   E   F

CO13

8

7

17

6

Sladbury's Old House

Wellcroft

Treasure Holt Farm

Pond House

Smythie's Farm

Picker's Ditch

Holland Brook

B1032

FRINTON RD

Liby

CO15

Burrsville Park

Cemy

Cemy

Sch

1 CUMBERLAND CT
2 SILVERDALE CT
3 MERRYMOUNT GDNS
4 ST BRELADES CT

Holland Park Prim Sch

VALLEY RD   B1027

Mast

CANTERS MEADOW CT

BONHAM

CLAYHALL RD

WYNDHAM CRES

Clacton Cty High Sch

Playing Field

Sports Gd

Shorefields Sch

1 HOVE CT
2 BOSCOMBE CT
3 THE LODGE
4 SUNDALE CL
5 SOUTHVIEW CT

Holland-on-Sea

5

16

4

170

1 CONNAUGHT CT
2 CONNAUGHT CL
3 HEYBRIDGE CT
4 WESTMINSTER CT
5 KNIGHTSBRIDGE CT

1 AVONDALE HO
2 HOLLAND HO
3 COTSWOLD CT
4 ASHLEY LODGE
5 REBECCA HO
6 OULTON HALL
7 HADLEIGH CT
8 WINDERMERE CT
9 AMBLESIDE CT

CLACTON-ON-SEA

1 SURREY CT
2 HAROLD RD
3 HARROLD CT
4 ROSEBANK CT
5 SEAVIEW CT
6 LANGTRY CT
7 THE TOWERS
8 TURRET HO

Colchester Inst

G   H   I

CO13

B1032

CO15

Nature Reserve

Holland Haven Country Park

8

7

17

6

Holland Bridge

CLACTON RD

FRINTON RD

Mast

Holland Haven

MANOR WAY

HAVEN AVE

THE ESPLANADE

3

15

2

1

14

21   G   H   22   I

18   A   B   19   C   D   20   E   F

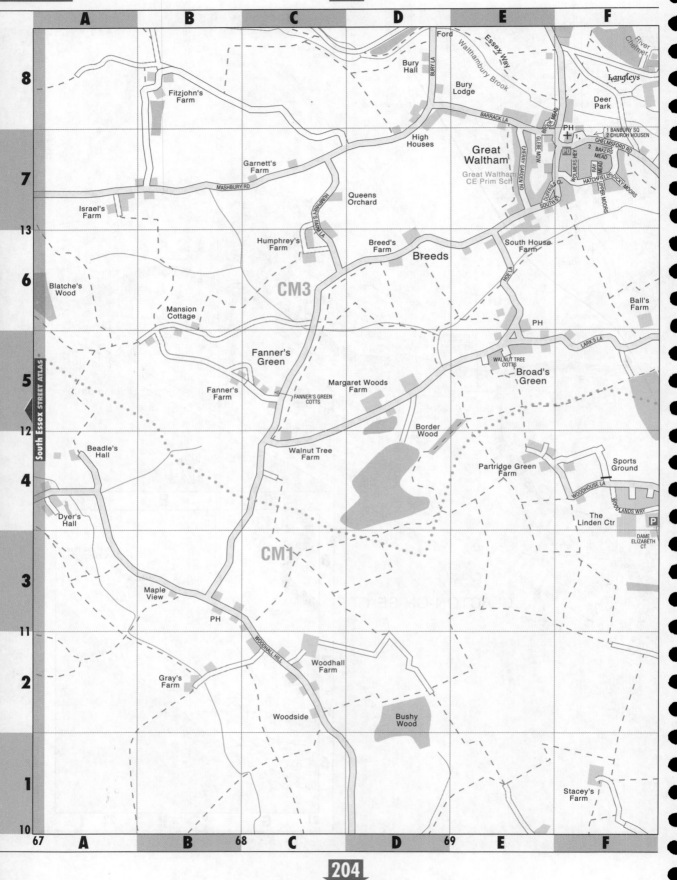

172

A B C D E F

8

7

13

6

CM3

5

12

4

3

CM1

11

2

1

10

67 A B 68 C D 69 E F

204

South Essex STREET ATLAS

Fitzjohn's Farm

Garnett's Farm

Israel's Farm

Mashbury Rd

Humphrey's Farm

Humphrey's Farm La

Queens Orchard

Breed's Farm

Breeds

South House Farm

Blatche's Wood

Mansion Cottage

Fanner's Green

Fanner's Farm

Fanner's Green Cotts

Margaret Woods Farm

Walnut Tree Cotts

Broad's Green

Lark's La

PH

Hoe La

Ball's Farm

Border Wood

Beadle's Hall

Walnut Tree Farm

Partridge Green Farm

Sports Ground

Woodhouse La

Woodlands Way

The Linden Ctr

Dame Elizabeth Ct

Dyer's Hall

Maple View

PH

Woodhall Hill

Gray's Farm

Woodhall Farm

Woodside

Bushy Wood

Stacey's Farm

Ford

Bury Hall

Bury La

Walthambury Brook

Essex Way

River Chelmer

Langleys

Deer Park

Bury Lodge

Barrack La

High Houses

Great Waltham

Great Waltham CE Prim Sch

Brook Mead

Glebe Mdw

Cherry Garden Rd

PH

PO

South St

Wlmers Hey

Dukes Cl

Ray Mead

Hatchfields

Upper Moors

Dicky Moors

Bakers Mead

Chelmsford Rd

1 Banbury Sq
2 Church Housen

1.

2

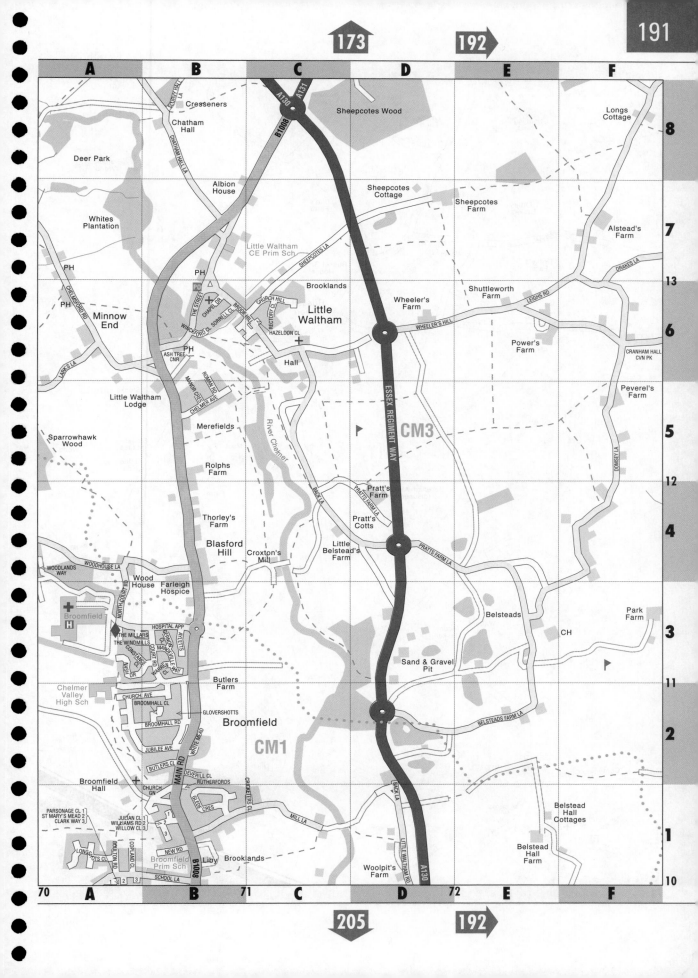

191 174

A B C D E F

8

Chopping's Wood

Noake's House

Noake's Farm

Lawns Farm

Little Drakes

BOREHAM RD

Bird's Farm

Ringer's Wood

7

DRAKES LA

Drake's Farm

Works

Russel Green House

13

Russell Green

6

Brent Hall

Stocks Farm

5

Mast

P

Works

Stocks Cottages

Little Holts

Porter's Wood

12

CM3

Boreham Airfield (disused)

Holts Farm

4

WALTHAM RD

Sand & Gravel Pit

Wallace's Farm Cottages

WALLACE'S LA

3

Park Farm

Walford House

Mount Maskall

11

2

The Grove

Brick House Farm

Boreham Ind Estl

Centenary Circle

GENERALS LA

BULLS LODGE COTTS

GWYN CL 1
ROSEMARY COTTS 2
ARMONDE CL 3
MEADOWSIDE CT 4
SEABROOK GDNS 5

A12

SHEARERS

B1137

1

New Hall Sch

P

+

Bulls Lodge

VILLIERS PL

CLEVES

ELM WAY

BRICK HOUSE

OAK COTTS

YON

B1137

MAIN RD

ST ANDREWS RD

BOLEYN WAY

CLAYPITS RD

ALLENS CL

PLANTATION RD

10

CM1

73 A B 74 C 75 D E F

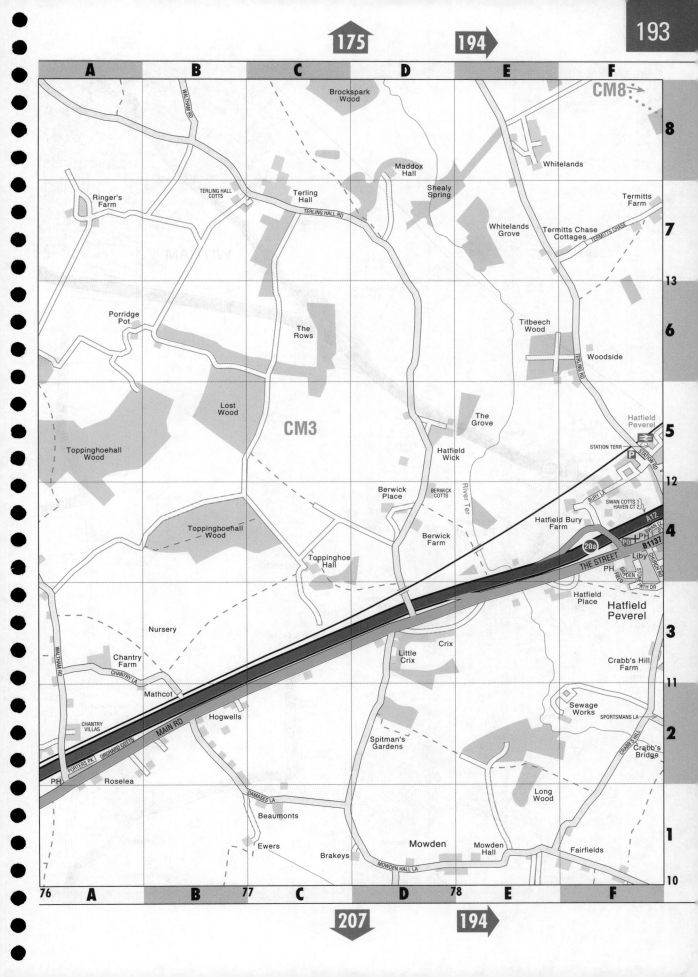

CM8

A B C D E F

8

Brockspark
Wood

Whitelands

Maddox
Hall

Shealy
Spring

Termitts
Farm

Ringer's
Farm

TERLING HALL
COTTS

Terling
Hall

Terling
Hall

TERLING HALL RD

Whitelands
Grove

Termitts Chase
Cottages

Termitts Chase

TERMITTS CHASE

7

13

Porridge
Pot

The Rows

Titbeech
Wood

Woodside

TERLING RD

6

MALDIW

Lost
Wood

CM3

The
Grove

Hatfield
Wick

Hatfield
Peverel

STATION TERR

STATION RD

P

5

Toppinghoehall
Wood

12

Berwick
Place

BERWICK
COTTS

River Ter

BURY LA

SWAN COTTS 1
HAVEN CT 2

A12

Toppinghoehall
Wood

Berwick
Farm

Hatfield Bury
Farm

PH

20a

THE STREET

PH

SWAN CL

POT

B1137

Liby

4

Toppinghoe
Hall

GLEBE
GREEN

STONE
PATH DR

CHURCH RD

Hatfield
Place

Hatfield
Peverel

Nursery

Crix

Crabb's Hill
Farm

3

WALTHAM RD

Chantry
Farm

CHANTRY LA

Little
Crix

11

Mathcot

Sewage
Works

SPORTSMANS LA

CRABB'S HILL

2

CHANTRY
VILLAS

Hogwells

Spitman's
Gardens

Crabb's
Bridge

MAIN RD

ORCHARD COTT'S

Long
Wood

PH

PORTERS PK.

Roselea

DAMASES LA

Beaumonts

Mowden

Mowden
Hall

Fairfields

1

Ewers

Brakeys

MOWDEN HALL LA

10

76 A B 77 C D 78 E F

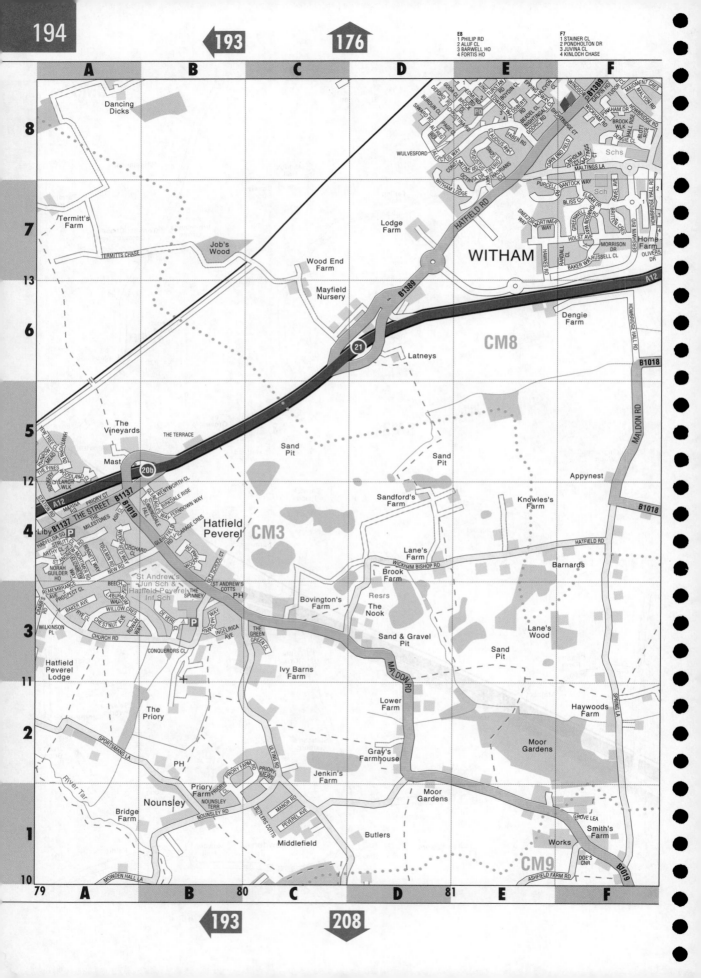

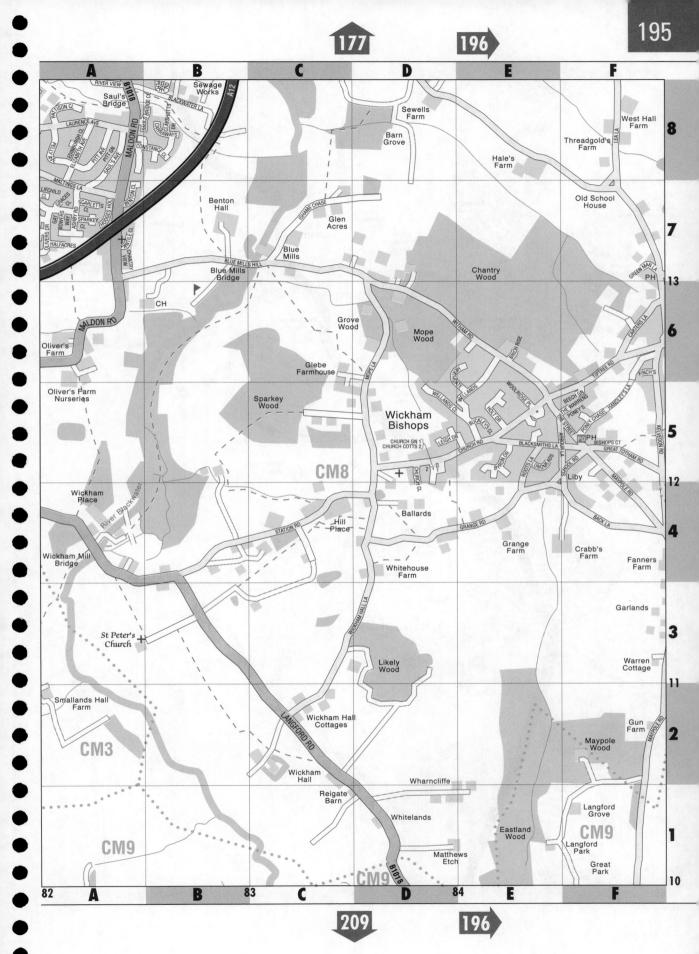

177
196

A   B   C   D   E   F

RIVER VIEW

Saul's
Bridge

Sewage
Works

BLACKWATER LA

A12

PATTISON CL
LAURENCE AVE
EDINBURGH CL
ELIZABETH AVE
PITT AVE
SAUL'S AVE
MALDON RD
PITT GN
CONSTANCE CL
PERRY
ISHAMS BRIDGE CL
CLARKHOTTS DR
CARRAWAYS
HODGES HOLT
PETTY AVE
MALTINGS LA
LIFCHILD CL
GRACES CL
GARY CL
BOWERS WAY
ASHBY RD
SPARKEY CL
OLIVERS DR
HALFACRES
PRITTLE CL
BENTON CL
CHANTRY VIEW

West Hall
Farm

Threadgold's
Farm

LEA LA

8

Sewells
Farm

Barn
Grove

Hale's
Farm

Old School
House

Benton
Hall

ISHAMS CHASE

Glen
Acres

7

Blue
Mills

GREEN MAN LA
PH

BLUE MILLS HILL

Blue Mills
Bridge

Chantry
Wood

13

CH

Grove
Wood

Mope
Wood

WITHAM RD

BIRCH RISE

CARTERS LA

6

MALDON RD

Oliver's
Farm

Glebe
Farmhouse

MOPE LA

TIPTREE RD

FINCH'S

Oliver's Farm
Nurseries

Sparkey
Wood

WELLANDS CL
WELLANDS
CATKIN CL
WOOLRIDGE PL
HOLT DR
BEECH GDN
THE WARRENS
PONEY'S
PONEY CHASE
HANDLEY'S LA
KELVEDON RD

Wickham
Bishops

CHURCH GN 1
CHURCH COTTS 2
LEIGH DR
BUCKLEY'S CL
CHURCH RD
BYRON DR
ROOTS LA
LONGMEADS
SCHOOL RD
BLACKSMITHS LA
PO
PH
BISHOPS CT
GREAT TOTHAM RD

CM8

5

Wickham
Place

River Blackwater

STATION RD

Hill
Place

Ballards

CHURCH CL
VD
2

Liby
MAYPOLE RD

12

GRANGE RD
BACK LA

Wickham Mill
Bridge

Whitehouse
Farm

Grange
Farm

Crabb's
Farm

Fanners
Farm

4

WICKHAM HALL LA

Garlands

St Peter's
Church

Likely
Wood

Warren
Cottage

3

Smallands Hall
Farm

LANGFORD RD

Wickham Hall
Cottages

Gun
Farm

MAYPOLE RD

11

CM3

Maypole
Wood

2

Wickham
Hall

Wharncliffe

Reigate
Barn

Langford
Grove

Langford
Park

CM9

Whitelands

Eastland
Wood

1

CM9

B1018

Matthews
Etch

Great
Park

CM9

10

82   A   B   83   C   D   84   E   F

209
196

195 178

A B C D E F

8

Round Wood

Shrub Hill Farm

MALDON RD B1022

CO5

Criers Wood

SEXTONS LA

HIGH RIDGE

Strowling Wood

BRAXTED LA

Spirits Hall

Great Totham

ROOKERY LA

Brick Kiln Farm

7

Shut Heath Wood

CM8

TIPTREE RD

Little Mountains Farm

KINGS RD

SPRING LA

BRICKSPRING LA

HILL RD

EATON WAY

Wheeler's Farm

Roughways Farm

13

Heath House

BRAXTED RD

Mountains Rd

PH

COLCHESTER RD

CHAPEL RD

Mount Pleasant

MOUNT LODGE CHASE

TOTHAM HILL GN

Lawns Farm

Moorah Farm

MACLARENS

ROUNDBUSH CNR

Roundbush Farm

6

BEACON HILL

Mountains

Mountains Grove

Plains Rd

Plains Farm

Beacon Hill

GOAT LODGE RD

Scripps Farm

Great Mountains Farm

Paynes Farm

BECKINGHAM RD

Hill Farm

5

Chasefield Farm

Goat Lodge Farm

Applebys Farm

Totham Hill

Great Totham Prim Sch

Bull Grove

CH

Fabian's Farm

12

WALDEN HOUSE RD

WALDEN CL

STAPLERS HEATH

STAPLERS WLK

STAPLERS CL

PH

MALDON RD

Walden House Farm

THE PADDOCKS

BURNS GN

HARVEY CL

HERDY WAY

SCHOLARS MEWS

SEAGERS

Great Totham

Spickets Wood

Spickets Brook

CM9

4

CATCHPOLE LA

WORTH

FOSTER RD

BROOK CT

THE CHASE

PLAYLE CHASE

MILLWAYS

SCHOOL RD

Sewage Works

PRINCE OF WALES RD

WOODSIDE

PH

ST PETERS WLK

WILLIS

ALMSHOUSES

BEADLE PL

HALL RD

MAYPOLE RD

Great Totham Hall

3

CAPTAINS WOOD RD

Bog Grove

Jepcrack's Farm

CHURCH RD

11

Captain's Wood

Godfrey Farm

2

BROAD STREET GREEN RD

Catchpole Brook

Sheepcoates Farm

SHEEPCOATES LA

Totham Lodge

South Wood

1

Home Farm

B1022

Middle Farm

10

85 A B 86 C D 87 E F

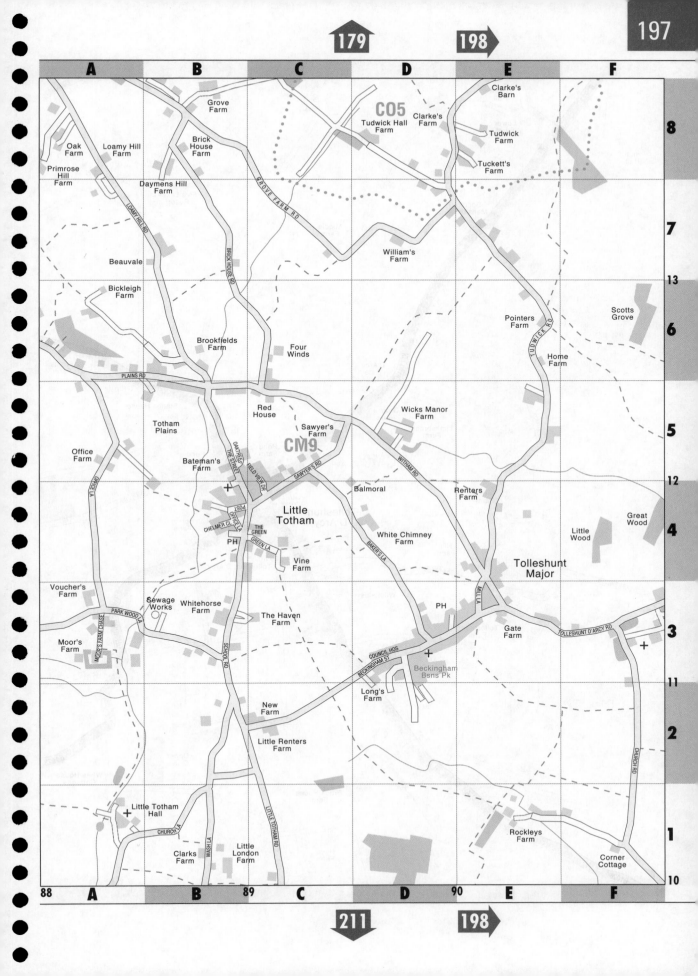

197
180

A **B** **C** **D** **E** **F**

8

Grove Hall

B1023

Blind La

Lower Farm

OXLEY HILL

High Hall

HONEYPOT LA

RECTORY RD

BARNHALL RD

Hotel

CH

Five Lakes Resort

7

Dodo Mansion

Middle Farm

13

6

KELVEDON RD

D'Arcy Gate

B1026

Profits Farm

STATION RD

Old Station House

Station Road Ind Est

Grout's Farm

Limesbrook Farm

Limes Brook

CM9

5

Pond Farm

Pond Farm

12

Frame Farm

Tolleshunt D'Arcy

MARGERY ALLINGHAM PL

SALTER'S MDW

VICARAGE CL

NORTH ST

SOUTH ST

PH

D'ARCY WAY

Spring Farm

CHAPEL RD

4

THE CHASE

Hill Farm

HARVESTERS

FESTIVAL GDNS

CHURCH ST

Tolleshunt D'Arcy St Nicholas Prim Sch

Tolleshunt D'Arcy Hall

B1023

BECKINGHAM RD

Bowstead Bridge

Cemy

Wildfields

TOLLESBURY RD

3

Bowstead Brook

Tolleshunts Farm

TOLLESHUNT D'ARCY RD

11

2

BROOK COTTS

Upper Grove

White House Cottages

B1023

MALDON RD

Brook House Farm

White House Farm

PASSEY LA

1

Hyde Farm

10

91

B1026

A

92

B

C

D

93

E

F

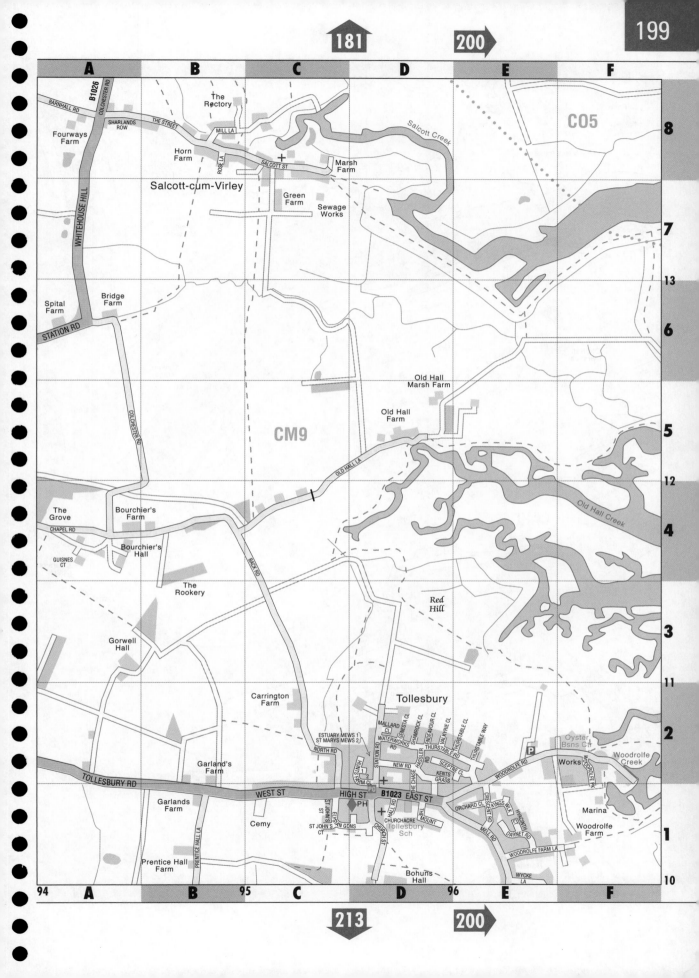

A B C D E F

CO5

B1026
BARNHALL RD
COLCHESTER RD
SHARLANDS ROW
THE STREET
Fourways Farm
WHITEHOUSE HILL
Horn Farm
ROSE LA
MILL LA
The Rectory
SALCOTT ST
Salcott-cum-Virley
Green Farm
Marsh Farm
Sewage Works
Salcott Creek

8

7

13

Spital Farm
Bridge Farm
STATION RD
COLCHESTER RD

Old Hall Marsh Farm
Old Hall Farm

CM9

6

5

The Grove
Bourchier's Farm
CHAPEL RD
Bourchier's Hall
GUISNES CT
The Rookery
BACK RD
OLD HALL LA
Red Hill
Old Hall Creek

12

4

Gorwell Hall

3

11

Carrington Farm
Tollesbury
MALLARD CL
GENESTA CL
SHAMROCK CL
ENDEAVOUR CL
VALKYRIE CL
THURSTABLE CL
THURSTABLE WAY
WATERWORKS RD
HASSLER
THE CHASE
SCEPTRE CL
KENTS GRASS
Oyster Bsns Ctr
Woodrolfe Creek

2

Garland's Farm
ESTUARY MEWS 1
ST MARYS MEWS 2
NORTH RD
STATION RD
NEW RD
HUNTS FARM CL
WOODROLFE RD
WOODROLFE PK
Works

TOLLESBURY RD
WEST ST
HIGH ST
PH
B1023
EAST ST
ORCHARD CL
CRESCENT RD
KINGS WLK
MELL RD
WYCKE LA
Marina
Woodrolfe Farm

Garlands Farm
Cemy
ST JOHN'S ST
ELYSIAN GDNS
ST JOHN'S CT
CHURCH ST
CHURCHACRE
Tollesbury Sch
HALL RD
HILL MOUNT
DARNET RD

1

Prentice Hall Farm
PRENTICE HALL LA
Bohuns Hall
WOODROLFE FARM LA
WYCKE LA

10

94 A B 95 C D 96 E F

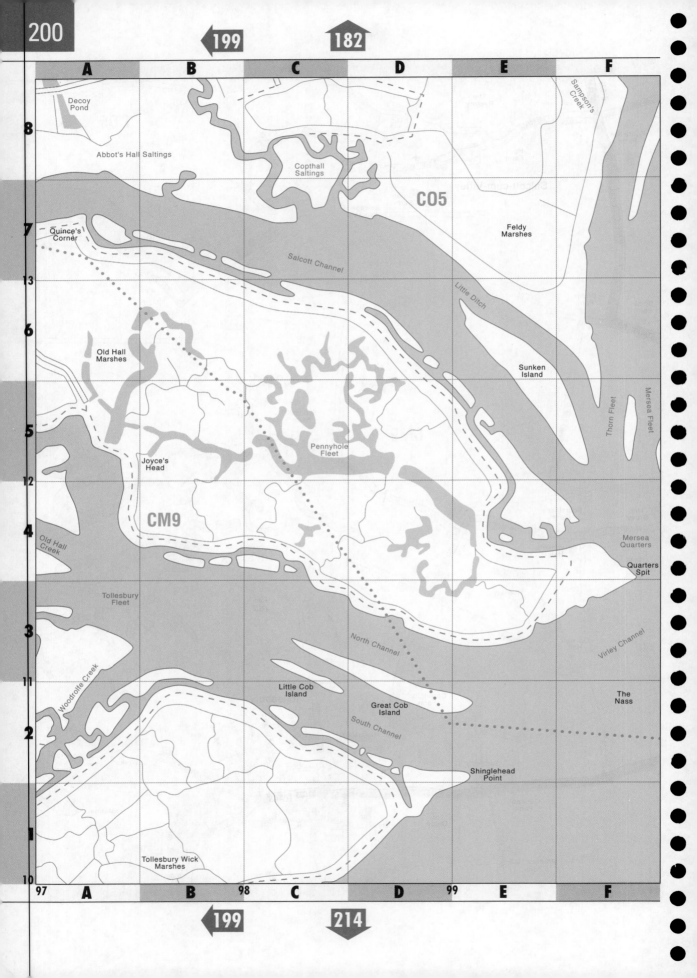

A B C D E F

8

Decoy
Pond

Abbot's Hall Saltings

Copthall
Saltings

CO5

7

Quince's
Corner

Feldy
Marshes

Sampson's
Creek

13

Salcott Channel

Little Ditch

6

Old Hall
Marshes

Sunken
Island

Thorn Fleet

Mersea Fleet

5

Joyce's
Head

Pennyhole
Fleet

12

CM9

Old Hall
Creek

Mersea
Quarters

Quarters
Spit

4

Tollesbury
Fleet

3

Woodrolfe Creek

North Channel

Virley Channel

11

Little Cob
Island

Great Cob
Island

The
Nass

2

South Channel

Shinglehead
Point

1

Tollesbury Wick
Marshes

10

97 A B 98 C D 99 E F

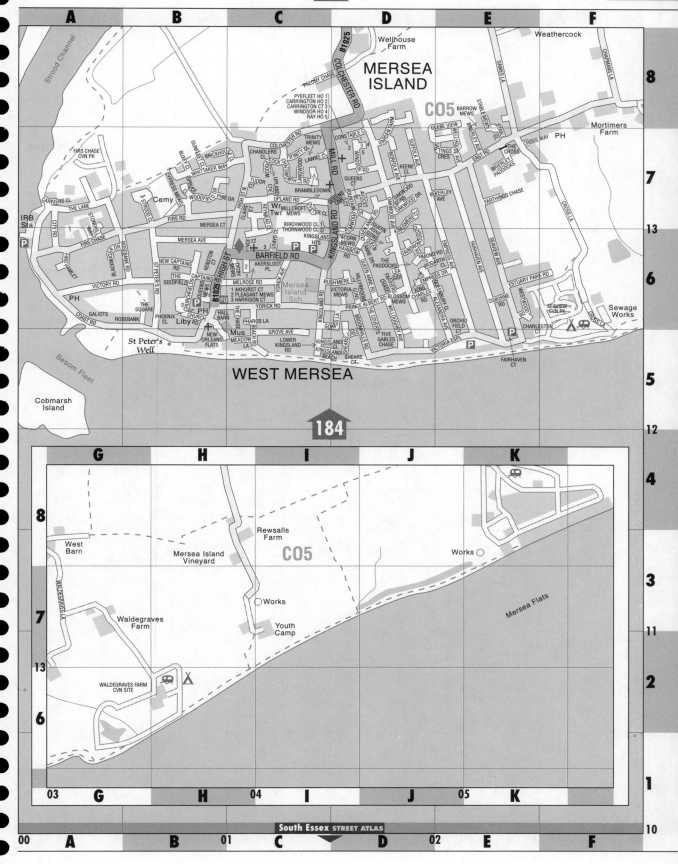

MERSEA ISLAND

CO5

Weathercock

Wellhouse Farm

Mortimers Farm

Strood Channel

FIRS CHASE CVN PK

IRB Sta

Cemy

WEST MERSEA

Besom Fleet

Cobmarsh Island

St Peter's Well

BARFIELD RD

Mersea Island Sch

1 AKHURST CT
2 PLEASANT MEWS
3 HARRISON CT

PYEFLEET HO 1
CARRINGTON HO 2
CARRINGTON CT 3
WINDSOR HO 4
RAY HO 5

Sewage Works

CO5

West Barn

Mersea Island Vineyard

Rewsalls Farm

Works

Waldegraves Farm

Works

Youth Camp

Mersea Flats

WALDEGRAVES LA

WALDEGRAVES FARM CVN SITE

186

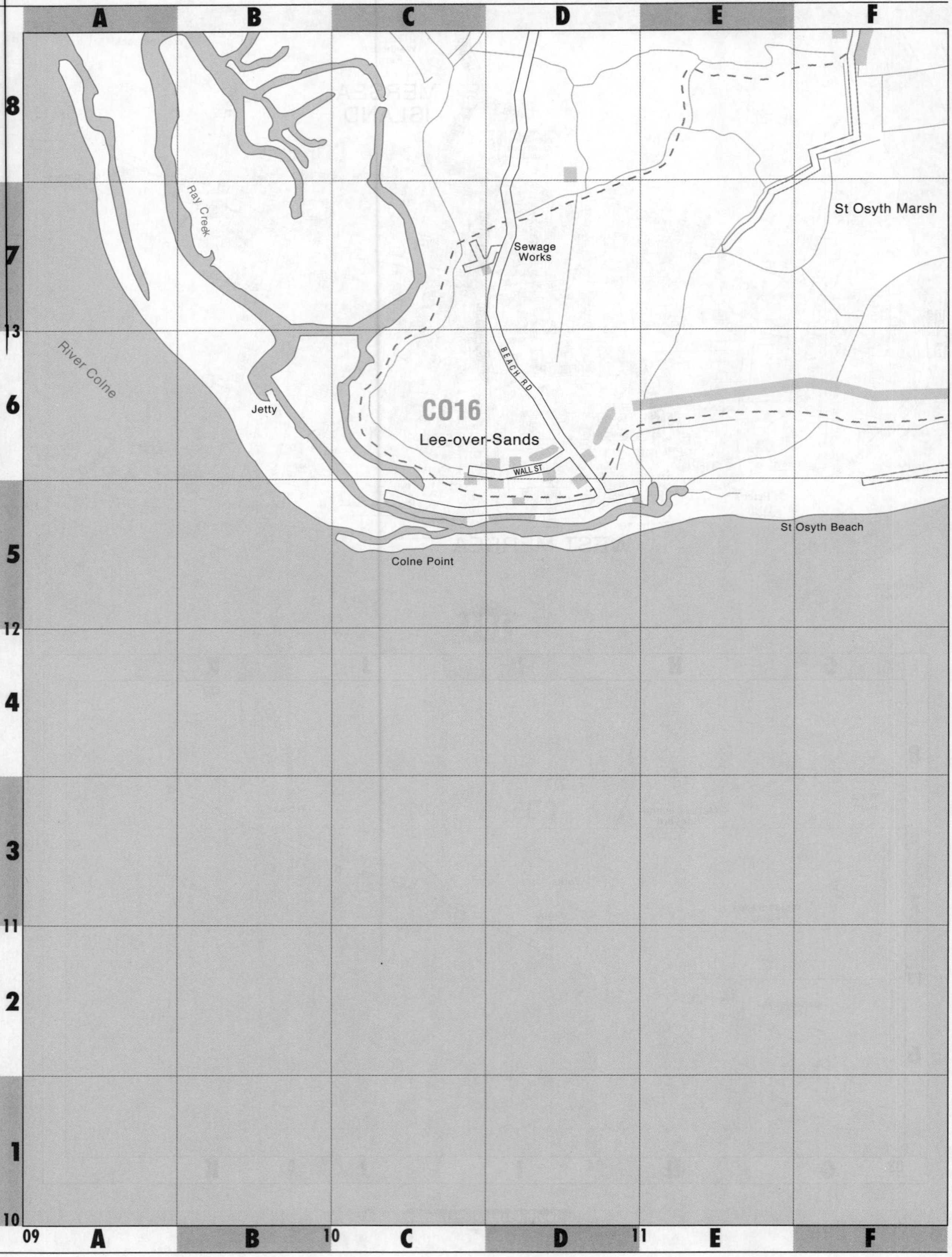

A B C D E F

8
7
13
6
5
12
4
3
11
2
1
10

09 A B 10 C D 11 E F

Ray Creek

River Colne

Jetty

Sewage
Works

BEACH RD

St Osyth Marsh

CO16
Lee-over-Sands

WALL ST

St Osyth Beach

Colne Point

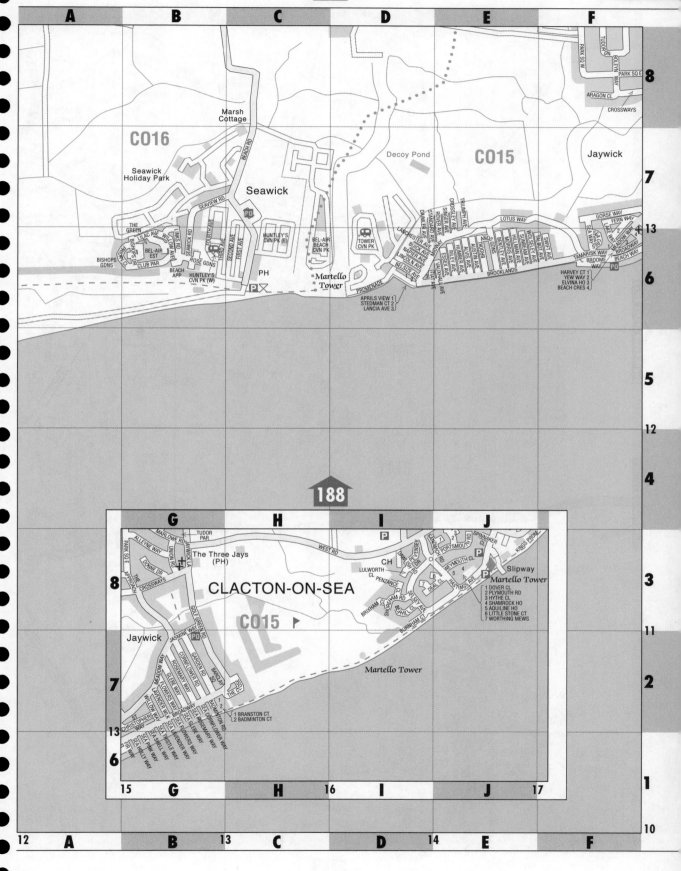

187

188

CO16

Marsh
Cottage

Seawick
Holiday Park

CO15

Jaywick

Seawick

Decoy Pond

THE
GREEN

BISHOPS
GDNS

BISHOPS DR
UNION RD

LILAC AVE

WILLOW AVE

BEL-AIR
EST

CLUB PAR

BEACH
APP

ROSE GDNS

HUNTLEY'S
CVN PK (W)

SEAVIEW RD

FOURTH AVE

THIRD AVE

SECOND AVE

FIRST AVE

WARWICK RD

BEACH RD

PO

HUNTLEY'S
CVN PK (E)

PH

P

BEL-AIR
BEACH
CVN PK

TOWER
CVN PK

Martello
Tower

PROMENADE

APRILS VIEW 1
STEDMAN CT 2
LANCIA AVE 3

LANCHESTER AVE

DAIMLER AVE

BUICK AVE

NAPIER AVE

LINCOLN AVE

BELSIZE AVE

STANDARD AVE

ROVER AVE

SINGER AVE

CROSSLEY AVE

TRIUMPH AVE

RILEY AVE

ESSEX AVE

ALVIS AVE

HUMBER AVE

AUSTIN AVE

VAUXHALL AVE

FIAT AVE

MORRIS AVE

BENTLEY AVE

RHODODB

SUNBEAM AVE

HILLMAN AVE

TALBOT AVE

WOLSELEY AVE

SWIFT AVE

LOTUS WAY

Brooklands

TAMARISK WAY

SEA WAY

LAKE WAY

GORSE WAY

FERN WAY

YEW WAY

BEACON WAY

BROADWAY

BROOME
WAY

BEACH WAY

PO

HARVEY CT 1
YEW WAY 2
ELVINA HO 3
BEACH CRES 4

PARK SQ W

PARK SQ E

BOLEYN WAY

TUDOR
GDNS

ARAGON CL

CROSSWAYS

8

7

13

6

5

12

4

CLACTON-ON-SEA

CO15

Jaywick

The Three Jays
(PH)

MARLOWE RD

ALLEYNE WAY

PARK SQ E

THE
APPROACH

THE
CROSSWAYS

DONNE DR

UNION RD

JAYWICK LA

TUDOR
PAR

GOLF GREEN RD

JASMINE WAY

PO

MEADOW WAY

LAVENDER WAY

WILLOW WAY

ROSEMARY WAY

FLOWERS WAY

CORNFLOWER RD

GARDEN RD

BROADWAY

BARCLAY
SQ

SEA BADMINTON RD

THE ESPL

BRANSTON CT 1
BADMINTON CT 2

WEST RD

P

LULWORTH
CL

PENZANCE

BRIXHAM CL

SHOREHAM CL

OXLEY DR

DAWLISH DR

DEAL CL

SELSEY AV

CH

HASTINGS AVE

PORTSMOUTH
RD

WEYMOUTH CL

SANDOWN
RD

SPINNAKER
CL

KINGS PROM

P

Martello Tower
Slipway

1 DOVER CL
2 PLYMOUTH RD
3 HYTHE CL
4 SHAMROCK HO
5 AQUILINE HO
6 LITTLE STONE CT
7 WORTHING MEWS

BURNHAM CL

Martello Tower

CHRISTOPHERS
WAY

SEA PINK WAY

SEA HOLLY WAY

FIR WAY

SEA SHELL WAY

SEA THISTLE WAY

SEA LAVENDER WAY

SEA ROSEMARY WAY

SEA CORNFLOWER WAY

SEA GLEBE WAY

8

3

11

7

2

13

6

1

10

A   B   C   D   E   F

G   H   I   J

15   G   H   16   I   J   17

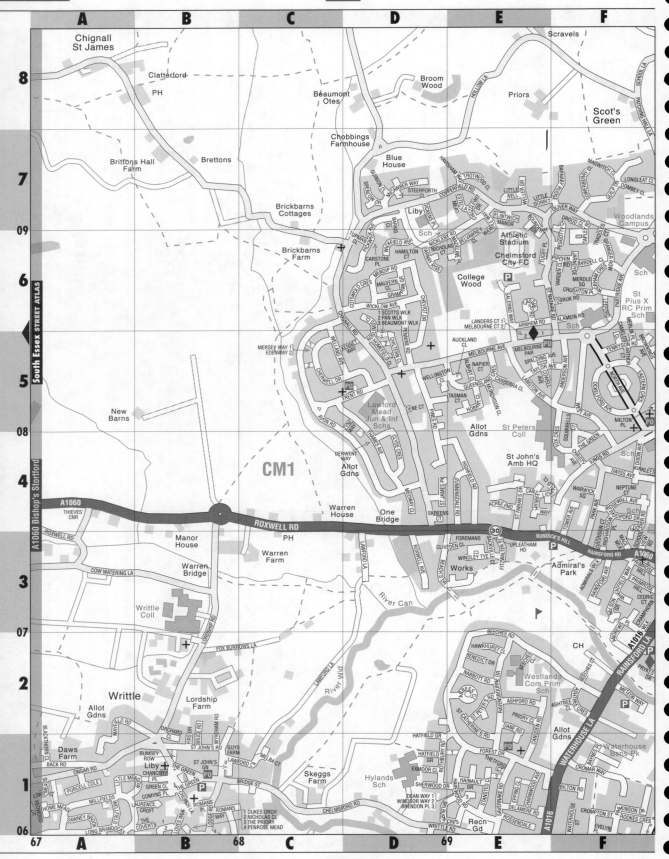

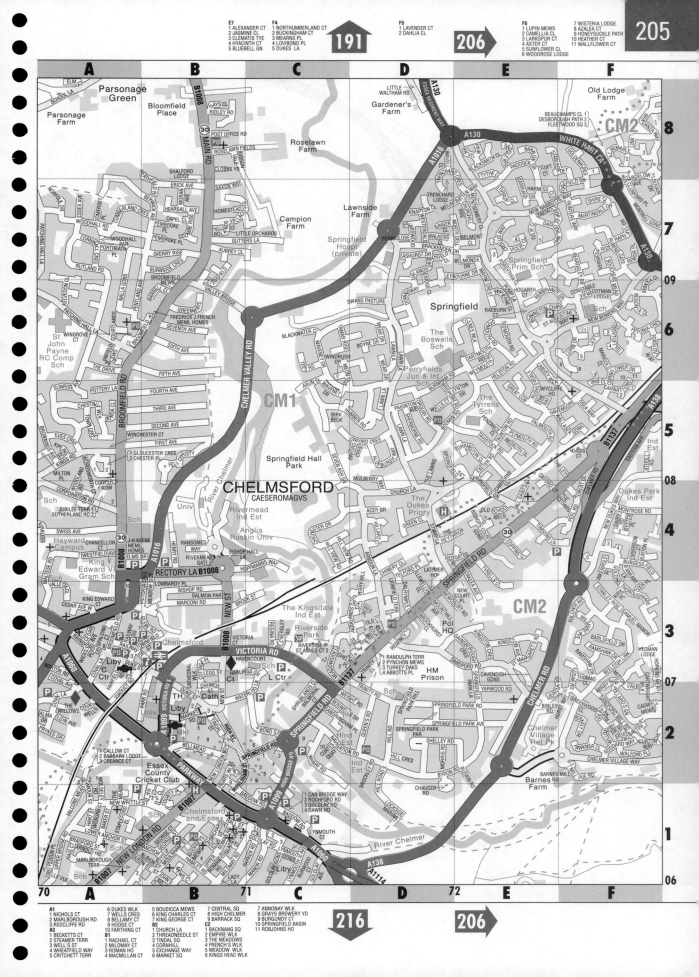

205 192

A B C D E F

8

CM1

7

09

6

5

08

4

3

07

2

1

06

A12

GENERALS LA

CHELMER RD

A138

MAIN RD

PAYNES LA

Tyrell Cottage

Boreham

The Old Rectory

Old Hall

CROMWELL CL
VILLIERS PL
OAK COTTS
B1137
ST ANDREWS
SUSSEX CL
HOLMANS
HULTON CL
BOONS CL
FALKLAND CL
BUTTERFIELD RD
FITZWALTER RD
HASELFOOT Sch
PLANTATION RD
RIVER COTTS
OLD FORGE RD
PH
THIRLAWN
TYSSEN MEAD
LEWIN CL
PO
JUNIPER RD
THE ARCHES
THE WILLOWS
CHURCH RD
CHURCH GN
WALKFARES
HOWARDS CL
ABERCORN HO
COOPERS 2
LONGS CRES
THE CHASE

A138
A130
Hotel
19
Service Area
DROVERS WAY
CHELMER RD
COLCHESTER RD
WINSFORD WAY
FORDSON RD
A130
PH
Hedgerows Bsns Pk
Sheepcotes
WHITE HART COTTS
SPRINGFIELD LYONS APP
SHEEPCOTES
LONEBARN LINK

Boreham House

Boreham Hall

Little Baddow Lock

WHITE HART LA
P
JACARANDA CL
OAK LODGE
TYE
ALYSSUM CL
LOBELIA CL
PRIMULA WAY
DAISY CL
POPPY GN
B1137
B1137
COLCHESTER RD
B1131

Stonham's Lock

Chelmer & Blackwater Navigation

CM3

TA Ctr
Springfield Lyons
Cuton Hall
CM2
CUTON DR
NEGG
TYE
TOWNSEND
BRYANT LINK
BORROW CHASE
ALLEN WAY
ALBRA MEAD
CORNELIUS VALE
WRIGHT MEAD
GEPPS
WIGGINS VIEW

Whitwell's Farm

Phillow's Farm

Dukes Park Ind Est
NEW DUKES WAY
BEAUFORT RD
ARGYLL RD
CUTON HALL LA
MONTROSE RD
RICHMOND RD
SUFFOLK
WILLIAMS
MURRELLS CL
BARTONS REACH
WINN DANK
BROOK END RD N
CONDOVER WAY
CHANCELLOR AVE
QUALE RD
ELDERS
WAR PATCH
GELDRS
CROZIER TERR
EGLINTON
Chelmer Village

Cuton Lock

Centenary Circle

River Chelmer

HERRINGHAM GN
GRAFTON
HARTLEY
SHEPPARD DR
DANKNER GATE
CLARENCE CL
WILKINS
BLACKBLDGE CL
Schs
PETERSBROOK
BROOK END RD
OLIVERS DR
PORTAL
BENNIERS PL
WHITMORE PL
WEBB CL
HARRINGTON MEAD
Prim Sch
Brookend

Hammond's Farm

HURRELLS LA
Ford
HAMMONDS RD

POCKLINGTON CL
LITTELL TWEED
COATES LQ
HOLLIS
DUIMORE
LANKIN CL
BLACKS
Prim Sch
BROOK END RD S
LEAPINGWELL CL
CHELMER VILLAGE WAY
WOODROFFE CL

Waterhall Meadows Nature Reserve

Hypermarket
PO
CHELMSFORD
VILLAGE SQ
HOPKINS MEAD
FAIRFAX MEAD
HOWARD DR
CURZON WAY
PALMERS CROFT
POLLARO'S GN
YELDHAM LOCK
YELDHAM GATE
COLYERS REACH
MARSTON
STORMS WAY
SAYWELL BROOK
SANDFORD BROOK
MILL RD

Grace's Wlk

Sewage Works

Rumbold's Farm

Sandford Mill Bridge

SANDFORD MILL RD

Works

A12

73 A B 74 C D 75 E F

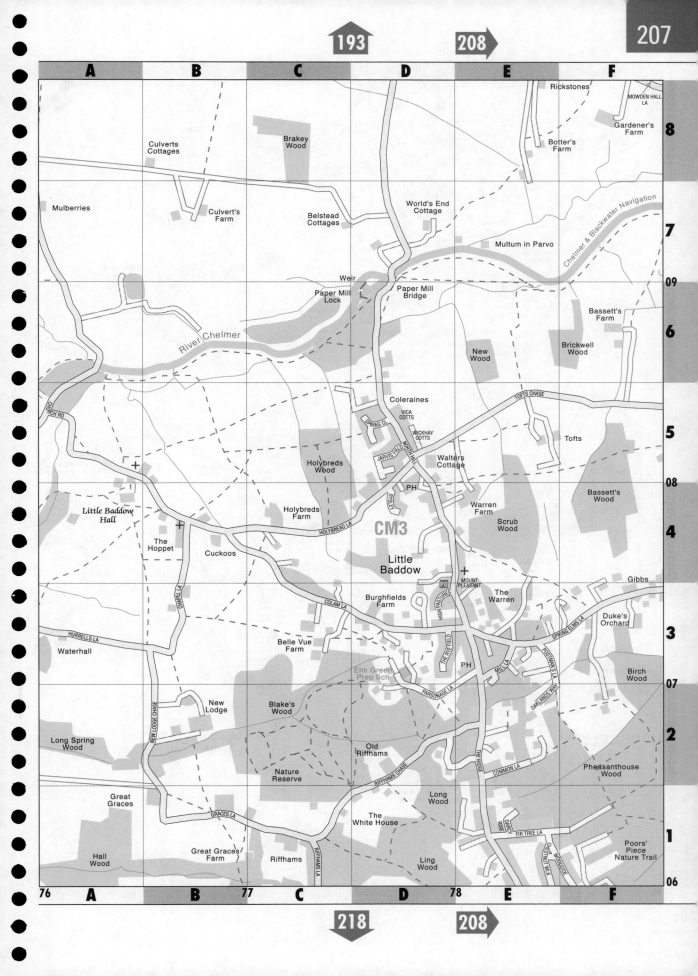

A B C D E F

8

7

09

6

5

08

4

07

3

2

1

06

Rickstones
MOWDEN HALL LA
Gardener's Farm
Culverts Cottages
Brakey Wood
Botter's Farm
Mulberries
Culvert's Farm
Belstead Cottages
World's End Cottage
Chelmer & Blackwater Navigation
Multum in Parvo
Weir
Paper Mill Lock
Paper Mill Bridge
Bassett's Farm
River Chelmer
New Wood
Brickwell Wood
Coleraines
TOFTS CHASE
VICA COTTS
SPRING CL
WICKHAY COTTS
Tofts
NORTH HILL
JARVIS FIELD
Holybreds Wood
Walters Cottage
Bassett's Wood
RISLEY
PH
Little Baddow Hall
Holybreds Farm
HOLYBREAD LA
CM3
Warren Farm
Scrub Wood
The Hoppet
Cuckoos
Little Baddow
MOUNT PLEASANT
The Warren
Gibbs
CHAPEL LA
Burghfields Farm
PO
Duke's Orchard
COLAM LA
HIGH PASTURES
SPRING ELMS LA
HURRELLS LA
Belle Vue Farm
THE RYE FIELD
PH
Birch Wood
Waterhall
Elm Green Prep Sch
PARSONAGE LA
MILL LA
POSTMAN'S LA
OAKLANDS WAY
07
New Lodge Chase
New Lodge
Blake's Wood
THE RIDGE
COMMON LA
Pheasanthouse Wood
Long Spring Wood
Old Riffhams
Nature Reserve
Long Wood
GRACES LA
Great Graces
The White House
RIFFHAMS CHASE
RIFFHAMS LA
DARCY RISE
FIR TREE LA
Poors' Piece Nature Trail
CHESTNUT WLK
WOODSIDE
Hall Wood
Great Graces Farm
Riffhams
Ling Wood

207 194

MOWDEN HALL LA
MALDON RD
B1019

8

Cardfield's Farm

Crouchman's

Fairwinds Farm

Ulting Grove

Ashfield Cottage

ASHFIELD FARM RD

River Ter

BUMFORDS LA

Bamfields

Wick Wood

CROUCHMAN'S FARM RD

7

Bumfords Bridge

ULTING HALL RD

Stammer's Farm

09

CHURCH RD

Ulting Wick

Ulting Hall

Southland's Farm

6

Ulting

Chelmer & Blackwater Navigation

THE CAUSEWAY

River Chelmer

ULTING LA

TOFTS CHASE

Retreat Farm

MANOR RD

5

Hoemill Bridge

Hoe Mill Barns

Manor Farm

08

Bassetts

Hoe Mill

HOE MILL RD

Raven's Farm

LITTLE LONDON LA

4

CM3

BASSETTS LA

West Bowers Farm

West Bowers Hall

WEST BOWERS RD

Little London Farm

Blue Mill

HOP GARDENS LA

Glendale

BLUE MILL LA

SPRING ELMS LA

Crossways

MEAD PASTURES

CURLING TYE LA

3

Spring Elms Poultry Farm

COMMON LA

ST NAUL'S RD

CM9

RECTORY RD

Whitehouse Farm

Woodhall

CH

LITTLE BADDOW RD

Gun Hill Farm

Woodham Walter CE Prim Sch

07

TOP RD

PH

THE STREET

PO

BROOK CL

CHURCH HILL

OAK FARM RD

2

Woodham Walter Common Nature Reserve

CH

The Wilderness

Woodham Walter

CHURCH CNR

The Warren House

Gravel Pit

HERBAGE PARK RD

1

Twitty Fee

TWITTY FEE

Oak Farm

06

OLD LONDON RD

207 219

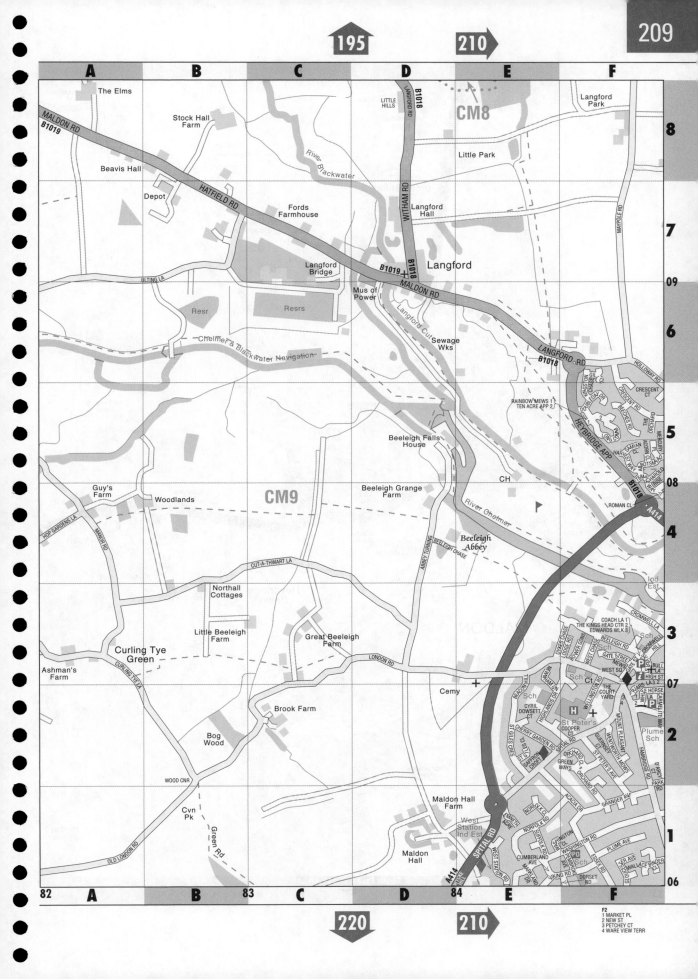

A1
1 LESLIE NEWNHAM CT
2 NIGHTINGALE CNR
3 SASSOON WAY
4 DRAYTON CL

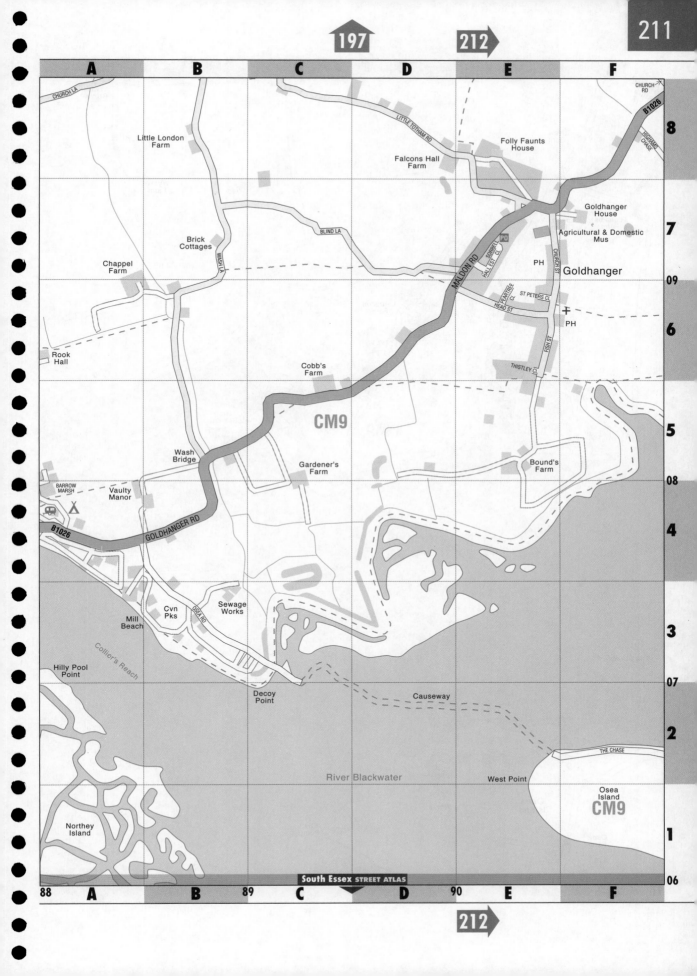

A   **B**   **C**   **D**   **E**   **F**

CHURCH LA

CHURCH RD

B1026

8

Little London Farm

LITTLE TOTHAM RD

Folly Faunts House

Falcons Hall Farm

HIGHAMS CHASE

Goldhanger House

BLIND LA

Brick Cottages

Agricultural & Domestic Mus

7

WASH LA

MALDON RD

SORREL CL

HALL EST CL

PO

PH

CHURCH ST

Goldhanger

09

Chappel Farm

PEARTREE CL

ST PETERS CL

HEAD ST

FISH ST

PH

6

Rook Hall

THISTLEY CL

Cobb's Farm

CM9

5

Gardener's Farm

Wash Bridge

Bound's Farm

08

BARROW MARSH

Vaulty Manor

GOLDHANGER RD

B1026

4

Cvn Pks

OSEA RD

Sewage Works

Mill Beach

3

Collier's Reach

Hilly Pool Point

07

Decoy Point

Causeway

2

THE CHASE

River Blackwater

West Point

Osea Island

CM9

Northey Island

1

06

88   **A**   **B**   89   **C**   **D**   90   **E**   **F**

MALDON RD
B1026

A B C D E F

8

New
Barn

JOYCE'S CHASE

HIGHAMS CHASE

7

Highams
Farm

Longwick
Farm

Bowstead Brook

Wycke
Farm

PAGES LA

Lower
Grove

09

JOYCE'S CHASE

6

Joyce's
Farm

Lauriston
Farm

LAURISTON
BGLWS

5

CM9

Gore
Saltings

08

4

Goldhanger Creek

River Blackwater

3

The Stumble

07

2

Osea Island

Works

THE CHASE

1

Osea
Farm

East
Point

Wr
Twr

06

91 A B 92 C D 93 E F

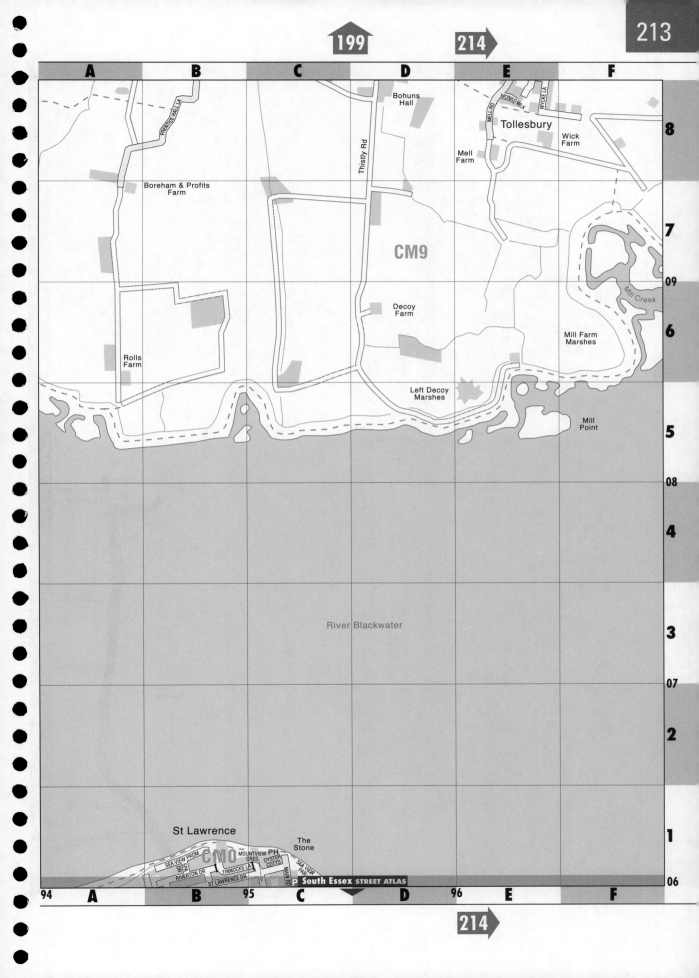

A B C D E F

8

Bohuns
Hall

MONKS WLK
WYCKE LA
MELL RD

Tollesbury

Wick
Farm

Mell
Farm

Thistly Rd

Boreham & Profits
Farm

7

CM9

09

Decoy
Farm

Mill Farm
Marshes

6

Mill Creek

Rolls
Farm

Left Decoy
Marshes

Mill
Point

5

08

4

River Blackwater

3

07

2

1

St Lawrence

The
Stone

CM0

SEA VIEW PROM
SPA
DR
MOUNTVIEW
CRES.
PH
OYSTER
COTTS
SEA VIEW
PAR
RIVERTON DR
TINNOCKS LA
ST LAWRENCE DR
MAIN RD

06

94 A B 95 C D 96 E F

CM9

River Blackwater

Jetty

Pewet
Island

South Essex STREET ATLAS

SHOEMENDERS
LA

B1021

Cvn
Pk
PARKER
CT

PO

Bradwell
Waterside

OLD
COASTGUARD
COTTS

PH

Mast

Marina

Bradwell Creek

TRUSSES RD

Westwick
Farm

WATERSIDE RD

WOODYARDS

Down
Westwick

CM0

Orplands

ORPLANDS
COTTS

Kennel
Barn

MALDON RD

B1021

MALDON RD

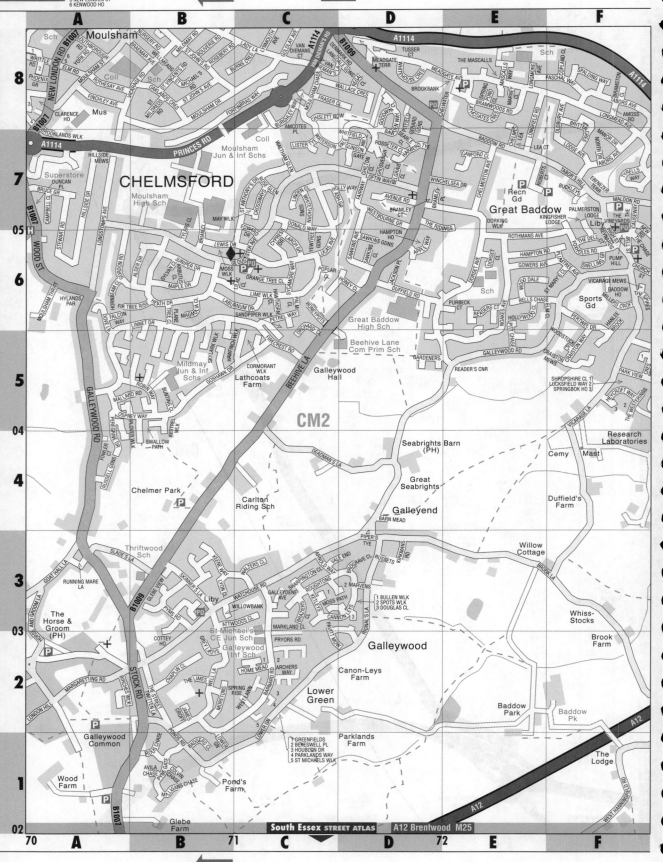

216

A8
1 CHERRYGARDEN LA
2 UPPER CHASE
3 DOUGLAS WLK
4 LAUREL GR
5 NEW LONDON CT
6 KENWOOD HO

215
205
215

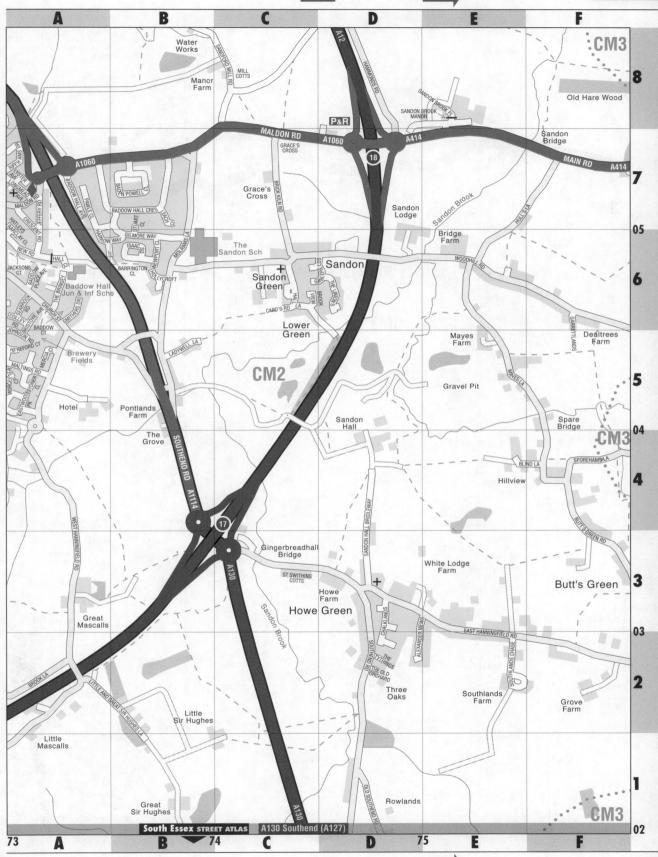

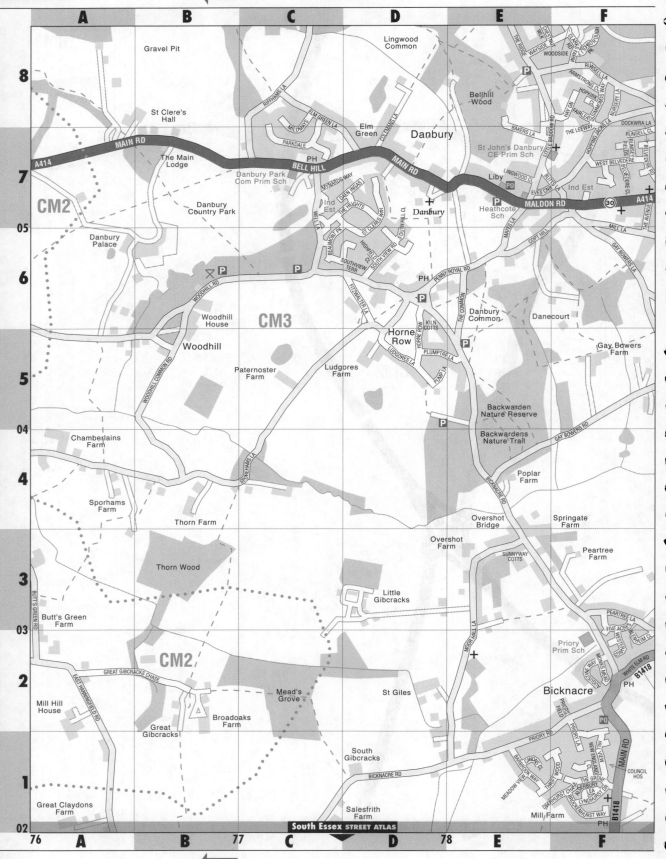

	A	B	C	D	E	F

8

Gravel Pit

St Clere's Hall

Lingwood Common

THE RIDGE
WAYSIDE
WOODSIDE
CHESTNUT WALK
CLARKS RD
THE BARROW

Bellhill Wood

7

MAIN RD
A414

The Main Lodge

Danbury Park Com Prim Sch

RIFFHAMS LA
MILDMAYS
PARKDALE
ELM GREEN LA
COLEMANS LA
Elm Green
PH
BELL HILL

MAIN RD

Danbury

St John's Danbury CE Prim Sch

Liby
PO
MALDON RD

Ind Est
A414
30

CM2

Danbury Palace

Danbury Country Park

MYNARDS WAY
DAEN INGAS
Ind Est
THE HEIGHTS
WILLIAM
ST CLERS WAY
SOUTH VIEW RD
Danbury

Heathcote Sch

MAYES LA
COPT HILL

05

BEAUMONT PK
HIGHFIELD
SOUTH VIEW RD

GAY BOWERS LA

6

WOODHILL RD
P

SOUTHVIEW TERR
FITZWALTER LA
PH
PENNY ROYAL RD
P

Danbury Common

Danecourt

Woodhill House

CM3

Woodhill

HORNE ROW
Horne Row
KILN COTTS
LUDGORES LA
PLUMPTRE LA
THE COMMON
PLUMP LA

Gay Bowers Farm

5

Paternoster Farm

Ludgores Farm

Backwarden Nature Reserve

04

Chamberlains Farm

P
Backwardens Nature Trail
GAY BOWERS RD

4

Sporhams Farm

Thorn Farm

SPORHAMS LA

BICKNACRE RD

Poplar Farm

Overshot Bridge

Springate Farm

3

Thorn Wood

Little Gibcracks

Overshot Farm

SUNNYWAY COTTS

Peartree Farm

PEARTREE LA
FIVE ACRES
BLENHEIM CL

Priory Prim Sch

03

BUTT'S GREEN RD
Butt's Green Farm

CM2

GREAT GIBCRACKS CHASE
EAST HANNINGFIELD RD

MOOR HALL LA

WHITE ELM RD
B1418
PH

2

Mill Hill House

Mead's Grove

St Giles

Bicknacre

PO

PRIORS FIELD
AUGUSTINE WAY
MONKS MEAD
PRIORY RD
PRIORY LA
NEW ENGLAND CL
HILL VIEW

Great Gibcracks
Broadoaks Farm

South Gibcracks

BICKNACRE RD

1

Great Claydons Farm

Salesfrith Farm

Mill Farm

Council Hos

MEADOW VIEW LA
THREE WOODS
BARROCK WAY
CANONS CL
THE GROVE
CHASE
PRIORY CHASE
LINDEN DR
DISPENHURST CHASE
BROCKENHURST WAY
B1418
MAIN RD
PH

02

76	A	B	77	C	D	78	E	F

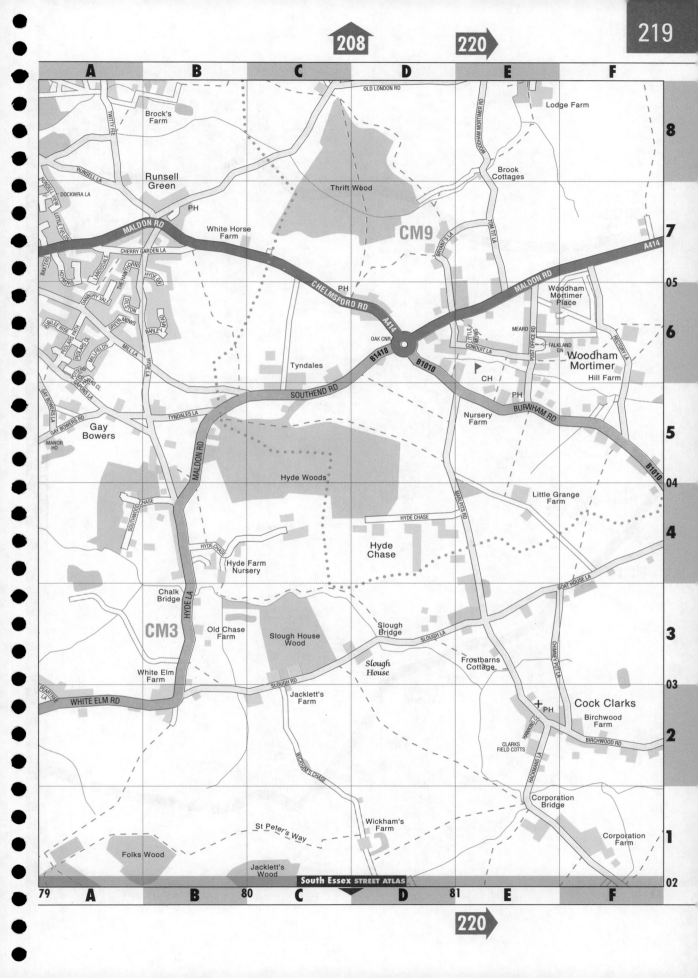

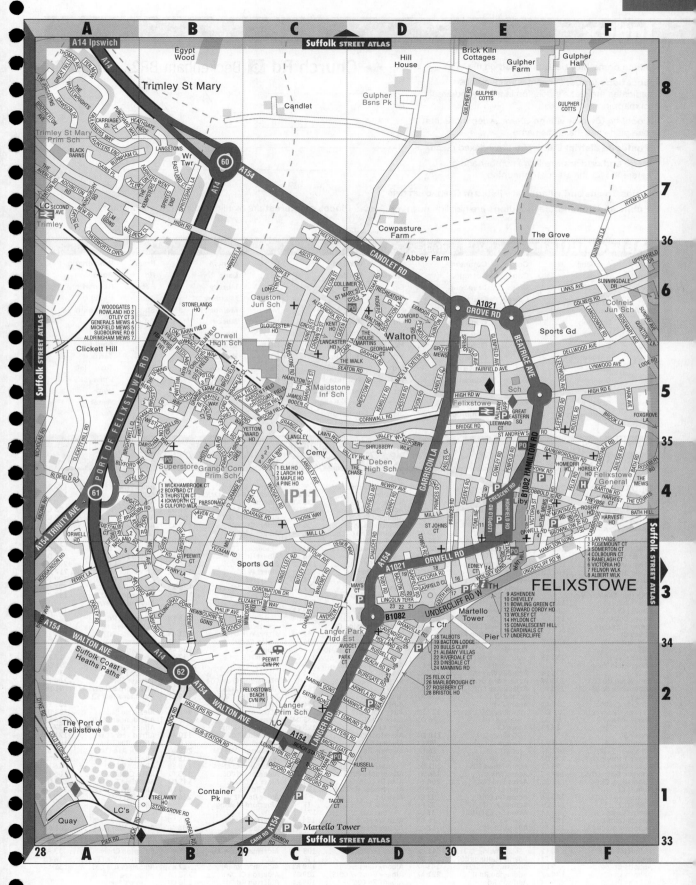

A14 Ipswich

Trimley St Mary

Egypt Wood

Candlet

Hill House

Brick Kiln Cottages

Gulpher Farm

Gulpher Hall

Gulpher Bsns Pk

GULPHER RD

GULPHER COTTS

GULPHER COTTS

8

Trimley St Mary Prim Sch

Wr Twr

60

A154

A14

7

LC SECOND AVE

Trimley

Cowpasture Farm

The Grove

36

CANDLET RD

Abbey Farm

6

A1021
GROVE RD

Colneis Jun Sch

Sports Gd

Clickett Hill

WOODGATES 1
ROWLAND HO 2
OTLEY CT 3
GENERALS MEWS 4
MICKFIELD MEWS 5
SUDBOURNE RD 6
ALDRINGHAM MEWS 7

STONELANDS HO

LONG BARN FIELD

Orwell High Sch

Causton Jun Sch

St Mary's Cres

Walton

BEATRICE AVE

Sch

PORT OF FELIXSTOWE RD

Maidstone Inf Sch

Felixstowe

Railway

GREAT EASTERN SQ

HIGH RD E

5

35

Grange Com Prim Sch

1 ELM HO
2 LARCH HO
3 MAPLE HO
4 PINE HO

Cemy

IP11

Deben High Sch

Felixstowe General

H

1 WICKHAMBROOK CT
2 BOXFORD CT
3 THURSTON CT
4 ICKWORTH CT
5 CULFORD WLK

Superstore

GARRISON LA

HAMILTON RD
B1082

THE MEWS

4

Liby

61

A154 TRINITY AVE

ORWELL HO

Sports Gd

ST JOHNS CT

ORWELL RD

A1021

FELIXSTOWE

1 LANYARDS
2 ROSEMOUNT CT
3 COLBOURN CT
4 RANELAGH CT
6 VICTORIA HO
7 FELNOR WLK
8 ALBERT WLK

3

Martello Tower

9 ASHENDEN
10 CHEVELEY
11 BOWLING GREEN CT
12 EDWARD CORDY HO
13 WOLSEY CT
14 HYLDON CT
15 CONVALESCENT HILL
16 CARDINALS CT
17 UNDERCLIFFE

WALTON AVE

A14

62

A154 WALTON AVE

Suffolk Coast & Heaths Paths

PEEWIT CVN PK

FELIXSTOWE BEACH CVN PK

Langer Park Ind Est

Langer Prim Sch

L Ctr

Pier

UNDERCLIFF RD W

34

18 TALBOTS
19 BACTON LODGE
20 BULLS CLIFF
21 ALBANY VILLAS
22 RIVERDALE CT
23 DINSDALE CT
24 MANNING RD

25 FELIX CT
26 MARLBOROUGH CT
27 ROSEBERY CT
28 BRISTOL HO

2

The Port of Felixstowe

Container Pk

LANGER RD

A154

1

Quay

LC's

Martello Tower

33

28 A   B   29   C   D   30   E   F   33

Index

Place name May be abbreviated on the map

Location number Present when a number indicates the place's position in a crowded area of mapping

Locality, town or village Shown when more than one place has the same name

Postcode district District for the indexed place

Page and grid square Page number and grid reference for the standard mapping

Church Rd 6 Beckenham BR2..........**53** C6

Cities, towns and villages are listed in CAPITAL LETTERS

Public and commercial buildings are highlighted in magenta   **Places of interest** are highlighted in blue with a star★

Abbreviations used in the index

Acad	Academy	Comm	Common	Gd	Ground	L	Leisure	Prom	Promenade
App	Approach	Cott	Cottage	Gdn	Garden	La	Lane	Rd	Road
Arc	Arcade	Cres	Crescent	Gn	Green	Liby	Library	Recn	Recreation
Ave	Avenue	Cswy	Causeway	Gr	Grove	Mdw	Meadow	Ret	Retail
Bglw	Bungalow	Ct	Court	H	Hall	Meml	Memorial	Sh	Shopping
Bldg	Building	Ctr	Centre	Ho	House	Mkt	Market	Sq	Square
Bsns, Bus	Business	Ctry	Country	Hospl	Hospital	Mus	Museum	St	Street
Bvd	Boulevard	Cty	County	HQ	Headquarters	Orch	Orchard	Sta	Station
Cath	Cathedral	Dr	Drive	Hts	Heights	Pal	Palace	Terr	Terrace
Cir	Circus	Dro	Drove	Ind	Industrial	Par	Parade	TH	Town Hall
Cl	Close	Ed	Education	Inst	Institute	Pas	Passage	Univ	University
Cnr	Corner	Emb	Embankment	Int	International	Pk	Park	Wk, Wlk	Walk
Coll	College	Est	Estate	Intc	Interchange	Pl	Place	Wr	Water
Com	Community	Ex	Exhibition	Junc	Junction	Prec	Precinct	Yd	Yard

Index of towns, villages, streets, hospitals, industrial estates, railway stations, schools, shopping centres, universities and places of interest

222 Abb–All

A

Abbas Wlk CO10 .... 34 C5
ABBERTON 163 A3
Abberton Rd
  Fingringhoe CO5 ...... 163 D3
  Layer de la H CO2 .... 162 C5
Abberton Resr Nature
  Reserve★ CO2 .... 161 F2
Abberton Wildfowl Visitor
  Ctr★ CO2 .... 161 E1
Abbess Cl CM1 .... 204 E2
Abbey Cotts CO11 .... 115 C7
Abbey Cres CO16 .... 142 A1
Abbey Ct
  Colchester CO2 .... 136 A5
  10 Ipswich IP1 .... 17 A7
ABBEY FIELD 135 E5
Abbey Field View
  CO2 .... 135 E4
Abbeygate Ho CO2 ...... 135 F6
Abbey Gate St 11 CO2 .. 135 F6
Abbey La
  Coggeshall CO6 ...... 131 A1
  Saffron Walden CB10. . 22 E1
Abbey Mdw CO9 .... 51 D2
Abbey Rd CO10 .... 15 E1
Abbey St
  Ickleton CB10 .... 3 A4
  Thorpe-le-S CO16 ..... 142 A1
Abbey Turning CM9 .... 209 D4
Abbey View CM6 .... 96 E2
Abbigail Gdns CO15 .... 189 B4
Abbotsbury Cl IP2 ...... 17 A1
Abbots Cl
  Clacton-on-S CO15...... 188 E6
  Wix CO11 .... 115 C5
Abbots Cotts CB9 .... 10 A4
Abbots Gdns CO16 ..... 187 C4
Abbotsmead CM9 .... 209 F5
Abbot's Rd CO2 .... 136 B3
Abbots Wick La CO5 .... 181 B3
Abbott Rd CO12 .... 90 F2
Abbott's Croft CB9 .... 9 F4
Abbotts Ct CB9 .... 9 E5
Abbotts La CO6 .... 134 A7
Abbotts Pl CM2 .... 205 D3
Abbotts Way CM23 ..... 145 E3

Abdy Ave CO12 .... 90 E2
Abell Way CM2 .... 206 B4
Abels Rd CO9 .... 103 D8
Abercorn Ct 11 CB9 ...... 8 F7
Abercorn Ho CM3 ...... 206 E8
Abercorn Way CM8 .... 177 A2
Aberdare Cl IP2 .... 17 B2
Abingdon Cl IP2 .... 17 A1
Abinger Cl CO16 .... 188 C6
Abington Pl 2 CB9 .... 9 A8
Abraham Dr CM8 ...... 156 E4
Abram's La SG8 .... 19 C4
Acacia Ave CO4 .... 136 E8
Acacia Cl IP3 .... 18 E1
Acacia Ct CO11 .... 60 D1
Acacia Dr
  Great Dunmow CM6 ... 123 C1
  Maldon CM9 .... 209 F1
Acacia Gdns CM8 ...... 177 B4
Accommodation Rd
  CO4 .... 109 D7
Acer Gr
  Chelmsford CM1 ...... 205 D4
  Ipswich IP8 .... 16 C1
Achilles Way CM7 ...... 128 B5
Achnacone Dr CO4 .... 109 C3
Acland Ave CO3 .... 135 B7
Acland Ct CO3 .... 135 A7
Acorn Ave
  Braintree CM7 .... 127 E2
  Halstead CO9 .... 76 D1
Acorn Cl
  Colchester CO4 ...... 110 C4
  Harwich CO12 .... 90 F1
  Ipswich IP2 .... 16 C2
  Maldon CM9 .... 209 F5
Acorn Mews CO5 ...... 201 D6
Acorn Wlk CO7 .... 166 A5
Acres End CM1 .... 204 E4
Acton Cl CO10 .... 33 F8
Acton Gn CO10 .... 33 E7
Acton La CO10 .... 33 F8
Acton Sq 4 CO10 ...... 33 E7
Adair Rd IP1 .... 16 D8
Adams Cl IP2 .... 17 C3
Adams Ct
  Halstead CO9 .... 76 D2
  Saffron Walden CB11.. 43 C8
Adams Maltings CM9.... 76 D2
Adderley Rd CM23 .... 145 F7
Addington Rd IP11..... 221 A7
Addison Rd
  Great Holland CO13...... 170 B5

Addison Rd continued
  Sudbury CO10 .... 34 B8
Adelaide Dr CO2 ...... 136 A1
Adelaide Rd IP4 .... 18 D6
Adelaide St CO12 ...... 90 F5
Admiral Rd IP8 .... 36 E8
Admirals The CO12 .... 91 D4
Admirals Wlk
  Chelmsford CM1 ...... 204 F3
  Wivenhoe CO7 .... 164 B8
Aerofoil Gr CO4 .... 109 D2
Aetheric Rd CM7 ...... 127 E3
Affleck Rd CO4 .... 136 E7
Agar Rd 9 CO14 ...... 171 C8
Agar Road App 10
  CO14 .... 171 C8
Agate Rd CO15 .... 188 F2
Agincourt Rd CO15 .... 188 D4
Agnes Silverside Cl
  Beerchurch CO2 ...... 162 F8
  Colchester CO2 ...... 135 F1
Agricultural/Domestic
  Mus★ CM9 .... 211 E7
Ainger Rd CO12 .... 90 E2
AINGERS GREEN 166 E5
Aingers Green Rd
  CO7 .... 167 A5
Ainslie Rd IP1 .... 17 A6
Aire Wlk CM8 .... 176 E2
Airey Hos CO10 .... 11 D1
Aisne Rd CO2 .... 135 D4
Ajax Cl CM7 .... 128 B5
Akersloot Pl CO5 ...... 201 C6
Akhurst Ct CO5 .... 201 C6
Alamein Rd
  Chelmsford CM1 ...... 204 F6
  Colchester CO2 ...... 135 C2
Alanbrooke Rd CO2..... 136 D2
Alan Dr CO16 .... 168 D1
Alan Hasler Ho CM6.... 150 D7
Alan Rd
  Ipswich IP3 .... 17 F4
  Witham CM8 .... 176 E1
Alan Way CO3 .... 134 F4
Albany Chase CO15 .... 189 B4
Albany Cl
  Chelmsford CM1 ...... 204 E5
  West Bergholt CO6 ... 108 E4
Albany Gdns CO2 ...... 136 D4
Albany Gdns E CO15 .. 189 B3
Albany Gdns W CO15... 189 B3
Albany Rd CO6 .... 108 E4
Albany The IP4 .... 17 E8

Albany Villas IP11 ..... 221 D3
Albemarle Gdns CM7... 128 C5
Albemarle Link CM2 ... 205 F8
Albemarle St CO12..... 91 D5
Albert Cotts CO7 .... 60 C2
Albert Ct CM7 .... 128 A3
Albert Gdns
  Clacton-on-S CO15..... 189 B3
  Coggeshall CO6 ...... 131 A2
Albert Ho IP2 .... 17 B4
Albertine Cl CO3 ...... 134 C6
Albert Pl CO6 .... 131 A2
Albert Rd
  Braintree CM7........ 128 A3
  Brightlingsea CO7 .... 186 A6
  Witham CM8 .... 177 A3
Albert St
  Colchester CO1 ...... 135 E8
  Harwich CO12 .... 91 D5
Albert Wlk IP11 .... 221 E4
Albion Ct CM2 .... 205 B1
Albion Gr CO2 .... 136 A5
Albion Hill IP4 .... 17 F7
Albion St CO5 .... 164 A8
Albra Mead CM2 ...... 206 B4
Albrighton Croft CO4 .. 110 C4
Alconbury CM23 .... 119 B1
Alcorns The CM24 ..... 119 E7
Aldeburgh Cl
  Clacton-on-S CO16..... 188 B4
  Haverhill CB9 .... 8 E7
Aldeburgh Gdns
  Colchester CO4 ...... 110 B4
  Ipswich IP4 .... 18 A6
Aldeburgh Way CM1 ... 205 D5
Alderbury Lea CM3 .... 218 F1
Alderbury Rd CM24 ... 119 E8
Aldercar Rd CO6 ...... 133 F1
Alder Cl CM23 .... 145 D4
Alde Rd CB9 .... 9 A8
Alder Dr CM2 .... 216 B6
Alderford Maltings
  CO9 .... 75 E8
Alderford St CO9 ...... 75 E8
Alderlee IP2 .... 36 F8
Alderman Blaxhill Sch
  CO2 .... 135 B3
Alderman Howe Lo
  CO4 .... 110 B4
Alderman Rd IP1 ...... 17 B5
Alderton Cl CM6 ...... 152 C6
Alderton Rd CO4 ...... 136 C8
Alder Way CO10 .... 33 F8

Alder Wlk CM8 .... 177 B4
ALDHAM 133 B8
Aldham Ct 18 CB9 .... 8 E7
Aldon Cl CO12 .... 90 C1
Aldous Cl CO7 .... 59 C4
Aldridge Cl CM2 ...... 206 A4
Aldringham Mews
  IP11 .... 221 B5
Alec Kay Ct CO2 ...... 135 C2
Aletha Farm Pl CO9.... 29 D6
Alexander Ct 1 CM1.... 205 E7
Alexander Mews CM2... 217 D2
Alexander Rd CM7 .... 127 E4
Alexandra Ave CO5 ... 201 E6
Alexandra Dr CO7 .... 137 C3
Alexandra Mews 7
  CM7 .... 128 A2
Alexandra Rd
  Clacton-on-S CO15..... 188 F3
  Colchester CO3 ...... 135 E6
  Felixstowe IP11...... 221 C6
  Harwich CO12 .... 91 D5
  Ipswich IP4 .... 17 E6
  Sible Hedingham CO9 .. 51 D1
  Sudbury CO10 .... 34 A7
  Weeley CO16 .... 140 F1
Alexandra St CO12 .... 91 D5
Alexandra Terr 9
  CO3 .... 135 E6
Alexia Ho CM6 .... 123 D1
Alefounder Cl CO4 .... 136 E6
Alfells Rd CO7 .... 137 F6
Alfred Terr CO14 ...... 171 C8
Alfreg Rd CM8 .... 194 D8
Alienor Ave CM7 .... 72 B1
Allectus Way CM8 .... 194 D8
Allenby Rd IP2 .... 16 F6
Allen Cotts CO6 .... 106 E5
Allen Ho CM7 .... 128 A3
Allendale Dr CO6 ..... 133 D4
Allen Ho CM7 .... 128 A3
Allens Cl CM3 .... 192 F1
Allen Way
  Chelmsford CM2 ...... 206 B4
  Point Clear B CO16 ... 186 A3
Alleyne Way CO15 .... 203 G8
Allfields CO12 .... 91 A2
All Hallows Ct IP3 ..... 18 A1
Allington Cl IP4 .... 17 F7
Allington Wlk CB9 ...... 8 E8
All Saints Ave CO3 .... 135 A4
All Saints CE Prim Sch
  Bishop's Stortford
  CM23 .... 146 B8

All Saints CE Prim Sch
continued
Great Oakley CO12 . . . . . **116** C3
Harwich CO12 . . . . **90** F3
Maldon CM9 . . . . **209** F3
All Saints Cl
Ashdon CB10 . . . . **23** F7
Bishop's Stortford
CM23 . . . . **146** A8
Chelmsford CM1 . . . . . . **205** E4
All Saints Maldon CE Prim
Sch CM9 . . . . **209** E2
All Saints' Rd IP1 . . . . . **17** A8
Allshots Enterprises
CO5 . . . . **157** B5
Alma Dr CM1 . . . . **205** A2
Alma Sq 4 CO11 . . . . . **86** D4
Alma St CO7 . . . . **164** B8
Almond Cl
Clacton-on-S CO15 . . . . . **188** C3
Tiptree CO5 . . . . **179** C6
Wivenhoe CO7 . . . . **137** C2
Almondhayes IP2 . . . . . **17** B3
Almond Way CO4 . . . . . **136** E8
ALMSHOUSE GREEN . . . **74** E7
Almshouses CO7 . . . . . **164** B8
Alnesbourn Cres IP3 . . . **38** D7
Alpe St IP1 . . . . **17** B7
Alpha Cl CM7 . . . . **128** A2
ALPHAMSTONE **54** F3
Alphamstone Rd CO8 . . . **55** B4
Alpha Pl
4 Bishop's Stortford
CM23 . . . . **145** F8
2 Saffron Walden CB11 . . . **22** E1
Alpha Rd CO16 . . . . **186** B3
Alpha Terr IP3 . . . . **18** E1
Alport Ave CO2 . . . . **135** C4
ALRESFORD **165** A8
Alresford Prim Sch
CO7 . . . . **165** B7
Alresford Rd CO7 . . . . . . **164** E8
Alresford Sta CO7 . . . . . . **165** A8
Alsa Bsns Pk CM24 . . . . . **93** F1
Alsa Gdns CM22 . . . . . . **94** C2
Alsa Leys CM22 . . . . . . **94** C2
Alsa St CM24 . . . . **93** F1
Alston Cres CO10 . . . . . . **2** E6
Alston Rd IP3 . . . . **17** F4
Alstons Ct IP3 . . . . **18** D1
Altbarn Cl CO4 . . . . **110** C5
Altbarn Rd CO2 . . . . **136** D5
Altitude Bsns Pk IP3 . . . . . **18** C1
Alton Dr CO3 . . . . **135** B6
Alton Gn IP9 . . . . **63** A2
Alton Hall La IP9 . . . . . . **61** F3
Alton Park Jun Sch
CO15 . . . . **188** D2
Alton Park La CO15 . . . . . **188** B1
Alton Park Rd CO15 . . . . . **188** D3
Alton Rd CO15 . . . . **188** E1
Alton Water (Resr)★
IP9 . . . . **62** A4
Alton Water Visitor Ctr★
IP9 . . . . **62** B3
Aluf Cl 2 CM8 . . . . **194** E8
Alverton Cl CM77 . . . . . . **154** B6
Alverton Way CO4 . . . . . **110** B3
Alvis Ave CO15 . . . . **203** E6
Alyssum Cl CM1 . . . . . . **206** A6
Alyssum Wlk CO4 . . . . . **136** D8
Amberley Cl CO7 . . . . . . **137** C1
Ambleside Ct CO15 . . . . . **189** A3
Ambridge Rd CO6 . . . . . **130** E3
Ambrose Ave CO3 . . . . . **134** F4
Ambrose Ct CO6 . . . . . . **133** D4
Ambrose Ho CO2 . . . . . . **135** D2
Amcotes Pl CM2 . . . . . . **216** C8
Amerells Rd CO16 . . . . . **168** C4
America Rd CO6 . . . . . . **105** C2
America St CM9 . . . . . . **210** A2
Amos Hill CO10 . . . . . . **54** B8
Amoss Rd CM2 . . . . **216** F8
Ancaster Rd IP2 . . . . . . **17** B4
Anchorage Hill CM9 . . . . **210** A3
Anchorage The CO12 . . . . **90** F5
Anchor Cvn Camp
CO16 . . . . **168** D2
Anchor End CO11 . . . . . **87** A4
Anchor Hill CO7 . . . . . . **164** B7
Anchor Ho CO2 . . . . **135** E2
Anchor La
Dedham CO7 . . . . **85** A4
Heybridge CM9 . . . . **210** A5
New Mistley CO11 . . . . . **87** A4
Anchor Rd
Clacton-on-S CO15 . . . . . **188** E3
Tiptree CO5 . . . . **179** C4
Anchor St
Bishop's Stortford
CM23 . . . . **146** A6
Chelmsford CM2 . . . . . . **205** B1
Ipswich IP3 . . . . **17** E4
Anderson Ave CM1 . . . . . **204** F5
Anderson Cl CM23 . . . . . **92** F2
Andover Cl CO15 . . . . . . **189** A6
Andrew Cl
Braintree CM7 . . . . **127** F5
Felixstowe IP11 . . . . . . **221** C3
Andrews Farm La
CM6 . . . . **123** C8
Andrews Pl CM1 . . . . . . **204** F3
Andros Cl IP3 . . . . **38** A8
Anemone Cl CO4 . . . . . . **109** C2
Angelgate CO12 . . . . . . **91** E6
Angelgate Cotts CO12 . . . **91** E6
Angel La
Glemsford CO10 . . . . . . **2** B4

Angel La continued
Great Dunmow CM6 . . . . **150** D8
17 Ipswich 1P4 . . . . **17** D5
Angel Mdw CO10 . . . . . . **2** B4
Anglefield CO15 . . . . . . **188** F2
Anglesea Rd
Ipswich IP1 . . . . **17** B7
Wivenhoe CO7 . . . . **164** C8
Anglesey Cl CM23 . . . . . **145** C7
Angle Side CM7 . . . . . . **128** B2
Anjou Cl CM2 . . . . **135** B3
Anita Cl E IP2 . . . . **16** E5
Anita Cl W IP2 . . . . **16** E5
Anjou Gn CM1 . . . . **206** A7
Annbrook Rd IP2 . . . . . . **16** E1
Ann Coles Cl CB9 . . . . . . **27** C6
Anne Cl CO7 . . . . **185** F6
Anne St IP11 . . . . **221** C3
Annonay Wlk 7 CM2 . . . . **205** C2
Ann St IP1 . . . . **17** B7
Ansgar Rd CB11 . . . . . . **43** E7
Anson Cl CO12 . . . . **91** A4
Anson Way CM7 . . . . . . **128** C4
Anthony Cl CO4 . . . . . . **110** D2
Antonia Cl CB9 . . . . **9** E7
Antonio Wlk CO4 . . . . . . **136** F7
Antonius Way CO4 . . . . . **110** B6
Anvil Way CM1 . . . . **205** B6
Anzani Ave IP11 . . . . . . **221** A4
Anzio Cres CO2 . . . . **135** C3
Apollo Ho IP2 . . . . **16** D1
Apollo Mews CO2 . . . . . . **135** C1
Appleby Cl IP2 . . . . **16** D1
Applegates Mdw CO9 . . . **29** F2
Appleton Fields CM23 . . . **145** E4
Appletree Cl CM77 . . . . . **155** F5
Apple Tree Cl CO9 . . . . . **77** A2
Appletree Hill Cotts
CM3 . . . . **172** D6
Appletree Wlk CM7 . . . . **128** A1
Apple Way CM2 . . . . **216** D6
Approach The CO15 . . . . . **203** G8
Apsley Ave CO15 . . . . . . **203** D6
Apsley Cl CM23 . . . . **145** F4
Apsley Ct 3 IP1 . . . . **17** A7
Apton Cl CM23 . . . . **145** F7
Apton Fields CM23 . . . . . **145** F6
Apton Rd CM23 . . . . **145** F7
Aquiline Ho CO15 . . . . . . **203** J8
Aragon Cl CO15 . . . . **203** F8
Aragon Rd
Great Leighs CM3 . . . . . **173** F7
Haverhill CB9 . . . . **8** D6
Arakan Cl CO2 . . . . **135** B1
Arbour La
Chelmsford CM1 . . . . . . **205** D4
Wickham Bishops CM8 . . . **195** F5
Arbour Way CO4 . . . . . . **110** C4
Arbutus Cl CM2 . . . . **216** B6
Arcade St 15 IP1 . . . . . . **17** C6
Arcade The CO15 . . . . . . **188** F2
Archangel Gdns IP2 . . . . **16** E4
Archer Cres CO5 . . . . . . **179** E5
Archers Way CM2 . . . . . **216** C2
Archery Fields CO15 . . . . **189** A5
Arden Cl CO4 . . . . **110** C3
Arderne Cl CO12 . . . . . . **90** F2
ARDLEIGH **111** E7
Ardleigh Cl CO7 . . . . . . **111** E8
ARDLEIGH HEATH **84** D1
Ardleigh Rd
Dedham CO7 . . . . **84** D3
Great Bromley CO7 . . . . . **112** B4
Little Bromley CO11 . . . . . **112** E5
Argents La CO3 . . . . **108** C2
Argyle Ct CO5 . . . . **158** C2
Argyle Rd CO16 . . . . **141** F2
Argyll Cl 1P4 . . . . **17** D6
Argyll Ct 10 CB9 . . . . **8** F7
Argyll Rd CM2 . . . . **206** A5
Ariel Cl CO4 . . . . **136** F7
ARKESDEN **41** E2
Arkesden Rd CB11 . . . . . **65** E6
Arkwright Rd IP2 . . . . . . **16** E7
Arlesford Ct CO4 . . . . . . **136** F4
Armidale Wlk CO4 . . . . . **136** A2
ARMIGERS **96** D6
Armiger Way CM8 . . . . . **177** B2
Armonde Cl CM3 . . . . . . **192** E1
Armond Rd CM8 . . . . . . **176** F3
Armourers Cl CM23 . . . . **145** B4
Armoury Rd CO6 . . . . . . **108** F4
Armstrong Cl CM3 . . . . . **218** F4
Armstrong Way CO9 . . . . **30** A2
Arnhem Gr CM7 . . . . . . **127** C5
Arnhem Rd CM1 . . . . . . **204** E6
Arnold Dr CO4 . . . . **136** E6
Arnold Ho CM2 . . . . **205** A1
Arnold Rd CO15 . . . . . . **188** D1
Arnold Villas CO5 . . . . . **179** C6
Arnold Way CM2 . . . . . . **216** C3
Arnstones Cl CO4 . . . . . . **136** C8
ARP Shelter Mus★ IP4 . . . **17** F5
Arras Sq 12 IP1 . . . . **17** C6
Arrow Rd CO4 . . . . **136** F7
Arrowsmith Wlk CO4 . . . . **110** A6
Arthur Ct CM1 . . . . **204** F5
Arthur St 5 CO2 . . . . . . **135** F6
Arthur's Terr IP4 . . . . . . **17** F4
Arthy Cl CM3 . . . . **194** A4
Artillery Dr CO12 . . . . . . **90** D1
Artillery St CO1 . . . . . . **136** B6
Arun Cl CM1 . . . . **205** C5
Arundel Way IP3 . . . . . . **18** E3

Arundel Wlk 1 CB9 . . . . . **8** E8
Arwela Rd IP11 . . . . **221** D2
Asbury Cl CO4 . . . . **136** D8
Ascot Cl CM23 . . . . **146** C8
Ascot Dr
Felixstowe IP11 . . . . . . **221** C6
Ipswich IP3 . . . . **18** B3
Ascot Gdns CO3 . . . . . . **134** E7
Ascot Mews CO15 . . . . . **189** C5
Ash Bglws CM7 . . . . **127** E3
Ashbury Dr CO6 . . . . . . **132** F3
Ashby Rd CM8 . . . . **195** A7
Ashby Rise CM23 . . . . . **119** B1
Ash Cl
Brightlingsea CO7 . . . . . **185** E7
Clacton-on-S CO15 . . . . . **188** C3
Hatfield Peverel CM3 . . . . **194** A4
Ipswich IP3 . . . . **18** F1
Ash Ct CO12 . . . . **90** E2
Ashdale CM23 . . . . **145** D4
ASHDON **6** B1
Ashdon Mus The★
CB10 . . . . **24** B8
Ashdon Prim Sch CB10 . . . **6** B1
Ashdon Rd
Ashdon CB10 . . . . **24** E3
Saffron Walden CB10 . . . . **23** C3
Ashdon Road Commercial
Ctr CB10 . . . . **23** A3
Ashdown Cl CM77 . . . . . **154** B8
Ashdown Way
Colchester CO4 . . . . **136** D7
Ipswich IP3 . . . . **18** D3
ASHEN **11** D1
Ashen Cl CO10 . . . . **11** D1
Ashenden IP11 . . . . **221** E4
Ashen Hill CO10 . . . . . . **11** C2
Ashen La CO10 . . . . **11** C3
Ashen Rd
Ashen CO10 . . . . **12** A1
Clare CO10 . . . . **12** B5
Ridgewell CO9 . . . . **29** B8
Ashes Cl CO14 . . . . **170** F8
Ashes Rd CM77 . . . . **155** F7
Ash Fall CM8 . . . . **177** A5
Ashfield Cl CM6 . . . . . . **123** C1
Ashfield Farm Rd
CM9 . . . . **208** D8
Ashfields Farm CM6 . . . . **149** B3
Ashford Rd CM1 . . . . . . **204** E2
Ash Gn CB10 . . . . **3** D1
Ash Gr
Blackheath CO2 . . . . . . **163** A8
Capel St M IP9 . . . . **35** A2
Great Cornard CO10 . . . . **34** C5
Great Dunmow CM6 . . . . **150** D7
Heybridge CM9 . . . . **210** C6
Wivenhoe CO7 . . . . **137** C3
Ash Ground Cl CO11 . . . . **86** D8
Ash Ho IP2 . . . . **16** D2
Ashlea Cl CB9 . . . . **9** B6
Ashlea Rd CB9 . . . . **9** B6
Ashley Ct CO12 . . . . **91** B3
Ashley Gdns CO3 . . . . . . **135** C6
Ashley Lo CO15 . . . . **189** A3
Ashley Rd CO12 . . . . **91** B3
Ashley St IP2 . . . . **17** C4
Ashlong Gr CO9 . . . . . . **76** E3
Ashlyn's Rd IP13 . . . . . . **170** E4
Ashmere Gr IP4 . . . . **17** F6
Ashmere Rise CO10 . . . . . **34** A8
Ashmole Dr CO13 . . . . . . **170** F6
Ashpole Rd CM7 . . . . . . **102** B1
Ash Rd CO7 . . . . **165** B8
Ash Rise CO9 . . . . **103** F8
Ashstead Cl CO16 . . . . . **188** B6
Ashton Cl IP2 . . . . **16** C2
Ashton Pl CM2 . . . . **206** A3
Ashtree Cl CM1 . . . . **204** F2
Ash Tree Cnr CM3 . . . . . **191** B6
Ashtree Cres CM1 . . . . . **204** F2
Ashurst Cl CO5 . . . . **163** F8
Ashurst Dr CM1 . . . . . . **205** D7
Ash Way CO3 . . . . **134** F3
Ashwells Mdw CO6 . . . . . **105** B6
Ashwin Ave CO6 . . . . . . **133** C4
Askins Rd CO7 . . . . **59** C3
Aspens The CM23 . . . . . **119** B3
Aspen Way
3 Colchester CO4 . . . . . **136** D8
Little Oakley CO12 . . . . . **117** B7
Aspin Mews CB10 . . . . . **22** E3
Asquith Dr CO4 . . . . **110** C5
Astell Ct CO13 . . . . **170** F4
Aster Cl
Bishop's Stortford
CM23 . . . . **145** D6
Clacton-on-S CO16 . . . . . **188** C4
Aster Ct 4 CM1 . . . . **205** F6
Aster Rd IP2 . . . . **16** E4
Astley Rd CO15 . . . . **188** D3
Ataka Rd IP11 . . . . **221** D6
Athelstan Rd CO3 . . . . . **135** C5
Atherton Rd IP2 . . . . . . **16** D2
Atholl Rd CM2 . . . . **205** F5
Atlantic Sq CM8 . . . . . . **177** A3
Atlas Bglws CO6 . . . . . . **105** A6
Atlas Ct CO6 . . . . **105** A7
Atlas Ho 3 IP4 . . . . **17** E6
Atlas Rd CO6 . . . . **104** F7
Atlas Works CO6 . . . . **105** B6
Attlee Gdns 7 CO1 . . . . . **136** A6
Attwood Cl CO4 . . . . **110** B5
Attwoods Cl CM2 . . . . . . **216** C3
Aubrey Buxton Nature
Reserve★ CM24 . . . . . **94** A1

Aubrey Cl CM1 . . . . **205** B7
Auckland Cl CM1 . . . . . . **204** E5
Audley Cl CM77 . . . . **154** B7
Audley Ct CB11 . . . . **22** D1
AUDLEY END
Castle Hedingham **52** E8
Saffron Walden **43** B8
Audley End House &
Gdns★ CB11 . . . . **22** B1
Audley End Miniature
Rly★ CB11 . . . . **43** A8
Audley End Rd CB11 . . . . **43** C8
Audley End Sta CB11 . . . . **42** F5
Audley Gr IP4 . . . . **18** F5
Audley Rd
Colchester CO3 . . . . **135** C5
Great Leighs CM3 . . . . . **173** F7
Saffron Walden CB11 . . . . **22** C1
Audley Way CO13 . . . . . . **171** B6
Audrey Gdns CM23 . . . . **145** F4
Audries Est CO14 . . . . . . **171** A8
Augusta Cl IP3 . . . . **38** E7
Augustine Way CM3 . . . . **218** F2
Augustus Cl
Colchester CO4 . . . . **110** B6
Haverhill CB9 . . . . **9** D7
Augustus Mews CM7 . . . . **127** E2
Augustus Way CM8 . . . . **194** B8
Austen Cl CM77 . . . . . . **155** A8
Austin Ave CO15 . . . . . . **203** B6
Austin St IP2 . . . . **17** C4
Auton Croft CB11 . . . . . . **43** D7
Autoway CO4 . . . . **110** C5
Autumn Cl CO16 . . . . . . **188** C5
Aveley Way CM9 . . . . . . **220** F8
Aveline Rd CO7 . . . . **111** E7
Avenue Pl CM23 . . . . . . **146** A6
Avenue Rd
Bishop's Stortford
CM23 . . . . **146** B6
Chelmsford CM2 . . . . . . **216** D7
Witham CM8 . . . . **177** A3
Avenue The
Braintree CM7 . . . . **127** F3
Clacton-on-S CO15 . . . . . **189** B7
Colchester CO3 . . . . **135** C6
Danbury CM3 . . . . **218** F7
Great Braxted CM8 . . . . . **178** A3
Great Dunmow CM6 . . . . **150** E8
Great Oakley CO12 . . . . . **116** B3
Ipswich IP1 . . . . **17** C8
Trimley St M IP11 . . . . . . **221** A7
Washbrook IP8 . . . . **35** F7
West Bergholt CO6 . . . . . **108** D3
Witham CM8 . . . . **177** A2
Wivenhoe CO7 . . . . **137** B1
Avignon Cl CO2 . . . . **136** B4
Avila Chase CM2 . . . . . . **216** B1
Avitus Way CO4 . . . . **110** B5
Avocet Cl
Frinton-on-S CO13 . . . . . **170** E6
Kelvedon CO5 . . . . **158** D2
West Mersea CO5 . . . . . **201** D7
Avocet Ct IP11 . . . . **221** D2
Avocet Way CM9 . . . . . . **210** C5
Avondale Ho CO15 . . . . . **189** A3
Avondale Rd
Clacton-on-S CO15 . . . . . **189** A3
Ipswich IP3 . . . . **18** A2
Avon Rd CM1 . . . . **204** C5
Avon Way CO4 . . . . **136** F6
Avon Way Ho CO4 . . . . . **136** F6
Avon Wlk CM8 . . . . **176** E3
Axial Way CO4 . . . . **110** B6
Aylesbury Dr
Great Notley CM77 . . . . . **154** C5
Holland-on-S CO15 . . . . . **189** F6
Ayletts CM1 . . . . **191** B3
Ayloffe Rd CO4 . . . . **110** C1
Aynsworth Ave CM23 . . . **119** B2
Azalea Ct
8 Chelmsford CM1 . . . . . **205** F6
Colchester CO4 . . . . **136** D8
Azalea Way CO16 . . . . . . **188** C4

B

Baburgh Ho CO10 . . . . . . **33** F7
Back Hamlet IP3 . . . . . . **17** E5
Back Hill
Hadstock CB1 . . . . **5** B6
Holbrook IP9 . . . . **62** E4
Back La
Broomfield CM1 . . . . . . **191** D1
Colchester CO3 . . . . **134** E7
Felixstowe IP11 . . . . . . **221** D5
Ford End CM3 . . . . **172** B6
Great Oakley CO12 . . . . . **116** C3
Ickleton CB10 . . . . **3** A3
Little Waltham CM3 . . . . . **191** C4
Ramsey CO12 . . . . **90** A1
Stisted CM77 . . . . **129** C7
Tattingstone IP9 . . . . . . **61** C6
Washbrook IP8 . . . . **35** E8
Wickham Bishops CM8 . . . **195** F4
Back La E CO7 . . . . **139** A6
Back La W CO7 . . . . **138** F7
Backnang Sq 1 CM2 . . . . **205** C2
Back Rd
Ardleigh CO7 . . . . **112** B5
Tollesbury CM9 . . . . . . **199** C4
Writtle CM1 . . . . **204** A1
Backwarden Nature
Reserve★ CM3 . . . . . . **218** E5
Backwardens Nature
Trail★ CM3 . . . . **218** E4

Back Waterside La
CO7 . . . . **185** F5
BACON END **149** F2
BACONEND GREEN **149** E4
Bacons Green Cotts
CO7 . . . . **58** E7
Bacon's La CO6 . . . . **106** C3
Bacton Lo IP11 . . . . **221** D3
Bacton Rd IP11 . . . . **221** D3
Baddow Ct CM2 . . . . **217** A6
Baddow Hall Ave
CM2 . . . . **217** A7
Baddow Hall Cres
CM2 . . . . **217** B7
Baddow Hall Inf Sch
CM2 . . . . **217** A6
Baddow Hall Jun Sch
CM2 . . . . **217** A6
Baddow Ho CM2 . . . . . . **216** F6
Baddow Pk CM2 . . . . **216** F2
Baddow Place Ave
CM2 . . . . **217** A6
Baddow Rd
Chelmsford CM2 . . . . . . **205** C1
Great Baddow CM2 . . . . . **216** E7
Baden Powell Cl CM2 . . . **217** B7
Baden Powell Dr CO3 . . . **135** A4
Bader Cl IP3 . . . . **18** C2
Badger Gr CM7 . . . . **128** B3
Badgers CM23 . . . . **145** E5
Badgers Bank IP2 . . . . . . **16** E1
Badgers Cl CM2 . . . . **216** B1
Badgers Gn CO6 . . . . . . **132** E3
Badgers Holt CO3 . . . . . . **134** D6
Badley Hall Rd CO7 . . . . **112** F2
Badminton Ct CO15 . . . . **203** G7
Badminton Rd CO15 . . . . **203** G7
Badshah Ave IP3 . . . . . . **18** B3
Bagshaw Rd CO12 . . . . . **91** D4
Bailey Bridge Rd CM7 . . . **127** E5
Bailey Cl
Haverhill CB9 . . . . **9** D7
Ipswich IP2 . . . . **16** E6
Bailey Dale CO3 . . . . . . **134** C4
BAILEY HILL **28** B5
Bailey La CO10 . . . . **12** C7
Bainbridge Dr CO5 . . . . . **179** C4
Baines Cl CO3 . . . . **135** A5
Baird Cl IP2 . . . . **16** F7
Baker Ave CM3 . . . . **194** A3
Baker Mews CM9 . . . . . . **210** A2
Baker Rd IP9 . . . . **91** A8
Bakers Almshouses
IP9 . . . . **61** F3
Bakers Ct
5 Bishop's Stortford
CM23 . . . . **146** A7
Colchester CO1 . . . . **109** E1
Bakers La
Danbury CM3 . . . . **218** E7
Felsted CM6 . . . . **152** C4
Baker's La
Colchester CO4 . . . . **109** A2
Great Notley CM77 . . . . . **154** D6
Tolleshunt Major CM9 . . . **197** D4
Bakers Mead CM3 . . . . . **190** F7
Baker's Rd CO10 . . . . . . **12** F2
Baker St CM2 . . . . **205** A1
Baker Way CM8 . . . . **194** F7
Bakery Ct CM24 . . . . **119** D6
Baldry Cl IP8 . . . . **16** C1
Baldwin's La CO6 . . . . . . **131** E8
Bale Cl CO3 . . . . **134** E4
Balfe Ct CO4 . . . . **136** E6
Balfour Terr IP3 . . . . **38** C8
Balkerne Gdns CO1 . . . . **135** E7
Balkerne Hill CO3 . . . . . **135** E7
Balkerne Pas CO1 . . . . . **135** E7
Ball Alley 3 CO1 . . . . . . **135** F7
Ballantyne Dr CO2 . . . . . **136** D5
Ballast Quay Rd
Fingringhoe CO5 . . . . . . **164** B6
Wivenhoe CO7 . . . . **137** D1
BALLINGDON **33** D6
Ballingdon Gr CO10 . . . . **33** D5
Ballingdon Hill CO10 . . . **33** C5
Ballingdon Hill Ind Est
CO10 . . . . **33** C6
Ballingdon St CO10 . . . . **33** D6
Ballingdon Trad Est
CO10 . . . . **33** C6
Ball La
Abberton CO2 . . . . **162** F5
Blackheath CO2 . . . . . . **163** B5
Ball's Chace CO8 . . . . . . **79** F2
Ball's Chace CO9 . . . . . . **76** F1
Ball's Farm CO7 . . . . . . **137** E7
Balmoral Ave CO15 . . . . **188** D3
Balmoral Cl IP2 . . . . **16** F1
Balmoral Ct
Braintree CM7 . . . . **128** C4
Chelmsford CM2 . . . . . . **205** C2
Balmoral Dr CB9 . . . . . . **8** E8
Balton Way CO12 . . . . . . **90** F2
BAMBER'S GREEN **121** F3
Bangs CB21 . . . . **7** A7
Banham Dr CO10 . . . . . . **33** F8
Banister Cl CO16 . . . . . . **188** C5
Bankart La CM2 . . . . **205** F4
Bank Bldgs 13 CO10 . . . . **33** E7
Bank Pas CO1 . . . . **135** E7
Bank Rd IP4 . . . . **17** E6
Banks Ct CM6 . . . . **150** D8
Bank St CM7 . . . . **127** F3
BANNISTER GREEN **152** F6

Bannister Green Villas
CM6 . . . . **152** E6
Banters La CM3 . . . . **154** B1
Bantock Way CM8 . . . . **194** F7
Bantoft Terr IP3 . . . . **18** C2
Barbary Lo CM2 . . . . **205** A2
Barbel Rd CO4 . . . . **110** F1
Barbour Gdns CO2 . . . . **134** F2
Barbrook La CO5 . . . . **179** D6
Barbrook Way CM3 . . . . . . **218** E1
Barclay CM2 . . . . **217** A6
Barclay Sq CO15 . . . . **203** G7
Bardell Cl CM1 . . . . **204** F6
Bardfield Ctr CM7 . . . . **72** B1
BARDFIELD END GREEN
. . . . **70** C2
Bardfield End Villas
CM6 . . . . **70** C2
Bardfield Rd
Bardfield Saling CM7 . . . . **99** F1
Colchester CO2 . . . . **136** A1
Finchingfield CM7 . . . . **72** C5
Thaxted CM6 . . . . **70** D2
BARDFIELD SALING **99** C2
Bardfield Way CO13 . . . . . . **170** F6
Bardsley Cl 2 CO4 . . . . . . **109** E2
Bardsley Rd 2 CO4 . . . . . . **109** E2
Barfield Rd CO5 . . . . **201** C6
Barfields Row CO5 . . . . **159** D2
Bargate La CO7 . . . . **85** C3
Baring-Gould Cotts
CO5 . . . . **184** D1
Barker Cl
Ipswich IP2 . . . . **16** D5
Lawford CO11 . . . . **86** B4
Steeple Bumpstead CB9 . . **27** B6
Barker Rd CO10 . . . . **15** E2
Barkers Terr CO7 . . . . **85** A5
Barkis Cl CM1 . . . . **204** D7
Barkstead Rd CO4 . . . . **110** C1
Barlee Cl CB11 . . . . **65** C3
Barley Cl CO11 . . . . **87** A4
Barley Ct
Saffron Walden CB11 . . . . . **22** D1
Wivenhoe CO7 . . . . **137** C3
Barleyfields CM8 . . . . **177** A1
Barleyhayes CL IP2 . . . . **17** B2
Barley Hills CM23 . . . . **145** E4
Barley Ho CO10 . . . . **15** B5
Barley Mead CM3 . . . . **219** B6
Barley Way CO3 . . . . **134** E5
Barlon Rd CO11 . . . . **112** F4
Barlow Road Cotts CB10 . . . **6** B2
Barlow's Reach CM2 . . . . . **206** A4
Barnaby Rudge CM1 . . . . . **204** F7
Barnard Cl CB11 . . . . **66** F8
Barnardiston Rd CO4 . . . . . **110** C1
Barnardiston Way
CM8 . . . . **176** F3
Barnard Rd CM2 . . . . **216** C2
Barnards Ct CB10 . . . . **22** B2
Barnards Field CM6 . . . . . . **70** B2
Barnards Orch CM77 . . . . . **126** F2
Barnards Yd CB10 . . . . **22** D1
Barnby Cl CB9 . . . . **8** C8
Barncroft Cl CO4 . . . . **110** B3
Barnes Farm Inf Sch
CM2 . . . . **206** A3
Barnes Farm Jun Sch
CM2 . . . . **206** A3
Barnes Mill Rd CM2 . . . . . . **205** F2
Barnett Reach CO14 . . . . . . **144** E2
Barnfield
Capel St M IP9 . . . . **35** B1
Feering CO5 . . . . **158** D3
Manningtree CO11 . . . . **86** D4
Barn Field IP11 . . . . **221** B6
Barnfield Cotts CM9 . . . . . . **210** B5
Barnfield Mews CM1 . . . . . **205** A6
Barnfield Pl CM8 . . . . **176** F1
Barnfield Rd CO6 . . . . **109** C6
Barnfields CO5 . . . . **163** F5
Barn Fields CO3 . . . . **134** C6
Barn Gn CM1 . . . . **205** E8
Barn Hall Ave CO2 . . . . **136** C4
Barnhall Rd CM9 . . . . **180** D2
Barnham Pl IP5 . . . . **18** F6
Barn La CO11 . . . . **112** F7
Barn Mead
Braintree CM7 . . . . **128** D2
Galleywood CM2 . . . . **216** D4
BARNSTON **151** A4
Barnston Gn CM6 . . . . **151** A4
Barn View Rd CO6 . . . . **131** A4
Baronia Croft CO4 . . . . **110** C3
Baron's Ct 5 CB9 . . . . **8** F7
Baron's La CM3, CM9 . . . . **220** E1
Barons The CM23 . . . . **145** D5
Baronswood Way
CO2 . . . . **135** D2
Barrack Cnr 5 IP1 . . . . . . **17** B6
Barrack La
Great Waltham CM3 . . . . . **190** E8
Harwich CO12 . . . . **91** E4
Ipswich IP1 . . . . **17** B6
Barrack Sq 9 CM2 . . . . . . **205** B2
Barrack St
Bradfield CO11 . . . . **114** D8
Colchester CO1 . . . . **136** B6
Barracks The CM7 . . . . **73** C3
Barr Cl CO7 . . . . **137** C1
Barrel Cl CO7 . . . . **139** C4
Barrells Down Rd
CM23 . . . . **118** E1
Barrett La 5 CM23 . . . . . . **145** F7

Barrington Cl
Great Baddow CM2 . . . . . **217** A6
Little Clacton CO16 . . . . . **168** C2
Barrington Gdns
CO15 . . . . **189** C5
Barrington Ho CO2 . . . . . . **136** A5
Barrington Rd CO2 . . . . . . **136** A5
Barrow Chase CM2 . . . . . . **206** B4
Barrow Marsh CM9 . . . . . . **211** A4
Barrow Mews CO5 . . . . . . **201** E8
Barryfields CM7 . . . . **100** E7
Bartholomew Cl CB10 . . . . **3** E2
Bartholomew Ct CO4 . . . . . **109** E3
BARTHOLOMEW GREEN
. . . . **153** E7
Bartholomew Rd 8
CM23 . . . . **145** F6
Bartholomew St IP4 . . . . . . **17** F6
Bartletts CB10 . . . . **22** D1
BARTLOW **6** B7
Bartlow Rd
Castle Camps CB21 . . . . **7** C4
Hadstock CB1 . . . . **5** D7
Barton Cl IP2 . . . . **16** E2
Barton Rd IP11 . . . . **221** F4
Bartram Ave N CM7 . . . . . **128** C3
Bartram Ave S CM7 . . . . . **128** C3
Barwell Ho 3 CM8 . . . . . . **194** E8
Barwell Way CM8 . . . . **177** B2
Basbow La 2 CM23 . . . . . **145** F7
Basin Rd CM9 . . . . **210** E3
Bassetts La CM3, CM9 . . . **208** A4
Bassingbourn Rd
CM24 . . . . **121** A3
Bassingham Cres
CO5 . . . . **179** E5
Bateman Rd CO7 . . . . **185** E8
Bateman's Rd CO16 . . . . . . **168** B4
Bates Rd CM9 . . . . **210** B4
Bath Ct CB9 . . . . **8** F6
Bath Hill IP11 . . . . **221** F4
Bath Rd IP11 . . . . **221** F4
BATH SIDE **91** D5
Bath St
Ipswich IP2 . . . . **17** D3
Wivenhoe CO7 . . . . **164** B8
Bathurst Cl 1 CO2 . . . . . . **136** A1
Battery La IP9 . . . . **91** B8
Batt Hall CO10 . . . . **33** B6
Battisford Dr CO16 . . . . . . **188** A4
Battle Rise CM9 . . . . **210** B4
Battlesbrook Rd CO2 . . . . . **136** D2
Bawden Way CM2 . . . . **216** D8
Bawdsey Cl CO16 . . . . **188** B3
Bawn Cl CM7 . . . . **128** A4
Bawtree Way CO3 . . . . **135** A5
Baxters CM3 . . . . **219** A7
Bayard Ave CO7 . . . . **185** F7
Bay Ct CO12 . . . . **91** D5
Bayley St CO9 . . . . **51** F4
Baynard Ave CM6 . . . . **151** B6
Baynard Gn CO2 . . . . **135** F4
Baynards Cres CO13 . . . . . **170** E6
Baynard's Prim Sch
CO5 . . . . **179** B7
Baynes Pl CM1 . . . . **204** F1
Bayning Ho CO7 . . . . **139** F8
Bay Rd CO12 . . . . **91** D4
Bays Dr CO9 . . . . **76** E2
Baytree Cl
Rayne CM77 . . . . **126** F2
Wix CO11 . . . . **115** C5
Bay View Cres
Harwich CO12 . . . . **90** C1
Little Oakley CO12 . . . . . . **117** C8
Beach App CO16 . . . . **203** B6
Beach Cres CO15 . . . . **203** F6
Beach Rd
Clacton-on-S CO15 . . . . . **188** F2
Harwich CO12 . . . . **91** C2
Lee-o-S CO16 . . . . **202** D6
Seawick CO16 . . . . **203** C7
St Osyth CO16 . . . . **187** B2
West Mersea CO5 . . . . . . **201** C5
Beach Rd W IP11 . . . . **221** D2
Beach's Dr CM1 . . . . **204** D3
Beach Station Rd
IP11 . . . . **221** C1
Beach Way CO15 . . . . **203** F6
Beacon Cl CO7 . . . . **185** E6
BEACON END **134** D6
Beacon End Ctyd
CO3 . . . . **134** C6
Beacon Field IP11 . . . . **221** C5
BEACON HILL **196** A6
Beacon Hill
Maldon CM9 . . . . **209** E2
Wickham Bishops CM8 . . . **196** A6
Beacon Hill Ave CO12 . . . . **91** E4
Beacon Hill Sch IP2 . . . . . . **16** F3
Beacon Hts CO16 . . . . **186** B2
Beaconsfield Ave
CO3 . . . . **135** E6
Beaconsfield Cl CO10 . . . . . **33** E8
Beaconsfield Ct 7 CB9 . . . **8** F7
Beaconsfield Rd
Clacton-on-S CO15 . . . . . **188** F3
Ipswich IP1 . . . . **16** F7
Sudbury CO10 . . . . **33** E8
Beacon Way
Colchester CO3 . . . . **134** C6
Point Clear B CO16 . . . . . **186** B2
Beadel Cl CM8 . . . . **194** E8
Beadle Pl CM9 . . . . **196** B3
Beadle Way CM3 . . . . **174** A6
Beadon Dr CM7 . . . . **128** A1
Beard's La CB11 . . . . **41** A4
Beardsley Dr CM1 . . . . **205** F7

Beard's Terr CO6 . . . . **131** A3
Bear St CO6 . . . . **56** A1
Bearwalden Bsns Pk
CB11 . . . . **42** F5
Beatrice Ave IP11 . . . . **221** E5
Beatrice Cl IP3 . . . . **18** A3
Beatrice Rd
Clacton-on-S CO15 . . . . . **188** E2
Walton-on-t-N CO14 . . . . **144** D2
Beatty Gdns CM7 . . . . **128** C4
Beatty Rd IP3 . . . . **18** B2
Beauchamps Cl CM1 . . . . . **205** F8
Beaufort Ct 5 CB9 . . . . **8** F7
Beaufort Gdns CM7 . . . . . **128** A4
Beaufort Rd CM2 . . . . **206** A4
Beaufort St IP1 . . . . **17** A7
Beaulieu Bvd CM1 . . . . . . **206** A7
BEAUMONT **141** F7
Beaumont Ave
Brightlingsea CO7 . . . . . . **186** A7
Clacton-on-S CO15 . . . . . **188** D3
Beaumont Cl
Colchester CO4 . . . . **109** F4
Walton-on-t-N CO14 . . . . **170** F7
Beaumont Hill CM6 . . . . . . **123** D2
Beaumont Pk CM3 . . . . . . **218** C6
Beaumont Pl CM7 . . . . **128** B3
Beaumont Rd CO12 . . . . . **116** C3
Beaumont Vale CB9 . . . . **9** B6
Beaumont Wlk CM1 . . . . . **204** D5
Beaver Cl CO3 . . . . **134** E7
Beaver Ct IP4 . . . . **18** B7
BEAZLEY END **101** C6
Beche Ho CO2 . . . . **135** E4
Beche Rd CO2 . . . . **136** B5
Becker Rd CO3 . . . . **134** E4
Beckers Green Prim Sch
CM7 . . . . **128** D2
Beckers Green Rd
CM7 . . . . **128** D2
Becketts Ct 1 CM1 . . . . . . **205** A3
Becketts La IP7 . . . . **57** D8
Beckford Rd CO11 . . . . **87** A4
Beckingham Bsns Pk
CM9 . . . . **197** D3
Beckingham Rd
Great Totham CM9 . . . . . **197** A2
Tolleshunt D'arcy CM9 . . . **198** C4
Beckingham St CM9 . . . . **197** D3
Beck Rd CB11 . . . . **22** D1
Becontree Cl CO15 . . . . . . **188** F8
Bedells Ave CM77 . . . . **155** B5
Bedford Cl
Braintree CM7 . . . . **128** B4
Tiptree CO5 . . . . **179** C5
Bedford Ct 9 CB9 . . . . **8** F7
Bedford Rd
Colchester CO4 . . . . **109** F5
Holland-on-S CO15 . . . . . **189** D5
Bedford St IP1 . . . . **17** B6
Bedwell Rd CM22 . . . . **94** B3
Beech Ave
Braintree CM7 . . . . **127** F5
Halstead CO9 . . . . **77** A2
Wivenhoe CO7 . . . . **137** B1
Beech Cl
Sproughton IP8 . . . . **16** A6
Takeley CM22 . . . . **148** C8
Beechcroft Ave CO13 . . . . . **170** D6
Beeches Cl
Chelmsford CM1 . . . . **204** E2
Saffron Walden CB11 . . . . . **43** C7
Beeches Ct CM1 . . . . **204** F2
Beeches Rd
Chelmsford CM1 . . . . **204** E2
Heybridge CM9 . . . . **209** F5
Beeches The
Ipswich IP3 . . . . **17** F4
Lawford CO11 . . . . **86** C3
Wendens Ambo CB11 . . . . **42** E6
Beech Gn CM8 . . . . **195** F5
Beech Gr
Fordham Heath CO3 . . . . **107** F1
Haverhill CB9 . . . . **8** F8
Ipswich IP3 . . . . **17** F3
Little Oakley CO12 . . . . . . **117** B7
Rushmere St A IP5 . . . . **18** F7
Sible Hedingham CO9 . . . . **51** D1
Beech Hill CO3 . . . . **135** A6
Beech Ho
Ipswich IP2 . . . . **16** D2
Saffron Walden CB10 . . . . . **22** E2
Beechholm 2 IP4 . . . . **17** E6
Beechlands CM23 . . . . **145** F5
Beech Rd
Great Cornard CO10 . . . . . **34** B6
Rivenhall CM8 . . . . **177** B7
Rushmere St A IP5 . . . . **18** F7
Beech Rise CM3 . . . . **194** A3
Beech Tree Lo CO3 . . . . . . **135** B7
Beechwood Cl CO2 . . . . . . **135** D2
Beehive Cl CO7 . . . . **59** C3
Beehive Cnr CO7 . . . . **59** C3
Beehive Ct CO1 . . . . **136** A6
Beehive Ho CM7 . . . . **127** E4
Beehive La CM2 . . . . **216** C5
Beehive Lane Com Prim
Sch CM2 . . . . **216** D5
Beeleigh Chase CM9 . . . . . **209** D4
Beeleigh Cl CM2 . . . . **136** A1
Beeleigh Link CM2 . . . . . . **205** F3
Beeleigh Rd CM9 . . . . **209** F3
BEERCHURCH **135** F1
Begonia Cl CM1 . . . . **205** F6
Begonia Pl CO16 . . . . **188** C4
Bekeswell La CM2 . . . . **215** F2

Bekeswell Pl CM2 . . . . . . **216** C2
Bel-Air Beach Cvn Pk
CO15 . . . . **203** C6
Bel-Air Est CO16 . . . . **203** A6
BELCHAMP OTTEN **31** C8
Belchamp Rd CO9 . . . . **30** B5
BELCHAMP ST PAUL **13** A2
Belchamp St Paul CE Prim
Sch CO10 . . . . **13** A1
BELCHAMP WALTER **31** F5
Belcham's La CB11 . . . . **93** E8
Beldams Cl CO16 . . . . **142** A1
Beldams Gate CM23 . . . . . **146** C6
Beldams La CM23 . . . . **146** B5
Belfry Rd IP3 . . . . **38** F7
Belgrave Ct
Chelmsford CM2 . . . . **216** D7
Ipswich IP4 . . . . **17** E8
Belgrave Ho 6 CM23 . . . . **146** B8
Belgrave Pl 1 CO1 . . . . . . **136** A7
Bellamy Cl CO13 . . . . **170** D6
Bellamy Ct 8 CM1 . . . . . . **205** A3
Bellamy Ho 3 CM7 . . . . . . **127** F2
Bell Cl
Colchester CO2 . . . . **136** D2
Ipswich IP2 . . . . **17** C4
Bell Coll CB11 . . . . **43** E8
Belle Vue CM2 . . . . **205** A1
Belle Vue Rd
Colchester CO1 . . . . **109** E1
Ipswich IP4 . . . . **17** F6
Sudbury CO10 . . . . **33** F7
Wivenhoe CO7 . . . . **137** C1
Bellevue Terr CO9 . . . . **76** E2
Bell Farm Ind Pk SG8 . . . . . **39** B2
Bellfield Ave CO7 . . . . **186** A7
Bellfield Cl
Brightlingsea CO7 . . . . . . **186** A8
Witham CM8 . . . . **176** F3
Bell Gn CO7 . . . . **186** A7
Bell Hill
Danbury CM3 . . . . **218** C7
Lamarsh CO8 . . . . **55** C3
Bellingham Bldgs
CB10 . . . . **22** D2
Bellingham Dr CO6 . . . . . . **133** E5
Bellingham Pl CO5 . . . . . . **158** C5
Bell La
Great Bardfield CM7 . . . . . **72** A2
Ipswich IP2 . . . . **17** C4
Nuthampstead SG8 . . . . . . **39** B2
Panfield CM7 . . . . **127** A7
2 Thaxted CM6 . . . . **70** A3
Bellmead CM1 . . . . **205** B2
Bells Chase CM2 . . . . **216** E6
Bells Cl CB11 . . . . **43** E6
BELL'S CORNER **56** E8
Bells Hill
Bishop's Stortford
CM23 . . . . **145** E7
Bures CO8 . . . . **80** A4
Bells La CO10 . . . . **2** C5
Bells Rd CO10 . . . . **31** F6
Bell St CM2 . . . . **216** F6
Belmans Ct CO12 . . . . **91** A2
Belmer Rd CM24 . . . . **120** D4
Belmonde Dr CM1 . . . . . . **205** E7
Belmont Cl CM1 . . . . **205** E7
Belmont Cres CO4 . . . . **110** C3
Belmont Ct 6 CB9 . . . . **8** F7
Belmont Hill CB11 . . . . **43** A1
Belmont Pl CO1 . . . . **136** C5
Belmont Rd IP2 . . . . **16** C1
Belsay Ct CB9 . . . . **8** D8
Belsize Ave CO15 . . . . **203** D6
BELSTEAD **36** C7
Belstead Ave IP2 . . . . **17** B3
Belstead Rd IP2 . . . . **17** A3
Belstead Sch IP8 . . . . **16** C2
Belsteads Farm La
CM3 . . . . **191** E2
Belvawney Cl CM1 . . . . . . **204** E6
Belvedere Cl CM3 . . . . **218** F7
Belvedere Ct
Chelmsford CM2 . . . . **215** F8
Maldon CM9 . . . . **220** F8
Belvedere Pl CM9 . . . . **220** F8
Belvedere Rd
Danbury CM3 . . . . **218** F7
Ipswich IP4 . . . . **17** F7
Belvoir Ct 4 CB9 . . . . **8** E8
Bembridge Cl CO15 . . . . . . **188** F8
Bemerton Cl CO3 . . . . **170** B6
Bemerton Gdns CO13 . . . . **170** C6
Benacre Rd IP3 . . . . **18** A2
Bench Barn Farm
CO10 . . . . **11** F7
Bendalls Ct 13 CO11 . . . . . **86** D4
Bendlowes Rd CM7 . . . . . . **72** C1
Benedict Dr CM1 . . . . **204** E2
Benedict Ho CO2 . . . . **135** E4
Benezet St IP1 . . . . **17** B6
Benfield Way CM7 . . . . **128** B2
Benhall Cl CO16 . . . . **188** A4
Benhooks Ave CM23 . . . . . **145** E5
Benhooks Pl 1 CM23 . . . . **145** E5
Bennet Cl CO4 . . . . **136** E6
Bennett Cl
Braintree CM7 . . . . **155** A8
Walton-on-t-N CO14 . . . . **171** A8
Bennett Rd IP1 . . . . **16** D8
Bennett's La CM6 . . . . **151** E2
Bennett Way CM3 . . . . **194** A4
Ben Sainty Ct CM8 . . . . . . **177** A2
Benskins Cl CM23 . . . . **92** A8
Bensusan Ct CO2 . . . . **135** B3

Bentall Cl CO9 . . . . **103** F8
Bentalls Complex The
CM9 . . . . **210** B5
BENTFIELD BOWER **119** C8
Bentfield End Cswy
CM24 . . . . **119** D7
Bentfield Gdns CM24 . . . . **119** D7
BENTFIELD GREEN **119** D8
Bentfield Pl CM24 . . . . . . **119** D7
Bentfield Prim Sch
CM24 . . . . **119** D8
Bentfield Rd CM24 . . . . . . **119** D7
Bent Hill IP11 . . . . **221** E3
Bent La IP4 . . . . **18** E8
Bentleigh Ct 5 CO1 . . . . . **136** D7
BENTLEY **60** E7
Bentley Ave CO15 . . . . **203** E6
Bentley CE Prim Sch
IP9 . . . . **60** F7
Bentley Cl CM23 . . . . **145** F5
Bentley Ct CO3 . . . . **135** C7
Bentley La
Belstead IP8 . . . . **36** C6
Stutton IP9 . . . . **61** E3
Bentley Rd
Little Bromley CO11 . . . . . **113** D3
Weeley Heath CO7,
CO16 . . . . **167** E6
Witham CM8 . . . . **176** E4
Benton Cl
Cressing CM77 . . . . **155** E6
Witham CM8 . . . . **195** A7
Berberis Wlk 5 CO4 . . . . **136** E7
Berbice La CM6 . . . . **123** D2
BERDEN **92** C8
BERECHURCH **135** F1
Berechurch Hall Rd
CO2 . . . . **162** D8
Berechurch Rd CO2 . . . . . **135** E2
Berefield Way 6 CO2 . . . . **136** A1
Bergamot Rd CB9 . . . . **8** C8
Bergen Ct CM9 . . . . **220** E8
Bergholt Rd
Brantham CO11 . . . . **86** B7
Colchester CO4 . . . . **109** D2
Beridge Rd CO9 . . . . **76** D2
Beriffe Pl CO7 . . . . **185** F7
Berkeley Cl IP4 . . . . **17** E8
Berkeley Gdns CO5 . . . . . . **163** F7
Berkeley Rd CO15 . . . . **188** F5
Berkely Dr CM2 . . . . **205** F2
Berkley Cl CO4 . . . . **110** C4
Bermuda Rd IP3 . . . . **38** E7
Bernard Cl CO13 . . . . **170** E6
Bernard Cres IP3 . . . . **18** B2
Berners End CM6 . . . . **151** B4
Berners St IP1 . . . . **17** B6
Bernside CM7 . . . . **127** F2
Berridge Ho CM9 . . . . **210** B2
Berrimans Cl CO4 . . . . **136** D6
Berry Cl IP3 . . . . **18** F1
Berryfield Cotts CO4 . . . . . **136** B7
Berry Terr 19 CO10 . . . . . . **33** E7
Bertram Ave CO16 . . . . . . **168** D1
Berwick Ave CM1 . . . . **205** B7
Berwick Cotts CM3 . . . . . . **193** D4
Beryl Rd CO12 . . . . **90** D1
Beslyns Rd CM7 . . . . **72** A3
Beta Terr IP3 . . . . **18** E1
Betjeman Cl CM7 . . . . **155** A8
Betony Wlk CB9 . . . . **8** D8
Betts Green Rd CO16 . . . . . **168** D5
Betty Cocker Gr CO10 . . . . . **34** B7
Betty Dent's Cnr
CO16 . . . . **141** C5
Beverley Ave CO5 . . . . **201** E7
Beverley Ct 5 IP4 . . . . **17** D6
Beverley Dr CO13 . . . . **170** E7
Beverley Rd
Colchester CO3 . . . . **135** D6
Ipswich IP4 . . . . **17** F8
Bevington Mews CM8 . . . . **177** B2
Bewick Ct CO9 . . . . **51** E2
Bexhill Cl CO15 . . . . **203** I8
Bexley Ave CO12 . . . . **90** F1
Bibb Way IP1 . . . . **17** A5
BICKNACRE **218** F2
Bicknacre Rd CM3 . . . . . . **218** F4
Bignells Croft CO4 . . . . . . **110** C4
Bigods La CM6 . . . . **123** D4
Bijou Cl CO5 . . . . **179** D6
Bilberry End CB1 . . . . **5** C7
Bilberry Rd IP3 . . . . **38** C7
Billers Chase CM1 . . . . . . **206** A4
Billy's La CO7 . . . . **58** D2
Bilsdale Cl CO4 . . . . **110** C4
Bilton Rd CM1 . . . . **204** F1
Binley Rd CM2 . . . . **205** F2
BIRCH **161** A4
BIRCHALL CORNER **84** C2
Birchalls CM24 . . . . **119** E8
BIRCHANGER **119** E2
Birchanger CE Prim Sch
CM23 . . . . **119** D2
Birchanger Ind Est
CM23 . . . . **119** B2
Birchanger La CM23 . . . . . **119** D2
Birch Ave
Great Bentley CO7 . . . . . . **166** E8
Harwich CO12 . . . . **91** B3
Birch Bsns Ctr CO2 . . . . . **161** A7
Birch CE Prim Sch
CO2 . . . . **161** A4
Birch Cl
Braintree CM7 . . . . **127** C2
Brightlingsea CO7 . . . . . . **185** E6
Clacton-on-S CO15 . . . . . **188** C3
Witham CM8 . . . . **177** A4

Birch Dr
Brantham CO11 60 D1
Halstead CO9 77 A2
Birches Cotts CO2 161 A2
Birches The CO13 170 E6
Birches Wlk CM2 216 A2
BIRCH GREEN 161 A2
Birch Rd
Birch CO2 161 A5
Great Dunmow CM6 123 B2
Layer de la H CO2 161 E5
Birch Rise CM8 195 E6
Birch St
Birch CO2 161 A3
Nayland CO6 56 A1
Birchway CO2 161 A2
Birchwood CM23 119 D2
Birchwood Cl
Tiptree CO5 179 F5
West Mersea CO5 201 D6
Birchwood High Sch CM23 146 C8
Birchwood Rd
Cock Clarks CM3 219 F2
Dedham CO7 84 B3
Langham CO4 84 A4
Birchwood Way CO5 179 F5
BIRDBROOK 28 B7
Birdbrook Rd CO9 28 A3
Birdbush Ave CB11 43 D7
Bird La CO5 179 E4
Birds Cl CB10 3 A3
Birk Beck CM1 205 C5
Birkdale Rise CM3 194 B4
Birkfield Cl IP2 17 A4
Birkfield Dr IP2 16 F2
Birkin Cl CO5 179 C3
Biscay Cl CB9 9 C7
Bishop Hall La CM1 205 B4
Bishop Mews IP8 16 B2
Bishop Rd
Chelmsford CM1 205 B3
Colchester CO2 135 A3
Bishops Ave CM7 128 B3
Bishop's Ave CM23 145 F3
Bishops' CE & RC Prim Sch The CM1 205 F6
Bishop's Cl [8] CB9 8 E8
Bishops Court Gdns CM2 205 E4
Bishops Ct CM8 195 F5
Bishop's Ct [7] CB9 8 E8
Bishops Dr CO16 203 B6
Bishopsgarth IP3 17 F4
Bishops Gdns CO16 203 A6
Bishop's Hill IP3 17 E4
Bishops La CO5 179 C7
Bishop's La CO9 54 B3
BISHOP'S PARK 145 B6
Bishops Park Coll CO16 188 A3
Bishops Park Way CM23 145 B7
BISHOP'S STORTFORD 145 D7
Bishop's Stortford Bsns Ctr CM23 146 A6
Bishop's Stortford Coll CM23 145 E7
Bishop's Stortford High Sch The CM23 145 F4
Bishop's Stortford Mus★ CM23 146 A6
Bishop's Stortford Sta CM23 146 A6
Bishop William Ward CE Prim Sch The CO6 109 B7
Bisley Cl CO16 188 B6
Bittern Cl
Ipswich IP2 16 E3
Kelvedon CO5 158 D2
Bixley Dr IP4 18 E5
Bixley La IP4 18 F5
Bixley Rd IP3 18 D3
Black Arches IP8 36 E8
Black Barns IP11 221 A7
Blackberry Rd CO3 134 C4
Black Boy La CO11 89 A4
Black Bread Cl CM7 128 D3
Blackbrook Rd CO6 109 C7
Black Buoy Hill CO7 164 B7
Blackbushe CM23 119 C1
Black Chapel La CM6 151 E1
Blackdown Ave IP5 18 F6
Blackfriars CO10 33 D6
Blackfriars Ct [8] IP4 17 D5
BLACKHALL 64 B4
BLACKHEATH 163 B8
Blackheath CO2 163 A8
Black Horse La IP1 17 C6
Blackhouse La CO10 34 C3
Black La CO7 71 F2
Blacklands Cl CB11 43 C7
Blackley La
Braintree CM3 153 F3
Great Notley CM77 154 A4
Blacklock CM2 206 A3
Blackman Way CM8 177 A1
BLACKMORE END 74 B2
BLACK NOTLEY 155 B5
Blacksmith Cl CM1 205 E8
Blacksmiths Cl CM23 145 B5
Blacksmith's Cnr CO6 109 B8
Blacksmith's Cnr CO4 83 D4
BLACKSMITH'S CORNER 36 C6
Blacksmiths Hill CO10 11 B4
Blacksmiths La
Bulmer Tye CO10 32 F2
Shudy Camps CB21 7 C6
Wickham Bishops CM8 195 E5
Blacksmith's La CO12 90 F2
Blackthorn Ave CO4 136 E7
Blackthorn Cl
Ipswich IP3 18 E1
Writtle CM1 204 A1
Blackthorn Rd
Harwich CO12 90 F2
Witham CM8 176 E4
Blackthorn Way CM9 180 A2
Blackwater Ave CO4 110 E1
Blackwater Cl
Chelmsford CM1 205 C6
Heybridge Basin CM9 210 E3
Blackwater Cotts CM77 129 D3
Blackwater Dr CO5 201 A6
Blackwater La CM8 195 B8
Blackwater Way CM7 128 A4
Blackwell Dr CM7 127 C4
Bladen Dr IP4 18 F5
Bladon Cl
Braintree CM7 127 E7
Tiptree CO5 179 E5
Blaine Dr CO13 170 F7
Blair Cl
Bishop's Stortford CM23 145 C7
Rushmere St A IP4 18 E5
Blair Par CB9 8 E8
Blake Cl CO11 86 B4
Blake Dr
Braintree CM7 128 C4
Clacton-on-S CO16 188 D6
BLAKE END 126 A2
Blake Rd CM8 176 F5
Blamsters Cres CO9 103 D8
Blamsters Rise CM6 97 A2
Blanchard Cl CO13 170 A7
Blanche St IP4 17 D6
Blandford Rd IP3 18 D3
Blaxhall Ct [17] CB9 8 E7
Blenheim Cl
Bicknacre CM3 218 F2
Braintree CM7 127 E7
Brantham CO11 60 D1
Blenheim Ct
Bishop's Stortford CM23 145 C7
Clacton-on-S CO15 188 D2
[4] Ipswich IP1 17 A7
Blenheim Dr CO2 163 A8
Blenheim Rd
Clacton-on-S CO15 188 D2
Ipswich IP1 17 A7
Blenheim Way CO5 179 F5
Blickling Cl IP2 17 B2
Blickling Rd CM77 154 C8
Blind La
Easthorpe CO2 160 B4
Eight Ash G CO6 134 A8
Goldhanger CM9 211 C7
Howe Green CM2 217 F4
Tolleshunt Knights CM9 180 B1
Bliss Cl CM8 194 F7
Blithe Ct CO7 164 B8
Blofield Rd IP11 221 A4
Blois Meadows Bsns Ctr CB9 27 C8
Blois Rd
Steeple Bumpstead CB9 27 D8
Sturmer CB9 9 F1
Bloom Cl CO13 170 F6
Bloomfield Ave CO13 170 E7
Bloomfield Ct CO10 12 B7
Bloomfield St IP4 18 B6
Blooms Hall La CO10 2 F8
Blossom Mews CO5 201 D6
Blott Rise CM8 194 F8
Bloyers Mews CO1 109 F1
Bluebell Ave CO16 188 C4
Bluebell Cl
Ipswich IP2 16 E4
Witham CM8 176 E3
Bluebell Gn [5] CM1 205 E7
Bluebell Way CO4 109 C2
Bluebridge Cotts CO9 77 A1
Bluebridge Ind Est CO9 77 B1
Bluegate La IP9 60 B7
Bluehouse Ave CO16 188 A4
Blue Mill La CM9 208 E4
Blue Mills Hill CM8 195 B7
Blue Rd CO5 179 C5
Bluestem Rd IP3 38 E8
Blundens The CO6 56 C6
Blunt's Hall Dr CM8 176 D1
Blunts Hall Rd CM8 176 D1
Blyford Rd CO16 188 A4
Blyford Way IP11 221 A4
Blyth Cl IP2 17 A1
Blyth Ct CB11 43 E8
Blythe La CO7 164 B8
Blyth's Mdw CM7 127 F3
Blyth's Way CM77 126 F2
Blythwood Gdns CM24 119 D6
Boadicea Cotts CO8 79 F6
Boadicea Way CO2 135 C4
Boars Tye Rd CM8 156 D6
Boat Ho The CO7 185 E5
Boat House Mews The CO10 12 B7
Boatman Cl IP8 36 E8
Bobbits La IP9 36 F8
Bobbits Way CO7 164 C8
Bober Ct CO2 163 B7
Bob Russell Ho CO2 136 A5
BOCKING 127 F4
BOCKING CHURCHSTREET 127 F8
Bocking Church Street Prim Sch CM7 127 F8
Bocking End CM7 127 F3
Bocking Pl CM7 127 F3
BOCKING'S ELM 188 B5
Bockings Elm Par CO16 188 B5
Bocking's Gr CO16 188 B5
Bocking Windmill★ CM7 128 A8
Bodiam Cl IP3 18 D4
Bodiam Rd IP3 18 D4
Bodiam Wlk [3] CB9 8 E8
Bodmin Rd CM1 205 D5
Bogmoor Rd SG8 39 A8
Bohun Cl CM3 173 F7
Bois Field Terr CO9 76 E2
Bois Hall Gdns CO9 76 F3
Boley Dr CO15 189 A4
Boleyns Ave CM7 127 F6
Boleyn Way
Boreham CM3 192 F1
Clacton-on-S CO15 203 F8
Haverhill CB9 8 D7
Boley Rd CO6 106 A8
Bolford St CM6 69 F2
Bolingbroke Cl CM3 173 F7
Bolsin Dr CO4 109 E4
Bolton La IP4 17 D6
Bond St
Chelmsford CM2 205 C2
Ipswich IP4 17 D5
Bonham Cl CO15 189 A5
Bonington Chase CM1 205 E6
Bonneting La CM23 92 B8
Bonnington Rd IP3 17 F1
Bonny Cres IP3 38 C8
Boone Pl CM8 177 A2
Boons Cl CM3 206 E8
BOOSE'S GREEN 77 F2
Booth Ave CO4 136 C8
Borda Cl CM1 205 A5
BOREHAM 206 E8
Borehamgate CO10 33 F7
Boreham Ind Est CM3 192 F2
Boreham Pl CO9 10 B2
Boreham Prim Sch CM3 206 F8
Boreham Rd
Great Leighs CM3 174 B7
Little Waltham CM3 174 B2
BORLEY 14 F3
BORLEY GREEN 14 D2
Borley Rd CO10 15 B4
Borough La CB11 43 D8
Borradale Ct CB9 27 B6
Borrowdale Ave IP4 17 E8
Boscawen Gdns CM7 128 C4
Boscombe Ct CO15 189 F6
Boss Hall Bsns Pk IP1 16 E7
Boss Hall Rd IP1 16 E7
Bostock Rd IP2 17 C1
Boston Rd IP4 17 F7
Boswells Dr CM2 205 C2
Boswells Sch The CM1 205 D6
Botanical Way CO16 187 A5
Botany Dr CM7 128 D3
Botany La CO16 168 B5
Bouchers Mead CM1 205 F7
Bouchiers Barn Visitors Ctr★ CO6 130 D7
Bouchiers Pl CO5 159 D2
Boudicca Mews [5] CM2 205 B1
Boudicca Wlk CO7 137 C3
Boulton Cotts CM9 210 B5
Boundary Cl CM23 146 A5
Boundary Rd
Bishop's Stortford CM23 146 A5
Colchester CO4 136 F4
Sturmer CB9 9 D5
Wivenhoe CO7 137 A4
Bounderby Gr CM1 204 E7
Bounstead Hill CO2 162 C5
Bounstead Rd CO2 162 D7
Bourchier Ave CM7 128 D5
Bourchier Way CO9 103 D8
Bournebridge Hill CO9 103 B6
Bourne Cl CO9 103 D8
Bourne Ct
Braintree CM7 128 D1
Colchester CO2 136 A4
Bourne Hill IP2 37 B7
Bourne Mill★ CO2 136 B4
Bournemouth Rd CO15 189 F6
Bourne Park Residential Pk IP2 17 B1
Bourne Rd
Colchester CO2 136 B4
Haverhill CB9 9 B8
West Bergholt CO6 108 E2
Bourne Terr IP2 37 B8
Bourne The CM23 146 A8
Bouverie Rd CM2 216 B8
Bovills Way CO16 168 C1
Bovingdon Rd CM7 101 D2
Bowdens La CO6 80 F7
Bower Gdns CM9 209 F3
Bower Hall Dr CB9 27 B6
Bower Hall La CO5 183 F1
Bowers Cl CM8 156 E3
Bowes Rd CO7 137 D1
Bowland Dr IP8 16 C1
Bowling Cl [14] CM23 145 F6
Bowling Green Ct IP11 221 E4
Bowmans Pk CO9 51 E4
Bowsers La CB10 5 C3
Bowthorpe Cl IP1 17 B7
Boxford Ct
Felixstowe IP11 221 A4
Haverhill CB9 8 E7
Boxhouse La CO7 84 C5
Box Mill La CO9 76 E3
BOXTED 82 F7
Boxted Ave CO16 188 C4
Boxted Church Rd CO6 82 C5
BOXTED CROSS 83 B5
Boxted Rd
Colchester CO4 109 E6
Great Horkesley CO6 82 C3
Boxted St Peter's CE Prim Sch CO4 82 F7
Boxted Straight Rd CO4 83 A5
Boyd Cl [1] CM23 146 B8
Boydell's Dairy Farm★ CM7 100 E8
Boydin Cl CM8 194 E8
Boydlands IP9 35 A1
Boyes Croft CM6 123 D1
Boyles Ct CO2 163 B7
Boyne Dr CM1 205 D6
Boysenberry Wlk IP3 38 C7
BOYTON END 70 C5
Boyton Rd IP3 18 B1
Boytons Acre CB11 43 D8
Boyton's La CB10 26 A1
Boyton Vineyard★ CO10 10 D5
Brackenbury Cl IP1 17 B8
Brackenden Dr CM1 205 D7
Brackenhayes Cl IP2 17 B3
Brackens The CO4 110 B3
Bracken Way CO5 163 B2
Brackley Cl IP11 221 C5
Bracks La CO6 131 F3
Bradbrook Cotts CO6 108 F4
Bradbury Dr CM7 127 D3
Braddy Ct CO5 158 C2
BRADFIELD 87 F2
BRADFIELD HEATH 114 D8
Bradfield Prim Sch CO11 87 E1
Bradfield Rd CO11 115 B7
Bradford Dr CO4 109 E2
Bradfords Ct CM7 128 A4
Bradford St
Braintree CM7 128 A4
Chelmsford CM2 205 A1
Brading Ave CO15 189 A7
Bradley Cl CM6 123 C2
Bradley Comm CM23 119 C3
Bradley Mews [1] CB10 22 F2
Bradley St [6] IP2 17 C4
BRADWELL 129 D2
Bradwell Ct CM77 155 C8
BRADWELL WATERSIDE 214 F4
Braeburn Dr CM9 210 A1
Braemar Ave CM2 216 B8
Braemore Cl CO4 110 D3
Braganza Way CM2 205 F8
Braggon's Hill IP29 2 B8
Braiding Cres CM7 128 C3
Brain Rd CM8 176 E3
BRAINTREE 128 B5
Braintree Cnr CO9 75 F6
Braintree Coll CM7 128 A5
Braintree Ent Ctr CM7 127 D5
Braintree Foyer The [7] CM7 127 F2
Braintree Mus & Heritage Ctr★ CM7 127 F3
Braintree Rd
Cressing CM77 155 E7
Felsted CM6 152 C6
Gosfield CO9 102 E5
Great Bardfield CM7 72 B1
Great Dunmow CM6 124 A1
Shalford CM7 100 E6
Terling CM3 174 E5
Wethersfield CM7 73 D2
Witham CM8 176 F4
Braintree Sta CM7 128 A2
Braintree Town FC CM7 128 C2
Brain Valley Ave CM77 155 B6
BRAISWICK 109 B2
Braiswick CO4 109 C2
Braiswick La CO4 109 D4
Braiswick Pl CO4 109 C3
Braithwaite Dr CO4 109 F2
Bramble Ct CM8 176 E4
Brambledown CO5 201 C7
Bramble Dr IP3 18 E1
Bramble La CM6 151 F8
Bramble Rd CM8 176 E4
Brambles CO14 171 B7
Brambles The
Bishop's Stortford CM23 145 C6
Brambles The *continued*
Braintree CM7 127 E3
Colchester CO3 134 F3
Bramble Tye CO12 90 D1
Bramblewood [1] IP8 16 C2
Bramford La IP1 16 F8
Bramford Rd IP1 16 E8
Bramhall Cl IP2 16 D1
Bramley Chase IP4 18 B7
Bramley Cl
Alresford CO7 165 B8
Braintree CM7 128 A1
Colchester CO3 135 B7
Bramley Cotts CM3 175 B2
Bramley Ct CM2 216 D7
Bramley Pl CM2 216 D7
Bramley Rd CB9 8 D7
Bramleys The CO6 131 A3
Bramston Cl CM2 216 F8
Bramston Gn CM8 176 F4
Bramston Wlk CM8 176 F4
Bramwoods Rd CM2 216 E8
Brancaster Dr CM77 154 C6
Brand Ct CM7 127 F7
Brand Dr CO5 163 B3
Brandon Rd
Braintree CM7 127 D2
Felixstowe IP11 221 A4
Brands Cl CO10 34 C5
BRAN END 124 D7
Bran End Fields CM6 124 D7
Bransby Gdns IP4 17 E7
Branscombe Cl CO13 170 E5
Branston Ct
Clacton-on-S, Jaywick CO15 203 G7
Clacton-on-S, Rush Green CO16 188 C4
Branston Rd CO15 188 D3
BRANTHAM 60 E1
Brantham Hill CO11 86 C8
Brantham Mill Ind Est CO11 86 B7
Braxted La
Great Braxted CM8 178 C1
Great Totham CM8, CM9 196 D8
Braxted Park Rd
Rivenhall End CM8 177 E4
Tiptree CO5, CM8 178 D2
Braxted Rd CM8 196 A6
Braybrooke Gdns CB11 43 D8
Braziers Cl CM2 216 C3
Braziers Quay CM23 146 A6
Brazier's Wood Rd IP3 38 B8
Breach La CM6 97 B2
Bream Ct CO4 110 F1
Brecon Cl IP2 17 B2
Bredfield Cl IP11 221 B5
Bree Ave CO6 132 E3
Brendon Ct CO5 179 D4
Brendon Dr
Halstead CO9 103 F8
Rushmere St A IP5 18 F6
Brendon Pl CM1 204 E1
Brent Cl
Frinton-on-S CO13 170 F7
Witham CM8 176 E2
Brent Hall Rd CM7 72 B6
BRENT PELHAM 64 B2
Brentwood Rd CO15 189 C6
Brett Cl IP1 16 E8
Bretten Cl CO16 188 A4
Brettenham Cres IP4 17 D8
Bretts Cotts CO5 178 F3
Brewers Cl CM23 145 C5
BREWER'S END 148 B7
Brewery Dr CO9 103 E8
Brewery Fields CM2 217 A5
Brewery La CM24 119 E7
Brewery Tower The [2] CO1 136 A7
Brewery Yd CM24 119 E7
Brewster Cl CO9 103 F8
Brewsters Ct CO12 91 D5
Breydon Way IP3 38 D7
Brian Bishop Cl CO14 171 B8
Brian Cl CM2 216 B6
Briardale Ave CO12 90 F3
Briarfields CO13 170 C8
Briarhayes Cl IP2 17 B3
Briar Rd CO7 112 B4
Briarsford Ind Est CM8 177 B1
Briarswood CM1 205 D7
Briarwood Ave CO15 189 F6
Briarwood End CO4 110 B3
Brices Way CO10 2 B5
Brickbarns CM3 173 F7
Brickburn Cl CM6 152 C4
Brick Cotts IP9 62 F4
BRICK END 121 E8
Brick End Villas CM6 121 E8
Brickfield Cl IP2 17 D3
Brickhouse Cl CO5 201 B7
BRICK HOUSE END 92 B5
Brick House La CM3 192 E1
Brickhouse Rd CO6 78 A3
Brick House Rd CM9 197 B7
Brick Kiln Cl CO6 131 A3
BRICKKILN GREEN 74 A4
Brick Kiln La
Great Horkesley CO6 109 C7
Rickling Green CB11 66 D1

Brick Kiln La *continued*
Stebbing CM6 124 D7
Thorrington CO7 165 E5
Brick Kiln Rd
Chelmsford CM2 217 C7
Colchester CO1 109 E1
Harkstead IP9 63 C5
Brick Kiln Way CM7 128 D2
Brickmakers La CO4 109 F2
Brickman's Hill CO11 87 D3
Brick Row SG8 19 D3
Brickspring La CM9 196 D7
Brick St CO3 108 B1
Brickwall Ct CO6 105 B6
Brickwall Farm CM77 129 C6
Bridewell Ind Est CO10 12 C8
Bridewell St CO10 12 C8
Bridgebrook Cl CO4 110 D1
Bridge Cottage★ CO7 85 D7
Bridge Cotts
Cavendish CO10 1 D2
Ridgewell CO9 29 B7
Bridge Croft CM3 172 F2
Bridge Ct
Maldon CM9 210 A3
Witham CM8 176 F1
BRIDGE END 72 B3
Bridge End CB11 43 A2
Bridge End La CM77 154 C8
Bridgefield Cl CO4 136 C7
Bridge Foot CO10 33 D6
Bridgeford Ho 13
CM23 145 F6
BRIDGE GREEN 41 B6
Bridge Hall Rd CM77 129 C3
Bridge Hill CO6 107 C7
Bridge Mdw CO5 158 D3
Bridge Pl CO11 86 C7
Bridge Rd IP11 221 E5
Bridge St
Bishop's Stortford
CM23 145 F7
Bures CO8 55 F1
Coggeshall CO6 130 F1
Finchingfield CM7 72 C6
Great Bardfield CM7 72 B2
Great Yeldham CO9 30 A1
Halstead CO9 76 E2
Ipswich IP1 17 C4
Saffron Walden CB10 22 D2
Witham CM8 176 F1
Writtle CM1 204 C1
Bridge Terr
Maldon CM9 210 A5
1 Sudbury CO10 33 F8
Bridge View IP3 17 F1
Bridgwater Rd IP2 16 D2
Bridlewalk CO3 134 D6
Bridleway The CO3 108 A1
Bridport Ave IP3 18 D3
Bridport Rd CM1 205 D5
Bridport Way CM7 128 D4
Brierley Ave CO5 201 E7
Brierley Paddocks
CO5 201 E7
Bright Cl CO16 188 D6
BRIGHTLINGSEA 185 D6
Brightlingsea Ct CO7 136 F4
Brightlingsea Inf Sch
CO7 185 E6
Brightlingsea Jun Sch
CO7 185 E6
Brightlingsea Mus
CO7 185 F6
Brightlingsea Rd
Thorrington CO7 165 E3
Wivenhoe CO7 137 C4
Brighton Rd CO15 189 F6
Bright Rd CM6 151 F6
Brightside CO13 170 E7
Brightwell Cl IP11 221 A4
Brimstone Ct CM7 154 E8
Brimstone Rd IP8 36 E8
Brindley Rd CO15 189 B8
Bringey The CM2 217 A6
Brinkley Cres CO4 110 D2
Brinkley Grove Prim Sch
CO4 110 B5
Brinkley Grove Rd
CO4 110 A5
Brinkley La CO4 110 B5
Brinkley Pl CO4 109 F3
Brisbane Rd IP4 18 D6
Brisbane Way CO2 136 A1
Brise Cl CM7 128 A1
Bristol Ct CM8 156 E3
Bristol Hill IP9 91 B8
Bristol Ho IP11 221 D2
Bristol Rd
Colchester CO1 136 A8
Ipswich IP4 18 A7
Bristowe Ave CM2 217 A6
Britannia Cres CO7 137 B1
Britannia Ct CO7 137 B1
Britannia Ho IP4 18 B5
Britannia Pl 3 CM23 145 E5
Britannia Rd IP4 18 B6
Britric Cl CM6 151 F6
Brittania Prim Sch IP4 18 B5
Brittany Way CO2 136 B4
Britten Cl CO4 136 E6
Britten Cres
Great Baddow CM2 216 F8
Witham CM8 194 F7
Brixham Cl CO15 203 I8
Brixton La CB11, CM23 93 B6
Broadcroft Cres CB9 8 F8
Broadfield CM23 118 F2
Broadfield Rd CM22 148 E7
Broadfields CO7 137 C3
BROAD GREEN
Chrishall 19 C4
Coggeshall 131 F3
Steeple Bumpstead 27 E8
Broad La CO6 82 C2
Broadlands CO13 170 E3
Broadlands Way
Colchester CO4 110 B1
Rushmere St A IP4 18 F5
Broadleaf Ave CM23 145 D4
Broad Mdw 3 IP8 16 C2
Broadmead Rd CO4 110 E1
Broadmere Cl CO15 189 E7
Broadmere Rd IP1 16 E8
Broad Oakes Cl CB10 44 E2
Broadoaks Cres CM7 128 D4
Broad Oaks Pk CO4 110 E3
Broad Oke IP1 17 B6
Broad Rd
Braintree CM7 128 B7
Wickham St P CO9 53 B8
BROAD'S GREEN 190 E5
Broad St CB9 8 F8
BROAD STREET GREEN
210 C7
Broad Street Green Rd
CM9 210 C7
Broadstrood CO16 187 B5
Broadwater Gdns IP9 91 A8
Broadway
Clacton-on-S CO15 203 G7
Glemsford CO10 2 B5
Silver End CM8 156 D4
Broadway Ct CM8 156 D5
Broadway The CM6 123 F3
Brock Cl
Tiptree CO5 179 E6
Witham CM8 194 E8
Brockenhurst Ct CO4 110 E1
Brockenhurst Way
CM3 218 F1
Brockham Cl CO16 188 B6
Brockley Cres IP1 16 D8
Brockley Rd CM2 205 D2
Brocks Mead CM6 122 E7
Brockwell La CO5 158 C1
Brograve Cl CM2 216 D3
BROKE HALL 18 D3
Broke Hall Com Prim Sch
IP4 18 E5
Broke Hall Gdns IP3 18 D4
Broke Hall Ho IP3 18 D3
Broman's La CO5 185 A2
Bromfield CB11 43 E8
Bromley Cl
Clacton-on-S CO16 188 D4
Ipswich IP2 17 C3
Bromley Cnr CO11 86 A2
BROMLEY CROSS 112 C3
Bromley Cross CO7 112 B3
Bromley Hts CO4 136 F8
Bromley La CB11 43 B1
Bromley Rd
Colchester CO7, CO4 111 C2
Elmstead Market CO7 138 B5
Frating Green CO7 139 A4
Lawford CO11 86 B2
Brompton Gdns CM9 220 E8
Bronte Cl CM7 155 A8
Bronte Rd CM8 176 F5
Bronze Ct CO9 76 F1
Brookbank CM2 216 E8
Brook Cl
Braintree CM7 127 C2
Great Totham CM9 196 A3
Tiptree CO5 179 F3
Woodham Walter CM9 208 D2
Brook Cotts
Boxted CO4 82 E5
Elmstead Market CO7 137 E5
Stansted Mountfitchet
CM24 119 E5
Tolleshunt D'arcy CM9 198 C2
Brookdale Ct 16 CO1 136 A6
Brooke Ave CB10 22 E2
Brooke Gdns CM23 146 C7
BROOKEND 124 D2
Brook End Rd CM2 206 B2
Brook End Rd N CM2 206 A4
Brook End Rd S CM2 206 B3
Brookes Nature Reserve★
CM77 103 E2
Brooke Sq CM9 210 A1
Brook Farm Cl
Bishop's Stortford
CM23 145 C3
Halstead CO9 77 A1
Brook Farm La IP9 62 D6
Brookfield Rd IP1 16 F8
Brookfields CM6 124 D7
Brook Hall Rd CO5 164 B5
Brookhampton St CB10 3 A5
Brook Hill
Little Waltham CM3 191 B6
North End CM6 151 E1
Brookhill Way IP4 18 F4
Brookhouse Bsns Pk
IP2 16 F6
Brookhouse Pl 3
CM23 145 F8
Brookhouse Rd CO6 132 B8
Brookhurst Cl CM2 205 D3
Brook La
Chelmsford CM2 206 B2
Felixstowe IP11 221 F5
Galleywood CM2 216 E3
Brookland CO5 179 C4
Brooklands
Clacton-on-S CO15 203 E6
Colchester CO1 136 B7
Brooklands Gdns
CO15 203 E6
Brooklands Prim Sch
CO11 86 D8
Brooklands Rd CO11 86 D8
Brooklands Rise CO11 86 D8
Brooklands Wlk CM2 216 A7
Brook Lo CO3 135 C6
Brooklyn Ct CO12 91 C3
Brooklyn Mews CO12 91 C3
Brooklyn Rd CO12 91 C3
Brook Mdw CO9 51 D1
Brook Mdws CO5 179 C4
Brook Mead CM3 190 E8
Brook Pl CO9 76 E1
Brook Rd
Aldham CO6 133 B7
Great Tey CO6 132 C7
Stansted Mountfitchet
CM24 119 E6
Tiptree CO5 179 F3
Tolleshunt Knights CM9,
CO5 180 A2
Brook Retail Pk CO16 188 E7
Brook Service Rd CB9 9 A7
Brooks Hall Rd IP1 17 A7
Brookside Cl CO2 136 B4
Brooksies CB11 40 F6
Brooks Malting 3
CO11 86 D4
Brook St
Chelmsford CM1 205 B3
Colchester CO1 136 B7
Colne Engaine CO6 77 F1
Dedham CO7 84 F7
Glemsford CO10 2 B6
Great Bardfield CM7 72 B2
Great Bromley CO7 112 E1
Little Dunmow CM6 151 D6
Manningtree CO11 86 D4
Wivenhoe CO7 164 C8
BROOK STREET 2 B6
Brook Street Bsns Ctr
CO1 136 B6
Brook Terr CO9 51 E1
Brook Vale CO16 187 B3
Brookview IP2 36 E8
Brook View
Chelmsford CM2 217 C6
Stansted Mountfitchet
CM24 119 E5
Thaxted CM6 70 A3
Brook Wlk CM8 194 F8
Broomclose Villas
CM7 100 E5
Broom Cres IP3 17 F1
Broome Gr CO7 137 B2
Broome Way CO15 203 F6
Broom Farm Rd CM22 94 C2
BROOMFIELD 191 B2
Broomfield CM8 156 C5
Broom Field IP11 221 C5
Broomfield Comm IP8 16 B6
Broomfield Cres CO7 137 B2
Broomfield Ctyd CB9 8 F8
Broomfield Hospl
CM1 191 A3
Broomfield Mews
CM1 205 B6
Broomfield Prim Sch
CM1 191 B1
Broomfield Rd CM1 205 A5
Broomgrove Inf & Jun
Schs CO7 137 B2
Broomhall Cl CM1 191 B2
Broomhall Rd CM1 191 B2
Broomhayes IP2 17 A2
Broomhill IP9 62 D6
Broom Hill Rd IP1 17 A8
Broomhills Ind Est
CM7 127 D2
Broomhills Rd CO5 201 D5
Broom Knoll CO7 60 C2
Broom St CO10 34 B5
Broom Way
Abberton CO5 163 B2
Capel St M IP9 35 B2
Brotherton Ave IP11 221 A8
Broton Dr CO9 76 E2
Brougham Glades
CO3 134 D5
Broughton Cl CO2 135 C4
Broughton Rd IP1 17 B7
Browning Cl CO3 134 F6
Browning Rd
Braintree CM7 155 A8
Brantham CO11 86 C7
Brownings Ave CM1 205 A5
Brownlow Rd IP11 221 F4
Brownsea Way CO3 135 A4
Brown's End Rd CM6 121 F7
BROXTED 95 F2
Bruce Gr CM2 216 A7
Bruce Rd CM1 204 B1
Bruff Cl CO4 109 E2
Bruff Dr CO14 171 A7
Bruff Rd IP2 17 C3
Bruges Cl CO12 91 A1
Brundells Rd CO7 139 A5
BRUNDON 15 C1
Brundon La CO10 33 C7
Brunel Ct CO4 110 C6
Brunel Rd
Braintree CM7 128 A1
Clacton-on-S CO15 189 B8
Ipswich IP2 16 F6
Brunel Way CO4 110 C6
Brunswick House Cut
CO11 87 A3
Brunswick Rd IP4 17 F8
Brunwin Rd CM77 126 F2
Brussels Cl CO12 91 B1
Bryanita Ct CO5 179 D5
Bryan Rd CM23 145 F8
Bryanstone Mews
CO3 134 E5
Bryant Link CM2 206 B4
Bryant's La CM9 219 D7
Bryon Ave IP11 221 A3
Bryony Cl CM8 176 D4
Buchan Cl CM7 155 A8
Buckenhoe Rd CB10 22 E3
Buckfast Ave CO13 170 D6
Buckfast Cl 5 IP2 17 A2
Buck Hill CM77 154 F6
Buckingham Ct 2
CM2 205 F4
Buckingham Dr CO4 136 E7
Buckingham Rd CB9 8 E6
Bucklesham Rd IP3 18 E2
Buckleys CM2 216 F7
Buckleys Cl CM8 195 E5
Buckley's La CO6 131 E6
Buck's Horns La IP8 36 B6
Bucks La CO10 12 B7
Buckwoods Rd CM7 128 A1
Buddleia Cl IP2 16 E4
Buddleia Ct CO7 137 A2
Buffett Way CO4 136 E6
Buglers Rise CM1 215 B8
Buick Ave CO15 203 D6
BUILDING END 40 B8
Building End Rd
Chrishall SG8 19 C1
Duddenhoe End SG8 40 B8
Bulford Cl CM77 155 D5
Bulford La CM77 155 C5
Bulford Mill La CM77 155 D5
Bullace Cl CO4 110 D3
Bullen Wlk CM2 216 C3
Bullfields CB11 67 A8
Bullfinch Cl
Colchester CO4 136 F8
Harwich CO12 90 E1
Bullfinch Dr CO9 77 A1
Bull Hill Rd CO15 188 F5
Bull La
Langley CB11 40 C2
Long Melford CO10 15 E8
Maldon CM9 210 A3
Tiptree CO5 179 C3
Bullocks La CO10 33 E6
Bullocks Terr CO10 33 E6
Bullock Wood Cl CO4 110 D4
Bull Rd IP3 18 B4
Bulls Cliff IP11 221 D3
Bulls Lodge Cotts
CM3 192 B1
BULMER 32 F5
Bulmer Rd CO10 33 C6
Bulmer Road Ind Est
CO10 33 C6
Bulmer St CO10 32 D4
BULMER TYE 32 F2
Bulrush Cl CM7 128 B1
Bulstrode Rd IP2 17 D4
Bulwer Rd IP1 17 A6
Bumfords La CM3,
CM9 208 A7
Bumpstead Rd CB9 9 B4
Bundick's Hill CM1 204 F3
Bungalows The CM8 176 F1
Bung Row CM8 178 C1
Bunting Cl CM2 216 B5
Buntingford Ct 2
CO2 136 A1
Bunting Rd IP2 16 D3
BUNTING'S GREEN 77 D1
Buntings The CO2 161 E4
Bunyan Rd CM7 127 E3
Burdun Cl CM8 194 D8
Bure Dr CM8 176 D3
Buregate Rd IP11 221 D2
BURES 79 E8
Bures CE Prim Sch
CO8 79 F8
Bures Ct 16 CB9 8 E7
Bures Ho CO8 79 F8
Bures Rd
Great Cornard CO10 34 B3
Nayland CO6 81 B8
Wakes Colne CO6 106 D7
West Bergholt CO6 108 D7
White Colne CO6 105 E8
Bures Sta CO8 79 E8
Burgate Cl CO16 188 A4
Burgate Lane Cotts
CO7 85 B3
Burgess Field CM2 205 F4
Burghley Ave CM23 145 C7
Burghley Cl
Great Notley CM77 154 B6
4 Ipswich IP2 17 A2
Burghley Way CM2 216 C8
Burgundy Ct 9 CM2 205 C2
Burkitts Ct 8 CO10 33 E7
Burkitts La CO10 33 E7
Burley Rd CM23 146 A4
Burlingham Ho IP2 17 B4
Burlington Rd
Colchester CO3 135 E6
Ipswich IP1 17 B6
Burmanny Cl CO15 188 C3
Burnell Gate CM1 206 A7
Burnells Way CM24 119 E7
Burnet Cl IP8 36 D8
Burnham Cl
Ipswich IP4 17 F7
Trimley St M IP11 221 A7
Walton-on-t-N CO14 171 B8
Burnham Ct CO15 203 I8
Burnham Lo IP4 18 A6
Burnham Rd
Chelmsford CM1 205 D5
Woodham Mortimer CM9,
CM3 219 E5
Burnsall Cl CB11 43 F8
Burns Ave CO3 134 F6
Burns Cl CM9 210 A1
Burns Cres CM2 216 C8
Burns Gn CM9 196 A4
Burnside Cres CM1 205 B7
Burnstie Rd CM6 152 F6
Burnt Dick Hill CO4 82 D7
BURNT HEATH 112 B4
Burnthouse Rd CO6 105 E2
Burnt Oak Cnr CO7 59 D1
Burr Cl CO12 90 C1
Burrell Rd IP2 17 C4
Burroughs Piece Rd
CO10 33 F7
Burrows Cl
Clacton-on-S CO16 188 D6
Lawford CO11 86 B4
Burrow's Rd CO6 105 B7
Burrs Rd CO15 189 A7
Burrsville Com Inf Sch
CO15 188 F6
BURRSVILLE PARK 189 A7
Burrswood Pl CM9 210 E3
Burstall Cl CO16 188 B4
Burstall La IP8 16 A6
Burton Cl CB9 8 E7
BURTON END 120 C4
Burton End CB9 8 E7
Burton End Prim Sch
CB9 8 D7
Burton Pl CM2 205 F4
BURTON'S GREEN 104 B2
Burton's Green Rd
CO9 104 B4
Burwood Ct CM2 205 C1
Bury Cl
Colchester CO1 136 A8
Marks Tey CO6 132 F4
Bury Farm Cotts CM9 220 F6
Bury Fields CM6 152 A5
Bury Gdns CB11 20 A4
Bury La
Chrishall SG8 19 D1
Great Waltham CM3 190 D8
Hatfield Peverel CM3 193 F4
Bury Lodge La
Great Hallingbury
CM22 147 C7
Stansted Mountfitchet
CM24 120 A2
Bury The CO16 187 A4
Bury Villas CM22 121 E3
Burywater Cotts CB11 42 F1
Bury Water La CB11 42 E1
Burywoods CO4 109 B3
Bushell Way CO13 170 E6
BUSH END 148 A4
Bushey Cl IP9 35 A1
Bushey Ley CM7 128 D3
Bush Gr CO10 33 C6
Bush Rd CB10 46 E2
BUSTARD GREEN 98 B6
Butcher Row CB10 22 D1
Butcher's Hill CB10 3 A4
Butchers La
Capel St M IP9 35 B1
Walton-on-t-N CO14 171 B7
Butchers Pasture
CM6 122 F5
Butcher's View CO5 182 E6
Bute Ct CB9 8 F6
Butler Cl CB11 22 E1
Butler Rd CO9 76 D2
Butlers Cl CM1 191 B2
Butlers Cotts CM3 194 C1
Butler's Hall La CM23 145 B3
Butlers La CB10 23 C5
Butler's La CO11 88 E1
Butlers Way CO9 30 A1
Butley Cl IP2 36 F8
Butley Ct 1 CB9 8 E6
Butley Rd IP11 221 C3
Buttercup Cl IP8 16 C2
Buttercup Wlk CM8 176 E4
Butterfield Rd CM3 206 E8
Butterfly Gdns IP4 18 E5
Butter Market IP1 17 C6
Buttermarket Sh Ctr 3
IP1 17 C5
Buttermere CM77 154 C7
Butt La
Maldon CM9 210 A3
Manuden CM23 92 E2
Buttleys La CM6 149 F8
Butt Rd
Colchester CO3 135 E5
Great Cornard CO10 34 B6
Stoke-by-N CO6 56 C5
BUTTS GREEN 64 E8

Butt's Green Rd CM2 . . . . 217 F3
Butts La CM3 . . . . 218 F7
Butts Way CM2 . . . . 215 E3
Buxey Cl CO5 . . . . 201 B7
Buxton Cotts CO6 . . . . 132 A3
Buxton Rd
  Coggeshall CO6 . . . . 130 F3
  Colchester CO2 . . . . 136 A3
Bylam La IP9 . . . . 63 C6
Byland Cl IP2 . . . . 17 A2
Bylands Cl CM23 . . . . 145 D6
Byng Cl CO16 . . . . 142 B1
Byng Cres CO16 . . . . 142 B1
Byng Ct CO2 . . . . 136 A1
Byng Gdns CM7 . . . . 128 C4
Byng Ho CO16 . . . . 142 B1
Bypass Rd CO16 . . . . 187 B5
Byrd's Farm La CB10 . . . . . . 22 E3
Byron Ave CO3 . . . . 134 F7
Byron Cl CM7 . . . . 155 A8
Byron Dr CM8 . . . . 195 E5
Byron Rd CM2 . . . . 205 D2

C

Cadenhouse Mews
  CO3 . . . . 134 E7
Caelum Dr CO2 . . . . 136 D5
Caernarvon Wlk CB9 . . . . . . .8 E8
Cage La
  Boxted CO4 . . . . 83 B4
  Felixstowe IP11 . . . . 221 D5
Cairns Rd CO2 . . . . 136 B2
Caithness Cl IP4 . . . . 18 B8
Calamint Rd CM8 . . . . 176 D3
Caldbeck Way CM77 . . . . . 154 C6
Caledonia Rd IP9 . . . . 91 B8
Calford Dr CB9 . . . . 8 C8
CALFORD GREEN 9 F7
CALIFORNIA 18 A6
California Cl CO4 . . . . 110 B4
California Rd CO11 . . . . 87 A4
Callis Ct CO10 . . . . 12 C8
Callis St CO10 . . . . 12 B8
Callisto Ct IP1 . . . . 16 D7
Callow Ct CM2 . . . . 205 A2
Callowood Croft CM3 . . . . 220 D1
Calverley Cl CM23 . . . . 145 E4
Calves La CO6 . . . . 56 B8
Camberley Rd IP4 . . . . 18 D7
Camberton Rd CM7 . . . . . 127 E6
Camborne Cl CM1 . . . . 205 E6
Cambrai Rd CO2 . . . . 135 D4
Cambria Cl CO11 . . . . 87 B3
Cambridge Ave CO9 . . . . . . 75 E8
Cambridge Cotts
  CM22 . . . . 148 B7
Cambridge Ct
  Clacton-on-S CO15 . . . . . 188 E4
  Frinton-on-S CO13 . . . . . 171 A4
Cambridge Dr IP2 . . . . 16 F1
Cambridge Ho CB9 . . . . .9 B6
Cambridge Rd
  Clacton-on-S CO15 . . . . . 188 E4
  Colchester CO3 . . . . 135 C5
  Felixstowe IP11 . . . . 221 E4
  Frinton-on-S CO13 . . . . . 171 A5
  Littlebury CB11 . . . . 21 F4
  Newport CB11 . . . . 43 A2
  Stansted Mountfitchet
  CM24 . . . . 119 E6
Cambridge Way CO8 . . . . . 79 F8
Camden Rd IP3 . . . . 18 B4
Camellia Ave CO4 . . . . 188 C4
Camellia Cl CM1 . . . . 205 E6
Camellia Cres CO16 . . . . . 188 C5
Camellia Ct CO4 . . . . 136 D8
Camelot Cl CM1 . . . . 204 F5
Camelot Mews CM7 . . . . . 127 E2
Cameron Cl
  Braintree CM7 . . . . 127 F8
  Long Melford CO10 . . . . . 15 C6
Camoise Cl CO9 . . . . 50 B7
Camomile Way CO4 . . . . . 109 C2
Campbell Cl CM2 . . . . 216 A4
Campbell Ct CO3 . . . . 135 D6
Campbell Dr CO4 . . . . 110 E2
Campbell Rd
  Ipswich IP3 . . . . 18 C1
  Witham CM8 . . . . 176 F5
Campernell Cl CO7 . . . . . . 185 F8
Campion Rd
  Colchester CO2 . . . . 136 A5
  Ipswich IP2 . . . . 16 F4
Campions Hill CO6 . . . . 81 D8
Campions The CM24 . . . . . 119 E8
Campion Way CM8 . . . . . . 176 E3
Camp Rd CO7 . . . . 139 A7
CAMPS END 7 A1
Camps Rd
  Bartlow CB21 . . . . 6 B7
  Haverhill CB9 . . . . 8 F7
  Helions Bumpstead CB9 . . . 8 B1
Camulodunum Way
  CO2 . . . . 135 C1
Camulus Cl
  [1] Braintree CM7 . . . . . . 128 A2
  Colchester CO2 . . . . 135 A2
Cam Way CM8 . . . . 176 D2
Camwood Gdns IP3 . . . . . . 18 B4
Canberra Cl
  Chelmsford CM1 . . . . 204 E5
  [9] Colchester CO2 . . . . . 136 A1
  Ipswich IP4 . . . . 18 D6
Can Bridge Way CM2 . . . . 205 C1
Candlet Gr IP11 . . . . 221 D5

Candlet Rd IP11 . . . . 221 D6
Candytuft Rd CM1 . . . . . . 205 F6
Canes Mill Ct CM7 . . . . . . 128 A5
Canfield CO23 . . . . 145 E8
Canfield Dr CM22 . . . . 148 E6
Canfield Rd
  Great Canfield CM6 . . . . . 149 D1
  Takeley CM22 . . . . 148 D5
Canford Cl CM2 . . . . 216 E7
Cangle Junc CB9 . . . . 9 A8
Canhams Rd CO10 . . . . 34 C5
Canham St [8] IP1 . . . . 17 B6
Cann Cl CO10 . . . . 15 D2
Cann Hall Prim Sch
  CO16 . . . . 188 D6
Canning St CO12 . . . . 91 D5
Cannock Mill Ct CO2 . . . . 136 C4
Cannon Circ CM2 . . . . 73 D6
Cannon Leys CM2 . . . . 216 D3
Cannon Rd
  Colchester CO1 . . . . 136 B6
  Little Dunmow CM6 . . . . 151 E6
Cannons Cl
  Bishop's Stortford
  CM23 . . . . 119 A1
  Colchester CO2 . . . . 135 D4
Cannons Mead CM24 . . . . 119 D7
Cannon St
  CM23 . . . . 119 A1
Cannon St CO1 . . . . 136 B6
Cannons The CO2 . . . . 135 D4
Canonium Mews CO5 . . . . 158 C2
Canons Cl CM3 . . . . 218 E1
Cansey La CO11 . . . . 114 E6
Canterbury Cl IP2 . . . . 36 F8
Canterbury Grange
  CM7 . . . . 127 F8
Canterbury Rd
  Colchester CO2 . . . . 136 A5
  Holland-on-S CO15 . . . . . 189 E5
  Sudbury CO10 . . . . 15 C2
Canterbury Way CM1 . . . . 204 E4
Canters Meadow Ct
  CO15 . . . . 189 A5
Cant Way CM7 . . . . 128 C5
Canuden Rd CM1 . . . . 204 E2
Canvey Wlk CM1 . . . . 205 E6
Canwick Gr CO2 . . . . 136 C4
Capel Cl
  Chelmsford CM1 . . . . 205 B7
  Rayne CM77 . . . . 126 F2
Capel Dr IP11 . . . . 221 A4
Capel Ho CO4 . . . . 109 F4
Capel Pk CO13 . . . . 170 E2
Capel Rd
  Colchester CO3 . . . . 135 C5
  Rayne CM77 . . . . 126 F2
CAPEL ST MARY 35 A2
Capel St Mary CE Prim
  Sch IP9 . . . . 35 A1
Caper La CO2 . . . . 160 F4
Capons La CM3 . . . . 219 A5
Cap Pillar Cl CO7 . . . . 137 B2
Capstan Pl CO4 . . . . 136 D5
Captains Ct CO5 . . . . 201 B8
Captains Wood Rd CM8,
  CM9 . . . . 196 A3
Caracalla Way CO4 . . . . . . 110 B6
Cardiff Ave IP2 . . . . 17 B2
Cardigan St IP1 . . . . 17 B7
Cardinal Cl CO4 . . . . 137 A4
Cardinal Pk IP1 . . . . 17 C5
Cardinals Ct IP11 . . . . 221 E4
Cardinal St IP1 . . . . 17 C5
Card's Rd CM2 . . . . 217 C6
Careless Ct [21] CM23 . . . . 145 F7
Carisbrooke Ave
  CO15 . . . . 189 A7
Carleton Ct CO5 . . . . 163 E8
Carlford Ct IP4 . . . . 18 B5
Carlisle Cl CO1 . . . . 136 A8
Carlton Cl CO9 . . . . 30 A2
Carlton Mews CO7 . . . . . . 164 A8
Carlton Rd CO15 . . . . 189 B5
Carlton Way IP4 . . . . 17 E8
Carmarthen Rd IP2 . . . . 17 A2
Carmelite Way CM9 . . . . . 209 F2
Carmel St CB10 . . . . 3 D2
Carmen St CB10 . . . . 3 D3
Carnarvon Rd CO15 . . . . . 188 F3
Carnation Cl CM1 . . . . 205 F5
Carnation Dr CB10 . . . . 22 F2
Carolbrook Rd IP2 . . . . 16 E1
Carolina Way CO5 . . . . . . 179 D5
Caroline Cl CO7 . . . . 137 C3
Carpenters Dr CM77 . . . . 154 B7
Carpenters The CM23 . . . . 145 B5
Carraways CM8 . . . . 195 B8
Carriage Cl IP11 . . . . 221 A8
Carriage Dr CM1 . . . . 205 E7
Carriers Cl CO5 . . . . 201 A7
Carriers Ct CO7 . . . . 59 D3
Carrigans CM23 . . . . 145 E8
Carrington Ct CO5 . . . . . . 201 D7
Carrington Ho CO5 . . . . . . 201 D7
Carringtons Rd CO7 . . . . . 112 D4
Carrington Way CM7 . . . . 127 F8
Carr Rd IP11 . . . . 221 C1
Carrs Rd CO15 . . . . 188 D3
Carr St IP4 . . . . 17 D6
Carsey Hill CB21 . . . . 7 B6
Carshalton End CO3 . . . . . 134 F4
Carsons Dr CO10 . . . . 34 D5
Carstone Pl CM1 . . . . 204 D4
Cartbridge Cl CO14 . . . . . 171 B8
Carters Cl CO16 . . . . 188 B3
Carters Croft CB10 . . . . 6 B1

Carters Ct [15] CO1 . . . . . . 136 A6
Carters Hill
  Boxted CO4 . . . . 83 A6
  Manuden CM23 . . . . 93 A1
Carters La
  Henham CM22 . . . . 94 F5
  Wickham Bishops CM8 . . 195 F6
Carters Leys CM23 . . . . . . 145 D8
Carters Vineyard ★
  CO4 . . . . 82 E5
Cartwright Wlk CM2 . . . . . 205 F2
Carus Cres CO4 . . . . 110 B5
Case La IP9 . . . . 60 D7
Cassino Rd
  Chelmsford CM1 . . . . 204 E6
  Colchester CO2 . . . . 135 C3
Castings The CO6 . . . . 105 A6
Castle Ave CM9 . . . . 8 E7
Castle Bailey [16] CO1 . . . . 135 F7
CASTLE CAMPS 7 E3
Castle Camps CE Prim Sch
  CB21 . . . . 7 E3
Castle Cl
  Castle Hedingham CO9 . . . 51 E4
  Great Leighs CM3 . . . . . . 173 F6
Castle Cross CB10 . . . . 22 E2
Castle Ct
  Clacton-on-S CO15 . . . . . 188 E3
  Colchester CO1 . . . . 135 F8
Castleden Way CM6 . . . . . 123 D2
Castlefields CM3 . . . . 173 F7
Castlegate St CO12 . . . . . . 91 E6
Castle Hill
  Dedham CO7 . . . . 84 F4
  Saffron Walden CB10 . . . . 22 D2
Castle Hill Mid Sch CB9 . . . 8 D7
Castle Hill Pk CO16 . . . . . 188 E7
Castle Ho ★ CO7 . . . . 85 A5
Castle La
  Castle Hedingham CO9 . . . 51 E4
  Haverhill CB9 . . . . 8 F8
Castle Manor Bsns &
  Enterprise Coll CB9 . . . . .8 E8
Castle Mdw CM9 . . . . 51 D2
Castle Rd
  Clacton-on-S CO15 . . . . . 188 E3
  Colchester CO1 . . . . 136 A7
Castle St
  Bishop's Stortford
  CM23 . . . . 145 F6
  Saffron Walden CB10 . . . . 22 D2
Castle View CM23 . . . . 146 A7
Castleward CO7 . . . . 164 C8
Castle Way CO16 . . . . 187 A4
Castle Wlk
  Haverhill CB9 . . . . 8 E8
  Stansted Mountfitchet
  CM24 . . . . 119 E6
Caswell Mews CM2 . . . . . . 205 F2
Catchpole Ct [12] CO10 . . . 33 E7
Catchpole La CM9 . . . . 196 A4
Catchpool Rd CO1 . . . . . . 135 F8
Caterham Cl CO16 . . . . . . 188 C6
Cates Cnr CB11 . . . . 22 E1
Cathedral CE Prim Sch
  The CM1 . . . . 205 C3
Cathedral Wlk CM1 . . . . . 205 B3
Catherine Cl CO15 . . . . . . 189 A5
Catherine Hunt Way
  CO2 . . . . 135 C2
Catherine May Ct
  CO15 . . . . 188 F3
Catherines CM3 . . . . 174 A6
CATMERE END 21 A3
Catons La CB10 . . . . 22 D2
Cat's La CO10 . . . . 34 A7
CATTAWADE 86 D7
Cattawade St CO11 . . . . . . 86 C7
Cattermole Ct CO16 . . . . . 188 B3
Catts Cl IP9 . . . . 61 F2
Cattsfield IP9 . . . . 61 F2
Cauldwell Ave IP4 . . . . 17 F6
Cauldwell Hall IP4 . . . . 17 F6
Cauldwell Hall Rd IP4 . . . . 18 A6
Causeway
  Felsted CM3 . . . . 152 F1
  Ford End CM3 . . . . 172 A4
CAUSEWAY END 152 C3
Causeway End Rd
  CM6 . . . . 152 C3
Causeway Reach
  CO15 . . . . 188 E7
Causeway The
  [1] Bishop's Stortford
  CM23 . . . . 146 A7
  Braintree CM7 . . . . 127 F4
  Brent Pelham SG9 . . . . . . 64 B1
  Colchester CO4 . . . . 110 C1
  Finchingfield CM7 . . . . . . 72 D6
  Great Baddow CM2 . . . . . 216 F7
  Great Dunmow CM6 . . . . 123 D4
  Great Horkesley CO6 . . . . 82 B2
  Halstead CO9 . . . . 76 E1
  Haverhill CB9 . . . . 8 E7
  Henham CB11 . . . . 68 B7
  Langley CB11 . . . . 40 C3
  Maldon CM9 . . . . 210 A4
  Ridgewell CO9 . . . . 28 F8
  Toppesfield CO9 . . . . 50 B7
  Ulting CM9 . . . . 208 B7
Causton Jun Sch
  IP11 . . . . 221 C6
Causton Rd CO1 . . . . 135 E8
Caustons Cl CO10 . . . . 34 C5
Cavalier Gr CO2 . . . . 136 A5

Cavell Ct CM23 . . . . 146 B6
Cavell Dr CM23 . . . . 146 B6
CAVENDISH 1 C1
Cavendish Ave CO2 . . . . . 136 C3
Cavendish CE Prim Sch
  CO10 . . . . 1 C2
Cavendish Cl
  [2] Haverhill CB9 . . . . 8 E6
  [8] Saffron Walden CB10 . . 22 F2
Cavendish Dr
  Clacton-on-S CO16 . . . . . 188 A4
  Lawford CO11 . . . . 86 B3
Cavendish Gdns
  Braintree CM7 . . . . 128 C5
  Chelmsford CM2 . . . . 205 E3
Cavendish Ho CB9 . . . . .8 F7
Cavendish La CO10 . . . . . . .1 F3
Cavendish Rd
  Clare CO10 . . . . 12 D7
  Felixstowe IP11 . . . . 221 D3
Cavendish St IP3 . . . . 17 F5
Cavendish Way CO10 . . . . 33 F7
Cawkell Cl CM24 . . . . 119 D7
Cawkwell Cl CM2 . . . . 206 A4
Caxton Cl CO5 . . . . 179 D4
Caxton Ct CO4 . . . . 110 C6
Caxton Pl CO9 . . . . 76 E2
Cecil Cl CM23 . . . . 146 D7
Cecilia St IP1 . . . . 17 C5
Cecil Rd IP1 . . . . 17 B7
Cedar Ave
  Brightlingsea CO7 . . . . . . 185 E7
  Chelmsford CM1 . . . . 205 A3
  Tiptree CO5 . . . . 179 C7
Cedar Ave W CM1 . . . . . . 205 A3
Cedar Chase CM9 . . . . 210 C5
Cedar Cl
  Brantham CO11 . . . . 60 D1
  Great Dunmow CM6 . . . . 123 A1
  Walton-on-t-N CO14 . . . . 171 A7
Cedar Cres CO11 . . . . 86 C3
Cedar Ct
  Bishop's Stortford
  CM23 . . . . 118 F1
  West Bergholt CO6 . . . . . 108 D5
Cedar Dr CM8 . . . . 177 A5
Cedar Ho IP2 . . . . 17 A3
Cedar Pk CM23 . . . . 145 D4
Cedars Rd [13] CO2 . . . . . 135 F6
Cedars The
  Chelmsford CM2 . . . . 205 F4
  Gosfield CO9 . . . . 102 E7
  Stansted Mountfitchet
  CM24 . . . . 119 D6
Cedar Way CO7 . . . . 166 E8
Cedric Ct CM1 . . . . 204 F3
Celandine Ct CO4 . . . . . . 109 C2
Celestion Dr IP3 . . . . 18 B4
Cemetery La
  East Bergholt CO7 . . . . . . 59 B2
  Ipswich IP4 . . . . 17 E8
Cemetery Rd
  Bishop's Stortford
  CM23 . . . . 145 F6
  Ipswich IP4 . . . . 17 E6
Centaury Cl CO3 . . . . 134 C7
Centenary Way CO15,
  CO16 . . . . 168 E1
Central Arc CB10 . . . . 22 D1
Central Ave
  Frinton-on-S CO13 . . . . . 171 A6
  Ipswich IP3 . . . . 38 E5
Central Ho CO12 . . . . 91 D4
Central Maltings The [5]
  CO11 . . . . 86 D4
Central Par CO15 . . . . 188 F2
Central Sq [7] CM1 . . . . . . 205 B2
Centre The
  [2] Colchester CO4 . . . . . 136 E7
  Halstead CO9 . . . . 76 E2
Centre The CO5 . . . . 179 D5
Centre The IP2 . . . . 17 A1
Centrum Ct IP2 . . . . 17 B4
Centurian Ho [2] CO2 . . . . 135 F6
Centurion Way CO2 . . . . . 135 A3
Century Dr CM7 . . . . 128 B2
Chadburn Rd CO10 . . . . . 15 D8
Chadwick Dr CM7 . . . . . . 127 E3
Chaffinch Dr CO2 . . . . 90 E1
Chaffinch Gdns CO4 . . . . 136 F8
Chaffinch Way CO9 . . . . . 77 A1
Chaffix CM6 . . . . 152 C6
Chaffix Cl CM6 . . . . 152 C6
Chainey Pieces [12] CB9 . . .8 F7
Chalfont Rd CO4 . . . . 110 C3
Chalfont Sq [15] IP4 . . . . . 17 D6
Chalklands
  Howe Green CM2 . . . . . . 217 D3
  Saffron Walden CB10 . . . . 22 E3
Chalkners Cl [2] IP9 . . . . . . 35 A1
Chalks Rd CM8 . . . . 176 F4
Chalkstone Mid Sch
  CB9 . . . . 9 A8
Chalkstone Way CB9 . . . . . 9 D7
Chalky La CB9 . . . . 19 D2
Challenge Way CO1 . . . . . 136 B6
Challis La CM7 . . . . 155 A8
Chalon St IP1 . . . . 17 B5
Chamberlain Ave
  CO14 . . . . 171 B7
Chamberlain Way IP8 . . . . 16 C2
Chamley Ct CO15 . . . . 189 D5
Chancellor Ave CM2 . . . . 206 B4
Chancellor Ct CM1 . . . . . . 205 A4
Chancellor Park Prim Sch
  CM2 . . . . 206 B3
Chancery Gr CO2 . . . . 163 A8
Chancery Pl CM1 . . . . 204 B1

Chancery Rd IP1 . . . . 17 B5
Chandlers Cl
  Bishop's Stortford
  CM23 . . . . 145 C4
  Clacton-on-S CO16 . . . . . 188 B3
  West Mersea CO5 . . . . . . 201 C7
Chandlers Quay CM9 . . . . 210 A3
Chandlers Row CO1 . . . . . 136 C5
Chaney Rd CO7 . . . . 137 A2
Chant Ct CO4 . . . . 110 D3
Chanterelle CO4 . . . . 110 B3
CHANTRY 16 E3
Chantry Cl
  Bishop's Stortford
  CM23 . . . . 145 E8
  Clacton-on-S CO16 . . . . . 188 E7
Chantry Dr CO6 . . . . 80 E4
Chantry Gn IP2 . . . . 16 D3
Chantry High Sch & Sixth
  Form Ctr IP2 . . . . 16 E3
Chantry Home Farm Pk
  IP2 . . . . 16 E5
Chantry La CM3 . . . . 193 A3
Chantry Mount CM23 . . . . 145 E8
Chantry Rd CM23 . . . . . . 145 E8
Chantry The
  [6] Bishop's Stortford
  CM23 . . . . 145 F8
  Colchester CO3 . . . . 135 C7
Chantry View CM8 . . . . . . 195 A7
Chantry Villas CM3 . . . . . 193 A2
Chanute Ave CM7 . . . . 73 D7
Chapel Cl IP9 . . . . 35 A1
Chapel Cnr CO6 . . . . 80 F4
Chapel Croft CO7 . . . . 111 E7
Chapel Cut CO11 . . . . 87 A4
Chapel Dr CM3 . . . . 191 B6
CHAPELEND 23 A8
CHAPEL END 121 C7
CHAPELEND WAY 28 B2
Chapel End Way CO9 . . . . 28 B2
Chapelfields CO13 . . . . . . 170 E6
Chapel Fields CM22 . . . . . 148 B7
Chapel Hill
  Belchamp Walter CO10 . . . 31 D4
  Braintree CM7 . . . . 128 B2
  Halstead CO7 . . . . 76 D2
  Stansted Mountfitchet
  CM24 . . . . 119 E6
Chapel Hill Bsns & Ret Pk
  CM77 . . . . 128 C1
Chapel La
  Belstead IP8 . . . . 36 C7
  Boxted CO4 . . . . 83 A3
  Colchester CO7 . . . . 111 B1
  Elmstead Market CO7 . . . 138 A6
  Great Bromley CO7 . . . . . 139 A5
  Great Cornard CO10 . . . . 34 C2
  Heybridge Basin CM9 . . . 210 E2
  Kirby Cross CO13 . . . . . . 170 A6
  Little Baddow CM3 . . . . . 207 B3
  Newport CB11 . . . . 67 A8
  St Osyth CO16 . . . . 187 A4
  Tendring CO16 . . . . 140 E8
  Thorington Street CO6 . . . 57 D6
  Thorrington CO7 . . . . 166 B5
  Tiptree CO5 . . . . 179 E5
  Washbrook IP8 . . . . 16 A1
  West Bergholt CO6 . . . . . 108 C3
Chapel Mews [18] IP4 . . . . 17 D6
Chapel Rd
  Beaumont CO16 . . . . 141 E7
  Boxted CO4 . . . . 83 A3
  Brightlingsea CO7 . . . . . . 186 A7
  Colchester CO3 . . . . 134 C6
  Great Totham CM9 . . . . . 196 D6
  Langham CO4 . . . . 83 D4
  Ridgewell CO9 . . . . 29 B7
  Tiptree CO5 . . . . 179 E4
  Tolleshunt D'arcy CM9 . . 198 D4
  West Bergholt CO6 . . . . . 108 E4
  Wivenhoe CO7 . . . . 164 B8
Chapel Rise CM77 . . . . . . 129 D2
Chapel Row [3] CM23 . . . . 145 F6
Chapel St N [2] CO2 . . . . . 135 E6
Chapel St S [3] CO2 . . . . . 135 E6
Chapel St
  Halstead CO9 . . . . 76 E2
  Rowhedge CO5 . . . . 164 A8
  Steeple Bumpstead CB9 . . 27 C7
  Stoke by C CO10 . . . . 11 A3
Chaplin Cl CM2 . . . . 216 B2
Chaplin Dr CO4 . . . . 110 D1
Chaplin Rd CO7 . . . . 59 D3
Chaplins CO13 . . . . 170 F7
Chapman La IP1 . . . . 17 B6
Chapman Pl CO4 . . . . 110 B6
Chapman Rd CO15 . . . . . . 188 F3
Chapmans La CO5 . . . . . . 201 F8
CHAPPEL 106 C5
Chappel CE Prim Sch
  CO6 . . . . 106 D5
Chappel Cnr CO6 . . . . 106 D6
Chappel Hill CO6 . . . . 106 C5
Chappel Rd
  Bures CO6, CO8 . . . . 79 E3
  Fordham CO6 . . . . 107 D7
  Great Tey CO6 . . . . 106 C1
Chappel & Wakes Colne
  Sta CO6 . . . . 106 D6
Chariot Dr CO2 . . . . 135 C7
Charlecote Rd CM77 . . . . 154 C7
Charles Ct
  Colchester CO3 . . . . 134 D6

Charles Ct continued
Wivenhoe CO7 . . . .**137** C3
Charles Cvn Pk CO16 . .**167** E8
Charles Hall CO4 . . . .**109** F4
Charles Ho CO1 . . . .**135** F8
Charles Pell Rd CO4 . . . .**136** E7
Charles Rd
Brightlingsea CO7 . . . . . .**185** F6
Felixstowe IP11 . . . .**221** C3
Charles Smith Ho
CO2 . . . .**136** A3
Charles St
Colchester CO1 . . . .**136** A6
Ipswich IP1 . . . .**17** C6
Charleston Ct CO5 . . . . .**201** E6
Charlotte Dr CO13 . . . . .**170** E6
Charlotte Way CM8 . . . .**177** B2
Charnock Cl CO13 . . . . .**170** F6
Charnwood Ave CM1 . . .**204** E1
Charnwood Ct IP2 . . . . . .**17** B4
Charrington Cl CB9 . . . .**9** C6
Charter Ct CO4 . . . .**110** C6
Charter Ho CM9 . . . .**210** A2
Charters The CM6 . . . . .**123** D2
Charter Way
Braintree CM7 . . . .**128** C1
Colchester CO4 . . . .**109** F4
Chartfield Dr CO13 . . . . .**170** D8
Chartwell Cl
Braintree CM7 . . . .**127** E7
Ipswich IP3 . . . .**18** A5
Chartwell Pl CM23 . . . . .**119** B1
Chase Ct
Colchester CO4 . . . .**136** D7
Harwich CO12 . . . .**90** E2
Chase La CO12 . . . .**90** E2
Chase Lane Prim Sch
CO12 . . . .**90** E2
Chaser Cl IP3 . . . .**38** C8
Chase Rd E CO7 . . . .**139** C8
Chase Rd W CO7 . . . .**139** A6
Chase The
Aldham CO6 . . . .**133** B8
Barnston CM6 . . . .**151** B4
Bishop's Stortford
CM23 . . . .**145** F6
Boreham CM3 . . . .**206** E8
Braintree CM7 . . . .**128** A7
Brantham CO11 . . . .**60** F1
Colchester CO1 . . . .**136** B7
6 Colchester, Greenstead
CO1 . . . .**136** D7
Elmstead Market CO7 . . . .**138** B6
Felixstowe IP11 . . . .**221** D4
Foxearth CO10 . . . .**14** C6
Goldhanger CM9 . . . .**212** A1
Great Baddow CM2 . . . . .**216** F6
Great Notley CM77 . . . . . .**154** C5
Great Tey CO6 . . . .**132** C8
Great Totham CM9 . . . . . .**196** A4
Henham CM22 . . . .**94** F6
Holland-on-S CO15 . . . . .**189** E5
Kelvedon CO5 . . . .**158** C2
Manningtree CO11 . . . .**86** D3
Steeple Bumpstead CB9 . . .**27** B7
Thaxted CM6 . . . .**70** A2
Tollesbury CM9 . . . .**199** D2
Tolleshunt D'arcy CM9 . . .**198** B4
West Mersea CO5 . . . . . .**201** C6
Chaseway CM8 . . . .**176** F5
Chaseway The CM7 . . . .**128** C2
Chase Way The
Colchester CO3 . . . .**109** C1
Colchester, Lexden CO3 . .**109** B1
Chaston Bsns Ctr
CO15 . . . .**188** F5
Chaters Hill CB10 . . . . . .**22** E2
Chatham Gn CM3 . . . . . .**173** D3
Chatham Hall La CM3 . . .**191** B8
Chatley Rd CM3 . . . .**173** F7
Chatsworth Ave CM77 . .**154** B7
Chatsworth Cl CM23 . . .**145** C7
Chatsworth Cres
Ipswich IP2 . . . .**17** B2
Trimley St M IP11 . . . .**221** A6
Chatsworth Dr IP4 . . . . . .**18** E5
Chatsworth Gdns
CO15 . . . .**188** D2
Chatsworth Rd CO5 . . . .**201** C7
CHATTER END **118** C2
Chattisham Rd IP8 . . . . . .**35** C8
Chaucer Cl CO15 . . . . . .**188** A1
Chaucer Cres CM7 . . . . .**155** A8
Chaucer Rd
Chelmsford CM2 . . . .**205** D1
Felixstowe IP11 . . . .**221** D3
Sudbury CO10 . . . .**15** D2
Chaucer Way CO3 . . . . .**134** F6
Chauntry Rd CB9 . . . .**8** F7
Chauntry The **2** CB9 . . . .**9** A7
Chedburgh Pl **3** CB9 . . . .**9** A8
Chedworth Pl IP9 . . . .**61** D7
Chelmer Ave CM3 . . . . . .**191** B5
Chelmer Cl
Kirby Cross CO13 . . . . . .**170** E7
Little Totham CM9 . . . . . .**197** B4
Chelmer Dr CM6 . . . .**150** E8
Chelmer Lea CM2 . . . . . .**216** E7
Chelmer Pl CM2 . . . .**205** D3
Chelmer Rd
Braintree CM7 . . . .**128** D1
Chelmsford CM2 . . . .**205** D1
Haverhill CB9 . . . .**9** B8
Witham CM8 . . . .**176** F2
Chelmer Terr CM9 . . . . .**210** B2

Chelmerton Ave CM2 . . .**216** E7
Chelmer Valley High Sch
CM1 . . . .**191** A2
Chelmer Valley Rd
CM1 . . . .**205** B5
CHELMER VILLAGE **206** B4
Chelmer Village Ret Pk
CM2 . . . .**205** E2
Chelmer Village Way
CM2 . . . .**206** A3
CHELMONDISTON **63** E8
Chelmondiston CE Prim
Sch IP9 . . . .**63** E7
CHELMSFORD **205** C4
Chelmsford Coll
Chelmsford CM2 . . . .**216** A8
Chelmsford CM2 . . . .**216** C7
Chelmsford Cty High Sch
for Girls CM1 . . . .**205** A4
Chelmsford & Essex Ctr
CM2 . . . .**205** B1
Chelmsford & Essex
Regiment Mus*
CM2 . . . .**216** A8
Chelmsford Ho CM6 . . . .**150** E7
Chelmsford New Model
Specl Sch, Hayward
Campus The CM1 . . . . . .**205** A4
Chelmsford New Model
Specl Sch, Woodlands
Campus The CM1 . . . . . .**204** F6
Chelmsford Rd
Barnston CM6 . . . .**151** A4
Felsted CM6 . . . .**152** B4
Great Dunmow CM6 . . . . .**150** E7
Great Waltham CM3 . . . . .**191** A6
Holland-on-S CO15 . . . . .**189** D6
Purleigh CM3 . . . .**220** C3
Woodham Mortimer
CM9 . . . .**219** C6
Writtle CM1 . . . .**204** C1
Chelmsford Road Ind Est
CM6 . . . .**150** E7
Chelmsford Sta CM1 . . . .**205** B3
Chelsea Ct CO15 . . . .**33** F7
Chelsea Mews **12**
CM7 . . . .**127** F2
Chelsea Rd CO10 . . . .**33** F7
Chelsworth Ave CO10 . . .**34** B7
Chelsworth Rd IP11 . . . . .**221** B5
Chelwater CM2 . . . .**216** D8
Chenies Gn CM23 . . . . . .**145** D6
Chepstow Rd IP11 . . . . . .**221** D5
Chequers CM23 . . . .**145** C8
Chequers Ct CM8 . . . . . .**177** B2
Chequers La
Glemsford CO10 . . . .**2** C6
Great Dunmow CM6 . . . . .**150** D8
Maldon CM9 . . . .**210** A2
Chequers Rd CO11 . . . . .**113** C6
Chequers The CO7 . . . . .**165** A7
Cheriton Rd CM7 . . . .**128** C1
Cherry Bglws **1** CM7 . . .**127** F3
Cherry Blossom Cl IP8 . . .**16** B2
Cherry Chase CO5 . . . . .**179** D4
Cherry Cres CM6 . . . .**123** C1
Cherrygarden La **1**
CM2 . . . .**216** A8
Cherry Garden La
Danbury CM3 . . . .**219** B7
Newport CB11 . . . .**66** F8
Cherry Garden Rd
Great Waltham CM3 . . . . .**190** E7
Maldon CM9 . . . .**209** E2
Cherry Gdns
Bishop's Stortford
CM23 . . . .**146** A8
Great Notley CM77 . . . . . .**154** D8
Haverhill CB9 . . . .**9** B5
CHERRY GREEN
(CHAURETH GREEN)
. . . .**95** E7
Cherry La CO9 . . . .**51** A8
Cherry Lane Gdns IP4 . . .**18** B7
Cherry Row CO3 . . . .**134** F5
Cherry Tree Ave
CO15 . . . .**188** C1
Cherry Tree Cl
Halstead CO9 . . . .**77** A2
Little Oakley CO12 . . . . . .**117** B7
Cherrytree Ct CO3 . . . . .**134** F5
Cherry Tree Ho CO5 . . . .**158** C3
Cherry Tree La
Abberton CO2 . . . .**162** F6
Blackheath CO2 . . . .**163** A7
Cherry Tree Prim Sch
CO2 . . . .**163** A8
Cherrytree Rd CO10 . . . . .**34** B7
Cherrytree Rise CM8 . . . .**177** A5
Cherry Trees CO15 . . . . .**188** F2
Cherrywood Dr CO3 . . . .**134** F5
Cherrywoods CO7 . . . . . .**166** D8
Chervil Cl CO5 . . . .**179** C4
Cherwell Dr CM1 . . . .**204** C5
Cheryl Ct CO15 . . . .**188** D1
Chesapeake Cl IP9 . . . . . .**63** F7
Chesapeake Rd IP3 . . . . . .**38** A8
Chesfield Cl CM23 . . . . . .**145** F5
Chesham Rd IP2 . . . .**17** B4
Chessington Gdns IP1 . . .**16** F8
Chess La CM8 . . . .**177** A2
Chester Camp CO16 . . . .**188** A4
Chester Ct **4** CB9 . . . .**8** E6
Chester Pl CM1 . . . .**205** A5
Chester Rd IP11 . . . .**221** D5
Chesterton Ct IP2 . . . .**16** F1
Chesterwall Mews
CO4 . . . .**109** D6

Chestnut Ave
Blackheath CO2 . . . .**163** A8
Clacton-on-S CO15 . . . . .**188** C3
Gosfield CO9 . . . .**102** E8
Great Notley CM77 . . . . . .**154** C7
Hatfield Peverel CM3 . . . .**194** A3
Heybridge CM9 . . . .**210** C6
Jaywick CO16 . . . .**188** A2
Kirby Cross CO13 . . . . . .**170** C6
Littlebury CB11 . . . .**21** C1
Chestnut Cl
Bishop's Stortford
CM23 . . . .**145** E6
Colchester CO6 . . . .**109** D5
Haverhill CB9 . . . .**8** F8
Chestnut Ct CB11 . . . .**67** A8
Chestnut Gr CM7 . . . .**127** E2
Chestnut Mews CM9 . . .**210** C6
Chestnut Rd
Alresford CO7 . . . .**165** B8
Glemsford CO10 . . . .**2** B5
Chestnuts The IP2 . . . . . .**16** C2
Chestnut Terr CO10 . . . . .**15** C8
Chestnut View CM6 . . . .**123** C1
Chestnut Way
Brightlingsea CO7 . . . . . .**185** E7
Takeley CM22 . . . .**148** C7
Tiptree CO5 . . . .**179** C7
Chestnut Wlk
Chelmsford CM1 . . . .**205** A5
Felsted CM6 . . . .**152** C6
Little Baddow CM3 . . . . . .**207** E1
Witham CM8 . . . .**177** B4
Chevalier Rd IP11 . . . . . .**221** F4
Chevallier St IP1 . . . .**17** A7
Cheveley IP11 . . . .**221** E4
Cheveling Rd CO2 . . . . . .**136** D2
Cheviot Dr CM1 . . . .**204** D6
Chevy Ct CO12 . . . .**90** C2
Cheyne Ct CO10 . . . .**33** E7
Chichester Ct CO3 . . . . .**135** A7
Chichester Dr CM1 . . . . .**205** C4
Chichester Rd CB11 . . . . .**43** E8
CHICKNEY **95** F4
Chickney Rd CM22 . . . . . .**95** C7
Chigborough Rd CM9 . . .**210** F6
Chignall Rd CM1 . . . .**204** D5
CHIGNALL ST JAMES
. . . .**204** A8
Chilburn Rd CO15 . . . . . .**189** A7
Childers Field IP11 . . . . . .**221** B5
Childwell Alley CO1 . . . . .**136** A6
Chilford Ct CM7 . . . .**127** D3
Chiltern Cl
Chelmsford CM1 . . . .**204** D5
Colchester CO1 . . . .**109** E1
Chilton Cl
Chelmsford CM2 . . . .**216** D7
Great Horkesley CO6 . . . .**109** A7
Chilton Cotts CO6 . . . . . .**80** E4
Chilton Ct
Ipswich IP2 . . . .**17** B3
Sudbury CO10 . . . .**34** A6
Chilton Ind Est CO10 . . . .**34** B8
Chilton Lodge Rd
CO10 . . . .**34** A7
Chilton Rd IP3 . . . .**18** C4
Chilton Rd Ind Est
CO10 . . . .**34** B8
Chimney Pot La CM3 . . . .**219** E3
Chimswell Way CB9 . . . . . .**8** C8
Chinery Cl CM1 . . . .**205** D4
Chingford Ave CO15 . . . .**188** F8
Chinnel La CB11 . . . .**42** D5
Chinnery Hill CM23 . . . . .**145** F5
Chinook CO4 . . . .**110** B4
Chippetts La CO3 . . . . . .**133** C7
Chippingdell CM8 . . . . . .**176** F4
CHIPPING HILL **176** F3
Chipping Hill
3 Halstead CO9 . . . .**76** F2
Witham CM8 . . . .**176** F3
Chipping Hill Inf Sch
CM8 . . . .**176** F3
Chipstead Wlk CO16 . . . .**188** C6
Chishill Rd SG8 . . . .**19** A4
Chislett Row CM2 . . . . . .**216** C8
Chittock Cl CO16 . . . .**188** B3
Chitts Hill CO3 . . . .**108** D1
Chivers Rd CB9 . . . .**8** D7
Choat's Cotts CO6 . . . . . .**107** E1
Choats Wood CO3 . . . . . .**107** F1
CHRISHALL **19** D3
Chrismund Way CO6 . . . .**106** C1
Christchurch Ct **4**
IP4 . . . .**17** D6
Christ Church Ct CO3 . . .**135** D5
Christchurch Mansion
(Mus)* IP4 . . . .**17** D6
Christchurch St IP4 . . . . . .**17** D6
Christian Sch The
CM22 . . . .**148** B7
Christina Rd CM8 . . . .**194** E8
Christine Chase CO3 . . . .**134** F5
Christmas Field CO9 . . . . .**51** D2
Christopher Ct **9**
CO10 . . . .**33** E7
Christopher Dr CO16 . . . .**168** D1
Christopher Jolly Ct
CO2 . . . .**135** F4
Christopher La CO10 . . . . .**33** E7
Christy Ave CM1 . . . .**204** F4
Churcacre CM9 . . . .**199** D1
Church Ave CM1 . . . .**191** A2
Church Chase CM8 . . . . .**178** A3
Church Cl
Cavendish CO10 . . . .**1** D2
Sproughton IP8 . . . .**16** A6

Church Cl continued
West Bergholt CO6 . . . . . .**108** E4
Wickham Bishops CM8 . . .**195** D5
Church Cnr CM9 . . . .**208** D2
Church Cotts CM8 . . . . . .**195** D5
Church Cres
Clacton-on-S CO15 . . . . .**188** F2
Sproughton IP8 . . . .**16** A6
Church Dr CM23 . . . .**92** B8
CHURCHEND **123** E2
CHURCH END
Ashdon **24** A7
Elsenham **95** F3
Church End
Great Dunmow CM6 . . . . .**123** E2
Panfield CM7 . . . .**127** B7
CHURCH END
Shalford **100** E1
Stebbing **124** F4
Church End Villas
CM6 . . . .**123** E3
Church Farm Way
CO4 . . . .**109** E4
Church Field
Ashdon CB10 . . . .**23** F7
Saffron Walden CB11 . . . . .**43** E7
Churchfield Rd
Coggeshall CO6 . . . .**131** A3
Walton-on-t-N CO14 . . . .**171** C8
Church Field Rd
Stutton IP9 . . . .**62** B2
Sudbury CO10 . . . .**34** C8
Churchfields
Stansted Mountfitchet
CM24 . . . .**119** F6
West Mersea CO5 . . . . . .**201** B6
Church Fields CO9 . . . . . .**29** F2
Churchfields Ave
CO3 . . . .**134** C4
Churchfields Dr CB9 . . . . .**27** B6
Churchfields Wlk CB9 . . . .**27** B6
Churchgate
Glemsford CO10 . . . .**2** C5
Thorpe-le-S CO16 . . . . . .**141** F1
Church Gdns CM6 . . . . . .**123** D2
Church Gn
Boreham CM3 . . . .**206** F8
Broomfield CM1 . . . .**191** B1
Coggeshall CO6 . . . .**131** A3
Hinxton CB10 . . . .**3** B7
Little Yeldham CO9 . . . . . .**30** D4
Wickham Bishops CM8 . . .**195** D5
Church Gr CO6 . . . .**133** B8
Church Hill
Ashdon CB10 . . . .**24** A8
Earls Colne CO6 . . . .**105** C6
Finchingfield CM7 . . . .**72** D6
Harwich CO12 . . . .**90** B1
Helions Bumpstead CB9 . . .**26** C8
Holbrook IP9 . . . .**62** D5
Lawford CO11 . . . .**85** F3
Little Waltham CM3 . . . . .**191** C6
Purleigh CM3 . . . .**220** E1
Radwinter CB10 . . . .**45** F7
Rowhedge CO5 . . . .**163** F8
White Notley CM8 . . . . . .**175** F8
Woodham Walter CM9 . . .**208** D2
Church Housen CM3 . . . .**190** F7
Churchill Ave
Halstead CO9 . . . .**77** A3
Ipswich IP4 . . . .**18** B5
Churchill Cl CO7 . . . .**185** F6
Churchill Cnr CM24 . . . . .**119** F5
Churchill Ct CO12 . . . .**91** A4
Churchill Dr CO10 . . . . . .**15** E2
Churchill Rd
Braintree CM7 . . . .**127** E7
Tiptree CO5 . . . .**179** F5
Churchill Rise CM1 . . . . .**205** D4
Churchill Terr CM7 . . . . .**127** E6
Churchill Way CO2 . . . . .**136** B4
Church La
Beaumont CO16 . . . .**142** A6
Belstead IP8 . . . .**36** A7
Bishop's Stortford
CM23 . . . .**145** D3
Braintree CM7 . . . .**127** F6
Brantham CO11 . . . .**60** E1
Castle Camps CB21 . . . .**7** F2
Castle Hedingham CO9 . . . .**51** E4
1 Chelmsford, Moulsham
CM1 . . . .**205** B2
Chelmsford, Springfield
CM1 . . . .**205** D4
Clare CO10 . . . .**12** B7
Colchester, Lexden
CO3 . . . .**135** A6
Colchester, Stanway
CO3 . . . .**134** A4
Copdock IP8 . . . .**35** F7
Debden CB11 . . . .**68** A7
East Mersea CO5 . . . .**184** E1
Elsenham CM22 . . . .**120** E8
Felixstowe IP11 . . . .**221** D6
Ford End CM3 . . . .**172** B6
Great Henny CO10 . . . .**54** D8
Great Holland CO13 . . . . .**170** B3
Great Leighs CM3 . . . . . .**173** D7
Great Tey CO6 . . . .**132** C4
Great Wigborough CO5 . . .**181** F4
Harkstead IP9 . . . .**63** B3
Harwich CO12 . . . .**91** E6
Little Totham CM9 . . . . . .**197** B1
Marks Tey CO6 . . . .**133** A4
Mistley CO11 . . . .**86** E4
Nayland CO6 . . . .**56** B1
Ridgewell CO9 . . . .**29** B6
Sproughton IP8 . . . .**16** B6

Church La continued
Takeley, Brewer's End
CM22 . . . .**148** B7
Takeley, Little Canfield
CM6 . . . .**149** B7
Toppesfield CO9 . . . .**50** B7
Washbrook IP8 . . . .**35** D8
Weeley Heath CO16 . . . . .**168** A7
Widdington CB11 . . . .**67** D4
Writtle CM1 . . . .**204** B1
Church Manor CM23 . . . .**146** B8
Churchmans Ho IP1 . . . . .**17** B5
Church Mdw CO10 . . . . . .**32** E5
Church Mdws CM7 . . . . .**127** F6
Church Mead CM8 . . . . . .**155** F1
Church Mews CM6 . . . . . .**56** B1
Church Path
Hadstock CB1 . . . .**5** B6
Saffron Walden CB10 . . . . .**22** D2
Church Pk CO10 . . . .**11** C3
Churchponds CO9 . . . .**51** E4
Church Rd
Alphamstone CO10 . . . . . .**54** C6
Alresford CO7 . . . .**165** B7
Bentley IP9 . . . .**60** F7
Black Notley CM77 . . . . . .**155** A6
Boxted CO4 . . . .**82** E6
Bradwell CM77 . . . .**129** E1
Brightlingsea CO7 . . . . . .**185** E8
Bulmer CO10 . . . .**32** F4
Capel St M IP9 . . . .**35** F1
Chrishall SG8 . . . .**19** D3
Clacton-on-S CO15 . . . . .**189** A3
Copford CO6 . . . .**133** E2
Cressing CM77 . . . .**156** A5
Elmstead Market CO7 . . . .**138** A7
Fingringhoe CO5 . . . .**164** A5
Fordham CO6 . . . .**107** D5
Frating Green CO7 . . . . . .**138** D2
Gosfield CO9 . . . .**102** E8
Great Cornard CO10 . . . . .**34** A5
Great Hallingbury
CM22 . . . .**146** D3
Great Notley CM77 . . . . . .**154** F6
Great Totham CM9 . . . . . .**196** E3
Great Yeldham CO9 . . . . . .**29** F2
Greenstead Green CO9 . . .**104** A5
Hatfield Peverel CM3 . . . .**194** A3
Hempstead CB10 . . . .**46** F8
Kelvedon CO5 . . . .**158** C2
Layer de la H CO2 . . . . . .**161** F4
Little Baddow CM3 . . . . . .**207** A5
Little Bentley CO7 . . . . . .**140** A5
Little Bromley CO11 . . . . .**113** B4
Pattiswick CM77 . . . .**129** F5
Peldon CO5 . . . .**182** D6
Rivenhall CM8 . . . .**157** B1
Shudy Camps CB21 . . . .**7** C5
Stambourne CO9 . . . .**28** D2
Stansted Mountfitchet
CM24 . . . .**119** F5
Stutton IP9 . . . .**62** A2
Tattingstone IP9 . . . .**61** C7
Terling CM3 . . . .**175** B2
Thorrington CO7 . . . .**166** A6
Tiptree CO5 . . . .**179** D5
Tolleshunt Major CM9 . . .**197** F2
Ulting CM9 . . . .**208** C6
Walton-on-t-N CO14 . . . .**171** C8
West Mersea CO5 . . . . . .**201** B6
Wickham Bishops CM8 . . .**195** E5
Wickham St P CO9 . . . . . .**53** B6
Wormingford CO6 . . . .**80** E5
Wrabness CO11 . . . .**88** F4
Church Rise CB9 . . . .**26** C8
Church Row CM6 . . . .**122** E3
Church Sq
Bures CO8 . . . .**55** F1
St Osyth CO16 . . . .**187** A4
Church St
Belchamp St P CO10 . . . . .**13** B3
Bishop's Stortford
CM23 . . . .**145** F7
Boxted CO4 . . . .**82** F7
Braintree CM7 . . . .**102** B1
Chelmondiston IP9 . . . . . .**63** E7
Chelmsford CM1 . . . .**205** B2
Clare CO10 . . . .**12** B7
Coggeshall CO6 . . . .**131** A2
Colchester CO1 . . . .**135** E7
Colne Engaine CO6 . . . . . .**78** A1
Gestingthorpe CO9 . . . . . .**31** E1
Goldhanger CM9 . . . .**211** E7
Great Baddow CM2 . . . . .**217** A6
Great Chesterford CB10 . . . .**3** D2
Great Dunmow CM6 . . . . .**123** D2
Great Maplestead CO9 . . . .**52** D1
Harwich CO12 . . . .**91** E6
Henham CM22 . . . .**94** F6
Ickleton CB10 . . . .**3** B4
Kelvedon CO5 . . . .**158** B2
Maldon CM9 . . . .**210** B2
Newport CB11 . . . .**43** A1
Rowhedge CO5 . . . .**164** A8
Saffron Walden CB10 . . . . .**22** D2
Sible Hedingham CO9 . . . . .**51** D1
Steeple Bumpstead CB9 . . .**27** B7
Stoke-by-N CO6 . . . .**56** D5
Sudbury CO10 . . . .**33** D6
Tollesbury CM9 . . . .**199** D1
Tolleshunt D'arcy CM9 . . .**198** D4
Wendens Ambo CB11 . . . .**42** E5
Witham CM8 . . . .**176** F4
CHURCH STREET **13** B3
Church Terr
Bures CO8 . . . .**55** F1
Stoke by C CO10 . . . .**10** D2

Church View
Ardleigh CO7 ... 111 E7
Colne Engaine CO6 ... 77 F1
Dedham CO7 ... 84 F3
Stoke by C CO10 ... 10 D3
Churchview Ct 12
CO14 ... 171 C8
Church Villas CO7 ... 186 A6
Churchwell Ave CO5 ... 160 A7
Church Wlk
Colchester CO1 ... 135 E7
Littlebury CB11 ... 21 F4
Maldon CM9 ... 209 F3
Sturmer CB9 ... 9 E4
5 Sudbury CO10 ... 33 E7
Churnwood Cl CO4 ... 110 D1
Churnwood Rd CO4 ... 110 D1
Chuzzlewit Dr CM1 ... 204 E7
Cinnabar Cl IP8 ... 36 E8
Cinque Port Rd CO7 ... 185 F7
Circular Rd E CO2 ... 135 F5
Circular Rd N CO2 ... 135 E5
Circular Rd S CO2 ... 135 E4
Circular Rd W CO2 ... 135 E5
Circus Sq CO2 ... 135 F3
City Rd CO5 ... 201 A6
Civic Dr IP1 ... 17 B6
Civic Ind Est CB9 ... 8 F5
Clachar Cl CM2 ... 206 A3
Clacton Comm CO15 ... 169 A1
Clacton Cty High Sch
CO15 ... 189 A4
Clacton & District Hospl
CO15 ... 188 E1
Clacton Factory Shopping
Village CO15 ... 169 A1
CLACTON-ON-SEA ... 189 B3
Clacton Rd
Bradfield CO11 ... 114 A6
Elmstead Market CO7 ... 138 C5
Great Holland CO13 ... 170 A2
Holland-on-S CO15 ... 189 F7
Little Oakley CO12 ... 117 B5
Mistley CO11 ... 86 E2
St Osyth CO16 ... 187 B4
Thorrington CO7 ... 166 C4
Weeley Heath CO16 ... 168 A6
Wivenhoe CO7 ... 137 C5
Wix CO11 ... 115 C5
Wix, Stones Green
CO12 ... 115 D1
Clacton Sta CO15 ... 188 F3
Claire Ct CO5 ... 201 C7
Claire Rd CO13 ... 170 B6
Clairmont Cl CM7 ... 127 F2
Clairmont Rd CO3 ... 134 E5
Clandon Ho CO13 ... 170 F4
Clapgate Dr CO16 ... 168 C2
Clapgate La IP3 ... 18 A2
Clapton Hall La
Great Dunmow CM6 ... 150 D5
Great Dunmow CM6 ... 150 E6
Clara Reeve Cl CO3 ... 134 F4
CLARE ... 12 C8
Clare Ancient House
Mus★ CO10 ... 12 B7
Clare Castle Ctry Pk★
CO10 ... 12 C7
Clare Cl CO9 ... 103 D7
Clare Com Prim Sch
CO10 ... 12 B8
Clare Ct CM6 ... 69 F3
Clare Mid Sch CO10 ... 12 C8
Claremont Hts CO1 ... 109 E1
Claremont Rd CO7 ... 164 C8
Clarence Cl CM2 ... 206 A4
Clarence Ho CM2 ... 216 A8
Clarence Rd
Clare CO10 ... 12 B8
Ipswich IP3 ... 18 B1
Stansted Mountfitchet
CM24 ... 119 E7
Sudbury CO10 ... 15 E1
Clarendon Pk CO15 ... 189 B5
Clarendon Rd
Haverhill CB9 ... 8 F6
Takeley CM6 ... 148 E7
Clarendon Way CO1 ... 109 E1
Clare Rd
Braintree CM7 ... 127 E2
Ipswich IP4 ... 17 F8
Tilbury Juxta Clare CO9 ... 30 A5
Clare Way CO16 ... 188 B5
Clarkesmead CO5 ... 179 C4
Clarke's Rd CO12 ... 90 F3
Clarkia Wlk CO4 ... 136 D7
Clarks Farm Rd CM3 ... 218 F8
Clarks Field Cotts
CM3 ... 219 E2
Clarkson St IP1 ... 17 B6
Clarks Wood Dr CM7 ... 128 D3
Clark Way CM1 ... 191 A1
Clatterbury La
Arkesden CB11 ... 41 E1
Clavering CB11 ... 65 D5
Claude Oliver Cl CO11 ... 86 A2
Claude St IP1 ... 17 C6
Claudian Cl CB9 ... 9 D7
Claud Ince Ave CM77 ... 155 E6
Claudius Ct CO1 ... 135 F8
Claudius Rd CO2 ... 136 A5
Claudius Way CM8 ... 194 E8
CLAVERING ... 65 C5
Clavering Prim Sch
CB11 ... 65 C4
Clavering Rd CM7 ... 127 F6
Claverton Way IP4 ... 18 E4
Claydon Cl CB21 ... 7 E4
Clayhall Rd CO15 ... 189 A5
Clay Hill CO10 ... 54 C8
Clay Hills CO9 ... 77 F8
Clayhive Dr CB9 ... 8 F7
Clay La
Stebbing CM6 ... 124 D7
St Osyth CO16 ... 187 C7
Clay Lane Gr CO4 ... 110 D4
Claypit Hill CM22 ... 120 E5
Clay Pit Piece CB11 ... 43 E6
Clay Pits CM7 ... 128 D3
Claypits Ave CO8 ... 80 A8
Claypits La CO10 ... 14 D5
Claypits Rd CM3 ... 192 F1
Claypits Villas CM6 ... 70 B2
Clay Pits Way CM7 ... 128 D3
Clayponds CM23 ... 146 B7
Clayshotts Dr CM8 ... 195 B8
Clays Mdw CB11 ... 21 F4
Clays Rd
Walton-on-t-N CO14 ... 171 A7
Walton-on-t-N CO14 ... 171 B7
Clayton Rd CO12 ... 90 C2
Claywall Bridge CB9 ... 27 C7
Claywall Cotts CB9 ... 27 C7
Clear Springs Chalet Site
CO12 ... 91 A1
Clearwater CO2 ... 136 B3
Clearwater Reach
CO15 ... 188 F2
Clearwing Cl IP8 ... 36 E8
Clees Hall CO8 ... 55 A1
Clematis Tye 3 CM1 ... 205 E7
Clematis Way CO4 ... 136 E7
Clementine Gdns IP4 ... 18 B5
Clement Mellish Ho 10
CO1 ... 135 F7
Clements Cl
Chelmsford CM2 ... 206 B3
Haverhill CB9 ... 8 F7
Clements Com Prim Sch
CB9 ... 8 F7
Clements Dr CB9 ... 8 F7
Clement's La CB9 ... 8 F7
Clench Cl 8 IP4 ... 17 D6
Clench Rd IP9 ... 62 D7
Clermont Ave CO10 ... 15 E2
Clevedon Cl CM77 ... 154 C7
Cleveland Cl CO4 ... 110 C4
Cleves Ct CM3 ... 192 E1
Cleves Rd CB9 ... 8 D6
Clibbon Ho CO10 ... 34 B6
Clicket Hill CO8 ... 80 B8
Clickett Hill Rd IP11 ... 221 A4
Cliff Cres CM7 ... 100 E7
Cliff Ct
Frinton-on-S CO13 ... 171 B6
Harwich CO12 ... 91 D3
Cliffield CM7 ... 100 E7
Cliff La IP3 ... 17 F3
Cliff Lane Prim Sch
IP3 ... 17 E3
Clifford Ct 9 CM23 ... 146 A7
Clifford Rd IP4 ... 17 F5
Clifford Road Air Raid
Shelter Mus★ IP4 ... 17 F5
Clifford Road Prim Sch
IP4 ... 17 F5
Cliff Par CO14 ... 144 E2
Cliff Rd
Harwich CO12 ... 91 D3
Holland-on-S CO15 ... 189 E5
Ipswich IP3 ... 17 E3
Cliff View Ct CO15 ... 189 C4
Cliff Way CO13 ... 171 B5
Clifton Ct 13 CO14 ... 171 C8
Cliftons Farm Dr CO10 ... 12 B7
Clifton Terr CO7 ... 164 B8
Clifton Way IP2 ... 16 D2
Clifton Wood IP9 ... 62 D6
Clingoe Ct CO4 ... 136 E5
Cliveden Cl CM1 ... 204 E3
Clive Rd CO1, CO2 ... 136 A6
Clobbs Yd CM1 ... 205 B8
Clockhouse Way CM7 ... 128 C2
CLODMORE HILL ... 41 C3
Cloes La CO16 ... 188 B4
Cloisters The
Braintree CM7 ... 128 A5
Kelvedon CO5 ... 158 B1
Cloncurry Gdns IP11 ... 221 B3
Clopton Dr CO10 ... 15 C6
Close The
Clacton-on-S CO15 ... 203 H7
Cressing CM77 ... 155 E6
Debden CB11 ... 68 B7
Frinton-on-S CO13 ... 170 E5
Great Dunmow CM6 ... 150 E7
Great Holland CO13 ... 170 A3
Harwich CO12 ... 91 A3
Sudbury CO10 ... 33 F8
Tattingstone IP9 ... 61 D7
Clouded Yellow Cl
CM7 ... 154 E8
Clough Rd CO4 ... 110 D6
Clovelly Cl IP4 ... 18 F4
Clover Ave CM23 ... 145 B6
Clover Cl IP2 ... 16 F4
Clover Ct
Colchester CO3 ... 134 D5
Great Cornard CO10 ... 34 C6
Clover Dr CO7 ... 166 A5
Clover Field CB9 ... 8 D8
Cloverlands CO4 ... 110 C2
Clovers 5 CO9 ... 76 D1
Clover Way CO7 ... 111 B5
Cluanie Orch CO10 ... 1 E1
Club Par CO16 ... 203 B6
Clump Field IP2 ... 16 F2
Clunford Pl CM1 ... 205 F7
Clyde Cres CM1 ... 204 D4
Clydesdale Rd CM7 ... 127 E2
Coach Ho The CO6 ... 105 A7
Coach House Way 10
CM8 ... 177 A2
Coach La CM9 ... 209 F3
Coachmans Ct 6 IP4 ... 17 C5
Coachmans Mead CM7 ... 72 C6
Coachman's Paddock
IP9 ... 62 D6
Coach Rd
Alresford CO7 ... 165 B8
Great Horkesley CO6 ... 109 A7
Hempstead CB10 ... 25 F2
Coan Ave CO15 ... 188 D1
Coastguard Cotts
CO14 ... 144 D1
Coast Rd CO5 ... 201 A6
Coates Cl CM9 ... 210 B4
Coates Lo CM2 ... 206 A3
Coates Quay CM2 ... 205 C2
Coats Hutton Rd CO2 ... 135 B3
Cobble Row CO3 ... 134 E6
Cobbold Mews 16 IP4 ... 17 D6
Cobbold Rd IP11 ... 221 E4
Cobbold St IP4 ... 17 D6
COBBS FENN ... 75 D7
Cobbs La CM22 ... 121 F3
Cobbs Pl CM1 ... 205 D3
Cobden Pl IP4 ... 17 D6
Cobham Rd IP3 ... 18 C2
COBLER'S GREEN ... 152 D4
Cockaynes La CO7 ... 138 A1
Cock & Bell La CO10 ... 15 C8
COCK CLARKS ... 219 F2
Cockett Wick La
CO16 ... 187 C1
COCK GREEN ... 152 E4
Cock La CB11 ... 64 F3
Cock Rd CO9 ... 53 B1
Cockrell's Rd CO6 ... 81 B4
Codham Little Park Dr
CM7 ... 101 C6
Cody Rd IP3 ... 18 C1
Coeur De Lion CO4 ... 109 F2
COGGESHALL ... 131 B3
COGGESHALL HAMLET
... 158 A8
Coggeshall Rd
Ardleigh CO7 ... 84 F2
Braintree CM7 ... 128 C3
Coggeshall CO6 ... 131 F3
Earls Colne CO6 ... 105 B3
Great Tey CO6 ... 132 B7
Kelvedon CO5 ... 158 B5
Marks Tey CO6 ... 132 C3
Coggeshall Rd (Feering)
CO5 ... 158 D7
Coggeshall Road
(Feering) CO6 ... 131 B1
Coggeshall Way CO9 ... 77 A2
Cogmore CB11 ... 41 B8
Cohen Cl CM77 ... 155 B5
Cohort Dr CO2 ... 135 A2
Cokers Cl CM77 ... 155 C5
Coke St CO12 ... 91 D5
Colam La CM3 ... 207 C3
Colbayns High Sch
CO15 ... 188 D4
Colbourn Ct IP11 ... 221 E4
COLCHESTER ... 135 C7
Colchester Bsns Ctr
CO1 ... 136 A6
Colchester Bsns Pk
CO4 ... 110 C6
Colchester Castle★
CO1 ... 135 F7
Colchester Castle Mus★
CO1 ... 135 F7
Colchester Cty High Sch
for Girls CO3 ... 135 B6
Colchester General Hospl
CO4 ... 109 E3
Colchester High Sch
CO3 ... 135 E6
Colchester Inst
Clacton-on-S CO15 ... 189 A2
Colchester CO3 ... 135 D8
Colchester Natural History
Mus★ CO3 ... 135 F7
Colchester Rd
Abberton CO5 ... 163 B1
Ardleigh CO7 ... 111 C6
Bures CO8 ... 79 F8
Chappel CO6 ... 106 E5
Chelmsford CM2 ... 206 A6
Coggeshall CO6 ... 131 D2
Dedham CO7 ... 84 E6
Elmstead Market CO7 ... 137 F6
Frating Green CO7 ... 139 E3
Great Bentley CO7,
CO16 ... 186 F8
Great Bromley CO7 ... 112 A3
Great Totham CM9 ... 196 D7
Great Wigborough CM9,
CO5 ... 181 C2
Halstead CO9 ... 77 A1
Heybridge CM9 ... 210 B5
Holland-on-S CO15 ... 189 D6
Ipswich IP4 ... 18 B8
Lawford CO11 ... 86 C3
Little Horkesley CO6 ... 81 B1
Peldon CO5 ... 183 B5
Salcott-c-V CM9 ... 199 A5
St Osyth CO16 ... 187 A5
Thorpe-le-S CO16 ... 141 D2
Colchester Rd *continued*
Tiptree CO5 ... 179 D7
Weeley CO16 ... 140 C2
West Bergholt CO6 ... 108 E4
West Mersea CO5 ... 201 C7
White Colne CO6 ... 105 E6
Witham CM8 ... 177 B3
Wivenhoe CO7 ... 137 B4
Wix CO12 ... 115 B3
Wix, Goose Green
CO11 ... 114 E4
Wormingford CO8 ... 80 A6
Colchester Ret Pk
CO3 ... 135 E7
Colchester Royal Gram
Sch CO3 ... 135 D6
Colchester Sta CO1 ... 109 E1
Colchester Town Sta
CO1 ... 136 A6
Colchester Zoo★
CO3 ... 134 C1
Cold Hall Chase CO7 ... 138 E6
Coldnailhurst Ave
CM7 ... 127 F5
Cold Store Rd IP11 ... 221 A1
COLE END ... 44 D6
Cole End La CB10 ... 44 D5
Cole Gn CO10 ... 13 A1
Cole Hill CM3 ... 174 B5
Colehills CB11 ... 65 C4
Colehills Cl CB11 ... 65 C4
Coleman Ct CO15 ... 188 F3
Colemans La CM3 ... 218 D7
Cole Ness Rd IP3 ... 38 A8
Coleridge Rd CM9 ... 210 A1
COLES GREEN ... 35 C8
Coles La CO14 ... 144 A1
Coles Oak La CO7 ... 84 C6
Colet Cres CO2 ... 135 F4
College Cl CM23 ... 145 D7
College Ct CO11 ... 86 C4
College Ho CM7 ... 127 E2
College Rd
Braintree CM7 ... 127 E2
Clacton-on-S CO15 ... 189 A3
College St IP4 ... 17 C5
Coller Rd CO12 ... 90 F5
Colles Brook Rd CO7 ... 166 F4
Colletts Chase CO6 ... 80 F4
Colley Rd CM2 ... 217 A6
Collier Row CB10 ... 6 B1
Colliers The CM9 ... 210 E3
Collimer Cl IP9 ... 63 E7
Collimer Ct IP11 ... 221 C6
Collindale Gdns CO15 ... 189 C5
Collingwood Ave IP3 ... 18 B3
Collingwood Cl CM7 ... 128 C5
Collingwood Fields
CO7 ... 59 B4
Collingwood Gn
CO15 ... 188 D1
Collingwood Rd
Clacton-on-S CO15 ... 188 D1
Colchester CO3 ... 134 E6
Witham CM8 ... 177 A2
Collins Cl 10 CM7 ... 127 F2
COLLINS CROSS ... 146 B8
Collins Cross CM23 ... 119 B1
Collinson's IP2 ... 16 D5
Collins Rd CO9 ... 53 D1
Collops Villas CM6 ... 125 A4
Collyers Ct CO1 ... 136 B7
Colne Bank Ave CO3 ... 135 D8
Colne Chase CM8 ... 176 E2
Colne Com Sch & Coll The
CO7 ... 185 E8
Colne Cswy CO2 ... 136 D5
Colne Ct
Braintree CM7 ... 128 C1
Rowhedge CO5 ... 164 A8
COLNE ENGAINE ... 77 F2
Colne Engaine CE Prim
Sch CO6 ... 78 A2
Colneford Hill CO6 ... 105 D7
Colne Ho CM9 ... 210 B5
Colneis Jun Sch IP11 ... 221 F6
Colneis Rd IP11 ... 221 F6
Colne Park Rd CO6 ... 105 D7
Colne Rd
Brightlingsea CO7 ... 185 E6
Bures CO8 ... 79 E8
Clacton-on-S CO15 ... 188 F2
Coggeshall CO6 ... 131 A6
Halstead CO9 ... 77 A2
Sible Hedingham CO9 ... 75 E8
Colne Rise CO5 ... 163 F8
Colne Springs CO9 ... 29 B6
Colne Terr CO7 ... 164 B8
Colne The CO7 ... 185 E5
Colne Valley Cl CO9 ... 76 D2
Colne Valley Farm Pk★
CO9 ... 51 D5
Colne Valley Rd CB9 ... 9 A7
Colne Valley Rly★ CO9 ... 51 C5
Colne View
Colchester CO2 ... 136 D2
Point Clear B CO16 ... 186 A2
Colne View Cotts
CO5 ... 163 D3
Colne View Ret Pk
CO1 ... 110 A1
Colne Way CO16 ... 185 F4
Colne Wlk CM7 ... 128 D1
Colneys Cl CO10 ... 15 D1
Colthorpe Rd CO15 ... 188 F8
Coltsfield CM24 ... 119 E8
Coltsfoot Ct CO4 ... 109 C2
Coltsfoot Rd IP2 ... 16 E4
Colts The CM23 ... 145 E4
Columbine Gdns
Ipswich IP2 ... 16 E5
Walton-on-t-N CO14 ... 171 B7
Columbine Mews
CO3 ... 134 C7
Columbines The CO10 ... 1 E2
Colville Cl CM77 ... 154 C7
Colvin Chase CM2 ... 216 B1
Colvin Cl CO3 ... 134 F7
Colyers Reach CM2 ... 206 A2
Colyn Pl CB10 ... 22 E3
Comac Yd CO15 ... 188 E5
Comma Cl CM7 ... 127 E1
Commerce Pk CO2 ... 136 D4
Commerce Way
Colchester CO2 ... 136 D4
Lawford CO11 ... 86 C5
Commercial Rd IP1 ... 17 B4
Commodity Ctr CM8 ... 177 F4
Common Hill CB10 ... 22 D2
Common La
Duddenhoe End SG8 ... 40 B7
Little Baddow CM3 ... 207 E2
Woodham Walter CM9 ... 208 B3
Common Quay IP2 ... 17 D5
Common St CO10 ... 12 B8
Commons The CO3 ... 135 A5
Common The CM3 ... 218 E6
Compass Ct 16 CO11 ... 86 D4
Compasses Rd CM77 ... 129 F5
Compton Mews 5
CO4 ... 136 C8
Compton Rd CO4 ... 136 C8
Comyns Cl CO4 ... 110 A6
Comyns Pl CM1 ... 204 B1
Conan Doyle Cl CM7 ... 155 A8
Conder Way CO2 ... 136 D4
Conduit La CM9 ... 219 E6
Coney Acre CB11 ... 93 D8
Conford Ho IP11 ... 221 D6
Congregation Ho 5
CO9 ... 76 F2
Conies Rd CO9 ... 103 D7
Conifer Cl
Alresford CO7 ... 164 F7
Colchester CO4 ... 136 E8
Conifer Ct 7 CM23 ... 145 F8
Conifer Way CM6 ... 123 C1
Coniston Cl CM77 ... 154 D6
Coniston Rd IP3 ... 18 B2
Coniston Sq IP3 ... 18 B2
Connaught Ave CO13 ... 170 F4
Connaught Cl
Clacton-on-S CO15 ... 189 B3
Colchester CO1 ... 136 C6
Connaught Ct CO15 ... 189 B3
Connaught Gdns CM7 ... 128 B4
Connaught Gdns E
CO15 ... 189 B4
Connaught Gdns W
CO15 ... 189 B3
Connaught Ho
Clacton-on-S CO15 ... 189 B4
Frinton-on-S CO13 ... 170 F5
Connaught Mews 2
CO13 ... 170 F5
Connaught Rd
Haverhill CB9 ... 8 E7
Little Clacton CO16 ... 168 C5
Conquerors Cl CM3 ... 194 B3
Conrad Rd CM8 ... 176 F5
Constable Ave CO16 ... 188 C6
Constable Cl
Lawford CO11 ... 86 B4
West Mersea CO5 ... 201 D7
Constable Ct
Brightlingsea CO7 ... 185 F7
Colchester CO2 ... 135 B3
Constable Ho CM7 ... 127 E3
Constable Rd
Felixstowe IP11 ... 221 F4
Ipswich IP4 ... 17 D8
Sudbury CO10 ... 33 E8
Constable View CM1 ... 205 F6
Constable Way CM77 ... 155 B5
Constance Cl
Broomfield CM1 ... 191 A3
Witham CM8 ... 195 B8
Constantine Rd
Colchester CO3 ... 135 D5
Ipswich IP1 ... 17 B5
Witham CM8 ... 194 E8
Constitution Hill
Ipswich IP1 ... 17 B8
Sudbury CO10 ... 33 F8
Convalescent Hill
IP11 ... 221 E3
Convent Hill CM7 ... 128 A5
Convent La CM7 ... 128 A5
Conway Cl
Halstead CO9 ... 103 D8
Haverhill CB9 ... 8 E8
Ipswich IP2 ... 17 B2
Wivenhoe CO7 ... 164 C8
Conyer Cl CM9 ... 220 F8
Cook Cl CO12 ... 90 F1
Cook Cres CO4 ... 136 E7
Cook Pl CM2 ... 205 F3
Cooks Cl CO9 ... 103 F8
Cook's Cnr CO11 ... 88 E2
Cook's Gn CO8 ... 55 B1
COOK'S GREEN ... 169 B2
Cook's Hall Rd CO6 ... 108 C3
Cooks Hill CO4 ... 83 B6

Cook's La
Colchester CO3 . . . . 134 F7
Great Bardfield CM7 . . . . 71 E4
West Bergholt CO3 . . . . . 134 E8
Coolyne Way CO15 . . . . . . 189 B7
Coombe Lo CO6 . . . . 105 B6
Coombe Rise CM1 . . . . . . 205 B7
Cooper Ct CM9 . . . . 209 F2
Cooper Dr CM7 . . . . 127 D4
Coopers CM3 . . . . 206 E8
Coopers Ave CM9 . . . . . . 210 D5
Coopers Cl CM23 . . . . 145 B4
Coopers Cres
Great Notley CM77 . . . . . 154 C8
West Bergholt CO6 . . . . . 108 F4
COOPER'S END 41 A5
Coopers End Rd
CM24 . . . . 121 A2
Coopers End Rdbt
CM24 . . . . 121 B3
Coopers La
Clacton-on-S CO15 . . . . . 188 C3
Great Leighs CM3 . . . . . . 173 F4
Cooper's La CO7 . . . . 84 F5
Cooper's Row CM1 . . . . . 205 A5
Coopers Villas CM22 . . . 121 B2
Cooper Wlk CO4 . . . . 136 D8
COPDOCK 35 F7
Copdock Prim Sch IP8 . . 35 F8
COPFORD 133 D4
Copford CE Prim Sch
CO6 . . . . 133 D2
Copford Ct CO6 . . . . 133 D3
COPFORD GREEN 133 C2
Copingford End CO6 . . . 133 D5
Copland Cl
Broomfield CM1 . . . . 191 A1
Great Baddow CM2 . . . . . 216 F8
Copleston High Sch
IP4 . . . . 18 C5
Copleston Rd IP4 . . . . . . 18 B5
Coploe Rd CB10 . . . . 3 A2
Coploe Rise CB10 . . . . 3 A3
Copperas Rd CO7 . . . . . . 185 F5
Copper Beeches CO3 . . 134 D5
Copper Ct CM7 . . . . 127 E1
Copperfield Rd
Chelmsford CM1 . . . . 204 E7
Ipswich IP2 . . . . 16 E5
Copperfields CB11 . . . . . 43 C8
Copper Gr IP8 . . . . 36 E8
Coppice Cl CM6 . . . . 123 D1
Coppice End CO4 . . . . . . 110 B3
Coppice Rd CO7 . . . . 165 B8
Coppice The
Bishop's Stortford
CM23 . . . . 145 E5
Clacton-on-S CO15 . . . . . 188 D1
Coppins Cl CM2 . . . . 205 E4
Coppins Green Prim Sch
CO15 . . . . 188 E5
Coppins Rd CO15 . . . . . . 188 D4
Coprolite St IP3 . . . . 17 E5
Copse The
Bishop's Stortford
CM23 . . . . 146 C8
Colchester CO4 . . . . 109 F3
Felsted CM6 . . . . 152 F6
Copthall Cl CM22 . . . . . 146 F4
Copthall La CM6 . . . . 70 B3
Copt Hall La CO5 . . . . . . 182 C3
Copt Hill CM3 . . . . 218 E6
Copy Hill CB9 . . . . 8 E3
Coral Dr IP1 . . . . 16 D8
Coralin Wlk CO4 . . . . 134 C6
Cordell Cl CO10 . . . . 15 D8
Cordell Pl CO10 . . . . 15 D8
Cordell Rd CO10 . . . . 15 D8
Corder Rd IP4 . . . . 17 D8
Cordwinders CO7 . . . . . . 59 F1
Coriander Rd CO5 . . . . . . 179 C4
Corinda Ho CO13 . . . . . . 170 F7
Coriolanus Cl CO2 . . . . . 135 A3
Cormorant Wlk CM2 . . . 216 C5
Cornard Mere Nature
Trail* CO10 . . . . 34 B3
Cornard Rd CO10 . . . . . . 33 F7
CORNARD TYE 34 E7
Cornel Cl CM8 . . . . 176 D4
Cornelius Vale CM2 . . . . 206 B4
Cornells La CB11 . . . . 67 E3
Corner Pk CB10 . . . . 22 E3
Cornerth Cres CO10 . . . . 34 B6
Cornflower Cl
Colchester CO3 . . . . 134 C7
Ipswich IP2 . . . . 16 E4
Cornflower Dr CM1 . . . . 205 F6
Cornflower Rd CO15 . . . 203 G7
Cornford Way CO11 . . . . 86 B4
Cornhill
4 Chelmsford CM1 . . . 205 B2
16 Ipswich IP1 . . . . 17 C6
Corniche The CM7 . . . . . 72 B1
Cornish Ct CO10 . . . . 34 A7
CORNISH HALL END 48 C5
Cornish Hall End Rd
Stambourne CO9 . . . . 28 A1
Steeple Bumpstead CM7,
CO9 . . . . 48 E8
Corn Mill Ct CB11 . . . . . . 43 E8
Cornwall Cres CM1 . . . . 205 A7
Cornwall Gdns CM7 . . . 128 B4
Cornwall Ho CM23 . . . . . 145 E4

Cornwallis Dr CO6 . . . . . 132 F3
Cornwallis Pl CB10 . . . . . 22 E3
Cornwallis Rd CB9 . . . . . . 8 F6
Cornwallis Terr IP4 . . . . . 17 F6
Cornwall Rd IP11 . . . . . . 221 D5
Coronation Ave
Braintree CM7 . . . . 127 F2
Colchester CO2 . . . . 136 A5
Coronation Dr IP11 . . . . 221 C3
Coronation Rd
Bishop's Stortford
CM23 . . . . 145 E5
Clacton-on-S CO15 . . . . . 188 C3
Ipswich IP4 . . . . 18 B5
Coronation Villas
CO16 . . . . 141 F7
Coronation Way
CM77 . . . . 155 D6
Corporal Lillie Cl CO10 . . 33 E6
Corporation Ave IP2 . . . . 37 A8
Corporation Rd CM1 . . . 205 A4
Corriander Dr CM22 . . . . 94 D2
Corry Ct **7** CO4 . . . . 136 D8
Corsellis Ho CO7 . . . . 137 B1
Cortoncroft Cl CO13 . . . 170 F7
Corton Rd IP3 . . . . 18 B1
Cotman Ave CO11 . . . . . . 86 B4
Cotman Lo CM1 . . . . 205 F6
Cotman Rd
Clacton-on-S CO16 . . . . . 188 D6
Colchester CO3 . . . . 135 A5
Ipswich IP3 . . . . 18 A1
Cotswold Cres CM1 . . . . 204 D6
Cotswold Ct
Clacton-on-S CO15 . . . . . 189 A3
Colchester CO4 . . . . 110 C4
Cotswold Dr CO10 . . . . . . 15 C6
Cotswold Rd CO15 . . . . . 188 F5
Cottage Dr CO2 . . . . 136 D3
Cottage Gn CO16 . . . . . . 188 C6
Cottage Gr CO16 . . . . . . 188 C6
Cottage Pl
Chelmsford CM1 . . . . 205 B3
3 Ipswich IP1 . . . . 17 B6
Cottage Wlk CO16 . . . . . 188 C6
Cottey Ho CM2 . . . . 216 B2
Cottingham Rd IP8 . . . . . 16 B1
Cottonwood Cl CO2 . . . . 135 D1
Coulsdon Cl CO16 . . . . . . 188 C6
Council Bglws CM7 . . . . 127 F7
Council Cotts
Great Holland CO13 . . . . 169 F3
Helions Bumpstead CB9 . . . 8 E1
Council Hos
Bicknacre CM3 . . . . 218 F1
Finchingfield CM7 . . . . . . 72 C6
Great Bromley CO7 . . . . . 139 A6
Hadstock CB1 . . . . 5 B6
Holbrook IP9 . . . . 62 D6
Peldon CO5 . . . . 182 E5
Shudy Camps CB21 . . . . . . 7 B6
Thorington Street CO6 . . . 57 B3
Thorpe-le-S CO16 . . . . . . 141 E2
Tolleshunt Major CM9 . . . 197 D3
Wakes Colne CO6 . . . . 79 C1
Wix CO11 . . . . 115 B5
Wrabness CO11 . . . . 88 F2
Council Houses
Cressing CM77 . . . . 156 A4
Great Bentley CO7 . . . . . 166 F5
COUNTESS CROSS 78 D3
Counting House La
CM6 . . . . 123 D1
County Pl CM2 . . . . 205 B1
Coupals Cl CB9 . . . . 9 C6
Coupals Com Prim Sch
CB9 . . . . 9 D7
Coupals Ct CB9 . . . . 9 C6
Coupals Rd CB9 . . . . 9 C6
Courtauld Cl CO9 . . . . . . 76 F1
Courtauld Homes of Rest
CO9 . . . . 76 E3
Courtauld Mews **1**
CM7 . . . . 127 F2
Courtauld Rd CM7 . . . . . 128 A4
Court Cl CM23 . . . . 145 E5
Court Eight CM8 . . . . 176 F5
Court Eighteen CM8 . . . . 176 F5
Court Eleven CM8 . . . . . . 176 F5
Courtenay Cl CO10 . . . . . 15 D2
Court Farm CO11 . . . . 61 A1
Court Fifteen CM8 . . . . . 176 F5
Court Five CM8 . . . . 176 F5
Court Four CM8 . . . . 176 F5
Court Fourteen CM8 . . . . 176 F5
Court Ind Est CM2 . . . . . 205 C2
Courtland Mews CM9 . . . 220 F8
Courtland Pl CM9 . . . . . . 220 F8
Courtlands
Chelmsford CM1 . . . . 205 A6
Halstead CO9 . . . . 103 D8
Tollesbury CM9 . . . . 199 E1
Walton-on-t-N CO14 . . . . 171 F1
Court Nine CM8 . . . . 176 F5
Court Nineteen CM8 . . . . 176 F5
Court One CM8 . . . . 176 F5
Court Rd CM1 . . . . 191 B3
Court Seven CM8 . . . . . . 176 F5
Court Seventeen CM8 . . . 176 F5
Court Six CM8 . . . . 176 F5
Court Sixteen CM8 . . . . . 176 F5
Court St CO6 . . . . 56 A1
Courts The IP11 . . . . 221 E6
Court Ten CM8 . . . . 176 F5
Court The CO7 . . . . 59 B2
Court Thirteen CM8 . . . . 176 F5
Court Three CM8 . . . . . . 176 F5
Court Twelve CM8 . . . . . 176 F5
Court Twenty CM8 . . . . . 176 F5
Court Two CM8 . . . . 176 F5

Courtyard Offices
CM8 . . . . 178 B3
Courtyard The
Braintree CM7 . . . . 128 A4
Ipswich IP1 . . . . 17 B7
Maldon CM9 . . . . 209 F2
Coval Ave CM1 . . . . 205 A3
Coval La CM1 . . . . 205 A2
Coval Wells CM1 . . . . . . 205 A2
Covehite Ct **3** CB9 . . . . . 8 E5
Coventry Cl CO1 . . . . 136 A8
Coverdale CM8 . . . . 176 E4
Coverts The
West Mersea CO5 . . . . . . 201 D6
Writtle CM1 . . . . 204 B1
Cowdray Ave CO1 . . . . . . 109 F1
Cowdray Cres CO1 . . . . . 135 F7
Cowdray Ctr The CO1 . . . 110 A1
Cowdrie Way CM2 . . . . . 206 B4
Cowell Ave CM1 . . . . 204 E5
Cowell St IP2 . . . . 17 C3
Cowels Farm La CM6 . . . . 97 E5
Cow La
Great Chesterford CB10 . . . 4 A5
Point Clear B CO16 . . . . . 186 C3
Cowley Rd IP11 . . . . 221 C6
Cowpar Mews CM7 . . . . 155 A8
Cowper St IP4 . . . . 18 B6
Cowslip Cl IP2 . . . . 16 E4
Cowslip Ct CO3 . . . . 134 C7
Coxhall Rd IP9 . . . . 36 E1
Cox La IP4 . . . . 17 D5
Cox Rd CO7 . . . . 165 B8
Coxs Cl CB9 . . . . 8 D7
Cox's Ct CO12 . . . . 91 E5
Cox's Gdns CM23 . . . . . . 145 E5
Cox's Hill CO11 . . . . 86 B4
Coytes Gdns **2** IP1 . . . . 17 C5
Crabbe St IP4 . . . . 18 A6
Crabbs Gn CM22 . . . . . . 148 C1
Crabb's Hill CM3 . . . . . . 193 F2
Crabs Croft CM7 . . . . . . 128 D1
Crabtree CO3 . . . . 170 C8
Crabtree Hill CB11 . . . . . 67 C3
Crabtree La CO6 . . . . 81 C1
Crabtrees CB11 . . . . 43 E8
Cracknell Ct CM7 . . . . . . 137 B2
Crafton Gn CM24 . . . . . . 119 E7
Craig Ct CO2 . . . . 135 B3
Craigfield Ave CO15 . . . 189 A6
Craig Ho CM7 . . . . 128 A3
CRAIG'S END 49 D8
Craig's Hill CO8 . . . . 79 E6
Craigs La CO8 . . . . 79 E6
Craiston Mews CM2 . . . . 216 F5
Craiston Way CM2 . . . . . 216 F5
Cramphorn Wlk CM1 . . . 204 E4
Cramswell Cl CB9 . . . . 8 E6
Cranberry Sq IP3 . . . . . . 38 C7
Cranborne Cl CO4 . . . . . 109 F2
Cranbrook La CO10 . . . . . . 2 F1
Crane Ave CO3 . . . . 134 B4
Crane Hill IP2 . . . . 16 E4
Crane's La CO5 . . . . 157 F1
Cranford Cl CO13 . . . . . . 170 E5
Cranham Hall Cvn Pk
CM3 . . . . 191 F6
Cranham Rd CM6 . . . . 95 F3
Cranleigh Cl CO16 . . . . . 188 B6
Cranmer Ct CO1 . . . . 136 A7
Cranmer Ho CM2 . . . . . . 215 F7
Cranmer's La CO6 . . . . . 131 E6
Cranmore Ct CM22 . . . . . 94 C2
Cranmoregreen La
CO10 . . . . 2 F3
Cranwell Cres IP3 . . . . . . 18 C1
Cranwell Gdns CM23 . . . 119 C1
Craven Dr CO4 . . . . 110 C3
CRAWLEY END 19 D4
Crawley End SG8 . . . . 19 D4
Crayfields CM6 . . . . 123 E1
Crayford Cl CM9 . . . . 220 E8
Crayford Rd CO10 . . . . . . 15 D2
Creance Ct CM2 . . . . 205 A2
Creasen Butt Cl CM9 . . . 210 A4
Credon Cl CO15 . . . . 188 F7
Credon Dr CO15 . . . . 188 F7
Creek Cotts CO14 . . . . . . 144 E4
Creekhurst Cl CO7 . . . . . 186 A6
Creek View CO5 . . . . 181 F2
Creffield Rd CO3 . . . . . . 135 D6
Crepping Hall Dr IP9 . . . . 61 F1
Crescent Ct CM9 . . . . . . 209 F5
Crescent Rd
Bishop's Stortford
CM23 . . . . 146 A6
Felixstowe IP11 . . . . 221 C6
Great Baddow CM2 . . . . . 217 A7
Heybridge CM9 . . . . 209 F5
Ipswich IP1 . . . . 17 B6
Crescent The
Clacton-on-S CO15 . . . . . 189 B7
Colchester CO4 . . . . 110 C7
Frinton-on-S CO13 . . . . . 170 F4
Gestingthorpe CO9 . . . . . 31 F2
Great Holland CO13 . . . . 170 A4
Great Horkesley CO6 . . . . 82 B1
Great Leighs CM3 . . . . . . 173 E5
Marks Tey CO6 . . . . 133 A3
Steeple Bumpstead CB9 . . 27 B7
Thorpe-le-S CO16 . . . . . . 141 F2
West Bergholt CO6 . . . . . 108 D5
Cressages Cl CM6 . . . . . 152 F6
Cress Croft CM7 . . . . 128 D1
CRESSING 156 A6

Cressing Prim Sch
CM77 . . . . 155 E6
Cressing Rd
Braintree CM7 . . . . 128 C2
Witham CM8 . . . . 176 D6
Cressing Sta CM77 . . . . . 155 D5
Cressing Temple Barns*
CM77 . . . . 155 B2
Crestlands CO7 . . . . 165 B7
Cricketers Cl
Broomfield CM1 . . . . 191 C1
Sudbury CO10 . . . . 33 E6
Cricketfield La CM23 . . . 145 E8
Cricket Hill Rd IP11 . . . . 221 B5
CRIPPLE CORNER 54 B2
Crispin Cl CB9 . . . . 8 D7
Critchett Terr **5** CM1 . . . 205 A3
Crittal Ct CM7 . . . . 127 D4
Crittall Cl CM8 . . . . 156 E4
Crittall Ct CM8 . . . . 177 A3
Crittall Dr CM7 . . . . 127 D4
Crittall Rd CM8 . . . . 177 B3
CRIX GREEN 153 D6
Crix Green Villas
CM6 . . . . 153 D6
Croasdaile Rd CM24 . . . . 119 E8
Croasdale Cl CM24 . . . . . 119 E8
Crocklands CO9 . . . . 104 A5
CROCKLEFORD HEATH
. . . . 111 C2
Crocus Cl
Clacton-on-S CO16 . . . . . 188 C4
Ipswich IP2 . . . . 16 F4
Crocus Fields CB10 . . . . . 22 E3
Crocus Way CM1 . . . . . . 205 E7
Croft Cl CM7 . . . . 128 A3
Croft Ct
Chelmsford CM1 . . . . 205 E8
20 Sudbury CO10 . . . . . . 33 E7
Crofters Wlk CM77 . . . . . 154 D8
Croft Ho **4** CO9 . . . . 76 F2
Croft La CB9 . . . . 9 B6
Crofton Cl CM2 . . . . 18 B7
Crofton Ho **6** CO10 . . . . 33 E8
Crofton Rd IP4 . . . . 18 B7
Croft Rd
Clacton-on-S CO15 . . . . . 188 D4
Kelvedon CO5 . . . . 158 B2
Sudbury CO10 . . . . 33 E8
Croftside CO8 . . . . 55 F1
Croft St IP2 . . . . 17 C3
Croft The
Bures CO8 . . . . 55 F1
Earls Colne CO6 . . . . 105 A6
Elsenham CM22 . . . . 94 C1
Glemsford CO10 . . . . 2 C4
Great Yeldham CO9 . . . . . 30 A2
Croft Villas CO10 . . . . 2 C3
Croft Way CM8 . . . . 177 A3
Cromarty Rd IP4 . . . . 18 B8
Cromar Way CM1 . . . . . . 204 F1
Crome Cl CO3 . . . . 135 A5
Crome Rd CO16 . . . . 188 D5
Cromer Mews CO4 . . . . . 109 E3
Cromer Rd IP1 . . . . 16 F8
Crompton Ho CM1 . . . . . 215 F8
Crompton Rd IP2 . . . . 16 F7
Crompton St CM1 . . . . . . 204 F1
Cromwell Cl
Bishop's Stortford
CM23 . . . . 145 B7
Boreham CM3 . . . . 206 D8
Cromwell Ct
11 Ipswich IP1 . . . . 17 C5
Maldon CM9 . . . . 210 A3
Cromwell Ctr CM8 . . . . . 177 B2
Cromwell Hill CM9 . . . . . 209 F3
Cromwell Ho CO4 . . . . . . 109 F4
Cromwell La CM9 . . . . . . 209 F3
Cromwell Pk CM6 . . . . . . 152 B5
Cromwell Rd
16 Colchester CO2 . . . . 135 F6
Little Dunmow CM6 . . . . 151 E6
Saffron Walden CB11 . . . . 43 E7
Cromwell Sq **8** IP1 . . . . 17 C5
Cromwell Way CM8 . . . . 176 F2
Croquet Gdns CO7 . . . . . 137 C1
Cross Cotts CO4 . . . . 83 B6
CROSS END 78 C4
Crossfield Rd CO15 . . . . . 188 E3
Crossfields
Halstead CO9 . . . . 103 F8
Stoke-by-N CO6 . . . . 56 C5
Crossfield Way CO3 . . . . 170 B6
Cross Field Way CO4 . . . . 83 B5
Crossgate Field IP11 . . . 221 C5
Cross Hill CO12 . . . . 116 D1
Cross La CO5 . . . . 201 F7
Crossley Ave CO15 . . . . . 203 E7
Crossley View CO15 . . . . 189 B3
Cross Rd
Maldon CM9 . . . . 210 A1
Witham CM8 . . . . 176 F5
Crossroads CO9 . . . . 31 E2
Cross St
Felixstowe IP11 . . . . 221 C6
Saffron Walden CB10 . . . . 22 D1
Sudbury CO10 . . . . 33 D7
Cross The
West Mersea CO5 . . . . . . 201 E7
Wivenhoe CO7 . . . . 137 D2
Crosstree Wlk CO2 . . . . . 136 A3
Cross Way CO5 . . . . 201 E7
Crossways
Chelmsford CM2 . . . . 216 C7
Clacton-on-S CO15 . . . . . 203 G8
Colne Engaine CO6 . . . . . 77 F1
Crotchets Cl IP9 . . . . 35 A1

Crouch Ct CM7 . . . . 128 D1
Crouch Dr CM8 . . . . 176 E2
CROUCH GREEN 51 C4
Crouchman's Farm Rd
CM9 . . . . 208 B3
Crouch St CO3 . . . . 135 E6
Croutel Rd IP11 . . . . 221 F5
Crowe Hall La IP9 . . . . . . 62 A1
Crowhall La CO11 . . . . . . 87 E1
Crowhurst Rd CO3 . . . . . 135 E7
Crowhurst Ct CO3 . . . . . . 135 E7
Crow La CO16 . . . . 141 A3
Crowland Cl **7** IP2 . . . . . 17 A2
Crowland Rd CB9 . . . . 8 F8
Crown Bays Rd CO4 . . . . 136 C8
Crownfield Rd CO10 . . . . . 2 B6
Crownfields CO7 . . . . 84 F6
Crown Gate CO4 . . . . 110 C6
Crown Hill CB10 . . . . 6 B1
Crown La
Harwich CO12 . . . . 91 D4
Tendring CO16 . . . . 140 D3
Crown La N CO7 . . . . 110 F7
Crown La S CO7 . . . . 111 A7
Crown Mdw CM7 . . . . . . 128 D4
Crown Rd CO15 . . . . 188 C1
Crown St
Castle Hedingham CO9 . . . 51 E4
Dedham CO7 . . . . 84 F6
Felixstowe IP11 . . . . 221 C6
Great Bardfield CM7 . . . . 72 B2
Ipswich IP1 . . . . 17 C6
Crown Terr CM23 . . . . . . 146 A7
Crow Pond Cotts
CM3 . . . . 175 C3
Crow Pond Rd CM3 . . . . 175 C3
CROW'S GREEN 125 E8
Crow St CM22 . . . . 94 F5
Croxall Ct CM8 . . . . 176 F2
Crozier Ave CM23 . . . . . 145 C8
Crozier Mews IP4 . . . . . . 18 B6
Crozier Terr CM2 . . . . . . 206 B4
Cruce Way CO16 . . . . 185 F3
Crummock Cl CM77 . . . . 154 C6
Crunch Croft CB9 . . . . 9 E5
Crusader Way CM7 . . . . 128 D2
Crushton Pl CM1 . . . . . . 204 F6
Cuckfield Ave IP3 . . . . . . 18 E3
Cuckoo Farm Bsns Pk
CO4 . . . . 110 A7
Cuckoo Hill
Bures CO8 . . . . 55 F1
Sible Hedingham CO9 . . . . 75 B8
Cuckoos La
Great Canfield CM6 . . . . 149 A3
Takeley CM6 . . . . 148 F2
Cuckoo Way CM77 . . . . . 154 C7
Cudmore Grove Ctry Pk*
CO5 . . . . 185 A1
Culford Pl IP3 . . . . 17 F4
Culford Wlk IP11 . . . . . . 221 A3
Cullingham Rd IP1 . . . . . 17 A5
Culver St E CO1 . . . . 135 F7
Culver St W CO1 . . . . 135 F7
Culvert Cl CO6 . . . . 130 F1
Culver Wlk **21** CO1 . . . . 135 F7
Cumberland Ave CO9 . . . 209 C1
Cumberland Cl CM7 . . . . 128 B4
Cumberland Cres
CM1 . . . . 205 A7
Cumberland Ct
Clacton-on-S CO15 . . . . . 189 B5
Colchester CO3 . . . . 135 D6
Cumberland St IP1 . . . . . 17 B7
Cumberland Twrs **9**
IP1 . . . . 17 A4
Cunningham Cl CO2 . . . . 136 A4
Cunnington Rd CM7 . . . . 128 C3
Cunobelin Way CO2 . . . . 135 A2
Cuppers Cl CM8 . . . . 176 E1
Curds Rd CO6 . . . . 105 A4
Curlew Cl
Clacton-on-S CO15 . . . . . 188 F6
Heybridge CM9 . . . . 210 C5
Kelvedon CO5 . . . . 158 D2
Curlew Croft CO4 . . . . . . 136 F8
Curlew Rd IP2 . . . . 16 D4
CURLING TYE GREEN
. . . . 209 A3
Curling Tye La
Maldon CM9 . . . . 209 A3
Woodham Walter CM9 . . 208 F3
Currants Farm Rd
CM7 . . . . 127 E5
Currents La CO12 . . . . . . 91 E6
Curriers' La IP1 . . . . 17 C5
Curtis Cl
Clacton-on-S CO16 . . . . . 188 B3
Ipswich IP8 . . . . 16 C1
Curzon Rd CO10 . . . . 34 B8
Curzon Way CM2 . . . . . . 206 A2
Cusak Rd CM2 . . . . 205 F3
Custerson Ct CB11 . . . . . 22 D1
Custerson Dr CM77 . . . . 155 B5
Custom House La
CO12 . . . . 91 D6
Cut-A-Thwart La
CM9 . . . . 209 C4
Cut Hedge CM77 . . . . . . 154 C6
Cuthedge La CO6 . . . . . . 157 D2
Cutlers Cl CM23 . . . . 145 C5
CUTLERS GREEN 69 D2
Cutlers La CO7 . . . . 59 D5
Cutler St IP1 . . . . 17 C5
Cutmore Pl CM2 . . . . 215 F8
Cuton Gr CM2 . . . . 206 B5
Cuton Hall La CM2 . . . . . 206 A5
Cut The CO5 . . . . 179 C5

Cut Throat La CM8 .... 177 A4
Cutting Dr CO9 .... 76 E1
Cygnet Ct
  [11] Bishop's Stortford
  CM23 .... 145 F6
  Sible Hedingham CO9 ..... 51 E1
Cygnet Wlk CO3 .... 134 C4
Cymbeline Way
  (Colchester By Pass)
  CO3 .... 135 B8
Cypress Ct CO15 .... 188 E7
Cypress Ct CM6 .... 123 B1
Cypress Dr CM2 .... 216 C6
Cypress Gr [5] CO4 ...... 136 F8
Cypress Mews CO5 ..... 201 B7
Cypress Rd CM8 .... 177 A4
Cyril Child Cl CO4 ...... 136 C2
Cyril Dowsett Ct CM9 ... 209 E2

D

Daen Ingas CM3 .... 218 D7
Daffodil Cl IP2 .... 16 E3
Daffodil Way CM1 ...... 205 E7
Dagnets La CM77 .... 154 D3
Dahlia Cl
  [2] Chelmsford CM1 ..... 205 F5
  Clacton-on-S CO16 ..... 188 C4
Dahlia Wlk CO4 .... 136 D7
Daimler Ave CO15 ...... 203 D6
Dains Pl IP11 .... 221 A7
DAIRY FARM MEADOW
  .... 186 C3
Dairyhouse La CO11 .... 114 C5
Dairy Rd CM2 .... 205 F4
Daisleys La CM3 .... 174 A2
Daisy Ct CM1 .... 206 A6
Daisy Green Rd CO3 .... 133 E8
Daisyley Rd CM6 ...... 98 B4
Dale Cl
  Colchester CO3 .... 134 B7
  Elmstead Market CO7 .... 138 A6
Dale Ct CO12 .... 91 A4
Dale Hall La IP1 .... 17 C8
Dale Ho CM7 .... 127 E4
Dales The CO12 .... 90 F1
Dales View IP8 .... 35 E8
Dales View Rd [1] IP1 ... 17 A8
Dale The CO7 .... 164 C4
Daleview Ave CO11 .... 115 C5
Dalham Pl [4] CB9 ..... 9 A8
Dalhams CO10 .... 1 C1
Dallwood Way CM7 .... 128 B3
Dalrymple Cl CM1 ..... 205 D3
Daltes La CO16 .... 187 C3
Dalton Gdns CM23 .... 145 E4
Dalton Rd IP1 .... 17 B6
Damant's Farm La
  CO16 .... 142 D1
Damases La CM3 ...... 193 C1
Damask Mews [9]
  CM7 .... 128 A2
Damask Rd CO3 .... 134 C7
Dame Elizabeth Ct
  CM1 .... 190 F3
Dame Johane Bradbury's
  Sch CB10 .... 22 F2
Dammant Ct [8] CO4 .... 136 D6
Dampier Ct CO6 .... 130 F3
Damselfly Rd IP3 ..... 38 C8
DANBURY 218 D7
Danbury Cl CO6 .... 132 F3
Danbury Ctry Pk*
  CM3 .... 218 B7
Danbury Park Com Prim
  Sch CM3 .... 218 C7
Danbury Vale CM3 .... 219 A6
Dancing Dicks La
  CM8 .... 176 A2
Dandalan Cl IP1 ...... 16 E8
Dane Acres CM23 ..... 145 D8
Dane Ho CM23 .... 145 D8
Dane O'Coys Rd CM23 .. 118 E1
Dane Pk CM23 .... 145 D8
Dane Rd CM1 .... 204 D4
Danes Ct CO10 ...... 34 B4
Dane St CM23 .... 146 A7
Daneum Holt CO10 ... 12 A6
Daniel Cole Rd CO2 ... 135 F4
Daniell Cl CO16 ..... 188 C6
Daniell Dr CO2 ...... 135 B2
Daniells Ho CO6 ..... 108 F4
Daniel Way CM1 ..... 156 E4
Dansie Ct [7] CO4 .... 136 C8
Daphne Cl CM77 ..... 154 C7
Daphne Ct [4] CO4 .... 136 D8
Dapifer Cl CO2 ...... 135 F4
Dapifer Dr CM7 ...... 128 C3
D'arcy Ave CM9 ...... 210 B1
D'arcy Ct CO13 ...... 170 F6
D'Arcy Ct CM9 .... 209 F2
D'Arcy Ho CO14 ...... 144 D2
D'arcy Hts CO2 ...... 136 C3
D'arcy Rd
  Colchester CO2 ...... 136 C3
  St Osyth CO16 ...... 187 B5
  Tiptree CO5 .... 179 F2
Darcy Rise CM3 ..... 207 E1
D'arcy Way
  Brightlingsea CO7 ... 185 E7
  Tolleshunt D'arcy CM9 .. 198 E4
Darina Cl CO3 ...... 134 B7
Darkhouse La CO5 .... 164 A8
Darnay Rise CM1 .... 204 D4
Darnel Way CO3 ..... 134 B7
Darnet Rd CM9 ..... 199 E4
Darrell Cl CM1 ..... 205 B6

Darrell Rd IP11 .... 221 B1
Darsham Cl IP11 ...... 221 B4
Dart Cl CM8 .... 176 D2
Darter Cl IP3 .... 38 C8
Dartmouth Rd CM1 .... 205 E6
Darwin Cl
  [5] Braintree CM7 .... 127 F1
  Colchester CO3 ...... 136 B1
Darwin Rd IP4 ...... 17 F5
Dashwood Cl IP8 .... 16 D1
Datchet Ho CO3 ..... 134 F7
Daundy Cl IP2 ...... 16 D5
Davall Cl CO12 ..... 90 C1
Davey Cl
  Colchester CO1 ..... 136 D6
  Ipswich IP3 .... 17 F1
Davidson Cl CO10 ... 34 D4
David Wright Cl CM6 .. 150 E7
Davies Cl CM7 ...... 128 A4
Davies Way CM6 .... 151 E6
Davy Rd CO15 ...... 189 C8
Dawes La CO5 ...... 201 E8
Dawlish Rd CO15 .... 203 J8
Dawn Ave IP3 ...... 17 F3
Dawnbrook Cl [1] IP2 .. 16 E1
Dawnford Cl CO3 .... 134 C7
Dawnford Ct CO3 .... 134 C7
Dawn Ho CM2 ..... 205 C1
Daws Cross CO8 .... 78 F6
Daw's Hall (Wildfowl
  Farm)* CO8 .... 55 B6
Dawson Cl CB10 .... 22 F2
Dawson Dr IP11 .... 221 A8
Dawson Way CM8 ... 194 F7
Daw St
  Birdbrook CO9 ..... 28 B7
  Finchingfield CM7 ... 72 E4
Days Cl CM1 .... 205 B8
Dazeley's La CO7 ... 85 F8
Dead La
  Ardleigh CO7 ..... 111 C8
  Great Bentley CO7 .. 166 F2
  Lawford CO11 ..... 86 C2
  Little Clacton CO16 .. 168 B2
Deadman's La CM2 .. 216 C4
Deal Cl
  Braintree CM7 ..... 127 E6
  Clacton-on-S CO15 ... 203 J8
Deal Way CO7 ...... 185 E8
Deanery Gdns CM7 .. 127 F7
Deanery Hill CM7 ... 127 E7
Deane's Cl CO12 ... 91 A2
Deanes Ct CO12 ... 91 A2
Deane's La CO12 ... 90 E1
Deanhill Ave CO15 .. 189 C5
Dean Rd CB21 ..... 6 B1
Dean Rogers Pl CM7 .. 127 F7
Dean St CO7 ...... 185 E7
Deans Wlk CM7 .... 127 F8
Dean Way CM1 .... 204 D1
DEBDEN 68 B7
Debden CE Prim Sch
  CB11 .... 68 B7
Debden Dr CB10 ... 44 E2
DEBDEN GREEN ... 68 F5
Debden Rd
  Newport CB11 .... 67 C8
  Saffron Walden CB11 .. 43 D8
  Saffron Walden CB11 .. 43 E6
Deben Cl CM8 .... 176 E2
Deben Cl CM7 .... 128 D1
Deben Dr CO10 ... 34 A8
Deben Rd
  Colchester CO4 ... 110 C1
  Haverhill CB9 ..... 9 B8
Deben Way IP11 ... 221 C3
Deben Wlk CO16 ... 188 C6
De Bohun Ct CB10 .. 22 E2
De Burgh Rd CO3 .. 134 E6
DEDHAM 84 F7
Dedham Ave CO16 .. 188 B5
Dedham CE Prim Sch
  CO7 .... 85 A6
Dedham Ct CO2 ... 136 B4
Dedham Hall Bsns Ctr
  CO7 .... 84 F7
DEDHAM HEATH ... 84 F4
Dedham Meade CO7 .. 84 F3
Dedham Pl [7] 1P4 .. 17 D5
Dedham Rd
  Ardleigh CO7 ..... 84 D1
  Boxted CO4 ...... 83 B6
  Langham CO4 ..... 84 A7
  Lawford CO11 .... 85 E4
  Stratford St M CO7 .. 58 L1
Deepdale Rd CO12 .. 91 A4
Deeping Wlk CO16 .. 187 B5
Deerhurst Chase CM3 .. 218 F1
Deerleap Way CM7 .. 128 D4
Deer Park Cl CO9 .. 51 F3
DEER'S GREEN 65 A4
Defoe Cres CO4 ... 109 E4
Deford Rd CM8 .... 194 D8
De Greys Cl CO10 .. 34 C5
Delamere Rd
  Chelmsford CM1 ... 204 E1
  Colchester CO3 .... 110 D3
Delius Wlk CO4 ... 136 E6
Dell La
  Bishop's Stortford, Hockerill
  CM23 .... 146 A7
  Little Hallingbury CM22 .. 146 B1
Dellows La CM22 ... 94 A2
Dells The [11] CM23 .. 145 F7
Dell The
  Colchester CO1 ... 136 A6
  Great Baddow CM2 .. 216 D6
  Great Cornard CO10 .. 34 A6

Dell The continued
  Great Dunmow CM6 .. 123 E1
Dellwood Ave IP11 ... 221 F5
DELVIN END 50 F3
Delvyn's La CO9 ... 52 C6
De Mandeville Rd
  CM22 .... 94 C2
De-Marci Ct CM7 .. 128 C3
Demoiselle Cres IP3 .. 38 C8
Dene Ct CM1 ..... 204 D5
Dengie Cl CM8 .... 194 F8
Denham Cl CO7 ... 164 C8
Denham Gdns IP9 .. 62 D6
Denholm Ct CM8 ... 194 F8
Denmark Bank CO6 .. 132 E3
Denmark Ho CM2 .. 216 D8
Denny Ct CM23 ... 119 B2
Denton Cl IP2 .... 16 D2
Denton's Terr CO7 .. 164 B8
Derby Cl IP4 ..... 18 A5
Derby Rd IP3 .... 18 A4
Derby Road Sta IP3 .. 18 A4
Dereham Ave IP3 .. 17 F3
Dereham Cl CO2 .. 135 C3
Derwent Gdns CO15 .. 189 C6
Derwent Rd
  Colchester CO4 ... 110 C4
  Ipswich IP3 ...... 17 F3
Derwent Way
  Chelmsford CM1 ... 204 D4
  Great Notley CM77 .. 154 C7
Desborough Path
  CM2 .... 205 F8
De Staunton Cl CO7 .. 165 B7
Devereaux Cl CO14 .. 170 F4
Devereaux Ct [1] IP4 .. 17 D6
Devereux Pl CO4 .. 109 C3
De Vere Ave CO9 .. 210 B1
De Vere Cl
  Hatfield Peverel CM3 .. 194 B3
  Wivenhoe CO7 ... 164 B8
De Vere Est CO7 .. 166 D8
De Vere La CO7 ... 164 B8
De Vere Prim Sch CO9 .. 51 E4
De Vere Rd
  Colchester CO3 ... 135 A5
  Earls Colne CO6 ... 104 F7
De Veres Rd [7] CO9 .. 76 D1
Devereux Ct CO15 .. 188 F3
Devereux Pl CO4 .. 109 C3
De Vere Way CO12 .. 90 F2
Deverill Cl CM1 .... 191 B2
De Vigier Ave CB10 .. 23 A2
Devlin Rd IP8 .... 16 B1
Devoils La [9] CM23 .. 145 F7
Devon Rd
  Colchester CO2 ... 135 B3
  Felixstowe IP11 .... 221 D5
Devonshire Gdns
  CM7 .... 128 B4
Devonshire Rd IP3 .. 17 F5
Devon Way
  Harwich CO12 .... 90 D2
  Holland-on-S CO15 .. 189 E7
Dewberry Cl [3] CO4 .. 136 D7
DEWES GREEN 64 F1
Dewes Green Rd
  Berden CM23 .... 92 A8
  Clavering CM23 ... 64 F1
Dewlands CM77 .... 155 B6
Deynes Rd CB11 ... 68 B7
Dhobi Pl IP1 ..... 17 F6
Dial Cnr CO7 ..... 166 E3
Dial La IP1 ...... 17 C6
Dial Rd CO7 ...... 166 E3
Diana Ho CO13 .... 170 E5
Diana Way CO15 ... 188 C2
Dickens Cl CM7 ... 155 A8
Dickenson Rd CO4 .. 109 E3
Dickens Pl CM1 ... 204 D7
Dickens Rd IP2 .... 16 D7
Dickett's Hill CO9 .. 51 B6
Dicksons Cnr CO7 .. 16 C7
Dicky Moors CM3 .. 190 F7
Didsbury Cl IP2 .... 16 D2
Digby Mews CO5 .. 201 C6
Digby Rd IP4 ..... 18 C7
Dilbridge Rd E CO4 .. 136 C8
Dilbridge Rd W CO4 .. 136 C8
Dillestone Ct CB9 .. 9 E5
Dillwyn St W IP1 ... 17 A6
Dillwyn St IP1 .... 17 A6
Dilston CM3 ...... 219 A6
Dimsdale Cres CM3 .. 146 B6
Dinants Cres CO6 .. 132 E3
Dingle The CO5 ... 164 B6
Dinsdale Cl [1] CO4 .. 136 C8
Dinsdale Ct IP11 ... 221 D3
Dismals The CM3 .. 175 B2
Distillery La CO2 .. 136 C4
Ditchingham Gr IP5 .. 18 F6
Ditton Way IP4 ... 18 B8
Dixon Ave
  Chelmsford CM1 ... 204 F4
  Clacton-on-S CO16 .. 188 C6
Dixon Cl CO11 .... 86 B4
Dixon Way CO7 ... 137 A2
Dobbies La CO6 ... 132 F3
Docker Ct CO2 .... 136 B4
Dockfield La CO7 .. 165 A2
Dock La CO12 .... 117 A4
Dock Rd IP11 .... 221 B2
Dock St IP2 ..... 17 C4
Dockwra La CM3 .. 219 A7
Doctor's La CO10 .. 11 D2
Docwra Rd CO5 ... 158 C2
Doddenhill Cl CB10 .. 22 E3
Dodmans [7] IP9 ... 35 A1

Doe's Cnr
  Halstead CO9 ..... 76 D5
  Hatfield Peverel CM9 .. 194 F1
Dog Chase CM7 ... 73 C3
Dogden La CM23 ... 92 E2
Doggetts La CO6 ... 132 F2
Doghouse Rd CM7 .. 129 F4
Dogs Head St [4] IP4 .. 17 C5
Dogwood Cl IP3 ... 18 D2
Dolby Rise CM2 ... 205 F2
Dolphin Ct CO13 .. 171 B6
Dolphin Way CM3 .. 146 A8
Dombey Cl CM1 ... 204 F7
Dombey Rd IP3 ... 16 F5
Domitian Cl CO4 .. 110 B6
Domsey Bank CO6 .. 132 E3
Domsey Chase CO6 .. 159 C8
Domsey La CM3 ... 191 F5
Doms La CM3 ..... 175 B2
Donald Way CM2 ... 216 C7
Donard Dr CO6 ... 108 D4
Don Ct CM8 ...... 176 D2
Donkey La CO7 ... 58 F1
Donne Dr CO15 ... 203 G8
Donyland Way CO5 .. 163 F8
Dooley Rd
  Felixstowe IP11 .... 221 A3
  Halstead CO9 ..... 76 D1
Dorchester End CO2 .. 136 B3
Dorchester Rd IP3 .. 18 D3
Dordell Ct CO9 ... 50 B8
Dorewards Ave CM7 .. 127 F7
Dorking Cres CO16 .. 188 C6
Dorking Wlk CM2 .. 216 E2
Dorlings The CO14 .. 171 C8
Dorothy Curtice Ct
  CO6 .... 133 E5
Dorothy Sayers Dr
  CM8 .... 177 A5
Dorset Ave CM2 ... 216 E6
Dorset Cl
  Great Baddow CM2 .. 216 E6
  Halstead CO9 ..... 76 E1
  Holland-on-S CO15 .. 189 E6
Dorset Ho [13] CM23 .. 145 F7
Dorset Rd CM9 ... 220 F8
Dorvis La CB10 ... 6 B1
Doubleday Cnr CO6 .. 130 F2
Doubleday Dr CM9 .. 209 F5
Doubleday Gdns CM7 .. 128 B5
Doucecroft Sch CO5 .. 158 C3
Douglas Cl CM2 ... 216 D3
Douglas Gr CM8 ... 176 D2
Douglas Rd
  Clacton-on-S CO15 .. 188 C4
  Harwich CO12 .... 91 B3
Douglas Wlk [3] CM2 .. 216 A8
Dove Cl
  Bishop's Stortford
  CM23 .... 145 E3
  Stansted Mountfitchet
  CM24 .... 119 E8
Dove Cotts CM22 .. 93 F3
Dove Cres CO12 ... 90 D2
Dovedale IP11 .... 221 B3
Dovedale Gdns CO15 .. 189 C6
Dove House Rd CB9 .. 9 A8
Dove La CM2 ..... 216 A6
Dover Cl
  Braintree CM7 ..... 127 E6
  Clacton-on-S CO15 .. 203 J8
DOVERCOURT 91 C4
Dovercourt Cvn Pk
  CO12 .... 91 A1
Dovercourt Sta CO12 .. 91 D4
Dover Rd
  Brightlingsea CO7 .. 185 F8
  Ipswich IP3 ...... 18 A4
Doves Ct CO7 .... 185 F6
Doves La CM6 .... 150 B2
Dove St IP4 ...... 17 E5
Dove Tree Ct CO3 .. 134 C5
Dowches Cotts CO5 .. 158 C2
Dowches Dr CO5 .. 158 C3
Dowches Gdns CO5 .. 158 C3
Dowding Cl CO2 ... 136 A4
Dowling Rd CO8 .. 79 F3
Downham Bvd IP3 .. 38 C8
Downing Cl IP2 ... 16 F2
Downs Cres
  Great Dunmow CM6 .. 123 C1
  Haverhill CB9 .... 8 F1
Downside Cl IP2 .. 36 F8
Downs Pl [2] CB9 .. 8 F1
Downs Rd CM9 ... 210 B3
Downs Terr CM6 .. 124 D6
Downs The
  Felixstowe IP11 .... 221 B5
  Great Dunmow CM6 .. 123 D1
Downsway CM1 ... 205 D6
Downton Dr CB9 .. 8 E8
Downton Wlk CO5 .. 179 D6
Dragon's Gn CB10 .. 23 D1
Drake Ave IP3 .... 18 B2
Drake Gdns CM7 .. 128 C4
Drakes App CO15 .. 188 A1
Drakes Cnr CO5 ... 181 F2
Drakes La
  Boreham CM3 ..... 192 B7
  Little Waltham CM3 .. 191 F7
Drake Sq N IP3 ... 18 B2
Drake Sq S IP3 ... 18 B2
Drake's Yd CB9 ... 9 A8
Drapers Chase
  Heybridge CM9 ... 210 D4
  Rayne CM7 ...... 153 D8
Drapers La CB9 ... 8 B2
Drapery Comm CO10 .. 2 B4

Dray Ct CO6 ...... 108 F4
Drayman's Cl CM23 .. 145 B5
Draymans Gr CM77 .. 154 C8
Draymans Way IP3 .. 17 E3
Drays The CO10 ... 15 B5
Drayton Cl [4] CM9 .. 210 A1
Dreys The CB10 ... 44 D8
Driberg Way CM7 .. 128 A1
Driffield Cl CO5 ... 158 D4
Drift The
  Dedham CO7 ...... 84 F7
  East Bergholt CO7 .. 60 C2
  Great Cornard CO10 .. 34 C5
  Ipswich, California IP4 .. 18 A6
  Ipswich, Priory Heath
  IP3 .... 18 C1
  Stutton IP9 ...... 62 C2
Driftway The IP4 ... 18 B6
Drive The
  Chelmsford CM1 ... 205 A6
  Clacton-on-S CO15 .. 189 B7
  Harwich CO12 .... 91 B2
  Rivenhall End CM8 .. 177 E6
  Thaxted CM6 ..... 69 F3
Drood Cl CM1 .... 204 F7
Drovers Way
  Bishop's Stortford
  CM23 .... 145 C5
  Chelmsford CM2 ... 206 B7
Druce The CB11 ... 65 D4
Drum Field CO7 ... 58 D1
Drury Dr CO10 ... 15 F2
Drury La
  [5] Braintree CM7 ... 127 F3
  Ridgewell CO9 .... 29 A6
Drury Lo CO2 .... 135 C4
Drury Rd CO2 .... 135 C5
Dry Dock CO7 .... 164 B8
Du Cane Pl [3] CM8 .. 177 A2
Duchess Cl CM23 .. 145 C7
DUCK END
  Bishop's Stortford .. 119 E1
  Finchingfield 72 D7
  Stebbing 98 D1
Duckend Farm La CM6 .. 97 C3
DUCKEND GREEN .. 126 F3
Ducketts Wharf [10]
  CM23 .... 145 F6
Duck St
  Little Easton CM6 .. 122 F5
  Wendens Ambo CB11 .. 42 E5
DUDDENHOE END .. 41 A6
Duddery Cl CB9 ... 9 B7
Duddery Hill CB9 .. 9 A7
Duddery Rd CB9 ... 9 A7
Dudley Cl
  Boreham CM3 ..... 192 E1
  Colchester CO2 ... 136 A4
Dudley Ct CO15 ... 189 A8
Dudley Rd
  Clacton-on-S CO15 .. 188 D3
  Earls Colne CO6 ... 104 F7
  Fingringhoe CO5 .. 163 E3
Duffield Dr CO4 ... 136 E7
Duffield Rd CM2 .. 216 D6
Duffries Cl CM3 .. 190 E7
Duffs Hill CO10 ... 2 B6
Dugard Ave CO3 .. 134 E4
Duggers La CM7 .. 128 A1
Dugmore Ave CO13 .. 170 C8
Dukes La [5] CM2 .. 205 F4
Dukes Orch CM1 .. 204 B1
Dukes Park Ind Est
  CM2 .... 205 F4
Dukes Priory Hospl The
  CM1 .... 205 D4
Dukes Rd CM7 ... 127 F5
Dukes Ride CM23 .. 145 C2
Duke St
  Brightlingsea CO7 .. 185 E6
  Chelmsford CM1 ... 205 B2
  Ipswich IP3 ...... 17 E4
Dukes Wlk [6] CM1 .. 205 A3
Dulverton Cotts CO3 .. 134 C4
Dulwich Cl CO15 .. 189 D4
Dulwich Rd CO15 .. 189 D5
Dumbarton Rd IP4 .. 18 C8
Dumfries Rd IP4 .. 18 C8
Dumney La
  Braintree, Hornells Corner
  CM3 .... 153 E2
  Braintree, Thistley Green
  CM6 .... 153 B3
  Great Leighs CM3 .. 173 E8
Dumont Ave CO16 .. 186 B2
Duncan Pl CM2 ... 216 A2
Duncan Rd CO2 ... 135 B4
Duncan Rise CO9 .. 29 F2
Dundee Ho IP4 ... 18 B8
Dunlin Cl CM9 ... 210 C5
Dunlin Ct CO5 ... 158 C2
Dunlin Rd IP2 .... 16 E2
Dunlop Rd IP2 .... 16 F6
Dunmore Rd CM2 .. 206 A3
Dunmow Rd
  Bishop's Stortford
  CM23 .... 146 C7
  Felsted CM6 ...... 125 F2
  Great Bardfield CM7 .. 98 F8
  Great Canfield CM6 .. 149 F1
  Great Hallingbury
  CM22 .... 147 C7
  Rayne CM77 ...... 126 B2
  Takeley CM22 ..... 148 C7
  Thaxted CM6 ..... 97 A7

Dunmow St Mary's Prim Sch CM6 . . . . 150 C8
Dunning Cl CO11 . . . . . . 114 C8
Dunnock Way CM7 . . . . . . 137 A7
Dunoon Cl CM7 . . . . . . 128 D4
Dunstable Dr CM7 . . . . . . 128 D3
Dunster Dr CB9 . . . . 8 E8
Dunthorne Rd CO4 . . . . . . 110 E2
Dunthorpe Rd CO16 . . . . . . 188 D6
Duntons Almshouses CO7 . . . . 84 F6
Dunwich Ct
  Colchester CO2 . . . . . . 135 F4
  Haverhill CB9 . . . . 8 C8
  Ipswich IP1 . . . . 16 E8
Dupont Cl CO16 . . . . . . 188 D6
Durand La CM6 . . . . . . 151 E6
Durham Cl CM7 . . . . 72 A1
Durham Sq CO1 . . . . . . 136 A7
DUTON HILL 96 E3
Duxford Rd CB10 . . . . 3 A7
Dyehouse Mdw CO10 . . . . . 15 B7
Dyers Ct CM23 . . . . . . 145 C5
DYER'S END 28 E1
Dyers Rd CO9 . . . . 28 E1
Dyer's Rd
  Colchester CO3 . . . . . . 134 C3
  Maldon CM9 . . . . 210 A2
Dyke Rd IP11 . . . . 221 A4
Dykes Chase CM9 . . . . . . 209 F2
Dyke St IP1 . . . . 17 C7
Dyne's Hall Rd CO9 . . . . . 76 C8

E

Eagle Ave CO14 . . . . . . 144 D1
Eaglegate 4 CO1 . . . . . . 136 A7
Eagle La CM7 . . . . 127 F6
Eagles CI IP11 . . . . . . 221 D4
Eagle St 3 IP4 . . . . . . 17 D5
Earlhams Cl CO12 . . . . . . 90 F1
Earlhams Mews CO12 . . . . 90 D1
Earls Cl CM23 . . . . . . 145 D6
EARLS COLNE 105 C7
Earls Colne Prim Sch CO6 . . . . 105 C6
Earls Colne Rd CO6 . . . . 106 A1
Earlsfield Dr CM2 . . . . . 205 F3
Earls Gn CB9 . . . . 8 C8
Earls Hall Dr CO16 . . . . 187 E5
Earlsmead CM8 . . . . . . 176 F3
Earlswood Lo CO14 . . . . 144 E3
Earlswood Way CO2 . . . . 135 D2
Eastacre CB10 . . . . 22 E2
East Anglian Rly Mus★ CO6 . . . . 106 D6
East Area IP1 . . . . 16 C7
East Bay CO1 . . . . 136 B7
EAST BERGHOLT 59 C2
East Bergholt CE Prim Sch CO7 . . . . 59 B3
East Bergholt High Sch CO7 . . . . 59 D3
East Bergholt Place Gdn★ CO7 . . . . 59 F1
Eastby Cl CB11 . . . . 43 F8
Eastcliff Ave CO15 . . . . . 189 B4
Eastcliff Ho CO14 . . . . . 144 D1
East Court Ho CO1 . . . . . 136 C7
East Dock Rd CO12 . . . . . 90 F6
EAST END 60 C2
Eastend La CM6, CM22 . . 121 C8
East End La CO7 . . . . . . 60 C2
East End Rd CO7 . . . . . . 60 A3
Easten Greene CO6 . . . . . 80 E4
Easterford Rd CO5 . . . . . 158 C2
Easterling Cl CO12 . . . . . 91 A4
Eastern App CM2 . . . . . 205 F5
Eastern Ave CB9 . . . . 8 F8
Eastern Cl IP4 . . . . 18 F4
Eastern Cres CM1 . . . . . 204 F5
Eastern Prom CO16 . . . . 185 F3
Eastern Rd CO7 . . . . . . 185 E6
East Essex Aviation Mus★ CO16 . . . . 185 E4
Eastgate CB10 . . . . 3 D2
Eastgate 13 IP4 . . . . . . 17 D6
East Gates Ind Est CO1 . . . . 136 B7
Eastgate St CO12 . . . . . 91 D6
EAST GORES 132 A4
East Gores Farm CO6 . . . 131 F4
East Gores Rd CO6 . . . . 131 F5
East Hanningfield Rd CM2 . . . . 217 E2
East Haven CO15 . . . . . 188 E5
East Hill CO1 . . . . 136 A7
EASTHORPE 160 B7
Easthorpe Rd
  Feering CO5 . . . . 159 D7
  Messing CO5 . . . . . . 159 F5
East La CO7 . . . . 85 B5
Eastland Ct IP11 . . . . . . 221 B4
East Lawn IP4 . . . . 18 C8
EAST MERSEA 184 F1
East Mersea Rd CO5 . . . 183 E1
East Mill CO9 . . . . 76 F2
East Mill Gn IP9 . . . . . . 60 E6
Easton Farm CM6 . . . . . 122 E6
Easton Rd CM8 . . . . . . 177 A3
Easton Way CO13 . . . . . 171 B6
East Rd
  Bishop's Stortford CM23 . . . . 146 B7

East Rd continued
  East Mersea CO5 . . . . 184 D1
  West Mersea CO5 . . . . 201 E7
East Row IP9 . . . . 62 D6
East Side CO4 . . . . 83 A4
East St
  Braintree CM7 . . . . . . 128 A3
  Coggeshall CO6 . . . . . 131 A2
  Colchester CO1 . . . . . 136 B7
  Harwich CO12 . . . . . . 91 D4
  Saffron Walden CB10 . . . 22 E1
  Sudbury CO10 . . . . . . 33 F8
  Tollesbury CM9 . . . . . 199 D1
  Wivenhoe CO7 . . . . . . 164 B7
East Stockwell St CO1 . . . . 135 F7
East Terr CO14 . . . . . . 144 D1
East View CM22 . . . . . . 148 C8
East View Cl CB10 . . . . . 45 F8
East Ward Mews CO1 . . . 136 C7
Eastways CM8 . . . . . . 177 B4
Eastways Ind Est CM8 . . 177 B4
Eastwood Dr CO4 . . . . . 110 B3
Eastwood Pk CM2 . . . . . 217 A5
Eaton Cl IP11 . . . . 221 C2
Eaton Cotts CO5 . . . . . 179 D7
Eaton Gdns IP11 . . . . . 221 C2
Eaton Ho 5 CM2 . . . . . 146 B8
Eaton Mews CO2 . . . . . 136 B3
Eaton Way CM9 . . . . . . 196 F2
Ebenezer Cl CM8 . . . . . 176 E5
Ebenezer Terr CM2 . . . . 216 F7
Ebony Cl CO2 . . . . 135 D2
Eccles Rd IP2 . . . . 16 D1
Eckersley Rd CM1 . . . . . 205 C3
Eden Cl CM8 . . . . 176 E3
Eden Rd
  Haverhill CB9 . . . . 9 A7
  Ipswich IP4 . . . . 18 B5
Edens Cl CM23 . . . . . . 146 B7
Edenside CO13 . . . . . . 170 E7
Edenway CM1 . . . . 204 C5
Edgefield Ave CO11 . . . . 86 B3
Edgeworth Rd IP2 . . . . . 16 E2
Edgware Rd CO16 . . . . . 188 D5
Edgworth Rd CO10 . . . . 33 E7
Edinburgh Cl CM8 . . . . . 195 A8
Edinburgh Gdns
  Bishop's Stortford CM23 . . . . 145 E6
  Braintree CM7 . . . . . . 128 C4
Edison Cl 3 CM7 . . . . . 127 F1
Edison Gdns CO4 . . . . . 110 C1
Edison Rd CO15 . . . . . . 189 F6
Edith Borthwick Sch The CM7 . . . . 127 F8
Edith Cavell Way CB9 . . . 27 C6
Edith Rd
  Clacton-on-S CO15 . . . 188 C4
  Kirby-le-S CO13 . . . . . 170 D8
Edmund Cl CB9 . . . . 8 F8
Edmund Gn CO9 . . . . . 102 E8
Edmund Rd CM8 . . . . . 194 E8
Edney Ct IP11 . . . . 221 E3
Edward Ave CO7 . . . . . 185 F7
Edward Bowden Ct CB10 . . . . 22 D1
Edward Bright Cl CM9 . . . . 210 A2
Edward Cl
  Ipswich IP1 . . . . 16 F8
  Little Clacton CO16 . . . 168 E5
Edward Cordy Ho IP11 . . . . 221 E3
Edward Dr CM2 . . . . . . 216 C7
Edward Ho CB10 . . . . . . 22 E3
Edward Marke Dr CO5 . . . . 163 B3
Edward Paxman Gdns 10 CO1 . . . . 136 C6
Edward Rd CO16 . . . . . 168 F7
Edward St CO12 . . . . . . 90 E5
Edwards Wlk CM9 . . . . . 209 F3
Edward Terr CO16 . . . . . 168 E5
Egerton Green Rd CO2 . . . . 135 A3
Egglestone Cl IP2 . . . . . 16 F1
Eggshall La CM7 . . . . . . 27 E2
Eglinton Dr CM2 . . . . . 206 B4
Egremont St CO10 . . . . . 2 B3
Egremont Way CO3 . . . . 134 C4
Egret Cres CO4 . . . . . . 137 A8
Ehringshausen Way CB9 . . 9 B7
Eider Ct CM23 . . . . . . 146 A6
Eight Acre La CO2 . . . . 135 C2
EIGHT ASH GREEN 134 B8
Eight Ash Green & Aldham CE Prim Sch CO3 . . . . 107 F1
Elderberry Gdns CM8 . . . 177 B4
Elder Field CM7 . . . . . . 154 B5
ELDER STREET 44 E1
Eld La CO1 . . . . 135 F7
Eldon Cl CO4 . . . . 110 E1
Eldred Ave CO2 . . . . . . 135 B3
Eldred Cl IP1 . . . . 16 D8
Eldred Ct CO10 . . . . . . 34 C4
Eldred Dr CO10 . . . . . . 34 C4
Eleanor Cl CO5 . . . . . . 179 D6
Eleanor Wlk CO5 . . . . . 179 D6
Eleventh Ave CM24 . . . . 120 B2
Elfrida Ho CO2 . . . . . . 135 B3
Elgar Dr CM8 . . . . 194 F7
Elgin Ave CM1 . . . . . . 205 A2
Elianore Rd CO3 . . . . . 135 B7
Eliot Way CM9 . . . . . . 210 A1
Elizabeth Ave CM8 . . . . 195 A8

Elizabeth Cl
  Colchester CO4 . . . . . 110 C4
  Saffron Walden CB10 . . . 22 F2
Elizabeth Ct
  Harwich CO12 . . . . . . 91 A3
  Ipswich IP3 . . . . 17 F5
  4 Sudbury CO10 . . . . 33 F8
  Walton-on-t-N CO14 . . . 144 E3
Elizabeth Rd
  Bishop's Stortford CM23 . . . . 145 E5
  Harwich CO12 . . . . . . 91 A3
Elizabeth Villas CO5 . . . 180 A2
Elizabeth Way
  Brightlingsea CO7 . . . . 185 F6
  Felixstowe IP11 . . . . . 221 C3
  Halstead CO9 . . . . . . 76 E2
  Hatfield Peverel CM3 . . 194 A4
  Heybridge CM9 . . . . . 210 A5
  Saffron Walden CB10 . . . 22 F2
  Sudbury CO10 . . . . . . 33 C5
  Wivenhoe CO7 . . . . . . 137 C3
Ellenborough Cl CM23 . . . . 145 D5
Ellenbrook Gn IP2 . . . . . 16 D1
Ellenbrook Rd IP2 . . . . . 16 D1
Ellen Way CM77 . . . . . . 154 D7
Elliot Pl CM7 . . . . 128 C3
Elliots Dr CO14 . . . . . . 171 B8
Elliott Ct CM23 . . . . . . 146 A8
Elliott St IP1 . . . . 17 A6
Ellis Rd
  Boxted CO4 . . . . 82 F3
  Bradfield CO11 . . . . . 114 D8
  Clacton-on-S CO15 . . . 188 E2
Elm Ave CM9 . . . . 210 C5
Elm Bglws CM7 . . . . . . 127 D4
Elmbrook Dr CM23 . . . . 145 E3
Elm Cl
  Alresford CO7 . . . . . . 165 B8
  Brantham CO11 . . . . . 60 D1
  Chelmsford CM1 . . . . 205 A8
  Elsenham CM22 . . . . . 94 C2
  Great Baddow CM2 . . . 216 F6
  Great Bentley CO7 . . . 166 E8
  Haverhill CB9 . . . . 8 F8
  Sible Hedingham CO9 . . 51 D2
  Takeley CM22 . . . . . . 148 C7
  Tiptree CO5 . . . . 179 C7
Elm Close Extension CM22 . . . . 148 C7
Elm Cres CO4 . . . . 136 D7
Elmcroft CO7 . . . . 138 A6
Elm Ct
  Elmdon CB11 . . . . . . 20 B4
  Sturmer CB9 . . . . 9 E5
Elmdale Dr CO11 . . . . . 86 D3
Elmden Ct CO15 . . . . . 188 E5
ELMDON 20 B4
Elmdon Pl 1 CB9 . . . . . . 9 B8
Elm Dr
  Brightlingsea CO7 . . . . 185 D7
  Halstead CO9 . . . . . . 76 F1
  Harwich CO12 . . . . . . 91 B3
Elm Est CO7 . . . . 59 C3
Elm Farm Cvn Pk CO16 . . . . 142 A1
Elmfield Cl CO15 . . . . . 189 E7
Elm Gdns IP11 . . . . . . 221 A7
Elm Gr
  Bishop's Stortford CM23 . . . . 146 B7
  Clacton-on-S CO15 . . . 188 F6
  Kirby Cross CO13 . . . . 170 D6
  Saffron Walden CB10 . . . 22 D1
  Wivenhoe CO7 . . . . . . 137 B1
Elm Green La CM3 . . . . 218 C8
Elm Green Prep Sch CM3 . . . . 207 D3
Elm Ho IP11 . . . . 221 C4
Elmhurst Cl CB9 . . . . . . 9 B7
Elmhurst Dr IP3 . . . . . . 17 F3
Elmhurst Rd CO12 . . . . . 91 A3
Elm La
  Capel St M IP9 . . . . . 35 A1
  Marks Tey CO5, CO6 . . 132 B2
  Washbrook IP8 . . . . . 35 E8
Elm Rd
  Bishop's Stortford CM23 . . . . 145 F8
  Chelmsford CM2 . . . . 216 A8
  East Bergholt CO7 . . . . 59 C3
  Great Dunmow CM6 . . . 123 C2
  Little Clacton CO16 . . . 168 C3
  Rushmere St A IP5 . . . 18 F7
  Sudbury CO10 . . . . . . 34 A7
Elm Rise CM8 . . . . 177 A5
Elms Dr CM1 . . . . 205 A4
Elms Hall Rd CO6 . . . . . 104 E8
Elm St IP1 . . . . 17 C6
ELMSTEAD HEATH 138 A2
ELMSTEAD MARKET . . . 138 A6
Elmstead Prim Sch CO7 . . . . 137 F6
Elmstead Rd
  Colchester CO4 . . . . . 136 E5
  Wivenhoe CO7 . . . . . . 137 D4
Elms The
  East Bergholt CO7 . . . . 60 C3
  Frinton-on-S CO13 . . . 170 F6
  Great Chesterford CB10 . . 3 E3
Elm Tree Ave CO13 . . . . 170 F7
Elm Tree Cl CO13 . . . . . 170 F7
Elm Way CM3 . . . . 192 E1
Elm Wlk CM77 . . . . . . 126 F2
Elmwood CO3 . . . . 134 D6
Elmwood Ave CO2 . . . . . 135 B2
Elmwood Dr CO5 . . . . . 201 D7

ELSENHAM 94 C1
Elsenham CE Prim Sch CM22 . . . . 94 D1
Elsenham Cross CM22 . . . 94 C1
Elsenham Hall CM22 . . . 120 C8
Elsenham Sta CM22 . . . . 94 C3
Elsham Dr CM2 . . . . . . 154 B6
Elsmere Rd IP1 . . . . . . 17 C8
Elstar La CO6 . . . . 109 B8
Elthorne Pk CO16 . . . . . 188 D4
Elton Park Bsns Ctr IP2 . . . . 16 E6
Elton Pk IP2 . . . . 16 D6
Elton Wlk CO15 . . . . . . 179 D6
Elvina Ho CO15 . . . . . . 203 F6
Elwes Cl CO4 . . . . 110 D1
Elwin Rd CO5 . . . . 179 D5
Ely Gdns CO1 . . . . 136 A7
Elysian Gdns CM9 . . . . . 199 C1
Embassy Ct CM9 . . . . . 210 A2
Emberson Ct CM2 . . . . . 205 F4
Emblems CM9 . . . . 123 C1
Embra Ct CO2 . . . . 136 B5
Emily Bray Ho IP4 . . . . . 17 F7
Emily May Ct CO12 . . . . 91 A3
Emlen St IP1 . . . . 17 A6
Emmanuel Cl IP2 . . . . . 16 F3
Emmerson Ho CM23 . . . 146 A5
Emneth Acre CM9 . . . . . 209 E1
Emperor Circ IP3 . . . . . 38 C8
Emperor Cl CM4 . . . . . 210 A5
Empire Bsns Pk CO15 . . . 188 E3
Empire Ct
  Clacton-on-S CO15 . . . 188 E3
  3 Frinton-on-S CO13 . . 170 F5
Empire Rd CO12 . . . . . 91 D3
Empire Wlk 2 CM2 . . . . 205 C2
Empress Ave CO5 . . . . . 201 E6
Empress Dr CO5 . . . . . 201 D6
Emson Cl CB10 . . . . . . 22 D2
Endean Ct CO7 . . . . . . 137 C2
Endeavour Cl CM9 . . . . . 199 D2
Endsleigh Ct CO3 . . . . . 135 C7
Endway The
  Great Easton CM6 . . . . 122 F7
  Steeple Bumpstead CB9 . . 27 C8
Engaines Prim Sch CO16 . . . . 168 C2
Engineers Sq CO4 . . . . . 109 D2
Engleric SG8 . . . . 19 D5
Enid Way CO4 . . . . 109 D2
Ennerdale Ave CM77 . . . 154 C6
Enoch Ho CO4 . . . . . . 136 E8
Enterprise Ct CM7 . . . . . 128 B2
Enterprise Ct CM8 . . . . . 177 A3
Enterprise Ho CO9 . . . . . 51 E2
Enville Way CO4 . . . . . . 110 B4
Epping Cl
  Chelmsford CM1 . . . . 204 E1
  Clacton-on-S CO16 . . . 188 D6
Epping Way CM8 . . . . . 176 E1
Epsom Cl CO16 . . . . . . 188 D6
Erbury Pl CO10 . . . . . . 12 B8
Erica Wlk CO4 . . . . 136 D7
Erick Ave CM1 . . . . 205 B7
Eridge Cl CM1 . . . . 205 D2
Eriswell Rd CO9 . . . . 9 B8
Erle Havard Rd CO6 . . . . 108 E4
Ernalds Cl CO6 . . . . . . 105 B7
Ernest Rd CO7 . . . . . . 137 C1
Ernleigh Rd IP4 . . . . . . 18 B6
Errington Rd CO3 . . . . . 135 D5
Erskine Rd CO11 . . . . . . 86 D4
Esplanade
  Frinton-on-S CO13 . . . 170 F3
  Harwich CO12 . . . . . . 91 E4
Esplanade Ct
  Frinton-on-S CO13 . . . 171 A5
  Harwich CO12 . . . . . . 91 E6
Esplanade The CO15 . . . 189 G6
Essex Ave
  Chelmsford CM1 . . . . 205 A7
  Clacton-on-S CO15 . . . 203 E6
  Sudbury CO10 . . . . . . 15 F2
Essex County Cricket Club★ CM2 . . . . 205 B2
Essex Cty Hospl CO3 . . . 135 D6
Essex Hall Rd CO1 . . . . 109 E1
Essex Hill CB11 . . . . . . 20 B2
Essex Knowle CO8 . . . . . 55 F1
Essex Rd
  Braintree CM7 . . . . . . 128 B4
  Maldon CM9 . . . . 209 F1
Essex Regiment Way CM3 . . . . 191 D5
Essex Way IP3 . . . . 18 E1
Essex Yeomanry Way CO3 . . . . 134 B7
Estate Yd The CM3 . . . . 175 C2
Estella Mead CM1 . . . . . 204 E7
Estuary Cl CO4 . . . . . . 109 E4
Estuary Cres
  Clacton-on-S CO15 . . . 188 D3
  Shotley Gate IP9 . . . . . 91 B8
Estuary Mews CM9 . . . . 199 D2
Estuary Park Rd CO5 . . . 201 E6
Estuary Rd IP9 . . . . . . 91 B8
Eton Ct CO13 . . . . 171 A5
Eton Rd
  Clacton-on-S CO15 . . . 188 F4
  Frinton-on-S CO13 . . . 171 A5
Eudo Ho CO2 . . . . 135 F4
Eudo Rd CO2 . . . . 135 C4
Europa Pk CM8 . . . . . . 177 A3
Europa Way
  Harwich CO12 . . . . . . 90 F4
  Ipswich IP1 . . . . 16 D7
Eustace Rd IP1 . . . . . . 16 E8

ELSENHAM 94 C1
Euston Ave IP4 . . . . . . 18 F6
Euston Ct IP11 . . . . . . 221 A4
Evabrook Cl IP2 . . . . . . 16 E1
Evelyn Pl CM1 . . . . 204 F1
Evelyn Rd CM3 . . . . . . 153 D4
Evelyn Wood Rd CM77 . . . . 155 E6
Everest Gdns CM23 . . . . 145 E6
Everest Way CM9 . . . . . 210 B5
Everett Ho CO1 . . . . . . 136 B6
Evergreen Dr CO4 . . . . . 110 D4
Everitt Rd CB10 . . . . . . 22 F2
Everitt Way CO9 . . . . . . 51 E2
Eves Cnr CM3 . . . . 218 E7
Eves Cres CM1 . . . . . . 205 A5
Eves Ct CO12 . . . . 90 D1
Evesham Cl IP2 . . . . . . 17 A2
Eves Orch CO8 . . . . . . 55 F1
Ewan Cl CO3 . . . . 134 C6
Ewan Way CO3 . . . . . . 134 C7
Ewell Hall Chase CO5 . . . 158 C1
Ewer Ct CO1 . . . . 136 A6
Exchange Way 5 CM1 . . . . 205 B2
Exeter Cl
  Braintree CM7 . . . . . . 128 B5
  Great Horkesley CO6 . . 109 C7
Exeter Ct 6 CB9 . . . . . . 8 E6
Exeter Dr CO1 . . . . 136 A7
Exeter Rd
  Chelmsford CM1 . . . . 205 E5
  Felixstowe IP11 . . . . . 221 D5
  Ipswich IP3 . . . . 18 B4
Exmoor Cl IP11 . . . . . . 204 D1
Exmoor Rd IP11 . . . . . . 221 D6

F

Faber Rd CM8 . . . . 194 E8
Fabians Cl CO6 . . . . . . 131 A3
Factory Hill CO5 . . . . . 179 E3
Factory La CO11 . . . . . . 86 C7
Factory La E CO9 . . . . . 76 E1
Factory La W CO9 . . . . . 76 E1
Factory Terr CO9 . . . . . 76 E2
Faggot Yd CM7 . . . . . . 127 F5
Fairbrother Ct 1 CO4 . . . . 136 D7
Fair Cl CO7 . . . . 186 A6
Fairclough Ave CO16 . . . 188 B3
Fairfax Hall CO4 . . . . . . 109 F4
Fairfax Mead CM2 . . . . . 206 A2
Fairfax Rd 17 CO2 . . . . 135 F6
Fairfield Ave IP11 . . . . . 221 E5
Fairfield Cl CO7 . . . . . . 139 A7
Fairfield Gdns 2 CO4 . . . . 136 C8
Fairfield Inf Sch IP11 . . . 221 E5
Fairfield Rd
  Braintree CM7 . . . . . . 127 F2
  Chelmsford CM1 . . . . 205 A3
  Clacton-on-S CO15 . . . 188 E4
  Ipswich IP3 . . . . 18 A2
Fairfields CM3 . . . . . . 220 D1
Fairfield Way CO9 . . . . . 76 F1
Fair Gn CO10 . . . . 2 B5
Fairhaven Ave CO5 . . . . 201 E6
Fairhaven Ct CO5 . . . . . 201 E5
Fairhead Rd N CO4 . . . . 136 C8
Fairhead Rd S 6 CO4 . . 136 C8
Faireleads CB10 . . . . . . 218 F8
Fair Leas CB10 . . . . . . 22 E3
Fairlop Cl CO15 . . . . . . 188 F8
FAIRSTEAD 175 B6
Fairstead Hall Rd CM3 . . . . 175 A5
Fairstead Rd CM3 . . . . . 175 C5
Fairway
  Bishop's Stortford CM23 . . . . 146 C6
  Chelmsford CM2 . . . . 216 D7
Fairways CO4 . . . . 109 B3
Fairways The IP4 . . . . . 18 E5
Fairycroft Rd CB10 . . . . 22 E1
Fairy Hall La CM77 . . . . 127 A1
Falcon Cl CB9 . . . . 9 C8
Falcon Cres CO1 . . . . . 136 B5
Falconer Rd CB9 . . . . . . 9 C5
Falconer St CM23 . . . . . 145 C5
Falcon Fields CM9 . . . . 220 F8
Falcon Mews CM9 . . . . . 220 F8
Falcons Mead CM2 . . . . 205 A1
Falcon Sq CO9 . . . . . . 51 F4
Falcon St
  Felixstowe IP11 . . . . . 221 C6
  Ipswich IP1 . . . . 17 C5
Falcon Way
  Chelmsford CM2 . . . . 216 A6
  Clacton-on-S CO15 . . . 188 F6
Fal Dr CM8 . . . . 176 E2
Falkland Cl CM3 . . . . . . 206 E8
Falkland Ct CM7 . . . . . . 128 B4
Falkland Gn CM9 . . . . . 219 E6
Falklands Dr 8 CO11 . . . 86 D4
Falklands Rd CO2 . . . . . 135 E3
Fallowden La CB10 . . . . 23 F8
Fallowfield Cl CO12 . . . . 90 F3
Fallowfield Ct 14 CB9 . . . 8 E7
Fallowfield Rd CO2 . . . . 135 C2
Falmouth Rd CM1 . . . . . 205 E5
Falstaff Cotts CM7 . . . . 60 F8
Fambridge Chase CM8 . . . . 155 F2
Fambridge Cl CM9 . . . . 210 A1
Fambridge Rd CM9 . . . . 209 F2
FANNER'S GREEN 190 C5

Fanner's Green Cotts
  CM3 . . . . 190 C5
Fanny's La CO16 . . . . . . 167 D2
Faraday Cl
  Braintree CM7 . . . . . . 127 F1
  Clacton-on-S CO15 . . . 169 A1
Faraday Rd IP4 . . . . 17 F5
Farford Field CO10 . . . . . 34 C5
Farina Cl IP1 . . . . 16 F7
Farm Dr CO6 . . . . 134 A8
Farmers Way CO16 . . . . 188 B3
Farmfield Rd CO6 . . . . . 106 B1
Farmleigh Ave CO15 . . . 188 F8
Farm Rd CO12 . . . . 116 D3
Farm Wlk CO7 . . . . 185 E8
FARNHAM 118 D6
Farnham CE Prim Sch
  CM23 . . . . 118 D6
FARNHAM GREEN 118 B7
Farriers Chase CO5 . . . . 201 D6
Farriers End CO5 . . . . . . 134 D5
Farriers Way CM77 . . . . 154 B7
Farriers Went IP11 . . . . 221 B7
Farrington Cl 3 CO1 . . . 136 C6
Farrow Rd CM1 . . . . 215 E7
Farthing Cl CM7 . . . . . . 128 D4
Farthing Ct 10 CM1 . . . . 205 A3
Farthing Rd IP1 . . . . 16 C7
Farthing Road Ind Est
  IP1 . . . . 16 C7
Farthings Chase CO5 . . . 201 D6
Farthings Went IP9 . . . . . 35 B2
FAR THORPE GREEN
  . . . . 141 C2
Fastnet Cl CB9 . . . . 9 D8
Faulds Wlk CO2 . . . . 136 A3
FAULKBOURNE 176 A4
Faulkbourne Rd CM8 . . . 176 D4
Faulkeners Way IP11 . . . 221 A8
Fawkner Cl CM2 . . . . . . 205 B2
Fawley Cl IP4 . . . . 18 C7
Fayrewood Dr CM3 . . . . 173 F7
Feather Cl CM7 . . . . 128 D3
Feathers Field IP11 . . . . 221 B5
Feedhams Cl CO7 . . . . . 137 C3
FEERING 158 E5
Feering CE Prim Sch
  CO5 . . . . 158 E4
Feering Hill CO5 . . . . . . 158 D3
Feering Mus★ CO5 . . . . 158 B1
Feering Rd CO6 . . . . 131 B3
Felaw St IP2 . . . . 17 D4
Felbrigg Ct CM77 . . . . . 154 B7
Felix Ct IP11 . . . . 221 D2
Felix Rd
  Felixstowe IP11 . . . . . 221 F4
  Ipswich IP3 . . . . 18 C2
FELIXSTOWE 221 F3
Felixstowe Beach Cvn Pk
  IP11 . . . . 221 C2
Felixstowe Cl CO16 . . . . 188 A4
Felixstowe General Hospl
  IP11 . . . . 221 F4
Felixstowe Rd IP3 . . . . . . 18 B3
Felixstowe Sta IP11 . . . . 221 E5
Fellbrigg Ave IP5 . . . . 18 F6
Fell Christy CM1 . . . . . . 205 B5
Fellowes Cl CO4 . . . . . . 109 F2
Felnor Wlk IP11 . . . . . . 221 E4
Felsted Cl CO2 . . . . 163 A8
FELSTED 152 B5
Felsted Almshouses
  CM6 . . . . 152 B6
Felsted Prep Sch
  CM6 . . . . 152 B5
Felsted Prim Sch
  CM6 . . . . 152 C6
Felsted Sch CM6 . . . . . . 152 C6
Felsted Vineyard★
  CM6 . . . . 151 C7
Feltwell Pl 2 CB9 . . . . 9 B8
Fen Bight Circ IP3 . . . . . . 38 C7
Fenbridge La CO7 . . . . . . 59 B1
Fen Farm Cvn Site
  CO5 . . . . 184 F1
Fen Field Units CB9 . . . . . 8 F5
Fen La CO7 . . . . 84 D1
Fenman Ct CM22 . . . . . . 94 C2
Fen Mdw IP11 . . . . 221 A8
Fenn Cl CO3 . . . . 139 A3
Fennel Cl CO15 . . . . 179 C5
Fennels Cl CB9 . . . . 9 A7
Fennes Rd CM7 . . . . 102 A3
Fennings Chase CO1 . . . 136 A7
Fenno Cl CO3 . . . . 134 F4
Fenn Rd CO9 . . . . 77 A1
Fen St CO6 . . . . 56 B1
Fenton Rd CB9 . . . . 9 B8
Fen View IP8 . . . . 35 E8
Fenwick Dr CO1 . . . . . . 136 B8
Ferdinand Wlk CO4 . . . . 136 F7
Ferguson Cl CB11 . . . . . . 23 A2
Ferndale CO15 . . . . 188 F7
Ferndale Rd CO12 . . . . . . 91 D5
Ferndown Rd CO13 . . . . 170 E5
Ferndown Way CM3 . . . 194 B4
Fern Gr IP9 . . . . 8 E8
Fernhayes Cl IP2 . . . . 17 A2
Fern Hill CO10 . . . . 2 B7
Fernie Rd CM7 . . . . 127 D2
Fernlea CO4 . . . . 109 C2
Fernlea Rd CO12 . . . . 91 D5
Fern Way CO15 . . . . 203 F7

Fernwood Ave CO15 . . . 189 F5
Ferry La IP11 . . . . 221 A3
Ferry Rd CO5 . . . . 164 B6
Festival Gdns CM9 . . . . 198 D4
Feverills Rd CO16 . . . . . 168 D4
Fiat Ave CO15 . . . . 203 D6
Fiddlers Folly CO3 . . . . . 107 E1
Fiddlers Hill CO3 . . . . . . 107 E2
Fiddlers La CO7 . . . . 59 C3
Field Ct CO4 . . . . 136 E6
Fieldgate Dock CO7 . . . . 185 E5
Field Gate La CM22 . . . . . 94 A3
Fields Cl CO16 . . . . 167 F6
Fields Farm Rd CO2 . . . . 162 B4
Fieldside CB11 . . . . 43 E7
Field View CO10 . . . . 33 F8
Field View Dr CM9 . . . . . 197 C4
Field Way CO7 . . . . 137 C2
Field Wlk CO14 . . . . 171 A8
Fifth Ave
  Chelmsford CM1 . . . . 205 B6
  Frinton-on-S CO13 . . . 170 E5
  Halstead CO9 . . . . 77 B1
  Stansted Mountfitchet
  CM24 . . . . 120 B2
Finbars Wlk IP4 . . . . 17 F5
Finborough Cl IP4 . . . . . . 18 F4
Finchdale CO15 . . . . 188 F6
Finch Dr
  Braintree CM7 . . . . . . 127 D4
  Great Bentley CO7 . . . 139 D1
Finch Hill CO10 . . . . 33 A7
FINCHINGFIELD 72 C5
Finchingfield CE Prim Sch
  CM7 . . . . 72 D6
Finchingfield Guildhall
  Mus★ CM7 . . . . 72 D6
Finchingfield Rd
  Stambourne CO9 . . . . . 49 C7
  Steeple Bumpstead CB9 27 C5
Finchingfield Way
  CO2 . . . . 163 A8
Finchley Ave CM2 . . . . . 216 A8
Finchley Rd IP4 . . . . 17 E6
Finch's CM8 . . . . 195 F6
Findley Cl IP9 . . . . 61 F2
Finer Cl CO16 . . . . 188 D2
FINGRINGHOE 163 F5
Fingringhoe CE Prim Sch
  CO5 . . . . 163 F5
Fingringhoe Rd
  Abberton CO5 . . . . . . 163 B3
  Colchester CO2, CO5 . . 136 D1
Fingringhoe Wick
Conservation Ctr★
  CO5 . . . . 164 D3
Fingringhoe Wick Nature
Reserve & Visitor Ctr★
  CO5 . . . . 164 D3
Finham Cl CO4 . . . . 136 F7
FINKLE GREEN 28 A5
Finsbury Pl IP7 . . . . 76 F2
Firebronds Rd IP9 . . . . . . 62 D5
Firecrest Rd CM2 . . . . . . 216 C5
Firefly Way IP3 . . . . 38 B8
Firlands CM23 . . . . 145 E6
Firlands Ho CM23 . . . . . 145 E6
Firlie Wlk CO2 . . . . 136 A2
Firmin Cl IP1 . . . . 17 A4
Firmins Ct CO6 . . . . 108 D4
Firs Chase CO5 . . . . 201 A6
Firs Chase Cvn Pk
  CO5 . . . . 201 A7
Firs Cvn Pk CO16 . . . . . 168 D2
Firs Dr CM1 . . . . 204 B1
Firs Hamlet CO5 . . . . . . 201 A6
Firs Rd
  Tiptree CO5 . . . . 179 D4
  West Mersea CO5 . . . . 201 B7
First Ave
  Chelmsford CM1 . . . . 205 B5
  Clacton-on-S CO15 . . . 189 B4
  Frinton-on-S CO13 . . . 170 E4
  Glemsford CO10 . . . . . . 2 C5
  Halstead CO9 . . . . 77 B1
  Harwich CO12 . . . . 91 C3
  Seawick CO16 . . . . . . 203 C6
  Stansted Mountfitchet
  CM24 . . . . 120 B2
  Walton-on-t-N CO14 . . 144 E3
  Weeley CO16 . . . . 140 F1
Firs The
  Gosfield CO9 . . . . 102 E8
  Layer de la H CO2 . . . 162 A6
Firstore Dr CO3 . . . . 134 E7
Fir Tree Cl CO4 . . . . 110 B4
Fir Tree Hill IP9 . . . . 62 E4
Fir Tree La CM3 . . . . 207 E1
Fir Tree Rise
  Chelmsford CM2 . . . . 216 B6
  Ipswich IP8 . . . . 16 C2
Fir Tree Wlk CM9 . . . . . 210 C5
Fir Way CO15 . . . . 203 G6
Firwood's Rd CO9 . . . . . 103 E8
Fishbane Cl IP3 . . . . 38 B8
Fisher Cl CB9 . . . . 9 D8
Fisher's La CO7 . . . . 60 C3
Fisher Way CM7 . . . . . . 128 C4
Fishmarket St CM6 . . . . . 70 A2
Fish Pond Hill IP9 . . . . . . 63 C3
Fishponds Hill CO6 . . . . . 81 F4
Fishponds La IP9 . . . . 62 E5
Fish St CM9 . . . . 211 E6
Fisin Wlk CO3 . . . . 134 E3
Fiske Ct CO15 . . . . 188 F2
Fitches Cres CM9 . . . . . 210 B1
Fitches Croft CO6 . . . . . 133 C4

Fitches Mews CM9 . . . . 210 B1
Fitzgerald Cl CO11 . . . . . 86 B4
Fitzgerald Cotts CO12 . . . 90 F2
Fitzgerald Ct IP4 . . . . 18 A5
Fitzgilbert Rd CO2 . . . . . 135 C4
Fitzmaurice Rd IP3 . . . . . 18 B3
Fitzpiers CO15 . . . . 22 E2
Fitzwalter La CM3 . . . . . 218 D6
Fitzwalter Pl
  Chelmsford CM1 . . . . 204 E3
  Great Dunmow CM6 . . 150 D8
Fitzwalter Rd
  Boreham CM3 . . . . . . 206 F8
  Colchester CO3 . . . . . 135 B6
  Little Dunmow CM6 . . . 151 E7
Fitzwilliam Cl IP2 . . . . 16 F2
Fitzwilliam Rd CO3 . . . . 135 B7
Five Acres
  Bicknacre CM3 . . . . . . 218 F3
  Holbrook IP9 . . . . 62 B1
  Stansted Mountfitchet
  CM24 . . . . 119 E8
  Walton-on-t-N CO14 . . 171 B8
Fiveash La CM77 . . . . . . 129 E1
Five Fields CO4 . . . . 136 E7
Five Gables Chase
  CO5 . . . . 201 D5
Five Ways CO3 . . . . 134 D4
Fiveways Ret Pk CO3 . . . 134 D4
FLACKS GREEN 175 B2
Flag Hill CO7 . . . . 186 F8
Flagstaff Rd CO2 . . . . . . 135 F6
Flail Cl CO7 . . . . 137 F6
Flanders Cl CM7 . . . . . . 127 E5
Flanders Field CO2 . . . . 136 B3
Flatford Dr CO16 . . . . . . 188 B5
Flatford La CO7 . . . . 85 D7
Flatford Mill (Field Ctr)★
  CO7 . . . . 85 D7
Flatford Rd
  East Bergholt CO7 . . . . 85 C8
  Haverhill CB9 . . . . 8 C8
Flavian Cl CB9 . . . . 9 D7
Flavius Way CO4 . . . . . . 110 A6
Flax La CO10 . . . . 2 C3
Fleetwood Ave
  Felixstowe IP11 . . . . . 221 F5
  Holland-on-S CO15 . . . 189 E7
Fleetwood Cl CO15 . . . . 189 E7
Fleetwood Rd IP11 . . . . 221 F5
Fleetwood Sq CM2 . . . . 205 F8
Fleming Cl 7 CM7 . . . . . 127 F1
Flemish Cotts The CO7 . . 84 F6
Flemish Ct CO1 . . . . 135 F8
Fletcher Rd IP3 . . . . 18 A1
Flint Cl IP2 . . . . 17 B2
Flintwich Manor CM1 . . . 204 E7
Flitch Ind Est The
  CM6 . . . . 150 D7
Flitch La CM6 . . . . 150 E7
Flixton Cl CO16 . . . . 188 A4
Flood La CO4 . . . . 110 C6
Flora Rd CM8 . . . . 176 D4
Florence Cotts CO7 . . . . 185 F6
Florence Rd CO14 . . . . . 144 E2
Florence Wlk 8
  CM23 . . . . 145 F8
Florie's Rd CO6 . . . . 131 F8
Flowers Way CO15 . . . . 203 G7
Foley Cotts CM7 . . . . . . 102 D3
Folkards La CO7 . . . . . . 185 F8
Folley The CO3 . . . . 134 D5
FOLLY GREEN 103 D1
Folly La IP8 . . . . 35 D4
Folly Mill La CM6 . . . . . . 96 E6
Folly The
  Layer de la H CO2 . . . 162 A5
  Tiptree CO5 . . . . 179 F2
  Wivenhoe CO7 . . . . . . 164 C7
Fonnereau Rd IP1 . . . . . . 17 C6
FORD END
  Clavering 64 E4
  Felsted 172 B7
Ford End CE Prim Sch
  CM3 . . . . 172 B6
FORDHAM 107 D5
Fordham All Saints CE
Prim Sch CO6 . . . . 107 D4
FORDHAM HEATH 107 C7
Fordham Pl IP4 . . . . 18 F5
Fordham Rd
  Bures CO6, CO8 . . . . . . 79 F2
  Wormingford CO6 . . . . . 80 E2
Ford La CO7 . . . . 165 A5
Ford Rd CO15 . . . . 188 D3
Fords La CO4 . . . . 109 D5
Fordson Rd CM2 . . . . . . 206 B6
Ford St CO6 . . . . 107 C2
Fordwater Cl CO9 . . . . . . 10 B3
Fordwich Rd CO7 . . . . . 165 E1
Forefield La CM6 . . . . . . 205 F7
Fore Field CM7 . . . . 128 D3
Fore Hamlet IP3 . . . . 17 E5
Foremans CM1 . . . . 204 E3
Foresight Rd CO2 . . . . . 136 D2
Fore St IP4 . . . . 17 D5
Forest Dr CM1 . . . . 204 E1
Forester Dr IP8 . . . . 36 E8
Foresters Ct CO7 . . . . . 137 B1
Foresthall Rd CM24 . . . . 119 E4
Forest Park Ave CO15 . . 188 F7
Forest Rd
  Colchester CO4 . . . . . 136 D7
  Witham CM8 . . . . 177 A5
Forfar Cl IP4 . . . . 18 B8

Forfields Way CM77 . . . 155 E6
Forge Cotts CO10 . . . . . . 13 E6
Forge Cres CM77 . . . . . 129 D3
Forge Ct CO7 . . . . 111 E7
Forges Cnr CO10 . . . . . . 13 E6
Forge St CO7 . . . . 85 A6
Former Horsehair Factory
  CO10 . . . . 2 C5
Fornham Ho IP4 . . . . 18 B6
Forres CO13 . . . . 170 F4
Forrest Ct IP4 . . . . 18 A7
FORRY'S GREEN 75 B6
Forsyth Dr CM7 . . . . . . 155 A8
Forsythia Cl CM1 . . . . . 205 E7
Forties Cl CB9 . . . . 9 D8
Fortinbras Way CM2 . . . 216 B8
Fortis CM8 . . . . 194 E8
Fortis Ho 4 CM8 . . . . . . 194 E8
Fortune Cl CM3 . . . . . . 174 A7
Fossetts La CO6 . . . . . . 107 F4
Foster Ct 2 CM8 . . . . . . 177 A2
Foster Rd
  Great Totham CM9 . . . 196 A4
  Harwich CO12 . . . . 90 E5
Foster's Cotts CM77 . . . 129 E1
Foundation St 13 IP4 . . . 17 C5
Foundry La
  Copford CO6 . . . . 133 D5
  Earls Colne CO6 . . . . . 105 B6
  Ipswich IP2 . . . . 17 C5
Fountain Ct
  Harwich CO12 . . . . 91 E5
  West Mersea CO5 . . . . 201 D7
Fountain La
  Copford CO6 . . . . 134 A1
  Easthorpe CO6 . . . . . . 160 F8
Fountains Rd IP2 . . . . 16 F1
Four Acres
  Great Chesterford CB10 . . 3 E3
  Saffron Walden CB11 . . 22 E1
Four Ashes CM7 . . . . 74 C1
Four Ash Hill CO9 . . . . . . 10 E1
Four Sisters CO7 . . . . 59 B5
Fourth Ave
  Chelmsford CM1 . . . . 205 B5
  Clacton-on-S CO15 . . . 189 C4
  Frinton-on-S CO13 . . . 170 F4
  Glemsford CO10 . . . . . . 2 B5
  Halstead CO9 . . . . 77 B1
  Seawick CO16 . . . . . . 203 B6
  Stansted Mountfitchet
  CM24 . . . . 120 B2
Fourways CM22 . . . . 94 C1
Fowe's La CO10 . . . . 31 B8
Fowler Ct CM2 . . . . 216 A4
Fowlers Arc CO13 . . . . . 170 F4
Fowlmere Rd SG8 . . . . . . 19 A6
Foxberry Gdns IP3 . . . . . 18 D5
Foxburrow Rd IP3 . . . . . . 18 F1
Fox Burrows La CM1 . . . 204 B2
Fox Cres CM1 . . . . 204 F4
Foxdells La CM23 . . . . . 118 F2
Foxden CM8 . . . . 177 D6
FOXEARTH 14 C6
Foxendale Folly CO3 . . . 134 C7
Foxes Cnr CO6 . . . . 107 D1
Foxes La
  Aldham CO3, CO6 . . . . 133 D8
  Ashen CO10 . . . . 11 D1
Foxes Rd CO10 . . . . 11 E1
Foxglove Cl
  Bishop's Stortford
  CM23 . . . . 145 C6
  Clacton-on-S CO15 . . . 188 F7
  Witham CM8 . . . . 176 D3
Foxglove Cres IP3 . . . . . . 18 E1
Foxglove Wlk 4 CO4 . . . 136 E7
Foxgrove La IP11 . . . . . . 221 F5
Foxhall Cl CO7 . . . . 59 C4
Foxhall Fields CO7 . . . . . 59 C3
Foxhall Rd IP3, IP4 . . . . . 18 D5
Foxholes Rd CM2 . . . . . 216 F6
Foxley Cl IP3 . . . . 18 D4
Foxley Dr CM23 . . . . . . 146 B8
Foxmead CM8 . . . . 177 D6
Fox St CO7 . . . . 110 F4
FOX STREET 110 F4
Foxtail Rd IP3 . . . . 38 E8
Foxwood Cl CO11 . . . . . . 85 C2
Foxwood Cres IP4 . . . . . . 18 F5
Fox Yd CO9 . . . . 53 C5
Frambury La CB11 . . . . . . 66 F8
Framlingham Ct 5
  IP1 . . . . 17 A8
Framlingham Way
  CM77 . . . . 154 C7
Frampton Rd IP3 . . . . 38 A8
Frances Cl CO7 . . . . 137 B2
Frances Gn CM1 . . . . . . 206 A7
Franciscan Way IP1 . . . . . 17 C5
Francis Cl
  Haverhill CB9 . . . . 8 F8
  Tiptree CO5 . . . . 179 C4
Francis Ct
  Copford CO6 . . . . 133 C4
  Silver End CM8 . . . . . 156 C5
Francis Kellerman Wlk
  CO3 . . . . 135 E7
Francis Rd
  Braintree CM7 . . . . . . 127 D2
  14 Sudbury CO10 . . . . 33 E7
Francis St CO7 . . . . 185 F5
Francis Way
  Colchester CO4 . . . . . 110 D1
  Silver End CM8 . . . . . 156 C4
Frank Clater Cl CO4 . . . . 136 C8
Franklin Rd IP3 . . . . 18 B2

Frank Naylor Ct 11
  CO1 . . . . 135 F7
Fraser Cl CM2 . . . . 216 C8
Fraser Rd IP1 . . . . 16 F7
Frating Abbey Farm Rd
  CO7 . . . . 166 C6
Frating Cross CO7 . . . . . 166 B7
Frating Ct CM7 . . . . 128 D1
FRATING GREEN 139 A3
Frating Hill CO7 . . . . . . 138 D3
Frating Rd
  Ardleigh CO7 . . . . 111 F6
  Great Bromley CO7 . . . 138 F6
  Thorrington CO7 . . . . . 166 A7
Fredrick J French Meml
Homes CM1 . . . . 205 B6
Fredricks Cl CO11 . . . . . 115 B5
Freebournes Ct 5
  CM8 . . . . 177 A2
Freebournes Rd CM8 . . . 177 B2
Freehold Rd IP4 . . . . 18 B6
Freeland Rd CO15 . . . . . 188 E1
Freelands
  Brightlingsea CO7 . . . . 186 C6
  Ipswich IP4 . . . . 18 B6
Freeman Cl CO4 . . . . . . 110 A6
Freeport Designer Outlet
  CM77 . . . . 128 C1
Freeport Office Village
  CM7 . . . . 128 B1
Freeport Sta 17 CM7 . . . 128 B1
Free Rodwell Ho CO11 . . . 86 F4
Freewood La CB11 . . . . . 20 B3
Freezes Barns CB9 . . . . . 27 B7
Fremantle Rd CO2 . . . . . 136 B1
FRENCHES GREEN 153 A6
French's Wlk 4 CM2 . . . 205 C2
Frensham Cl CO3 . . . . . 134 D7
Frere Ct CM23 . . . . 118 F1
Frere Way CO5 . . . . 164 B6
Freshfields CO12 . . . . 90 F1
Freshfields Rd CO12 . . . . 91 A4
Freshwater Cres CM9 . . 210 B4
Freshwater La CO15 . . . 188 F7
Freshwell Gdns CB10 . . . 22 C2
Freshwell St CB10 . . . . . 22 D2
FRESTON 37 E3
Freston Hill IP9 . . . . 37 E4
Freston Rd IP3 . . . . 38 C8
Freston St IP9 . . . . 37 E3
Friars IP9 . . . . 60 B8
Friars Bridge Rd IP1 . . . . 17 B5
Friars Cl
  Clacton-on-S CO15 . . . 188 E6
  Colchester CO4 . . . . . 110 C2
  Sible Hedingham CO9 . . 51 D2
  Wivenhoe CO7 . . . . . . 164 C8
Friar's Cotts CM77 . . . . 154 B4
Friars Ct
  Colchester CO2 . . . . . 136 C3
  15 Sudbury CO10 . . . . 33 E7
Friars Ctyd 1 IP1 . . . . . . 17 C5
Friars Grove Jun & Inf
Schs CO4 . . . . 110 C2
Friars La
  Braintree CM7 . . . . . . 127 A4
  Maldon CM9 . . . . 209 F2
Friars Mead CB9 . . . . 9 F4
Friars St
  Ipswich IP1 . . . . 17 C5
  Sudbury CO10 . . . . 33 E7
Friars Wlk CM2 . . . . 205 B1
Friars Wood CM23 . . . . 146 C8
Friary Fields CM9 . . . . . 210 A2
Friday Wood Gn CO2 . . . 162 F8
Friedberg Ave CM23 . . . 145 D4
Friends Field CO8 . . . . . . 55 F1
Friends Sch CB11 . . . . . . 43 D8
Friends Wlk CB11 . . . . . . 43 D7
Friesian Cl CM7 . . . . . . 127 D2
Frietuna Rd CO13 . . . . . 170 E6
Frinton Ct CO13 . . . . . . 170 F3
Frinton Lo CO13 . . . . . . 171 A4
FRINTON-ON-SEA 170 D5
Frinton-on-Sea Prim Sch
  CO13 . . . . 170 E5
Frinton Rd
  Holland-on-S CO15 . . . 189 E6
  Kirby Cross CO13 . . . . 170 D6
  Thorpe-le-S CO16 . . . . 142 B1
Frinton Sta CO13 . . . . . 170 F5
Fritillary Cl IP8 . . . . 36 E8
Fritton Cl IP2 . . . . 17 A1
Fritton Ct 19 CB9 . . . . 8 E7
Frobisher Dr CO15 . . . . 187 F1
Frobisher Prim Sch
  CO15 . . . . 187 F1
Frobisher Rd
  Harwich CO12 . . . . 90 F1
  Ipswich IP3 . . . . 17 E1
Frobisher Way CM7 . . . . 128 C4
Frogge St CB10 . . . . 3 B3
Frog Hall Cl CO5 . . . . . . 164 B6
Frog Mdw CO7 . . . . 84 F7
Fronk's Ave CO12 . . . . . . 91 C2
Fronk's Rd CO12 . . . . 91 B2
Front Rd IP3 . . . . 38 D8
Frowick La CO16 . . . . . . 167 B2
Fryatt Ave CO12 . . . . 91 A4
Fryatt Hospl CO12 . . . . . 91 A3
Fuchsia Ct 6 CO4 . . . . . 136 D8
Fuchsia La IP4 . . . . 18 A5
Fuchsia Way CO16 . . . . 188 C5
Fulcher Ave CM2 . . . . . . 205 F3
Fulfen Way CB11 . . . . . . 43 D7

Fullbridge CM9 . . . . **210** A3
Fuller Ct **3** CM23 . . . . **146** A7
Fuller's Almshouses
CM24 . . . . **119** F6
Fuller's Cl CO5 . . . . **158** B2
Fullers Ct CM7 . . . . **128** A3
FULLER'S END **120** D8
Fullers Gate CO5 . . . . . . **158** B2
Fullers Rd CO2 . . . . **136** D2
FULLER STREET **174** D4
Fulmar Cl CO4 . . . . **137** A8
Fulton Cres CM23 . . . . . **146** C8
Furneaux La CO5 . . . . . . **163** F5
Furness Cl IP2 . . . . **36** F8
Furriers CM23 . . . . **145** C5
Furrow Cl CO3 . . . . **134** E5
FURTHER FORD END **64** D6
Further Mdw CM1 . . . . . . **215** A8
Furze Cres CO7 . . . . **165** A7
Furze La CO7 . . . . **139** A5

G

Gablefields CM2 . . . . . . **217** D6
Gable Ho IP4 . . . . **17** F6
Gables The CB9 . . . .**9** F4
Gabriel Ho CM6 . . . . **150** D8
Gaces Acre CB11 . . . . **43** A1
Gadwall Reach CO5 . . . . **158** D2
Gager Dr CO5 . . . . **179** E5
Gage's Rd
Belchamp St P CO10 . . . . **13** A1
Little Yeldham C10 . . . . . . **30** F8
Gaiger Cl CM1 . . . . **205** D7
GAINSBOROUGH **38** B8
Gainsborough Cl
Clacton-on-S CO16 . . . . **188** B6
West Mersea CO5 . . . . . **201** D6
Gainsborough Cres
CM2 . . . . **205** E3
Gainsborough Ct **17**
CO10 . . . . **33** E7
Gainsborough Dr CO11 . . **86** C4
Gainsborough La IP3 . . . . **37** F7
Gainsborough Rd
Black Notley CM77 . . . . **155** A4
Colchester CO3 . . . . . . **135** B5
Felixstowe IP11 . . . . **221** F4
Ipswich IP4 . . . . **17** D8
Sudbury CO10 . . . . **33** E8
Gainsborough's House
Mus★ CO10 . . . . **33** E7
Gainsborough St CO10 . . **33** E7
Gainsford Ave CO15 . . . **189** B4
GAINSFORD END **49** F4
Gainsford End Rd CO9 . . **50** B6
Galiots CO5 . . . . **201** A6
Gall End La CM24 . . . . . . **119** F7
Galleydene Ave CM2 . . . **216** C3
GALLEYEND **216** D4
GALLEYWOOD **216** D2
Galleywood Inf Sch
CM2 . . . . **216** C2
Galleywood Rd
Chelmsford CM2 . . . . . . **216** A5
Great Baddow CM2 . . . . **216** E5
Galliford Rd CM9 . . . . . . **210** A4
Galliford Road Ind Est
CM9 . . . . **210** A4
Galloway Cl **1** CM23 . . **145** F8
Galloway Dr CO16 . . . . . **168** D3
Galloway Rd CM23 . . . . . **118** F1
GALLOWS GREEN
Fordham Heath **107** C1
Great Easton **97** F2
Gallows Green Rd CM6 . . **97** F2
Gallows Hill CB11 . . . . . . **43** C7
Galpin Ho CM8 . . . . **194** F8
Galsworthy Cl CM7 . . . . **155** A7
GAMBLES GREEN **175** A2
Gamma Terr IP3 . . . . **18** E1
Gandish Cl CO7 . . . . **59** D1
Gandish Rd CO7 . . . . **59** E2
Ganges Rd IP9 . . . . **91** B8
Gannet Cl CB9 . . . .**9** C8
Gannet Rd IP2 . . . . **16** D7
Ganymede Cl IP1 . . . . **16** D7
Gaol La CO10 . . . . **33** E7
Gap The
Arkesden CB11 . . . . **41** F1
Holland-on-S CO15 . . . . **189** G6
Garden Cotts CO6 . . . . . **131** A2
Garden Ct CO13 . . . . **170** F3
Garden Dr CO3 . . . . **134** E6
Gardeners CM2 . . . . **216** D5
Gardeners Rd CO9 . . . . . . **76** F1
Gardeners Row CO6 . . . . **131** A2
Garden Farm CO5 . . . . . **201** D6
Garden Field
Felixstowe IP11 . . . . **221** C5
Hatfield Peverel CM3 . . . **193** F4
Garden Field Cotts
CO6 . . . . **81** E5
Garden Fields
Great Tey CO6 . . . . **132** C8
Stebbing CM6 . . . . **124** D6
Gardenia Pl CO16 . . . . . . **188** B4
Gardenia Wlk CO4 . . . . . **136** E7
Garden Pl CO10 . . . . **33** D7
Garden Rd
Clacton-on-S CO15 . . . . **203** G7
Walton-on-t-N CO14 . . . . **171** A7
Garden Terr CO9 . . . . **76** F2
Garfield Cl IP11 . . . . **221** D3

Garfield Rd IP11 . . . . **221** D3
Garland Rd CO12 . . . . **90** F5
Garling Wlk CO6 . . . . **108** E3
Garnets Mead CM3. . . . . **175** B3
Garnetts CM22 . . . . **148** B8
Garnetts Bglws CM6 . . . . **152** C5
Garnetts La CM6 . . . . **152** C6
Garnetts Villas CM6 . . . . **152** C5
Garnons Chase CO6 . . . . . **81** A5
Garret Pl CO6 . . . . **108** F4
Garrettlands CM2 . . . . . . **217** F6
Garrison La IP11 . . . . **221** D4
Garrods IP9 . . . . **35** B1
Garthwood Cl CO6 . . . . . **108** E4
Gascoigne Rd CO4 . . . . . **136** C8
Gasfield **14** CO11 . . . . . . **86** D4
Gasgoine Ho CO4 . . . . . . **109** F4
Gaston End CO7 . . . . **59** C3
Gaston St CO7 . . . . **59** C3
Gatacre Ct CO2 . . . . **135** B3
Gatacre Rd IP1 . . . . **17** A7
Gatefield Cl CO14 . . . . . . **170** F7
Gatefield Ct CO14 . . . . . . **170** F7
Gatehouse Villas CM6 . . . **150** E7
Gatekeeper Cl
8 Braintree CM7 . . . . . **127** F1
Ipswich IP8 . . . . **36** E8
Gate Street Mews
CM9 . . . . **209** F3
Gatwick Cl IP11 . . . . **119** B1
Gauden Rd CM7 . . . . **127** C1
Gavin Way CO4 . . . . **110** B6
Gawlers CM23 . . . . **92** B8
GAY BOWERS **219** B1
Gay Bowers La CM3 . . . . **218** F6
Gay Bowers Rd CM3 . . . . **218** F4
Gay Bowers Way CM8 . . . **195** A2
Gaye St **1** IP1 . . . . **17** B6
Gazelle Ct CO4 . . . . **110** C4
Geetons The CO5 . . . . . . **163** C3
Generals La CM3 . . . . **192** B3
Generals Mews IP11 . . . . **221** B5
Genesta Cl CM9 . . . . **199** D2
Geneva Rd IP1 . . . . **17** B7
Genevyll Cl CO10 . . . .**1** D2
Gentian Ct CO4 . . . . **109** C2
Geoff Seaden Cl **2**
CO1 . . . . **136** C6
George Ave CO7 . . . . **185** F7
George Cl CO15 . . . . **188** C2
George Ct CM2 . . . . **205** B1
George Cut CO7 . . . . **185** F6
George Frost Cl IP4 . . . . . **17** D7
George Gent Cl CB9 . . . . . **27** B6
George Green Bglws
CM22 . . . . **146** B1
George La CO10 . . . .**2** B3
George Rd CM7 . . . . **127** D2
George St
Chelmsford CM2 . . . . . . **205** B1
12 Colchester CO1 . . . . **135** F7
Harwich CO12 . . . . **91** D6
Saffron Walden CB10. . . . **22** D1
George Williams Way
CO1 . . . . **136** A6
George Yard Sh Ctr **8**
CM7 . . . . **127** F3
Georgian Ct IP11 . . . . . . **221** D5
Georgian Ho CM7 . . . . . . **128** A4
Gepp Pl CM2 . . . . **206** B4
Geralds Ave IP4 . . . . **18** A5
Geranium Cl CO16 . . . . . **188** C4
Geranium Wlk CO4 . . . . . **136** D7
Gerard Ave CM23 . . . . . . **145** E4
Gerard Gdns CM2 . . . . . . **216** D8
Gerard Rd CO16 . . . . **188** C6
Gernon Cl CM1 . . . . **191** B3
Gernon Rd CO7 . . . . **111** E7
Gershwin Bvd CM8. . . . . **194** F7
GESTINGTHORPE **31** E1
Gestingthorpe Rd
CO10 . . . . **31** F4
Gibbons Ct CM6 . . . . **123** D1
Gibbons St **3** IP1 . . . . . . **17** A4
Gibbs Field CM23 . . . . . . **145** D5
Gibson Cl
Ipswich IP3 . . . . **18** C2
Saffron Walden CB10. . . . **22** D1
Gibson Gdns CB10 . . . . . . **22** D1
Gibson Rd CO9 . . . . **51** D1
Gibson Vale CM1 . . . . . . **205** B8
Gibson Way CB10 . . . . **22** D1
Giffins Cl CM7 . . . . **127** F1
Gifford Cl IP9 . . . . **62** D5
Giffords Pl IP4 . . . . **18** A7
Gilberd Cl CO4 . . . . **110** C6
Gilberd Ho CO3 . . . . **135** A4
Gilberd Rd CO2 . . . . **136** B4
Gilberd Sch The CO4. . . . **110** B5
Gilbert Rd CO10 . . . . **12** B8
Gilbert Way CM7. . . . . . . **128** C5
Gilbey Ave CM23 . . . . . . **146** B6
Gilbey Cotts CM22 . . . . . . **94** C1
Gilbey Cres CM24 . . . . . . **119** E8
Gilbey Gn CB11 . . . . **42** F1
Gilchrist Way CM7 . . . . . **127** E4
Gilderdale Cl CO4. . . . . . **110** C6
Gilders Way CO16. . . . . . **188** C5
Gill Cl CM9 . . . . **209** F6
Gilmore Way CM2. . . . . . **217** B6
Gilpin Way CM77. . . . . . . **154** C7
Gilson Cl CM2 . . . . **205** F2
Gilwell Park Cl CO3 . . . . **135** A4
Gimson Cl CM8 . . . . **176** F2

Gippeswyk Ave IP2 . . . . . **17** A4
Gippeswyk Rd IP2 . . . . . . **17** B4
Gipping Cl CB9 . . . .**8** E6
Gipping Way IP8 . . . . **16** B6
Gipsy La CM23, CM24 . . . **119** C4
Girling St CO10 . . . . **33** E8
Girton Rd CB9 . . . .**9** B7
Girton Way IP2 . . . . **16** F1
Glade The CO4 . . . . **110** F2
Gladeview CO15 . . . . **188** F7
Gladiator Way CO2 . . . . . **135** A2
Gladstone Ct CM2 . . . . . **205** B1
Gladstone Rd
Colchester CO1 . . . . **136** B5
Tiptree CO5 . . . . **179** D4
Gladwin Rd CO2 . . . . **135** D4
Glamis Cl CB9 . . . .**8** D8
Glamorgan Rd IP2 . . . . . . **17** B1
Glastonbury Cl IP2 . . . . . . **16** F1
Glebe Ave CM7 . . . . **127** F6
Glebe Cl
Elmstead Market CO7 . . . **138** A4
Sproughton IP8 . . . . **16** B6
Tattingstone IP9 . . . . **61** C7
Wix CO11 . . . . **115** C5
Glebe Cres
Broomfield CM1 . . . . **191** B1
Witham CM8 . . . . **176** E4
Glebe Ct CM23 . . . . **146** B8
Glebe End
Capel St M IP9 . . . . **35** B2
Elsenham CM22 . . . . **94** D1
Glebefield Rd CM3 . . . . . **194** B4
Glebe Gdns CO5 . . . . **158** E5
Glebe La
Chelmondiston IP9 . . . . . **63** A8
Little Easton CM6 . . . . . **122** F5
Woolverstone IP9 . . . . . . **38** B1
Glebelands CO6 . . . . **82** B1
Glebe Mdw CM3 . . . . **190** E7
Glebe Rd
Chelmsford CM1 . . . . . . **205** B3
Colchester CO2 . . . . **135** C2
Heybridge CM9 . . . . **210** C5
Kelvedon CO5 . . . . **158** B2
Tiptree CO5 . . . . **179** C5
Glebe The
Elmdon CB11 . . . . **20** A4
Elsenham CM22 . . . . **94** C1
Peldon CO5 . . . . **182** E5
Purleigh CM3. . . . . **220** D1
Saffron Walden CB11. . . . . **43** F7
Glebe View
Galleywood CM2 . . . . . . **216** B3
West Mersea CO5 . . . . . **201** E8
Glebe Way
Clacton-on-S CO15 . . . . **203** G7
Frinton-on-S CO13 . . . . . **170** F5
Glemham Dr IP4. . . . . **18** F4
GLEMSFORD **2** C4
Glemsford Pl IP11 . . . . . . **221** B3
Glemsford Com Prim Sch
CO10. . . . .**2** B5
Glemsford Pl **3** CB9 . . . . . .**9** B8
Glen Ave CO3. . . . . **135** B7
Glenavon Rd IP4 . . . . **18** D7
Glencoe Rd IP4. . . . . **18** C8
Glendale Gr CO4. . . . . . . **110** C3
Gleneagles Dr IP4 . . . . . . **18** D5
Gleneagles Way CM3. . . . **194** B4
Gleneley Ct CO13 . . . . . . **170** F3
Glenfield Ave IP11 . . . . . **221** E5
Glenhurst Ave IP4 . . . . . . **18** A8
Glenside CO10 . . . . **34** A6
Glentress Ct CO4 . . . . **110** D3
Glenway Cl CO6 . . . . **82** B1
Glenway Ct CO6 . . . . **82** B1
Glisson Sq CO2 . . . . **135** B4
Globe Cl CO5 . . . . **179** D6
Globe Cres CM23 . . . . . . **118** D6
Globe Wlk CO5 . . . . **179** D6
Globe Yd **4** CO10 . . . . . . **33** E8
Gloucester Ave
Chelmsford CM2 . . . . . . **216** C6
Colchester CO2 . . . . **135** C3
Maldon CM9. . . . . **209** F1
Gloucester Cres CM1. . . . **205** A5
Gloucester Gdns CM7 . . . **128** B4
Gloucester Ho IP11 . . . . . **221** C6
Gloucester Rd
Haverhill CB9. . . . .**8** F6
Ipswich IP3 . . . . **18** B2
Gloucester Way CO10 . . . **15** D2
Glovers CM3. . . . . **173** F7
Glovershotts CM1. . . . . . **191** B2
Goat Hall La
Chelmsford CM2 . . . . . . **215** F3
Galleywood CM2 . . . . . . **216** A3
Goat House La CM3 . . . . . **219** F4
Goat Lodge Rd CM8,
CM9. . . . . **196** A5
Goda Cl CM8 . . . . **194** D8
Goddard Way
Chelmsford CM2 . . . . . . **205** F2
Saffron Walden CB10. . . . **22** E3
Godfreys Mews CM7 . . . . **205** B1
Godfrey Way CM6. . . . . . **123** C1
Godlings Way CM7. . . . . . **127** F2
Godmans La CO6 . . . . **132** E3
Godric Pl CM7 . . . . **127** E3
Godric Rd CM8 . . . . **194** E8
Godwin Cl CO9 . . . . **76** D1
Godwit Ct CO5 . . . . **158** D2
Goff's La CO16 . . . . **141** F8
Goings La CO5 . . . . **201** D6
Gold Cl CM22 . . . . **94** B3
Goldcrest Cl CO4 . . . . . . **137** A8

Goldcrest Ct IP2. . . . . **16** D3
Goldcrest Rd IP2 . . . . **16** C3
Goldenacres CM1 . . . . . . **205** F8
Golden Dawn Way
CO4 . . . . **109** E2
Golden La
Radwinter CB10. . . . . **25** A2
Thorpe-le-S CO16 . . . . . **141** F3
Golden Lion La CO12. . . . **91** E6
Goldenlonds CO6 . . . . **56** C5
Golden Noble Hill
CO1. . . . . **136** A6
Goldfinch Cl CO4 . . . . . . **136** F7
GOLDHANGER **211** F7
Goldhanger Ct CM7 . . . . **128** D1
Goldhanger Rd CM9 . . . . **210** D4
Goldingham Dr CM7 . . . . **155** A7
Goldings CM3. . . . . **146** B8
Golding Thoroughfare
CM2 . . . . **205** F3
Golding Way
Glemsford CO10 . . . .**2** B4
St Osyth CO16 . . . . **187** A5
Goldlay Ave CM2. . . . . . . **216** C8
Goldlay Gdns CM2 . . . . . **205** C1
Goldlay Rd CM2. . . . . **205** C1
Golds Nursery Bsns Pk
CM22 . . . . **94** C3
Gold St CB10 . . . . **22** D1
Golf Green Rd CO15 . . . . **203** G8
Goodchild Way CO9. . . . . **30** A2
Goodey Cl CO1 . . . . **136** A6
Goodier Rd CM1 . . . . **204** F4
Goodlake Cl CO12. . . . . . . **90** F2
Goodliffe Pk CM23 . . . . . **119** B2
Goodmans La CM3 . . . . . **173** F4
Goodwin Cl CM2 . . . . **216** D8
Goodwins Cl CB11 . . . . . . **21** E3
Goodwin Stile CM23 . . . . **145** D5
Goodwyns Mews CO7 . . . **166** E8
Goojerat Rd CO2 . . . . **135** D5
GOOSE GREEN
Tendring Green **140** E7
Wix **114** E3
Gordian Wlk CO4 . . . . . . **110** B5
Gordon Dr CO4 . . . . **110** C5
Gordon Rd
Chelmsford CM2 . . . . . . **216** A6
Harwich CO12 . . . . **91** B2
Ipswich IP4 . . . . **18** A7
Gordon Way CO12 . . . . . . **91** B2
Gorefield Rd CM22,
CM24 . . . . **121** B5
Gorefield Rdbt CM24 . . . **121** B4
Gore La CM77 . . . . **127** A2
Gore Rd CM77 . . . . **127** A2
Gore Terr CM77. . . . . **127** A2
Goring Ho CO4 . . . . **109** E4
Goring Rd
Colchester CO4 . . . . **110** C1
Ipswich IP4 . . . . **18** C6
Gorsehayes IP2. . . . . **17** B3
Gorse La
Clacton-on-S CO15 . . . . **189** A8
Tiptree CO5 . . . . **179** C4
Gorse Lane Ind Est
CO15. . . . . **189** B8
Gorse Rd IP3 . . . . **18** B2
Gorse Way
Clacton-on-S CO15 . . . . **203** F7
Colchester CO3 . . . . **134** D4
Gorse Wlk CO4 . . . . **136** D7
Gosbecks Bsns Pk
CO2. . . . . **135** B2
Gosbecks Prim Sch
CO2. . . . . **135** A3
Gosbecks Rd CO2 . . . . . . **135** A2
Gosbecks View CO2. . . . . **135** A2
GOSFIELD **102** E7
Gosfield Com Prim Sch
CO9. . . . . **102** E8
Gosfield Hall★ CO9 . . . . **102** C8
Gosford Ct CO10 . . . . **12** B8
Goshawk Dr CM2 . . . . . . **216** B5
Goslings The CM8 . . . . . . **156** C5
Gouldings Ave CO14 . . . . **171** B8
Goulds Rd CO8 . . . . **54** F2
Goul La CB10 . . . . **22** D1
Goulton Rd CM1 . . . . **191** A1
Government Ct CO12. . . . . **91** E5
Gowers Ave CM2 . . . . . . **216** E6
Gowers End CO10 . . . .**2** C5
Gower St IP2 . . . . **17** C4
Goyfield Ave IP11 . . . . . . **221** D4
Grace Gdns CM23 . . . . . . **145** E4
Graces Cl CM8 . . . . **195** A7
Grace's Cross CM2 . . . . . **217** C2
Graces La CM3 . . . . **207** B1
Graces Wlk CO13 . . . . . . **171** A6
Grafton Pl CM2 . . . . **206** A4
Grafton Rd CO12 . . . . **91** D4
Grafton Way IP1 . . . . **17** C5
Graham Ave IP1 . . . . **17** B8
Graham Rd
Felixstowe IP11 . . . . **221** D5
Ipswich IP1 . . . . **17** B7
Grailands CM23. . . . . **145** D8
Grammar School Pl **11**
CO10 . . . . **33** E7
Grampian Gr CM1 . . . . . . **204** D6
Granaries CM9. . . . . **210** A3

Granary Ct
12 Colchester CO1 . . . . **136** C6
Great Dunmow CM6 . . . . **150** D7
Granary The
Bures CO8 . . . . **55** F1
Clare CO10 . . . . **12** B6
Granchester Ct CO4. . . . . **110** C4
Grand Ct CO13 . . . . **170** F3
Grand The CO13 . . . . **170** F3
Grange Cl
Felixstowe IP11 . . . . **221** C5
Halstead CO9. . . . . **103** E7
Walton-on-t-N CO14 . . . . **171** A7
Grange Com Prim Sch
IP11 . . . . **221** B4
Grange Ct
Chelmsford CM2 . . . . . . **215** F7
Clacton-on-S CO16. . . . . **188** A4
Grange Farm CO2. . . . . . **136** D4
Grange Farm Ave
IP11 . . . . **221** B5
Grange Farm Rd CO2 . . . **136** D4
Grange Hill CO6 . . . . **130** F1
Grange La CM6 . . . . **151** C7
Grange Mill CO6 . . . . **130** F1
Grange Pk CM23 . . . . **118** F1
Granger Ave CM9 . . . . . . **209** F1
Grange Rd
Bishop's Stortford
CM23 . . . . **146** A7
Felixstowe IP11 . . . . **221** B4
Great Horkesley CO6 . . . **109** B7
Harwich CO12 . . . . **91** A3
Ickleton CB10 . . . . **20** A8
Ipswich IP4 . . . . **17** E6
Lawford CO11 . . . . **85** F1
Little Bromley CO11. . . . . **112** E7
Tiptree CO5 . . . . **179** A6
Wickham Bishops CM8 . . **195** E4
Granger Row CM1 . . . . . . **204** F6
Grangeside CM23 . . . . . . **119** A2
Grange The CM23 . . . . . . **118** F1
Grange Way CO2. . . . . . . **136** D3
Grange Way Bsns Pk
CO2. . . . . **136** D3
Grange Wlk CM23 . . . . . . **146** A7
GRANSMORE GREEN
. . . . **125** F1
Granta Cl CB10 . . . .**3** D1
Granta Cotts CB10 . . . .**3** C2
Grantham Ave CM7 . . . . . **154** B7
Grantham Cres IP2 . . . . . . **17** A4
Grantham Ct CO1 . . . . . . **136** A7
Grantham Rd CO6. . . . . . **109** B7
Grantley Cl CO6 . . . . **133** D5
Grants Ct CO14 . . . . **171** C8
Granville Cl CO6 . . . . **108** E3
Granville Rd
Clacton-on-S CO15. . . . . **188** F3
Colchester CO1 . . . . **136** B5
Felixstowe IP11 . . . . **221** D3
Granville St **2** IP1 . . . . . . **17** B6
Granville Way CO7 . . . . . **186** A7
Grasby Cl CO7 . . . . **137** B2
Grasmere Cl
Great Notley CM77 . . . . **154** C6
Ipswich IP3 . . . . **18** B1
Grasmere Gdns CO13 . . . **170** F7
Grassfields CO13 . . . . . . **170** E6
GRASS GREEN **29** B1
Grassmere CO4. . . . . **110** B5
Gratian Cl CO4. . . . . **110** B5
Gravel Ct CO6 . . . . **130** F2
Gravel Hill CO6 . . . . **56** A2
Gravel Hill Way CO12 . . . . **90** F1
Gravel Pit La CO11 . . . . . . **60** E2
Gravel The CO6. . . . . **130** F2
Grayling Cl CM7 . . . . **127** E1
Grayling Dr CO4 . . . . **110** F1
Grayling Rd IP8 . . . . **36** E8
Gray Rd CO3. . . . . **135** D6
Grays Brewery Yd **8**
CM2 . . . . **205** C2
Grays Cl CO5 . . . . **201** C6
Gray's Cotts CO1 . . . . **136** B7
Grays Ct CM23 . . . . **145** E8
Gray's La CM7 . . . . **73** E4
Grays Mead CO9 . . . . **51** D2
GREAT BADDOW **216** E7
Great Baddow High Sch
CM2 . . . . **216** D6
GREAT BARDFIELD **72** C1
Great Bardfield Cage★
CM7 . . . . **72** B2
Great Bardfield Cottage
Mus★ CM7 . . . . **72** A1
Great Bardfield Prim Sch
CM7 . . . . **72** B2
GREAT BENTLEY **166** D8
Great Bentley Prim Sch
CO7. . . . . **166** E7
Great Bentley Rd
CO7. . . . . **166** A8
Great Bentley Sta
CO7. . . . . **166** E7
Great Bradfords Jun & Inf
Schs CM7 . . . . **128** B4
GREAT BRAXTED **178** C1
GREAT BROMLEY **112** F1
GREAT CANFIELD **149** C1
GREAT CHESTERFORD **3** D2
Great Chesterford CE Prim
Sch CB10. . . . .**3** D2
Great Chesterford Ct
CB10. . . . .**3** C2
Great Chesterford Sta
CB10. . . . .**3** C1
GREAT CLACTON **188** E5

Great Clacton CE Jun Sch
  CO15 . . . . .188 F6
Great Cob CM1 ⁙ 205 E5
Great Colman St �14
  1P4 . . . . .17 D6
GREAT CORNARD 34 B5
Great Cornard Ctry Pk★
  CO10 . . . . .34 C3
Great Cornard Mid Sch
  CO10 . . . . .34 C4
Great Cornard Upper Sch
  & Tech Coll CO10 . . . .34 B4
GREAT DAWKINS 25 F4
GREAT DUNMOW 150 C7
Great Dunmow Mus★
  CM6 . . . . .123 D1
Great Dunmow Prim Sch
  CM6 . . . . .123 B1
Great Eastern Cl
  CM23 . . . . .146 A6
Great Eastern Ct
  CO14 . . . . .171 C7
Great Eastern Rd CO10 . . . .33 F7
Great Eastern Sq
  IP11 . . . . .221 E5
GREAT EASTON 122 F7
Great Easton CE Prim Sch
  CM6 . . . . .123 A8
Greate House Farm Rd
  CO2 . . . . .162 A6
Great Field IP11 . . . . . .221 A8
Great Gibcracks Chase
  CM2 . . . . .218 A2
Great Gipping St IP1 . . . . .17 B5
Great Hadham Rd
  CM23 . . . . .145 C5
GREAT HALLINGBURY
   . . . . .146 E4
Great Harrods CO14 . .171 A7
Great Havers Ct
  CM23 . . . . .145 E5
GREAT HENNY 54 C8
GREAT HOLLAND 170 A3
Great Holland Common Rd
  CO13 . . . . .169 D2
Great Holland Ct
  CO13 . . . . .170 A3
GREAT HORKESLEY 82 A1
GREAT LEIGHS 173 E7
Great Leighs Prim Sch
  CM3 . . . . .174 A7
GREAT MAPLESTEAD 52 D2
GREAT NOTLEY 154 B8
Great Notley Ave
  CM77 . . . . .154 C5
Great Notley Country Park
  & Doscovery Ctr★
  CM77 . . . . .154 A7
GREAT OAKLEY 116 C4
Great Oak Ct CO9 . . . . .30 A1
Great Pitchers CO6 . . . .105 A7
Great Priory Cotts
  CM7 . . . . .127 C8
GREAT SALING 126 A8
GREAT SAMPFORD 47 B4
Great Sampford Prim Sch
  CB10 . . . . .47 A3
Great Sq �10 CM7 . . . .127 F3
GREAT TEY 132 C8
Great Tey CE Prim Sch
  CO6 . . . . .106 C1
Great Tey Rd CO6 . . . .132 C4
GREAT TOTHAM 196 C4
Great Totham Prim Sch
  CM9 . . . . .196 A5
Great Totham Rd
  CM8 . . . . .195 F5
Great Tufts IP9 . . . . . . .35 B1
GREAT WALTHAM 190 E7
Great Waltham CE Prim
  Sch CM3 . . . . .190 E7
Great Whip St IP2 . . . . .17 C4
GREAT WIGBOROUGH
   . . . . .181 F3
GREAT YELDHAM 30 A1
Great Yeldham Rd
  CO9 . . . . .50 D7
Grebe Cl IP2 . . . . .16 E2
Greenacres
  Clacton-on-S CO15 . . . .189 A5
  Coggeshall CO6 . . . . . .130 F1
  Colchester CO4 . . . . . .109 E3
Greenacres Cvn Pk
  CO12 . . . . .91 A1
Green Acres Rd CO2 . . . .162 A5
Green Cl
  Chelmsford CM1 . . . . . .205 D4
  Hatfield Peverel CM3 . . .194 C3
  Writtle CM1 . . . . .204 B1
Green Cnr CO7 . . . . . . .139 E1
Green Ct CO6 . . . . .104 F7
Green End La CO13 . . . .170 B5
Greene View CM7 . . . . . .155 B8
Green Farm Rd CO6 . . . .78 B2
Greenfield CM8 . . . . . . .177 A1
Greenfield Cotts CO4 . . . .82 E6
Greenfield Dr CO6 . . . .106 B1
Greenfield Hos
  Birch CO2 . . . . .161 A3
  Birch Green CO2 . . . . . .160 F3
Greenfields
  Galleywood CM2 . . . . .216 C2
  Gosfield CO9 . . . . .102 F4
  Stansted Mountfitchet
  CM24 . . . . .119 E7
Greenfields Way CB9 . . . .8 E6
Greenfinch Ave IP2 . . . .16 D3
Greenfinch End CO4 . . . .136 F8

Greenford Rd CO15 . . . . .188 C3
Greengates Mobile Home
  Pk CO16 . . . . .168 C4
Greenhill Pk CM23 . . . .145 D5
Greenhurst Rd CO7 . . . .186 A6
Greenhythe Ct CO4 . . . .136 D6
Green La
  Aldham CO6 . . . . .107 C1
  Ardleigh CO7 . . . . .111 D6
  Black Notley CM8 . . . . .155 B3
  Boxted CO4 . . . . .82 D5
  Colchester CO4 . . . . . .110 C1
  Colchester, Crockleford Heath
  CO7 . . . . .111 C1
  Great Dunmow CM6 . . .150 C8
  Great Horkesley CO6 . . .109 C6
  Great Notley CM8 . . . . .154 F7
  Little Totham CM9 . . . .197 C4
  Stratford St M CO7 . . . .58 C4
  Tattingstone IP9 . . . . . . .61 D7
  Tiptree CO5 . . . . .179 D6
  Tolleshunt Knights CO5 . .179 E1
  Walton-on-t-N CO14 . . .144 D2
  Weeley Heath CO16 . . . .168 A6
Greenland Gr CO16 . . . .186 D3
Greenlawns Cvn Pk
  CO16 . . . . .168 C2
Green Man La CM8 . . . . .195 F4
Green Mdws CM3 . . . . .219 A6
Green Oak Glade IP8 . . .36 D8
Greensmill CO11 . . . . . . .86 C5
Greenspire Gr IP8 . . . . .16 B2
Green St CM6 . . . . .148 F2
GREENSTEAD 136 E6
Greenstead Ct CO1 . . . .136 D6
GREENSTEAD GREEN
   . . . . .104 A5
Greenstead Rd CO1 . . . .136 D7
Greenstead Rdbt CO4 . . .136 D6
Greens The IP4 . . . . .18 F4
Greens Yd CO13 . . . . . .170 F5
Green's Yd CO1 . . . . . . .135 E7
GREEN THE 155 C4
Green The
  Bishop's Stortford
  CM23 . . . . .145 F4
  Chelmsford CM1 . . . . . .204 F4
  Chrishall SG8 . . . . .19 D3
  Clacton-on-S CO16 . . . .188 B2
  Colne Engaine CO6 . . . . .78 A2
  Feering CO5 . . . . .158 E5
  Great Bentley CO7 . . . . .166 D8
  Hatfield Peverel CM3 . . .194 C3
  Little Totham CM9 . . . .197 C4
  Mistley CO11 . . . . .86 F4
  Saffron Walden CB10 . . .22 D3
  Seawick CO16 . . . . .203 B6
  Stanstead CO10 . . . . .2 E7
  Wickham St P CO9 . . . . .53 C5
  Writtle CM1 . . . . .204 B1
Greenview Pk CO15 . . . .189 A7
Greenway
  Bishop's Stortford
  CM23 . . . . .146 C6
  Frinton-on-S CO13 . . . .170 F5
Green Way CO6 . . . . . . .78 A2
Greenway Cl CO15 . . . .189 B7
Greenway Gdns
  CM77 . . . . .154 D7
Greenways
  Chelmsford CM1 . . . . . .205 B6
  Feering CO5 . . . . .158 D3
  Gosfield CO9 . . . . .102 F7
  Maldon CM9 . . . . .209 F2
  Saffron Walden CB11 . . . .43 E7
Greenways Cl IP1 . . . . . .17 B8
Greenways The CO6 . . . .131 A3
Greenway The CO15 . . . .189 B7
Greenwell Rd CM8 . . . . .194 F7
GREENWICH 17 E1
Greenwich Bsns Pk
  IP3 . . . . .17 E2
Greenwich Cl IP3 . . . . . .17 E2
Greenwich Rd IP3 . . . . . .17 E2
Greenwood Cl
  Chelmsford CM2 . . . . . .205 F2
  Haverhill CB9 . . . . .8 E7
Greenwood Gr CO4 . . . .110 C3
Gregory St CO10 . . . . . .33 E7
Grenadier Rd CB9 . . . . . .8 C8
Grendel Way CO15 . . . .189 F6
Grenfell Ave CO15 . . . . .189 E6
Grenfell Cl CO4 . . . . . . .110 C1
Grenville Rd
  Braintree CM7 . . . . . . .127 E2
  Sudbury CO10 . . . . .15 F2
Gresham Ct IP1 . . . . . . .17 B8
Gresham Pl CM7 . . . . . .127 F4
Gresley Cl CO4 . . . . . . .109 F2
Gresley Dr ⁅2⁆ CM7 . . . .128 A2
Gresley Gdns IP2 . . . . . .17 C3
Gretna Gdns IP4 . . . . . . .18 B8
Greville Ct CO14 . . . . . .144 E2
Grey Friars Rd ⁅10⁆ IP1 . . .17 C5
Greyhound Hill CO4 . . . .83 E5
Greyhound Rd CO10 . . . . .2 B3
Grey Ladys CM2 . . . . . .216 B2
Greys Cl CO10 . . . . .1 C1
Greys Hollow CB11 . . . . . .93 D8
Greystones Cl CO3 . . . . .135 A3
Grieves Ct CO3 . . . . . . .134 C4
Griffin Ct IP2 . . . . .17 D3
Grimston Rd CO2 . . . . .136 A4
Grimston Way CO14 . . . .171 B7
Grimwade Cl CO11 . . . . .86 D7
Grimwade St 1P4 . . . . . .17 D5

Grimwood Cnr ⁅18⁆
  CO10 . . . . .33 E7
Grindle The IP8 . . . . . . .16 A7
Groome Ct ⁅2⁆ CO4 . . . .136 D7
Groom Ho CO15 . . . . . .188 E4
Groom Pk CO15 . . . . . .188 E4
Groomside ⁅5⁆ CM7 . . . .128 A2
Grooms La CM8 . . . . . . .156 E4
Grosvenor
  Bishop's Stortford
  CM23 . . . . .145 D4
  Chelmsford CM2 . . . . . .216 D2
  Ipswich IP4 . . . . .17 E8
  Tiptree CO5 . . . . .179 D5
Grosvenor Ct IP3 . . . . . .18 B1
Grosvenor Ho ⁅4⁆
  CM23 . . . . .146 B8
Grosvenor Pl CO1 . . . . .136 B7
Grosvenor Rd CO10 . . . .15 D2
Grove Ave
  Walton-on-t-N CO14 . . .171 B8
  West Mersea CO5 . . . . . .201 C5
Grove Cotts ⁅1⁆ CM8 . . . .177 A2
Grove Ctr The CM8 . . . . .177 A1
Grove Farm Rd
  Little Totham CM9 . . . .197 C7
  Tiptree CO5, CM9 . . . . .179 A1
Grove Field CM7 . . . . . .102 C1
Grove Hill
  Belstead IP8 . . . . .36 C7
  Dedham CO7 . . . . .84 D4
  Langham CO4 . . . . .83 F5
  Stansted Mountfitchet
  CM24 . . . . .119 F7
Grove La
  Chelmondiston IP9 . . . . .63 E5
  Ipswich IP5 . . . . .17 E5
Grove Lea CM9 . . . . . . .194 F1
Grove Mews IP11 . . . . . .221 D5
Grove Orch CM7 . . . . . .102 C1
Groves Cl CO4 . . . . . . .109 E2
Grove The
  Bicknacre CM3 . . . . . . .218 F1
  Clacton-on-S CO15 . . . .188 F2
  Earls Colne CO6 . . . . . .105 B6
  Great Hallingbury
  CM22 . . . . .146 F4
  Witham CM8 . . . . .177 A2
Grove Villas CM7 . . . . . .126 A8
Grove Wlk IP8 . . . . .36 D8
Gryme's Dyke Ct CO3 . . .134 D6
Gryme's Dyke Way
  CO3 . . . . .134 E3
Gryphon Way CO2 . . . . .135 E3
Gryps Cl CO2 . . . . .135 E1
GUBBION'S GREEN 174 B8
Guelph's La CM6 . . . . . . .70 A3
Guernsey Cl CM9 . . . . . .209 F2
Guernsey Way CM7 . . . .127 D2
Guildford Rd CO1 . . . . .136 A8
Guildhall Way CB10 . . . .24 A7
Guinea Cl CM7 . . . . . . .128 D4
Guisnes Ct CM9 . . . . . .199 A4
Guithavon Ct CM8 . . . . .176 F2
Guithavon Rd CM8 . . . .176 F1
Guithavon Rise CM8 . . . .176 F2
Guithavon St CM8 . . . . .176 F2
Guithavon Valley
  CM8 . . . . .176 F2
Gull Cl CO16 . . . . .142 D4
Gull Ct CO16 . . . . .141 F7
Gulls Croft CM7 . . . . . .128 D3
Gull's La CO7 . . . . .85 A3
Gulpher Bsns Pk
  IP11 . . . . .221 D8
Gulpher Cotts IP11 . . . .221 E8
Gulpher Rd IP11 . . . . . .221 E8
Gunfleet Cl CO5 . . . . . .201 B7
Gunfleet Ct CO15 . . . . .189 C4
Gun Hill CO7 . . . . .84 C7
Gunson Gate CM2 . . . . .216 D7
Gurdon Rd CO2 . . . . . . .135 F3
Gurney Benham Cl
  CO2 . . . . .135 B4
Gurton Rd CO6 . . . . . . .131 A3
Gusford Com Prim Sch
  IP2 . . . . .16 D1
Gutteridge Hall La
  CO16 . . . . .167 E7
Gutters La CM1 . . . . . . .205 C7
Guy Cook Cl CO10 . . . . .34 C4
Guys Farm CM1 . . . . . .204 B1
Gwendoline Cl IP4 . . . . .18 F4
Gwent Ho IP2 . . . . .17 B3
Gwyn Cl CM3 . . . . .192 E1
Gwynne Rd CO12 . . . . . .91 D4
Gymnasium St IP1 . . . . .17 B7
Gypsy La
  Feering CO5 . . . . .159 C6
  Little Dunmow CM6 . . . .151 E7
  Sudbury CO10 . . . . .33 C6

H

Hackmans La CM3 . . . . .219 E2
Haddon Pk CO1 . . . . . . .136 C5
Hadfelda Sq CM3 . . . . .194 A4
Hadfield Dr CM7 . . . . . .155 B5
Hadham Ct CM23 . . . . .145 C8
Hadham Gr CM23 . . . . .145 C8
Hadham Rd CM23 . . . . .145 D8
Hadleigh Ct
  Clacton-on-S CO15 . . . .189 A3
  ⁅4⁆ Saffron Walden CB10 . . .22 F2
Hadleigh Rd
  Clacton-on-S CO16 . . . .188 B4
  East Bergholt CO7 . . . . .59 B3
  Frinton-on-S CO13 . . . .171 A5
  Ipswich IP2 . . . . .16 D5
  Stratford St M CO7 . . . .58 A6
Hadleigh Road Ind Est
  IP2 . . . . .16 F7
Hadley Cl CM7 . . . . . . .102 B1
Hadrian Cl
  Colchester CO4 . . . . . .110 B6
  Haverhill CB9 . . . . .9 D7
Hadrians Cl CM8 . . . . . .194 E8
Hadrians Way CM9 . . . . .210 A4
HADSTOCK 5 C6
Hadstock Rd CB1 . . . . . . .5 B8
Haggars La CO7 . . . . . .138 F3
Haggers Cl CB10 . . . . .3 D2
Haig Ct CM2 . . . . .205 A1
Hailes Wood CM22 . . . . .94 D1
Hailes Wood Cl CM22 . . . .94 D1
Hainault Gr CM1 . . . . . .204 E1
Hakewill Way CO4 . . . . .109 C3
Halcyon Cl CM8 . . . . . .176 F1
Hale Cl IP2 . . . . .16 D2
Halesowen Cl IP2 . . . . . .36 F8
Hale Way CO4 . . . . .110 B6
Halfacres CM8 . . . . . . .195 A7
Half Acres CM23 . . . . . .145 E6
Half Moon Yd CO10 . . . .12 B7
Halford Ct ⁅6⁆ IP8 . . . . .16 C2
Halfway Cotts CO5 . . . .158 B6
Half Way Cotts CO5 . . . .158 B6
Halifax Prim Sch IP2 . . . .17 B2
Halifax Rd IP2 . . . . .17 B2
Halifax Way CO6 . . . . . .104 F2
Hall Barn CO5 . . . . .201 B6
Hall Barns CM24 . . . . . .119 D7
Hall Bridge Rise CM9 . . .210 C4
Hall Chase CM3 . . . . . .133 B3
Hall Cl
  Great Baddow CM2 . . . .217 A1
  Henham CM22 . . . . .94 F5
Hall Cres CO15 . . . . . . .189 F6
Hallcroft Chase CO4 . . . .110 C4
Hall Cut CO7 . . . . .185 F6
Hall Dr CO9 . . . . .102 D8
Hall Est CM9 . . . . .211 E7
Hall Farm Cl CO5 . . . . .158 E4
Hallfield CB11 . . . . .66 E1
Hall Field IP11 . . . . . . .221 C5
Hallingbury Cl CM22 . . .146 B1
Hallingbury Rd CM22,
  CM23 . . . . .146 B4
HALLINGBURY STREET
   . . . . .147 A4
Halliwell Rd IP4 . . . . . . .18 B6
Hall La
  Chelmsford CM2 . . . . . .217 C6
  Harwich CO12 . . . . .91 A2
  Ridgewell CO9 . . . . .29 B6
  Thorpe-le-S CO16 . . . . .169 B8
  Walton-on-t-N CO14 . . .144 D2
Hall Pond Way IP11 . . . .221 C5
Hall Rd
  Belchamp Walter CO10 . . .32 A6
  Borley CO10 . . . . .15 A3
  Bures CO8 . . . . .79 E5
  Copford CO6 . . . . .133 E4
  Elsenham CM22 . . . . . . .94 D1
  Fordham CO6 . . . . .107 D5
  Great Bromley CO7 . . . .112 C2
  Great Totham CM9 . . . .196 C3
  Maldon CM9 . . . . .210 B4
  Panfield CM7 . . . . .127 A6
  Tiptree CO5 . . . . .179 C3
  Tollesbury CM9 . . . . . .199 D1
  West Bergholt CO6 . . . . .108 D5
Hall Rise
  Sudbury CO10 . . . . .33 C6
  Witham CM8 . . . . .194 F8
Hall Road Cotts CO6 . . . .108 D6
Hall St
  Chelmsford CM2 . . . . . .205 B1
  Long Melford CO10 . . . . .15 C8
Hall View Rd CO7 . . . . .166 E7
Hall Villas CM7 . . . . .72 B1
HALSTEAD 76 D2
Halstead Bsns Ctr CO9 . . .76 E1
Halstead Hospl CO9 . . . .76 E3
Halstead Rd
  Braintree CM7 . . . . . . .102 E3
  Colchester CO3 . . . . . .134 D7
  Earls Colne CO6 . . . . . .104 F7
  Eight Ash G CO6 . . . . . .134 A8
  Fordham CO6 . . . . .107 B3
  Fordham Heath CO6 . . . .107 E1
  Gosfield CO9 . . . . .75 F1
  Kirby Cross CO13 . . . . .170 B7
  Kirby-le-S CO13 . . . . . .170 C8
  Sible Hedingham CO9 . . .76 B6
Halstead Pl CM9 . . . . . .220 F8
Halton Cres IP3 . . . . . . .18 C1

Gre–Har 235

Hamble Cl CM8 . . . . . . .176 E2
Hamel Way CB11 . . . . . .67 D4
Hamford Cl CO14 . . . . . .144 D2
Hamford Dr CO12 . . . . .116 C3
Hamford Prim Sch
  CO14 . . . . .170 F7
Hamilton Ct
  Brightlingsea CO7 . . . . .186 A7
  Chelmsford CM1 . . . . . .204 C8
  Clacton-on-S CO15 . . . .189 E6
Hamilton Gdns IP11 . . . .221 F3
Hamilton Ho IP4 . . . . . .18 A7
Hamilton Mews ⁅3⁆
  CB10 . . . . .22 F2
Hamilton Prim Sch
  CO3 . . . . .135 D5
Hamilton Rd
  Colchester CO3 . . . . . .135 D5
  Felixstowe IP11 . . . . . .221 E4
  Great Holland CO13 . . . .170 A5
  Ipswich IP3 . . . . .18 B3
  Sudbury CO10 . . . . .33 E7
  Takeley CM6 . . . . .148 F7
  Wivenhoe CO7 . . . . . . .164 B8
Hamilton St
  Felixstowe IP11 . . . . . .221 C5
  Harwich CO12 . . . . .90 F1
Hamlet Ct CO8 . . . . .79 E8
Hamlet Dr CO4 . . . . . . .136 F7
Hamlet Rd
  Chelmsford CM2 . . . . . .205 B1
  Haverhill CB9 . . . . .9 B7
Hammond Ct ⁅1⁆ CO13 . .170 F5
Hammonds Rd CM3 . . . .206 E3
HAMPERDEN END 68 D3
Hampit Rd CB11 . . . . . . .41 D2
HAMPITS 41 D2
Hampstead Ave CO16 . . .188 D5
Hampton Ho CM2 . . . . .216 D6
Hampton Rd
  Great Baddow CM2 . . . .216 E6
  Ipswich IP1 . . . . .16 F7
Hamsters Cl CO9 . . . . . . .77 F8
Hanbury Gdns CO4 . . . . .110 B5
Hanbury Rd CM1 . . . . . .215 E8
Hance La CM77 . . . . . . .126 F2
Hanchetts Orch CM6 . . . .70 A3
HANCHETT VILLAGE 8 B8
Handel Wlk CO4 . . . . . .136 E6
Handford Hall Prim Sch
  IP1 . . . . .17 A6
Handford Cut IP1 . . . . . .17 A6
Handford Pl CO3 . . . . . .135 D6
Handford Rd IP1 . . . . . . .17 A6
Handley's La CM8 . . . . .195 F5
Handy Fisher Ct CO3 . . . .135 B4
Hankin Ave CO12 . . . . . .90 C1
Hanlee Brook CM2 . . . . .216 F6
Hanningfield Way
  CO4 . . . . .110 B5
Hanover Bridge CO5 . . . .158 F5
Hanover Ct
  Braintree CM7 . . . . . . .127 F8
  Harwich CO12 . . . . .91 C3
  Ipswich IP4 . . . . .17 E6
  Sudbury CO10 . . . . .33 D6
  Walton-on-t-N CO14 . . .171 A8
  Witham CM8 . . . . .177 B1
Hanover Pl CB10 . . . . . .22 C1
Hanover Sq CO5 . . . . . .158 F6
Hanwell Cl CO16 . . . . . .188 D5
Ha'penny Dr IP9 . . . . . . .62 D5
Ha'penny Field IP9 . . . . . .62 D5
Ha'penny Pier Visitor Ctr★
  CO12 . . . . .91 D6
Happy Gdns CO5 . . . . . .179 A8
Harberd Tye CM2 . . . . . .216 D7
Harborough Hall Rd
  CO5 . . . . .159 E2
Harbour Cres CO12 . . . . .91 E5
Hardies Point CO2 . . . . .136 D5
Hardings Cl CO6 . . . . . .133 B8
Hardings Yd CO7 . . . . . .164 B7
Hard The CO7 . . . . .185 F5
Hardwick Cl
  Great Notley CM77 . . . .154 B7
  Rushmere St A IP4 . . . .18 E5
Hardwick Rd CB9 . . . . . . .9 B8
Hardy Cl
  Braintree CM7 . . . . . . .155 A8
  Brantham CO11 . . . . . . .86 C7
Hardy Ct CO10 . . . . .15 F2
HARDY'S GREEN 160 E6
Harebell Cl CO4 . . . . . . .110 B3
Harebell Dr CM8 . . . . . .176 E3
Harebell Rd IP2 . . . . . . .16 F4
HARE GREEN 139 A6
Hares Wlk CO10 . . . . . . .33 F8
Harewood Rd CM1 . . . . .204 E1
Harewood Terr ⁅20⁆ CB9 . . .8 E7
Harfred Ave CM9 . . . . . .210 E3
Hargrave Cl CM24 . . . . .119 E8
Harkilees Way CM7 . . . .127 F5
HARKSTEAD 63 B2
Harkstead La
  Chelmondiston IP9 . . . . .63 A7
  Woolverstone IP9 . . . . . .38 A1
Harkstead Rd IP9 . . . . . .62 F3
Harland St IP2 . . . . .17 C3
Harlings Gr CM1 . . . . . .205 C3
Harmans Yd CM6 . . . . . .150 D8
Harman Wlk CO16 . . . . .188 C5
Harness Cl CM1 . . . . . . .205 E7
Harnham Dr CM77 . . . . .154 C7

Harold Cl C09 . . . . **76** F1
Harold Collins Pl CO1 . . **136** B7
Haslers La CM6 . . . . **150** B8
Harold Gr CO13 . . . . **170** F4
Harold Rd
  Braintree CM7 . . . . **127** E2
  Clacton-on-S CO15 . . . . . . **188** F3
  Frinton-on-S CO13 . . . . . **170** F4
Harold Rise CM9 . . . . **209** F5
Harold Sims Ho CO6 . . . . **105** B7
Harold Way CO13 . . . . . . **170** F4
Harp Close Rd CO10 . . . . . **33** F8
Harpers Way CO16 . . . . . **188** A3
Harp La CO10 . . . . **12** C8
Harp Meadow La
  CO2 . . . . **135** D4
Harpur's Rd CO10 . . . . **2** B4
Harrier Cl IP3 . . . . **18** B1
Harrington Cl
  7 Bishop's Stortford
  CM23 . . . . **146** A7
  Tiptree CO5 . . . . **179** B5
Harrington Mead
  CM2 . . . . **206** B3
Harris Gn CM6 . . . . **150** E7
Harrison Ct
  Chelmsford CM1 . . . . . . **204** F3
  West Mersea CO5 . . . . . . **201** C4
Harrison Dr CM7 . . . . . . **128** A1
Harrison Ho CO12 . . . . . . **91** D4
Harrison Rd CO2 . . . . . . **135** F3
Harrisons CM23 . . . . **119** D2
Harrold Ct CO15 . . . . . . **189** A2
Harrow Cl IP4 . . . . **18** A5
HARROWCROSS **75** C8
Harrow Hill CO9 . . . . **49** F6
Harrow Rd
  Clacton-on-S CO15 . . . . . **188** F4
  Haverhill CB9 . . . . **8** E7
Harrow Way CM2 . . . . . . **217** A6
Harsnett Rd CO1 . . . . . . **136** B5
Hartest Way CO10 . . . . . **34** B6
HARTFORD END **172** D8
Hartley Cl CM2 . . . . **206** A4
Hartley St IP2 . . . . **17** C4
Hart's La CO7 . . . . **84** B2
Hart St CM2 . . . . **205** A1
Harvard Ct CO4 . . . . **110** B4
Harvest Cl CO6 . . . . **133** B4
Harvest Ct
  Feering CO5 . . . . **158** E4
  Felixstowe IP11 . . . . **221** F4
Harvest End CO3 . . . . . . **134** D5
Harvesters CM9 . . . . **198** D4
Harvesters' Way CO6 . . . **132** B8
Harvest Fields CM22 . . . . **148** B3
Harvest Ho IP11 . . . . . . **221** F4
Harvest Way
  Elmstead Market CO7 . . . **137** F6
  Maldon CM9 . . . . **209** F5
Harvey Cl CO11 . . . . **86** C4
Harvey Cres CO3 . . . . . . **134** C4
Harvey Ct CO15 . . . . . . **203** E5
Harvey Rd
  Colchester CO2 . . . . **135** B2
  Great Totham CM9 . . . . **196** A4
  Wivenhoe CO7 . . . . **137** C1
Harvey St CO9 . . . . **76** F1
Harvey Way
  Hempstead CB10 . . . . **25** F1
  Saffron Walden CB10 . . . . **22** F2
Harwell Cl CM7 . . . . **128** D4
HARWICH **91** E5
Harwich Com Prim Sch
  CO12 . . . . **91** A4
Harwich Crane The ★
  CO12 . . . . **91** E5
Harwich Ct CO4 . . . . . . **136** F4
Harwich Gateway Retail
  Pk CO12 . . . . **91** A4
Harwich Ind Est CO12 . . . . **90** F5
Harwich International Port
  CO12 . . . . **90** F6
Harwich Parkeston Quay
  Sta CO12 . . . . **90** F6
Harwich Rd
  Ardleigh CO7 . . . . **111** F8
  Beaumont CO16 . . . . . . **141** F7
  Bradfield CO11 . . . . **87** F2
  Colchester CO7 . . . . . . **110** F3
  Colchester, Greenstead
   CO1 . . . . **136** C7
  Dedham CO7 . . . . **84** F1
  Great Bromley CO7 . . . . **139** C6
  Great Oakley CO12 . . . . **116** D5
  Lawford CO11 . . . . **85** C2
  Little Bentley CO7 . . . . . **113** E1
  Little Clacton CO16 . . . . **168** E6
  Little Oakley CO12 . . . . **117** C7
  New Mistley CO11 . . . . . . **87** B3
  Wix CO11, CO12 . . . . . . **116** A4
  Wix, Wix Green CO11 . . . **115** D5
  Wrabness CO11 . . . . **88** D2
Harwich Sch The CO12 . . **91** A2
Harwich Town Sta
  CO12 . . . . **91** D5
Harwood Cl CO2 . . . . . . **136** A4
Haselfoot Rd CM3 . . . . . **206** F8
Haskell Mews CM7 . . . . . **155** A8
Haslar Pl CM6 . . . . **150** D8
Haslemere CM23 . . . . . . **146** A4
Haslemere Dr IP4 . . . . . . **17** E7
Haslemere Gdns
  CO13 . . . . **170** F7
Haslemere Ind Est
  CM23 . . . . **146** A4
Hasler Rd CM9 . . . . **199** D2
Haslers La CM6 . . . . **150** B8
Hastings Ave CO15 . . . . . **203** J8
Hastings Pl CO7 . . . . . . **185** F8
Hastings Rd CO3 . . . . . . **135** A4
Hatchcroft Gdns CO7 . . . **138** A6
Hatcher Cres CO2 . . . . . **136** C5
Hatchfields CM3 . . . . . . **190** F4
Hatfield Forest (Ctry Pk) ★
  CM22 . . . . **147** D3
Hatfield Forest Nature
  Trail ★ CM22 . . . . **147** E5
Hatfield Gr CM1 . . . . . . **204** D1
HATFIELD PEVEREL . . **194** B4
Hatfield Peverel Inf Sch
  CM3 . . . . **194** B3
Hatfield Peverel St
  Andrew's Jun Sch
  CM3 . . . . **194** B3
Hatfield Peverel Sta
  CM3 . . . . **193** F5
Hatfield Rd
  Hatfield Peverel CM8 . . . **194** F4
  Ipswich IP3 . . . . **18** A3
  Langford CM9 . . . . **209** B7
  Terling CM3 . . . . **175** D3
  Witham CM8 . . . . **194** E7
Hatherley Ct CB10 . . . . . . **22** E2
Hatleys CM2 . . . . **217** A4
Haubourdin Ct CO9 . . . . . **77** A2
Haughley Dr IP4 . . . . **18** F6
Hauliers Rd IP11 . . . . . . **221** B2
Haven Ave CO15 . . . . . . **189** G6
Haven Cl IP11 . . . . **221** B4
Havencourt CM1 . . . . . . **205** B3
Havencroft Ct **3**
  CO14 . . . . **171** C8
Haven Ct CM3 . . . . **193** F4
Havengore CM1 . . . . **205** F5
Haven Rd CO2 . . . . **136** D4
Havens The IP3 . . . . **38** C1
Haven The CO12 . . . . **90** F3
Havenvale CO15 . . . . **188** E4
Havergate Rd IP3 . . . . . . **38** D8
HAVERHILL **9** C7
Haverhill Rd
  Castle Camps CB21 . . . . . . **7** E5
  Helions Bumpstead CB9 . . **8** D1
  Steeple Bumpstead CB9 . . **27** C8
Havering Cl
  Clacton-on-S CO15 . . . . . **188** E7
  Colchester CO4 . . . . . . **110** B1
Havers La CM23 . . . . . . **145** F5
Havers Par CM23 . . . . . **145** F5
Havisham Way CM1 . . . . **204** E3
Hawbridge IP9 . . . . **35** A2
Hawbush Rd CM77 . . . . . **155** F5
Hawes St IP2 . . . . **17** D3
Hawfinch Rd CO2 . . . . . **162** A5
Hawfinch Wlk CM2 . . . . **216** B5
Hawkendon Rd CO16 . . . **188** A4
Hawke Rd IP3 . . . . **17** E1
Hawkes La IP11 . . . . **221** B6
Hawkes Rd
  Coggeshall CO6 . . . . . . **130** F3
  Witham CM8 . . . . **194** E7
Hawkesway CO15 . . . . . **188** F6
Hawkhurst Cl CM1 . . . . . **204** E2
Hawkins Cl CM3 . . . . . . **219** E2
Hawkins Ct CO10 . . . . . . **15** F2
HAWKIN'S HILL **71** E7
Hawkins Rd
  Alresford CO7 . . . . **165** B8
  Colchester CO2 . . . . . . **136** D5
Hawkins Way CM7 . . . . . **128** C4
Hawks Cl CM3 . . . . **219** A6
HAWKSPUR GREEN . . . **71** D5
Hawkwood Rd CO9 . . . . . **75** D8
Hawlmark End CO6 . . . . **132** E3
Hawthorn Ave CO4 . . . . **136** E7
Hawthorn Cl
  Chelmsford CM2 . . . . . . **216** C6
  Halstead CO9 . . . . **77** A2
  Takeley CM22 . . . . **148** C7
Hawthorn Dr IP2 . . . . . . **16** C3
Hawthorne Rise CM8 . . . **177** A5
Hawthornes CM3 . . . . . . **220** M1
Hawthorn Rd
  Clacton-on-S CO15 . . . . . **188** E6
  Great Cornard CO10 . . . . **34** B7
  Hatfield Peverel CM3 . . . **194** A5
  Tolleshunt Knights
   CM9 . . . . **180** A2
Hawthorn Rise CM23 . . . **145** F3
Hawthorns
  Kirby Cross CO13 . . . . . **170** F7
  Sible Hedingham CO9 . . . . **51** D2
Hawthorns The CM3 . . . **219** A4
Haycocks Farm CO5 . . . . **183** F1
Haycocks La CO5 . . . . . . **183** F1
Haycroft CM23 . . . . **146** C7
Haye La CO5 . . . . **163** C4
Hayes Cl CM2 . . . . **205** B1
Hayes Rd CO15 . . . . . . **188** E3
Hay Gn CM3 . . . . **218** D8
Hayhill Rd IP4 . . . . **17** E7
Hayhouse Rd CO6 . . . . . **105** A6
Hay La N CM7 . . . . **128** C3
Hay La S CM7 . . . . **128** C3
Hayley Bell Gdns
  CM23 . . . . **145** F3
Hayman Rd IP3 . . . . **17** F1
Haymeads La CM23 . . . . **146** C6
Haynes Green Rd
  CO5 . . . . **180** A8

Haytor Cl CM7 . . . . **128** C2
Haywain The CO3 . . . . . **134** D5
Hayward Ct CO1 . . . . . . **136** C7
Hazel Cl
  Great Dunmow CM6 . . . **123** C1
  Haverhill CB9 . . . . **8** E7
  Thorrington CO7 . . . . . **166** A5
  Witham CM8 . . . . **177** A4
Hazeldon Cl CM3 . . . . . . **191** C6
Hazel Dr IP3 . . . . **18** F1
HAZELEIGH **220** A4
Hazeleigh Hall La
  CM3 . . . . **220** C4
Hazelend Rd CM23 . . . . **119** B4
Hazel Gr CM7 . . . . **127** E1
Hazell Ave CO2 . . . . **135** B2
Hazel Mews CO7 . . . . . . **185** E7
HAZEL STUB **8** C7
Hazelton Rd CO4 . . . . . . **110** D1
Hazelville Cl CO12 . . . . . . **90** E1
Hazelwood Cres
  CO16 . . . . **168** C1
Hazelwood Ct CM9 . . . . **210** B6
Hazlemere Jun & Inf Schs
  CO4 . . . . **136** E8
Hazlemere Rd CO15 . . . . **189** C4
Headgate CO1 . . . . **135** E6
Headgate Bldg **1**
  CO2 . . . . **135** E6
Headingham Cl **3** IP2 . . **17** A2
Head La CO10 . . . . **34** B5
Headland Ave CB9 . . . . . . **8** E7
Head St
  Colchester CO1 . . . . . . **135** E7
  Goldhanger CM9 . . . . . **211** E6
  Halstead CO9 . . . . **76** F2
  Rowhedge CO5 . . . . . . **163** F8
Head Way CO10 . . . . **15** E2
Heards La
  Cornish Hall End CM7 . . . **48** C6
  Cornish Hall End CM7 . . . **48** D5
Hearsall Ave CM1 . . . . . **205** B7
Heath Bsns Pk CO2 . . . . **136** D3
Heath Cl CO7 . . . . **59** D3
Heathcote Sch CM3 . . . . **218** C4
Heath Cotts CO3 . . . . . . **107** F1
Heath Dr CM2 . . . . **216** B6
Heather Cl
  Bishop's Stortford
   CM23 . . . . **145** D6
  Clacton-on-S CO15 . . . . . **189** B7
  Layer de la H CO2 . . . . . **161** F5
Heather Ct **10** CM1 . . . . **205** F6
Heather Dr CO3 . . . . . . **134** F5
Heatherhayes IP2 . . . . . . **17** A3
Heathfield Rd
  Chelmsford CM1 . . . . . . **205** B7
  Holbrook IP9 . . . . **62** D5
Heathfields CO6 . . . . . . **134** B8
Heathfields Ho CO2 . . . . **136** C3
Heathgate CM8 . . . . **195** D6
Heathgate Piece
  IP11 . . . . **221** A8
Heath La IP4 . . . . **18** C5
Heathlands CO7 . . . . . . **166** A5
Heathlands CE Prim Sch
  CO6 . . . . **108** E4
Heathlands Pk IP4 . . . . . . **18** E4
Heath Rd
  Alresford CO7 . . . . **165** B8
  Bradfield CO11 . . . . **114** D3
  Colchester CO3 . . . . . . **134** F5
  Colchester, Stanway Green
   CO3 . . . . **134** D4
  East Bergholt CO7 . . . . . . **59** D3
  Fordham Heath CO3 . . . **108** A1
  Ipswich IP4 . . . . **18** D6
  New Mistley CO11 . . . . . . **87** B2
  Rowhedge CO5 . . . . . . **163** F8
  St Osyth Heath CO16 . . . **167** E1
  Tendring CO16 . . . . **140** E7
  Wivenhoe CO7 . . . . **137** B2
Heath Row CM23 . . . . . **119** B1
Heath Sch The CO3 . . . . **134** D5
Heathside CO6 . . . . **108** E4
Heathside Sch IP4 . . . . . . **18** D6
Heath The
  Dedham CO7 . . . . **85** A4
  Layer de la H CO2 . . . . . **162** A6
Heatley Way CO4 . . . . . **136** F8
Heaton Way CO5 . . . . . **179** D6
HECKFORDBRIDGE **161** B8
Heckford's Rd CO7 . . . . **139** E2
Heckworth Cl CO4 . . . . . **110** C6
Hedge Dr CO2 . . . . **135** B3
Hedgelands CO6 . . . . . . **133** D5
Hedgerows CO3 . . . . . . **134** D6
Hedgerows Bsns Pk
  CM2 . . . . **206** A6
Hedgerows The CM23 . . . **146** B6
Hedingham Castle ★
  CO9 . . . . **51** F4
Hedingham Pl CO9 . . . . . **51** E1
Hedingham Rd
  Bulmer Tye CO10 . . . . . . **32** C1
  Gosfield CO9 . . . . **75** E3
  Halstead CO9 . . . . **76** E3
  Wickham St P CO9 . . . . . **53** A7
Hedingham Sch CO9 . . . . **51** D3
Heights The CM3 . . . . . **218** D7
Helena Rd IP3 . . . . **17** E3
Helena Romanes Sch &
  Sixth Form Ctr CM6 . . . **123** C3
Helen Ewing Pl CO2 . . . . **135** F1
Helen How CM3 . . . . . . **173** F7
Helford Ct CM8 . . . . . . **176** D2

HELIONS BUMPSTEAD
  . . . . **26** C8
Helions Bumpstead Rd
  CB9 . . . . **9** A5
Helions Park Ave CB9 . . . . **9** A7
Helions Park Gdns CB9 . . . **9** A7
Helions Park Gr CB9 . . . . . **9** A7
Helions Rd CB9 . . . . **27** A6
Helions Service Rd CB9 . . . **9** A7
Helions Wlk CB9 . . . . **9** A7
HELLMAN'S CROSS . . . **148** F2
Helm Cl CO2 . . . . **109** C7
Helston Rd CM1 . . . . . . **205** E6
Hemingway Rd CM8 . . . . **176** F5
Hemlock Cl CM8 . . . . . . **177** A4
Hemmings Ct CM9 . . . . . **220** E8
HEMPSTEAD **25** F1
Hendon Cl CO16 . . . . . . **188** D5
Hengrave Cl IP2 . . . . **17** A2
HENHAM **94** F6
Henham Rd
  Debden CB11 . . . . **68** E3
  Elsenham CM22 . . . . **94** E3
Henham & Ugley Prim Sch
  CM22 . . . . **94** F5
Hening Ave IP3 . . . . **38** D8
Hening Rd IP3 . . . . **38** D8
Henley Ct
  Colchester CO3 . . . . . . **134** F6
  Manningtree CO11 . . . . . . **86** C4
Henley Rd IP1 . . . . **17** C8
Henniker Gate CM2 . . . . **206** A4
Henniker Rd IP1 . . . . **16** D8
Henny Back Rd CO8 . . . . . **54** E4
Henny Rd CO8 . . . . **55** B5
HENNY STREET **33** F1
Henrietta Cl CO7 . . . . . . **137** C3
Henry Cl
  Clacton-on-S CO15 . . . . . **188** C2
  Haverhill CB9 . . . . **8** D6
Henry Dixon Rd CM8 . . . **177** C4
Henry Laver Ct CO3 . . . . **135** E7
Henry Rd
  Chelmsford CM1 . . . . . . **205** B4
  Ipswich IP3 . . . . **18** B1
Henslow Rd IP4 . . . . **18** B5
Henstead Gdns IP3 . . . . . **18** A2
Herald Cl CM23 . . . . . . **145** D6
Herbage Park Rd
  CM9 . . . . **208** D1
Herbert Rd CO15 . . . . . . **188** E3
Hereford Ct
  Clacton-on-S CO15 . . . . . **189** E5
  Great Baddow CM2 . . . . **217** A5
Hereford Dr CM7 . . . . . **128** D5
Hereford Rd
  Colchester CO1 . . . . . . **136** A8
  Holland-on-S CO15 . . . . . **189** E6
Hereward Cl CO7 . . . . . . **137** C3
Hereward Way CM7 . . . . . **73** C3
Hering Dr CM9 . . . . **210** C4
Heriot Way CM9 . . . . . . **196** B4
Heritage Mus The ★
  CO6 . . . . **105** A6
Hermitage Ct CM24 . . . . **119** D7
Hermitage Ho CM24 . . . . **119** D7
Heron Cl CO3 . . . . **134** B4
Heron Ct CM23 . . . . . . **146** A7
Heron Glade CO15 . . . . **188** F7
Heron Rd
  Ipswich IP2 . . . . **16** E3
  Kelvedon CO5 . . . . **158** D2
Heronsgate CO13 . . . . . **170** F6
Heron Way
  Frinton-on-S CO13 . . . . . **170** E6
  Heybridge CM9 . . . . . . **210** C5
Herrick Pl CO3 . . . . **135** A6
Herringham Gn CM2 . . . **206** A4
Herring's Way CO6 . . . . **107** D6
Hertford La SG8, CB11 . . **19** E5
Hertfordshire & Essex
  High Sch The CM23 . . . **146** B7
Herts & Essex Com Hospl
  CM23 . . . . **146** B6
Hervey St IP4 . . . . **17** D7
Hervilly Way CO14 . . . . **171** C8
Heseltine Ct CO15 . . . . . **189** B3
Hesper Rd CO2 . . . . **136** C5
Hetherington Cl CO2 . . . **163** A8
Hewes Cl CO4 . . . . **136** F7
Hewitt Rd CO12 . . . . **90** C1
Hewitt Wlk **6** CM8 . . . . **177** A4
HEYBRIDGE **210** B6
Heybridge App CM9 . . . . **209** F5
HEYBRIDGE BASIN . . . **210** D3
Heybridge Ct CO15 . . . . **189** B3
Heybridge House Ind Est
  CM9 . . . . **210** B4
Heybridge Prim Sch
  CM9 . . . . **210** C5
Heybridge St CM9 . . . . . **210** B5
Heycroft Dr CM77 . . . . . **155** E5
Heycroft Way
  Great Baddow CM2 . . . . **216** F5
  Tiptree CO5 . . . . **179** D6
HEYDON **19** A5
Heydon La
  Chrishall SG8 . . . . **19** B5
  Elmdon CB11 . . . . **19** F4
Heymeads Ct CM9 . . . . . **210** A5
Heythrop The CM2 . . . . **205** D4
Heywood Cl IP2 . . . . **16** E1
Heywood Ct CM9 . . . . . **210** B6
Heywood La CM6 . . . . . . **150** D7
Heywood Way CM9 . . . . **210** B6
Hickford Hill CO10 . . . . . **12** D6
Hickory Ave CO4 . . . . . . **136** D7

Hicks Way CB9 . . . . **9** E5
Hidcote Way CM77 . . . . **154** B7
HIGHAM **58** B4
Higham Hill CO7, IP7 . . . **58** A8
Higham Lodge Cotts
  CO7 . . . . **58** B5
Higham Rd CO7 . . . . **58** C3
Highams Chase CM9 . . . **212** A8
Highbank CO10 . . . . **2** B5
Highbirch Rd CO16 . . . . **167** D3
High Bridge Rd CM2 . . . **205** C1
Highbury Terr **1** CO9 . . . **76** F2
Highbury Way CO10 . . . . **34** B5
High Chelmer **8** CM1 . . **205** B2
High Cl SG8 . . . . **19** A5
Highclere Rd
  Colchester CO4 . . . . . . **110** B4
  Great Notley CM77 . . . . **154** B6
High Croft CO6 . . . . **78** A2
High Cross La CM6 . . . . . **149** B5
High Cross La E CM6 . . . **149** E6
High Cross Villas
  CM6 . . . . **149** C6
High Easter Rd CM6 . . . . **150** F2
Highfield CO10 . . . . **12** D7
Highfield Ave
  Bishop's Stortford
   CM23 . . . . **146** C6
  Harwich CO12 . . . . **91** B3
Highfield Cl
  Braintree CM7 . . . . **128** A6
  Danbury CM3 . . . . **218** D6
Highfield Ct CO12 . . . . . . **91** B3
Highfield Dr CO3 . . . . . . **135** C7
Highfield Holiday Pk
  Clacton-on-S CO16 . . . . . **188** E8
  Little Clacton CO15 . . . . **168** F1
Highfield Rd
  Chelmsford CM1 . . . . . . **204** E4
  Felixstowe IP11 . . . . **221** E4
  Sudbury CO10 . . . . **34** A8
Highfields
  Bentley IP9 . . . . **60** E6
  Debden CB11 . . . . **68** B7
  Great Yeldham CO9 . . . . . **30** A2
  Halstead CO9 . . . . **103** F8
  Henham CM22 . . . . **94** F6
  Langley CB11 . . . . **40** D2
  Saffron Walden CB10 . . . . **22** E2
High Fields CM6 . . . . . . **150** D8
Highfields La CO3 . . . . . **178** E7
Highfields Prim Sch
  CO11 . . . . **86** C4
Highfields Rd CM8 . . . . . **176** E1
Highfield Stile Rd
  CM7 . . . . **128** A6
HIGH GARRETT **102** D2
High Garrett CM7 . . . . . **102** C2
Highgates CO9 . . . . **102** E8
High La CM24 . . . . **119** F8
Highland Rd CM23 . . . . **145** F3
Highlands CO9 . . . . **75** E1
Highlands Dr CM9 . . . . . **209** E2
Highlands Gr CO15 . . . . **189** A7
Highlands Pk CO15 . . . . **189** A7
High Lift Villas CO4 . . . . . **83** D8
High Mdw CM6 . . . . **150** C8
Highmead CM24 . . . . . . **119** E8
High Oaks CO12 . . . . **90** B2
HIGH PARK CORNER
  . . . . **164** C6
High Pastures CM3 . . . . **207** D3
High Rd
  Layer de la H CO2 . . . . . **161** F5
  Trimley St M IP11 . . . . . **221** B7
High Rd E IP11 . . . . **221** F5
High Rd W IP11 . . . . **221** D5
High Ridge CM8 . . . . . . **196** C8
High St N CO5 . . . . **201** C7
High St
  Bishop's Stortford
   CM23 . . . . **145** F7
  Braintree CM7 . . . . **127** F3
  Brightlingsea CO7 . . . . . **185** F6
  Bures CO8 . . . . **55** F1
  Castle Camps CB21 . . . . . **7** E3
  Cavendish CO10 . . . . **1** D2
  Chelmsford CM1 . . . . . . **205** B2
  Chrishall SG8 . . . . **19** D3
  Clacton-on-S CO15 . . . . . **188** F2
  Clare CO10 . . . . **12** B7
  Clavering CB11 . . . . **65** D4
  Colchester CO1 . . . . . . **135** F7
  Debden CB11 . . . . **68** B7
  Dedham CO7 . . . . **84** F7
  Earls Colne CO6 . . . . . . **105** B6
  Elsenham CM22 . . . . **94** D1
  Felixstowe IP11 . . . . **221** C6
  Great Baddow CM2 . . . . **216** F6
  Great Bardfield CM7 . . . . **72** A1
  Great Chesterford CB10 . . . **3** E2
  Great Dunmow CM6 . . . **150** D8
  Great Oakley CO12 . . . . **116** C4
  Halstead CO9 . . . . **76** E2
  Harwich CO12 . . . . **91** D4
  Haverhill CB9 . . . . **9** A7
  Hempstead CB10 . . . . . . **25** F1
  Henham CM22 . . . . **94** F5
  Hinxton CB10 . . . . **3** B7
  Ipswich IP1 . . . . **17** C6
  Kelvedon CO5 . . . . **158** C2
  Langham CO4 . . . . **83** D4
  Littlebury CB11 . . . . **21** F4
  Little Chesterford CB10 . . **21** F8
  Maldon CM9 . . . . **210** A2
  Manningtree CO11 . . . . . . **86** D4
  Mistley CO11 . . . . **86** F4

High St *continued*
Nayland CO6 . . . . 56 B1
Newport CB11 . . . . 67 A8
Rowhedge CO5 . . . . 164 A8
Saffron Walden CB10 . . . . 22 D1
Sproughton IP8 . . . . 16 A6
Stebbing CM6 . . . . 124 E5
Thorpe-le-S CO16 . . . . . 141 F1
Tollesbury CM9 . . . . 199 D1
Walton-on-t-N CO14 . . . . 171 A8
West Mersea CO5 . . . . . . 201 B6
Wethersfield CM7 . . . . . . 73 C3
Widdington CB11 . . . . . . 67 D4
Wivenhoe CO7 . . . . 164 B8
High Stile CM6 . . . . 150 C8
HIGHSTREET GREEN 51 A2
High Tree La CO14 . . . . . 144 D2
High View CM23 . . . . . . 119 D3
High View Ave CO15 . . . 188 E6
Highview CO10 . . . . 15 E2
High View Cl CO15 . . . . 188 E6
High View Rd IP1 . . . . . . 16 D8
Highwoods App CO4 . . . 110 C4
Highwoods Com Prim Sch
CO4 . . . . 110 B4
High Woods Country Park
Visitor Ctr** CO4 . . . . . 109 F3
High Woods Ctry Pk*
CO4 . . . . 110 A3
Highwoods Sq CO4 . . . . 110 B4
Hildabrook Cl [2] IP2 . . . 16 E1
Hillary Cl
Bradwell CM77 . . . . 129 D2
Chelmsford CM1 . . . . . . 205 D4
Heybridge CM9 . . . . 210 B5
Ipswich IP1 . . . . 18 A5
Hill Cl CO10 . . . . 15 D8
Hill Cotts CO7 . . . . 166 E1
Hill Cres CM2 . . . . 205 D2
Hillcrest
Clacton-on-S CO15 . . . . 189 A6
Kirby-le-S CO13 . . . . . . 170 D8
Hill Crest Cotts CO4 . . . . 83 E6
Hillcrest Cotts CO5 . . . . 163 B3
Hillcrest Ct CO12 . . . . . . 91 C3
Hillcrest Rd CO10 . . . . . . 15 E2
Hill Farm La IP9 . . . . 63 F7
Hillfield CO5 . . . . 158 D7
HILL GREEN 65 E6
Hill House Ct CO7 . . . . . 186 A7
Hillhouse La CO16 . . . . . 141 B3
Hill House Rd IP3 . . . . . . 17 E5
Hilliards Rd CO7 . . . . . . 113 C2
Hillie Bunnies CO6 . . . . 105 B7
Hill La CB9 . . . . 9 F4
Hillman Ave CO15 . . . . . 203 E6
Hillmead Prim Sch
CM23 . . . . 145 C7
Hill Rd
Chelmsford CM2 . . . . . . 205 D2
Clacton-on-S CO15 . . . . 188 E6
Coggeshall CO6 . . . . . . 131 B2
Harwich CO12 . . . . 91 C4
Hempstead CB10 . . . . . . 46 D8
Ramsey CO12 . . . . 116 E8
Hill Rd S CM2 . . . . 205 D2
Hillridge CO4 . . . . 110 B3
Hills Cl CM7 . . . . 127 F4
Hills Cres CO3 . . . . 135 A5
Hillside CO13 . . . . 170 E4
Hillside Ave CM23 . . . . . 146 A7
Hillside Com Prim Sch
IP2 . . . . 17 C3
Hillside Cotts
Birchanger CM23 . . . . . . 119 C3
Ipswich IP9 . . . . 37 E4
Sudbury CO10 . . . . 34 A7
Hillside Cres
Holland-on-S CO15 . . . . 189 C5
Ipswich IP3 . . . . 18 C3
Hillside End CM23 . . . . . 119 C3
Hillside Gdns CM7 . . . . . 127 F1
Hillside Gr CM2 . . . . 216 A7
Hillside Ho [2] CM7 . . . . 127 F1
Hillside Mews CM2 . . . . 216 A7
Hillside Rd CO10 . . . . . . 34 A7
Hillside Specl Sch
CO10 . . . . 15 F1
Hillside Terr [1] CM7 . . . 127 F1
Hillsleigh Mews CO1 . . . 136 A7
Hills Rd CO9 . . . . 75 D8
Hill St CB10 . . . . 22 D1
Hillston Cl CO2 . . . . 136 B2
Hill Terr CO10 . . . . 12 C8
Hilltop Cl CO2 . . . . 136 D4
Hilltop Cres CO16 . . . . . 140 F1
Hill Top La CB11 . . . . . . 43 E7
Hilltop Rise CO16 . . . . . 140 E1
Hill View CM3 . . . . 218 F1
HillView CO1 . . . . 163 F8
Hill View Rd CM1 . . . . . 205 C4
Hillybroom Gdns CO5 . . 201 D6
Hilton CO11 . . . . 86 D4
Hilton Rd IP3 . . . . 18 C1
Hilton Way CO9 . . . . 75 E8
Hilton Wlk CO9 . . . . 75 E8
Hines Cl CO6 . . . . 133 B8
Hines Rd IP3 . . . . 18 A4
Hintlesham Cl IP4 . . . . . . 18 F5
Hintlesham Dr IP11 . . . . 221 B5
HINXTON 3 B7
Hinxton Mill* CB10 . . . . . 3 A7
Hinxton Rd CB10 . . . . 3 A7
Hipkins CM23 . . . . 145 E4
Histon Cl IP5 . . . . 18 F7
Hitcham Rd CO6 . . . . . . 130 F3
Hitchcock Pl CO10 . . . . . 15 E1

Hitch Common Rd
CB11 . . . . 66 F8
Hitchin Mews CM7 . . . . 155 B8
HMS Ganges Assoc Mus*
CO12 . . . . 91 B3
Hobart Cl CM1 . . . . 204 E5
Hobbs Dr CO4 . . . . 83 A5
Hobbs La CO10 . . . . 2 D1
Hoblongs Ind Est
CM6 . . . . 150 E6
HOCKERILL 146 A6
Hockerill Anglo-European
Coll CM23 . . . . 146 B7
Hockerill Ct [6] CM23 . . 146 A7
Hockerill St CM23 . . . . . 146 A7
Hockley Cl CB21 . . . . 7 B5
Hockney Gdns IP3 . . . . . 38 A8
Hodge Ct [9] CM1 . . . . . 205 A3
Hodges Holt CM8 . . . . . 195 A7
Hodgkinson Rd IP11 . . . 221 A3
Hoe Dr CM1 . . . . 135 A5
Hoe La
Great Waltham CM3 . . . 190 E6
Pentlow CO10 . . . . 13 F8
Hoe Mill Rd CM9 . . . . . . 208 E4
Hoffmanns Way CM1 . . 205 B4
Hogarth Cl CO5 . . . . 201 D6
Hogarth Ct CM1 . . . . . . 205 E6
Hogarth End CO13 . . . . . 170 E7
Hogarth Rd IP3 . . . . 18 A1
Hogarth Sq IP3 . . . . 18 A1
Hog's La SG8 . . . . 19 D3
Holborough Cl CO4 . . . . 136 F7
HOLBROOK 62 D5
Holbrook Cl CO16 . . . . . 188 B4
Holbrook Cres IP11 . . . . 221 B4
Holbrooke Wlk CO5 . . . . 179 E5
Holbrook High Sch
IP9 . . . . 62 D6
Holbrook Prim Sch
IP9 . . . . 62 D6
Holbrook Rd
Harkstead IP9 . . . . 63 A2
Haverhill CB9 . . . . 8 E6
Ipswich IP3 . . . . 17 F1
Stutton IP9 . . . . 62 A3
Holcombe Cres IP2 . . . . 16 D2
Holden Cl
Braintree CM7 . . . . 128 A2
Ipswich IP3 . . . . 17 D3
HOLDEN END 6 B2
Holden Rd CO4 . . . . 109 F2
HOLDER'S GREEN 97 E6
Holdsworth Cl CO10 . . . . 2 B3
Holkham Cl IP4 . . . . 18 F5
Holland Haven Ctry Pk*
CO15 . . . . 189 I8
Holland Haven Prim Sch
CO15 . . . . 189 E6
Holland Ho CO15 . . . . . . 189 A3
Holland Lo CO15 . . . . . . 188 F3
HOLLAND-ON-SAND 189 F5
Holland Park Prim Sch
CO15 . . . . 189 B5
Holland Pk CO15 . . . . . . 189 B4
Holland Pl CO13 . . . . . . 170 E3
Holland Rd
Clacton-on-S, Rush Green
CO15 . . . . 188 F2
Felixstowe IP11 . . . . 221 D3
Frinton-on-S CO13 . . . . 170 E3
Holland-on-S CO15 . . . . 189 B4
Ipswich IP4 . . . . 17 F6
Kirby Cross CO13 . . . . . 170 B6
Little Clacton CO16 . . . . 168 E2
Hollands Rd CB9 . . . . 9 A6
Holland Villas CO13 . . . . 170 A3
Holledge Cres CO13 . . . 170 E6
Hollesley Ave CB9 . . . . . 8 C8
Hollies Rd CM77 . . . . . . 129 C3
Holliland Croft CO6 . . . . 132 C8
Hollington Gr CO2 . . . . . 161 A3
Hollis Lock CM2 . . . . . . 206 A3
Holliwell Cl CO3 . . . . . . 134 D6
Holloway Rd CM9 . . . . . 210 A5
Hollow La
Broomfield CM1 . . . . . . 204 E8
Bures CO8 . . . . 55 F3
Chelmondiston IP9 . . . . . 63 F7
Hollow Rd
Ashen CO10 . . . . 11 E3
Braintree CM6 . . . . 153 B4
Chrishall SG8 . . . . 19 D2
Elmdon CB11 . . . . 20 C4
Kelvedon CO5 . . . . 157 F2
Washbrook IP8 . . . . 35 D8
Widdington CB11 . . . . . 67 C3
Hollybank CM8 . . . . 176 F1
Holly Blue Cl IP8 . . . . . . 36 E8
Holly Brook CM7 . . . . . . 128 A4
Holly Bush Cnr CO7 . . . . 58 C5
HOLLYBUSH HILL 166 F1
Hollybush Hill CO7 . . . . 166 E3
Holly Cl
Colchester CO2 . . . . . . 135 C2
Great Dunmow CM6 . . . 123 C1
Ipswich IP8 . . . . 18 F1
Holly Cotts CO7 . . . . 60 C2
Holly Ct CO15 . . . . 188 E4
Hollycroft CM2 . . . . 217 B6
Hollyhock Rd CB10 . . . . 22 E2
Holly La
Belstead IP8 . . . . 36 C7
Great Horkesley CO6 . . . 82 C4
Stutton IP9 . . . . 61 E3
Hollymead Cl CO4 . . . . . 109 F3
Holly Oaks CO6 . . . . 80 E4

Holly Rd
Colchester CO3 . . . . . . 134 C4
Ipswich IP1 . . . . 17 B7
Rushmere St A IP5 . . . . . 18 F7
Hollytree Ct CO2 . . . . . . 135 C3
Hollytrees Mus* CO1 . . . 135 F7
Hollyview Cl CO16 . . . . . 140 F5
Holly Way
Chelmsford CM2 . . . . . . 216 D7
Elmstead Market CO7 . . 138 C4
Tiptree CO5 . . . . 179 C5
Holly Wlk CM8 . . . . 177 B5
Hollywood Cl CO16 . . . . 216 E6
Holman Cres CO3 . . . . . 135 A4
Holman Rd CO9 . . . . 103 E8
Holmans CM3 . . . . 206 E8
Holmbrook Way CO13 . . 170 E5
Holm Dr CM6 . . . . 123 B1
Holme Oaks Ct IP3 . . . . . 17 F3
Holme Rd CO9 . . . . 103 E8
Holmoak IP9 . . . . 62 D6
Holm Oak CO2 . . . . 136 A3
Holmwood Cl CO16 . . . . 188 B6
Holmwood Ho IP4 . . . . . 17 F6
Holmwood House Prep
Sch CO3 . . . . 134 D8
Holst Ave CM8 . . . . 194 F7
Holt Dr
Blackheath CO2 . . . . . . 163 A7
Wickham Bishops CM8 . . 195 E5
HOLTON ST MARY 58 F6
Holt's Rd CO6 . . . . 81 B3
Holybread La CM3 . . . . . 207 C4
Holy Family RC Prim Sch
CM8 . . . . 194 F7
Holyrood IP2 . . . . 90 F2
Holyrood Cl IP2 . . . . 16 F2
Holy Trinity CE Prim Sch
CO9 . . . . 76 D2
Holy Trinity CE St Nicholas
CE Prim Sch SG8 . . . . . 19 C3
Holywells Cl IP3 . . . . 17 E4
Holywells Ct IP3 . . . . . . 18 B1
Holywells High Sch
IP3 . . . . 18 C1
Holywells Rd IP3 . . . . . . 17 E3
Homebridge CB10 . . . . . 47 A3
Home Cl CB9 . . . . 27 C7
Homedale Cotts CO4 . . . 83 B6
Home Farm La
Ardleigh CO7 . . . . 112 A8
Dedham CO7 . . . . 85 A1
Home Farm Prim Sch
CO3 . . . . 134 F6
Homefield IP9 . . . . 35 B1
Homefield Cl CM1 . . . . . 204 D5
Homefield Rd
Colchester CO2 . . . . . . 135 C1
Haverhill CB9 . . . . 8 F5
Witham CM8 . . . . 177 A4
Homefield Road Units
CB9 . . . . 8 F5
Homefield Way
Cressing CM77 . . . . 155 D7
Earls Colne CO6 . . . . . . 105 A7
Homelands Ct CO14 . . . 171 A7
Homelea CO11 . . . . 144 D1
Homelye Chase CM6 . . . 124 B1
Home Mead
Galleywood CM2 . . . . . 216 C2
Writtle CM1 . . . . 204 A1
Homeorr Ho IP11 . . . . . 221 F4
Homerton Cl CO15 . . . . 188 F8
Homestead CM1 . . . . . . 205 B7
Homestead Sch CO4 . . . 83 E4
Homeweave Ho CO6 . . . 130 F2
Homey Bridge Rd CO6 . . 56 C8
Homing Rd CO16 . . . . . . 168 C4
Honeybourne CM23 . . . . 145 E4
Honey Cl CM2 . . . . 216 D6
Honeycroft CO11 . . . . . . 86 B3
Honey La CB11 . . . . 64 F3
Honey Pot Hall CO15 . . . 188 F3
Honeypot La
Little Clacton CO16 . . . . 168 A4
Little Clacton CO16 . . . . 168 B4
Tolleshunt Knights CM9 . 180 B1
Wix CO11 . . . . 114 F3
Honeypots CM2 . . . . 216 C6
Honeysuckle Cl CM23 . . 145 C6
Honeysuckle Gdns IP2 . . 16 E4
Honeysuckle Path [9]
CM1 . . . . 205 F6
Honeysuckle Way
Colchester CO4 . . . . . . 136 E8
Thorrington CO7 . . . . . . 166 A5
Witham CM8 . . . . 176 D4
Honeywood Ave CO6 . . . 131 A3
Honeywood Rd CO9 . . . . 77 A3
Honorius Dr CO4 . . . . . . 110 B6
Honor Link CM1 . . . . . . 206 A7
Honywood Cl CO6 . . . . . 132 E3
Honywood Com Science
Sch CO6 . . . . 131 A3
Honywood Rd CO3 . . . . 135 D6
Honywood Way CO13 . . 170 F7
Hood Gdns CM7 . . . . . . 128 C4
Hood Rd IP3 . . . . 17 E1
Hope Ct IP3 . . . . 17 E4
HOPE END GREEN 148 C3
Hop Fields CB11 . . . . . . 43 E8
Hop Gardens La CM9 . . . 208 F4
Hopgrounds The CM7 . . 72 D6
Hopkins Cl
Chelmsford CM2 . . . . . . 206 A3
Kirby Cross CO13 . . . . . 170 F6
Hopkin's La CO12 . . . . . 91 D6
Hopkins Mead CM2 . . . . 206 A2

Hopkirk Cl CM3 . . . . . . 218 F8
Hop Mdw CO7 . . . . 59 B2
Hopping Jacks La
CM3 . . . . 218 F7
Hoppit Mead CM7 . . . . . 127 F1
Hopton Rise CB9 . . . . . . 8 B8
Horace Eves Cl [1] CB9 . . 8 F8
Hordle Pl CO12 . . . . 91 D4
Hordle St CO12 . . . . 91 D4
HORKESLEY HEATH 109 B7
Horkesley Hill CO6 . . . . . 82 A7
Horkesley Rd
Great Horkesley CO4 . . . 109 E8
Nayland CO6 . . . . 56 A1
Horley IP2 . . . . 16 E4
Horley Cl CO15 . . . . 188 C6
Hornbeam Cl
Chelmsford CM2 . . . . . . 216 A6
Colchester CO2 . . . . . . 135 D2
Hornbeams The CO12 . . 117 B7
Hornbeam Wlk CM8 . . . 177 A4
Horn Book CB10 . . . . . . 22 F1
HORNELLS CORNER 153 E2
HORNE ROW 218 D5
Horne Row CM3 . . . . . . 218 D5
Horner Pl [4] CM8 . . . . . 177 A2
HORNESTREET 83 D5
Horn Hill CO9 . . . . 75 C5
Hornsea Villas CM6 . . . . 124 D7
Horrocks Cl CO2 . . . . . . 136 A4
Horse & Groom La
CM2 . . . . 216 A3
Horse Pond Cl CO10 . . . 34 C4
Horseshoe Cl CB11 . . . . 20 B4
Horseshoe La CB9 . . . . . 8 E7
Horsey Rd CO13 . . . . . . 170 C8
Horsham Ave IP3 . . . . . . 18 D3
Horsley Cross CO11 . . . . 114 A3
HORSLEYCROSS STREET
. . . . 114 A6
Horsley Ho IP11 . . . . 221 F4
Horton Cl CM9 . . . . 210 A1
Hospital App CM1 . . . . . 191 B3
Hospital Field CM77 . . . . 155 B5
Hospital La CO3 . . . . 135 D6
Hospital Rd CO3 . . . . . . 135 D6
Hossack Rd IP3 . . . . 38 A8
Houblon Dr CM2 . . . . . . 216 C2
Houchin's La CO6 . . . . . 131 E3
Houghton Pl IP4 . . . . . . 18 F5
Houldings Garage
CM9 . . . . 210 B5
House Martins The
IP11 . . . . 221 D6
House on the Hill Toy Mus
The* CM24 . . . . 119 F7
Hove Ct CO15 . . . . 189 F6
Howard Ave CO12 . . . . . 90 F2
Howard Cl
Braintree CM7 . . . . 128 C3
Haverhill CB9 . . . . 8 D7
Howard Dr CM2 . . . . . . 206 A2
Howard Ho IP2 . . . . 17 A4
Howard Rd
Holland-on-S CO15 . . . . 189 C4
Saffron Walden CB10 . . . 22 E2
Howards Cl CM3 . . . . . . 206 E8
Howards Croft CO4 . . . . 109 D5
Howard St IP4 . . . . 18 B6
Howard Vyse Ct CO15 . . 188 E5
Howbridge CE Jun Sch
CM8 . . . . 194 F8
Howbridge Hall Rd
Witham CM8 . . . . 194 F6
Witham CM8 . . . . 194 F7
Howbridge Inf Sch The
CM8 . . . . 194 F8
Howbridge Rd CM8 . . . . 194 F8
Howe Ave IP3 . . . . 18 C3
Howe Chase CO9 . . . . . . 76 E4
Howe Cl CO4 . . . . 136 D7
HOWE GREEN
Bishop's Stortford 146 D2
Chelmsford 217 D3
Howe Green House Sch
CM22 . . . . 146 D2
Howe La CB10 . . . . 47 A5
HOWE STREET
Finchingfield 48 F1
Great Waltham 172 F2
Howlets Terr IP9 . . . . 63 E7
HOWLETT END 45 B2
Hoxter Way CO10 . . . . . 15 E2
Hoxton Cl CO16 . . . . . . 188 D5
Hoynors CM3 . . . . 219 A7
Hubbards Chase
CO14 . . . . 171 B8
Hubert Rd CO3 . . . . 135 B8
Hub The CM77 . . . . 154 A8
Huckleberry Cres IP3 . . . 38 C7
Hucklesbury Ave
CO15 . . . . 189 E7
Hudson Cl
Clacton-on-S CO16 . . . . 188 C5
Harwich CO12 . . . . 91 A1
Haverhill CB9 . . . . 9 C6
Hudson's Hill CM7 . . . . . 73 D4
Hudsons La CO6 . . . . . . 57 B5
Hugh Dickson Rd CO4 . . 109 E2
Hughes Cnr CO7 . . . . . . 59 A4
Hughes Rd CO7 . . . . 59 A4
Hughes Stanton Way
CO11 . . . . 86 B4
Hugh Villas CM23 . . . . . 146 A5
Hull La CM3 . . . . 175 A2
Hull's La CM2 . . . . 217 E2
Hulton Cl CM3 . . . . 206 E8
Hulver Ct IP3 . . . . 18 B2

Humber Ave CO15 . . . . . 203 E6
Humber Doucy La IP4 . . 18 D8
Humber Rd
Chelmsford CM1 . . . . . . 205 C5
Witham CM8 . . . . 176 D2
Humphrey's Farm La
CM3 . . . . 190 C7
Humphry Rd CO10 . . . . . 33 E8
Hundon Pl [4] CB9 . . . . . 9 B8
Hundred La CO4 . . . . . . 83 C4
Hungerdown La CO11 . . 85 E1
Hunnable Ind Est CO9 . . 50 F8
Hunnable Rd CM7 . . . . . 127 C2
Hunt Ave CM9 . . . . 210 B5
Hunt Cl CO5 . . . . 158 C4
Hunt Dr CO16 . . . . 188 D6
Hunter Dr
Braintree CM7 . . . . 128 C2
Lawford CO11 . . . . 86 A3
Hunter Rd IP3 . . . . 38 C8
Hunters Chase CO13 . . . 170 A7
Hunter's Chase CO7 . . . 84 E2
Hunters Cnr CO3 . . . . . . 134 F5
Hunters Ct CM23 . . . . . . 94 C2
Hunters End IP11 . . . . . 221 A7
Hunters Ridge CO4 . . . . 110 B4
Hunters Way
Chelmsford CM1 . . . . . . 205 F7
Saffron Walden CB11 . . . 43 D7
Huntingdon Way
CO15 . . . . 188 E6
Hunting Gate CO1 . . . . . 136 C7
Huntley's Cvn Pk (E)
CO16 . . . . 203 C6
Huntley's Cvn Pk (W)
CO16 . . . . 203 B6
Hunt Rd CO6 . . . . 105 A6
Hunt's Cl CM1 . . . . 215 B8
Hunt's Dr CM1 . . . . 215 B8
Hunts Farm Cl CM9 . . . . 199 D2
Hunts Hill CO10 . . . . 2 B4
Hunts La CB10 . . . . 3 B7
Hunts Yd CO6 . . . . 105 B6
Hunt Way CO13 . . . . . . 170 E6
Hunwicke Rd CO4 . . . . . 136 E7
Hurnard Dr CO3 . . . . . . 135 A7
Hurn Gr CM23 . . . . 119 C1
Hurrell Down
Boreham CM3 . . . . 192 F1
Colchester CO4 . . . . . . 110 A4
Hurrells La CM3 . . . . . . 206 F3
Hurricane Pl IP3 . . . . . . 18 C1
Hurst Cl
Bishop's Stortford
CM23 . . . . 145 E7
Brightlingsea CO7 . . . . . 186 A6
HURST GREEN 186 A6
Hurst Way CM2 . . . . 205 F2
Hutchinson Cl CO5 . . . . 179 D4
Hutland Rd IP4 . . . . 17 F7
Hutley Dr [3] CO4 . . . . . 109 E2
Huxtables La CO3 . . . . . 108 A1
Hyacinth Cl
Clacton-on-S CO16 . . . . 188 C4
Tollesbury CM9 . . . . . . 199 E1
Hyacinth Ct [4] CM1 . . . 205 E7
Hyams La IP9 . . . . 62 D5
Hyam's La IP9 . . . . 61 F1
HYDE CHASE 219 D4
Hyde Chase
Danbury CM3 . . . . 219 B4
Woodham Mortimer
CM9 . . . . 219 D4
Hyde Gn CM3 . . . . 219 B7
Hyde La
Blackmore End CM7 . . . 74 B2
Danbury CM3 . . . . 219 B6
Hyde Park Cnr CO10 . . . 1 D2
Hyde Rd CO10 . . . . 33 E7
Hyde The CB11 . . . . 65 C8
Hydewood Rd CO9 . . . . 30 B3
Hyem's La IP11 . . . . 221 F7
Hylands Cl CM6 . . . . . . 151 A4
Hylands Par CM2 . . . . . 216 A6
Hylands Sch CM1 . . . . . 204 D1
Hyldon Ct IP11 . . . . 221 E3
Hyll Cl CB10 . . . . 3 D3
Hyntle Cl IP2 . . . . 16 E5
Hyperion Ct IP1 . . . . 16 D8
Hythe Cl
Braintree CM7 . . . . 127 E6
Clacton-on-S CO15 . . . . 203 J8
Hythe Gr CO2 . . . . 165 E1
Hythe Hill CO1 . . . . 136 C6
Hythe Quay CO2 . . . . . . 136 D5
Hythe Sta CO4 . . . . 136 D6
Hythe Station Rd
CO2 . . . . 136 D6
HYTHE THE
Colchester 136 C5
Maldon 210 B2
Hythe The CM9 . . . . 210 B2

I

Iceni Way CO2 . . . . 135 B3
ICKLETON 3 A4
Ickleton Pl [5] CB9 . . . . . 9 B8
Ickleton Rd
Elmdon CB11 . . . . 20 A4
Great Chesterford CB10 . 3 C2
Hinxton CB10 . . . . 3 B6
Icknield Cl CB10 . . . . 3 A3
Ickworth Cl CM77 . . . . . 154 C7

Ickworth Cres IP4 . . . . 18 F5
Ickworth Ct IP11 . . . . 221 A3
Iconfield Pk CO12. . . . . 91 A4
Ilex Cl CO2 . . . . 135 D2
Imogen Cl 4 CO4. . . . . . . 136 F8
Imperial Ct CO15. . . . . 188 E1
Imphal Cl CO2 . . . . 135 C1
Ingarfield Rd CO15. . . . . . 189 E6
Ingelow Gdns IP4. . . . . 18 B6
Ingelrica Ave CM3 . . . . . . 194 B3
Ingestre St CO12. . . . . 91 D4
Ingham Rd CB9 . . . . .9 B8
Inglenook CO15. . . . . 189 B7
Ingleside Ct CB10. . . . . 22 D1
Inglis Rd CO3. . . . . 135 D6
Ingram Mews CM7. . . . . . 155 B8
Ingram's Piece CO7. . . . . . 111 E8
Ingram's Well CO10. . . . . . . 33 F7
Ingram's Well Rd CO10. . . . 33 F7
Inkerman Row 3 CO10. . . 33 E8
Inkerpole Pl CM2 . . . . 205 F4
Innes End 4 IP8. . . . . 16 C2
Innham Hill CO9 . . . . 75 C6
Inverness Cl CO1 . . . . 136 A8
INWORTH 178 F8
Inworth La CO6. . . . . 79 D2
Inworth Rd CO5. . . . . 158 E3
Inworth Wlk 5 CO2. . . . . . 136 A1
Iona Wlk CO5. . . . . 164 A8
IP Central 20 IP4. . . . . 17 D5
IPSWICH 17 C7
Ipswich High Sch IP9. . . . . 38 C2
Ipswich Hospl IP4 . . . . 18 C6
Ipswich Mus* IP1. . . . . 17 C6
Ipswich Prep Sch IP1. . . . . 17 B7
Ipswich Rd
  Ardleigh CO7 . . . . 83 F1
  Brantham CO11. . . . . 60 E2
  Colchester CO4 . . . . 110 C3
  Dedham CO7 . . . . 84 B6
  Harkstead IP9. . . . . 63 B3
  Holbrook IP9 . . . . 62 E6
  Holland-on-S CO15 . . . . 189 D6
  Ipswich IP10 . . . . 38 F6
  Stratford St M CO7 . . . . . 58 E2
Ipswich Sch IP1 . . . . 17 C7
Ipswich Sta IP2 . . . . 17 B4
Ipswich Transport Mus*
  IP3 . . . . 18 C2
Ireland Rd IP3 . . . . 17 F1
Ireton Rd CO4 . . . . 109 F4
Ireton Rd CO3 . . . . 135 D5
Iris Cl
  Chelmsford CM1 . . . . 205 F5
  Ipswich IP2 . . . . 16 F5
Irlam Rd IP2 . . . . 16 D1
Iron Latch La CO3. . . . . . . 134 C8
Ironside Wlk CO11. . . . . 86 C4
Iron View CM7. . . . . 128 C2
Irvine Rd CO3. . . . . 135 C5
Irving Cl CM23 . . . . 145 D4
Isaac Sq CM2 . . . . 217 B6
Isbourne Rd CO4. . . . . 136 F7
Isham Pl IP3 . . . . 17 E4
Ishams Chase CM8 . . . . . . 195 C7
Island Ct CM23 . . . . 146 A5
Island La CO13. . . . . 143 E1
Island Rd CO14 . . . . 143 E4
Ivanhoe CO13. . . . . 170 E3
Ivor Brown Ct CO4 . . . . . . 110 B4
Ivry St IP1. . . . . 17 B7
Ivy Cotts CM6. . . . . 123 C4
Ivy La CO5. . . . . 185 B3
Ivy Lodge Rd CO6. . . . . . 109 C8
Ivy Todd Hill CB11 . . . . 68 A8
Ixworth CB9 . . . . 8 E6

J

Jacaranda Cl CM1 . . . . . . 206 A6
Jack Andrews Dr
  CO4 . . . . 110 C5
Jack Branch Ct CO15. . . . . 188 E2
Jack Hatch Way CO7. . . . . 137 A3
Jack's La CM22 . . . . 148 D7
Jackson Ho CO4 . . . . 110 B6
Jackson Pl CM2 . . . . 216 D6
Jackson Rd CO15 . . . . 188 E2
Jacksons Ct CM2 . . . . 217 A6
Jackson's La CB10 . . . . 3 D3
Jackson Sq 10 CM23 . . . . 145 F7
Jackson's Sq CB10 . . . . 3 D3
Jackson Wlk CO2. . . . . 136 B3
Jacobs Cl CO10 . . . . 34 B5
Jacobs Ct CO7. . . . . 185 F6
Jacquard Way 6
  CM7 . . . . 128 A2
Jacqueline Ct CO3. . . . . . . 135 A7
Jacques Hall Sch
  CO11. . . . . 88 A3
Jaggard's Rd CO6. . . . . . . 131 A3
James Boden Cl IP11 . . . . 221 C5
James Carter Rd CO3 . . . . 134 F3
James Cl CO7 . . . . 137 C3
James Croft CM2. . . . . 216 B2
James Gdns CO6. . . . . 187 B5
James Hatfield Ho IP2. . . . 17 D4
Jameson Pl 5 CO10 . . . . 33 E8
Jameson Rd CO15 . . . . . . 188 C3
James Parnell Dr
  CO2 . . . . 135 F1
James Rd CO15 . . . . 188 C2
James St
  Brightlingsea CO7 . . . . . . 185 F6

James St continued
  Colchester CO1 . . . . 136 A6
James Wicks Ct CO3 . . . . 135 E7
Janebrook Rd IP2 . . . . 16 E2
JANKE'S GREEN 106 E8
Janmead CM8 . . . . 177 A3
Janus Cl CB9 . . . . 9 D6
Japonica Ct CO15. . . . . . . 189 C4
Jaques Cl CO10. . . . . 2 C5
Jarmin Rd CO1 . . . . 135 F8
Jarndyce CM1 . . . . 204 F6
Jarvis Field CM3 . . . . 207 D5
Jasmin Cl CM23. . . . . 145 C6
Jasmine Cl
  2 Chelmsford CM1 . . . . 205 E7
  Colchester CO4 . . . . 136 E8
  Ipswich IP2. . . . . 16 F3
Jasmine Way CO15. . . . . . 203 G7
JASPER'S GREEN 100 E2
Jay Cl
  Great Notley CM77 . . . . . 154 D8
  Haverhill CB9. . . . . 9 C7
Jaymar Ct 9 CM7. . . . . . 127 F2
Jayrest Ctr CO3. . . . . 134 E4
Jays La CO6 . . . . 132 F3
Jays The CO4. . . . . 110 C3
JAYWICK 203 F7
Jaywick La CO15,
  CO16. . . . . 188 A3
Jaywick Rd CB9 . . . . 9 A8
Jeans La CM23. . . . . 145 E2
Jeffcut Rd CM2. . . . . 205 E2
Jefferies Rd IP4 . . . . 17 E6
Jefferson Cl CO3 . . . . 134 E5
Jeffery Rd CM2 . . . . 217 A7
Jeffrey Cl CO3. . . . . 134 F5
Jeffreys Ct CM77. . . . . 155 E6
Jeffrey's Rd CM77 . . . . . . 155 E6
Jekylls La CM7. . . . . 48 D4
Jellicoe Way CM7. . . . . . . 128 C4
Jenkins Dr CM22. . . . . 94 C3
Jenkins Hill CO11. . . . . 87 C3
Jenkins La CM22. . . . . 146 C5
Jenner Cl CM7. . . . . 127 F1
Jenner Mead CM2 . . . . . . 206 A3
Jennings Cl 1 CO1 . . . . 136 C6
Jermyns Cl IP9 . . . . 35 B2
Jersey Rd CM9 . . . . 210 B1
Jersey Way CM7. . . . . 127 D2
Jervis Cl IP9 . . . . 62 D5
Jervis Rd CM23. . . . . 145 F6
Jessica Cl CO4. . . . . 136 F7
Jessop Cl CO15. . . . . 189 A8
Jimmy's La CO11 . . . . 60 F2
Joes Rd CO10. . . . . 34 F6
John Ball Wlk 2 CO1 . . . 135 F7
John Barr Ho CM7 . . . . . . 127 B7
John Bird Ct CO1 . . . . 109 F1
John Bramston Sch The
  CM8 . . . . 176 F1
John Bunyan Inf Sch
  CM7 . . . . 127 E4
John Bunyan Jun Sch
  CM7 . . . . 127 E4
John Crouch Ct CO12 . . . 91 C3
John Dane Player Ct 5
  CO10 . . . . 22 E1
John Dyde Cl CM23 . . . . . 146 A6
John English Ave
  CM7 . . . . 127 E4
John Hammond Cl
  CO2 . . . . 162 F8
John Harper St 4
  CO1 . . . . 135 E8
John Henry Keene Meml
  Homes CM2 . . . . 205 A4
John Kavanagh Ct 1
  CO1 . . . . 136 A6
John Kent Ave CO2 . . . . . 135 B2
John King Ct CO7 . . . . 185 F6
John Lawrence Wlk
  CO2 . . . . 135 F1
John Raven Ct CO5 . . . . . 179 D6
John Ray Gdns CM77. . . . 155 B5
John Ray Inf Sch
  CM7 . . . . 154 F8
John Ray Jun Sch
  CM7 . . . . 154 F8
John Ray St CM7. . . . . 128 A3
Johnson Cl
  Braintree CM7. . . . . 155 A7
  Ipswich IP2. . . . . 17 C3
Johnson Rd
  Great Baddow CM2. . . . . 217 A5
  St Osyth CO16. . . . . 187 B4
Johnson's Dr CO7 . . . . 138 A6
Johnsons Yd CB11. . . . . 22 D2
Johns Rd CM23 . . . . 119 A1
John St
  Brightlingsea CO7 . . . . . . 185 F6
  Ipswich IP3. . . . . 17 C6
Johnston Cl
  Halstead CO9. . . . . 103 F8
  Holland-on-S CO15 . . . . 189 E5
John Tibauld Ct CB9 . . . . . 27 B6
John Weston Nature
  Reserve* CO14. . . . . 144 D6
Jollyboys La N CM6 . . . . . 152 C4
Jollyboys La S CM6 . . . . . 152 C4
Jonathan Feedham Ct
  CO7 . . . . 137 B1
Jonquil Way CO4 . . . . 109 C2
Jordan Cl CB11. . . . . 43 E8
Joscelyn's Yd 11
  CM23 . . . . 146 A7
Joseph Gdns CM8. . . . . . . 156 E4
Josselin Cl CO6. . . . . 105 B7
Josselyns The IP11 . . . . . . 221 A8

Jovian Way
  Colchester CO4 . . . . 110 B6
  Ipswich IP1. . . . . 16 D7
Joyce Brooks Ho
  CO3 . . . . 135 D6
Joyce's Chase CM9 . . . . . 212 A8
Jubilee Ave
  Broomfield CM1. . . . . . . 191 B2
  Clacton-on-S CO16. . . . . 188 E8
Jubilee Cl
  Colchester CO3 . . . . 134 D6
  Harwich CO12. . . . . 90 E2
Jubilee Cott 12 CM23. . . . 146 A7
Jubilee Ct
  Great Dunmow CM6 . . . . 123 C1
  Sible Hedingham CO9 . . . 75 E8
  Tiptree CO5 . . . . 179 D4
  Walton-on-t-N CO14 . . . . 171 C7
Jubilee End CO11. . . . . 86 C5
Jubilee La CO7 . . . . 111 C3
Jubilee Rd CO10 . . . . 33 F8
Jubilee Rise CM3 . . . . 219 A6
Jubilee Terr CM1 . . . . 205 A4
Jubilee Way CO13 . . . . . . 170 F6
Jubilee Wks CB11 . . . . 65 E6
Jubilee Wlk 3 CB9 . . . . 9 A7
Judge CM2 . . . . 206 B4
Julian Ave CO4 . . . . 110 B6
Julian Rd
  Broomfield CM1. . . . . . . 191 B1
  Haverhill CB9. . . . . 9 D7
Julien Court Rd CM7. . . . . 128 A4
Juniper Cl CO9 . . . . 103 D8
Juniper Cres CM8. . . . . . . 177 A4
Juniper Ct CM6 . . . . 123 B1
Juniper Dr CM2. . . . . 216 B6
Juniper Rd
  Boreham CM3 . . . . 206 F8
  Colchester CO3 . . . . 134 D5
Juniper Way CO4 . . . . 136 D8
Juno Mews CO2 . . . . 135 C1
Jupes Hill CO7. . . . . 85 C4
Jupe's Hill CO6 . . . . 79 D1
Jupiter Cl CB9 . . . . 9 D6
Jupiter Rd IP4. . . . . 18 B7
Justinian Cl CB9 . . . . 9 D6
Jutland Ct CO10 . . . . 33 F7
Juvina Cl 3 CM8 . . . . . . 194 E7

K

Kale Croft CO3 . . . . 134 D5
Kangels The CB11 . . . . 43 D8
Kate Daniels Ho CO16. . . . 140 F1
Kate's La CB10. . . . . 24 C8
Katherine Semar Inf Sch
  CB11. . . . . 43 E6
Katherine Semar Jun Sch
  CB11. . . . . 43 E6
Kay Cl CM3 . . . . 174 A7
Kayla Ct 6 CO3. . . . . 135 E6
Keable Rd CO6 . . . . 132 E3
Keating Cl CO11. . . . . 86 B4
Keats Ave CM7 . . . . 154 F8
Keats Rd CO3. . . . . 134 F6
Kebbles CO10 . . . . 2 B6
Keble Cl CO3 . . . . 135 D6
Kedington Hill CO10 . . . . . . 34 B2
Keeble Cl CO5 . . . . 179 C6
Keeble Ct CO7 . . . . 166 E7
Keeble Pk CM9 . . . . 220 F8
Keeble's Yd 7 CB9 . . . . . . 9 A8
Keeble Way CM7. . . . . 128 A3
Keelars La CO7. . . . . 137 E2
Keelers Way CO6 . . . . 109 B7
Keene Cl CO5. . . . . 201 D7
Keene Way CM2 . . . . 216 B3
Keepers Gn CO4 . . . . 109 B3
Keep The 3 CB9. . . . . 8 E7
Keith Cl CO15. . . . . 189 B8
Kelly Rd IP2 . . . . 16 E5
Kelso Cl CO6 . . . . 109 C6
KELVEDON 158 D2
Kelvedon Cl CM1 . . . . 205 A6
Kelvedon Dr IP4 . . . . 18 F5
Kelvedon Hall La CO5 . . . 178 E5
Kelvedon Rd
  Coggeshall CO6 . . . . 158 A8
  Kelvedon CO5. . . . . 158 F2
  Messing CO5 . . . . 159 C2
  Tiptree CO5 . . . . 179 B7
  Tollesunt D'arcy CM9 . . . 198 C6
  Wickham Bishops CM8 . . 195 F5
Kelvedon St Mary's CE
  Prim Sch CO5 . . . . 158 C2
Kelvedon Sta CO5. . . . . . . 158 C3
Kelvin Ct CO13. . . . . 170 F3
Kemball St IP4. . . . . 18 A5
Kempe Rd CM7 . . . . 72 D6
Kempson Dr CO10 . . . . 34 C5
Kempsters The IP11 . . . . . 221 B7
Kempton Pk CO16 . . . . . . 168 B5
Kemsley Rd
  Earls Colne CO6. . . . . . . 105 A6
  Felixstowe IP11. . . . . . . 221 D5
Ken Cooke Ct 4 CO1. . . . 135 F7
Kendall CE Prim Sch
  CO1. . . . . 136 C4
Kendall Rd CO1. . . . . 136 A6
Kendall Terr CO1 . . . . 136 A6
Kendall's Almshouses 3
  CO1. . . . . 136 A6
Kenilworth Gr CO16 . . . . . 142 A2
Kenilworth Rd CO15 . . . . 189 E6
Kennedy Cl IP4 . . . . 18 A6
Kennedy Way CO15 . . . . . 189 A5
Kennels The CO6 . . . . 104 F6

Kennet Way CM1 . . . . 204 D5
Kensington Rd IP1. . . . . . . 17 A8
Kenston Ct CO5. . . . . 201 B6
Kent Cl CO7 . . . . 185 F7
Kent Cres CM23. . . . . 145 E4
Kentford Rd IP11. . . . . 221 A4
Kent Gdns CM7 . . . . 128 B4
Kent Ho IP11 . . . . 221 C6
Kentings The CM7 . . . . . . 127 E2
Kentmere Cl CO4 . . . . 110 E2
Kent's Ave CO15. . . . . 189 E6
Kents Grass CM9. . . . . . . 199 D2
Kents Yd CB11. . . . . 21 F4
Kentwell Cl IP4 . . . . 18 F4
Kenwood Ho 6 CM2 . . . . 216 A8
Kenworthy Rd CM7 . . . . . 127 F2
Kenyon Cl CO7 . . . . 58 D1
Kenyon St IP2 . . . . 17 C4
Kerby Rise CM2. . . . . 205 F2
Kerridge's Cut CO11 . . . . . 87 A4
Kerry Ct CO1 . . . . 136 C7
Kersey Ave CO10. . . . . 34 B6
Kersey Ct CO2 . . . . 135 C3
Kersey Dr CO16. . . . . 188 B5
Kersey Rd IP11 . . . . 221 B3
Kessler Ave CM7 . . . . 73 D7
Kesteven Rd IP2 . . . . 17 B4
Kestrel Gdns CM23 . . . . . 145 C6
Kestrel Rd
  Haverhill CB9. . . . . 9 C7
  Ipswich IP2. . . . . 16 D3
Kestrel Rise CO9. . . . . 76 F1
Kestrel Way CO15 . . . . . . 188 F6
Kestrel Wlk CM2. . . . . 216 B5
Keswick Ave CO15 . . . . . . 189 C6
Keswick Cl CO13 . . . . 170 F7
Ketley Cl CO5 . . . . 179 E5
Ketleys CM7 . . . . 216 C3
Ketleys View CM7. . . . . . . 127 A7
Kettlebaston Way IP4. . . . . 17 B7
Kew La CO13 . . . . 170 A4
Key Ct CO15 . . . . 188 E3
Keyes Way CM7. . . . . 128 C4
Keymer Way CO3 . . . . 134 F4
Keynes Way CO12. . . . . . . 90 F1
Key Rd CO15. . . . . 188 E3
Key St IP4 . . . . 17 D5
Khartoum Rd IP4 . . . . 17 F7
Khartoum Villas CO7. . . . . 111 E8
Kidder Rd CM77 . . . . 126 F1
Kilburn Gdns CO15. . . . . . 188 D5
Kildermorie Cl CO4 . . . . . . 110 D3
KILLEM'S GREEN 40 A4
Kilmaine Rd CO12. . . . . . . 90 F2
Kiln Barn Ave CO15 . . . . . 188 F7
Kiln Cotts
  Danbury CM3. . . . . 218 D6
  Dedham CO7 . . . . 84 F5
Kiln Dr CO10. . . . . 34 B6
Kiln Field IP11 . . . . 221 B5
Kiln La CO11. . . . . 86 D4
Kilns Hill CO6. . . . . 130 F5
Kiltie Rd CO5 . . . . 179 E5
Kimberley Cl CM23 . . . . . 146 A5
Kimberley Rd CO1 . . . . . . 136 B5
Kincaid Rd CO16. . . . . 187 A4
King Charles Ct 6
  CM2. . . . . 205 B1
King Charles Rd CO5. . . . . 201 D6
King Coel Cl CO3. . . . . . . 134 D7
King Edward Cl CM1 . . . . 205 A3
King Edward Ind Pk
  CO2. . . . . 136 D5
King Edward Quay
  CO2. . . . . 136 D5
King Edward Rd CO3 . . . . . 18 B3
King Edward VI Gram Sch
  CM1 . . . . 205 A3
King Edward VII Dr
  IP9. . . . . 91 C8
King Edward VI's
  Almshouses CB11 . . . . . 22 D1
King Edward Way
  CM8 . . . . 194 E8
Kingfisher Ave IP2. . . . . . . 16 E3
Kingfisher Cl
  Colchester CO4 . . . . 136 F8
  Haverhill CB9. . . . . 9 C8
  Heybridge CM9 . . . . 210 C5
Kingfisher Dr CO12 . . . . . . 90 E1
Kingfisher Gate CM7 . . . . 128 A5
Kingfisher Lo CM2 . . . . . . 216 F7
Kingfisher Mdws CO9 . . . . 76 F1
Kingfishers CO15 . . . . 188 F6
Kingfisher Way
  Bishop's Stortford
  CM23 . . . . 146 A7
  Kelvedon CO5 . . . . 158 C2
King George Ct 7
  CM2 . . . . 205 B1
King George Rd CO2 . . . . 135 F4
King George's Ave
  CO12 . . . . 91 B4
King George's Pl
  CM9 . . . . 210 A2
King Georges View
  CM7 . . . . 128 C2
King George V Meml
  Homes IP3 . . . . 17 F3
King Harold Rd CO3. . . . . 135 A4
Kings Acre CO6. . . . . 130 F2
Kings Ave
  Clacton-on-S CO15. . . . . 189 D5
  Ipswich IP4. . . . . 17 E5
Kingsbridge Cl CM7. . . . . . 127 E4
Kingsbridge Rd CM23 . . . 146 A8
Kingsbury Cl CO6 . . . . 132 F3
Kingsbury Rd IP11. . . . . . . 221 A7

Kingsbury Wlk CO10 . . . . . 34 C5
Kings Chase CM8 . . . . . . 177 A1
Kings Cl CO11 . . . . 86 C4
King's Cl CO5. . . . . 187 A3
King's Cotts CM23 . . . . . . 146 A6
Kings Ct CM23 . . . . 146 A8
King's Ct CO4 . . . . 110 B6
Kings Ct
  Harwich CO12. . . . . 91 B3
  Holland-on-S CO15 . . . . 189 E5
King's Ct CM6 . . . . 123 D1
Kingsdale Ind Est The
  CM1 . . . . 205 C3
Kingsfield Ave IP1. . . . . 17 D8
Kings Fleet Rd IP11. . . . . . 221 C3
Kingsford Ct CO2 . . . . 135 B3
Kingsford Dr CM2. . . . . . . 206 B4
King's Ford Jun & Inf Schs
  CO2. . . . . 135 C3
Kingsgate Dr IP4 . . . . 17 F8
Kings Gdns CO5 . . . . 158 E4
Kings Head Ct 1 CO1 . . . 135 E8
Kings Head Ctr The
  CM9 . . . . 209 F3
King's Head St CO12 . . . . 91 E6
Kings Head Wlk 6
  CM2 . . . . 205 C2
Kings Hill CO10. . . . . 34 A6
Kings Ho CO13. . . . . 171 A4
Kings La CM77. . . . . 129 A6
King's La
  Elmdon CB11 . . . . 20 A3
  Long Melford CO10 . . . . . 15 F7
Kingsland Beach CO5. . . . 201 C5
Kingsland Cl CO5. . . . . . . 201 C5
Kingsland Hts CO5. . . . . . 201 C6
Kingsland Rd CO5 . . . . . . 201 D6
Kingsman Dr CO16. . . . . . 188 C5
Kings Mdw CO10. . . . . 34 A6
Kings Mead CO9 . . . . 78 A7
Kingsmead Hall CO3 . . . . 134 F5
Kingsmead Ho CO3 . . . . . 134 F5
Kings Meadow Ct
  CO5. . . . . 158 C3
Kings Meadow Rd
  CO1. . . . . 135 F8
Kingsmead Pk CM7 . . . . . 128 C4
Kingsmead Rd CM23 . . . . 146 A8
Kingsmere Cl CO5 . . . . . . 201 D7
Kings Mews CO7. . . . . 137 C4
Kings Par CO15 . . . . 189 E5
Kings Prom CO15 . . . . . . 203 J8
King's Quay St CO12 . . . . 91 E6
Kings Quay St CO12 . . . . . 91 E6
Kings Rd
  Braintree CM7. . . . . 127 E6
  Chelmsford CM1 . . . . 204 F4
  Glemsford CO10 . . . . 2 B5
  Great Totham CM9. . . . . 196 D7
  Halstead CO9. . . . . 76 E1
King's Rd
  Clacton-on-S CO15. . . . . 188 D1
  Harwich CO12. . . . . 91 B3
Kings Reach CO14 . . . . . . 144 D1
Kings Road Prim Sch
  CM1 . . . . 204 F4
King St
  Bishop's Stortford
  CM23 . . . . 145 F7
  Bradfield CO11. . . . . 114 C8
  Castle Hedingham CO9 . . 51 F4
  Felixstowe IP11. . . . . . . 221 C6
  14 Ipswich IP1. . . . . 17 C6
  Maldon CM9. . . . . 210 A1
  Saffron Walden CB10 . . . 22 D1
  Sudbury CO10 . . . . 33 E7
King Stephen Rd CO1 . . . 136 B6
Kingston Ave CM2 . . . . . . 205 E3
Kingston Chase CM9 . . . . 209 F5
Kingston Cres CM2 . . . . . 205 E3
Kingston Mews CO15. . . . 188 C3
Kingston Rd IP1. . . . . 16 F8
King Street Mews 1
  CM23 . . . . 145 F7
Kingsway
  Harwich CO12. . . . . 91 D4
  Tiptree CO5 . . . . 179 C6
King's Way IP3 . . . . 18 C2
Kings Wlk CM9 . . . . 199 E1
Kingswode Hoe Sch
  CO3. . . . . 135 C7
Kingswood Rd CO4. . . . . . 109 F4
Kingwell Ave CO15. . . . . . 188 E5
Kinlett Cl CO4 . . . . 110 B4
Kinloch Chase 4
  CM8 . . . . 194 F7
Kino Rd CO14. . . . . 171 D8
Kipling Cl CM1. . . . . 205 A5
Kipling Way CM7 . . . . 155 A8
Kirby Cl IP4 . . . . 18 A7
KIRBY CROSS 170 B7
Kirby Cross Sta CO13 . . . 170 B6
Kirby Hall Rd CO9. . . . . . . 51 D5
KIRBY-LE-SOKEN 170 C8
Kirby Prim Sch CO13. . . . 170 B7
Kirby Rd
  Great Holland CO13. . . . 170 B5
  Walton-on-t-N CO14 . . . . 171 B8
Kirby St IP4 . . . . 18 A6
Kirkbaye CO13. . . . . 170 E6
Kirkham Cl IP2 . . . . 17 A2
Kirkhurst Cl CO7. . . . . 186 A6
Kirklees CM1 . . . . 204 F4
Kirkley Ct CB9. . . . . 8 C8
Kirkmans Rd CM2 . . . . . . 216 D3
Kirk Pl CM2. . . . . 205 F3
Kirkton Cl IP9. . . . . 91 A8
Kirtling Pl 12 CB9. . . . . 9 B8

Kitchener Rd IP1 . . . . 16 F8
Kitchener Way IP9 . . . . 91 A8
Kitchen Field CM7 . . . . . . 128 D3
Kittiwake Cl IP2 . . . . 16 E3
Kittiwake Dr CM9 . . . . . . 210 C5
Knapton Cl CM1 . . . . 205 D7
Knebworth Ct CM23 . . . . 145 D6
Knevett Cl CO4 . . . . 109 E3
Knightsbridge Cl CO2 . . 135 C3
Knightsbridge Ct
CO15 . . . . 189 B3
Knights Cl
Bishop's Stortford
CM23 . . . . 145 C8
Lawford CO11 . . . . 86 C4
Tiptree CO5 . . . . 179 F3
Knight's Ct **2** CB9 . . . . 8 E7
Knights Field CO2 . . . . . . 136 A5
Knights Rd
Braintree CM7 . . . . 128 D1
Coggeshall CO6 . . . . 130 F2
Knights Row CM23 . . . . . 145 E6
Knights Way CM6 . . . . . . 123 D1
Knole La CB11 . . . . 41 A7
Knowles Cl CO9 . . . . 76 E1
KNOWL GREEN 30 E8
Knox Ct CO15 . . . . 188 E5
Knox Gdns CO15 . . . . 188 E5
Knox Rd CO15 . . . . 188 E5
Knutsford Cl IP8 . . . . 16 C1
Kohima Rd CO2 . . . . 135 B1
Kreswell Gr CO12 . . . . 91 B2
Kynaston Pl CM8 . . . . 177 B2
Kynaston Rd CM7 . . . . . . 127 A7

L

Laburnum Cl
Clacton-on-S CO15 . . . . 188 C3
Great Bentley CO7 . . . . 166 F8
2 Ipswich, Chantry IP8 . . 16 C2
Ipswich, Warren Heath
IP3 . . . . 18 E2
Laburnum Cres CO13 . . . 170 D6
Laburnum Dr CM2 . . . . . 216 C6
Laburnum Gr CO4 . . . . . . 136 E6
Laburnum Rd CM6 . . . . . 123 B1
Laburnum Way
Hatfield Peverel CM3 . . 194 A4
Witham CM8 . . . . 177 A5
Lacewing Cl IP8 . . . . 36 E8
Lacey St IP4 . . . . 17 E6
Lackford Pl IP3 . . . . 38 C8
Ladbrook Dr CO2 . . . . . . 136 A3
Ladbrooke Rd CO16 . . . . 188 D6
Ladell Cl CO3 . . . . 134 E3
Lady D'Arcy Charity
Almshouses **3** CO1 . . . 135 F6
Ladygate CB9 . . . . 8 E6
Lady La
Chelmsford CM2 . . . . . 216 C8
6 Ipswich IP1 . . . . 17 B6
Ladysmith Ave CO1 . . . . 185 E6
Ladysmith Cotts CM6 . . 152 C4
Ladywell La CM2 . . . . 217 B5
Ladywood Rd IP4 . . . . 18 C7
Laing Rd CO4 . . . . 136 E6
Lake Ave CO15 . . . . 188 C3
Lake Mead CM9 . . . . 210 C3
Lakeside Cl IP2 . . . . 16 E2
Lakeside Rd IP2 . . . . 16 E2
Lakeside Wlk CO3 . . . . . . 134 C4
Lakes Ind Pk CM7 . . . . . 128 B2
Lakes Mdw CO6 . . . . 131 A2
Lakes Rd CM7 . . . . 128 B2
Lake Way CO15 . . . . 203 F6
Lake Wlk CO15 . . . . 188 C3
Lakewood CO7 . . . . 112 E1
Lakforth CO10 . . . . 15 D8
Lakin Cl CM2 . . . . 206 A3
LAMARSH 55 B4
Lamarsh Hill
Bures CO8 . . . . 55 E1
Lamarsh CO8 . . . . 55 B6
Lamarsh Rd CO8 . . . . 55 A4
LAMB CORNER 84 D4
Lambert Cross CB10 . . . . 22 E3
Lamberts Orch CM7 . . . . 127 D4
Lambert's Rd CO6 . . . . . 105 F3
Lambeth Cl IP1 . . . . 16 F8
Lambeth Wlk CO15 . . . . . 188 E5
Lamb La CO9 . . . . 75 D7
Lambourne Cl
Clacton-on-S CO15 . . . . 188 F8
Colchester CO3 . . . . . . 134 C4
Lambourne Gr CM9 . . . . 220 F8
Lammas Dr CM7 . . . . 128 D3
Lammas Way CO7 . . . . . . 137 C2
Lancaster Ct
5 Braintree CM7 . . . . . 128 B2
Frinton-on-S CO13 . . . . 171 A5
Lancaster Gdns E
CO15 . . . . 189 A3
Lancaster Gdns W
CO15 . . . . 189 A3
Lancaster Ho IP11 . . . . . 221 C6
Lancaster Rd
5 Ipswich IP4 . . . . 17 E6
Sudbury CO10 . . . . 15 D2
Lancaster Way
Bishop's Stortford
CM23 . . . . 145 C6
Braintree CM7 . . . . 127 E4
Earls Colne CO6 . . . . . . 104 F2
Lanchester Ave CO15 . . 203 D6
Lancia Ave CO15 . . . . . . 203 D6

Lancing Ave IP4 . . . . 18 A8
Land Cl CO16 . . . . 188 C5
Landermere Rd CO16 . . . 142 B2
Landers Ct CM1 . . . . 204 E5
Landisdale CM3 . . . . 219 A7
Land La CO1 . . . . 136 A7
Landscape View CB11 . . . 43 D6
Landsdown Rd CO10 . . . . 34 A8
Landseer Cl IP3 . . . . 18 A1
Landseer Ct
Clacton-on-S CO15 . . . . 188 F2
Haverhill CB9 . . . . 8 F6
Landseer Rd
Colchester CO3 . . . . . . 135 B5
Ipswich IP3 . . . . 17 E2
Lanercost Rd IP2 . . . . 17 A1
Lane Rd CO6 . . . . 106 B7
Lane The
Mistley CO11 . . . . 86 F4
West Mersea CO5 . . . . . 201 A7
Langale CM77 . . . . 154 C8
Langale Dr CO4 . . . . 110 B4
Langale Gdns CM2 . . . . 216 D8
LANGENHOE 163 B2
Langenhoe Com Prim Sch
CO5 . . . . 163 B2
Langenhoe Hall La
CO5 . . . . 183 C7
Langenhoe Pk CO5 . . . . 163 B2
Langer Park Ind Est
IP11 . . . . 221 D3
Langer Prim Sch
IP11 . . . . 221 C2
Langer Rd IP11 . . . . 221 C2
LANGFORD 209 D7
Langford Rd
Heybridge CM9 . . . . . . 209 F6
Wickham Bishops CM8,
CM9 . . . . 195 C2
LANGHAM 83 F4
Langham Dr CO16 . . . . . 188 B2
Langham La CO4 . . . . 83 B2
LANGHAM MOOR 83 C4
Langham Pl CO4 . . . . 110 B3
Langham Prim Sch
CO4 . . . . 83 F4
Langham Rd CO4 . . . . . . 82 F1
LANGLEY 40 C2
Langley Ave
Felixstowe IP11 . . . . . . 221 C5
Wethersfield CM7 . . . . . 73 D7
Langley Cl
Felixstowe IP11 . . . . . . 221 C5
Harwich CO12 . . . . 91 C3
LANGLEY GREEN 158 F8
Langley Hill CO8 . . . . 55 C3
Langleys CO6 . . . . 106 C1
Langstons IP11 . . . . 221 B7
Langton Ave CM1 . . . . . . 204 E5
Langton Ct CB11 . . . . 189 A2
Languidic Cl CO10 . . . . . . 34 C6
Langwood CO5 . . . . 201 C7
Lanham Farm Rd
CM77 . . . . 156 A8
LANHAM GREEN 156 A8
Lanham Green Rd
CM77 . . . . 156 A7
Lansdowne Cl CO5 . . . . . 179 C4
Lansdowne Rd
Felixstowe IP11 . . . . . . 221 F6
Ipswich IP4 . . . . 18 A5
Lanvalley Rd CO3 . . . . . . 134 C4
Lanyards IP11 . . . . 221 F4
Lapwing Dr
Heybridge CM9 . . . . . . 210 C5
Kelvedon CO5 . . . . 158 D2
Lapwing Rd IP2 . . . . 16 D3
Larch Cl CO4 . . . . 136 D8
Larches The CM3 . . . . . . 206 E8
Larch Gr
Chelmsford CM2 . . . . . 216 C6
Witham CM8 . . . . 177 A5
Larch Ho IP11 . . . . 221 C4
Larch Way CM6 . . . . 123 B1
Larch Wlk
Hatfield Peverel CM3 . . 194 A4
Heybridge CM9 . . . . . . 210 C6
Larchwood CM23 . . . . . . 145 D6
Larchwood Cl IP2 . . . . . . 16 C5
Larkfield Rd CO7 . . . . . . 139 D1
Larkhill Rise IP4 . . . . 18 E5
Lark Rise CO10 . . . . 33 D5
Larkrise Prim Sch
CM2 . . . . 216 E6
Larks Cl CB9 . . . . 9 C7
Larksfield Cres CO12 . . . 91 B4
Larksfield Rd IP9 . . . . 62 A2
Lark's La
Broomfield CM3 . . . . . 191 A6
Great Waltham CM3 . . 190 F5
Larkspur Cl
Bishop's Stortford
CM23 . . . . 145 D6
Witham CM8 . . . . 176 E4
Larkspur Ct **3** CM1 . . . . 205 F6
Larkspur Rd IP2 . . . . 16 F3
Larks Rise CO9 . . . . 77 A1
Larksway
Bishop's Stortford
CM23 . . . . 145 C6
Felixstowe IP11 . . . . . . 221 B3
Larkway CO13 . . . . 170 E7
Larman Ct CO11 . . . . 86 C7
Larneys The CO13 . . . . . 170 E7
La Salle CI IP3 . . . . 17 B3
Latchmore Bank
CM22 . . . . 146 B2

Lathcoates Cres CM2 . . 216 E8
Lathe Ct CO4 . . . . 136 D6
Latimer Ho CM1 . . . . 205 D3
Lattice Ave IP4 . . . . 18 C6
LATTINFORD HILL 59 D6
Laud Mews IP3 . . . . 18 A2
Launceston Cl CM2 . . . . 136 B1
Laundry Gdns CO10 . . . . 33 D6
Laurel Ave CO12 . . . . 90 F2
Laurel Cl CO15 . . . . 189 B7
Laurel Ct CO4 . . . . 136 E8
Laurel Dr
Great Dunmow CM6 . . 123 B1
Long Melford CO10 . . . . 15 C7
Laurel Gr **4** CM2 . . . . . . 216 A8
Laurelhayes IP2 . . . . 17 A3
Laurels The
Braintree CM7 . . . . 128 A3
Great Notley CM77 . . . 154 C8
Laurence Ave CM8 . . . . . 195 A8
Laurence Cl CO7 . . . . 137 F6
Laurence Croft CM1 . . . . 204 B1
Lauriston Bglws CM9 . . . 212 C6
Lavender Cl
Bishop's Stortford
CM23 . . . . 145 D6
Tiptree CO5 . . . . 179 C4
Witham CM8 . . . . 176 E4
Lavender Ct **1** CM1 . . . . 205 F5
Lavender Field
Haverhill CB9 . . . . 8 D8
6 Saffron Walden CB10 . . 22 F2
Lavender Hill IP2 . . . . 16 F4
Lavender Way CO4 . . . . . 109 C2
Lavender Wlk CO15 . . . . 203 G7
Lavenham CI CO16 . . . . . 188 B4
Lavenham Ct CO2 . . . . . 135 C2
Lavenham Rd IP2 . . . . . . 16 E5
LAWFORD 86 B3
Lawford CE Prim Sch
CO11 . . . . 86 B2
Lawford La
Chelmsford CM1 . . . . . 204 D3
Writtle CM1 . . . . 204 C1
Lawford Mead Inf Sch
CM1 . . . . 204 D5
Lawford Mead Jun Sch
CM1 . . . . 204 D5
Lawford Pl
Lawford CO11 . . . . 86 A3
Rushmere St A IP4 . . . . 18 F5
Lawling Ave CM9 . . . . . . 210 C5
Lawn Chase CM8 . . . . . . 176 F1
Lawn La CM1 . . . . 205 D6
Lawns Cl CO5 . . . . 201 C7
Lawns The
Chelmsford CM1 . . . . . 205 D5
Ipswich IP1 . . . . 18 C8
Lawn Way IP11 . . . . 221 C5
Laws Cl CB11 . . . . 43 D7
Lawshall's Hill CO6 . . . . . 78 D1
Laxton Cl CO3 . . . . 135 A4
Laxton Gr CO13 . . . . 170 A6
Laxton Rd CO7 . . . . 165 B8
LAYER BRETON 161 B1
Layer Breton Hill CO2 . . 161 B1
Layer Cross CO2 . . . . . . 161 F5
Layer Ct CO2 . . . . 135 D4
LAYER DE LA HAYE 161 E5
Layer de la Haye CE Prim
Sch CO2 . . . . 161 F5
LAYER MARNEY 180 D8
Layer Marney Twr★
CO5 . . . . 180 D8
Layer Rd
Abberton CO5 . . . . 163 A3
Colchester CO2 . . . . . . 135 C3
Great Wigborough CO5 . 181 E5
Haverhill CB9 . . . . 8 E7
Malting Green CO5 . . . 162 E4
Layzell Croft CO10 . . . . . 34 C4
Leach Cl CM2 . . . . 217 B7
Lea Cl
Bishop's Stortford
CM23 . . . . 119 B1
Braintree CM7 . . . . 128 D1
Lea Ct CM2 . . . . 216 E2
Lea Gr CM23 . . . . 119 B1
Lea La CM8 . . . . 177 F2
Leam Cl CO4 . . . . 136 F1
Leapingwell Cl CM2 . . . . 206 A3
Lea Side CO5 . . . . 201 D6
Leas La CO2 . . . . 161 D6
Leas The CO13 . . . . 171 B6
Leather La
6 Braintree CM7 . . . . . 127 F3
Great Yeldham CO9 . . . 30 A1
Haverhill CB9 . . . . 8 E7
Le Cateau Rd CO2 . . . . . 135 E6
Leech's La CO4 . . . . 109 D4
Leeford CM1 . . . . 204 D6
LEE-OVER-SANDS 202 C6
Lee Rd
Harwich CO12 . . . . 91 C3
Ipswich IP3 . . . . 17 F9
Lees Ct CO10 . . . . 2 B4
Lees The CM6 . . . . 70 A3
Leeway The CM3 . . . . . . 218 F7
Lee Wick La CO16 . . . . . 186 D2
Leez La CM3 . . . . 152 E2
Leez Priory★ CM3 . . . . . 153 A2
Legerton Cotts CO6 . . . . 79 C1
Legg St CM1 . . . . 205 B3
Legions Way CM23 . . . . . 146 A8

Leicester Cl
Colchester CO1 . . . . . . 136 A8
Ipswich IP2 . . . . 16 F1
Jaywick CO15 . . . . 187 F1
Leicester Ct CM8 . . . . . . 156 D3
Leigh Dr
Elsenham CM22 . . . . . . 94 C1
Wickham Bishops CM8 . 195 D5
Leighs Rd CM3 . . . . 191 E6
Leighton Rd IP3 . . . . 38 A8
Leighton Sq IP3 . . . . 38 A8
Leiston Rd CB9 . . . . 8 E7
Lely Rd IP3 . . . . 37 F8
Lemons Hill IP9 . . . . 61 D8
Leonard Mews CM7 . . . . 155 B8
Leopold Gdns IP4 . . . . . . 18 B8
Leopold Rd
Felixstowe IP11 . . . . . . 221 E4
Ipswich IP4 . . . . 18 A8
Les Bois CO2 . . . . 162 A5
Leslie Newnham Ct **1**
CM9 . . . . 210 A1
Leslie Rd IP3 . . . . 18 D1
Lethe Gr
Blackheath CO2 . . . . . . 163 A8
Colchester CO2 . . . . . . 162 F8
Letton Cl IP9 . . . . 35 A1
LEVEL'S GREEN 118 C5
Levens Way CM77 . . . . . 154 C6
Levington Rd
Felixstowe IP11 . . . . . . 221 C5
Ipswich IP3 . . . . 18 A3
Lewes Cl IP3 . . . . 18 E3
Lewin Pl CM3 . . . . 206 E8
Lewis Dr CM2 . . . . 216 B6
Lewis La IP9 . . . . 61 E2
LEXDEN 135 A7
Lexden Cl CO3 . . . . 135 C7
Lexden Gr CO3 . . . . 134 F7
Lexden Grange CO3 . . . . 135 B7
Lexden Mews CO3 . . . . . 134 F7
Lexden Park Ho CO3 . . . 135 A7
Lexden Pl CO3 . . . . 134 E7
Lexden Prim Sch CO3 . . 134 E6
Lexden Springs Sch
CO3 . . . . 134 E7
Lexden Rd
Colchester CO3 . . . . . . 135 B7
West Bergholt CO6 . . . 108 D4
Leybourne Dr CM1 . . . . . 205 E7
Leyfield CM77 . . . . 155 D7
Ley Field
Marks Tey CO6 . . . . . . 132 E3
Takeley CM22 . . . . 148 C7
Leyfields CM77 . . . . 126 F1
Leys Dr CO16 . . . . 168 C1
Leyside CM77 . . . . 126 F2
Leys Rd CO7 . . . . 137 C3
Leys The
Chelmsford CM2 . . . . . 205 F5
Wimbish CB10 . . . . 45 C3
Ley The CM7 . . . . 128 D1
Leyton Ct CO15 . . . . 188 F8
Leywood Cl CM7 . . . . . . 128 D2
Libius Dr CO4 . . . . 110 A5
Lichfield Cl
Chelmsford CM1 . . . . . 204 E4
Colchester CO1 . . . . . . 136 A8
Lidgate Ct IP11 . . . . 221 A4
Lichfild Cl CM8 . . . . 195 A7
Lie Field CM7 . . . . 128 D3
Lightship Way CO2 . . . . . 136 D5
Lilac Ave CO16 . . . . 203 B6
Lilac Cl CM2 . . . . 216 C6
Lilac Ct CO7 . . . . 137 A2
Lilac Tree Cl CO4 . . . . . . 136 E8
Lilian Impey Dr CO4 . . . . 110 B5
Lilley's La CO7 . . . . 112 D4
Lillies The CM7 . . . . 102 B1
Lilly Cnr CB9 . . . . 27 A6
Lily Cl CM1 . . . . 205 F6
Limbourne Dr CM9 . . . . 210 D5
Lime Ave
Colchester CO4 . . . . . . 136 D8
Harwich CO12 . . . . 91 B3
Limebrook Way CM9 . . . 220 E7
Lime Cl
Clacton-on-S CO15 . . . . 188 C3
Witham CM8 . . . . 177 A5
Limefields CB10 . . . . 22 D4
Lime Gr CB9 . . . . 9 C5
Lime Gr CO10 . . . . 33 C5
Limekiln La CM24 . . . . . 119 C5
Limes Cres CM23 . . . . . 146 A7
Lime St CO7 . . . . 185 F5
Limes The
Ardleigh CO7 . . . . 111 F7
Clacton-on-S CO15 . . . 189 A3
Colchester CO3 . . . . . . 135 B7
Galleywood CO2 . . . . . 216 B2
Gosfield CO9 . . . . 102 E7
Long Melford CO10 . . . 15 C7
Tattingstone IP9 . . . . . . 61 B6
Limetree Dr IP3 . . . . 18 D2
Lime Tree Hill CM6 . . . . 123 D2
Lime Tree Pl IP11 . . . . . . 16 E7
Lime Wlk CM2 . . . . 216 C6
Limington Ct IP3 . . . . . . 17 E5
Lincoln Ave CO15 . . . . . 203 D6
Lincoln Cl CM23 . . . . . . 145 D5
Lincoln La CO6 . . . . 82 C1
Lincoln Terr IP11 . . . . . . 221 D3
Lincoln Way CO1 . . . . . . 136 A8
Lindbergh Rd IP3 . . . . . . 18 C2
Linden Cl
Chelmsford CM2 . . . . . 216 C6
Colchester CO4 . . . . . . 110 E1
Lawford CO11 . . . . 86 B3

Linden Dr CO15 . . . . 188 E7
Lindens The
Bishop's Stortford
CM23 . . . . 145 F6
Braintree CM7 . . . . 128 A1
Colchester CO3 . . . . . . 135 B7
Halstead CO9 . . . . 103 F6
Lindisfarne Cl IP2 . . . . . . 17 A1
Lindisfarne Ct CM9 . . . . 220 E8
LINDSELL 98 A3
Lindsell La CM6 . . . . 98 B2
Lindsey Ave CO10 . . . . . . 34 B6
Lindsey Cl CM23 . . . . . . 118 F1
Lindsey Ct CO10 . . . . 34 B6
Lindsey Rd
Bishop's Stortford
CM23 . . . . 118 F1
Ipswich IP4 . . . . 18 C7
Line Cotts CO4 . . . . 83 A4
Linfold Cl CM7 . . . . 128 D4
Linford Mews CM9 . . . . 220 E8
Ling's La IP9 . . . . 63 D5
Lingwood Cl CM3 . . . . . 218 E7
Link Cl CO4 . . . . 109 E4
Link La IP9 . . . . 60 D6
Link Rd
Bishop's Stortford
CM23 . . . . 145 F8
Brightlingsea CO7 . . . . 186 A6
Capel St M IP9 . . . . 35 A1
Clacton-on-S CO15 . . . 188 D2
Halstead CO9 . . . . 103 D8
Links Ave IP11 . . . . 221 F6
Links Bsns Ctr The
CM23 . . . . 146 C2
Links Cl CO10 . . . . 2 C5
Links Dr CM2 . . . . 215 F7
Linksfield IP5 . . . . 18 E7
Linksfield Gdns IP5 . . . . 18 F7
Linkside CO13 . . . . 170 E3
Linkside Rd CM23 . . . . . 146 C6
Links Rd
Cressing CM77 . . . . . . 156 C7
Seawick CO16 . . . . 203 B6
Link The IP9 . . . . 60 D6
Link Way CM23 . . . . 145 E6
Linley Gdns CO15 . . . . . 188 D2
Linnet Dr CM2 . . . . 216 B6
Linnet Rd IP2 . . . . 16 D4
Linnets CO15 . . . . 188 F6
Linnetts La CB9 . . . . 10 A4
Linnet Way CO7 . . . . 166 D8
Linstead Cl CO16 . . . . . . 188 A4
Linton Cl CB11 . . . . 43 E4
Linton Pl **13** CB9 . . . . 9 B8
Linton Rd CB1 . . . . 5 B7
Lintons The CM2 . . . . . . 217 D6
Lionel Hurst Cl CO10 . . . 34 C5
Lionfield Terr CM1 . . . . . 205 D3
Lion Mdw CB9 . . . . 27 B7
Lion Rd CO10 . . . . 2 B5
Lion St IP1 . . . . 17 C6
Lion Wlk **20** CO1 . . . . . . 135 F7
Lisle Ho
Colchester, Lexden
CO3 . . . . 135 A7
Colchester, Mile End
CO4 . . . . 109 E4
Lisle Rd CO2 . . . . 136 A5
Lister Rd CM7 . . . . 154 F8
Lister Tye CM2 . . . . 216 C7
List Ho CO10 . . . . 15 C8
LISTON 15 A6
LISTON GARDENS 14 E8
Listonhall Chase CO9 . . . 75 B5
Liston La CO10 . . . . 15 B6
Litchborough Pk CM3 . . 218 E8
Litchfield CO12 . . . . 90 E2
Litchfield Cl CO15 . . . . . 188 E5
Littell Tweed CM2 . . . . . 206 A3
LITTLE BADDOW 207 D4
Little Baddow Rd
Danbury CM3 . . . . 218 E7
Woodham Walter CM9 . 208 C3
Little Bakers CO14 . . . . . 171 A7
LITTLE BENTLEY 139 E8
Little Bentley Rd
CO16 . . . . 114 B1
Little Bradfords CM7 . . . 128 A4
LITTLE BRAISWICK 109 C4
Little Bramford La IP1 . . 17 A7
LITTLE BRAXTED 177 D2
Little Braxted La CM8 . . 177 C3
LITTLE BROMLEY 113 B6
Little Bromley Rd
Ardleigh CO7 . . . . 112 B7
Great Bromley CO7 . . . 112 F3
Little Bentley CO7 . . . . 113 E1
LITTLEBURY 21 E4
Littlebury Gdns CO2 . . . 136 C4
LITTLEBURY GREEN 20 F2
Littlebury Green Rd
CB11 . . . . 21 D3
LITTLE CAMBRIDGE 97 B3
LITTLE CANFIELD 149 B7
LITTLE CHESTERFORD
. . . . 21 F8
LITTLE CHISHILL 39 E7
Little Chishill Rd SG8 . . . 39 E8
Little Church St CO12 . . 91 D6
LITTLE CLACTON 168 D3
Little Clacton Rd
Clacton-on-S CO16 . . . 188 B2
Great Holland CO13 . . . 169 E2
LITTLE CORNARD 34 E3

Littlecotes CO4 . . . . 109 D4
Little Croft St IP2 . . . . 17 C3
Little Dorrit CM1 . . . . . . 204 D7
LITTLE DUNMOW 151 D7
LITTLE EASTON 122 F5
Littlefield CO7 . . . . 137 C1
Littlefield Rd CO2 . . . . . . 135 C5
Little Fields CM3 . . . . . . 219 A7
Little Foxburrows
CO2 . . . . 135 E4
Littlegarth Sch CO6 . . . . . 82 B7
Little Gipping St 7
IP1 . . . . 17 B6
Little Gr 4 IP9 . . . . 35 A1
Little & Great Sir Hughes
La CM2 . . . . 217 B2
Little Gulls 6 IP9 . . . . . . 35 A1
LITTLE HALLINGBURY
. . . . 146 B1
Little Harrods CO14 . . . . 171 A7
LITTLE HENHAM 67 C1
Little Hills CM9 . . . . 209 D8
LITTLE HORKESLEY 81 E4
Little Horkesley Rd
CO6 . . . . 81 A4
Little Hyde Cl CO9 . . . . . . 30 A2
Little Hyde Rd CO9 . . . . . . 30 A2
Little Larchmount
CB11 . . . . 43 D8
LITTLE LEIGHS 173 E6
LITTLE LONDON
Berden 92 D7
Feering 158 F4
Finchingfield 48 C3
Little London Hill 72 D8
Little London La CM9 . . . 208 D2
LITTLE MAPLESTEAD 53 B1
Little Mdw CM1 . . . . 204 A1
Little Mdws CM9 . . . . . . 219 E6
Little Nell CM1 . . . . 204 E7
LITTLE OAKLEY 117 B7
Little Orch IP9 . . . . 62 D5
Little Orchards CM1 . . . . 205 B7
Little Paddocks CM7 . . . . 127 F1
Little Pasture Cl CM7 . . . 127 D4
Little St Mary's CO10 . . . . 15 C7
LITTLE SAMPFORD 71 D8
Little's Cres IP2 . . . . 17 C4
Little Sq 7 CM7 . . . . . . 127 F3
Little Stile CM1 . . . . 215 A8
Little Stone Ct CO15 . . . . 203 J8
LITTLE TEY 132 C4
Little Tey Rd CO5 . . . . . . 158 F7
LITTLE TOTHAM 197 C4
Little Totham Rd
CM9 . . . . 211 D8
Little Tufts IP9 . . . . 35 B1
LITTLE WALDEN 22 F8
Little Walden Rd CB10 . . . 22 E5
LITTLE WALTHAM 191 C6
Little Waltham CE Prim
Sch CM3 . . . . 191 B7
Little Waltham Rd
CM1 . . . . 191 D1
Little Whip St 2 IP2 . . . . 17 C4
LITTLE WIGBOROUGH
. . . . 182 B4
Little Wood CO13 . . . . . . 170 E6
Little Wood Mews
CO4 . . . . 109 D2
LITTLE YELDHAM 30 E4
Little Yeldham Rd CO9 . . . 30 C3
LITTLEY GREEN 172 F7
Livery Mews CM6 . . . . . . 124 E5
Llewellyn Cl CM1 . . . . . . 205 D3
Lloyd Rd IP9 . . . . 91 A8
Lloyds Ave 7 IP1 . . . . . . 17 C6
Loamy Hill Rd
Little Totham CM9 . . . . 197 A7
Tiptree CO5 . . . . 178 F1
Loates Pasture CM24 . . . 119 D8
Lobelia Cl CM1 . . . . 206 A6
Locarno Rd IP3 . . . . 18 B3
Lockhart Ave CO3 . . . . . . 135 C7
Lock Hill CM9 . . . . 210 E2
Lockram La
Witham CM8 . . . . 176 F2
7 Witham CM8 . . . . . . 177 A2
Lock Rd CO9 . . . . 103 E8
Lockside Marina CM2 . . . 205 D1
Lodge Ave CM2 . . . . 216 F7
Lodge Cl
Clacton-on-S CO15 . . . . 188 E4
Little Oakley CO12 . . . . 117 C8
Lodge Cres CM3 . . . . . . 206 E7
Lodge Ct CO6 . . . . 108 F4
Lodge Farm La CO16 . . . . 187 D4
Lodge Farm Rd CO10 . . . . 2 C3
Lodge La
Abberton CO5 . . . . 163 D1
Ardleigh CO7 . . . . 111 B6
Ardleigh CO7 . . . . 111 C6
Brightlingsea CO7 . . . . 185 E7
Langham CO4 . . . . 110 D8
Peldon CO5 . . . . 182 E7
Purleigh CM3 . . . . 220 C2
Tendring CO16 . . . . . . 140 F6
Lodge Rd
Braintree CM7 . . . . 127 F1
Brightlingsea CO7 . . . . 185 E8
Little Clacton CO16 . . . 169 A5
Little Oakley CO12 . . . . 117 C8
Maldon CM9 . . . . 209 F3
Messing CO5 . . . . 159 D3
Thorpe-le-S CO16 . . . . 168 F6

Lodge Rd continued
Woodham Mortimer CM3,
CM9 . . . . 220 B5
Writtle CM1 . . . . 215 A8
Lodge The CO15 . . . . 189 F6
Loftin Way CM2 . . . . 216 D7
Loganberry Rd IP3 . . . . . . 38 C7
Lombard Ct IP4 . . . . 17 F7
Lombardy Pk IP2 . . . . 17 B1
Lombardy Pl CM1 . . . . . . 205 B3
Lombardy Rd CO10 . . . . . 15 D2
Lonbarn Hill CO11 . . . . . . 88 A2
London Hill
Chelmsford CM2 . . . . . 215 F2
Galleywood CM2 . . . . . 216 A2
London Land Cotts
CO6 . . . . 80 E4
London Rd
Bishop's Stortford
CM23 . . . . 146 A5
Braintree CM7 . . . . 127 C1
Capel St M IP9 . . . . 35 B1
Chelmsford CM2 . . . . . 215 E6
Clacton-on-S CO15 . . . . 188 E7
Colchester CO3 . . . . . . 134 D6
Copford CO3, CO6 . . . . 133 D4
Feering CO5 . . . . 159 B7
Great Chesterford CB10 . . 3 D2
Great Horkesley CO6 . . . 81 F2
Great Notley CM77 . . . . 154 D6
Ipswich, Chantry IP2 . . . 16 C3
Ipswich, Chantry IP2 . . . 16 F5
Ipswich IP1 . . . . 17 A6
Kelvedon CO5 . . . . 158 B1
Littlebury CB11 . . . . 22 A1
Maldon CM9 . . . . 209 D3
Marks Tey CO6 . . . . . . 133 A3
Newport CB11 . . . . 67 A6
Saffron Walden CB11 . . . 43 D8
Washbrook IP8 . . . . 35 E6
Wendens Ambo CB11 . . . 42 F4
London Stansted Airport
CM24 . . . . 121 A4
Lone Barn Ct IP1 . . . . 16 D8
Lonebarn Link CM2 . . . . . 206 B5
Longacre
Chelmsford CM1 . . . . . 215 E8
Colchester CO4 . . . . . . 109 C2
Longacre Rd CM77 . . . . . 155 E6
Longacres CM7 . . . . 128 A1
Long Acres CO5 . . . . 158 F6
Long Border Rd
Great Hallingbury CM22,
CM24 . . . . 147 C8
Takeley CM24 . . . . 120 E1
Long Brandocks CM1 . . . 204 A1
Long Comm CM9 . . . . . . 209 F5
Longcroft
Felixstowe IP11 . . . . . . 221 C6
Hempstead CB10 . . . . . . 46 E8
Takeley CM22 . . . . 148 C7
Longcroft CM24 . . . . 119 D8
Longcroft Rd CO4 . . . . . . 136 C8
Longedryve CO2 . . . . 135 C4
Longfellow Rd CM9 . . . . . 210 A1
Longfield IP11 . . . . 221 B6
Longfield Rd
Capel St M IP9 . . . . 35 B2
Great Baddow CM2 . . . . 216 E8
Longfields CO16 . . . . 187 B4
Long Gdns CO9 . . . . 53 F5
Long Gn
Braintree CM77 . . . . . . 155 E8
Marks Tey CO6 . . . . . . 132 E3
Long Green La CM7 . . . . . 99 C2
Longhedges CB11 . . . . . . 22 E1
Long Horse Croft CB11 . . . 43 E7
Long La
Arkesden CB11 . . . . 41 E5
Great Holland CO13 . . . 170 C3
Rayne CM7 . . . . 153 F8
Long La CM7 . . . . 153 F8
Longleaf Dr CM7 . . . . . . 155 A8
Longleat Cl CM1 . . . . . . 204 F7
Long Ley CB11 . . . . 40 D2
Long Mdw
Bishop's Stortford
CM23 . . . . 145 D6
Great Notley CM77 . . . . 154 B5
Long Mdws CO12 . . . . . . 90 F2
Longmead Ave CM2 . . . . 216 F8
Longmeads CM8 . . . . . . 195 E5
Longmeads Cl CM1 . . . . . 204 A1
LONG MELFORD 15 D7
Long Melford CE Prim Sch
CO10 . . . . 15 C7
Longmore Ave CM2 . . . . 216 E8
Long Pastures CO10 . . . . . 2 C3
Long Perry IP9 . . . . 35 B1
Long Rd CO11 . . . . 86 C3
Long Rd E CO7 . . . . 85 B3
Long Rd W CO7 . . . . 84 E3
Longridge CO4 . . . . 136 F8
Longship Way CM9 . . . . . 220 E8
Longshots Cl CM1 . . . . . . 191 A1
Longs La CM3 . . . . 173 F1
Long St IP5 . . . . 17 E5
Longstomps Ave CM2 . . . 216 A7
Longstraw Cl CO3 . . . . . . 134 D6
Long Wyre St CO1 . . . . . . 135 F7
Lonsdale 4 IP2 . . . . 17 C4
Lonsdale Cl IP2 . . . . 17 F7
Lonsdale Rd CO16 . . . . . . 142 A2
Looe Rd IP11 . . . . 221 F5
Loompits Way CB11 . . . . . 43 D7
Loppys Hill 1 CM24 . . . . 119 E6
Loraine Way IP8 . . . . 16 A8
Lord Holland Rd CO2 . . . . 135 F3

Lords Ave CM23 . . . . 145 B7
Lords Cl CB10 . . . . 23 D1
Lord's Croft La CB9 . . . . . . 9 A8
Lordship Rd CM1 . . . . . . 204 B3
Lordsland La CM77 . . . . . 103 C1
Lordswood Rd CO2 . . . . . 135 C2
Lorkin's La CO10 . . . . 54 C4
Lorkin Way CO6 . . . . 108 F4
Lott's Rd CO16 . . . . 168 B4
Lotus Way CO15 . . . . 203 E7
Louise Cl CO14 . . . . 144 E3
Louise CO7 . . . . 84 E4
Louvain Dr CM1 . . . . 205 F7
Louvain Rd CO12 . . . . 91 A1
Loveday Cl SG8 . . . . 19 D3
Love La CO7 . . . . 185 F8
Lovers La IP9 . . . . 63 C4
Lover's La CO7 . . . . 167 A7
Loves La CO7 . . . . 204 B1
Love Way CO16 . . . . 188 C6
Lovibond Pl 4 CM2 . . . . 205 F4
Lowe Chase CO14 . . . . . . 171 B8
Lowefields CO6 . . . . 105 D5
Lower Anchor St
CM2 . . . . 205 A1
Lower Barn Farm
CO16 . . . . 142 B5
Lower Brook Mews 14
IP1 . . . . 17 C5
Lower Brook St IP4 . . . . . 17 C5
Lower Cotts CO15 . . . . . . 64 A2
Lower Dales View Rd 3
IP1 . . . . 17 A8
Lower Downs Slade
CB9 . . . . 9 A8
Lower Farm Rd CO4,
CO6 . . . . 57 B1
Lower Gn
Galleywood CM2 . . . . . 216 C2
Stoke by N CO6 . . . . . . 11 C4
Wakes Colne CO6 . . . . . 79 C1
LOWER GREEN
Blackmore End 74 B3
Galleywood 216 C2
Great Baddow 217 C6
Langley 40 B1
Radwinter 45 E2
Lower Green Ho CO7 . . . . 185 F6
Lower Harlings IP9 . . . . . 91 A8
LOWER HOLBROOK 62 F3
Lower Holt St CO6 . . . . . 105 D6
Lower Houses Rd IP9 . . . . 63 D2
Lower King CM7 . . . . 128 D1
Lower Kingsland Rd
CO5 . . . . 201 C5
Lower Langley CO6 . . . . . 106 C1
Lower Marine Par
CO12 . . . . 91 C3
Lower Mill Field CM6 . . . 150 E7
Lower Orwell St IP4 . . . . . 17 D5
Lower Park Cres
CM23 . . . . 145 F5
Lower Park Rd CO7 . . . . . 185 E6
LOWER POND STREET
. . . . 40 F8
Lower Rd
Birch CO2 . . . . 161 A5
Birch Green CO2 . . . . . 181 A8
Borley CO10 . . . . 15 B3
Glemsford CO10 . . . . . . 2 B2
Peldon CO5 . . . . 182 D5
Wormingford CO8, CO6 . 80 B5
Lower Sq CB10 . . . . 22 D2
Lower St
Cavendish CO10 . . . . . . 1 D1
Sproughton IP8 . . . . . . 16 A7
Stanstead CO10 . . . . 2 E6
Stanstead Mountfitchet
CM24 . . . . 119 F7
Stutton IP9 . . . . 62 A2
LOWER STREET 62 A1
Low Lighthouse Maritime
Mus* CO12 . . . . 91 E5
Low Rd CO12 . . . . 90 E1
Lowry Gdns IP3 . . . . 38 A8
Low St CO10 . . . . 2 C6
Luard Way
Birch CO2 . . . . 161 A3
Witham CM8 . . . . 176 F1
Lubberhedges La
CM6 . . . . 125 B8
Lucas Ave
Chelmsford CM2 . . . . . 216 C6
Fordham CO6 . . . . 107 D5
Lucas Hall CO4 . . . . 109 F4
Lucas Ho CO3 . . . . 135 A7
Lucas Rd
18 Colchester CO2 . . . . 135 F6
Sudbury CO10 . . . . 33 F7
Lucas's La CO16 . . . . 141 D6
Lucerne Rd CO7 . . . . 138 A6
Lucerne Way CM1 . . . . . 215 B8
Luces La CO9 . . . . 51 F4
Lucius Cres CM2 . . . . . . 110 B6
Lucksfield Way CM2 . . . . 216 F5
Luck's La CM3 . . . . 172 F2
Lucy Cl CO3 . . . . 134 C6
Lucy La N CO3 . . . . 134 B7
Lucy La S CO3 . . . . 134 C7
Ludgores La CM3 . . . . . . 218 D5
Ludham Hall La
CM77 . . . . 154 D7
Luff Way CO13 . . . . 170 F7
Lufkin Rd CO4 . . . . 109 F3
Lugar Cl CO4 . . . . 136 E6
Lukin's Dr CM6 . . . . 150 D7
Lulworth Ave IP3 . . . . 18 D3
Lulworth Cl CO15 . . . . . . 203 I8

Lulworth Dr CB9 . . . . 8 E8
Lumber Leys CO14 . . . . . 171 A7
Lundy Cl CB9 . . . . 9 D7
Lunnish Hill CO12 . . . . . . 89 F2
Lupin Cl CM1 . . . . 205 F6
Lupin Mews 1 CM1 . . . . 205 F6
Lupin Rd IP2 . . . . 16 E5
Lupin Way CO16 . . . . 188 C4
Lushington Ave CO13 . . . 170 E6
Lushington Rd CO11 . . . . . 86 C4
Luther Dr CO5 . . . . 179 E5
Luther Rd IP2 . . . . 17 C4
Lutus Cl CO10 . . . . 12 A6
Lydgate Cl CO11 . . . . 86 B4
Lydia Dr CO16 . . . . 186 A2
Lymington Ave CO15 . . . . 189 A8
Lyndcroft CM77 . . . . 154 B3
Lyndersewood Farm
CM77 . . . . 154 B3
Lyndersewood La CM77,
CM3 . . . . 154 B2
Lyndhaven Ct CO15 . . . . . 189 C4
Lyndhurst Ave IP4 . . . . . . 18 D5
Lyndhurst Dr CM3 . . . . . 218 F1
Lyndhurst Rd CO15 . . . . . 189 C4
Lynmouth Ave CM2 . . . . . 205 C1
Lynmouth Ct CM2 . . . . . 205 C1
Lynmouth Gdns CM2 . . . 205 C1
Lynnbrook Cl IP2 . . . . 16 E1
Lynne Cl CO13 . . . . 170 E6
Lynton Cl CO12 . . . . 91 B4
Lynton Cl CM23 . . . . 145 E4
Lynton Dr CM1 . . . . 205 E5
Lynwood Ave IP11 . . . . . 221 F5
Lyon Cl
Clacton-on-S CO15 . . . . 189 A4
Galleywood CM2 . . . . . 216 B3
Lyons Hall Prim Sch
CM7 . . . . 128 C4
Lyons Hall Rd CM7 . . . . . 128 D8
Lysander Rd IP3 . . . . 38 C8
Lyster Ave CM2 . . . . 217 A7

M

Mabbitt Way CO4 . . . . . . 110 B5
Maberly Ct CB10 . . . . 22 D2
Macbeth Cl CO4 . . . . 136 F7
MacDonough Cotts
CO12 . . . . 91 E5
MACE GREEN 35 C7
Mace Wlk CM1 . . . . 204 F3
Mackay Ct CO2 . . . . 136 B1
Maclarens CM8 . . . . 196 A6
Macmillan Ct 4 CM2 . . . 205 B1
McNamara Ct 6 IP4 . . . . 17 E6
Madeira Rd CO15 . . . . . . 189 D4
Madeline Pl CM1 . . . . . . 204 E6
Madgements Rd
CM77 . . . . 129 C8
Magazine Farm Way
CO3 . . . . 135 A6
Magdalen Cl CO15 . . . . . 188 E4
Magdalen Ct CO15 . . . . . 188 E4
Magdalene Cl IP2 . . . . 16 F2
Magdalene Cres CM8 . . . 156 D3
Magdalen Gn
Colchester CO1 . . . . . . 136 B6
Thaxted CM6 . . . . 70 B2
Magdalen Rd CO15 . . . . . 188 E4
Magdalen St CO1 . . . . . . 136 A6
MAGGOTS END 92 D4
Maginley Cres IP5 . . . . . . 18 F6
Magnaville Rd CM23 . . . . 145 E4
Magnolia Cl
Chelmsford CM2 . . . . . 216 B6
Witham CM8 . . . . 177 A5
Magnolia Dr CO4 . . . . . . 136 F8
Magnus Dr CO4 . . . . 110 B6
Magpie Cl
Harwich CO12 . . . . 90 E1
Ipswich IP8 . . . . 16 C2
Magwitch Cl CM1 . . . . . . 204 F7
Maidenburgh St CO1 . . . 135 F7
MAIDENHALL 17 B2
Maidenhall App IP2 . . . . . 17 B3
Maidenhall Gn IP2 . . . . . . 17 B2
Maidment Cres CM8 . . . . 194 F8
Maidstone Inf Sch
IP11 . . . . 221 C5
Maidstone Rd IP11 . . . . . 221 C5
Mailers La CM23 . . . . 92 F2
Main Rd
Boreham CM3 . . . . 192 F1
Braintree CM3 . . . . 153 D4
Broomfield CM1 . . . . . . 191 B2
Chelmondiston IP9 . . . . . 63 D7
Chelmsford CM2 . . . . . 217 F7
Danbury CM3 . . . . 218 A7
Danbury CM3 . . . . 218 D7
Frating Green CO7 . . . . 138 E3
Great Holland CO13 . . . 170 A3
Great Leighs CM3 . . . . 173 F7
Harwich, Bath Side CO12 . 91 E5
Harwich, Dovercourt
CO12 . . . . 91 B3
Ramsey CO12 . . . . 90 A1
Rushmere St A IP5 . . . . 18 F8
Woolverstone IP9 . . . . . 38 B2
Wormingford CO6 . . . . . 80 F4
Main St CB21 . . . . 6 F6
Mais Ct IP2 . . . . 16 F2
Maitland Ct CO13 . . . . . . 170 F4
Maitland Rd CM24 . . . . . 119 E6
Majendie La CO9 . . . . 51 F4
Makemores CM77 . . . . . 126 F2
Makins Rd CO12 . . . . 90 F5
MALDON 210 B3

Maldon Court Prep Sch
CM9 . . . . 209 F3
Maldon Ct
8 Colchester CO3 . . . . 135 E6
Great Cornard CO10 . . . 34 B7
Maldon & District
Agricultural & Domestic
Mus* CM9 . . . . 211 E7
Maldon District Mus*
CM9 . . . . 210 B2
Maldon Prim Sch
CM9 . . . . 210 A2
Maldon Rd
Birch Green CO2 . . . . . 160 E4
Bradwell Waterside
CM0 . . . . 214 F1
Colchester, Abbey Field
CO3 . . . . 135 D5
Colchester, Stanway Green
CO3 . . . . 134 D1
Danbury, Gay Bowers
CM3 . . . . 219 B5
Danbury, Runsell Green
CM3 . . . . 219 B7
Goldhanger CM9 . . . . . 211 E2
Great Baddow CM2 . . . . 217 C7
Great Totham CM9 . . . . 196 B4
Great Wigborough CO5 . 181 E2
Hatfield Peverel CM3,
CM9 . . . . 194 D3
Kelvedon CO5 . . . . 158 C1
Langford CM9 . . . . 209 D6
Maldon CM9 . . . . 210 A1
Tiptree CO5 . . . . 179 B3
Witham CM8 . . . . 195 A6
Woodham Mortimer
CM9 . . . . 219 E6
Maldon Way CO16 . . . . . 188 B4
Malin Cl CB9 . . . . 9 D7
Mallard Cl
Great Notley CM77 . . . . 154 C5
Kelvedon CO5 . . . . 158 C3
Layer de la H CO2 . . . . 162 A5
Tollesbury CM9 . . . . . . 199 D2
Mallard Ct
Bishop's Stortford
CM23 . . . . 146 A6
Ipswich IP2 . . . . 16 F3
Mallard Rd CM2 . . . . 216 A5
Mallard Way
Great Cornard CO10 . . . 34 C5
Ipswich IP2 . . . . 16 E3
Mallowhayes Cl IP2 . . . . . 17 B3
Mallows Field CO9 . . . . . . 76 F2
MALLOWS GREEN 92 D2
Mallows Green Rd
CM23 . . . . 92 D1
Mallows La CO9 . . . . 49 F3
Mallow Wlk CB9 . . . . 8 D8
Malmesbury Cl IP2 . . . . . . 17 A1
Maltese Rd CM1 . . . . 205 A4
Malthouse Rd CO11 . . . . . 86 D4
Malthouse The CO10 . . . . 15 B5
Malting Cotts CB9 . . . . . . 9 F4
Malting Farm La CO7 . . . . 84 D2
MALTING GREEN 162 B5
Malting Green Rd
CO2 . . . . 162 A5
Malting La
Clare CO10 . . . . 12 B7
Kirby-le-S CO13 . . . . . 143 C1
Malting Rd
Colchester CO2 . . . . . . 135 C1
Peldon CO5 . . . . 182 E6
Maltings Cl CO8 . . . . 55 E1
Maltings Ct CM8 . . . . . . 194 F8
Maltings La CM8 . . . . . . 194 F8
Maltings Rd
Brightlingsea CO7 . . . . 165 E1
Great Baddow CM2 . . . . 217 A5
Maltings The
Cavendish CO10 . . . . . . 1 D2
Great Dunmow CM6 . . . 123 D1
Great Easton CM6 . . . . 96 A2
Ramsey CO12 . . . . 116 E8
Rayne CM77 . . . . 127 A2
Saffron Walden CB10 . . . 22 D1
Thaxted CM6 . . . . 70 A2
Maltings View CM7 . . . . . 128 A3
Maltings Wharf CO11 . . . . 86 D4
Malting Terr IP2 . . . . 17 D4
Malting Yd CO7 . . . . 164 B8
Maltings Park Rd
CO6 . . . . 108 F4
Malvern Cl
Chelmsford CM1 . . . . . 204 D6
Ipswich IP3 . . . . 18 B4
Rushmere St A IP5 . . . . 18 F7
Malvern Way CO6 . . . . . . 109 B7
Malyon Cl CM7 . . . . 127 E3
Malyon Rd CM8 . . . . 194 F8
Manchester Rd
Holland-on-S CO15 . . . . 189 E6
Ipswich IP2 . . . . 16 D2
Mandeville Rd
Marks Tey CO6 . . . . . . 132 E3
Saffron Walden CB11 . . . 43 D8
Mandeville Way
Broomfield CM1 . . . . . . 191 B3
Kirby Cross CO13 . . . . . 170 F6
Mandeville Wlk CM6 . . . . 151 E6
Mandy Cl IP4 . . . . 18 A6
Manfield 2 CO9 . . . . 76 F2
Manfield Gdns CO16 . . . . 187 B5
Manning Rd IP11 . . . . . . 221 D3
Mannings Cl CB11 . . . . . . 43 E7
Mannings La IP9 . . . . 38 A2
Mannington Cl IP4 . . . . . . 18 F5

MANNINGTREE 86 E4
Manningtree Ct CO7 136 F4
Manningtree High Sch CO11 86 B3
Manningtree Mus★ CO11 86 D4
Manningtree Rd
Brantham CO11 86 A8
Dedham CO7 85 B6
East Bergholt CO7 59 F1
Little Bentley CO7 139 F8
Stutton IP9 61 F2
Manningtree Sta CO11 86 A5
Manor Cl
Cavendish CO10 1 C2
Great Horkesley CO6 109 C7
Manor Cres CM3 191 B5
Manor Dr CM2 216 F7
Manor Farm Cl CB9 9 B7
Manor Fields Prim Sch CM23 145 D5
Manor Ho CM3 219 A5
Manor House Way CO7 185 E8
Manor La
Great Chesterford CB10 3 D2
Harwich CO12 91 B2
Stutton IP9 61 E2
Manor Links CM23 146 C7
Manor Mews CO7 185 E7
Manor Par CO7 185 F7
Manor Pl CM7 128 A3
Manor Rd
Bishop's Stortford CM23 146 A7
Chelmsford CM2 205 C1
Colchester CO3 135 E7
Felixstowe IP11 221 C1
Great Holland CO13 170 A3
Harwich CO12 91 B3
Hatfield Peverel CM3 194 C1
Haverhill CB9 9 B7
Ipswich IP4 17 D8
Little Easton CM6 122 F5
Maldon CM9 209 A4
Stansted Mountfitchet CM24 119 E5
Sudbury CO10 15 E1
West Bergholt CO6 108 E5
Witham CM8 177 A4
Wivenhoe CO7 137 C1
Woodham Walter CM9 208 E5
Manors CM8 156 D4
Manor St CM7 128 A3
Manors Way CM8 156 C4
Manor Way CO15 189 G6
Mansard Ct CO15 189 C5
Mansbrook Bvd IP3 38 D7
Man's Cross CO9 29 E2
Manse Chase CM9 210 A1
Manse Gdns CM6 150 D8
Mansfield Twrs CO15 188 F2
Manston Dr CM23 119 B1
MANUDEN 92 F2
Manuden Prim Sch CM23 93 A2
Manwick Rd IP11 221 D2
Maple Ave
Bishop's Stortford CM23 145 D8
Braintree CM7 127 D2
Heybridge CM9 210 C6
Maple Cl
Bishop's Stortford CM23 145 D8
Clacton-on-S CO15 188 C3
Halstead CO9 77 A2
Harwich CO12 91 B3
Ipswich IP2 17 A3
Maple Dr
Chelmsford CM2 216 B6
Kirby Cross CO13 170 D6
Witham CM8 177 A5
MAPLE END 45 D7
Maple Gr CM23 145 D8
Maple Ho IP11 221 C4
Maple La CB10 45 C5
Maple Leaf CO5 179 C7
Maple Rd CO10 34 B5
Maple Spring CM23 145 D8
Maplestead Ct CO9 53 D2
Maples The IP4 18 E8
Maple Way
Colchester CO2 136 A4
Great Dunmow CM6 123 B1
Maplin Ct CO15 189 D4
Marasca End CO2 163 A7
Maraschino Cres CO2 163 A7
Marbled White Dr IP8 36 E8
Marconi Rd CM1 205 B3
Marcus Cl
Colchester CO4 110 B6
Haverhill CB9 8 D7
Marennes Cres CO7 185 E7
Mareth Rd CO2 135 C2
Margaret Cl CO7 186 A6
Margaret Rd CO1 135 F8
Margaret St
Felixstowe IP11 221 C5
Thaxted CM6 70 A3
Margaretting Rd
Chelmsford CM2 215 F1
Galleywood CM2 216 A2
Writtle CM1 215 A6
Margaret Way CB10 22 D1
Margate Rd IP3 18 C3
Margery Allingham Pl CM9 198 D4
Margrave Gdns [4] CM23 145 E5
Marguerite Way CM23 145 C6
Maria Ct CO2 136 C5
Maria St CO12 91 D5
Marigold Ave
Clacton-on-S CO16 188 C4
Ipswich IP2 16 E3
Marigold Cl
Chelmsford CM1 205 F6
Colchester CO4 136 E8
Marina Gdns
Clacton-on-S CO15 189 C5
Felixstowe IP11 221 C2
Marina Mews [1] CO14 171 C8
Marina Point CO15 188 D1
Marina Rd CM3 194 A4
Marine Bldgs [14] CO14 171 C8
Marine Ct
Clacton-on-S CO15 188 E1
Frinton-on-S CO13 170 F4
Marine Par CO12 91 D3
Marine Par E CO15 189 B3
Marine Par W CO15 188 E1
Mariners The CO12 91 C3
Marion Ave CO15 188 E6
Mario Way CO2 135 F3
Maritime Ave CM9 210 E3
Maritime Ct [12] IP4 17 D5
Market Cl CO1 135 E8
Market End CO6 130 F2
Market Field Sch CO7 138 A5
Market Gr CO9 30 A1
Market Hill
Clare CO10 12 B7
Coggeshall CO6 131 A2
Halstead CO9 76 E2
Haverhill CB9 9 A8
Maldon CM9 210 A3
Saffron Walden CB10 22 D2
Sudbury CO10 33 E7
Market Hill Ct CM9 210 A3
Market Pl
[12] Braintree CM7 127 F3
Great Dunmow CM6 123 D1
[1] Maldon CM9 209 F2
Saffron Walden CB10 22 D2
Market Pl The CO16 168 F7
Market Rd CM1 205 B2
Market Row CB10 22 D1
Market Sq
[6] Bishop's Stortford CM23 145 F7
[6] Chelmsford CM1 205 B2
Market St
[7] Bishop's Stortford CM23 145 F7
[11] Braintree CM7 127 F3
Harwich CO12 91 E6
Saffron Walden CB10 22 D2
Market Wlk CB10 22 D1
Marking's Field CB10 22 E2
Markland Cl CM2 216 C3
Markland Dr CM9 209 E1
Marks Gdns CM7 128 C3
Marks Hall Ctry Est★ CO6 130 E7
Marks Hall Rd CO6 130 E6
MARKS TEY 132 E4
Marks Tey Rdbt CO6 133 A4
Marks Tey Sta CO6 133 B4
Markwells CM22 94 D2
Marlborough Cl
Bishop's Stortford CM23 145 F5
Clacton-on-S CO15 188 C3
Marlborough Ct
Felixstowe IP11 221 D2
Haverhill CB9 8 E7
Marlborough Dr CO10 33 F8
Marlborough Rd
Braintree CM7 128 A4
[2] Chelmsford CM2 205 A1
Ipswich IP4 18 A6
Marlborough Terr CM2 205 A1
Marlowe Cl CM7 155 A8
Marlowe Rd
Clacton-on-S CO15 203 G8
Jaywick CO15 188 A1
Marlowe Way CO3 134 F6
Marlpits Rd CM3, CM9 219 E4
Marney Cl CM2 216 E8
Marney Way CO13 171 B6
Marquis Cl CM23 145 B7
Marram Cl CO3 134 B6
Marriages Yd CO1 136 B7
Marsden Ct CO3 134 E4
Marshall Cl CO5 158 D4
Marshalls Piece CM6 124 D6
Marshalls Rd CM7 127 E1
Marshbarns CM23 145 C8
Marsh Cres CO5 164 A8
Marsh Farm La CO7 166 D3
Marsh Rd CO6, CO7 57 E6
Marsh Way CO7 185 E6
Marston Beck CM2 206 A2
Martello Cvn Pk CO14 171 C8
Martello Rd [8] CO14 171 C8
Marten's La CO6 56 F8
Martens Mdw CM7 128 D3
Martin End CO2 162 A5
Martinet Gn IP3 18 C1
Martingale Dr CM1 205 F7
Martin Rd IP2 17 C4
Martinsdale CO15 188 F6
Martins Mews CB9 8 C8
Martin's Rd CO9 76 E1
Martyns Rise CO10 15 C5
Marvens CM2 216 D3
Marvens The IP8 16 A1
Maryborough Gr CO2 136 B2
Mary Frank Ho CO4 136 C8
Mary La N CO7 139 A8
Maryland Ct [1] CO2 136 A1
Marylands CO13 170 E3
Mary La S CO7 139 B6
Mary McArthur Pl CM24 119 E8
Maryon Rd IP3 18 B1
Mary Park Gdns CM23 145 F4
Mary Ruck Way CM77 155 B5
Marys Ho CO5 158 C2
Mary Warner Rd CO7 111 E7
Mascalls The CM2 216 E8
Mascalls Way CM2 216 E8
Mascot Ct CO15 188 F5
Mascot Sq CO4 136 D5
Masefield Dr CO3 134 F6
Masefield Rd CM7 155 A8
Mashay Rd CO9 30 D5
Mashbury Rd CM3 190 B7
Mason Cl CO2 135 B3
Mason Rd
Clacton-on-S CO16 188 B3
Colchester CO1 109 F1
Masons Cl IP4 17 F6
Masons Ct
Bishop's Stortford CM23 145 E7
Stansted Mountfitchet CM24 119 D6
Massingham Dr CO6 105 A6
Masterlord Bsns Pk IP3 18 E1
Masterman Wharf [12] CM23 145 F7
Matchett Dr CO4 110 B6
Matching La CM23 145 D8
Matfield Cl CM1 205 D7
Mathams Dr CM23 145 D5
Mather Way IP2 17 D4
Mathews Cl CO9 77 A3
Matilda Way CM6 151 E6
Matlock Cl [8] IP2 16 C2
Matson Rd IP1 16 F8
Matthews Cl CO7 58 C1
Maude St IP3 17 E4
Maudlyn Rd CO1, CO4 136 C6
Maurice Cl CB10 45 B1
Maximus Dr CO4 110 B6
Mayberry Wlk CO2 136 A3
Maybury Cl CO6 132 F3
Maybury Rd IP3 18 B1
Mayda Cl CO9 76 D1
Mayes Cl CM23 146 D8
Mayes La
Chelmsford CM2 217 E5
Danbury CM3 218 E6
Harwich CO12 90 C1
Mayes Pl CM6 97 A6
Mayfair Ct CO15 188 F3
Mayfield Cl CO4 110 C2
Mayfield Pk CM23 145 D3
Mayfield Rd
Ipswich IP4 18 C7
Writtle CM1 204 A2
Mayflower Ave CO12 91 E5
Mayflower Cl CO3 134 D6
Mayflower Gdns CM23 145 B6
Mayflower Ho CO12 91 D6
Mayflower Prim Sch The CO12 91 B4
Mayflower Way CO10 15 F2
Mayfly Cl IP8 36 E8
Mayford Way CO16 188 B6
Mayland Cl CM9 210 D4
Mayland Rd CM8 177 A2
Maylands Dr CM77 154 D8
Maynard Cl CM6 123 D1
Maynards Villas CM6 122 F5
Mayne Crest CM1 205 E6
Maypole Cl CB11 43 C7
Maypole Dr CO16 187 B4
MAYPOLE GREEN 135 D1
Maypole Green Rd CO2 135 C1
Maypole Rd
Tiptree CO5 179 C6
Wickham Bishops CM8, CM9 195 F2
Maypole Terr CB9 9 A7
Maypole The CM6 69 F3
May Rd IP3 18 C2
Mays Ct IP11 221 D3
Maysent Ave CM7 127 F5
May's La CO7 84 E4
Maytree Ct CO5 179 C6
Maytree Gdns CM22 94 B3
May Wlk
Chelmsford CM2 216 C7
Elsenham CM24 94 A1
Maze Green Hts CM23 145 C7
Maze Green Rd CM23 145 D7
Mazers Ct [14] CM7 127 F2
Mazoe Cl CM23 145 F5
Mazoe Rd CM23 145 F5
Meachen Rd CO2 136 C5
Mead Ct
Clacton-on-S CO15 188 E3
Stansted Mountfitchet CM24 119 D7
Meadgate Ave CM2 216 D8
Meadgate Prim Sch CM2 216 E8
Meadgate Terr CM2 216 D8
Meadowbrook Ct CO1 136 B7
Meadow Brown Ct CM7 127 E1
Meadow Cl
Chelmondiston IP9 63 F7
Clacton-on-S CO15 189 B7
Elmstead Market CO7 137 F6
Great Bromley CO7 139 A6
Halstead CO9 103 F8
Panfield CM7 127 A7
Meadow Cres IP3 18 F1
Meadowcroft CM24 119 E7
Meadowcroft Way CO13 170 F7
MEADOWEND 29 C5
Meadowford CB11 42 F1
Meadow Grass Cl CO3 134 B6
Meadow La
Sudbury CO10 33 E7
West Mersea CO5 201 C5
Meadowlands CM23 119 A2
Meadow Pk CM7 154 E8
Meadow Pl CO10 33 E6
Meadow Rd
Colchester CO2 135 D1
Great Chesterford CB10 3 D3
Meadowside
Braintree CM7 127 E5
Chelmsford CM2 205 C3
Meadow Side CM1 205 B3
Meadowside Ct CM3 192 E1
Meadowside Gdns IP4 18 E8
Meadows The
Bishop's Stortford CM23 145 E5
[3] Chelmsford CM2 205 C2
Meadowsweet Cl CM23 145 C6
Meadowvale Cl IP4 17 F7
Meadow View
Bicknacre CM3 218 E1
Great Bardfield CM7 72 B2
Kirby-le-S CO13 143 D1
St Osyth CO16 187 B4
Tiptree CO5 179 B5
Meadow View Cl CO3 134 E5
Meadow View Rd CO10 33 D5
Meadow Way
Abberton CO5 163 B2
Black Notley CM77 155 C5
Clacton-on-S CO15 203 G7
Meadow Wlk [5] CM2 205 C2
Mead Pastures CM9 208 D3
Mead Path CM2 215 F8
Meadside CM7 73 B3
Meads The
Chelmsford CM2 205 A1
Stansted Mountfitchet CM24 119 F6
Wicken Bonhunt CB11 66 A7
Mead The
Brightlingsea CO7 185 F8
Great Cornard CO10 34 B4
Great Dunmow CM6 123 C2
Thaxted CM6 70 A3
Meadway
Gosfield CO9 102 E8
Lawford CO11 86 B3
Maldon CM9 210 B1
Meard CM9 219 E6
Mearns Pl [3] CM2 205 F4
Mede Way CO7 137 C3
Medina Bsns Ctr CB11 22 F1
Medlar Cl CM8 177 A4
Medley Rd CM77 126 F2
Medusa Ct
Harwich CO12 91 B2
Holland-on-S CO15 189 E5
Medway Ave CM8 176 D2
Medway Cl CM1 204 D4
Medway Rd IP3 17 F2
Meekings Rd CO10 34 B8
Meers The CO13 170 E6
MEESDEN 64 A6
Meeson Mdws CM9 220 E8
Meeting Field CO10 15 C7
Meeting La
East Mersea CO5 184 C1
Ridgewell CO9 29 B7
Meeting Wlk CB9 9 B7
Meggy Tye CM2 206 B5
Megs Way CM7 128 B2
Melba Ct CM1 204 C1
Melbourne Ave CM1 204 E5
Melbourne Chase CO2 136 B1
Melbourne Ct CM1 204 E5
Melbourne Par CM1 204 E5
Melbourne Park Prim Sch CM1 204 F6
Melbourne Rd
Clacton-on-S CO15 188 E4
Ipswich IP4 18 D7
Melford Cl IP4 18 F5
Melford Gr CM77 154 B7
Melford Rd
Cavendish CO10 1 E2
Melford Rd continued
Sudbury CO10 15 D2
Melford Way IP11 221 A3
Mellings CO6 130 F3
Mellis Ct IP11 221 B5
Mellor Chase CO3 134 E7
Mell Rd CM9 199 E1
Melplash Cl IP3 18 E4
Melplash Rd IP3 18 E4
Melrose Gdns
Clacton-on-S CO15 189 C5
Ipswich IP4 18 B8
Melrose Rd CO5 201 C6
Melso Cl CO10 34 A5
Melton Cl CO16 188 A4
Melville Rd IP4 17 F5
Memnon Ct CO2 135 F3
Menai Ct IP1 17 B7
Mendip Dr IP5 18 F6
Mendip Rd CM1 204 D6
Mendlesham Cl CO16 188 B4
Menin Rd CO2 135 D4
Menish Way CM2 206 A3
Meon Cl CM1 205 C6
Meopham Ct CO2 136 B4
Mercantile Ho [1] CO1 135 F6
Mercers Ave CM23 145 C4
Mercers Row CB10 22 D1
Mercers Way [2] CO1 135 E8
Mercia Cl CM2 217 A5
Mercury Cl CO2 135 A3
Mercury Pl CM9 209 F5
Merdle Sq CM1 204 F6
Meredith Rd CO15 188 E3
Merediths Cl CO7 164 B8
Mere Gdns IP4 18 F4
Meriden Ct CO15 189 A5
Merivale Cl CO11 86 C3
Merivale Rd CO11 86 B3
Merlin Ct IP2 17 B4
Merlin End CO4 110 F1
Merlin Pl CM1 204 F5
Merlin Rd IP2 16 C3
Merriam Cl CO11 86 D8
Merrilees Cres CO15 189 D6
Merrill Hts IP2 17 C3
Merrill Pl [2] CM23 145 E5
Merrion Cl [7] IP2 16 C2
Merrymount Gdns CO15 189 B5
Mersea Ave CO5 201 B6
Mersea Ct CO5 201 B7
Mersea Fleet Way CM7 128 C1
Mersea Island Mus★ CO5 201 B6
Mersea Island Sch CO5 201 C6
Mersea Island Vineyard★ CO5 201 H8
Mersea Point Nature Reserve★ CO5 185 C3
Mersea Rd
Abberton CO2, CO5 163 B5
Colchester CO2 136 A3
Peldon CO5 182 F5
Mersea View CO16 186 A3
Mersey Rd
Ipswich IP3 17 F2
Witham CM8 176 E2
Mersey Way CM1 204 C5
Merstham Dr CO16 188 C6
Merton Ct CO2 163 A7
Merton Pl CB11 21 E4
Messines Rd CO2 135 D5
MESSING 159 D3
Messing-cum-Inworth Prim Sch CO5 159 C2
Messing Gn CO5 159 D2
Meteor Way CM1 204 F2
Mews Ct CM2 205 B1
Mews The
Bishop's Stortford CM22 146 A3
Felixstowe IP11 221 E4
Felixstowe IP11 221 F4
Frinton-on-S CO13 171 A5
Harwich CO12 91 C3
Panfield CM7 126 A7
Stansted Mountfitchet CM24 119 F7
Meyrick Cres CO2 135 F5
Micawber Way CM1 204 D7
Michaels Rd CM23 119 B2
Michaelstowe Cl CO12 90 C2
Michaelstowe Dr CO12 90 C2
Mickfield Mews IP11 221 B5
Micklegate Rd IP11 221 C1
Middleborough CO1 135 E8
Middlefield CO9 76 F1
Middlefield Rd CO11 87 A3
Middle Gn CO6 79 C1
Middle King CM7 128 D1
Middle Mill Rd CO1 135 F8
Middle Row [5] CM23 145 F6
Middleside Cvn Pk CM24 120 A4
Middle St CB11 65 C4
MIDDLETON 33 E4
Middleton Cl
Clacton-on-S CO16 188 D6
Ipswich IP2 16 D2
Middleton Rd CO10 33 D5
Middle Way CO10 15 D8
MIDDLEWICK 136 B2

Middlewick Cl 4
CO2 . . . . **136** A1
Midguard Way CM9 . . . **220** F8
Midland Cl CO2 . . . . **135** F4
Midland Ho CO12 . . . . **91** C4
Midway CO15 . . . . **203** E6
Midway Rd CO2 . . . . **135** C2
Milbank CM7 . . . . **206** B4
Milburn Cres CM1 . . . . . **204** D1
MILCH HILL **153** E5
Milch La CM3 . . . . **153** E6
Mildenhall Pl 14 CB9 . . . . .**9** B8
Milden Rd IP2 . . . . **16** E5
Mildmay Cl CM6 . . . . **151** E7
Mildmay Ct 2 CM1 . . . . **205** B1
Mildmay Inf Sch CM2 . . **216** B5
Mildmay Jun Sch
CM2 . . . . **216** B5
Mildmay Rd
Chelmsford CM2 . . . . . . **205** B1
Ipswich IP3 . . . . **18** B1
Mildmays CM3 . . . . **218** C2
MILE END **109** E3
Mile End IP1 . . . . **17** A6
Mile End Rd CO4 . . . . . . **109** E3
Miles Cl CO3 . . . . **134** C6
Milestones The CM3 . . **194** A4
Milford CO7 . . . . **137** D1
Military Ct 10 CO1 . . . . . **136** A6
Military Rd CO1 . . . . **136** A5
Military Way CO12 . . . . . **90** C1
Mill Apartments The
CO1 . . . . **136** B7
Millars The CM1 . . . . **191** A3
Millbridge Rd CM8 . . . . **176** F2
Mill Chase
Halstead CO9 . . . . **76** F2
Steeple Bumpstead CB9 . . **27** C5
Mill Cl
Elsenham CM22 . . . . **94** C1
Felixstowe IP11 . . . . **221** B4
Great Bardfield CM7 . . . . **72** B2
Harwich CO12 . . . . **91** C4
Tiptree CO5 . . . . **179** C6
Mill Cotts CM2 . . . . **217** C8
Millcroft CM23 . . . . **119** A1
Millcroft Mews CO5 . . . **201** C7
Mill Cswy SG8 . . . . **19** C5
Mill Ct
Braintree CM7 . . . . **128** B2
St Osyth CO16 . . . . **186** F4
Takeley CM6 . . . . **149** E7
Milldene Prim Sch
CO5 . . . . **179** D6
MILL END **123** B4
Mill End CM6 . . . . **70** A2
MILLEND GREEN **97** B1
Millennium Way CM7 . . **155** D8
Miller's Barn Rd
CO15 . . . . **188** A1
Millers Cl
Bishop's Stortford
CM23 . . . . **145** C5
Braintree CM7 . . . . **128** A8
Colchester CO3 . . . . **134** C6
Great Horkesley CO6 . . . **109** B7
Miller's Cl CM6 . . . . **151** A4
Millers Croft
Great Baddow CM2 . . . . **216** F6
Great Dunmow CM6 . . . . **123** E1
Millers Dr CM77 . . . . . . **154** C7
Millers La CO3 . . . . **134** D6
Millers Mead CO5 . . . . . **158** E4
Millers Reach CO11 . . . . **87** A4
Millers Row CM7 . . . . . . **48** C6
Millers View IP1 . . . . **16** F7
Mill Field
Barnston CM6 . . . . **151** A4
Chelmondiston IP9 . . . . . **63** E8
Millfield Gdns IP4 . . . . . **18** A6
Millfields
Danbury CM3 . . . . **219** A6
Stansted Mountfitchet
CM24 . . . . **119** E6
Tiptree CO5 . . . . **179** C6
Writtle CM1 . . . . **204** A1
Millfields Prim Sch
CO7 . . . . **137** D1
Millfields Way CB9 . . . .**9** B8
MILL GREEN
Haverhill **7** D7
Little Bentley **140** A8
Mill Hill
Braintree CM7 . . . . **128** B2
Chelmsford CM2 . . . . . . **215** F2
Farnham CM23 . . . . **118** E5
Harwich CO12 . . . . **91** C3
Haverhill CB9 . . . .**9** A7
Lawford CO11 . . . . **85** D4
Manningtree CO11 . . . . . . **86** C4
Purleigh CM3 . . . . **220** C1
Stansted Mountfitchet
CM24 . . . . **119** E6
Sudbury CO10 . . . . **33** D7
Wormingford CO6 . . . . . . **80** E6
Mill House Cotts
CO12 . . . . **116** D4
Millhouse Villas CM6 . . **151** A4
Milligans Chase CM2 . . **216** B1
Milliners Way CM23 . . . **145** C4
Mill La
Ardleigh CO7 . . . . **112** B4
Birch CO2 . . . . **161** A3
Bradfield CO11 . . . . **87** D2
Brent Pelham SG9 . . . . . . **64** A5

Mill La *continued*
Broomfield CM1 . . . . **191** C1
Cavendish CO10 . . . . **13** B8
Chelmondiston IP9 . . . . . **63** E7
Clavering CB11 . . . . **65** B6
Coggeshall CO5 . . . . **131** F1
Colne Engaine CO6 . . . . . **105** B8
Cressing CM77 . . . . **155** D5
Danbury CM3 . . . . **219** A6
Dedham CO7 . . . . **84** F7
Felixstowe IP11 . . . . **221** C4
Finchingfield CM7 . . . . . . **48** F3
Ford End CM3 . . . . **172** D7
Great Dunmow CM6 . . . . **123** D1
Great Holland CO13 . . . . **169** E3
Great Leighs CM3 . . . . . . **174** B7
Great Leighs CM77 . . . . . **154** C1
Great Maplestead CO9 . . . **76** E8
Great Yeldham CO9 . . . . . **30** A3
Harwich CO12 . . . . **91** D3
Hinxton CB10 . . . .**3** A7
Ickleton CB10 . . . .**3** B4
Layer de la H CO2 . . . . . **162** B5
Little Baddow CM3 . . . . . **207** E3
Littlebury CB11 . . . . **21** F4
Maldon CM9 . . . . **210** A3
Manningtree CO11 . . . . . . **86** D4
Pebmarsh CO9 . . . . **78** A7
Purleigh CM3 . . . . **220** C1
Rayne CM7 . . . . **153** E8
Saffron Walden CB10 . . . . **22** F2
Salcott-c-V CM9 . . . . **199** B8
Stebbing CM6 . . . . **124** E5
Stoke-by-N CO6 . . . . **56** D7
Sudbury CO10 . . . . **33** D7
Terling CM3 . . . . **175** A3
Thorington Street CO6 . . . **57** C4
Thorpe-le-S CO16 . . . . . **141** F1
Tolleshunt Major CM9 . . **197** E3
Walton-on-t-N CO14 . . . **171** C8
Washbrook IP8 . . . . **16** A1
Weeley Heath CO16 . . . . **168** A6
Witham CM8 . . . . **176** F1
Mill Lane Cl CO16 . . . . . **168** A6
Mill on the Gn CO7 . . . . **166** E8
Mill Park Dr CM7 . . . . . **128** B1
Mill Rd
Birdbrook CO9 . . . . **10** E2
Boxted CO4 . . . . **82** F4
Clare CO10 . . . . **12** C7
Colchester CO4 . . . . **109** F4
Debden CB11 . . . . **68** B8
East Bergholt CO7 . . . . . . **59** E2
Elder Street CB10 . . . . . . **45** B3
Felsted CM6 . . . . **152** A4
Finchingfield CM7 . . . . . . **72** D5
Fordham CO6 . . . . **107** D4
Foxearth CO10 . . . . **14** C5
Great Bardfield CM7 . . . . **72** B2
Great Totham CM9 . . . . . **196** D7
Haverhill CB9 . . . .**9** A7
Helions Bumpstead CB9 . . **26** C8
Henham CM22 . . . . **94** E4
Maldon CM9 . . . . **210** A4
Marks Tey CO6 . . . . **133** C4
North End CM6 . . . . **151** F2
Ridgewell CO9 . . . . **29** B6
Stambourne CO9 . . . . **28** C3
West Mersea CO5 . . . . . . **201** D7
Mill Rise IP9 . . . . **62** D5
Mill Road Cotts CB10 . . **45** B3
Mill Road Dr IP3 . . . . **18** F1
Mill Side CM24 . . . . **119** E6
Millside Ind Est CM23 . . **146** A5
Mills La CO10 . . . . **15** C4
Millson Bank CM2 . . . . . **206** A4
Mills Rd CO10 . . . . **34** A8
Mill St
Bishop's Stortford
CM23 . . . . **146** A5
Brightlingsea CO7 . . . . . **186** A6
Colchester CO1 . . . . **136** A6
Nayland CO6 . . . . **56** B1
Stoke-by-N CO6 . . . . **56** D8
St Osyth CO16 . . . . **186** F4
Mills The IP4 . . . . **18** E8
MILL STREET **56** D7
Mill Tye CO10 . . . . **34** A4
Mill Vale Lo CM8 . . . . . . **176** F2
Mill View
Bradwell CM77 . . . . **129** D3
Great Chesterford CB10 . . . .**3** C2
Mill Vue Rd CM2 . . . . . . **205** F2
Millways CM9 . . . . **196** B4
Mill Wlk CO5 . . . . **179** C6
Millwrights CO5 . . . . . . **179** C6
Milner Rd CO10 . . . . **34** B8
Milner St IP4 . . . . **17** E5
Milton Ave CM7 . . . . . . **155** A4
Milton Cl CO3 . . . . **134** F6
Milton Ct CO15 . . . . **189** E6
Milton Pl CM1 . . . . **205** A5
Milton Rd
Harwich CO12 . . . . **91** D4
Lawford CO11 . . . . **86** B2
Witham CM8 . . . . **176** F5
Milton St IP4 . . . . **18** B6
Mimosa Cl CM1 . . . . **205** F6
Mimosa Ct CO4 . . . . **136** E8
Minden Rd CO10 . . . . . . **33** F7
Minerva Cl
Harwich CO12 . . . . **90** F1
Haverhill CB9 . . . .**9** D6
Minerva End CO2 . . . . . **135** C1
MINNOW END **191** A6
Minos Way IP1 . . . . **16** D8
Minsmere Dr CO16 . . . . **188** C6

Minsmere Rd IP3 . . . . . . **38** D8
Minsmere Way CO10 . . . **34** C6
Minster Way CM9 . . . . . **220** E8
Minters Cotts CO11 . . . **115** C5
Miranda Wlk CO4 . . . . . **136** E7
Mirosa Dr CM9 . . . . **210** B1
Mission La CO7 . . . . **60** B3
MISTLEY **86** F4
MISTLEY HEATH **87** B2
Mistley Norman CE Prim
Sch CO11 . . . . **87** A4
Mistley Place Pk★
CO11 . . . . **86** E4
Mistley Sta CO11 . . . . . . **86** F4
Mistley Twrs★ CO11 . . . . **86** F5
Mitchell Ave CO9 . . . . . . **76** E1
Mitchell Circ CM7 . . . . . . **73** C6
Mitre Gdns CM23 . . . . . **146** A4
Mitre Way IP3 . . . . **17** F4
Mitton Vale CM2 . . . . . . **205** F2
Moat Farm CO9 . . . . **28** B7
Moat Farm Chase
CM8 . . . . **176** F3
Moat Farm Cl IP4 . . . . . . **17** F8
Moat Fields CO6 . . . . . . **107** D6
Moat La CO8 . . . . **55** A4
Moat Rd
Birdbrook CO9 . . . . **28** C7
Fordham CO6 . . . . **107** D6
Moat Wlk CB9 . . . .**8** E3
Modlen Rd CO14 . . . . . . **171** B7
Moffat Ave IP4 . . . . **18** B8
Mole Hall La CB11 . . . . . **67** F3
Mole Hall Wildlife Pk★
CB11 . . . . **67** F3
MOLEHILL GREEN
Elsenham **121** D6
Great Notley **153** C4
Molehill Green Cotts
CM22 . . . . **121** C6
Molehill Green Rdbt
CM22 . . . . **121** C5
Molrams La CM2 . . . . . . **217** B6
Monarch Cl CB9 . . . .**8** C8
Monarch Way IP8 . . . . . . **36** D8
Monkdowns Rd CO6 . . . **131** B3
Monken Hadley CM7 . . . **128** B8
Monklands Ct 2 CO9 . . . **76** D1
Monk's Cnr CB10 . . . . . . **47** B4
Monks Ct CM8 . . . . **176** E3
Monks Gate IP8 . . . . **16** A6
Monks Hill CB11 . . . . **43** F8
Monk's La CO7 . . . . **84** D4
Monks Lodge Rd CO9 . . . **52** D2
Monks Mead CM3 . . . . . **218** F2
Monks Rd CO6 . . . . **105** B7
MONK STREET **97** B6
Monks Wlk CM9 . . . . . . **213** E8
Monkswick Ave CO2 . . . **135** F1
Monkwick Jun & Inf Schs
CO2 . . . . **136** A2
Monmouth IP2 . . . . **17** B1
Mons Rd CO2 . . . . **135** D4
Montague Rd IP11 . . . . . **221** F4
Montagu Gdns CM1 . . . **205** F7
Monton Rise IP2 . . . . **16** D2
Montrose Ct IP3 . . . . **17** F4
Montrose Rd CM2 . . . . . **206** A4
Moonhall Bsns Pk CB9 . . .**9** A5
Moon Hall La CB9 . . . .**9** A6
Moorfield Ct CM8 . . . . . **176** F1
Moor Hall La
Bishop's Stortford
CM23 . . . . **145** C3
Bishop's Stortford, Thorley
CM23 . . . . **145** B3
Danbury CM3 . . . . **218** E2
Moorhouse Gn CO7 . . . . **111** E8
Moorings The CM23 . . . **146** A5
Moor Rd
Great Tey CO6 . . . . **132** C8
Langham CO4 . . . . **83** D4
Moors Cl
Feering CO5 . . . . **158** E5
Great Bentley CO7 . . . . . **139** E1
Moors Croft CM7 . . . . . . **128** D3
Moor's Farm Chase
CM9 . . . . **197** A3
Moorsfield CO10 . . . . . . **34** B4
Moorside CO1 . . . . **136** B7
Moors La
Little Dunmow CM6 . . . . **151** D7
Rayne CM7 . . . . **126** D3
Moor's La CO7 . . . . **139** E1
Moors The CM6 . . . . **151** D7
Mope La CM8 . . . . **195** D6
Moran Ave CM1 . . . . **205** B7
Morant Rd CO1 . . . . **136** B5
Morebarn Rd CO7 . . . . . **112** E2
Morecombe Ct IP4 . . . . . **18** A7
Morella Cl CO7 . . . . **166** E8
Morello Ct CO2 . . . . **163** A7
Moretons CM2 . . . . **216** B2
Morland Ct CO6 . . . . **82** B1
Morland Prim Sch IP3 . . **38** A8
Morland Rd IP3 . . . . **37** F8
Morley Rd
Halstead CO9 . . . . **76** F2

Morley Rd *continued*
Tiptree CO5 . . . . **179** D4
Morleys Rd CO6 . . . . . . **105** A6
Mornington Ave 2
IP1 . . . . **17** A8
Morris Ave CO15 . . . . . . **203** E6
MORRIS GREEN **74** C8
Morris Harp CB10 . . . . . . **22** E3
Morrison Dr CM8 . . . . . . **194** F7
Morris Rd CM2 . . . . **205** D2
Morrow La CO1 . . . . **112** A6
Mors End CO7 . . . . **58** D2
Morses La CO7 . . . . **165** F1
Morten Rd CO1 . . . . **135** E8
Mortimer Gdns CO4 . . . **110** B6
Mortimer Rd CM3 . . . . . **194** A4
Mortimer Way CM8 . . . **194** E7
Morton Rd CM9 . . . . . . **196** A4
Morton Way CO9 . . . . **77** A3
Mossfield Cl CO3 . . . . . . **135** C6
Moss Path CM2 . . . . **216** C3
Moss Rd
Colchester CO3 . . . . **134** E4
Witham CM8 . . . . **177** B3
Moss Way CO6 . . . . **108** E3
Moss Wlk CM2 . . . . **216** B6
Mottram Cl 9 IP2 . . . . . . **16** C2
Motts Cl CM7 . . . . **127** E4
Motts La CM8 . . . . **177** B4
Mott's La CO6 . . . . **132** D4
Motts Yd CM6 . . . . **124** E5
Moules La CB1 . . . .**5** C6
MOULSHAM **216** A8
Moulsham Chase
CM2 . . . . **216** C8
Moulsham Dr CM2 . . . . **216** B8
Moulsham Hall La
Braintree CM3 . . . . **153** F2
Great Leighs CM3 . . . . . **154** A1
Moulsham High Sch
CM2 . . . . **216** B7
Moulsham Inf Sch
CM2 . . . . **216** B7
Moulsham Jun Sch
CM2 . . . . **216** B7
Moulsham St
Chelmsford CM1 . . . . . . **205** B2
Chelmsford, Moulsham
CM2 . . . . **205** B1
Moulsham Thrift CM2 . . **216** A6
Moulton Cl CO10 . . . . . . **33** F8
Moulton Ash CO4 . . . . . . **110** C2
Mountain's Farm Rd
CM6 . . . . **150** C3
Mountains Rd CM8,
CM9 . . . . **196** C2
Mountbatten Cl CO10 . . **15** F2
Mountbatten Ct
Braintree CM7 . . . . **128** B4
7 Ipswich IP3 . . . . **17** A7
Mountbatten Dr CO2 . . **136** B4
Mountbatten Rd
Braintree CM7 . . . . **128** C4
Sudbury CO10 . . . . **15** F2
Mountbatten Way
CM1 . . . . **205** E7
MOUNT BURES **79** F5
Mount Dr
Ipswich IP3 . . . . **18** F1
Stansted Mountfitchet
CM24 . . . . **119** E5
Mountfitchet Castle &
Norman Village★
CM24 . . . . **119** F6
Mountfitchet Mathematics
& Computing Coll The
CM24 . . . . **119** F4
Mountfitchet Rd
CM24 . . . . **119** E5
Mount Hill CO9 . . . . **76** D1
Mounthill Ave CM2 . . . . **205** D3
Mount Lodge Chase
CM9 . . . . **196** E6
Mount Pleasant
Great Totham CM9 . . . . . **196** E6
Halstead CO9 . . . . **76** E1
Little Baddow CM3 . . . . . **207** E4
Maldon CM9 . . . . **209** F2
Mount Pleasant Cotts
CB11 . . . . **43** D8
Mount Pleasant Rd
CB11 . . . . **43** E8
Mount Rd
Braintree CM7 . . . . **128** A3
Coggeshall CO6 . . . . **131** B2
Haverhill CB9 . . . .**9** B7
Mount Rise 4 CO9 . . . . . **76** D1
Mount The
Colchester CO3 . . . . **134** F6
Tollesbury CM9 . . . . **199** D1
Mountview Rd CO15 . . . **189** A5
Moverons La CO7 . . . . . **165** C2
MOWDEN **193** D1
Mowden Hall La
Hatfield Peverel CM3 . . . **193** D1
Ulting CM3 . . . . **208** A8
Mowlands IP9 . . . . **35** B1
Moy Rd CO2 . . . . **136** A1
Moze Cross CO12 . . . . . **116** D2
Mulberries The 8
CM7 . . . . **128** A2
Mulberry Ave CO2 . . . . . **136** A4
Mulberry Cotts CO6 . . . **160** C8
Mulberry Ct CM23 . . . . . **146** A5
Mulberry Gdns CM8 . . . **177** A4
Mulberry Harbour Way
CO7 . . . . **164** B8
Mulberry Rd IP3 . . . . **38** C7

Mulberry Way CM1 . . . . **205** D4
Mullins Rd CM7 . . . . **127** F6
Multon Lea CM1 . . . . . . **206** A7
Mumford Cl CO6 . . . . . . **108** E4
Mumford Rd
Ipswich IP1 . . . . **16** E8
West Bergholt CO6 . . . . . **108** D4
Mumfords La CO13 . . . . **170** A7
Mundon Rd CM7 . . . . . . **128** D1
Munnings Cl IP3 . . . . **38** B8
Munnings Dr CO16 . . . . **188** B6
Munnings Rd CO3 . . . . . **135** A5
Munnings Way CO11 . . . **86** B5
Munro Rd CM8 . . . . **176** F5
Murchison Cl CM1 . . . . . **204** E5
Murray Cl CM7 . . . . **127** F6
Murrayfield Com Prim Sch
IP3 . . . . **18** A2
Murray Rd IP3 . . . . **18** A3
Murrell Lock CM2 . . . . . **206** A4
Murrills Rd IP3 . . . . **18** F1
Murton Slade 6 CB9 . . . . .**9** A8
Muscade Cl CO5 . . . . . . **179** D6
Museum St
14 Colchester CO1 . . . . . **135** F7
Ipswich IP1 . . . . **17** C6
Saffron Walden CB10 . . . . **22** D2
Musgrave Cl CO12 . . . . . **90** F1
Musk Cl CO3 . . . . **134** D7
Mus of Power★ CM9 . . . **209** D6
Mustard Gapp CB9 . . . .**9** C7
Muswell Wlk CO16 . . . . **188** D5
Mutlow Cl CB11 . . . . **42** F5
Mutlow Hill CB11 . . . . . . **42** F5
Myddylton Pl CB10 . . . . . **22** D2
Myland Hall Chase
CO4 . . . . **110** C3
Myland Prim Sch
CO4 . . . . **109** E4
Mynards Way CM3 . . . . **218** C7
Myneer Pk CO6 . . . . **131** B2
Myrtle Gr CO2 . . . . **136** B5
Myrtle Rd IP3 . . . . **17** E4
Myson Way CM23 . . . . . **146** B7
Mytchett Cl CO16 . . . . . **188** B6

N

Nabbott Rd CM1 . . . . . . **204** E2
Nacton Cres IP3 . . . . **18** B2
Nacton Rd
Felixstowe IP11 . . . . **221** C1
Ipswich, Racecourse IP3 . . **18** B2
Ipswich, Rose Hill IP3 . . . . **18** A2
Nails 15 CM23 . . . . **145** F7
Nails Lane Ho 23
CM23 . . . . **145** F7
Nalla Gdns CM1 . . . . . . **205** A6
Nancy Smith Cl CO2 . . . **135** F5
Nansen Rd
Holland-on-S CO15 . . . . **189** D6
Ipswich IP3 . . . . **18** B2
Napier Ave CO15 . . . . . . **203** D6
Napier Ct CM1 . . . . **204** E5
Napier Rd CO2 . . . . **135** F6
Narvik Cl CM9 . . . . **220** E8
Nash Cl
Colchester CO3 . . . . **135** B5
Lawford CO11 . . . . **86** B5
Nash Ct CO9 . . . . **76** F1
Nash Dr CM1 . . . . **191** A3
Nash Gdns IP3 . . . . **38** B8
Nassau Rd CO16 . . . . . . **187** B4
Nathan Ct CO2 . . . . **163** B8
National Wireless &
Televion Mus The★
CO12 . . . . **91** E5
Nats La CB11 . . . . **42** E6
Navarre St 4 IP1 . . . . **17** C6
Navigation Pl CM9 . . . . **210** B4
Navigation Rd CM2 . . . . **205** C2
NAYLAND **56** B1
Nayland Dr CO16 . . . . . . **188** B4
Nayland Prim Sch CO6 . . **56** A1
Nayland Rd
Bures CO8 . . . . **79** F8
Colchester CO6 . . . . **109** D6
Felixstowe IP11 . . . . **221** A4
Great Horkesley CO6 . . . . **82** B4
Haverhill CB9 . . . .**8** E6
West Bergholt CO6 . . . . . **108** D7
Nayling Rd CM7 . . . . **127** C2
Nazecliff Gdns CO14 . . . **144** E3
Naze Ct CO14 . . . . **144** E3
Naze Marine Holiday Pk
CO14 . . . . **144** D2
Naze Nature Trail The★
CO14 . . . . **144** E4
Naze Park Rd CO14 . . . . **144** E2
Neale Rd CO9 . . . . **76** E1
Neale St IP1 . . . . **17** C6
Neasden Ave CO16 . . . . **188** D5
Neath Dr IP2 . . . . **17** A1
Needle Cnr IP9 . . . . **63** D1
Nelson Ct CO7 . . . . **186** A7
Nelson Gdns CM7 . . . . . **128** C4
Nelson Gr CM1 . . . . **204** F3
Nelson Ho IP3 . . . . **18** D4
Nelson Rd
Bishop's Stortford
CM23 . . . . **146** A5
Clacton-on-S CO15 . . . . **188** E1
Colchester CO3 . . . . **134** E6
Harwich CO12 . . . . **91** D4
Ipswich IP3 . . . . **18** A7
Nelson's Ave IP9 . . . . **38** C1
Nelson St CO7 . . . . **185** F6

Nene Dr IP3 . . . . 38 D7
Neptune Ct
  Chelmsford CM1 . . . . . . 204 F4
  5 Colchester CO1 . . . 136 C6
Neptune Quay IP4 . . . . . 17 D5
Neptune Sq IP4 . . . . 17 D5
Ness Wlk CM8 . . . . 176 D2
Nether Ct CO9 . . . . 77 A1
Nethergate St CO10 . . . . 12 B7
Nether Hill CO9, CO10 . . 31 D3
Nether Rd CO10 . . . . 1 D2
Netley Cl IP2 . . . . 36 F8
Nettleditch CB11 . . . . . . 21 E4
Neville Rd CB10 . . . . 22 E2
Newark Cl IP2 . . . . 16 F1
New Barn La CM22 . . . . . 146 D1
Newbarn Rd CO6 . . . . . . 106 B1
Newbiggen St CM6 . . . . . 69 F3
Newbourne Gdns
  IP11 . . . . 221 B3
New Bowers Way
  CM1 . . . . 205 F6
Newbridge Hill CO6 . . . . 108 D2
Newbridge Rd
  Birch CO5 . . . . 180 A6
  Tiptree CO5 . . . . 179 F5
Newbury Cl CM23 . . . . . . 145 E8
Newbury Ho IP4 . . . . 18 B6
Newbury Rd IP4 . . . . 18 C6
Newby Dr IP4 . . . . 18 F5
New Captains Rd CO5 . . . 201 B6
New Cardinal St IP1 . . . . 17 B5
Newcastle Ave CO3 . . . . . 134 F4
New Church Rd CO6 . . . . 108 E4
Newcomen Way CO4 . . . . 110 C6
New Cotts
  Great Tey CO6 . . . . 132 C8
  Wakes Colne CO6 . . . . . 106 C6
New Court Pl CM2 . . . . . . 205 E3
Newcourt Rd CM2 . . . . . . 205 D3
Newcroft **1** CB10 . . . . . 22 E1
New Cut
  Bures CO8 . . . . 79 E8
  Glemsford CO10 . . . . . . 2 B3
  Great Bentley CO7 . . . . 166 E8
  Layer de la H CO2 . . . . 161 F5
New Cut E IP2, IP3 . . . . . 17 D4
New Cut W IP2 . . . . 17 D4
New Dukes Way CM2 . . . . 205 F4
New England Cl CM3 . . . . 218 F1
New Farm Lo CO3 . . . . . . 134 D5
New Farm Rd CO3 . . . . . . 134 D6
Newgate St **5** CO14 . . . 171 C8
New Hall Cotts CO7 . . . . . 58 F7
New Hall Sch CM3 . . . . . . 192 A1
New Hall Vineyards★
  CM3 . . . . 220 D2
Newhaven La CO12 . . . . . 91 D6
New House La CB10 . . . . . 24 C3
Newhouse Rd CO6 . . . . . . 104 F5
Newhythe CO3 . . . . 134 E7
Newington Gdns
  CO15 . . . . 188 F8
New Kiln Rd CO3 . . . . 135 C7
New La
  Feering CO5 . . . . 158 F5
  Holbrook IP9 . . . . 63 A5
Newland Ave CM7 . . . . . . 72 B1
Newland Ct CM8 . . . . 176 F1
Newland Pl CM8 . . . . 177 A1
Newlands Dr CM8 . . . . . . 177 A2
Newlands La CO6 . . . . . . 56 B1
Newlands Prec **8**
  CM8 . . . . 177 A2
Newlands Spring Prim Sch
  CM1 . . . . 204 D7
Newland St CM8 . . . . 177 A2
New Lodge Chase
  CM3 . . . . 207 B2
New London Ct **5**
  CM2 . . . . 216 A8
New London Rd CM2 . . . . 205 A1
Newmain Rd CO2 . . . . . . 135 E3
Newman Dr CO4 . . . . 83 A4
Newmans Est CO15 . . . . . 188 D3
Newman's Rd CO10 . . . . . 33 F8
Newmarket Rd CB10 . . . . 3 C3
Newmill La
  Brantham CO11 . . . . . . 61 A1
  Stutton CO11 . . . . 87 A8
NEW MISTLEY 87 B4
New Nabbotts Way
  CM1 . . . . 205 E7
Newnham Cl CM7 . . . . . . 127 C2
Newnham Ct IP2 . . . . 16 E2
Newnham Gn CM9 . . . . . . 209 E3
New Orleans Flats
  CO5 . . . . 201 B5
New Park Gdns CO7 . . . . . 185 F7
New Park St CO1 . . . . 136 B6
Newpasture La CM6 . . . . . 125 C5
New Path CM23 . . . . 145 F6
New Pier St **7** CO14 . . . 171 C8
New Pk CO9 . . . . 51 F3
New Place Ho IP2 . . . . . . 17 A4
New Pond La CB10 . . . . . . 22 C2
NEWPORT 43 A1
Newport Cl
  Great Baddow CM2 . . . . 217 B6
  Harwich CO12 . . . . 91 A1
Newport Dr
  Clacton-on-S CO15 . . . . 189 A7
  Rickling Green CB11 . . . 66 F4
Newport Free Gram Sch
  CB11 . . . . 42 F1
NEWPORT POND 67 A7
Newport Prim Sch
  CB11 . . . . 66 F7

Newport Rd CB11 . . . . . . 43 C7
Newport Sta CB11 . . . . . . 67 A8
Newport Way CO13 . . . . . 171 A6
Newpots Cl CO5 . . . . 182 D5
Newpots La CO5 . . . . 182 E5
New Queens Rd CO10 . . . . 15 E1
New Rd
  Aldham CO6 . . . . 107 B2
  Broomfield CM1 . . . . . . 191 B1
  Colchester CO3 . . . . . . 134 D6
  Elsenham CM22 . . . . . . 94 C2
  Gosfield CO9 . . . . 102 C5
  Great Baddow CM2 . . . . 217 A6
  Hatfield Peverel CM3 . . . 194 A4
  Hinxton CB10 . . . . 3 B6
  Kelvedon CO5 . . . . 158 C2
  Long Melford CO10 . . . . 15 C7
  Messing CO5 . . . . 159 C1
  Mistley CO11 . . . . 86 E4
  Rayne CM7 . . . . 127 A1
  Saffron Walden CB10 . . . 22 E1
  Shudy Camps CB21 . . . . 7 C7
  Terling CM3 . . . . 175 C3
  Tiptree CO5 . . . . 179 D5
  Tollesbury CM9 . . . . . . 199 D2
  Trimley St M IP11 . . . . . 221 A7
New Road Terr CM77 . . . . 126 F1
New Row CB21 . . . . 7 E4
Newry Ave IP11 . . . . 221 D4
Newson St IP1 . . . . 17 B7
New St
  Braintree CM7 . . . . 127 F2
  Brightlingsea CO7 . . . . 185 F6
  Chelmsford CM1 . . . . . 205 B3
  Glemsford CO10 . . . . . . 2 A5
  Great Dunmow CM6 . . . 150 D8
  Halstead CO9 . . . . 76 E1
  2 Maldon CM9 . . . . . 209 F2
  Sudbury CO10 . . . . 33 E8
New Street Fields
  CM6 . . . . 150 D8
New Thorpe Ave
  CO16 . . . . 142 A2
Newton Cl **4** CM7 . . . . 127 F1
Newton Croft CO10 . . . . . 34 A7
Newton Gdns CO16 . . . . . 187 A5
Newton Gn CM6 . . . . 123 C1
Newton Hall CM6 . . . . . . 123 B1
Newton Pl **18** CB9 . . . . 9 B8
Newton Rd
  Harwich CO12 . . . . 91 A3
  Ipswich IP3 . . . . 18 A4
  Sudbury CO10 . . . . 34 A7
Newton St **10** IP4 . . . . 17 D6
Newton Way CO16 . . . . . . 187 B5
NEWTOWN 158 C3
NEW TOWN 145 F6
Newtown Rd CM23 . . . . . . 145 F6
New Town Rd
  Colchester CO1 . . . . . . 136 A6
  Thorpe-le-S CO16 . . . . . 141 F2
New Village CO11 . . . . . . 86 C7
New Way
  Ipswich IP2 . . . . 16 F6
  Point Clear B CO16 . . . . 185 F3
New Writtle St CM2 . . . . . 205 B1
Nexus The CO1 . . . . 135 E8
Nicholas Cl CM1 . . . . 204 B1
Nicholas Ct
  Chelmsford, Scot's Green
    CM1 . . . . 204 D6
  Witham CM8 . . . . 176 C2
Nicholas Rd IP11 . . . . 221 A4
Nichols Cl CO11 . . . . 86 B3
Nichols Cnr CO7 . . . . 112 A5
Nichols Ct **1** CM2 . . . . . 205 A1
Nichols Gr CM7 . . . . 128 C3
Nicholsons Gr CO1 . . . . . . 136 A6
Nickleby Rd CM1 . . . . 204 D6
Nien-Oord CO16 . . . . 188 C4
Nightingale Cl
  Clacton-on-S CO15 . . . . 188 F5
  Colchester CO4 . . . . . . 137 A8
  Harwich CO12 . . . . 90 F1
  Witham CM8 . . . . 194 B4
Nightingale Cnr
  Layer de la H CO2 . . . . . 162 A6
  2 Maldon CM9 . . . . . 210 A1
Nightingale Ct CO2 . . . . . 163 A8
Nightingale Hill CO4 . . . . 83 F6
Nightingale Mews **2**
  CB10 . . . . 22 F2
Nightingale Pl CO3 . . . . . 134 C4
Nightingale Rd IP3 . . . . . 38 A8
Nightingales CM23 . . . . . 146 B7
Nightingale Sq IP3 . . . . . 38 A8
Nightingale Way
  CO15 . . . . 188 F5
Nineacres CM7 . . . . 128 A1
Nine Acres IP2 . . . . 16 D5
Ninth Ave CM24 . . . . 120 B2
Noah's Ark La CO10 . . . . . 33 D7
Noakes Ave CM2 . . . . 216 E6
Noaks Rd IP7 . . . . 58 D8
Nobles The CM3 . . . . 145 D6
Nonancourt Way CO6 . . . . 105 A6
Nonesuch Mdw CO10 . . . . 33 E6
Nonsuch Mdw CO10 . . . . . 33 E7
Nook The CO7 . . . . 164 C8
Norah Guilder Ho
  CM3 . . . . 194 A4
Norbury Cl CO6 . . . . 132 C3
Norbury Rd IP4 . . . . 18 B8
Nordic Lo CM9 . . . . 220 F8
Norfolk Ave
  Clacton-on-S CO15 . . . . 189 E7
  West Mersea CO5 . . . . . 201 D7

Norfolk Cl CM9 . . . . 209 E1
Norfolk Cres CO4 . . . . . . 110 B1
Norfolk Dr CM1 . . . . 205 A7
Norfolk Gdns CM7 . . . . . . 128 B4
Norfolk Rd
  Ipswich IP4 . . . . 17 D6
  Maldon CM9 . . . . 209 E1
Norfolk Way CM23 . . . . . . 145 F5
Norman Ave CM23 . . . . . . 145 D6
Norman Cl
  Marks Tey CO6 . . . . 132 E3
  St Osyth CO16 . . . . 187 A4
Norman Cres IP3 . . . . . . 18 A2
Norman Ct CM24 . . . . . . 119 E7
Normandie Way CO8 . . . . 79 E8
Normandy Ave CO2 . . . . . 136 A3
Norman Hill CM3 . . . . . . 175 B2
Norman Rd
  Clacton-on-S CO15 . . . . 189 E6
  Manningtree CO11 . . . . 86 D4
Normansfield CM6 . . . . . 150 E7
Norman's Way CM24 . . . . 119 E7
Norman Way
  Colchester, Lexden
    CO3 . . . . 135 B6
  Colchester, Shrub End
    CO3 . . . . 135 B4
  Point Clear B CO16 . . . . 185 F3
Norris Cl
  Bishop's Stortford
    CM23 . . . . 146 C7
  Braintree CM7 . . . . 128 C5
Northampton Cl CM7 . . . . 128 D5
Northampton Mdw
  CM7 . . . . 72 B2
North Ave
  Chelmsford CM1 . . . . . 204 F5
  Haverhill CB9 . . . . 8 E8
Northbourne Rd
  CO15 . . . . 188 F4
North Cl IP4 . . . . 17 E8
North Court Rd CM1 . . . . 191 A3
North Cres CB9 . . . . 27 B7
Northcroft CO10 . . . . 33 E7
North Dell CM1 . . . . 205 E7
North Dr CM2 . . . . 216 F7
NORTHEND 22 A3
NORTH END
  Felsted 151 F2
  Great Yeldham 30 F3
North End Rd
  Gestingthorpe CO9,
    CO10 . . . . 31 C2
  Hinxton CB10 . . . . 3 B8
  Little Yeldham CO9 . . . . 30 D2
Northern App CO4 . . . . . . 109 E3
Northern Rd CO10 . . . . . . 34 B8
Northey View CM9 . . . . . . 210 C3
Northfield CM7 . . . . 72 B3
Northfield Gdns CO4 . . . . 110 A4
Northfield Rd CB11 . . . . . 43 E8
Northfields CM24 . . . . . . 119 E7
Northgate End CM23 . . . . 145 F8
Northgate Prim Sch
  CM23 . . . . 145 E8
Northgate St
  Colchester CO1 . . . . . . 135 F8
  Ipswich IP1 . . . . 17 C6
North Hall Rd
  Henham CM22 . . . . 94 B7
  Rickling Green CB11 . . . 67 A2
North Hill
  Colchester CO1 . . . . . . 135 E7
  Little Baddow CM3 . . . . 207 D5
North Hill Gdns **1** IP4 . . 17 E6
North Hill Rd IP4 . . . . . . 17 E6
North Ho CO13 . . . . 170 F4
North La CO6 . . . . 133 B5
North Lawn IP4 . . . . 18 C8
North Mill Pl CO9 . . . . . . 76 E3
Northolt Ave CM23 . . . . . 119 B1
North Prim Sch CO1 . . . . 135 E8
North Rd
  Belchamp Walter CO10 . . 31 F4
  Brightlingsea CO7 . . . . 185 F7
  Clacton-on-S CO15 . . . . 188 F5
  Great Yeldham CO9 . . . . 30 A2
  Takeley CM22 . . . . 148 C8
  Tollesbury CM9 . . . . . . 199 C2
North Rise CO10 . . . . 34 A6
North Sea View CO12 . . . . 90 F2
North St
  4 Bishop's Stortford
    CM23 . . . . 145 F7
  Great Dunmow CM6 . . . 123 D1
  Maldon CM9 . . . . 210 B2
  Manningtree CO11 . . . . 86 D4
  Steeple Bumpstead CB9 . . 27 B7
  Sudbury CO10 . . . . 33 E8
  Tolleshunt D'arcy CM9 . . 198 E5
  Walton-on-t-N CO14 . . . 171 C8
North Station Rd CO1 . . . . 135 E8
North Street Par **1**
  CO10 . . . . 33 E7
North Terr **5** CM23 . . . . 145 F8
Northumberland Cl
  CM7 . . . . 128 B4
Northumberland Ct **1**
  CM2 . . . . 205 F4
North View Cotts
  CO6 . . . . 109 B7
North Wall CO16 . . . . 186 A3
NORTON END 42 E4
Norton Rd
  Chelmsford CM1 . . . . . 205 A3
  Haverhill CB9 . . . . 8 E6
Norway Cres CO12 . . . . . . 90 F3

Norwich Cl
  Clacton-on-S CO16 . . . . 188 E6
  Colchester CO1 . . . . . . 136 A8
Norwich Ct **2** IP1 . . . . . 17 A7
Norwich Rd IP1 . . . . 17 A7
Norwood Ave CO15 . . . . . 189 B5
Norwood Way CO14 . . . . . 171 A7
NOSTERFIELD END 7 F5
Notcutts CO7 . . . . 59 E1
Notley Gn CM77 . . . . 154 B6
Notley Green Prim Sch
  CM77 . . . . 154 C8
Notley High Sch CM7 . . . . 154 E8
Notley Rd CM7 . . . . 154 E8
Nottage Cl CO7 . . . . 164 C8
Nottage Cres CM7 . . . . . . 127 E3
Nottidge Rd IP4 . . . . 17 E6
Nottingham Rd CO15 . . . . 189 E6
NOUNSLEY 194 B1
Nounsley Rd CM3 . . . . . . 194 B1
Nounsley Terr CM3 . . . . . 194 B1
Nunnery St CO9 . . . . 51 D4
Nunns Cl CO6 . . . . 131 A2
Nunn's Rd CO1 . . . . 135 E7
Nun's Mdw CO9 . . . . 102 E7
Nuns Wlk CO9 . . . . 29 F1
Nunty's La
  Greenstead Green
    CO9 . . . . 104 A1
  Pattiswick CM77 . . . . . . 129 F8
Nursery Cl
  Bishop's Stortford
    CM23 . . . . 145 F6
  Colchester CO3 . . . . . . 134 C5
Nursery Dr CM7 . . . . 128 A5
Nursery La CM3 . . . . 218 F8
Nursery Rd
  Bishop's Stortford
    CM23 . . . . 145 F6
  Chelmsford CM2 . . . . . 216 B8
  Great Cornard CO10 . . . 34 B5
Nursery Rise CM6 . . . . . . 150 D7
Nursery Wlk IP11 . . . . . . 221 D5
NUTHAMPSTEAD 39 A2

O

Oakapple Cl CO2 . . . . 135 D1
Oak Ave CO16 . . . . 188 A2
Oak Bglws CM7 . . . . 127 E3
Oak Bsns Pk CO16 . . . . . . 141 F8
Oak Cl
  Clacton-on-S CO15 . . . . 188 E6
  Felixstowe IP11 . . . . . . 221 C4
  Rushmere St A IP4 . . . . 18 E7
  Thorpe-le-S CO16 . . . . . 142 A1
  West Bergholt CO6 . . . . 108 E4
Oak Cnr
  Beaumont CO16 . . . . . . 141 F8
  Woodham Mortimer
    CM9 . . . . 219 D6
Oak Cotts CM3 . . . . 206 E8
Oak Eggar Chase IP8 . . . . 36 D8
Oak Fall CM7 . . . . 177 A5
Oak Farm Rd CM9 . . . . . . 208 F1
Oakfield CM6 . . . . 125 A4
Oakfield Dr CO4 . . . . 83 A5
Oakfield La CM3 . . . . 175 A2
Oakfield Rd
  Belstead IP8 . . . . 36 A7
  Washbrook IP8 . . . . 35 F6
Oakfield Wood Nature
  Reserve★ CO11 . . . . . . 88 D4
Oak Gr CO2 . . . . 16 A6
Oak Hall CM23 . . . . 145 E8
Oakhaven CO12 . . . . 90 F1
Oak Hill
  Beazley End CM7 . . . . . 101 A8
  Wethersfield CM7 . . . . . 73 F1
Oak Hill La IP2 . . . . 17 B3
Oak Ho
  Ipswich IP1 . . . . 16 D2
  Stutton IP9 . . . . 61 F2
Oak Ind Pk CM6 . . . . 150 F6
Oakland Rd CO12 . . . . . . 91 C3
Oaklands Ave CO3 . . . . . . 134 E5
Oaklands Cl
  Bishop's Stortford
    CM23 . . . . 119 B2
  Great Notley CM77 . . . . 154 D8
Oaklands Cres CM23 . . . . 216 B8
Oaklands Dr CM23 . . . . . . 119 B2
Oaklands Inf Sch
  CM2 . . . . 216 B8
Oaklands Pk CM23 . . . . . . 119 B2
Oaklands Way CM23 . . . . . 207 E2
Oaklea Ave CM2 . . . . 205 E3
Oaklee IP2 . . . . 17 A1
Oakleigh Ct CM23 . . . . . . 145 E6
Oakleigh Rd CO15 . . . . . . 188 F8
Oakley Cross CO12 . . . . . . 117 B7
Oakley Rd
  Braintree CM7 . . . . 127 F7
  Harwich CO12 . . . . 90 D1
  Wix CO11 . . . . 115 C5
Oak Lodge Tye CM1 . . . . . 206 A6
Oak Manor View CM3 . . . . 173 F7
Oakmead Rd CO16 . . . . . . 186 B3
Oak Rd
  Chappel CO6 . . . . 106 B3
  Great Cornard CO10 . . . 34 B6
  Halstead CO9 . . . . 103 D7
  Heybridge CM9 . . . . . . 210 B6
  Little Maplestead CO9 . . 77 A8
  Pebmarsh CO9 . . . . 77 F8
  Rivenhall CM8 . . . . 177 C6
  Tiptree CO5 . . . . 179 C7

Oak Ridge CO12 . . . . 117 B7
Oakroyd Ave CM6 . . . . . . 150 E8
Oakroyd Ho CM6 . . . . . . 150 E8
Oaks Com Prim Sch The
  IP2 . . . . 16 E3
Oaks Dr CO3 . . . . 135 D7
Oaks End CO2 . . . . 162 A6
Oaks Hospl The CO4 . . . . 109 E3
Oaksmere Gdns IP2 . . . . . 17 A2
Oaks Pl CM23 . . . . 109 E2
Oak St CM23 . . . . 145 F6
Oaks The CO13 . . . . 170 F6
Oakstead Cl IP4 . . . . 18 A6
Oak Tree Cotts CO6 . . . . . 133 B8
Oak Tree Rd CO7 . . . . 165 B8
Oaktrees CM9 . . . . 197 B5
Oakview CO17 . . . . 90 F1
Oak View Cvn Pk
  CM24 . . . . 120 A4
Oak Wlk CO9 . . . . 51 D2
Oakwood Ave
  Clacton-on-S CO15 . . . . 189 E7
  West Mersea CO5 . . . . . 201 D7
Oakwood Bsns Pk
  CO15 . . . . 169 A1
Oakwood Cl CO13 . . . . . . 170 E6
Oakwood Dr CO5 . . . . 201 D7
Oakwood Gdns CO5 . . . . . 201 D7
Oakwood Inf Sch
  CO15 . . . . 188 D2
Oak Yd CO9 . . . . 76 D2
Oasis Ct CM1 . . . . 205 F5
Oasthouse Ct CB10 . . . . . 22 D1
Oast House Spinney
  CM7 . . . . 127 F6
Oatfield Cl CO3 . . . . 134 D6
Oatlands CO7 . . . . 137 F6
Oban St IP1 . . . . 17 B7
Oberon Cl CO4 . . . . 136 F7
Obrey Way CM23 . . . . 145 E3
Observation Ct IP1 . . . . . 17 B5
Observer Way CO5 . . . . . . 158 C4
Ocean View CO14 . . . . . . 171 D8
Ockelford Ave CM1 . . . . . 204 F5
Ockendon Way CO14 . . . . 171 A8
Octavia Dr CM8 . . . . 194 E7
Oddcroft CO6 . . . . 77 F1
Odin Lo CM9 . . . . 220 F8
Office La CM9 . . . . 197 A4
Old Barn Rd CO8 . . . . 80 A6
Old Bell Cl CM23 . . . . 119 D6
Oldbury Ave CM2 . . . . . . 216 F8
Old Burylodge La
  CM24 . . . . 120 A4
Old Camps Castle CB21 . . 7 E3
Old Cattle Market **5**
  IP4 . . . . 17 C5
Old Church La
  Bulmer CO10 . . . . 32 F3
  Bulmer Tye CO10 . . . . . 32 F2
  West Bergholt CO6 . . . . 108 D5
Old Clements La CB9 . . . . 8 F7
Old Coach Rd CO1 . . . . . . 136 B7
Old Coastguard Cotts
  CM0 . . . . 214 E4
Old Convent The CO5 . . . . 158 B1
Old Court Ho **2**
  CM24 . . . . 119 E6
Old Court Rd CM2 . . . . . . 205 D3
Old Ct
  Chelmsford CM2 . . . . . 205 D3
  Long Melford CO10 . . . . 15 D8
Olde Forge CO7 . . . . 165 E4
Old Ferry Rd CO7 . . . . . . 164 B8
Oldfield Rd IP8 . . . . 16 B1
Old Forge CO7 . . . . 137 C2
Old Forge Rd
  Boreham CM3 . . . . 206 E8
  Layer de la H CO2 . . . . 161 F5
Old Foundry Rd IP4 . . . . . 17 D6
Old Hall Cl CB9 . . . . 27 C7
Old Hall La
  Capel St M IP9 . . . . 35 F3
  Tollesbury CM9 . . . . . . 199 C5
  Walton-on-t-N CO14 . . . 144 E3
OLD HEATH 136 C3
Old Heath Com Prim Sch
  CO2 . . . . 136 D3
Old Heath Rd CO1,
  CO2 . . . . 136 C4
Old House La CO4 . . . . . . 83 B2
Old House Rd CO16 . . . . . 109 A8
Oldhouse Villas CM22 . . . 148 C8
Old Ipswich Rd CO7 . . . . . 110 E7
Old Library The **15**
  CO11 . . . . 86 D4
Old London Rd
  Capel St M IP9 . . . . 59 F7
  Woodham Walter CM9 . . 208 E1
Old Maltings The **2**
  CM23 . . . . 146 A2
Old Market Ct **3** CO10 . . 33 E7
Old Market Pl **2** CO10 . . 33 E7
OLD MEAD 94 D4
Old Mead La CM22 . . . . . 94 D4
Old Mead Rd CM22 . . . . . 94 C5
Old Mill Chase CM7 . . . . . 73 C3
Old Mill Cl CM9 . . . . 210 A3
Old Mill La CO5 . . . . 158 C2
Old Mill Rd
  Langham CO4 . . . . 83 D5
  Saffron Walden CB11 . . . 43 E8
Old Moors CM3 . . . . 173 F7

Old Orchard The
CM2 . . . . .217 D2
Old Parsonage Ct
CM8 . . . . .176 F2
Old Parsonage Way
CO13 . . . . .170 F5
Old Pier St CO14 . . . . .171 C8
Old Rd
  Clacton-on-S CO15 . . . . . . .188 E4
  Coggeshall CO6, CO5 . . . . .131 E1
  Frinton-on-S CO13 . . . . . . .170 F4
  Pattiswick CM77 . . . . .129 F5
  Wickham St P CO9 . . . . .53 D5
Old Rectory Ct CO6 . . . . . .133 A4
Old River La CM23 . . . . . . .145 F7
Old Rope Wlk CB9 . . . . .8 E7
Old Rose Gdns CO4 . . . . . .109 D4
Old St The IP9 . . . . .35 B1
Old School Cl CO16 . . . . . .187 A4
Old School Ct
  Brightlingsea CO7 . . . . .185 E6
  Hatfield Peverel CM3 . . . . . .194 B3
Old School Field CM1 . . . .205 E4
Old School Ho IP9 . . . . . . .91 B8
Old School Ho The
  CO5 . . . . .164 A8
Old School La CO10 . . . . . .138 A6
Old School Yd CB11 . . . . . . .43 D8
Old Southend Rd
  CM2 . . . . .217 D1
Old Vicarage Rd CO12 . . . . .91 C3
Old Vicarage The CM7 . . . . .72 E6
Old Way CO13 . . . . .170 F4
Olive Gr CO2 . . . . .135 C2
Oliver Cl CM9 . . . . .210 B4
Oliver Pl CM8 . . . . .177 B2
Olivers Cl
  Clacton-on-S CO15 . . . . . . .188 E4
  Long Melford CO10 . . . . .15 D7
Olivers Ct CO15 . . . . .188 E4
Olivers Dr CM8 . . . . .195 A7
Olivers La CO2 . . . . .135 A1
Olivers Rd CO15 . . . . .188 E4
Oliver Way CM1 . . . . .204 F7
Oliveswood Rd CM6 . . . . . .150 D7
Olley Wlk CO5 . . . . .179 E6
OLMSTEAD GREEN 25 E7
Ongar Cl CO16 . . . . .188 B4
Ongar Rd
  Great Dunmow CM6 . . . . . .150 D6
  Writtle CM1 . . . . .204 B1
Ongar Road Trad Est
  CM6 . . . . .150 E7
Onslow Cotts CO5 . . . . . . .160 A4
Onslow Cres CO2 . . . . .136 B1
ONSLOW GREEN 151 C2
Opal Ave IP1 . . . . .16 D8
Ophir Rd CO7 . . . . .185 F5
Orange St CM6 . . . . .70 A2
Orange Tree Cl CM2 . . . . . .216 C6
Orchard Ave CO9 . . . . .76 D2
Orchard Cl
  Chelmsford CM2 . . . . .216 C6
  Clacton-on-S CO16 . . . . . . .188 C5
  Copford CO6 . . . . .133 D2
  Elmstead Market CO7 . . . . .138 A6
  Great Oakley CO12 . . . . . . .116 C3
  Hatfield Peverel CM3 . . . . . .194 A4
  Haverhill CB9 . . . . .8 F7
  Maldon CM9 . . . . .209 F2
  Newport CB11 . . . . .66 F8
  Ramsey CO12 . . . . .90 A2
  Ridgewell CO9 . . . . .29 B6
  Saffron Walden CB11 . . . . . .43 D7
  Thaxted CM6 . . . . .70 A3
  Tollesbury CM9 . . . . .199 E1
  Writtle CM1 . . . . .204 B1
Orchard Cotts
  Boreham CM3 . . . . .193 A2
  Langham CO4 . . . . .83 F3
  Little Horkesley CO6 . . . . . .81 E5
Orchard Ct CO3 . . . . .135 C7
Orchard Dr
  Braintree CM7 . . . . .128 A4
  Great Holland CO13 . . . . . .170 A4
Orchard Gate IP2 . . . . .16 C5
Orchard Gdns CO4 . . . . . . .136 B8
Orchard Gr IP5 . . . . .18 F7
Orchard Lo CO5 . . . . .179 D4
Orchard Mews CO5 . . . . . .179 C4
Orchard Pightle CB1 . . . . . .5 C6
Orchard Pl
  Colchester CO4 . . . . .109 F4
  Sudbury CO10 . . . . .33 D6
Orchard Rd
  Alresford CO7 . . . . .165 B8
  Bishop's Stortford
   CM23 . . . . .119 B3
  3 Colchester CO1 . . . . . . .135 E8
  Kelvedon CO5 . . . . .158 C3
  Maldon CM9 . . . . .209 F2
Orchards CM8 . . . . .176 F1
Orchard St
  Chelmsford CM2 . . . . .205 B1
  9 Ipswich IP4 . . . . .17 D6
Orchard The
  Felsted CM6 . . . . .152 C5
  Maldon CM9 . . . . .209 F4
Orchard Way CO10 . . . . . . .2 B3
Orchid Ave CM8 . . . . .176 E4
Orchid Cl
  Ipswich IP2 . . . . .16 E4
  Takeley CM22 . . . . .148 B7
Orchid Field Ct CO5 . . . . . .201 E6
Orford Cres CM1 . . . . .205 D5

Orford Ho CM22 . . . . .93 F3
Orford Rd
  Felixstowe IP11 . . . . .221 C1
  Haverhill CB9 . . . . .8 F6
Orford St IP1 . . . . .17 B7
Oriel Cl CO10 . . . . .34 B6
Oriole Way CM23 . . . . .145 C6
Orion Way CM7 . . . . .128 B4
Orkney Cl CB9 . . . . .9 D7
Orlando Cl CO14 . . . . .171 C8
Ormonde Cl CO6 . . . . .108 E4
Orpen Cl CO6 . . . . .108 D4
Orpen's Hill CO2 . . . . .161 A5
Orplands Cotts CM0 . . . . . .214 F1
Orrin Wlk 6 CO4 . . . . .109 E2
Orsino Wlk CO4 . . . . .136 F7
Orvis La CO7 . . . . .59 E1
Orwell Bsns Ctr IP3 . . . . . .17 E2
Orwell Cl CO4 . . . . .110 E1
Orwell Country Pk★
  IP10 . . . . .38 B6
Orwell Ct 1 IP4 . . . . .17 D5
Orwell Ctry Pk★ IP3 . . . . . .37 F8
Orwell Gdns IP2 . . . . .17 A3
Orwell High Sch IP11 . . . . .221 C5
Orwell Ho IP11 . . . . .221 A4
Orwell Hts IP2 . . . . .16 E2
Orwell Pl
  Chelmondiston IP9 . . . . .63 F7
  2 Ipswich IP4 . . . . .17 D5
Orwell Rd
  Clacton-on-S CO15 . . . . . . .188 F2
  Felixstowe IP11 . . . . .221 D3
  Harwich CO12 . . . . .91 D4
  Ipswich IP3 . . . . .18 A4
Orwell Ret Pk IP2 . . . . .16 F5
Orwell Rise IP9 . . . . .63 F8
Orwell Way CO16 . . . . .188 C6
Orwell Wlk CM8 . . . . .176 E3
Osbert Rd CM8 . . . . .194 E8
Osborne Cl CO15 . . . . .189 A7
Osborne Rd
  Ipswich IP3 . . . . .18 A4
  West Mersea CO5 . . . . .201 E6
Osbornes Ct CO7 . . . . .185 F6
Osborne St CO2 . . . . .135 F6
Osbourne Gdns 5
  CM23 . . . . .145 E5
Osea Rd CM9 . . . . .211 B3
Osea Way CM1 . . . . .205 F5
Osier Cl CO3 . . . . .134 D6
Osier Pl 3 CB9 . . . . .8 F8
Osmond Cl CM77 . . . . .155 B5
Osprey Cl CO3 . . . . .134 B4
Osprey Rd CB9 . . . . .9 C7
Ospreys CO15 . . . . .188 F6
Osprey Way CM2 . . . . .216 A5
Ostler Cl CM23 . . . . .145 C4
Ostler's Gn CB11 . . . . .41 B5
Othello Cl CO4 . . . . .136 F8
Otho Dr CO4 . . . . .110 A6
Otley Ct IP11 . . . . .221 B5
Otten Rd CO10 . . . . .13 B1
Ottershaw Way CO16 . . . . .188 B6
Oulton Cl CO12 . . . . .90 F3
Oulton Hall CO15 . . . . .189 A3
Oulton Rd IP3 . . . . .17 E2
Our Lady Immaculate RC
  Prim Sch CM2 . . . . .205 A1
Ouse Chase CM8 . . . . .176 D2
OUTER PART OF TOWN
  EASTWARD 91 E6
OUTER PART OF TOWN
  WESTWARD 91 D6
Outpart Eastward
  CO12 . . . . .91 E6
Overchurch Cl CB9 . . . . .8 F7
Overhall Hill CO6 . . . . .78 C2
Over Hall La CB10 . . . . .6 D2
Overstone Ct CO2 . . . . .135 C3
OVINGTON 12 B1
Ovington Pl 16 CB9 . . . . .9 B8
Owen Ward Cl CO2 . . . . . . .135 A3
Owl's Hill CM3 . . . . .175 B3
Owls Retreat 1 CM4 . . . . . .136 F8
Oxborrow Cl CO13 . . . . . . .170 A6
Oxcroft CM23 . . . . .145 F3
OXEN END 98 E6
Oxenford Cl CO12 . . . . .90 F1
Oxford Cl CO10 . . . . .34 A6
Oxford Cres CO15 . . . . .188 F4
Oxford Ct
  Chelmsford CM2 . . . . .205 E4
  Colchester CO3 . . . . .135 D6
  Earls Colne CO6 . . . . .105 B6
Oxford Ho CB9 . . . . .9 B6
Oxford House Sch
  CO3 . . . . .135 D6
Oxford La CO10 . . . . .51 D2
Oxford Mdw CO9 . . . . .51 D2
Oxford Pl CO6 . . . . .105 B6
Oxford Rd
  Clacton-on-S CO15 . . . . . . .188 F4
  Colchester CO3 . . . . .135 D6
  Frinton-on-S CO13 . . . . . . .171 A5
  Halstead CO9 . . . . .76 D1
  Ipswich IP4 . . . . .17 E5
  Manningtree CO11 . . . . .86 D4
OXLEY GREEN 180 A1
Oxley Hill
  Abberton CO5 . . . . .163 A3
  Tolleshunt D'arcy CM9 . . . . .198 B8
Tolleshunt Knights
  CM9 . . . . .180 A1
Oxley Ho CM77 . . . . .155 B5
Oxley Parker Dr CO4 . . . . . .110 A6
Oxleys CB11 . . . . .65 C3
Oxlip Rd CM8 . . . . .176 E4

Oxney Villas CM6 . . . . .152 D6
Oxton Cl CO5 . . . . .164 A8
Ox Yd CO5 . . . . .102 E7
Oyster Bsns Ctr CM9 . . . . .199 F2
Oyster Cl CO5 . . . . .201 C7
Oyster Cotts CM0 . . . . .213 C1
Oyster Pk CO1 . . . . .136 D6
Oyster Pl CM2 . . . . .205 F4
Oyster Tank Rd CO7 . . . . . .185 E5
Ozier Ct CB11 . . . . .43 E7
Ozier Fields CO9 . . . . .103 F8
Oziers CM22 . . . . .94 C2

P

Packard Ave IP3 . . . . .18 B2
Packards La CO6 . . . . .80 F1
Packe Cl CO5 . . . . .158 D4
Padbrook Ct IP3 . . . . .17 F5
Paddock Cl CO12 . . . . .91 C4
Paddock Dr CM1 . . . . .205 E8
Paddocks The
  Abberton CO5 . . . . .163 A2
  Ashen CO10 . . . . .11 D1
  Bures CO8 . . . . .79 E8
  Great Bentley CO7 . . . . .166 F5
  Great Totham CM9 . . . . .196 A4
  West Mersea CO5 . . . . .201 D6
  Witham CM8 . . . . .177 A2
Paddock The CM23 . . . . . . .145 D3
Paddock Way CO7 . . . . .137 C3
Padua Ho IP4 . . . . .17 F6
Paeony Chase CO5 . . . . . . .201 C8
Page Cl CM8 . . . . .194 D8
Page Rd CO15 . . . . .188 E3
Pages Cl CM23 . . . . .145 D5
Pages La CM9 . . . . .198 F1
Paget Ct CM22 . . . . .94 C1
Paget Rd
  Ipswich IP1 . . . . .17 B7
  Rowhedge CO5 . . . . .163 F8
  Wivenhoe CO7 . . . . .164 C8
Paignton Ave CM1 . . . . .205 D5
Pakenham Pl 18 CB9 . . . . . . .9 B8
Palace Gdns CM23 . . . . . . .145 E5
PALE GREEN 8 D1
Palfrey Hts CO11 . . . . .86 D8
Pallant Chase CO6 . . . . . . .134 A8
Pallister Rd CO15 . . . . .188 F2
Palm Cl
  Chelmsford CM2 . . . . .216 C6
  Witham CM8 . . . . .177 A5
Palmers Croft CM2 . . . . . . .206 A2
Palmers La
  8 Bishop's Stortford
   CM23 . . . . .145 F7
  Chrishall SG8 . . . . .19 C3
Palmerston Ct 7 IP4 . . . . . .17 E6
Palmerston Lo CM2 . . . . . . .216 F7
Palmerston Rd
  Ipswich IP4 . . . . .17 E6
  Thorpe-le-S CO16 . . . . .142 A2
Palmerswent Cl CO10 . . . . .15 D8
Pamela Gdns CM23 . . . . . . .145 F3
Pampas Cl CO4 . . . . .110 A4
PANFIELD 127 B7
Panfield La CM7 . . . . .127 E5
Pannells Ash CO10 . . . . . . .11 D1
Pannels Cl CO10 . . . . .2 B4
Pantile Cl CM8 . . . . .195 A7
Pantlings La CO5 . . . . .158 A5
Panton Cres 7 CO4 . . . . . . .136 E7
Panton Mews CM7 . . . . . . .155 A8
Pan Wlk CM1 . . . . .204 D5
Papermill Cotts CO9 . . . . . .76 E2
Papillon Ho CO1 . . . . .135 E7
Papillon Rd CO3 . . . . .135 E7
Parade Dr CO12 . . . . .90 C1
Parade Rd IP4 . . . . .17 F7
Parade The
  Colchester CO2 . . . . .136 A1
  Kirby Cross CO13 . . . . .170 B6
  Walton-on-t-N CO14 . . . . . .171 C8
Paradise Rd CM1 . . . . .215 B8
Pardoe Pl IP4 . . . . .18 E5
Park Ave
  Bishop's Stortford
   CM23 . . . . .145 F3
  Chelmsford CM1 . . . . .204 F4
  Felixstowe IP11 . . . . .221 F5
Park Bvd CO15 . . . . .189 E6
Park Chase CO16 . . . . .187 D6
Park Cl CO10 . . . . .34 A8
Park Cotts
  Gosfield CO9 . . . . .102 E8
  Manningtree CO11 . . . . .86 D3
  St Osyth CO16 . . . . .187 A5
Park Ct
  Felixstowe IP11 . . . . .221 D2
  Harwich CO12 . . . . .91 D4
  Sible Hedingham CO9 . . . . . .51 D1
Parkdale CM3 . . . . .218 C7
Park Dr
  Braintree CM7 . . . . .155 A8
  Brightlingsea CO7 . . . . .185 E7
  Halstead CO9 . . . . .76 E1
  Maldon CM9 . . . . .210 B1
  Tiptree CO5 . . . . .179 F5
Parker Ct CM0 . . . . .214 F4
Parker Rd
  Chelmsford CM2 . . . . .205 C1
  Colchester CO4 . . . . .110 B6
Parker's Way CO6 . . . . .56 A1
Parker Way CO9 . . . . .103 E8
PARKESTON 90 E5
Parkeston Rd
  Felixstowe IP11 . . . . .221 B4

Parkeston Rd *continued*
  Harwich CO12 . . . . .90 F4
  Harwich, Upper Dovercourt
   CO12 . . . . .91 A4
Park Farm CB10 . . . . .3 F6
Park Farm Ind Est SG8 . . . .39 C2
Park Farm La SG8 . . . . .39 C2
Parkfields CO9 . . . . .51 D1
Parkfield St CO5 . . . . .163 F7
Parkgate Cnr CO16 . . . . . . .169 A2
Park Gate Rd CM8 . . . . .157 B3
PARK GREEN 92 B6
Parkhall Rd
  Beazley End CM7 . . . . .101 E7
  Gosfield CO9 . . . . .102 B7
Parkinson Dr CM1 . . . . .204 F1
Parkins The IP9 . . . . .35 C2
Park La
  Bishop's Stortford
   CM23 . . . . .145 F4
  Bulmer Tye CO10 . . . . .32 F2
  Castle Camps CB21 . . . . .7 F3
  Earls Colne CO6 . . . . .105 B6
  Glemsford CO10 . . . . .2 D4
  Gosfield CO9 . . . . .102 F7
  Langham CO4 . . . . .83 E3
  Langley CB11 . . . . .40 A3
  Saffron Walden CB10 . . . . . .22 D1
  Tiptree CO5 . . . . .179 F5
  Tolleshunt Knights CM9 . . . .180 B3
  Toppesfield CO9 . . . . .50 B7
Parkland Ct CO1 . . . . .136 C5
Parklands
  Braintree CM7 . . . . .155 A8
  Coggeshall CO6 . . . . .131 A2
Parklands Cl CO10 . . . . .2 C5
Parklands Ct CO16 . . . . . . .188 B3
Parklands Dr CM1 . . . . .205 D3
Parklands Way CM2 . . . . . .216 C2
Park N IP4 . . . . .17 D8
Park Lane Cl CO6 . . . . .105 B6
Park Rd
  Ardleigh CO7 . . . . .111 F3
  Chelmsford CM1 . . . . .205 B2
  Clacton-on-S CO15 . . . . . . .188 D2
  Colchester CO3 . . . . .135 C6
  East Bergholt CO7 . . . . .60 B2
  Elsenham CM22 . . . . .94 D1
  Ford End CM3 . . . . .172 A3
  Great Chesterford CB10 . . . . .3 D5
  Harwich CO12 . . . . .91 D4
  Haverhill CB9 . . . . .8 D8
  Ipswich IP1 . . . . .17 C8
  Little Bentley CO7 . . . . .139 D8
  Little Easton CM6 . . . . .122 F3
  Little Horkesley CO6 . . . . . .82 B8
  Maldon CM9 . . . . .209 F2
  Rivenhall CM8 . . . . .157 A2
  Stansted Mountfitchet
   CM24 . . . . .119 E6
  Stoke-by-N CO6 . . . . .56 E4
  St Osyth CO16 . . . . .187 B4
  Sudbury CO10 . . . . .34 A8
  Wivenhoe CO7 . . . . .164 C8
  Wivenhoe, Wivenhoe Park
   CO4 . . . . .137 A4
Parkside
  Haverhill CB9 . . . . .8 F6
  Saffron Walden CB10 . . . . . .22 C1
Park Side CM6 . . . . .124 D6
Parkside Ave IP4 . . . . .17 D7
Parkside Quarter
  CO1 . . . . .135 E8
Park Sq E
  Clacton-on-S CO15 . . . . . . .203 G8
  Jaywick CO15 . . . . .188 A1
Park Sq W
  Clacton-on-S CO15 . . . . . . .203 F8
  Jaywick CO15 . . . . .187 F1
Park St
  Stoke-by-N CO6 . . . . .56 D5
  Thaxted CM6 . . . . .70 A2
Parkstone Rdbt CO12 . . . . . .90 F4
Park Terr
  Harwich CO12 . . . . .91 D4
  Long Melford CO10 . . . . .15 C7
Park The CO11 . . . . .86 D3
Park Vale Cl CO9 . . . . .51 E4
Park View CO10 . . . . .12 C7
Park View Cres CM2 . . . . . .216 F5
Park View Rd IP1 . . . . .17 B8
Parkway
  Chelmsford CM1 CM2 . . . . .205 B2
  Shudy Camps CB21 . . . . .7 C6
Parkway Mid Sch CB9 . . . . . .8 D8
Park Way CO15 . . . . .188 D1
Parkwood IP1 . . . . .17 C7
Parkwood Ave CO7 . . . . . . .137 B1
Parkwood Dr CO10 . . . . .15 E2
Park Wood La CM9 . . . . . . .197 A3
Parley Beams Cotts
  CO9 . . . . .104 D7
Parliament Rd IP4 . . . . .18 B5
Parmenter Dr CO10 . . . . . . .34 C5
Parnell Cl CO2 . . . . .136 A2
PARNEY HEATH 84 B4
Parnham Pl IP4 . . . . .18 F5
Parr Cl
  Braintree CM7 . . . . .128 D4
  Jaywick CO15 . . . . .187 F1
Parr Dr CO3 . . . . .134 E4
Parrington Way CO11 . . . . .86 A3
Parr Rd CB9 . . . . .8 D6
Parry Dr CO16 . . . . .188 C5
Parsonage Cl
  Broomfield CM1 . . . . .191 A1
  Felixstowe IP11 . . . . .221 B4

Parsonage Downs
  CM6 . . . . .123 C3
Parsonage Farm La
  CB10 . . . . .47 B4
Parsonage Farm Trad Est
  CM24 . . . . .119 F3
Parsonage Gdns 6 CB9 . . . . .8 E7
Parsonage Gr CO8 . . . . .79 E8
PARSONAGE GREEN 205 A8
Parsonage La
  Barnston CM6 . . . . .151 D3
  Bishop's Stortford
   CM23 . . . . .146 C8
  Clavering CB11 . . . . .65 B3
  Elder Street CB10 . . . . .44 F3
  Howe Street CM3 . . . . .172 F2
  Little Baddow CM3 . . . . . . .207 D2
  Stansted Mountfitchet
   CM24 . . . . .119 F4
  Tendring CO16 . . . . .140 E8
Parsonage Rd CM22 . . . . . .148 C8
Parsonage St CO9 . . . . .76 F1
Parsonage Terr CM7 . . . . . .72 D6
Parsons Ct 7 CO9 . . . . .76 F2
Parson's Field CO7 . . . . . . .85 A6
PARSON'S HEATH 110 D1
Parson's Heath CO4 . . . . . .110 E2
Parsons Heath CE Prim
  Sch CO4 . . . . .110 E2
Parsons Hill CO7 . . . . .138 F8
Parson's Hill CO3 . . . . .135 A6
Parsons La CO1 . . . . .136 C6
Parsonson Ct CO4 . . . . .110 D1
Parsons Yd 10 CM11 . . . . . .86 D4
Partridge Ave CM2 . . . . . . .204 F6
Partridge Cl CO12 . . . . .116 D4
Partridge Dr CO6 . . . . .107 D5
Partridge Rd IP2 . . . . .16 E3
Partridge Way CO3 . . . . . . .134 C4
Paschal Way CM2 . . . . .216 F8
Pashford Pl IP3 . . . . .38 C8
Pashlers Alley CO10 . . . . . . .12 B7
Paske Ave CB9 . . . . .8 F7
Pasture Rd CM8 . . . . .177 B1
Pastures The
  Rushmere St A IP4 . . . . .18 F5
  Takeley CM22 . . . . .148 B7
Patching Hall La CM1 . . . . .205 A6
Paternoster Row 6
  CO14 . . . . .171 C8
Pathfields Rd CO15 . . . . . . .188 D4
Path The CO7 . . . . .166 E8
Pathway The CO13 . . . . . . .170 E6
Patmore Cl CM23 . . . . .145 C8
Patmore Rd CO4 . . . . .110 D1
Patricia Gdns CM23 . . . . . .145 E5
Patten Cl CO6 . . . . .132 F3
Pattern Bush Cl CO11 . . . . .86 D8
Patteson Rd IP3 . . . . .17 E4
Patticroft CO10 . . . . .2 B6
Pattinson Wlk CO6 . . . . . . .109 B8
Pattison Cl CM8 . . . . .195 A8
PATTISWICK 129 F5
Pattock's La CO6 . . . . .106 C2
Pattrick's La CO12 . . . . .91 C4
Pauline Cl CO15 . . . . .189 B6
Pauline St 7 IP2 . . . . .17 C4
Paulk Hall La CM3 . . . . .174 A5
Pauls Cres CO7 . . . . .137 F6
Paul Spendlove Ct
  CO4 . . . . .110 E1
Pauls Way CO15 . . . . .188 A1
Pavilion Ct CB9 . . . . .9 B7
Pavitt Mdw CM2 . . . . .216 C2
Pawle Cl CM2 . . . . .217 A7
Paxman Ave CO2 . . . . .135 A3
Paxton Rd CO15 . . . . .189 B8
Paycocke's Ho★ CO6 . . . . .130 F1
Paycocke Way CO6 . . . . . . .131 A3
Paynes La CM3 . . . . .206 C8
Payne's La CO11 . . . . .113 C3
Peacehaven CO13 . . . . .171 A5
Peace Rd CO3 . . . . .134 C7
Peacock Cl
  Braintree CM7 . . . . .127 F1
  5 Ipswich IP8 . . . . .16 C2
Peacocks Cl CO10 . . . . .1 C2
Peacocks Rd CO10 . . . . .1 C2
Peake Ave CO13 . . . . .170 A6
Peakes Cl CO5 . . . . .179 B4
Peal Rd CB11 . . . . .43 F7
Pearce Manor CM2 . . . . . . .215 F8
Pearce Rd IP3 . . . . .18 A5
Pearl Dr CM7 . . . . .128 C3
Pearl Rd IP1 . . . . .16 D8
Pearmains CM3 . . . . .173 F7
Pearmain Way CO3 . . . . . . .134 C4
Pearmain Wlk CB9 . . . . .8 C8
Pearse Way IP3 . . . . .18 E1
Pearson Rd IP3 . . . . .18 C5
Pearsons Cl CO10 . . . . .2 B4
Peartree Bsns Ctr
  CO3 . . . . .134 C2
Peartree Cl
  Braintree CM7 . . . . .128 A1
  Goldhanger CM9 . . . . .211 E6
Pear Tree Cl CO9 . . . . .77 A3
Pear Tree Ct CO5 . . . . .179 D4
Peartree Hill CO8 . . . . .80 A5
Peartree La CM3 . . . . .218 F3
Peartree Rd CO3 . . . . .134 E4
Peartree Way CO16 . . . . . . .168 C2
Peaslands Rd CB11 . . . . . . .43 E8
Peasleys Yd CM23 . . . . .146 B7
PEBMARSH 78 B7
Pebmarsh Cl CO2 . . . . .163 A8

Pebmarsh Rd
Alphamstone CO8 54 E2
Colne Engaine CO6 77 F2
Pecockes Cl CO10 34 C5
Peddars Ct CO10 15 C7
Pedder's Cl CO3 134 F3
Pedlars Cl CM3 219 A6
Pedlars Path CM3 219 A6
Pedler's Cnr CO11 86 D2
Peek's Cnr CO6 105 D5
Peel Cres CM7 127 E3
Peel Rd CM2 205 F4
Peel St 5 IP1 17 C6
Peers Sq CM2 206 A4
Peerswood Rd CO2 135 D2
Peewit Ct IP11 221 B3
Peewit Cvn Pk IP11 221 C2
Peewit Hill IP11 221 B3
Peewit Rd IP2 16 C3
Pegasus Way
Braintree CM7 127 E5
Colchester CO4 110 C1
Peggotty Cl CM1 204 F6
Peggy's Wlk CB11 21 E3
Peg Millar's La CM3 175 E5
PELDON 182 E6
Peldon Cres CO5 182 E5
Peldon Rd
Abberton CO5 182 E7
Great Wigborough CO5 182 A3
Pelham Cl CO12 90 F2
Pelham Rd CB11 65 C4
Pelham's La 18 CO1 135 F7
Pelican Cl IP2 16 E3
Pelly Ave CM8 195 A8
Pembroke Ave CM9 209 F1
Pembroke Cl
Colchester CO2 136 C3
Ipswich IP2 17 B3
Pembroke Gdns CO15 189 E6
Pembroke Pl
Chelmsford CM1 205 B7
Sudbury CO10 15 D2
Pendleton Rd IP2 16 D1
Penfold Rd
Clacton-on-S CO15 188 E2
Felixstowe IP11 221 E4
Penhaligon Ct 9
CM8 177 A2
Peninsula Bsns Ctr The
IP9 37 B5
Penlan Hall La CO6 107 B5
Penn Cl IP9 35 B2
Pennine Rd CM1 204 D5
Pennington La CM22,
CM24 93 D2
Penningtons CM23 145 C5
Penn Mews CM7 155 A8
Pennsylvania La CO5 179 C5
Penny Cnr IP1 16 C8
Penny La IP3 18 F1
Penny Mdw IP9 35 A1
Pennypot Cnr CO9 103 B6
Pennypot Cotts CO9 103 B5
Pennyroyal Cres CM8 176 E4
Pennyroyal Gdns IP2 16 E4
Penny Royal Rd CM3 218 D6
Pennystone Rd CB11 43 E8
Penrice Cl CO4 136 E6
Penrice Ct CO14 144 D1
Penrose Mead CM1 215 B8
Penryn Rd IP5 18 F7
Penshurst Pl CM77 154 B6
Penshurst Rd IP3 18 D4
Penticton Rd CM7 127 D2
Pentland Ave CM1 205 A6
PENTLOW 13 F6
Pentlow Dr CO10 1 E1
Pentlow Hawke Cl CB9 9 B7
Pentlow Hill CO10 14 A8
Pentlow La CO10 1 E1
Pentlow Ridge CO10 13 F6
PENTLOW STREET 14 A8
Penzance Cl
Chelmsford CM1 205 E5
Clacton-on-S CO15 203 I8
Penzance Rd IP5 18 F6
Peppercorn Cl CO4 109 F2
Peppercorn Way IP2 17 D3
Pepper's Rd CO4 82 E1
Pepples La
Debden CB10 69 A8
Elder Street CB10 45 A1
Pepys St CO12 91 D5
Percival Rd
Kirby-le-S CO13 143 D1
Walton-on-t-N CO14 144 D2
Percy Ruse Cl CO10 34 B7
Peregrine Cl
Bishop's Stortford
CM23 145 D6
Clacton-on-S CO15 188 F7
Peregrine Ct CO4 136 F8
Peregrine Dr CM2 216 A4
Perkins Way IP3 17 F1
Perriclose CM1 205 D7
Perrin Pl CM2 205 A1
Perryfields CO10 34 B4
Perryfields Jun & Inf Sch
CM1 205 D6
PERRY GREEN 129 D1
Perry Hill CM1 205 D3
Perry La CO4 84 A4
Perry Rd
Little Dunmow CM6 151 E6
Tiptree CO5 179 C5
Witham CM8 177 B1
Perry Way CM8 177 B1
Persardi Ct CO2 163 A7
Pershore End CO3 134 E5
Perth Cl CO2 136 A1
Pertwee Cl CO7 185 E8
Pertwee Dr CM2 216 F6
Pertwees Ct CO1 136 C6
Pertwee Way CO5 163 B2
Pesthouse La CO12 116 D3
Petchey Ct 3 CM9 209 F2
Peter Bruff Ave CO16 188 C5
Peterfield's La CO9 102 F5
Peterhouse Cl IP2 16 F2
Petersfield CM1 205 B7
Peter's Gr IP9 35 A1
Peters Ho CO5 158 C2
Petlands CB10 22 F8
Peto Ave CO4 109 F2
Petrebrook CM2 206 A3
Petrel Way CM2 216 C6
Petrolea Cl CO4 109 F1
Petronius Way CO4 110 B5
Pettit La CM77 156 A4
Petts La CB10 4 E1
Pettwood Gdns IP9 62 D6
Petunia Cres CM1 205 F6
Petworth Cl
Great Notley CM77 154 B7
Wivenhoe CO7 164 C8
Pevensey Dr CO15 203 I8
Peverel Ave CM3 194 C1
Peverells Rd CB10 44 D1
Pewterers Ave CM23 145 C4
PHARISEE GREEN 150 A5
Pharos La CO5 201 C6
Pheasant Rd IP2 16 E3
Pheasant Rise IP8 35 F8
Philbrick Cl CO1 136 C5
Philip Ave IP11 221 B3
Philip Cl CO14 171 A8
Philip Morant Sch & Coll
CO3 135 B5
Philip Rd
Ipswich IP2 17 C4
1 Witham CM8 194 E8
Philips Cl CM77 126 F2
Philips Rd CM77 126 F2
Phillip Rd CO7 164 B8
Phillips Chase CM7 128 A5
Phillips Field Rd CO10 34 A5
PHILPOT END 150 A2
Philpot End La CM6 150 B4
Phoenix Cl CO5 201 B6
Phoenix Ct CO2 136 D5
Phoenix Ct 21 CO10 33 E7
Phoenix Gr CM2 216 A8
Phoenix Ind Pk CO12 91 A4
Phoenix Pavilions
CO12 91 C2
Phoenix Rd IP4 18 A7
Phoenix Sq CO4 110 C5
Piccotts La CM7 126 B8
Pickers Way CO15 189 E7
Pickford Wlk CO4 136 F7
Pickpocket La CM77 154 D6
Pickwick Ave CM1 204 D6
Pickwick Rd IP2 16 E5
Pier App CO14 171 C8
Pier Ave CO15 188 E2
Pierce Glade CO5 179 C5
Pier Gap CO15 188 F2
Pier Rd IP11 221 A1
Pierrefitte Way CM7 127 E3
Pigeon's La IP8 16 A3
Pightle The
Capel St M IP9 35 B2
Finchingfield CM7 72 D6
Haverhill CB9 9 A8
Pightle Way CO14 171 A7
Pig La CM22 146 A3
Pigotts Way CM23 145 E5
PIG STREET 168 E6
Pilborough Way CO3 134 E3
Pilcox Hall La CO16 140 D8
Pilgrim Cl CM7 127 F5
Pilgrims Cl CB10 3 D2
Pilgrims Ct CO8 55 F1
Pimblett Row CM22 94 F5
Pimpernel Rd IP2 16 F3
Pincey Rd CM24 120 F3
Pincey Rdbt CM24 121 A3
Pinchpools Rd CM23 93 A3
Pine Ave
Great Dunmow CM6 123 B1
Ipswich IP1 17 B8
Pine Cl
Brantham CO11 86 D8
Great Bentley CO7 166 F8
Pinecroft Gdns CO4 110 B3
Pinecroft Rise CO10 33 D5
Pine Dr IP3 18 F1
Pine Gr
Bishop's Stortford
CM23 146 B6
West Mersea CO5 201 B7
Witham CM8 177 A5
Pine Ho IP11 221 C4
Pinelands CM23 118 F1
Pines Hill CM24 119 D5
Pines Rd CM1 204 D5
Pines The CM3 194 A5
Pinetree Cl IP5 18 F7
Pine Tree Ct CO4 136 E8
Pine View Rd IP1 17 A8
Pinewood Cl
Clacton-on-S CO15 188 E7
Kirby Cross CO13 170 D6
Pinhoe Dr CB9 8 C8
Pinkeneys SG8 19 D5
Pinkham Dr CM8 194 F8
Pink La CM3 175 D7
Pinkney Cl CB10 44 E2
Pinkuah La CO10 13 F6
Pin Mill Cl IP2 16 C1
Pinmill Rd IP9 63 F8
Pinner's Cross SG8 39 A7
Pintail Cl IP2 16 E3
Pintail Cres CM77 154 C6
Pioneer Pl 8 CO1 136 A6
Pipchin Rd CM1 204 F6
Piperell Way CB9 9 A5
Piperell Way Units CB9 9 A5
Piper Rd CO3 135 B7
Pipers Cl CB9 9 C6
Piper's Tye CM2 216 D3
Pipers Vale Cl IP3 17 E1
Piper's Vale Com Prim Sch
IP3 17 F1
Pippins The
Colchester CO4 136 C8
Glemsford CO10 2 C4
Halstead CO9 76 D2
Pirie Rd CO6 108 E3
Pitcairn Rd IP1 16 E8
Pitfield CM2 216 D8
Pitfield Ho CM7 127 D4
Pit La CO5 179 C6
Pitmire La CO8 55 B6
Pitt Ave CM8 195 A8
Pitt Chase CM2 216 E5
Pitt Gn CM8 195 A8
Pitts End CO7 59 D3
Place Farm Com Prim Sch
CB9 8 F8
Place Farm Ct CO2 136 D2
Plains Farm Cl CO7 110 D6
Plains Field CM7 128 D1
Plains Rd
Great Totham CM9 196 F6
Little Totham CM9 197 A6
PLAISTOW GREEN 103 D5
Plaistow Green Rd
CO9 103 C5
Plaiters Way CM7 128 D3
Plane Tree Cl CM2 216 B6
Plane View Cl CO16 188 B2
Plantation Cl CB11 43 E6
Plantation Rd CM3 192 F1
Planton Way CO7 185 E6
Platters Cl IP3 38 B7
Platters Rd IP11 221 C2
Plaw Hatch Cl CM23 146 B8
Plaw Hatch Cnr
CM23 146 D8
Players Ct CM6 152 C6
Playfield Rd IP9 35 B1
Playford Ct 2 CO10 33 E8
Playford Rd IP4 18 E8
Playle Chase CM9 196 B4
Pleasant Mews CO5 201 C6
Pleasant Rd CM23 145 E8
Pleasant Row 13 IP4 17 D5
Pleasant Valley CB11 43 D7
PLEDGDON GREEN 95 C3
Pleshey Rd CM3 172 B5
Plough Cnr CO16 168 C4
Plough Dr CO3 135 A5
Plough La CO10 33 D7
Ploughmans Cl CM23 145 C5
Ploughmans Headland
CO3 134 E5
Ploughmans La CM77 154 C8
Plough Rd CO7 166 E6
Plough St IP3 17 E4
Plover Cl CO13 170 E6
Plover Rd IP2 16 E2
Plover Wlk CM2 216 B5
Plowright Ho 5 CO1 135 E8
Plume Ave
Colchester CO3 135 A4
Maldon CM9 209 F1
Plume Sch CM9 209 F2
Plume Sch (Lower)
CM9 210 A2
Plummers Rd CO6 107 E7
Plumptre La CM3 218 D5
Plums La CM7 99 E4
Plum St CO10 2 A6
Plumtree Ave CM2 216 F6
Plymouth Rd
Chelmsford CM1 205 E5
Clacton-on-S CO15 203 J8
Felixstowe IP11 221 D6
Pochard Way CM77 154 C5
Pocklington Cl CM2 206 A3
Podsbrook Ho CM8 176 F2
Pod's Brook Rd CM7 127 D2
Pods La CM77 126 D2
POINT CLEAR 186 A3
POINT CLEAR BAY 185 F3
**Point Clear Bay Holiday
Cvn Pk** CO16 185 F3
Point Clear Rd CO16 186 D3
Pointwell La CO6 158 A8
Pole Barn La CO13 170 F5
Polecat Rd CM77 155 F5
Pole La CM8 155 C3
Pollard Ct IP2 16 D2
Pollard's Gn CM2 205 F2
Pollards Villas CM7 99 D2
Pollard Wlk CO16 188 C5
Polley Cl CO13 170 E7
Polstead St CO6 56 D5
Polstead Way CO16 188 B4
Pond Chase CO3 135 B4
Pond Cl IP11 221 B5
Pond Cotts IP9 61 E2
Pond Cross Cotts CB11 67 A8
Pond Cross Farm CB11 67 A8
Pond Cross Way CB11 67 A8
Ponders Rd CO6 107 C4
Pondfield Rd CO4 110 D1
Pondfields CM6 123 D1
Pondholton Dr 2
CM8 194 F7
Pond House La CO15 189 D8
Pond La CM24 119 D7
Ponds Rd CM2 216 B1
Pondtail Ct CO13 170 C6
Poney Chase CM8 195 F5
Poney's CM8 195 F5
Pontisbright Cotts
CO6 106 E6
Poole Cl IP3 18 D3
Poole St
Cavendish CO10 1 C1
Great Yeldham CO9 51 B6
Pooley's Yd IP2 17 B4
Poore St CB11 65 F8
**Poors' Piece Nature
Trail★** CM3 207 F1
Poperinghe Rd CO2 135 F4
Popes Ct CB9 9 E5
Pope's La CO3 135 E7
Pope's Rd CO6 106 D4
Poplar Cl
Chelmsford CM2 216 C6
Clacton-on-S CO15 188 B2
Great Yeldham CO9 30 A1
Halstead CO9 103 F8
Witham CM8 177 A5
Poplar Cotts CO5 160 C1
Poplar Ct CO10 34 B7
Poplar Grove Chase
CM9 210 B8
Poplar Hall Cl CO1 109 E1
Poplar La IP8 16 B3
Poplar Rd CO10 34 B7
Poplars Cl CO7 165 B7
Poplars The
Brantham CO11 60 D2
Colchester CO3 134 E5
Great Dunmow CM6 123 C2
Great Hallingbury
CM22 146 F4
Poplar Way CO13 170 D6
Poppy Cl IP2 16 F4
Poppy Gdns CO2 136 C3
Poppy Gn CM1 206 A6
Pork La CO13 169 E5
Portal Prec CO1 135 F7
Porter Rd IP3 18 F1
Porters Brook Wlk
CO4 110 C2
Porter's Cl CO3 107 F2
Porter's Cotts CO3 107 F1
Porters Field CM7 127 D4
Porter's La CO3 107 F2
Porters Pk CM3 193 A2
Porter Way CO16 188 B3
Port La
Bishop's Stortford
CM22 146 B2
Colchester CO1 136 B5
Portland Ave CO12 91 C3
Portland Cl CM7 128 B3
Portland Cres CO12 91 C3
Portland Ho CO13 170 F5
Portland Pl 17 CM23 145 F7
Portland Rd
Bishop's Stortford
CM23 145 F7
15 Colchester CO2 135 F6
Portlight Cl CO11 87 A4
Portman Rd IP1 17 B6
Portman Road (Ipswich
Town FC) IP1 17 B5
Portmans Walk Ind Ctr
IP1 17 A5
Portman's Wlk IP1 17 A5
Portobello Rd CO14 171 C8
Port Of Felixstowe Rd
IP11 221 A4
Portreath Pl CM1 205 A7
Portsmouth Rd CO15 203 J8
Portway CM2 206 B4
Portway Ct CO9 76 F3
Posford Ct CO4 109 F4
Postman's La CM3 207 E3
Post Mill Cl IP4 17 F6
Post Office Cnr IP9 61 F2
Post Office La
Glemsford CO10 2 B5
Little Totham CM9 197 B4
Post Office Rd
Chelmsford CM1 205 B8
Woodham Mortimer
CM9 219 E6
POTASH 60 E8
Potash Cotts IP9 60 E8
Potash La IP9 60 E8
Pot Kiln Chase CO9 31 F2
Pot Kiln Prim Sch
CO10 34 B6
Pot Kiln Rd CO10 34 B6
Pot Kilns The CO10 34 C6
Potters Cl CM3 219 A6
Potter St
Bishop's Stortford
CM23 145 F7
Sible Hedingham CO9 75 E7
Pottery La
Castle Hedingham CO9 51 F3
Chelmsford CM1 205 A5
Poulteney Rd CM24 119 E8
Pound Farm Dr CO12 91 A3
Poundfield Cl CO7 165 B7
Poundfield Ho CO7 138 A5
Pound Fields CM1 215 B8
Pound Gate CM6 124 D6
Pound Hill Villas CM6 151 E8
Pound La IP9 59 F8
Pound Wlk CB10 22 E2
Powell Cl CO5 179 E5
POWERS HALL END 176 D3
Powers Hall End CM8 176 E3
Powers Hall Inf Sch
CM8 176 D3
Powers Hall Jun Sch
CM8 176 D3
Powling Rd IP3 18 A2
Pownall Cres CO2 135 F4
Pownall Rd IP3 17 E4
Poynter Pl CO13 170 E7
Prail Ct CO6 130 F2
Pratts Farm La CM3 191 D4
Pratt's La IP9 38 A2
Prentice Hall La CM9 213 B8
Prentice Mews IP3 38 C8
Prentice Way IP3 18 B4
President Rd CO3 134 E5
Preston Rd CO15 189 D5
Prestwick Dr CM23 119 B1
Pretoria Rd CO9 76 F2
Prettygate Inf Sch
CO3 135 B4
Prettygate Jun Sch
CO3 135 B4
Prettygate Rd CO3 135 A4
Pretyman Rd
Felixstowe IP11 221 C1
Ipswich IP3 18 B3
Prime's Cl CB10 22 D1
Primrose Cl CM23 145 C6
Primrose Hill
Chelmsford CM1 204 F3
Haverhill CB9 8 F7
Holbrook IP9 62 D4
Ipswich IP2 16 F4
Primrose La
Ramsey CO12 89 A1
Tiptree CO5 179 C6
Primrose Pl CM8 176 E4
Primrose Rd CO15 189 E6
Primrose Wlk
Colchester CO4 136 E7
Maldon CM9 210 B1
Primula Cl CO16 188 C4
Primula Way CM1 206 A6
Prince Albert Rd CO5 201 D6
Prince Charles Cl
Clacton-on-S CO15 188 C1
Sudbury CO10 33 F8
Prince Charles Rd
CO2 136 A2
Princel La CO7 84 F7
Princel Mews CO7 84 F7
Prince Of Wales Dr
IP2 17 B2
Prince of Wales Ind Est
CO6 133 B4
Prince Of Wales Rd CM8,
CM9 196 A3
Prince of Wales Rdbt
CO6 133 B4
Prince Philip Ave
CO15 188 C1
Prince Philip Rd CO2 136 A1
Princes Ct CM23 145 C7
Prince's Espl CO14 144 D1
Princes Gate CM23 145 C7
Princes Gdns IP11 221 D4
Princes Rd
Chelmsford CM2 216 B7
Clacton-on-S CO15 189 D5
Felixstowe IP11 221 E4
Harwich CO12 91 B3
Maldon CM9 210 A2
Princess Anne Cl
CO15 188 C1
Princess Dr CO4 110 C5
Princess St CO12 90 F5
Princes St IP1 17 B5
Princess Way CB9 8 E8
Prince St CO10 33 E8
Princes Well CB10 45 F7
Princethorpe Rd IP3 18 C4
Princeton Mews CO4 110 B4
Prior Cl CO9 103 D8
Priors 8 CM23 146 A7
Priors Field CM3 218 F2
Prior's Hall Barn★
CB11 67 D4
Priors Way CO6 131 A3
Prior's Wood Rd
CM22 148 C7
Prior Way CO4 109 E2
Priory Ave CB9 8 F7
Priory Cl
Chelmsford CM1 204 E2
Hatfield Peverel CM3 194 B1
Ickleton CB10 3 A3
Seawick CO16 203 A6
Priory Cotts CO2 160 E6
Priory Ct
Bishop's Stortford
CM23 145 F7
Colchester CO1 135 E7
Hatfield Peverel CM3 194 A4
Ipswich IP10 38 C6

Priory Dr CM24 . . . . 119 E5
Priory Farm Rd CM3 . . . . . 194 B2
Priory Gdns CO10 . . . . 33 E6
PRIORY HEATH 18 D1
Priory La
  Bicknacre CM3. . . . . 218 F1
  Great Notley CM77 . . . . . 154 C8
Priory Mews CM3 . . . . 194 C2
Priory Pk
  Ipswich IP10 . . . . 38 B6
  St Osyth CO16 . . . . 187 A4
Priory Prim Sch CM3 . . . . 218 F2
Priory Rd
  Bicknacre CM3. . . . . 218 E1
  Chappel CO6 . . . . 106 B3
  Clacton-on-S CO15. . . . . 188 E3
  Sudbury CO10 . . . . 15 D1
  Tiptree CO5 . . . . 178 F3
Priory St
  Colchester CO1 . . . . 136 A7
  Earls Colne CO6. . . . . . . 105 B7
Priory The CM1 . . . . 215 B8
Priory Wlk
  23 Colchester CO1 . . . . 135 F7
  Sudbury CO10 . . . . 33 F8
Priory Wood CO9 . . . . 51 E4
Priory Wood Rdbt
  CM22 . . . . 147 A8
Prittlewell Cl IP2 . . . . 16 F1
Proctor Cl CO5 . . . . 163 B2
Proctors Way CM23 . . . . . 146 A4
Proctor Way CO6 . . . . 132 E3
Progress Ct CM7 . . . . 127 E3
Progress Way CO16 . . . . . 168 C1
Promenade
  Clacton-on-S CO15. . . . . 203 D6
  Harwich CO12 . . . . 91 E4
  Harwich, Dovercourt
   CO12. . . . . 91 C2
Promenade Way CO7 . . . . 185 E5
Propelair Way CO4. . . . . . 109 D2
Prospect Cl CM3 . . . . 194 A3
Prospect Hill CO10. . . . . . . 34 D3
Prospect Pk CO13. . . . . . . 170 A5
Prospect Pl CB11 . . . . 22 F1
Prospect Rd IP1 . . . . 17 A7
Prospect St **1** IP1 . . . . . . 17 A6
Prospero Cl CO4. . . . . 136 F8
Provan Ct IP3 . . . . 18 B4
Provence Cl CO3. . . . . 134 C7
Providence La IP1 . . . . 17 A7
Providence Pl CO1 . . . . . . 136 B6
Providence St **6** IP1. . . . . 17 C6
Prunus Ct CO2. . . . . 163 A7
Prykes Dr CM1 . . . . 205 A2
Pryor Cl CM8 . . . . 177 A1
Pryors CO15 CM23 . . . . . . 146 A6
Pryors Rd CM2. . . . . 216 C2
Pudding La CO2 . . . . 161 B3
Puffinsdale CO15 . . . . 188 F5
Pulford Pl CM6 . . . . 124 C7
Pulpitfield Cl CO14. . . . . . 171 A8
Pumphill SG9. . . . . 64 A2
Pump Hill
  Great Baddow CM2 . . . . 216 F6
  St Osyth CO16 . . . . 187 D4
Pump Hill Cvn Pk
  CO16 . . . . 187 C4
Pump Ho The **13**
  CM23 . . . . 146 A7
Pump La
  Chelmsford CM1 . . . . . . 205 E6
  Danbury CM3. . . . . 218 D5
  Purleigh CM3 . . . . 220 D1
Pumpyard Cotts CO9. . . . . 31 E1
Punchard Way IP11 . . . . . 221 A8
Punders Field CM7. . . . . . 128 D1
Purbeck Ct
  4 Colchester CO1 . . . . 136 D7
  Great Baddow CM2 . . . . 216 E6
Purcell Cl CO4 . . . . 136 E6
Purcell Cole CM1 . . . . 204 A1
Purcell Rd CM8 . . . . 194 B4
Purdis Ave IP3 . . . . 18 F2
Purdis Farm La IP3 . . . . . . 18 F2
PURLEIGH 220 C1
Purleigh Com Prim Sch
  CM3 . . . . 220 D1
Purleigh Prim Sch
  CM3 . . . . 220 D1
Purley Way CO16 . . . . 188 B6
Purplett Ho IP2. . . . . 17 A4
Purplett St IP2 . . . . 17 A4
Purvis Way CO4. . . . . 110 B5
Putticks La CO7. . . . . 59 E3
PUTTOCK END 31 C6
PUTTOCK'S END 148 E4
Pyecat's Cnr CO7. . . . . . . 137 C7
Pye Cnr CO9. . . . . 51 E4
Pyefleet Cl
  Brightlingsea CO7 . . . . . 185 E7
  Fingringhoe CO5 . . . . . . 164 C6
Pyefleet Ho CO5 . . . . 201 C6
Pyefleet View CO5 . . . . . . 163 B3
Pye Gdns CM23 . . . . 145 E8
Pyesand CO13 . . . . 170 C8
PYE'S GREEN 153 C5
Pygot Pl CM7 . . . . 127 E4
Pyms Rd CM2. . . . . 216 B3
Pynchbek CM23. . . . . 145 E3
Pynchon Mews CM1 . . . . 205 D3
Pyne Gate CM2 . . . . 216 B1

Q

QM Ind Pk IP3. . . . . 18 C1
Quadling St IP1 . . . . 17 C5
Quadrangle Ctr The
  IP3 . . . . 18 C1
Quaker's La CB9 . . . . 9 A7
Quale Rd CM2 . . . . 206 B4
Quantock Cl IP5 . . . . 18 F7
Quay Ctyd **2** CO11 . . . . . 86 D4
Quay La
  Beaumont CO16 . . . . . . 142 B5
  Kirby-le-S CO13 . . . . 143 D1
  Sudbury CO10 . . . . 33 E6
Quayside Dr CO2 . . . . 136 D5
Quayside Ind Est CM9. . . 210 A4
Quay St
  1 Manningtree CO11. . . . 86 D4
  Wivenhoe CO7 . . . . 164 B8
Quay The
  Harwich CO12 . . . . 91 D6
  Wivenhoe CO7. . . . . 164 B8
Quay Theatre★ CO10 . . . . 33 E6
Queech La IP9 . . . . 87 C8
Queech The IP9 . . . . 35 B2
Queen Anne Dr CO5. . . . . 201 D6
Queen Anne Gdns
  CO5 . . . . 201 D6
Queen Anne Rd CO5 . . . . 201 D7
Queenborough Gr
  CM77 . . . . 154 C8
Queenborough La
  Great Notley CM77 . . . . 154 C8
  Rayne CM77. . . . . 154 B8
Queenbury Cl CO5 . . . . . . 201 E6
Queen Edith Dr CB9. . . . . . 27 B6
Queen Elizabeth Ave
  CO15 . . . . 188 C1
Queen Elizabeth Way
  CO2 . . . . 136 A2
Queen Mary Ave CO2. . . . 135 F4
Queen's Ave CM9 . . . . . . 210 A1
Queensberry Rd IP3 . . . . . 18 A1
Queensbury Ave CO6. . . . 133 D5
Queens Cl
  Stanstead Mountfitchet
   CM24 . . . . 119 E8
  Sudbury CO10 . . . . 33 E8
Queenscliffe Rd IP2 . . . . . . 17 A3
Queens Cnr CO5 . . . . 201 D7
Queen's Cotts CO5 . . . . . 105 B7
Queens Cres CM23 . . . . . 145 E5
Queens Ct
  5 Sudbury CO10 . . . . . 33 F8
  West Mersea CO5 . . . . . 201 D7
Queen's Ct
  Clacton-on-S CO15. . . . . 189 D4
  6 Haverhill CB9. . . . . . . 8 E4
Queensgate Dr IP4 . . . . . . 17 F8
Queen's Gdns CM7 . . . . . 127 E7
Queen's Head Rd CO4. . . . 82 E3
Queen's No CO13 . . . . 170 F4
Queensland Cres
  CM1 . . . . 204 E5
Queensland Dr CO2 . . . . . 136 A1
Queens Mews CO5 . . . . . 201 B6
Queens Rd
  Braintree CM7. . . . . 127 F5
  Sudbury CO10 . . . . 33 E8
Queen's Rd
  Chelmsford CM2 . . . . . . 205 D2
  Clacton-on-S CO15. . . . . 188 D1
  Colchester CO3 . . . . 135 C6
  Earls Colne CO6. . . . . . . 105 B7
  Felixstowe IP11. . . . . 221 E4
  Frinton-on-S CO13. . . . . 170 F4
  Harwich CO12 . . . . 91 A2
  West Bergholt CO6 . . . . 108 D3
  Wivenhoe CO7. . . . . 164 C8
Queens Sq **5** CB9 . . . . . . 9 A8
Queen's Sq IP3 . . . . 18 B2
Queen St
  Brightlingsea CO7 . . . . . 185 F6
  Castle Hedingham CO9 . . 51 E3
  Chelmsford CM2 . . . . . . 205 A1
  Coggeshall CO6 . . . . 131 A2
  Colchester CO1 . . . . 135 F7
  Felixstowe IP11. . . . . 221 C6
  Great Oakley CO12 . . . . 116 C4
  Haverhill CB9. . . . . 9 A8
  Ipswich IP1. . . . . 17 C5
  Maldon CM9. . . . . 210 A2
  Sible Hedingham CO9 . . . 75 F6
Queens Terr CO10 . . . . 34 A7
Queensway
  Clacton-on-S CO15. . . . . 189 D5
  Great Cornard CO10 . . . . 34 B5
  Haverhill CB9. . . . . 8 E8
  Lawford CO11 . . . . 86 C4
  Tiptree CO5. . . . . 179 C6
Queen's Way IP3 . . . . 18 B2
Queen Victoria Dr IP9 . . . 91 B8
QUENDON 66 F2
Quendon Pl **17** CB9 . . . . . 9 B8
Quendon Way CO13 . . . . . 171 A6
Quentin Cl IP1 . . . . 16 E8
Quickset Rd CB11 . . . . 20 C5
Quicksie Hill CB11 . . . . 41 E2
Quilberry Dr CM77 . . . . . . 154 D8
Quilp Dr CM1 . . . . 204 F7
Quilter Dr IP8 . . . . 16 C1
Quilter Rd IP11 . . . . 221 F1
Quilters Cl CO15 . . . . 189 F6
Quilter's Gn CO6 . . . . 107 D6
Quince Cl CO11 . . . . 60 D1
Quince Ct CO5 . . . . 179 D4
Quinion Cl CM1 . . . . 204 D7

Quintons Cnr CO7. . . . . . . 59 D4
Quinton's La IP11 . . . . . . 221 F7
Quintons Rd CO7 . . . . 59 D4

R

R A Butler Jun & Inf Schs
  CB11. . . . . 22 E1
RACECOURSE 18 B2
Rachael Ct **1** CM2. . . . . . 205 B1
Rachael Gdns CM8. . . . . . 156 E4
Rachel Ct **6** IP4. . . . . 17 D6
Radcliffe Dr IP2 . . . . 16 D2
Radiator Rd CO10. . . . . 34 A5
RADLEY'S END 97 A2
Radveld Chase CO3 . . . . . 134 E4
RADWINTER 45 F8
Radwinter CE Prim Sch
  CB10. . . . . 45 F7
RADWINTER END 25 B4
Radwinter Rd
  Ashdon CB10 . . . . 24 B7
  Saffron Walden CB10. . . . 23 B1
  Sewards End CB10. . . . . . 23 F1
Raeburn Cl CO13. . . . . . . 170 F7
Raeburn Ct CM1. . . . . 205 E6
Raeburn Rd IP3 . . . . 18 A1
Raeburn Rd S IP3 . . . . 17 F1
Raglan Mews CO15 . . . . . 188 C3
Raglan Rd CO13 . . . . 171 A5
Ragley Cl CM77 . . . . 154 B6
Raile Wlk CO10 . . . . 15 D8
Railey Rd CB11 . . . . 43 E8
Railway App IP11. . . . . . . 221 E5
Railway Cotts
  Thorpe-le-S CO16 . . . . . 168 F7
  Wendens Ambo CB11 . . . 42 F5
Railway Sq CM1 . . . . 205 A3
Railway St
  Braintree CM7. . . . . 128 A3
  Chelmsford CM1 . . . . . . 205 A3
  Manningtree CO11. . . . . . 86 D4
Railway Terr
  Clacton-on-S CO15. . . . . 188 F3
  11 Manningtree CO11. . . 86 D4
Rainbow Ct **1** CO12 . . . . . 91 D4
Rainbow Mead CM3. . . . . 194 A5
Rainbow Mews CM9 . . . . 209 F5
Rainbow Rd CO5. . . . . 201 D6
Rainbow Way CO6 . . . . 77 F1
Raine Ave CB9 . . . . 8 D8
Rainham Way CO13 . . . . . 171 B6
Rainsborowe Rd CO2 . . . . 135 C4
Rainsford Ave CM1. . . . . . 204 F3
Rainsford La CM1. . . . . . . 204 F2
Rainsford Rd
  Chelmsford CM1 . . . . . . 204 F3
  Stansted Mountfitchet
   CM24 . . . . 119 E8
Rambler Cl CO3. . . . . 134 D7
Rampart Cotts CO6 . . . . . 109 B7
Ramparts Cl CO6 . . . . 109 B7
Ramplings Ave CO15 . . . . 188 E5
Ramsden Cl CO15. . . . . . . 189 A5
RAMSEY 90 A2
Ramsey Cl
  Heybridge CM9 . . . . 210 D4
  Ipswich IP2. . . . . 17 A1
Ramsey Mews CO2. . . . . . 136 A4
Ramsey Rd
  Halstead CO9. . . . . 103 D8
  Harwich CO12 . . . . 90 C2
Ramsey Sch (Priory Hall)
  The CO9 . . . . 77 A2
Ramsey Sch The CO9. . . . . 77 A2
Ramsgate Dr IP3 . . . . 18 B3
Ramshaw Dr CM2. . . . . . . 205 F3
Rana Ct CM7 . . . . 127 F4
Rana Dr CM7 . . . . 127 F4
Randall Cl
  Great Dunmow CM6 . . . . 123 D1
  Witham CM8 . . . . 194 F1
Randolph Ave CM7. . . . . . . 73 C6
Randolph Cl
  Ipswich IP4. . . . . 18 B5
  Maldon CM9. . . . . 220 F8
Rands Way IP3 . . . . 18 B2
Randulph Terr CM1. . . . . . 205 D3
Randwell Cl IP4 . . . . 18 B5
Ranelagh Ct IP11 . . . . 221 E4
Ranelagh Prim Sch
  IP2 . . . . 16 F5
Ranelagh Rd
  Felixstowe IP11. . . . . 221 E4
  Ipswich IP2. . . . . 17 A5
Ranger Hts **4** CM7. . . . . . 127 C7
Ranger Wlk CO2 . . . . 136 B3
Rangoon Cl CO2 . . . . 135 B1
RANK'S GREEN 174 D8
Ransome Cl IP8 . . . . 16 A6
Ransome Cres IP3 . . . . 18 B2
Ransome Rd IP3 . . . . 18 B3
Ransomes Europark
  IP3 . . . . 38 E8
Ransomes Way
  Chelmsford CM1 . . . . . . 205 B4
  Ipswich IP3. . . . . 38 D8
Ransom Rd CO5 . . . . 179 C5
Ranulf Rd CM6. . . . . 151 E6
Ranulph Way CM3 . . . . . . 194 B3
Raphael Dr CM1 . . . . 205 F7
Rapier St IP2. . . . . 17 C3
Ratcliff Ct CO5. . . . . 158 B2
Ratcliffe Ct
  Colchester CO1 . . . . 136 B8
  Frinton-on-S CO13. . . . . 170 F5
Ratcliffe Rd CO3. . . . . 134 E6

Rat Hill IP9. . . . . 63 F2
Ravel Ave CM8. . . . . 194 F7
Ravens Ave CO9 . . . . 76 F1
Ravensbourne Dr
  CM1 . . . . 204 E2
Ravens Cres CM6 . . . . 152 E6
Ravenscroft Prim Sch
  CO16. . . . . 188 B4
Ravensdale CO15 . . . . 188 F6
Ravenswood **11** CO1 . . . . 136 A6
Ravenswood Ave IP3 . . . . . 38 C8
Ravenswood Com Prim
  Sch IP3 . . . . 38 C8
Ravenswood Way IP3. . . . . 38 B8
Raven Way CO4 . . . . 109 E4
Rawden Cl CO12 . . . . 91 B4
Rawlings Cres CO4. . . . . . 110 B5
Rawstorn Rd CO3 . . . . . . 135 E7
Ray Ave CO12 . . . . 91 A3
Raycliff Ave CO15 . . . . . . 188 E7
RAYDON 58 E8
Raydon Way CO10 . . . . 34 C6
Rayfield Cl CM6. . . . . 151 A4
Rayhaven CO12 . . . . 90 D2
Ray Ho CO5 . . . . 201 D7
Ray La
  Harwich CO12 . . . . 90 E5
  Ramsey CO12 . . . . 90 A3
Rayleigh Cl
  Braintree CM7. . . . . 128 C4
  Colchester CO4 . . . . 110 B1
Rayleigh Mans CO2 . . . . . 135 C5
Rayleighs The CO2 . . . . . . 135 C5
Ray Mead CM3. . . . . 190 F7
Rayments Bglws CB10. . . . 45 E3
Raymouth Ho CO2 . . . . . . 135 E2
RAYNE 126 E2
Rayne Hall Farm Ind Est
  CM77 . . . . 127 A2
Rayne Prim Sch
  CM77 . . . . 126 F2
Rayne Rd CM7 . . . . 127 D3
Rayner Rd CO2 . . . . 135 B4
Rayners Ct CO4 . . . . 83 F4
Rayner Way CO9 . . . . 76 E1
Raynham Cl CM23. . . . . . 146 C7
Raynham Rd CM23 . . . . . 146 B8
Raynhams CB10 . . . . 22 D1
Ray The CM1 . . . . 205 E6
Reade Rd IP9. . . . . 62 D5
Reader's Cnr CM2 . . . . . . 216 E5
Readers Ct CM2 . . . . 216 E6
Reading Rd IP4. . . . . 18 B7
Reaper Rd CO3 . . . . 135 A5
Rebecca Gdns CM8 . . . . . 156 E4
Rebecca Ho CO15 . . . . . . 189 A3
Rebecca Meade CM6. . . . 122 F8
Rebow Rd
  Harwich CO12 . . . . 91 A2
  Wivenhoe CO7. . . . . 164 B8
Rebow St CO1 . . . . 136 B6
Reckitts Cl CO15 . . . . 189 B4
Recreation Cl IP11. . . . . . 221 D6
Recreation Ground
  Sible Hedingham CO9 . . . 75 E8
  Stansted Mountfitchet
   CM24 . . . . 119 E6
Recreation Ho CO2 . . . . . 136 B5
Recreation La IP11 . . . . . 221 D6
Recreation Rd
  Clacton-on-S CO15. . . . . 188 F3
  Colchester CO1 . . . . 136 C5
  Haverhill CB9. . . . . 8 F7
  Sible Hedingham CO9 . . . 75 D8
Recreation Way
  Brightlingsea CO7 . . . . . 185 F7
  Ipswich IP3. . . . . 18 B2
Recreation Wlk CO10 . . . . 34 C5
Rectory Cl
  Bishop's Stortford
   CM23 . . . . 145 D3
  5 Colchester CO4. . . . . 109 C2
  Glemsford CO10 . . . . 2 B5
  Littlebury CB11 . . . . 21 F4
  Little Waltham CM3 . . . . 191 C6
Rectory Cotts CO7 . . . . . . 138 F1
Rectory Dr CM23. . . . . . . 118 D6
Rectory Field IP9 . . . . 63 E7
Rectory Hill
  East Bergholt CO7 . . . . . . 59 C1
  Stoke-by-N CO6 . . . . 56 D7
  Wivenhoe CO7. . . . . 137 C1
Rectory La
  Abberton CO5 . . . . 163 A3
  Ashdon CB10 . . . . 6 A1
  Brantham CO11 . . . . 60 E1
  Chelmsford CM1 . . . . . . 205 B4
  Farnham CM23 . . . . 118 D6
  Great Leighs CM3 . . . . . 173 D7
  Ramsey CO12 . . . . 90 A1
  Rivenhall CM8 . . . . 177 A6
  Wickham St P CO9. . . . . . 53 C6
  Woodham Mortimer
   CM9 . . . . 219 F6
Rectory Mdw CM77 . . . . . 129 C2
Rectory Mdws CO9. . . . . . . 51 D1
Rectory Rd
  Aldham CO6. . . . . 132 F7
  Copford CO6 . . . . 133 C1
  Frating Green CO7. . . . . . 138 F1
  Great Henny CO10. . . . . . 33 E4
  Great Holland CO13. . . . 170 A3
  Harkstead IP9 . . . . 63 C2
  Ipswich IP2. . . . . 17 C4
  Langham CO4 . . . . 83 F7
  Little Bentley CO7 . . . . . 139 E8
  Little Oakley CO12. . . . . 117 A7
  Rowhedge CO5 . . . . 163 E8

Rectory Rd continued
  Sible Hedingham CO9 . . . . 51 D1
  Stisted CM77 . . . . 129 B7
  Tiptree CO5. . . . . 179 C5
  Tolleshunt Knights
   CM9 . . . . 180 C1
  Weeley Heath CO16 . . . . 167 F3
  Wivenhoe CO7. . . . . 137 C2
  Woodham Walter CM9. . 208 D3
  Wrabness CO11. . . . . 89 A3
  Writtle CM1 . . . . 215 B8
Redan St IP1 . . . . 17 B7
Red Barn La CO12. . . . . . . 116 B2
Red Barn Rd CO7 . . . . 185 F6
Redbridge Rd CO15 . . . . . 188 F8
Redcliffe Rd **3** CM2 . . . . 205 A1
Reddells Cl **3** CO10. . . . . . 33 F8
Reddings Cl CB11 . . . . 43 E7
Rede Way CO10. . . . . 34 C6
Redgate La IP9 . . . . 37 D5
Redgates La CB10. . . . . 23 E3
Redgates Pl CM2 . . . . 205 D4
Redhill Cl IP1 . . . . 16 F8
Red House La
  Great Cornard CO10 . . . . 34 A4
  Sudbury CO10 . . . . 33 E7
Red La IP9 . . . . 60 A8
Red Lion Ct **4** CM23 . . . . 146 A7
Red Lion Yd **17** CO1 . . . . 135 F7
Redmayne Dr CM2. . . . . . 215 F8
Redmill CO3. . . . . 135 A3
Redrose Wlk CO16 . . . . . . 188 C4
Redruth Cl CM1. . . . . 205 E6
Redshank Cl CB9 . . . . 9 C7
Redshank Dr CM9. . . . . . . 210 C5
Redvers Cl CM23. . . . . . . 119 A2
Redwing Cl IP2. . . . . 16 D3
Redwood Cl
  Colchester CO4 . . . . 110 E1
  Witham CM8 . . . . 177 A5
Redwood Ct **2** CO4 . . . . . 136 E8
Redwoods The CM23 . . . . 145 D8
Reed Cl CO16 . . . . 188 C5
Reedland Way IP11. . . . . . 221 B5
Reeds La CB9. . . . . 9 A8
Refinery Rd CO12 . . . . 90 E5
Regal Cl CM2 . . . . 216 D8
Regency Cl
  Bishop's Stortford
   CM23 . . . . 145 E7
  Chelmsford CM2 . . . . . . 205 D3
Regency Ct
  Heybridge CM9 . . . . 210 A5
  Ipswich IP3. . . . . 17 F5
Regency Gn CO3 . . . . 135 A4
Regency Lo CO15 . . . . 188 E5
Regent Cl CO7. . . . . 185 F8
Regent Ct CO5. . . . . 164 A8
Regent Rd CO7 . . . . 185 F7
Regents Cl CO4. . . . . 110 C5
Regent St
  Ipswich IP4. . . . . 17 E6
  9 Manningtree CO11. . . . 86 D4
  Rowhedge CO5 . . . . 164 A8
Regimental Way CO12. . . . 90 C1
Regina Cl IP4 . . . . 18 B5
Regina Rd CM1 . . . . 205 C3
Reigate Ave CO16. . . . . . . 188 D6
Reigate Cl IP3 . . . . 18 B3
Rembrandt Gr CM1 . . . . . 205 E6
Rembrandt Way CO3. . . . . 135 B5
Rembrow Rd IP9 . . . . 35 A1
Remembrance Ave
  CM3 . . . . 194 A3
Remercie Rd CO11. . . . . . . 87 A4
Remus Cl CO4 . . . . 109 F5
Rendlesham Ct **8** IP1. . . . 17 A7
Rendlesham Rd
  Felixstowe IP11. . . . . 221 B5
  Ipswich IP1. . . . . 17 A6
Renfrew Rd IP4 . . . . 18 B8
Rennie Pl CM2. . . . . 206 B3
Rennie Wlk CM9 . . . . 210 C4
Renoir Pl CM1 . . . . 205 F7
Retreat The
  West Bergholt CO6 . . . . 108 D3
  Witham CM8 . . . . 177 A1
Reuben Wlk CO6. . . . . 105 B6
Reverdy Ho CO2 . . . . 135 E2
Rex Mott Ct CM8. . . . . . . 176 F2
Reydon Cl CB9. . . . . 8 C8
Reydon Ho IP3 . . . . 18 A2
Reymead Cl CO5. . . . . 201 C6
Reynard Copse CM23. . . . 118 F1
Reynard Hts CO4 . . . . 136 C8
Reynards Cl CO13. . . . . . . 170 D6
Reynards Copse CO4. . . . 110 A3
Reynards Ct CM2 . . . . 216 F6
Reynolds Ave
  Colchester CO3 . . . . 135 B5
  Ipswich IP3. . . . . 38 A8
Reynolds Ct IP11 . . . . 221 B5
Reynolds Rd IP3 . . . . 18 A1
Rhodes Ave CM23 . . . . . . 145 F5
Riby Rd IP11 . . . . 221 D3
Rice Bridge Ind Est
  CO16. . . . . 169 A7
Richard Ave
  Brightlingsea CO7 . . . . . 185 F6
  Wivenhoe CO7. . . . . 137 C3
Richard Burn Way
  CO10 . . . . 15 E2
Richard de Clare Com
  Prim Sch CO9 . . . . 76 F1
Richards Cl CM8 . . . . 176 F1
Richardson Pl CM1 . . . . . 204 F4

Richardson Rd CO7 . . . . 59 D3
Richardsons La IP9 . . . . . . 63 D8
Richardson Wlk
  Colchester CO3 . . . . 134 F5
  Witham CM8 . . . . 177 B2
Richards Wlk CO15 . . . . . . 188 A1
Richard Whittington Prim
  Sch CM23 . . . . 145 E4
Rich CI CM3 . . . . 173 F7
Riche CI CM6 . . . . 152 B5
Richmond CI CM23 . . . . . . 145 C7
Richmond Cres CO12 . . . . . 91 B2
Richmond Dr CO15 . . . . . . 188 A1
Richmond Ho 19 IP4 . . . . . . 17 D5
Richmond Rd
  Chelmsford CM2 . . . . . . 206 A4
  Ipswich IP1 . . . . 16 F8
  West Mersea CO5 . . . . . . 201 D6
RICHMOND'S GREEN 97 D7
RICKLING 66 B3
Rickling CE Prim Sch
  CB11 . . . . 93 E8
RICKLING GREEN 93 D8
Rickling Green Rd
  Quendon CB11 . . . . 66 E1
  Rickling Green CB11 . . . . . 93 E8
Rickling Rd CB11 . . . . 66 B6
Rickstones Rd CM8 . . . . . 177 A6
Rickstones Sch The
  CM8 . . . . 176 F6
Riddiford Dr CM1 . . . . . . 204 F4
Riddles Dr CO4 . . . . 109 F2
Ridge The
  Braintree CM7 . . . . 128 B6
  Little Baddow CM3 . . . . . 207 E2
  Walton-on-t-N CO14 . . . . 171 B8
Ridgeway CO4 . . . . 110 A4
Ridgeway The
  Braintree CM7 . . . . 128 A1
  Harwich CO12 . . . . 91 B3
RIDGEWELL 29 B7
Ridgewell Ave CM1 . . . . . 204 F4
Ridgewell CE Prim Sch
  CO9 . . . . 29 B6
Ridgewell Rd
  Ashen CO10 . . . . 11 C1
  Birdbrook CO9 . . . . 10 E2
  Great Yeldham CO9 . . . . . 29 E3
Ridgewell Way CO2 . . . . . 135 F1
Ridings Ave CM77 . . . . . . 154 B7
Ridings The
  Bishop's Stortford
    CM23 . . . . 145 D4
  Great Baddow CM2 . . . . . 216 D7
Ridlands CI CM77 . . . . . . 155 E6
Ridley Gdns CM22 . . . . . . 94 C2
Ridley Rd CM1 . . . . 205 B8
Riffhams Chase CM3 . . . . 207 D2
Riffhams Dr CM2 . . . . 217 A7
Riffhams La
  Danbury CM3 . . . . 218 C8
  Little Baddow CM3 . . . . . 207 C1
Rifle Hill CM7 . . . . 127 F1
Rifle Hill Works CM7 . . . . 127 F1
Rigby Ave CO11 . . . . 87 A3
Rignal's La CM2 . . . . 216 D3
Riley Ave CO15 . . . . 203 E6
Rimini CI CO2 . . . . 135 C3
Ringham Rd IP4 . . . . 18 A6
RINGTAIL GREEN 172 B5
Ripley CI CO16 . . . . 188 B6
Rippers Ct CO9 . . . . 51 E2
Ripple Way CO4 . . . . 110 B1
Risby CI
  Clacton-on-S CO16 . . . . . 188 A4
  Ipswich IP4 . . . . 18 B6
Rise The CO6 . . . . 134 A8
Ritabrook Rd IP2 . . . . 16 E1
RIVENHALL 177 B8
Rivenhall CE Prim Sch
  CM8 . . . . 177 B8
RIVENHALL END 177 E6
Riverbank CI CO10 . . . . . . 12 C1
River CI CO9 . . . . 76 F1
River Cotts CM3 . . . . 206 F8
Riverdale Ct IP11 . . . . . . 221 D3
River Hill
  Ipswich IP8 . . . . 16 C8
  Terling CM3 . . . . 175 B3
River Hill Cotts CM3 . . . . 175 B3
River Mead CM7 . . . . 128 A4
Rivermead Gate CM1 . . . . 205 B4
Rivermead Ind Est
  CM1 . . . . 205 B4
Rivers Ho CO14 . . . . 144 D2
Riverside
  Bishop's Stortford
    CM23 . . . . 145 F7
  Bradwell CM77 . . . . 129 D3
  Chelmsford CM2 . . . . . . 205 C3
  Great Dunmow CM6 . . . . 123 C1
Riverside Ave E CO11 . . . . 86 C5
Riverside Ave W CO11 . . . . 86 C5
Riverside Bsns Pk
  Earls Colne CO6 . . . . 104 F8
  Stansted Mountfitchet
    CM24 . . . . 119 E6
Riverside Cotts CO11 . . . . . 86 C7
Riverside Ct CO9 . . . . 76 E2
Riverside Ind Est CM9 . . . 209 F3
Riverside Ind Pk IP2 . . . . . 17 D3
Riverside Maltings
  CO6 . . . . 130 F1
Riverside Pk CM1 . . . . . . 205 C3
Riverside Rd IP1 . . . . 16 F7
Riverside Way
  Kelvedon CO5 . . . . 158 C2
  Sible Hedingham CO9 . . . . 51 E1

Riverside Wlk
  16 Bishop's Stortford
    CM23 . . . . 145 F7
  Colchester CO1 . . . . 135 E8
Rivers St IP4 . . . . 17 F7
Riverton Dr CM0 . . . . 213 B1
River View
  Braintree CM7 . . . . 127 F1
  Holbrook IP9 . . . . 62 D5
  Manningtree CO11 . . . . . . 86 C4
  Witham CM8 . . . . 195 A8
River View Rd IP9 . . . . . . 63 B2
Rivish La CO10 . . . . 15 C7
Roach Vale CO4 . . . . 110 E1
Roach Vale Prim Sch
  CO4 . . . . 110 E1
Roast Gn CB11 . . . . 64 F6
Robeck Rd IP3 . . . . 17 F1
Robert CI CM2 . . . . 205 F4
Roberts Ct CM2 . . . . 216 E7
Robert's Hill CO8 . . . . 79 F3
Roberts Rd CO1, CO2 . . . . 136 A5
Robert Suckling Ct
  CB9 . . . . 27 B6
Robert Wallace CI
  CM23 . . . . 118 F1
Robert Way CO7 . . . . 137 C3
Robin CI
  Great Bentley CO7 . . . . . 166 D8
  Haverhill CB9 . . . . 9 C7
Robin Cres CO3 . . . . 134 B4
Robin Dr IP2 . . . . 16 D3
ROBINHOOD END 49 B6
Robinia Ct 1 CO4 . . . . . . 136 E7
Robin Jeffrey Ct 18
  CM23 . . . . 145 F6
Robinsbridge Rd CO6 . . . . 130 F2
Robinsdale CO15 . . . . 188 F6
Robinson CI CM23 . . . . . . 145 F5
Robinson Rd CO7 . . . . . . 186 A7
Robin Way
  Chelmsford CM2 . . . . . . 216 B5
  Sudbury CO10 . . . . 33 C5
Robjohns Ho 11 CM2 . . . . 205 C2
Robjohns Rd CM1 . . . . . . 215 E8
Robletts Way CO6 . . . . . . 80 E4
Rochdale Way CO4 . . . . . 136 E6
Rochelle CI CM6 . . . . 70 A3
Rochester CI CM7 . . . . . . 128 C4
Rochester Ct CB10 . . . . . . 22 F2
Rochester Way CO10 . . . . . 15 D2
Rochford CI CM24 . . . . . . 119 E5
Rochford Ho CO14 . . . . . . 144 E2
Rochford Rd
  Bishop's Stortford
    CM23 . . . . 119 C1
  Chelmsford CM2 . . . . . . 205 C1
  St Osyth CO16 . . . . 187 B4
Rochford Way
  Frinton-on-S CO13 . . . . . 170 F7
  Walton-on-t-N CO14 . . . . 171 A7
Rockall CI CB9 . . . . 9 D7
Rockells Farm★ CB11 . . . . 41 B5
Rockhampton Wlk 10
  CO2 . . . . 136 A1
Rockingham CI CO4 . . . . . 110 D3
RODBRIDGE CORNER 15 C4
Rodbridge Hill CO10 . . . . . 15 B5
Rodbridge Nature
  Reserve★ CO10 . . . . 15 B4
Roddam CI CO3 . . . . 135 C6
Roding Ct CM7 . . . . 128 C1
Rodney Gdns CM7 . . . . . . 128 C4
Rodney Way CM1 . . . . . . 215 E7
Rogation CI CO3 . . . . 134 D6
Roger Browning Ho 25
  CO1 . . . . 135 F7
Rogers CI IP11 . . . . 221 D6
ROGERS END 6 B1
Rokell Way CO13 . . . . . . 170 F6
Rolands CI CM1 . . . . 205 B7
Rollerworld★ CO1 . . . . . . 136 B7
Rolley La CO5 . . . . 158 C2
Rolph CE Prim Sch
  CO16 . . . . 141 F1
Rolph CI CO16 . . . . 142 A2
Rolphs Cotts CM8 . . . . . . 156 D5
ROLPHY GREEN 172 A4
Roman Ct CM9 . . . . 209 F4
Roman Ct
  Braintree CM7 . . . . 128 C4
  Saffron Walden CB11 . . . . 43 E7
Roman Hill CO2 . . . . 163 B7
Roman Ho 8 CM2 . . . . . . 205 B1
Romanhurst CM9 . . . . . . 210 A4
Roman La CM24 . . . . 120 B2
Roman Rd
  Chelmsford CM2 . . . . . . 205 B1
  Colchester CO1 . . . . 136 A7
  Little Waltham CM3 . . . . . 191 B5
Romans Pl CM1 . . . . 204 B1
Romans Way CM1 . . . . . . 204 B1
Roman Way
  Colchester CO2 . . . . 135 E3
  Haverhill CB9 . . . . 9 D7
  Littlebury CB11 . . . . 21 F4
  Long Melford CO10 . . . . . 15 C4
  Point Clear B CO16 . . . . . 186 A3
Romford Ct CO4 . . . . 136 B8
Romney CI
  Braintree CM7 . . . . 127 E6
  Brightlingsea CO7 . . . . . . 165 E4
  Clacton-on-S CO16 . . . . . 188 D5
  Kirby Cross CO13 . . . . . . 170 E7
Romney Rd IP3 . . . . 38 A3
Romulus CI CO4 . . . . 109 F5
Ronald Rd CO9 . . . . 103 E8

ROOK END 68 A5
Rook End La CB11 . . . . . . 68 B5
Rookeries The CO6 . . . . . . 133 B4
Rookery Chase CO7 . . . . . 84 E2
Rookery CI
  Great Chesterford CB10 . . . 3 D3
  Hatfield Peverel CM3 . . . . 194 A5
Rookery La
  Great Totham CM9 . . . . . 196 E2
  Tiptree CO5 . . . . 179 C7
  Wendens Ambo CB11 . . . . 42 E4
Rookery The
  Lawford CO11 . . . . 86 C4
  Stansted Mountfitchet
    CM24 . . . . 119 E8
Rookes CB10 . . . . 22 D3
Rookes Cres CM1 . . . . . . 215 F8
Rookwood CI CO15 . . . . . 188 D7
Rookwood Way CB9 . . . . . . 9 A6
Roosevelt Way CO2 . . . . . 136 B4
Roos Hill Debden Rd
  CB11 . . . . 43 E5
Roothings The CM9 . . . . . 210 B3
Roots La CM8 . . . . 195 E5
Roper CI CO4 . . . . 110 B6
Roper Ct IP4 . . . . 18 C5
Roper's Chase CM1 . . . . . 215 A7
Ropers La CO10 . . . . 15 B5
Rope Wlk
  Ipswich IP4 . . . . 17 E5
  Maldon CM9 . . . . 210 A1
Rosabelle Ave CO7 . . . . . 137 B1
Rosalind CI CO4 . . . . 136 F7
Rose Acre CO7 . . . . 58 F6
Rose Allen Ave CO2 . . . . . 162 F8
Rose Ave CO3 . . . . 134 C4
Rosebank
  Harwich CO12 . . . . 91 A3
  West Mersea CO5 . . . . . 201 B6
Rosebank Ct CO15 . . . . . . 189 A2
Rosebank Rd CO5 . . . . . . 201 B6
Rosebay CI CM8 . . . . 176 D3
Rosebery CM23 . . . . 146 C6
Rosebery Ave CO1 . . . . . . 136 A7
Rosebery Ct IP11 . . . . . . 221 D2
Rosebery Rd
  Chelmsford CM2 . . . . . . 216 B8
  Felixstowe IP11 . . . . 221 F4
  Ipswich IP4 . . . . 17 F5
Rose Cotts
  Brent Pelham SG9 . . . . . . 64 A5
  Great Sampford CM7 . . . . 47 E5
Rose Cres CO4 . . . . 109 D2
Rosecroft CI CO15 . . . . . . 188 E6
Rose & Crown Wlk
  CB10 . . . . 22 D2
Rose Ct CO2 . . . . 163 B8
Rosedale Cotts CO3 . . . . . 133 F5
Rosefinch CI CB9 . . . . 9 C7
Rose Gdns
  Braintree CM7 . . . . 128 A2
  Seawick CO16 . . . . 203 B6
Rose Glen CM2 . . . . 216 C7
ROSE GREEN 106 E5
Rose Green Cotts
  CO6 . . . . 106 E5
ROSE HILL 18 A4
Rose Hill CM7 . . . . 128 A2
Rosehill Cres IP3 . . . . 17 F4
Rose Hill Prim Sch
  IP3 . . . . 18 A4
Rosehill Rd IP3 . . . . 17 F4
Rose Ho 12 CO1 . . . . 136 A6
Rose La
  Great Chesterford CB10 . . . 3 E2
  Ipswich IP1, IP4 . . . . 17 C5
  Salcott-c-V CM9 . . . . . . 199 B8
  Wivenhoe CO7 . . . . 164 B7
Roseland Ct CO15 . . . . . . 188 F3
Roselawn Fields CM1 . . . . 205 B8
Rosemary Ave
  Braintree CM7 . . . . 127 F4
  Felixstowe IP11 . . . . 221 F6
Rosemary CI
  Great Dunmow CM6 . . . . 123 C1
  Tiptree CO5 . . . . 179 C5
Rosemary Cotts CM3 . . . . 192 E1
Rosemary Cres
  Clacton-on-S CO15 . . . . . 188 F2
  Great Dunmow CM6 . . . . 123 C1
  Tiptree CO5 . . . . 179 C5
Rosemary Ct
  2 Colchester CO4 . . . . . 136 D8
  Tiptree CO5 . . . . 179 C5
Rosemary Gdns CO10 . . . . 15 F2
Rosemary La
  Castle Hedingham CO9 . . . 52 A5
  Great Dunmow CM6 . . . . 123 C1
  Halstead CO9 . . . . 76 E2
  Stebbing CM6 . . . . 124 C7
  Thorrington CO7 . . . . . . 166 B5
Rosemary Rd CO15 . . . . . 188 F2
Rosemary Rd W CO15 . . . 188 E2
Rosemary Way CO15 . . . . 203 G7
Rosemount Ct IP11 . . . . . 221 F4
Rosery Ho IP11 . . . . 221 F4
Rosery Mews CO13 . . . . . 170 A4
Rosetta CI CO7 . . . . 137 B2
Rose Wlk CO9 . . . . 29 B6
Rosewood CI CO4 . . . . . . 110 A4
Roslings CI CM1 . . . . 204 D5
Ross CI
  Haverhill CB9 . . . . 9 D7
  Saffron Walden CB11 . . . . 43 E6
Rossendale CM1 . . . . 204 E1
Rossendale CI CO4 . . . . . . 110 D3
Rosseter CI CM2 . . . . 216 D7

Rosslyn Terr CO5 . . . . . . 158 C3
Rotary Way CO3 . . . . 135 E8
Rothbury Rd CM1 . . . . . . 204 D1
Rothesay Ave CM2 . . . . . . 216 A8
Rothmans Ave CM2 . . . . . 216 E6
ROTTEN END 101 A7
Roughtons CM2 . . . . 216 C3
Roundacre CO9 . . . . 103 E8
Roundbush Cnr
  Birch Green CO5 . . . . . . 160 D3
  Great Totham CM9 . . . . . 196 D6
Roundbush Rd CO5 . . . . . 160 D2
Round CI CO3 . . . . 135 B7
Round Coppice Rd
  Great Hallingbury
    CM24 . . . . 147 A8
  Stansted Mountfitchet
    CM24 . . . . 120 B1
Roundridge Rd IP9 . . . . . . 35 B2
Roundwood Rd IP4 . . . . . . 18 A7
Rous Chase CM2 . . . . 216 B1
Rouse Way CO1 . . . . 136 B7
Routh Ave IP3 . . . . 18 F1
Rover Ave CO15 . . . . 203 E6
Rowallan CI CO3 . . . . 135 A3
Rowan Chase CO5 . . . . . . 179 C6
Rowan CI
  Clacton-on-S CO15 . . . . . 188 C3
  Colchester CO3 . . . . 134 D4
  Great Bentley CO7 . . . . . 166 D4
  Harwich CO12 . . . . 91 B3
  Ipswich IP3 . . . . 18 D2
Rowan Dr CM9 . . . . 210 C5
Rowanhayes CI IP2 . . . . . . 17 B3
Rowan Pl CO1 . . . . 109 E1
Rowan Way
  Great Dunmow CM6 . . . . 123 C1
  Hatfield Peverel CM3 . . . . 194 A3
  Witham CM8 . . . . 177 A5
ROW GREEN 154 D6
ROW HEATH 167 F4
ROWHEDGE 163 F8
Rowhedge Ct CO7 . . . . . . 136 F4
Rowhedge Ferry Rd
  CO7 . . . . 164 A8
Rowhedge Rd CO2,
  CO5 . . . . 136 E1
Rowherns La CO7 . . . . . . 139 F4
Rowland Ho IP11 . . . . . . 221 B5
Rowland's Yd CO12 . . . . . 90 E2
Rowley CI CO11 . . . . 86 C4
Rowley Cotts The CO6 . . . . 56 D5
Rowley Ct CB9 . . . . 9 E5
Rowley Hill CO7 . . . . 9 E5
Rowney Ave CB10 . . . . . . 44 E2
Rowntree Way CB11 . . . . . 43 D7
Row The
  Hadstock CB1 . . . . 5 B7
  Stratford St M CO7 . . . . . 58 C2
Roxborough CI CO6 . . . . . 132 E3
Roxburghe Rd CO16 . . . . 167 F6
Roxwell Ave CM1 . . . . . . 204 D3
Roxwell Rd
  Chelmsford CM1 . . . . . . 204 C4
  Writtle CM1 . . . . 204 A4
Royal Ct
  Colchester CO4 . . . . 110 E1
  Maldon CM9 . . . . 210 A1
Royal Hospital Sch
  IP9 . . . . 62 D3
Royal Oak Gdns 6
  CM23 . . . . 145 F6
Royal Sq CO7 . . . . 84 F7
Roy Ave IP3 . . . . 18 B5
Roydon Way CO13 . . . . . 170 F6
Royston Dr IP2 . . . . 16 D2
Royston La CB11 . . . . 20 C6
Royston Rd CB11 . . . . . . 42 C5
Ruaton Dr CO16 . . . . 188 C4
Rubens Gate CM1 . . . . . . 205 F7
Rubens Rd IP3 . . . . 18 A1
Rudd Ct CO4 . . . . 110 F1
Rudkin Rd CO4 . . . . 109 F5
Rudlands IP8 . . . . 16 C1
RUDLEY GREEN 220 C2
Rudsdale Way CO3 . . . . . 134 F5
Rue De Jeunes 6
  CM7 . . . . 127 F2
Ruffels Field CM6 . . . . . . 124 E4
Ruffles Rd CB9 . . . . 9 C7
Rugby Rd CO10 . . . . 34 B4
Rugosa CI CO3 . . . . 134 C5
Rumballs Ct CM23 . . . . . . 145 C4
Rumsey Fields CM3 . . . . . 218 F7
Rumsey Row CM1 . . . . . . 204 B1
Runnacles St CM8 . . . . . . 156 C5
Runnacles Way IP11 . . . . 221 B5
Running Mare La
  CM2 . . . . 216 A3
Runsell CI CM3 . . . . 218 F7
RUNSELL GREEN 219 B7
Runsell La CM3 . . . . 218 F8
Runsell View CM3 . . . . . . 219 A7
Rurik Ct CM9 . . . . 220 B8
Rushbury CI IP4 . . . . 18 B8
Rush CI IP4 . . . . 18 F4
Rushes Ct CM23 . . . . 146 A5
RUSH GREEN 188 B6
Rush Green Rd CO16 . . . . 188 B2
Rush La CM22 . . . . 94 C1
Rushleigh Gn CM23 . . . . . 145 D4
Rushleydale CM1 . . . . 205 E6
RUSHLEY GREEN 51 F6
Rushmere CI CO5 . . . . . . 201 D6
Rushmere Pl 11 CB9 . . . . . 9 B8
Rushmere Rd IP4 . . . . 18 B7
RUSHMERE ST ANDREW
  . . . . 18 E7

Rushmere St
  Ipswich IP4, IP5 . . . . 18 D8
  Rushmere St A IP5 . . . . . 18 E8
Rushmoor Dr CM7 . . . . . 128 B1
Ruskin CI CO13 . . . . 170 E7
Ruskin Rd
  Chelmsford CM2 . . . . . . 205 E2
  Ipswich IP1 . . . . 17 F5
Ruskins The CM77 . . . . . . 126 E1
Russell CI CM8 . . . . 194 F7
Russell Ct
  Colchester CO2 . . . . 136 B4
  Felixstowe IP11 . . . . 221 C1
Russell Gdns CM2 . . . . . . 216 A4
RUSSELL GREEN 192 D6
Russell Rd
  Clacton-on-S CO15 . . . . . 189 A3
  Felixstowe IP11 . . . . 221 D2
  Ipswich IP1 . . . . 17 B5
Russell's Rd
  Gosfield CO9 . . . . 76 A1
  Halstead CO9 . . . . 103 B8
Russell Way CM1 . . . . . . 215 E7
Russet CI CM7 . . . . 128 A1
Russets CM2 . . . . 216 D3
Russett CI CB9 . . . . 8 C8
Rustic CI CM7 . . . . 128 C3
Rutherfords CM1 . . . . . . 191 B1
Rutland Ave CO2 . . . . 135 B3
Rutland Ct 11 CB9 . . . . 8 E7
Rutland Gdns CM7 . . . . . 128 A4
Rutland Pl CM7 . . . . 72 B2
Rutland Rd CM1 . . . . 205 A7
Rydal Way CM77 . . . . . . 154 C6
Rydal Wlk IP3 . . . . 18 C2
Ryde Ave CO15 . . . . 189 A8
Rye CI
  Brightlingsea CO7 . . . . . . 165 E1
  Colchester CO3 . . . . 134 E5
  Hatfield Peverel CM3 . . . . 194 A3
  Ipswich IP3 . . . . 18 D4
Rye Ct 3 CB9 . . . . 8 F7
Rye Field The CM3 . . . . . 207 D3
Ryegate Rd CO1 . . . . 135 F7
Rye Grass Way CM7 . . . . 128 B1
Rye Hills CO9 . . . . 103 F8
Rye La CO2 . . . . 162 A4
Rye Mill La CO5 . . . . 158 D4
Ryes La CO10 . . . . 33 A2
Rye St CM23 . . . . 118 F1
Rylands IP9 . . . . 35 A2
Ryle The CM1 . . . . 215 A8
Rylstone Way CB11 . . . . . 43 F8
Rysley CM3 . . . . 207 D4

S

Sacketts Grove Cvn Pk
  CO15 . . . . 187 F2
Sackett's Grove Cvn Pk
  CO16 . . . . 188 A2
Sackville CI CM1 . . . . 204 E3
Sackville Way CO6 . . . . . . 108 D4
Saddle Mews CO3 . . . . . . 134 E6
Saddle Rise CM1 . . . . . . 205 E8
Saddlers CI
  Bishop's Stortford
    CM23 . . . . 145 C4
  Great Notley CM77 . . . . . 154 B7
Sadds Yd CO15 . . . . 188 F3
Sadler CI CO2 . . . . 136 B4
Sadlers CI CO13 . . . . 170 C6
Saffron Bsns Ctr CB10 . . . 22 F2
Saffron CI CM7 . . . . 73 C3
Saffron Croft CM9 . . . . . 209 E2
Saffron Ct CB11 . . . . 22 D1
Saffron Gdns CM7 . . . . . . 73 C3
SAFFRON WALDEN 22 E3
Saffron Walden Cty High
  Sch CB11 . . . . 43 C8
Saffron Walden Mus★
  CB10 . . . . 22 D2
Saffron Waldon Hospl
  CB11 . . . . 23 A2
Saffron Way CO5 . . . . . . 179 C4
Saffron Wlk CM7 . . . . 73 B3
Sagehayes CI IP2 . . . . . . 17 B3
Sage Rd CO2 . . . . 136 A2
Sages CM22 . . . . 94 F5
Sages End Rd CB9 . . . . . . 26 B8
Sage Wlk CO5 . . . . 179 C4
Saines Rd CM6 . . . . 151 E6
St Agnes Way IP5 . . . . . . 18 F6
St Alban's RC High Sch
  IP4 . . . . 18 C7
St Alban's Rd
  Clacton-on-S CO15 . . . . . 189 A3
  Colchester CO3 . . . . 135 D7
St Andrew's Ave
  Colchester CO4 . . . . 136 D6
  Wivenhoe CO7 . . . . 137 A5
St Andrew's CE Prim Sch
  Bulmer CO10 . . . . 32 F3
  Great Yeldham CO9 . . . . . 29 F2
  Halstead CO9 . . . . 77 A3
  Marks Tey CO6 . . . . 132 E3
  Weeley CO16 . . . . 167 F8
  Wormingford CO6 . . . . . . 80 E5
St Andrews CI
  Alresford CO7 . . . . 165 E1
  Ipswich IP4 . . . . 18 D5
St Andrew's Cotts
  CM3 . . . . 194 B3

St Andrews Ct ■3
CO4 . . . .**136** C8
St Andrew's Dr IP9 . . . . . **63** E7
St Andrews Gdns
CO4 . . . .**136** C8
St Andrew's Jun & Inf
Schs CO4 . . . .**136** D7
St Andrews Pl CO7 . . . . .**165** E1
St Andrews Rd
Boreham CM3 . . . .**192** F1
Great Cornard CO10 . . . .**34** A6
Halstead CO9 . . . .**76** F1
St Andrew's Rd
Clacton-on-S CO15 . . . . .**188** E3
Felixstowe IP11 . . . .**221** E5
Hatfield Peverel CM3 . . .**194** A4
Weeley CO16 . . . .**140** F1
St Andrew's Rise CO4 . .**32** E5
St Andrew Wlk IP4 . . . . .**18** F6
St Annes Cl CO6 . . . . . .**131** B2
St Annes Rd CM1 . . . . . .**205** C3
St Anne's Rd CO4 . . . . . .**136** C8
St Anne's Sch CM2 . . . . .**205** A1
St Anns Rd CO15 . . . . . .**188** E4
St Anthonys Cres IP4 . . .**17** F6
St Anthony's Dr CM2 . . .**216** C7
St Aubins Cl CO15 . . . . .**189** B4
St Aubyns Rd IP4 . . . . . .**18** A5
St Augustine Cl CM6 . . .**151** F6
St Augustine Mews
CO1 . . . .**136** A7
St Augustine Rd IP3 . . . .**18** D4
St Augustine's Gdns
IP3 . . . .**18** C3
St Augustine's Way
CM1 . . . .**205** F6
St Austell Rd CO4 . . . . .**110** D2
St Austin's La CO12 . . . .**91** E6
St Bartholomew Cl
CO4 . . . .**110** C3
St Bartholomews La
CO10 . . . .**15** D2
St Benedict's RC Coll
CO3 . . . .**135** B6
St Bernard Rd CO4 . . . .**110** D2
St Botolph's Church Wlk
■7 CO2 . . . .**135** F6
St Botolph's Cir ■8
CO2 . . . .**135** F6
St Botolph's Pl ■1 CB9 . .**8** F7
St Botolph's St ■6
CO2 . . . .**135** F6
St Botolph's Terr ■11
CO13 . . . .**171** C8
St Botolph's Way CB9 . . .**8** F8
St Brelades Ct CO15 . . .**189** B5
St Bride Ct CO4 . . . .**110** D2
St Catherines Cl CO2 . . .**135** D1
St Catherines Ct
CM23 . . . .**145** E7
St Catherine's Ct IP2 . . .**16** E1
St Catherine's Rd
Chelmsford CM1 . . . . . .**204** E2
Long Melford CO10 . . . . .**15** C7
St Cedd's Sch CM1 . . . . .**205** A4
St Christopher Ct
CO4 . . . .**110** D2
St Christopher Rd
CO4 . . . .**110** D2
St Christophers Way
CO15 . . . .**203** G7
St Clair Cl CO15 . . . . . .**188** F8
St Clair's Dr CO16 . . . . .**187** B5
St Clair's Rd CO16 . . . . .**187** B5
St Clare Dr CO3 . . . .**135** A7
St Clare Rd CO3 . . . . . .**135** A6
St Clare's RC Prim Sch
CO16 . . . .**188** B4
St Clement Rd CO4 . . . .**110** D4
St Clements CM6 . . . . . .**70** A2
St Clement's Church La ■18
IP4 . . . .**17** D5
St Clement's Ct CO16 . .**188** B5
St Clement's Hospl IP3 . .**18** B4
St Cleres Hall La
CO16 . . . .**187** B3
St Cleres Way CM3 . . . .**218** D7
St Columb Cl CO4 . . . . .**110** C2
St Cyrus Rd CO4 . . . . . .**110** D3
St Davids Cl CO4 . . . . . .**136** C7
St David's Rd IP3 . . . . . .**18** B3
St Denis Cl CO12 . . . . . .**91** A1
St Dominic Rd CO4 . . . .**110** D2
St Edmundsbury Ho
IP4 . . . .**17** F6
St Edmunds Cl CO12 . . .**91** A1
St Edmunds Croft
CM6 . . . .**123** E1
St Edmund's Ct CO4 . . .**136** C8
St Edmunds Fields
CM6 . . . .**123** E2
St Edmund's Hill CO8,
CO10 . . . .**55** D6
St Edmunds Ho CO4 . . .**136** E8
St Edmunds La
Bures CO8 . . . .**55** F1
Great Dunmow CM6 . . . .**123** E1
St Edmund's Pl IP1 . . . . .**17** C8
St Edmund's Rd
Felixstowe IP11 . . . .**221** D2
Ipswich IP1 . . . .**17** B8
St Fabian's Dr CM1 . . . .**204** E4
St Faith Rd CO4 . . . .**110** D2
St Felix RC Prim Sch
CB9 . . . .**8** D7

St Fillan Rd CO4 . . . . . .**110** D2
St Francis RC Prim Sch
Braintree CM7 . . . .**127** E4
Maldon CM9 . . . .**209** F3
St George's Ave CO12 . . .**91** C2
St George's CE Prim Sch
CO7 . . . .**112** E1
St Georges Cl CM9 . . . .**210** E1
St Georges Cl CO7 . . . .**112** E1
St George's Ct CM8 . . . .**176** F1
St George's Ct ■17 IP1 . .**17** C6
St George's Inf Sch
CO2 . . . .**136** A4
St Georges New Town
Jun Sch CO2 . . . .**136** A5
St George's St IP1 . . . . . .**17** C6
St Giles CE Prim Sch
CO9 . . . .**52** D2
St Giles Cl
Great Maplestead CO9 . . .**52** D2
Maldon CM9 . . . .**209** E2
St Giles Cres CM9 . . . . .**209** E2
St Gregory CE Prim Sch
CO10 . . . .**33** D7
St Gregory's Ct CO10 . . .**33** D8
St Helena Mews CO3 . . .**135** D5
St Helena Rd CO3 . . . . .**135** D5
St Helena Sch CO3 . . . . .**135** D8
St Helens Ave CO15 . . . .**189** A8
St Helen's Gn CO12 . . . .**91** E5
St Helen's La ■7 CO1 . .**135** F7
St Helen's Prim Sch
IP4 . . . .**17** E6
St Helen's St IP4 . . . .**17** D6
St Helier Cl CO15 . . . . .**189** B4
St Ives Cl CO16 . . . .**188** B3
St Ives Rd CO5 . . . .**182** C6
St James' CE Prim Sch
CO1 . . . .**136** A7
St James Ct
Brightlingsea CO7 . . . . .**185** E6
Clacton-on-S CO15 . . . . .**188** E1
Haverhill CB9 . . . .**8** E8
St James's ■5 CO1 . . . .**136** A7
St James' Ct ■5 CO1 . . .**136** A7
St James Pk CM1 . . . . . .**204** D4
St James Rd CM7 . . . . .**127** F5
St James' Rise CO1 . . . .**136** A7
St James's St CO9 . . . . . .**51** F4
St James Way CM23 . . .**145** C3
St Jean Wlk CO5 . . . . . .**179** D6
St John Gdns CO15 . . . .**188** E6
St John Payne RC Comp
Sch CM1 . . . .**205** A6
St Johns Ave CM7 . . . . .**127** F2
St John's Ave
Chelmsford CM2 . . . . . .**216** B8
■12 Colchester CO2 . . . . .**135** F6
St John's CE Prim Sch
Colchester CO4 . . . .**110** D4
Ipswich IP4 . . . .**18** A4
St Johns Cl
Great Chesterford CB10 . . .**3** D2
Saffron Walden CB11 . . . .**43** D7
St John's Cl CO4 . . . . . .**110** D4
St John's Cres CM24 . . .**119** E7
St Johns Ct IP11 . . . . . .**221** D4
St John's Ct
Ipswich IP4 . . . .**18** B6
Tollesbury CM9 . . . .**199** C1
St John's Danbury CE
Prim Sch CM3 . . . .**218** E7
St John's Gn
Colchester CO2 . . . .**135** F6
Writtle CM1 . . . .**204** B1
St John's Green Prim Sch
CO2 . . . .**135** F6
St John's Hospl CM2 . . .**215** F6
St John's La CM24 . . . . .**119** E7
St John's Pl ■14 CO2 . . .**135** F6
St John's Rd
Chelmsford CM2 . . . . . .**216** B8
Clacton-on-S CO16 . . . . .**188** C5
Colchester CO4 . . . .**110** D3
Ipswich IP4 . . . .**18** A6
Stansted Mountfitchet
CM24 . . . .**119** E7
Wivenhoe CO7 . . . .**164** C7
Writtle CM1 . . . .**204** B1
St John's St
Colchester CO2 . . . .**135** F6
Tollesbury CM9 . . . .**199** C1
St John's Terr CM7 . . . . .**72** B2
St John The Baptist CE
Prim Sch CO9 . . . .**78** B8
St Joseph Rd CO4 . . . . .**110** C3
St Joseph's Coll IP2 . . . .**17** A3
St Joseph's Prim Sch
CO10 . . . .**33** E8
St Joseph's RC Prim Sch
Bishop's Stortford
CM23 . . . .**145** E6
Harwich CO12 . . . .**91** B2
St Jude Gdns CO4 . . . . .**110** D2
St Judes Cl CO4 . . . .**110** D2
St Julian Gr CO1 . . . . . .**136** A6
ST LAWRENCE **213** B1
St Lawrence CE Prim Sch
CO2 . . . .**163** F8
St Lawrence Ct ■3
CM7 . . . .**127** F3
St Lawrence Dr CM0 . . .**213** B1
St Lawrence Rd CO4 . . .**110** D2
St Leonards Cl CB11 . . . .**43** A2
St Leonard's Hospl
CO10 . . . .**33** F7
St Leonards Rd IP3 . . . . .**18** B3

St Leonard's Rd CO1 . . .**136** C6
St Leonards School Ho ■8
CO1 . . . .**136** C6
St Leonards Terr ■7
CO1 . . . .**136** C6
St Luke's CE Prim Sch
CO5 . . . .**179** D5
St Luke's Chase CO5 . . .**179** D5
St Luke's Cl CO14 . . . . .**110** D2
St Margaret's CE Prim Sch
Ipswich IP4 . . . .**17** D6
Toppesfield CO9 . . . .**50** C7
St Margaret's Cross
CO4 . . . .**83** F4
St Margaret's Ct
CO16 . . . .**188** C4
St Margaret's Gn ■2
1P4 . . . .**17** D6
St Margaret's Plain ■1
1P4 . . . .**17** D6
St Margaret's Rd CM2 . .**205** E3
St Margaret's Sch
CO9 . . . .**102** D8
St Margaret's St 1P4 . . . .**17** D6
St Mark Dr CO4 . . . .**110** D2
St Marks RC Prim Sch
IP2 . . . .**16** F3
St Marks Rd CO15 . . . . .**188** E4
St Martins Cl CO15 . . . .**188** E4
St Mary Magdalen Ho
CO1 . . . .**136** B6
St Mary's Art Ctr ★
CO1 . . . .**135** E7
St Mary's Cath ★ CM1 . .**205** B2
St Mary's CE Foundation
Prim Sch CM24 . . . . . .**119** E7
St Mary's CE Prim Sch
Ardleigh CO7 . . . .**111** E7
Saffron Walden CB10 . . . .**22** D2
St Mary's Cl
Great Baddow CM2 . . . .**216** F6
Panfield CM7 . . . .**127** B7
St Mary's Cotts CO10 . . . .**2** C5
St Mary's Cres IP11 . . . .**221** D6
St Mary's Ct CO15 . . . . .**188** E3
St Mary's Ct CM9 . . . . .**210** B2
St Mary's Dr CM24 . . . .**119** F5
St Marys Fields CO3 . . .**135** E7
St Mary's La CM9 . . . . .**210** B2
St Marys Mead CM1 . . .**191** A1
St Marys Mews
Frinton-on-S CO13 . . . . .**171** A5
Tollesbury CM9 . . . .**199** D3
St Mary's Pl IP6 . . . .**151** D7
St Mary's RC Prim Sch
IP4 . . . .**17** F7
St Mary's RC Sch
CM23 . . . .**145** E7
St Mary's Rd
Braintree CM7 . . . .**128** B3
Clacton-on-S CO15 . . . . .**188** E4
Frinton-on-S CO13 . . . . .**171** A5
Great Bentley CO7 . . . . .**166** F6
Ipswich IP4 . . . .**17** F7
Kelvedon CO5 . . . .**158** C2
Rivenhall CM8 . . . .**177** B7
St Mary's Sch
Colchester CO3 . . . .**135** C7
Copford CO3 . . . .**133** F5
St Mary's Sq CO5 . . . . .**158** B1
St Marys Terr CO3 . . . . .**135** D6
St Marys View CB10 . . . .**22** E4
St Mary's Villas CM7 . . .**72** B1
St Mary's Wlk CM9 . . . . .**27** B6
St Mathew's Ho ■4 IP1 . .**17** B6
St Matthew's CE Prim Sch
IP1 . . . .**17** B6
St Matthew's St IP1 . . . . .**17** B6
St Michael's CE Jun Sch
CM2 . . . .**216** C2
St Michael's CE Prim Sch
Bishop's Stortford
CM23 . . . .**145** F7
Braintree CM7 . . . .**127** D2
St Michael's Chase
CO6 . . . .**133** D2
St Michaels Ct ■6
CO11 . . . .**86** D4
St Michael's Ct ■11
CM7 . . . .**127** F2
St Michael's Hospl
CM7 . . . .**127** E3
St Michael's La ■2
CM7 . . . .**127** F2
ST MICHAEL'S MEAD
CM23 . . . .**145** C5
St Michaels Mews ■5
CM7 . . . .**127** F2
St Michael's Prim Sch
CO2 . . . .**135** C1
St Michaels Rd CO2 . . . .**135** D1
St Michael's Rd
Braintree CM7 . . . .**127** F2
Chelmsford CM2 . . . . . .**216** B8
Harwich CO12 . . . .**91** B2
Thorpe-le-S CO16 . . . . . .**141** F2
St Michaels Wlk CM2 . . .**216** C2
St Mildreds Rd CM2 . . . .**216** B8
St Monance Way CO4 . . .**110** D2
St Nazaire Rd CM1 . . . . .**204** E6
St Neots Cl CO4 . . . .**110** D2
St Nicholas Cl CM8 . . . .**176** F4
St Nicholas Ct
Harwich CO12 . . . .**91** D6
■15 Ipswich IP1 . . . .**17** C5
St Nicholas Field CM23 . .**92** B8
St Nicholas' Gdns
CM7 . . . .**127** F8

St Nicholas Pas ■16
CO1 . . . .**135** F7
St Nicholas Rd CM8 . . . .**176** F4
St Nicholas Rdbt CO12 . .**91** A4
St Nicholas St
■22 Colchester CO1 . . . .**135** F7
Ipswich IP1 . . . .**17** C5
St Nicholas Way CO6 . . .**131** C3
ST OSYTH **187** B4
St Osyth CE Prim Sch
Clacton-on-S CO15 . . . . .**188** E3
St Osyth CO16 . . . .**187** B4
St Osyth Cl IP2 . . . .**36** F8
ST OSYTH HEATH **167** D1
St Osyth Priory ★
CO16 . . . .**187** A4
St Osyth Rd
Alresford CO7 . . . .**165** D7
Clacton-on-S CO15 . . . . .**188** B3
Little Clacton CO16 . . . . .**168** B1
St Osyth Rd E CO16 . . . .**168** C2
St Osyth Rd W CO16 . . .**168** C1
St Pauls Mews CM9 . . . .**210** C4
St Paul's Rd
Clacton-on-S CO15 . . . . .**189** A3
Colchester CO1 . . . .**135** C8
St Peter's Ave CM9 . . . .**209** F2
St Peter's CE Prim Sch
Coggeshall CO6 . . . . . .**131** B2
Sible Hedingham CO9 . . .**75** D8
St Peters Cl CM9 . . . . . .**211** E6
St Peter's Cl CM7 . . . . .**127** F4
St Peters Coll CM1 . . . .**204** E5
St Peters Ct
Clacton-on-S CO15 . . . . .**189** B5
Clare CO10 . . . .**12** B7
Colchester CO1 . . . .**135** E8
■10 Sudbury CO10 . . . . . .**33** E7
St Peter's Hospl CM9 . . .**209** F2
St Peter's-In-the-Fields
CM7 . . . .**127** F4
St Peter's Rd
Braintree CM7 . . . .**127** F4
Chelmsford CM1 . . . . . .**204** E2
Coggeshall CO6 . . . . . .**131** B2
West Mersea CO5 . . . . .**201** B6
St Peter's St
Colchester CO1 . . . .**135** F8
Ipswich IP1 . . . .**17** C5
St Peters View CO5 . . . . .**51** D1
St Peter's Wlk CM9 . . . .**196** B3
St Peter's Wlk CM7 . . . .**127** F4
St Philip's Priory Sch
CM2 . . . .**216** A8
St Philomena's Sch
CO13 . . . .**170** F5
St Pius X RC Prim Sch
CM1 . . . .**204** F6
St Runwalds St ■9
CO1 . . . .**135** F7
St Saviour Cl CO4 . . . . .**110** D2
St Stephens La ■13 IP1 . .**17** C6
St Swithins Cotts
CM2 . . . .**217** C3
St Teresa's RC Prim Sch
CO3 . . . .**134** E5
St Thomas Cl CO4 . . . . .**110** D2
St Thomas More RC Prim
Sch CB11 . . . .**43** E8
St Thomas More's RC Prim
Sch CO1 . . . .**136** A7
St Valery CM22 . . . .**148** C7
St Vincent Chase
CM7 . . . .**128** B5
St Vincent Rd CO15 . . . .**188** E1
St Vincents Rd CM2 . . . .**216** B8
Sainty Cl CO7 . . . .**164** C8
Salamanca Way CO2 . . .**135** C2
Salary Cl CO4 . . . .**110** F1
Salcombe Rd CM7 . . . . .**128** C1
Salcott Creek Ct CM7 . . .**128** D1
SALCOTT-CUM-VIRLEY
CM9 . . . .**199** B7
Salcott St CM9 . . . .**199** C8
Salehurst Rd IP3 . . . .**18** E3
Salerno Cres CO2 . . . . .**135** C2
Salerno Way CM1 . . . . .**204** E6
Saling Hall Gdns ★
CM7 . . . .**126** A8
Salisbury Ave CO3 . . . . .**135** E6
Salisbury Cl CM23 . . . . .**145** F5
Salisbury Ct
Clacton-on-S CO15 . . . . .**189** D5
■2 Haverhill CB9 . . . .**8** F7
Salisbury Rd
Clacton-on-S CO15 . . . . .**189** D5
Ipswich IP3 . . . .**18** A4
Salisbury Terr ■1 CO10 . .**33** E8
Sallows Cl IP1 . . . .**16** F7
Salmet Cl IP2 . . . .**17** A3
Salmon Cl CO3 . . . .**134** F4
Salmon Par CM1 . . . . . .**205** B3
Salmons Cl CM6 . . . . . .**151** A5
Salmon's Cnr CO6 . . . . .**132** A3
Salmon's La CO6 . . . . . .**132** A4
Saltcote Maltings
CM9 . . . .**210** E4
Salter Cl CO3 . . . .**135** E7
Salter Pl CM2 . . . .**205** F2
Salters CM23 . . . .**145** C4
Salters Hall Mews
CO10 . . . .**33** D7
Salter's Mdw CM9 . . . . .**198** D4
Salthouse St ■16 IP4 . . . .**17** D5
Saltings Cres CO5 . . . . .**201** D4
Salvia Cl CO16 . . . .**188** C4
Samford Cl IP9 . . . .**62** D7
Samford Ct IP9 . . . .**61** D7

Samford Pl IP8 . . . .**16** B6
Samian Cl CM9 . . . .**209** F5
Samphire Cl CM8 . . . . . .**176** D3
Sampson Dr CO10 . . . . . .**15** D8
Sampson's La CO5 . . . . .**182** F3
Samson's Cnr CO7 . . . . .**185** E8
Samsons Cl CO7 . . . . . .**185** E8
Samson's Cnr CO7 . . . . .**165** D1
Samson's Rd CO7 . . . . . .**165** E1
Samuel Ct IP4 . . . .**17** D6
Samuel Manor CM2 . . . .**205** F3
Sanderling Gdns CM9 . . .**210** C5
Sanders Cl CM24 . . . . . .**119** D7
Sanders Dr CO3 . . . .**135** B7
Sanderson Mews CO5 . . .**163** F8
Sandford Cl CO7 . . . . . .**164** C8
Sandford Mill Rd
Chelmsford CM2 . . . . . .**205** F2
Chelmsford CM2 . . . . . .**206** B2
Great Baddow CM2 . . . .**217** C8
Sandford Rd CM2 . . . . . .**205** E3
Sandhills Cotts CM7 . . . . .**73** D1
Sandhurst Ave IP3 . . . . . .**17** F4
Sandle Rd CM23 . . . . . .**146** A7
Sandling Cres IP4 . . . . . .**18** E5
Sandlings The IP3 . . . . . .**18** D1
Sandmartin Cres CO3 . . .**134** C4
SANDON **217** D6
Sandon Brook Manor
CM2 . . . .**217** E8
Sandon Brook Pl
CM2 . . . .**217** E8
Sandon Cl CO6 . . . .**109** C7
SANDON GREEN **217** C6
Sandon Hall Bridleway
CM2 . . . .**217** D4
Sandon Hill CM3 . . . . . .**172** A6
Sandon Sch The CM2 . . .**217** B6
Sandown Cl CO15 . . . . .**189** A8
Sandpiper Cl
Colchester CO4 . . . .**137** A8
Haverhill CB9 . . . .**9** C8
Heybridge CM9 . . . .**210** C5
Sandpiper Ct ■16
CM23 . . . .**145** F6
Sandpiper Rd IP2 . . . . . .**16** E2
Sandpiper Wlk CM2 . . . .**216** C6
Sandpit Cl IP4 . . . .**18** F5
Sandpit La ■9 CM7 . . . .**127** D4
Sandra Ct ■5 CO2 . . . . .**135** E6
Sandringham Cl IP2 . . . . .**16** F2
Sandringham Ct CO10 . . .**34** A7
Sandringham Dr CO2 . . .**136** A4
Sandringham Gdns ■6
CM23 . . . .**145** E5
Sandringham Pl CM2 . . .**205** C4
Sandwich Cl CM7 . . . . . .**127** E6
Sandwich Rd
Brightlingsea CO7 . . . . .**185** F8
Clacton-on-S CO15 . . . . .**203** J8
Sandy Hill CO6 . . . .**80** D5
Sandyhill La IP3 . . . .**17** E1
Sandy La
Bulmer CO10 . . . .**32** F5
Sudbury CO10 . . . .**33** B5
Santiago Cotts CO7 . . . .**185** E6
Sapling Pl IP4 . . . .**18** E5
Sapphire Cl IP1 . . . .**16** D8
Saran Ct CO7 . . . .**137** A2
Sarcel CM77 . . . .**129** C6
Sargeant Cl CO2 . . . . . .**136** B3
Sarre Way CO7 . . . .**185** E8
Sassoon Way ■3 CM9 . . .**210** A1
Saturn Rd IP1 . . . .**16** D8
Saul's Ave CM8 . . . .**195** A8
Sauls Bridge Cl CM8 . . .**195** A8
Saunders Ave CM7 . . . . .**127** E3
Saunders Cl CM22 . . . . . .**94** C1
Savernake Rd CM1 . . . . .**204** E1
Saville Cl CB11 . . . .**65** C4
Saville St CO14 . . . .**144** C1
Savill Rd CO2 . . . .**136** C2
Sawkins Ave CM2 . . . . . .**216** D6
Sawkins Cl
Abberton CO5 . . . .**163** B2
Chelmsford CM2 . . . . . .**216** D6
Sawkins Gdns CM2 . . . .**216** D6
Sawney Brook CM1 . . . .**204** A1
Sawpit La CM23 . . . .**92** D7
Sawston Cl IP2 . . . .**17** A2
Sawyers Cl ■3 IP9 . . . . . .**35** A1
Sawyer's Rd CM9 . . . . . .**197** C5
Saxmundham Way
CO16 . . . .**188** A3
Saxon Bank CM7 . . . . . .**128** B2
Saxon Cl
Colchester CO3 . . . .**134** F4
Halstead CO9 . . . .**76** F2
Saxon Ct CM9 . . . .**210** A3
Saxon Dr CM8 . . . .**176** E3
Saxon La IP8 . . . .**35** D7
Saxon Way
Chelmsford CM1 . . . . . .**205** B7
Holland-on-S CO15 . . . . .**189** F6
Maldon CM9 . . . .**210** B1
Point Clear B CO16 . . . . .**185** F3
Saffron Walden CB11 . . . .**22** C1
Saxstead Dr CO16 . . . . .**188** A4
Sayers Ho CO7 . . . .**185** F6
Saywell Brook CM2 . . . .**206** A2
Scarfe's Cnr CO6 . . . .**82** B4
Scarfe Way CO4 . . . . . .**136** E6
Scarletts Chase CO6 . . .**108** E6
Scarletts Cl CM8 . . . . . .**195** A7
Scarletts Rd CO1 . . . . . .**136** C4
Sceptre Cl CM9 . . . .**199** D2
Scholars Mews CM9 . . . .**196** B3

School Barn Cotts
CO10 . . . . 13 E7
School Chase CO9 . . . 103 E8
School Cl IP9 . . . . 35 A1
School Ct CO12 . . . . . . 91 D4
Schoolfield
Birdbrook CO9 . . . . 28 A6
Glemsford CO10 . . . . 2 B5
SCHOOL GREEN 74 A3
School Hill
Birch CO2. . . . . 161 A4
Washbrook IP8 . . . . 35 F8
School Ho
13 Colchester CO1 . . . 136 A6
Shalford CM7 . . . . 100 E5
School La
Birch CO2. . . . . 161 A3
Brantham CO11 . . . . . . 60 D1
Broomfield CM1 . . . . . 191 B1
Chelmsford CM1 . . . . . 204 F8
Dedham CO7 . . . . 84 F7
Duddenhoe End CB11 . . 41 A7
East Bergholt CO7 . . . . . 59 B3
Great Bentley CO7 . . . . 166 A8
Great Horkesley CO6. . . 82 A2
Great Leighs CM3 . . . . 173 F8
Great Wigborough CO5 . . 181 F3
Haverhill CB9 . . . . 8 E7
Henham CM22 . . . . . . 94 F5
Lawford CO11 . . . . . . 86 A2
Little Horkesley CO6 . . 81 D5
Mistley CO11 . . . . 86 F4
Newport CB11 . . . . . . 42 F1
Stratford St M CO7 . . . 58 D2
Takeley CM22 . . . . . . 121 D6
West Bergholt CO6 . . . 108 E4
School Mews CO6 . . . 130 F2
School Rd
Blackmore End CM7 . . 74 C2
Colchester CO2 . . . . . 136 A2
Copford CO6 . . . . 133 D3
Elmstead Market CO7 . . 138 A4
Frinton-on-S CO13 . . . 170 E5
Great Oakley CO12 . . . 116 C3
Great Totham CM9. . . . 196 B3
Langham CO4 . . . . . . 83 E4
Little Horkesley CO6 . . 81 D4
Little Maplestead CO9 . . 77 B8
Little Totham CM9 . . . 197 B3
Little Yeldham CO9. . . . 30 D3
Messing CO5 . . . . 159 D2
Pentlow CO10 . . . . . . 13 F6
Rayne CM7. . . . . 153 E8
Shotley Gate IP9 . . . . 91 B8
Sible Hedingham CO9 . . 75 D8
Silver End CM8 . . . . . 156 E3
Tattingstone IP9 . . . . 36 D1
Tendring CO16 . . . . . 140 E6
Wickham Bishops CM8 . . 195 F5
Wickham St P CO9 . . . 53 C5
School St
Foxearth CO10 . . . . . 14 D6
Great Chesterford CB10 . . 3 D2
Stoke-by-N CO6 . . . . . 56 D5
Sudbury CO10 . . . . . . 33 E7
School View CM7 . . . 127 E2
School View Rd CM1 . . 204 F3
School Villas
Great Easton CM6 . . . . 123 A4
Henham CM6 . . . . 95 F2
Lindsell CM6 . . . . 97 F4
Takeley CM22 . . . . . . 121 C6
School Wlk CM7 . . . . 127 F3
Schreiber Rd IP4 . . . . 18 B7
Scofield Ct CO10. . . . 34 A6
Scotland St CO6 . . . . 56 E6
SCOTLAND STREET . . 56 D6
SCOT'S GREEN 204 F8
Scott Ave CM7 . . . . . 73 D6
Scott Cl CM7 . . . . . . 155 A8
Scott Dr CO3 . . . . . . 134 F6
Scott Rd
Bishop's Stortford
CM23 . . . . 145 A6
Ipswich IP3 . . . . 18 B1
Scotts Wlk CM1. . . . . 204 D5
Scraley Rd CM9. . . . . 210 E6
Scrips CO6 . . . . 157 F6
Scrip's Rd CO6 . . . . . 158 A7
Scrivener Dr IP2. . . . 16 C2
Scurvy Hall La
Howe Street CM3 . . . . 173 C1
Little Waltham CM3 . . 191 B8
Scylla Cl CM9 . . . . . . 210 C6
Scythe Way CO3 . . . . 134 F4
Seabrook Gdns CM3 . . 192 F1
Seabrook Rd CM2. . . . 217 A6
Seabrooks The CO10. . . 2 B3
Sea Cornflower Way
CO15 . . . . 203 G7
Sea Cres CO15 . . . . . 203 F6
Seafield Ave CO11 . . . 87 B4
Seafield Rd CO12 . . . 91 B2
Seafields Gdns CO15 . . 189 C5
Seafields Rd CO15 . . . 189 C5
Sea Flowers Way
CO15 . . . . 203 G7
Seagers CM9. . . . . . . 196 B4
Sea Glebe Way CO15 . . 203 G7
Sea Holly Way CO15 . . 203 G6
Sea King Cres CO4 . . . 110 B4
Sea Lavender Way
CO15 . . . . 203 G7
Sea Pink Way CO15 . . 203 G6
Sea Rd IP11 . . . . 221 D4
Searle Cl CM2 . . . . . . 216 D7
Searles Cotts CO6 . . . 133 C4
Searle Way CO6 . . . . . 108 B1

Sea Rosemary Way
CO15 . . . . 203 G7
Sea Shell Way CO15. . . 203 G6
Sea Thistle Way
CO15 . . . . 203 G7
Seaton Cl CO11 . . . . . 86 B3
Seaton Rd IP11 . . . . . 221 D5
Seaview Ave
Little Oakley CO12. . . . 117 C7
West Mersea CO5 . . . . 201 E6
Seaview Ct CO15 . . . . 189 A2
Seaview Cvn Pk CO5 . . 201 E6
Seaview Gdns CO7 . . . 185 F7
Seaview Hts CO14. . . . 171 C7
Sea View Par CM0 . . . 213 C1
Sea View Prom CM0 . . 213 B1
Seaview Rd
Brightlingsea CO7 . . . . 185 F7
Seawick CO16 . . . . . . 203 B7
Seaview Terr CO16. . . . 186 A3
Sea Way CO15 . . . . . 203 F6
SEAWICK 203 C7
Seawick Rd CO16 . . . . 203 B6
Sebastian Cl CO4 . . . . 136 F7
Seckford Ct IP4 . . . . . 18 F5
Second Ave
Chelmsford CM1 . . . . 205 B5
Clacton-on-S CO15 . . . 189 B4
Frinton-on-S CO13 . . . 170 E3
Glemsford CO10 . . . . . 2 C5
Halstead CO9 . . . . . . 77 B1
Harwich CO12 . . . . . . 91 C3
Seawick CO16 . . . . . . 203 C6
Stansted Mountfitchet
CM24 . . . . 120 B2
Sudbury CO10 . . . . . . 15 F1
Trimley St M IP11 . . . . 221 A7
Walton-on-t-N CO14 . . 144 E3
Weeley CO16 . . . . . . 167 F8
Secundus Dr CO2 . . . . 135 F3
Seden Ct CO15. . . . . . 169 B1
Sedgefield Way CM7 . . 128 B1
Sedop Cl CB11. . . . . . 43 D7
Seedbed Ctr CO4 . . . . 110 C4
Seedfield The CO5 . . . 201 B6
Selby Cl CO2 . . . . . . 135 D1
Seldon Rd CO5 . . . . . 179 D5
Selhurst Ct CO14. . . . 170 F7
Selkirk Rd IP4. . . . . . 18 B8
Selsey Ave CO15 . . . . 203 I8
Selvale Way IP11 . . . . 221 C4
Selwyn Cl IP2 . . . . . . 17 C4
Septimus Dr CO4 . . . . 110 A5
Serenus Ct 12 IP1. . . . 17 C5
Serpentine Rd IP3 . . . 18 C2
Serpentine Wlk CO1 . . 109 E1
Servite Ho IP4. . . . . . 17 F6
Seven Ash Gn CM1. . . 205 C5
Seven Devils La CB11 . . 43 D6
SEVEN STAR GREEN . . 133 F8
Seventh Ave
Chelmsford CM1 . . . . 205 B6
Stansted Mountfitchet
CM24 . . . . 120 B2
Severalls La CO4. . . . . 110 B6
Severn Rd
Clacton-on-S CO15 . . . 188 F5
Ipswich IP3 . . . . 17 F5
SEWARDS END 23 E1
Sewell's La CO10 . . . . 13 B1
Sexton Cl CO2 . . . . . . 163 B8
Sextons La CM6. . . . . 178 B1
Seymore Dr CB9 . . . . 8 D7
Seymour Rd
Ipswich IP2 . . . . 17 C4
Jaywick IP17 . . . . 187 F1
Seymour St CM2. . . . . 205 A4
Shackleton Cl CO12. . . 90 F1
Shackleton Gdns
CM23 . . . . 145 E6
Shackleton Rd IP3. . . . 18 B3
Shackleton Sq IP3. . . . 18 B3
SHAFTENHOE END . . . 39 B8
Shaftenhoe End Rd
SG8 . . . . 39 B8
Shaftesbury Ave CO12. . 91 B4
Shaftesbury Ct 10 IP9 . . 8 E7
Shaftesbury Sq 4 IP4 . . 17 D5
Shafto Rd IP1 . . . . . . 16 E8
Shair La
Great Bentley CO7. . . . 167 B8
Weeley CO16 . . . . . . 140 B2
Shakespeare Cl CM7 . . 155 A7
Shakespeare Dr CM23 . . 210 A1
Shakespeare Rd CO3. . . 134 F6
Shakeston Cl CM1 . . . 215 B8
Shalfleet Ct CO15 . . . 188 F8
SHALFORD 100 E7
SHALFORD GREEN . . . 100 C3
Shalford Lo CM1. . . . . 205 B8
Shalford Prim Sch
CM7 . . . . 100 E5
Shalford Rd CM77. . . . 126 C3
Shalom Hall★ CO11 . . 181 B8
Shamrock Ave IP2. . . . 16 E4
Shamrock Cl CM9. . . . 199 D2
Shamrock Ho CO15 . . . 203 J8
Shangani Rd CM23. . . . 145 F5
Shanklin Cl CO15 . . . 189 A8
Shannon Cl CB9 . . . . 9 D7
Shannon Rd IP3 . . . . . 38 A8
Shardelow Ave CM1. . . 206 A8
Shardloes Bsns Pk
CM77 . . . . 156 A6
Shardlowe's Farm CO9. . 75 E1
Sharlands Row CM9. . . 199 A8
Sharpington Cl CM2 . . 216 C3
Shatters Rd CO2 . . . . 161 A1

Shaw Cl CO13 . . . . . . 170 F7
Shaw Dr CM7. . . . . . . 73 D7
Shawlands Ave CO10. . . 34 B7
Shaw Rd
Long Melford CO10 . . . . 15 D8
Witham CM8 . . . . 176 F5
Shearers The CM3 . . . 145 C4
Shearers Way CM3. . . . 192 F1
Shearman St 1 CB9 . . . 9 A7
Shears Cres CO5. . . . . 201 D5
Shears Ct CO5 . . . . . . 201 D5
Sheds La CB10. . . . . . 22 E2
Sheene Gr CM7 . . . . . 128 D5
Sheepbarn La CM9. . . . 196 F2
Sheepcote La CO5 . . . 92 E3
Sheepcotes CM2. . . . . 206 B5
Sheepcotes La
Little Waltham CM3 . . . 191 C7
Silver End CM8 . . . . . 156 E5
Sheepcot Rd CO9 . . . . 51 F3
Sheepen Pl CO3 . . . . . 135 E8
Sheepen Rd CO3. . . . . 135 D8
Sheepshead Hill CO10. . 34 C6
Sheering Wlk CO2 . . . . 135 F2
Sheerwater Mews
CO4 . . . . 137 A8
Sheldrake Dr IP2 . . . . 16 E2
Sheldrick Link CM2 . . . 206 B4
Shellcroft CO6 . . . . . . 77 F1
Shellduck Cres CM77. . . 154 C5
Shelley Ave
Great Cornard CO10 . . . 34 B6
Tiptree CO5 . . . . 179 E5
Shelley La CO16 . . . . . 168 F2
Shelley Rd
Chelmsford CM2 . . . . 205 D2
Clacton-on-S CO16. . . . 188 A5
Colchester CO3 . . . . . 134 F6
Shelley St 5 IP2. . . . . 17 C4
Shelley Wlk CM7. . . . . 155 A8
Sheltons The CO13. . . . 170 B6
Shenley Rd IP3 . . . . . 18 B1
Shepherd Dr
Colchester CO4 . . . . . 109 E3
Ipswich IP8. . . . . 16 C2
Shepherds La CM23 . . . 145 C4
Shepherds Croft CO3 . . 134 D5
Shepherds Ct 15 CB9. . . 8 E7
Shepherds La CO6 . . . . 2 A6
Shepherds Way CB10 . . 22 F2
Sheppard Cl CO16 . . . 188 D6
Sheppard Dr CM2. . . . 206 A4
Sherborne Rd CM1. . . . 205 D5
Sherbourne Ct CO13 . . 170 F7
Sherbourne Rd CO4. . . 136 F7
Sheridan Wlk CO3 . . . 134 F6
Sheriffs Way CO15 . . . 188 F7
Sheringham Dr CM7 . . 154 C7
Sherrington Rd IP1. . . . 17 A4
Sherwood Cl CO4. . . . 136 D7
Sherwood Ct 20 CM23 . . 145 F7
Sherwood Dr
Chelmsford CM1 . . . . 204 D1
Clacton-on-S CO15. . . . 188 E6
Sherwood Way CO5. . . 158 D4
Shetland Cl IP4. . . . . . 18 A8
Shetland Rd CB9. . . . . 9 D8
Shewell Wlk CO1 . . . . 135 E7
Shillito Cl CO3. . . . . . 134 F3
Shimbrooks CM3 . . . . 173 F7
Ship La CO11. . . . . . . 87 E3
Ship Launch Rd IP3 . . . 17 E3
Shipwrights The CO7 . . 164 B8
Shipyard Est CO7 . . . . 185 F5
Shire Cl CM1 . . . . . . 205 F7
Shire Ct CB9 . . . . 8 E7
Shire Hall Yd 10 IP4 . . . 17 D5
Shire Hill CB11 . . . . . 22 F1
Shire Hill Ind Est CB11. . 22 F1
Shire La CB10. . . . . . . 44 A8
Shires Cl CM77 . . . . . 154 B7
Shirley Ct CO15 . . . . . 188 A1
Shoebridge's Hill CO7. . 84 E6
Shoemenders La CM0. . 214 E4
Shop La CO5 . . . . 184 F3
Shop Rd CO11 . . . . . . 113 B6
Shops The CM8 . . . . . 156 D4
Shorefields CO15 . . . . 189 B4
Shoreham Rd CO15 . . . 203 I8
Shore La
Bradfield CO11 . . . . . 87 E3
Harkstead IP9 . . . . . . 63 A2
Shortcroft CM23. . . . . 146 D7
Short Cut Rd CO1 . . . . 135 E7
Short La CO13 . . . . . . 170 C3
Shortlands IP8 . . . . . . 16 D1
Shortlands PI CM23 . . . 145 F8
Shortridge Ct CM8. . . . 194 F8
Short Wyre St 24 CO1 . . 135 F7
Shotley La
Clacton-on-S CO16. . . . 188 A3
Felixstowe IP11 . . . . . 221 B4
Ipswich IP2. . . . . 16 C2
SHOTLEY GATE 91 A8
Shotley Mews CB9. . . . 8 C8
Shropshire Cl CM2. . . . 216 F5
Shrubbery Cl IP11 . . . 221 D4
SHRUB END 135 A3
Shrub End Rd CO3 . . . 135 B4
Shrubland Ct CO15. . . . 189 B5
Shrubland Dr IP4. . . . 18 F5
Shrubland Rd
6 Colchester CO2 . . . 136 A6
New Mistley CO11. . . . 87 A3
Shrublands CB10 . . . . 22 E3
Shrublands Cl CM2 . . . 205 C2
SHUDY CAMPS 7 B6

Shums Hill CO13 . . . . 170 C8
Shut La CO6 . . . . 105 B6
Siam Pl CO1. . . . . . . 33 E7
SIBLE HEDINGHAM . . . 51 E1
SIBLEY'S GREEN 97 B5
Sidegate Ave IP4 . . . . 18 A8
Sidegate La IP4 . . . . . 18 A8
Sidegate Prim Sch IP4. . 18 A8
Sidings Pl 3 CM7. . . . . 128 A2
Sidings The CO10 . . . . 2 C2
Sidmouth Rd CM1 . . . 205 E6
Sidney Pl CM1 . . . . . . 206 A7
Sidney Terr CM23 . . . . 145 F6
Siena Mews CO2. . . . . 136 B4
Siggin's La CB1 . . . . . 5 D7
Silcock Cl CO4. . . . . . 110 C2
Silcott St CO7 . . . . . . 185 E6
Silent St IP1 . . . . 17 C5
Silk Factory Row CO10. . 2 B6
Silk St IP4 . . . . 17 D6
Silks Way CM7 . . . . . 127 F2
Sillett Cl CO16 . . . . . . 188 D6
Siloam Pl IP3 . . . . . . 17 E4
Silvanus Cl CO3. . . . . 135 D6
Silverdale Ct CO15 . . . 189 B5
Silver Dawn Touring Pk
CO16 . . . . 188 A4
SILVER END 156 E4
Silver End Prim Sch
CM8 . . . . 156 E3
Silver Leys IP9 . . . . . . 60 E6
Silver Row CB11 . . . . . 42 F5
Silver St
Maldon CM9. . . . . . . 209 F3
Silver End CM8 . . . . . 156 E4
Stansted Mountfitchet
CM24 . . . . 119 D6
Wethersfield CM7 . . . . 73 B3
Silverthorn Cl CO5. . . . 179 F5
Silverthorne Cl CO2. . . 136 A3
Silvester Way CM2. . . . 206 B4
Simmonds Way CM3 . . 218 F8
Simon Ho IP4 . . . . . . 17 F6
Simons Flats CO5 . . . . 179 C7
Simons La CO1 . . . . . . 136 B6
Simpson Cl IP3. . . . . . 17 F1
Sims Cl CO6 . . . . 105 B7
Sinclair Cl CO4. . . . . . 109 F2
Sinclair Dr IP2 . . . . . . 17 C3
Singer Ave CO15 . . . . 203 E7
Singleton Ct CO10 . . . 34 A5
Sinnington End CO4 . . . 110 C4
Sioux Cl CO4 . . . . . . 110 C4
Sir Alf Ramsey Way
IP1 . . . . 17 B5
Sir Charles Lucas Arts Coll
CO4 . . . . 136 E8
Sirdar Rd IP1. . . . . . . 17 A4
Sir Isaac's Wlk CO1 . . . 135 F7
Siskin Cl CO4. . . . . . . 136 F8
Sittang Cl CO2 . . . . . 135 C1
Sitwell Cl CO11 . . . . . 86 B4
Siward Rd CM8 . . . . . 194 D8
Six Bells Ct CM7 . . . . 127 F5
Sixth Ave
Chelmsford CM1 . . . . 205 B6
Stansted Mountfitchet
CM24 . . . . 120 C3
Sixth Form Coll The
CO1. . . . . 135 E7
Skate's Hill CO10 . . . . 2 B2
Skeins Way CB11 . . . . 65 C4
Skelmersdale Rd
CO15 . . . . 188 F3
Skelton Cl CO11 . . . . . 86 C4
Skerry Rise CM1 . . . . 205 B7
Skiddaw Cl CM77 . . . . 154 D7
Skighaugh CO12 . . . . 141 C8
Skinner's La CM2 . . . . 216 B3
Skinners St CM23 . . . . 145 C4
Skipper Ct CM7 . . . . . 154 F8
Skipper Rd IP8 . . . . . . 36 E8
Skitts Hill CM7. . . . . . 128 A1
Skitts Hill Ind Est
CM7 . . . . 128 B1
Skreens Ct CM1. . . . . 204 D4
SKYE GREEN 131 E1
Sky Hall Hill CO4. . . . . 83 D7
Skylark La IP8 . . . . . . 16 C2
Skylark Wlk CM2. . . . . 216 B5
Skyrmans Fee CO13. . . 170 E6
Sladburys La CO15 . . . 189 D8
Sladbury's La CO15 . . . 189 C6
Slade Rd CO15. . . . . . 189 C6
Slades Cl CO10 . . . . . . 2 C5
Slade's La CM2 . . . . . 216 A3
Slade St 14 IP4 . . . . . 17 D5
Slade The CB10 . . . . . 22 F1
Slate CO9 . . . . 76 F1
Slaters Cl CO13 . . . . . 170 E6
Sleaford Cl IP2 . . . . . . 17 A3
Slipes Cnr CO11 . . . . . 87 C1
Sloeberry Rd IP3 . . . . 38 C7
Sloe Hill CO9 . . . . . . 76 C2
Slough Farm Rd CO9 . . 76 D2
Slough House Cl
CM7 . . . . 128 D1
Slough La
Ardleigh CO7 . . . . . . 111 D4
Cock Clarks CM3 . . . . 219 D3
Elmstead Market CO7 . . 137 B6
Slough Rd
Brantham CO7, CO11. . . 60 D2
Danbury CM3 . . . . . . 219 C3
Slushy La IP9. . . . . . . 63 B3
Smaley La CO10 . . . . . 15 C8
Smallbridge Entry CO8. . 80 D8

Smallwood Rd CO2 . . . 135 B3
Smart St 11 1P4. . . . . 17 D5
Smeaton Cl CO4 . . . . . 110 C5
Smeetham Hall La
CO10 . . . . 32 E6
Smithers Cl IP9 . . . . . 35 A1
Smithers Dr CM2 . . . . 217 A6
Smiths Cotts CM22. . . . 93 E4
SMITH'S END 39 A8
Smith's End La SG8 . . . 39 A8
Smiths Field
Colchester CO1 . . . . . 136 C5
Rayne CM77. . . . . . . 126 F2
Smiths Gn CB11 . . . . . 68 C6
SMITH'S GREEN
Steeple Bumpstead . . . 26 F4
Takeley. 148 D7
Smith's Green Cotts
CB9 . . . . 27 A5
Smythe Cl CO15 . . . . . 188 C6
SMYTHE'S GREEN 160 C2
Smythies Ave CO1 . . . 136 A7
Snakes La
Stansted Mountfitchet
CM24 . . . . 93 F2
Ugley CM22 . . . . 94 A2
Snape Cl CO16 . . . . . . 188 A4
Snape Way CO13. . . . . 170 F7
Sneating Hall La
CO13 . . . . 169 E8
Sneezor Way CM8 . . . . 194 E7
Snelling Gr CM2 . . . . . 216 F6
Sniveller's La CO5 . . . 157 D3
Snowberry Ct CM7. . . . 128 B3
Snowberry Gr CO2 . . . 136 A3
Snowcroft IP9. . . . . . . 35 A1
Snowdon Ct 5 CB9. . . . 8 E6
Snowdon Rd IP2 . . . . . 17 B2
Snowdrop Cl
Bishop's Stortford
CM23 . . . . 145 C6
Chelmsford CM1 . . . . 205 E7
Witham CM8 . . . . 176 E4
Snow Hill La CO6 . . . . 57 D5
Snowley Par CM23 . . . . 119 B1
Snows Way CO11 . . . . 86 D8
Soane St IP4. . . . . . . 17 D6
Sodbury Ho CO15 . . . . 188 F5
Soft Rd CO10 . . . . 31 F5
Soils The CO12 . . . . . 116 C5
Solway Ct 3 CO4 . . . . 136 E8
Somerset Cl CO2 . . . . 135 B3
Somerset Ct 9 CB9 . . . 8 E7
Somerset Pl CM1 . . . . 205 A7
Somerset Rd IP4 . . . . . 17 F8
Somerset Way CO15 . . 187 F1
Somers Rd CO3 . . . . . 135 A4
Somerton Ct IP11 . . . . 221 F4
Sonell Ct CO7 . . . . . . 137 B2
Songers Cotts CO4. . . . 83 B6
Sorrel Cl
Colchester CO4 . . . . . 109 C2
Ipswich IP2 . . . . 16 F3
Sorrel Gr CM77 . . . . . 154 B7
Sorrel Horse Mews 22
1P4 . . . . 17 D5
Sorrell Cl
Goldhanger CM9 . . . . 211 E7
Little Waltham CM3 . . 191 B6
Sorrel Wlk CB9 . . . . . 8 D8
South Area IP1 . . . . . . 16 C7
Southborough Rd
CM2 . . . . 216 A8
South Cl
Halstead CO9. . . . . . . 103 E8
Ipswich IP4 . . . . 17 E8
St Osyth CO16 . . . . . 187 B4
Southcliff CO14. . . . . . 171 C7
Southcliff Ct
Clacton-on-S CO15. . . . 189 A4
Walton-on-t-N CO14 . . 171 C7
Southcliff Hall CO15 . . 188 F2
Southcliff Pk CO15 . . . 189 A4
Southcliff Prom CO14. . 171 C7
Southcote Rd CM8 . . . 176 F4
Southcroft Cl CO13 . . . 170 C6
Southend Rd
Great Baddow CM2 . . . 217 B4
Howe Green CM2 . . . . 217 D2
Woodham Mortimer
CM9 . . . . 219 C5
Southey Cl CM9. . . . . 210 D4
SOUTHEY GREEN 75 D5
Southfield CB10 . . . . . 3 A3
Southfields CO7 . . . . . 84 F6
Southgate Cres CO5 . . . 179 C5
Southgate Gdns CO10 . . 15 C6
Southgate Rd IP8. . . . . 16 B1
Southgates Ind Pk
CB10 . . . . 43 F7
Southgate St CO10. . . . 15 C6
South Gn CB11 . . . . . 67 D4
SOUTH GREEN 164 A5
Southgreen Gdns
CO16 . . . . 188 C4
South Green Rd CO5 . . 163 F3
SOUTH HEATH 167 A3
South Heath Rd CO7. . . 166 F3
South Hill IP11 . . . . . 221 D3
South Hill Cl CM3 . . . . 218 C4
South Ho CO13 . . . . . 170 F4
Southland Cl CO4. . . . 110 C1
Southlands Chase
CM2 . . . . 217 E2
Southmill Ct CM23 . . . 146 A6

Southmill Rd CM23 ......146 A5
Southmill Trad Ctr
　CM23 ....146 A6
South Primrose Hill
　CM1 ....204 F3
South Rd
　Bishop's Stortford
　CM23 ....146 A4
　Saffron Walden CB11......22 E1
　Takeley CM22 ....148 C8
South St Commercial Ctr
　1 CM23................145 F6
South St
　Bishop's Stortford
　CM23 ....145 F6
　Braintree CM7 ....127 F2
　Colchester CO2 ....135 E6
　Great Chesterford CB10 ....3 D2
　Great Waltham CM3 .....190 E7
　Ipswich IP1 ....17 B7
　Manningtree CO11........86 D4
　Tolleshunt D'arcy CM9 ..198 D4
South Strand CO11........86 C5
South Suffolk Bsns Ctr
　CO10. ....34 A7
Southview **10** CM7 ......128 A2
South View CM6 ....150 C8
Southview Dr
　Holland-on-S CO15 ......189 F6
　Walton-on-t-N CO14 .....171 C7
South View Gn IP9. ....60 E6
Southview Rd CM3........218 D6
Southview Sch CM6. ......176 F6
Southview Terr CM3 ......218 D6
Southway
　Brightlingsea CO7 ......185 F7
　Colchester CO1, CO3....135 E6
Southwold Way CO16 .....188 A5
Southwood Chase
　CM3. ....219 A4
Sovereign Cl CM7. ....128 D4
Sovereign Cres CO3.......135 C6
Sovereign Ctr IP1 ....16 C7
Sowerberry Cl CM1 ....204 F7
Spa Dr CM0 ....213 B1
SPAIN'S END 47 E6
Spains Hall Rd CM7 ....72 C8
Spalding Ave CM1 ....204 E5
Spalding Cl CM7 ....127 E4
Spalding Ct CM1 ....205 A3
Spalding Way CM2 ....216 F8
Spanbies Rd CO7 ....58 D2
Spansey Ct **1** CO9 ......76 D1
Spa Rd
　Feering CO5 ....158 E4
　Witham CM8 ....176 E2
Sparepenny La N CB10 ....47 A4
Sparepenny La S CB10 ....47 B4
Sparkey Cl CM8. ....195 A7
Sparks La CO9 ....29 A6
Spar La CM3. ....220 C3
Sparling Cl CO2 ....135 C2
Sparlings The CO13 ....170 C8
Sparrow Cl CO9. ....75 D8
Sparrow Rd CO10 ....34 B6
Sparrows Cnr CO12 ....116 E5
Sparrowsend Cotts
　CB11. ....43 A4
Sparrowsend Hill CB11....43 A5
Sparrows Herne
　CO15. ....188 F6
Sparrows Ho CO7. ....185 E6
Spartan Cl CB9 ....8 C8
Speckled Wood Cl IP8 ....36 D8
Speckled Wood Ct
　CM7 ....154 E8
Speedwell Cl CM8 ....176 D4
Speedwell Rd
　Colchester CO2 ....136 D2
　Ipswich IP2 ....16 F4
Spencer Cl
　Elsenham CM22..........94 C3
　Stansted Mountfitchet
　CM24 ....119 C6
Spencer Ho CM24.........119 D7
Spencer Rd
　Great Chesterford CB10 ....3 D3
　Thorpe-le-S CO16 ....142 A2
Spencers Piece CO4 ....83 E4
Spencer Sq CM7. ....127 F8
Spendells Cl CO14 ....144 D2
Spendells Ho CO14. ......144 E2
Spenlow Dr CM1 ....204 D7
Spennells The CO16.......142 A2
Spenser Way CO15.......187 F1
Spicers La CO10 ....15 C8
Spike The **7** CB10 ....22 F2
Spindle Rd CB9 ....8 D8
Spindle Wood CO4 ....110 B4
Spindrift Way CO7 ....164 B8
Spinks La CM8. ....176 F1
Spinnaker Cl CO15 ....203 J8
Spinnaker Dr CM9 ....210 E3
Spinnel's Hill CO11 ....88 B1
Spinnel's La
　Wix CO11................115 D7
　Wrabness CO11..........88 C1
Spinner Cl IP1............16 D8
Spinneyfields CO5 ....179 D6
Spinney The
　Braintree CM7 ....128 C1
　Earls Colne CO6.........105 A6
　Hatfield Peverel CM3 ...194 B3
　Jaywick CO15 ....188 A2
　Long Melford CO10 ......15 C7
Spinney The continued
　Newport CB11 ....67 A7
　Rushmere St A IP4 ....18 F4
　Stansted Mountfitchet
　CM24 ....119 E6
Spires The
　Bishop's Stortford
　CM23 ....145 D7
　Great Baddow CM2 .....216 F6
Spiritus Ho CO2 ....136 D5
Spital Rd
　Maldon CM9.............209 F2
　Maldon CM9.............220 D7
Spitfire Cl IP3 ....18 B1
Sporehams La
　Danbury CM3............218 C4
　Howe Green CM2, CM3..217 A4
Sportsmans La CM3.......194 A2
Sportsway CO1 ....135 F8
Spots Wlk CM2 ....216 D3
Spout La CO10. ....55 D7
Spratts La CO11 ....113 B4
Springbank Ave CO15 ....86 B3
Springbok Ho CM2........216 F5
Spring Chase
　Brightlingsea CO7 ......185 E7
　Wivenhoe CO7...........137 B2
Spring Cl
　Clacton-on-S CO16......188 C5
　Colchester CO4 ....110 C3
　Little Baddow CM3 .....207 D5
Spring Cotts CB9 ....9 C6
Spring Elms La CM3.......207 F3
Springett Pl CM77 ....155 E6
Springett's Hill CO8. .....55 D2
SPRINGFIELD 205 E6
Springfield Ave IP11 .....221 E5
Springfield Basin **10**
　CM2 ....205 C2
Springfield Cotts
　CM9. ....210 B5
Springfield Ct
　Bishop's Stortford
　CM23 ....145 E8
　Clacton-on-S CO15......188 C3
Springfield Gn CM1 ......205 E4
Springfield Hospl (private)
　CM1. ....205 D7
Springfield Inf Sch IP1 ...16 F8
Springfield Jun Sch
　IP1 ....16 F8
Springfield La IP1 ....16 F8
Springfield Lyons App
　CM2 ....206 A5
Springfield Mdws
　CO16 ....168 C3
Springfield Park Ave
　CM2 ....205 E2
Springfield Park Hill
　CM2 ....205 D2
Springfield Park La
　CM2 ....205 E2
Springfield Park Par
　CM2 ....205 D2
Springfield Park Rd
　CM2 ....205 E2
Springfield Pl CM1. ......205 E6
Springfield Prim Sch
　CM1 ....205 D7
Springfield Rd
　Chelmsford CM1 ....205 E4
　Sudbury CO10 ....15 E1
Springfields
　Braintree CM77 ....127 C2
　Brightlingsea CO7 ......185 F7
　Great Dunmow CM6 ....150 D8
Springfields Dr CO2.......135 A3
Springfield Terr **2**
　CO10 ....33 F8
Spring Gardens Rd
　CO6 ....106 E6
Spring Gdns CO10 ....15 C8
Springham Dr CO4........110 A6
Spring Hill CB11 ....22 A1
Springhill Cl CO7 ....138 E8
Springhill Rd CB11 ....43 D8
Springhurst Cl IP4........17 F6
Spring La
　Colchester CO3 ....135 A7
　Colchester, Lexden
　CO3. ....135 A8
　Eight Ash G CO3 ....108 B1
　Great Totham CM9......196 D7
　Hatfield Peverel CM3,
　CM9 ....194 F2
　Maldon CM9.............210 B4
　West Bergholt CO6 .....108 E3
　Wivenhoe CO7...........137 B2
Springland Cl IP4.........18 A6
Springlands Way CO10 ...15 F2
Spring Lane Rdbt
　CO3. ....135 A7
Spring Mdw CO16 ....2 B6
Springmead CM77 ....154 D7
Spring Meadow Prim Sch
　CO12. ....91 A3
Spring Pond Cl CM2 ......216 D3
Spring Rd
　Brightlingsea CO7 ......185 F7
　Ipswich IP4..............18 A6
　St Osyth CO16 ....187 A3
　Tiptree CO5 ....179 C4
Spring Rise
　Galleywood CM2 ....216 C2
　Haverhill CB9. ....9 C6
Spring Sedge CO3.........134 C7
Springtail Rd IP8 ....36 E8
Springvalley La CO7 .....111 C4
Spring Way CO9 ....51 E1
SPRINGWELL 22 A7
Springwell Rd CB10,
　CB11. ....22 A5
Springwood Ct CM7......127 D3
Springwood Dr CM7 .....127 C4
Springwood Ind Est
　CM7 ....127 D3
Sprites End IP11..........221 B7
Spriteshall La IP11 ....221 B7
Sprites La IP8, IP2........16 C2
Sprites Prim Sch IP2 .....16 C2
SPROUGHTON 16 A6
Sproughton Bsns Pk
　IP1 ....16 C8
Sproughton CE Prim Sch
　IP8 ....16 B6
Sproughton Ct IP8........16 A6
Sproughton Rd IP1 ....16 D7
Spruce Ave
　Colchester CO4 ....136 E8
　Great Dunmow CM6 ....123 B1
Spruce Cl
　West Mersea CO5 ....201 B7
　Witham CM8 ....177 A4
Spurgeon Cl CO9 ....51 E1
Spurgeon Pl CO5 ....158 C2
Spurgeon St CO1 ....136 C6
Square The
　Colchester CO2 ....135 B3
　Heybridge CM9 ....210 A5
　Stansted Mountfitchet
　CM22 ....93 F3
　West Mersea CO5 ....201 B6
　Widdington CB11........67 D4
Squires Cl CM23 ....145 C8
Squires Ct CO6 ....105 B6
Squire's Ct **1** CB9 ....8 E7
Squirrells Ct CM1. ....204 F5
Squirrels Ct **1** CM23 ...145 F8
Squirrels Field CO4 ....109 F5
Squirrels The IP9. ....35 A2
Stable Cl
　Colchester CO3 ....134 E6
　West Mersea CO5 ....201 E7
Stablecroft CM1 ....205 E8
Stablefield Rd CO14......171 A7
Stable Mews CO5.........201 E8
Stable Yard Cotts
　CM6 ....122 C4
Stacey Ct **9** CM23 ......145 F6
Stackyard The CB10. ......3 A3
Stacy Ct CM6 ....123 C1
Stafford Cl CO13 ....170 E6
Stafford Cres CM7 ....128 D4
Stafford Ho CM23 ....145 F5
STAFFORD'S CORNER
　 ....181 B5
Stainer Cl **1** CM8.......194 F7
Stainers CM23 ....145 C5
Stalin Rd CO2 ....136 B4
Stallards Cres CO13......170 E6
STAMBOURNE 28 D3
STAMBOURNE GREEN
　 ....28 A1
Stambourne Rd
　Great Yeldham CO9 .....29 D3
　Ridgewell CO9 ....28 F5
　Toppesfield CO9 ....50 B8
Stambridge Rd CO15 .....188 D5
Stamford Cl IP2 ....36 F8
Stammers Rd CO4........109 F4
STANBROOK 96 E7
Standard Ave CO15 ......203 D6
Standard Rd **9** CO1....136 C6
Standley Rd CO14. ....144 D1
Standrums CM6 ....150 D8
Stane Cl CM23 ....118 F1
Stane Field CO6 ....132 E3
Stanes Rd CM7 ....127 F6
Stanfield Cl CO3 ....134 E3
Stanfield Mdw CM8 .....155 F1
Stanley Ave
　Brightlingsea CO7 ......186 A7
　Ipswich IP3..............18 A4
Stanley Drapkin Prim Sch
　CB9 ....27 B6
Stanley Rd
　Clacton-on-S CO15......188 C2
　Felixstowe IP11.........221 E3
　Great Chesterford CB10 ....3 E3
　Halstead CO9. ....76 D2
　Sudbury CO10 ....33 C1
　Wivenhoe CO7...........137 C1
Stanley Rise CM2 ....205 E4
Stanleys Farm Rd
　CB11 ....43 F8
Stanley Wood Ave
　CO10 ....15 F1
Stanley Wooster Way
　CO4 ....136 E7
Stanmore Cl CO16 ....188 D5
Stanmore Way CO16 .....187 B4
Stannard Way CO10 ......34 A6
STANSTED 2 F7
Stanstead Pl CO9 ....103 F8
Stanstead Rd CO9 ....103 F8
Stansted Airport Sta
　CM24 ....121 B4
Stansted Cl CM1 ....204 E1
Stansted Ctyd CM24......121 B1
STANSTED
　MOUNTFITCHET 119 C8
Stansted Mountfitchet Sta
　CM24 ....119 E6
Stansted Rd
　Birchanger CM23........119 C4
Stansted Rd continued
　Bishop's Stortford
　CM23 ....119 B2
　Colchester CO2 ....136 A1
　Elsenham CM22..........94 C1
Stansted Way CO13 .....171 A6
Stanstrete Field
　CM77 ....154 B5
Stanton Pl **9** CB9........9 B8
STANWAY 134 C5
Stanway Cl CO10. ....2 C5
Stanway Ctr The CO3. ...134 E4
Stanway Fiveways Prim
　Sch CO3 ....134 D5
STANWAY GREEN 134 D3
Stanway Prim Sch
　CO3. ....134 C6
Stanway Sch The
　CO3. ....134 D5
Stanwell St **9** CO2.....135 F6
Stanwyn Ave CO15 ......188 E3
Stapleford Cl CM2 ....205 A1
Staplers Cl CM9 ....196 B4
Staplers Heath CM9......196 B4
Staplers Wlk CM9........196 B4
Starfield Cl IP4...........18 B6
Star La
　Great Dunmow CM6 ....123 D1
　Ipswich IP4..............17 D5
Starling Ct **17** CM23 ...145 F6
STARLING'S GREEN 64 F3
Starling's Hill CO9 ....75 E4
Star Mead CM6 ....70 A2
Starr Rd CM22 ....94 F5
START HILL 147 A7
Station App
　Braintree CM7 ....128 A2
　Frinton-on-S CO13......170 F5
Station Hill CO8 ....79 E8
Station La CO12 ....91 C4
Station Rd
　Alresford CO7 ....165 A8
　Ardleigh CO7 ....111 E7
　Bentley IP9 ....60 E6
　Birdbrook CO9 ....10 D1
　Bishop's Stortford
　CM23 ....146 A2
　Bradfield CO11 ....87 E3
　Braintree CM7 ....127 F2
　Brightlingsea CO7 ......185 E6
　Clacton-on-S CO15......188 F3
　Clare CO10 ....12 C7
　Colne Engaine CO6 ......77 A3
　Cressing CM8 ....156 A3
　Earls Colne CO6. ....105 A2
　Elsenham CM22..........94 C2
　Felsted CM6. ....151 F6
　Great Bentley CO7......166 E8
　Great Dunmow CM6 ....150 E8
　Harwich, Bath Side CO12..91 E5
　Harwich CO12. ....90 F5
　Harwich, Dovercourt
　CO12. ....91 D4
　Hatfield Peverel CM3 ...193 F5
　Haverhill CB9. ....9 A8
　Kelvedon CO5 ....158 C3
　Kirby Cross CO13 ....170 B6
　Long Melford CO10 ......15 C3
　Maldon CM9.............210 A3
　Manningtree CO11.......86 D5
　Marks Tey CO6...........133 B4
　Newport CB11 ....67 A8
　Rayne CM77 ....126 F1
　Saffron Walden CB11....22 D1
　Sible Hedingham CO9 ....51 E2
　Stansted Mountfitchet
　CM24 ....119 E6
　Sudbury CO10 ....33 E7
　Takeley CM22 ....148 C7
　Thorpe-le-S CO16 ....168 F8
　Thorrington CO7 ....166 A6
　Tiptree CO5 ....179 C4
　Tollesbury CM9 ....199 D2
　Tolleshunt D'arcy CM9 ..198 E5
　Trimley St M IP11 ....221 A7
　Wakes Colne CO6 ....106 D6
　Wendens Ambo CB11 ....42 F5
　White Notley CM8 ......155 F2
　Wickham Bishops CM8 ..195 C4
　Witham CM8 ....177 A3
　Wivenhoe CO7...........164 B8
　Wrabness CO11..........88 F3
Station Road Ind Est
　Great Dunmow CM6 ....150 E7
　Tolleshunt D'arcy CM9 ..198 D5
Station St
　Ipswich IP2..............17 C3
　Saffron Walden CB11....22 D1
　Walton-on-t-N CO14 ....171 C6
Station Terr CM3 ....193 F5
Station Yd IP2. ....17 B4
Steamer Terr **2** CM1 ..205 A3
Steam Mill Rd CO11......114 B8
Stebbens Way CM9 ......210 B4
STEBBING 124 E5
STEBBING GREEN 125 C3
Stebbing Prim Sch
　CM6 ....124 E5
Stebbing Rd CM6 ....152 B7
Stedman Ct CO15 ....203 D6
Steed Cres CO2 ....136 A5
Steeds Mdw CO10 ....15 C8
Steele Cl CO6.............132 F3
STEEPLE BUMPSTEAD
　 ....27 B8
Steeple Bumpstead Rd
　CB9 ....26 E7
Steeple Cl CM9 ....210 D5
Steeple View CM23 ......145 F6
Steerforth Cl CM1 ....204 D7
Stella Maris IP2 ....16 D5
Stepfield CM8 ....177 B2
Stephen Cl
　Haverhill CB9............8 F8
　Long Melford CO10 ......15 B5
Stephen Cranfield Cl
　CO5 ....164 A7
Stephen Marshall Ave
　CM7 ....72 C6
Stephen Neville Ct
　CB11 ....43 D8
Stephen's Ct IP4 ....18 B6
Stephenson Rd
　Braintree CM7 ....128 A1
　Clacton-on-S CO15......189 B8
　Colchester CO7 ....110 D6
Stephenson Rd W
　CO15 ....169 A1
Sterling Cl CO3 ....134 E5
Sterling Complex IP1.....16 D7
Stevens Cl CO4 ....109 E3
Stevens La CM6...........152 F6
Stevenson Rd IP1. ....17 B6
Stevens Rd CM8 ....176 E1
Stevens Wlk CO4 ....136 F7
STEVENTON END 6 C2
Stewards Cl CO13 ....170 F7
Stewart Rd CM2 ....216 A6
Stewarts The CM23 ......145 E6
Stewarts Way CM23 .....92 F2
STICKLING GREEN 65 C6
Stilemans Wood CM7 ....128 D1
Stiles The CM9 ....210 E3
Stirling Dr CB9 ....8 E8
Stirrup Cl CM1. ....205 E7
Stirrup Mews CO3 ....134 E6
STISTED 129 C6
Stisted CE Prim Sch
　CM77 ....129 B6
Stivvy's Rd CM9. ....208 C3
Stock Chase CM9 ....210 B5
Stockhouse Cl CM9 ......180 B2
Stockhouse Rd CO5......180 B7
STOCKING GREEN 24 C1
Stocking La SG8 ....39 C1
Stockley Cl CB9. ....9 C7
Stockman Terr CM77.....154 C8
Stockmen Field CM23 ....145 C5
Stockmers End **1** IP9 ...35 A1
Stock Rd CM2 ....216 B2
STOCKS GREEN 158 F6
STOCKSTREET 130 B2
Stock Terr CM9 ....210 B5
Stockwell **5** CO1 ....135 F7
STOKE 17 D3
Stokeash Cl CO16 ....188 A3
Stokebridge Maltings **1**
　IP2. ....17 C4
STOKE BY CLARE 11 C4
STOKE-BY-NAYLAND 56 E5
Stoke-by-Nayland Mid
　Sch CO6 ....56 C6
Stoke-by-Nayland Prim
　Sch CO6 ....56 C5
Stoke Coll CO10 ....11 C3
Stoke Hall Rd IP2.........17 C4
Stoke High Sch IP2 ....17 C2
STOKE HILL 17 B4
STOKE PARK 17 A1
Stoke Park Dr IP2 ....17 A1
Stoke Park Gdns IP2......17 A1
Stoke Quay IP2. ....17 D4
Stoke Rd
　Clare CO10 ....12 A6
　Nayland CO6 ....56 B2
Stoke St IP2. ....17 C4
Stokes The CO14. ....171 B8
Stonebridge Hill CO6 ....104 E7
Stonechat Rd IP2. ....16 D2
Stone Cl CM7.............127 F2
Stone Cotts
　Great Maplestead CO9 ...52 D2
　Greenstead Green CO9 ..104 A5
Stonecrop CO4 ....109 C2
Stonegrove Rd IP11......221 B1
Stone Hall CO10 ....12 B7
Stonehall Dr CO16 ....168 D1
Stonehall La CO12........115 B1
Stoneham St CO6.........130 F2
Stonehill Way CO5 ....201 A6
Stone La
　Tiptree CO5 ....179 A2
　Wrabness CO11..........88 F5
Stonelands Ho IP11.......221 B6
Stoneleigh Pk CO3. ......134 F4
Stone Lodge La IP2. ......17 A3
Stone Lodge La W IP2 ....16 F3
Stone Lodge Wlk IP2 .....17 B3
Stone Path Dr CM3 ....193 F3
Stone Rd CO7 ....113 B1
STONES GREEN 115 D2
Stones Green Rd
　CO12 ....114 E2
Stone's Green Rd
　CO12 ....115 E2
Stoney Comm CM24......119 E5
Stoney Common Rd
　CM24 ....119 D5
Stoneyfield Dr CM24 ....119 E6
Stoney La CO7............186 A8
Stoney Pl CM24...........119 E5
Stonham Ave CO16.......188 A4
Stony La CM6.............70 A2
Stopes Ho **3** CO1.......136 A7
Stopford Ct **2** IP1.......17 A6
Stores Rd CO5 ....179 C6

Storms Way CM2 206 B2
Stortford Hall Ind Pk CM23 146 B7
Stortford Hall Pk CM23 146 B8
Stortford Hall Rd 3 CM23 146 B8
STORTFORD PARK 145 C8
Stortford Rd
Clavering CB11 65 C4
Great Dunmow CM6 123 C1
Takeley CM6 149 D7
Stort Lo CM23 145 D8
Stort Rd CM23 145 F6
Stort Valley Ind Pk CM23 119 B2
Stour Ave IP11 221 C3
Stour Cl
Glemsford CO10 2 C2
Harwich CO12 90 D2
Stour Ct CM7 128 D1
Stourdale Cl CO11 86 A3
Stour Estuary Nature Reserve* CO12 89 C3
Stour Gdns CO10 34 B4
Stour Gn CO10 12 B6
Stour Rd CO12 91 D5
Stourside IP9 91 A8
Stour St
Cavendish CO10 13 C8
Manningtree CO11 86 D4
Sudbury CO10 33 E7
Stourton Rd CM8 176 E3
Stour Vale
Clare CO10 12 A6
Stoke by C CO10 10 D2
Stour Valley Rd CB9 9 B7
Stourview Ave CO11 87 A4
Stourview Cl CO11 87 B4
Stour View Ct CO12 91 D5
Stour Wlk CO4 110 E2
Stow Ct CO4 109 F5
Stradbroke Rd IP4 18 A7
Straight Rd
Boxted CO4 82 F2
Bradfield CO11 87 C1
Colchester CO3 134 F5
Great Bentley CO7 167 A4
Straight Way CO2 161 A2
Strand The IP2 37 C8
Stranger's Cnr CO7 185 D8
Strasbourg Sq 6 CB9 9 B8
Stratford Pl 4 CO14 171 C8
Stratford Rd
Clacton-on-S CO15 189 D6
Dedham CO7 84 D7
STRATFORD ST MARY 58 C2
Stratford St Mary Prim Sch CO7 58 C1
Strawberry Cl CM7 128 A1
Strawberry Fields CB9 8 D7
Strawberry La CO5 179 F3
Strawbrook Hill CM3 173 E4
Straw La CO10 33 D7
Street Farm Bglws CO11 61 A2
Street The
Ardleigh CO7 111 E8
Ashen CO10 11 D1
Belchamp Otten CO10 31 C8
Belstead IP8 36 C6
Berden CM23 92 B8
Birdbrook CO9 28 B7
Bradfield CO11 87 E1
Bradwell CM77 129 D3
Brantham CO11 61 A1
Bulmer CO10 32 E5
Capel St M IP9 35 A1
Chappel CO6 106 D5
Cressing CM77 156 A6
East Bergholt CO7 59 B2
Feering CO5 158 E5
Foxearth CO10 14 C6
Galleywood CM2 216 B2
Gosfield CO9 102 E7
Great Hallingbury CM22 147 B4
Great Henny CO10 33 E3
Great Tey CO6 132 C8
Harkstead IP9 63 B2
Hatfield Peverel CM3 193 F4
Holbrook IP9 62 D6
Kirby-le-S CO13 143 B1
Little Clacton CO16 168 C3
Little Dunmow CM6 151 D7
Little Totham CM9 197 B5
Little Waltham CM3 191 B6
Maldon CM9 210 B4
Manuden CM23 92 F2
Messing CO5 159 D2
Pebmarsh CO9 78 A8
Pentlow CO10 14 A8
Purleigh CM3, CM9 220 F1
Ramsey CO12 90 A1
Rayne CM77 126 F2
Salcott-c-V CM9 199 B8
Shalford CM7 100 E7
Stisted CM77 129 C6
Stoke by C CO10 11 B3
Stratford St M CO7 84 C8
Tendring CO16 140 E5
Terling CM3 175 C2
Tiptree CO5 179 A8
Toppesfield CO9 50 B7
Washbrook IP8 35 F8
Weeley CO16 140 F1
Wherstead IP9 37 B6

Street The *continued*
White Notley CM8 155 E1
Wickham Bishops CM8 195 F5
Woodham Walter CM9 208 D2
Stretford Ct CM8 156 D3
STRETHALL 20 F4
Strethall Rd CB11 21 C4
Strickmere CO7 58 D2
Strood Cl CO5 201 B7
Strood The CO5 183 C3
Strudwick Cl 15 CM7 127 F2
Strutt Cl CM3 194 A4
Stuart Cl
Great Baddow CM2 217 B6
Ipswich IP4 17 F7
Stuart Ct 2 CM7 128 B2
Stuart Ho CO1 135 F8
Stuart Pawsey Ct CO7 137 C1
Stuarts Dr CO10 34 A7
Stuarts Way CM7 128 B2
Stubbs Cl
Ipswich IP3 18 A1
Kirby Cross CO13 170 E7
Lawford CO11 86 B4
Stubbs La CM7 128 C1
Studd's La CO4 109 D4
Stump Cross CB10 3 C5
Stump La CM1 205 D4
Stump's Cross CO9 29 A2
Sturdee Ave IP3 18 B3
STURMER 9 F4
Sturmer Ct 3 CO2 136 A1
Sturmer End Ind Est CB9 9 C6
Sturmer Rd
Haverhill, Calford Green CB9 9 F7
Haverhill CB9 9 C6
Sturrick La CO7 139 D1
STUTTON 61 F2
Stutton CE Prim Sch IP9 62 A2
Stutton Cl IP9 62 A2
Stutton Gn IP9 62 C1
Stutton La IP9 61 C5
Stutton Rd CO11 61 A2
Styles CM7 71 D2
Sub-Station Rd IP11 221 B2
Sucklings Yd CB9 27 C7
SUCKSTED GREEN 96 A6
Sudbourne Ave CO16 188 A4
Sudbourne Rd IP11 221 B5
SUDBURY 33 D8
Sudbury Rd
Bulmer CO10 32 F6
Bures CO8 55 F1
Castle Hedingham CO9 52 B4
Felixstowe IP11 221 A4
Gestingthorpe CO9 31 F2
Great Cornard CO10 34 F7
Great Maplestead CO9 53 C2
Halstead CO9 76 F3
Long Melford CO10 15 C3
Stoke-by-N CO6 56 C6
Sudbury Sta CO10 33 F7
Sudbury Upper Sch & Arts Coll CO10 15 F1
Sue Ryder Foundation Mus* CO10 1 D1
Suffolk Ave CO5 201 D7
Suffolk Cl
Clacton-on-S CO15 189 E7
Colchester CO4 110 B1
Suffolk Coll
Ipswich IP1 17 C6
Ipswich IP4 17 E5
Suffolk Coll (Argyll St Annexe) IP4 17 D6
Suffolk Dr CM2 206 A4
Suffolk Knowle CO8 55 F1
Suffolk Rd
Ipswich IP4 17 D7
Maldon CM9 209 E1
Sudbury CO10 33 E8
Suffolk Ret Pk IP1 17 A6
Suffolk Ski Ctr* IP2 37 B8
Suffolk Sq CO10 33 E8
Suffolk St CO14 171 C8
Sugar La CO9 74 E7
Sulleys Hill IP7 58 B8
Sullivan Cl CO4 136 E6
Summercroft Prim Sch CM23 146 C8
Summerfield Cl IP4 18 D8
Summerfield Ct IP4 18 D8
Summerfields CO9 51 E1
Summerhill Rd CB11 43 D8
Summerleaze Ct CM77 154 D7
Sunbank CM6 150 E7
Sunbeam Ave CO15 203 E6
Sunbeam Cl CO5 164 A8
Sunbury Way CM9 220 F8
Sundale Cl CO15 189 F6
Sunfield Cl IP4 18 B6
Sunflower Cl 5 CM1 205 F6
Sun Lido Square Gdns CM77 127 C2
Sunningdale CM23 145 E6
Sunningdale Ave
Felixstowe IP11 221 F6
Ipswich IP4 18 D5
Sunningdale Dr IP11 221 F6
Sunningdale Fall CM3 194 B4
Sunningdale Rd CM1 204 E4

Sunningdale Way CO13 170 E7
Sunnyfields Rd CM7 102 D2
Sunny Point CO14 144 E3
Sunnyside
Braintree CM7 127 E3
Stansted Mountfitchet CM24 119 E6
Sunnyside Rd CO6 107 D5
Sunnyside Way CO16 168 C1
Sunnyway Cotts CM3 218 E3
Sunray Ave IP11 221 F6
Sunrise Ave CM1 205 A5
Surbiton Rd IP1 16 F8
SURREX 131 E2
Surrex Cotts CO6 131 D2
Surrex Farm Units CO6 131 D2
Surrey Ct CO15 189 A2
Surrey La CO5 179 C4
Surrey Rd
Felixstowe IP11 221 D4
Ipswich IP1 17 A6
Sussex Cl CM3 206 F8
Sussex Gdns CO15 189 E6
Sussex Rd CO3 135 C7
Sutherland Ho CM1 205 A4
Sutor Cl CM8 176 E1
Sutton Mead CM2 206 A4
Sutton Park Ave CO3 135 A3
Swains Croft CO10 32 E5
Swallow Cl
Harwich CO12 90 E1
Layer de la H CO2 162 A5
Swallow Ct CM23 146 A6
Swallowdale
Clacton-on-S CO15 188 F6
Colchester CO2 136 C3
Swallow Field CO6 105 B6
Swallow Path CM2 216 B5
Swallow Rd IP2 16 C3
Swallow's Row CO7 167 B8
Swallow's Row CO7 140 B1
Swallowtail Cl IP8 36 E8
Swallow Wlk CO9 76 F1
Swanbridge Ind Pk CM8 177 B3
Swan Chase CO9 75 E8
Swan Cl
Colchester CO4 136 E5
Hatfield Peverel CM3 193 F4
Swan Cotts CM3 193 F4
Swan Ct
2 Bishop's Stortford CM23 145 F6
Maldon CM9 210 B4
New Mistley CO11 87 A3
Sible Hedingham CO9 75 E8
Swan Dale CO15 188 F7
Swan Farm Mews IP8 16 A1
Swanfield CO10 15 C7
Swan Gr CO6 106 C5
Swan Hill IP8 16 A2
Swan La
Haverhill CB9 9 A8
Long Melford CO10 15 C7
Swan Mdw CO7 58 C1
Swan Pas 13 CO1 135 F7
Swan Rd CO16 141 D5
Swanscomb Rd CO6 105 F4
Swansea Ave IP2 17 B1
Swan Side CM7 127 F3
Swans Pasture CM1 205 D6
Swan St
Chappel CO6 106 C3
Kelvedon CO5 158 D3
Sible Hedingham CO9 51 E1
SWAN STREET 106 C3
Swan Vale Ind Est CM8 177 B3
Swan Yd CO6 131 A2
Swatchway Cl IP3 38 B8
Swaynes CO7 58 C2
Sweden Cl CO12 90 F4
Swedish Est CO11 115 B5
Sweet Briar CM23 145 B6
Sweet Briar Rd CO3 134 C7
Sweet Mead CB10 22 E3
Swift Ave
Clacton-on-S CO15 203 F6
Colchester CO3 134 C4
Swift Cl CM7 155 A7
Swinbourne Dr CM7 127 D3
Swinton Cl IP2 16 D1
Swiss Ave CM1 205 A4
Sworders Yd 3 CM23 145 F7
Sycamore Cl
Ipswich IP8 16 C1
Takeley CM22 148 C7
Witham CM8 177 A5
Sycamore Cnr CM7 127 E1
Sycamore Ho IP4 18 A6
Sycamore Pl CO7 166 E8
Sycamore Rd
Colchester CO4 136 D8
Great Cornard CO10 34 B7
Heybridge CM9 210 C6
Sycamores The CM23 146 B6
Sycamore Way
Brantham CO11 60 D1
Chelmsford CM2 216 C6
Clacton-on-S CO15 188 C3
Kirby Cross CO13 170 D6
Sydner Cl CM2 217 A5
Sydney St
Brightlingsea CO7 185 F6
Colchester CO2 136 B1
Syers Field CM7 74 B2

Sylvan Cl CM2 216 B6
Symmons Cl CM77 126 F1
Symonds Ct 6 CO9 76 F2
Syringa Ct 6 CO4 136 E7

T

Taber Pl CM8 177 B3
Tabor Ave CM7 127 E3
Tabor Cl CO7 185 F8
Tabor Rd CO1 136 C7
Tabors Ave CM2 216 F8
Tabor Science Coll CM7 127 D4
Tabor's Hill CM2 216 F7
Tacket St IP4 17 D5
Tacon Ct IP11 221 C1
Tacon Rd IP11 221 C1
Tailors CM23 145 B5
Tailors Cl CM77 154 C8
Tait Mews CM9 210 A2
TAKELEY 148 C8
Takeley Bsns Ctr CM22 148 C7
Takeley Pk CM22 148 C6
Takeley Prim Sch CM22 148 C8
TAKELEY STREET 147 E7
Talavera Cres CO2 135 C2
Talbot Ave CO15 203 F6
Talbot Rd
Little Clacton CO16 168 C4
Sudbury CO10 15 F2
Talbots IP11 221 D3
Talbot St CO12 91 D5
Talcott Rd CO2 136 A2
Talisman Cl CO5 179 D6
Talisman Wlk CO5 179 D6
Tall Trees CO4 109 E3
Tall Trees Cvn Pk CM24 120 A4
Tally Ho CO4 110 B4
Tally Ho Cnr CO7 58 D1
Talmash Gdns IP2 17 A4
Tamar Ave CM8 176 E2
Tamarisk Way
Clacton-on-S CO15 203 F6
Colchester CO4 136 E8
Tamar Rise CM1 205 C6
Tambour Cl CO6 132 C8
Tamdown Way CM7 127 C4
Tamworth Chase CO2 136 A2
Tangerine Cl CO4 136 D6
Tan La CO16 168 F4
Tanner Cl CO16 188 B3
Tanners Mdw CM7 128 D2
Tanners View IP1 16 F7
Tanners Way CB10 22 E1
Tanton Rd CM6 151 E6
Tanyard The CM6 70 A2
Tapestry Ct CO6 105 B6
Tapestry Wlk CM7 128 D2
Tapley Rd CM1 204 F7
Tapsworth Cl CO16 188 D5
Tapwoods CO3 135 A7
Tara Cl CO4 110 D1
Tarragona Mews CO2 136 B4
Tarragon Cl CO5 179 C4
Tarrett Dr 11 CO1 136 C6
Tasman Ct CM1 204 E5
Tasmania Rd IP4 18 D6
Tasman Rd CB9 9 C7
Tattersall Way CM1 215 E7
TATTINGSTONE 61 C7
Tattingstone CE Prim Sch IP9 61 D7
Taunton Rd
Chelmsford CM1 205 E5
Felixstowe IP11 221 D6
Taverners Wlk CM8 176 F4
Tavern St IP1 17 C6
Tavistock Rd CM1 205 E5
Tawell Mews CO5 179 D5
Tawney Cl IP9 35 A1
Tawneys Ride CO8 80 A8
Tayberry Pl IP3 38 C7
Taylor Ave CM1 204 E5
Taylor Ct CO1 135 F7
Taylor Dr CO11 86 C4
Taylors End Rd CM24 120 E1
Taylor's Rd CO5 163 F8
Tayspill Ct CO2 135 B3
Teak Wlk CM8 177 A4
Teal Cl
Colchester CO4 137 A8
Great Notley CM77 154 B5
Ipswich IP2 16 D3
Teal Way CO5 158 D2
Teapot Cnr IP7 57 E8
Tedder Cl CO2 136 A4
Tees Cl CM8 176 E2
Tees Rd CM1 205 C6
Teign Dr CM8 176 D2
Telford Pl CM1 205 D4
Telford Rd
Braintree CM7 128 A1
Clacton-on-S CO15 189 C8
Telford Way CO4 110 D6
Temperance Yd CO6 105 B6
Templar Rd CM7 128 D2
Templars Ct CM8 176 F4
Templar's Ct CB9 8 E7
Templars Inf Sch CM8 176 F5
Templars Jun Sch CM8 176 F5
Temple Cl CO13 171 A6

Temple Ct CO4 110 D2
TEMPLE END 14 B4
Temple La CM8, CM77 156 C3
Templemead CM8 176 F3
Temple Pattle CO11 86 C7
Temple Rd
Colchester CO2 135 A2
Ipswich IP3 18 C4
Templeton Ct CM7 128 A3
Temple Way CM9 209 F5
Templewood Rd CO4 110 E1
Ten Acre App CM9 209 F5
Tenby Rd IP2 17 B1
TENDRING 140 F5
TENDRING GREEN 140 E8
TENDRING HEATH 114 D1
Tendring Prim Sch CO16 140 F6
Tendring Rd
Little Bentley CO7 140 A8
Thorpe-le-S CO16 141 D4
Tendring Tech Coll
Thorpe-le-S CO16 142 A1
Walton-on-t-N CO13 171 A7
Tennyson Cl CM7 154 F8
Tennyson Rd
Chelmsford CM1 204 F5
Ipswich IP4 17 F5
Tenpenny Hill CO7 165 E5
Tenter Cl CM7 127 F5
Tenterfield CM6 150 E8
Tenter Field CO7 58 D1
Tenterfield Rd CM9 210 A2
Tenterfields CB11 42 F1
Tenth Ave CM24 120 C2
TERLING 175 D3
Terling CE Prim Sch CM3 175 C3
Terling Cl CO2 136 A1
Terling Hall Cotts CM3 193 B7
Terling Hall Rd CM3 193 C7
Terling Rd
Hatfield Peverel CM3 193 F6
Witham CM8 176 B3
Terminal Rd N CM22, CM24 121 B4
Terminal Rd S CM22, CM24 121 B4
Termitts Chase CM3 194 A7
Tern Cl
Haverhill CB9 9 C7
Kelvedon CO5 158 D3
Terndale CO15 188 F6
Tern Mews CO7 164 B8
Tern Rd IP2 16 E2
Terrace Hall Chase CO6 109 D6
Terrace The
Cavendish CO10 1 D1
Felsted CM6 152 B5
Hatfield Peverel CM3 194 B5
Terra Cotta Pl CO10 2 E8
Tew Cl CO5 179 D5
Tewkesbury Rd CO15 188 F4
Tey Rd
Aldham CO6 106 E1
Coggeshall CO6 131 C4
Earls Colne CO6 105 D4
Tey Road Cl CO6 105 D6
Thackeray Cl CM7 155 A8
Thames Ave CM1 204 D4
Thames Cl CM7 128 D1
Thanet Rd IP4 18 B6
Thanet Wlk CO5 164 A8
Thatchers Dr CO7 137 F6
Thatchers The CM23 145 C5
Thatchers Way CM77 154 C8
THAXTED 70 A3
Thaxted Prim Sch CM6 70 A2
Thaxted Rd
Debden CB11 68 C6
Elder Street CB10 44 C4
Saffron Walden CB10 43 F8
Thaxted CB10 69 E8
Thaxted Wlk CO2 163 A8
Thebe Cl IP1 16 D8
Theberton Rd IP3 18 B1
The Bglws CM7 100 F5
THE HEATH 61 B6
Thelma Dr CO7 166 A5
Thelsford Wlk CO4 136 F7
Theobalds Cl CO10 15 B5
Thetford Ct CM1 204 E1
Thetford Rd 1 IP1 17 A7
Thieves' Cnr CM1 204 A4
Third Ave
Chelmsford CM1 205 B5
Clacton-on-S CO15 189 C4
Frinton-on-S CO13 170 E4
Glemsford CO10 2 C5
Halstead CO9 77 B1
Harwich CO12 91 C3
Seawick CO16 203 B6
Stansted Mountfitchet CM24 120 B2
Walton-on-t-N CO14 144 E3
Thirlmere Cl CM77 154 D7
Thirslet Dr CM9 210 C4
Thirtle Cl CO16 188 D6
Thistle Cl IP2 16 F4
Thistledown
Colchester CO4 110 B3
Panfield CM7 127 A7
Thistley Cl CM9 211 E6

Thistley Cres CB11 . . . . . . 66 E1
THISTLEY GREEN
Braintree 128 B7
Felsted. 153 A3
Thistley Green Rd
CM7. . . . . 128 B7
Thomas Ave IP11. . . . . . 221 A8
Thomas Bell Rd CO6 . . . 105 A6
Thomas Benold Wlk
CO2. . . . . 162 F8
Thomas Cl CM2. . . . . . . 205 F3
Thomas Heskin Ct 🔟
CM23. . . . . 146 A7
Thomas Lord Audley Sch
& Language Coll The
CO2. . . . . 135 F2
Thomas Rd CO15 . . . . . . 188 D4
Thomas St CO7 . . . . 185 F6
Thomas Wakley Cl
CO4. . . . . 109 F5
Thompson Ave CO3 . . . . 134 F6
Thompson Rd IP1 . . . . . . 16 F8
Thorington Cl CM7 . . . . . 154 C6
THORINGTON STREET
. . . . 57 B4
THORLEY 145 D2
Thorley Hall Stables
CM23 . . . . 145 D2
Thorley High CM23. . . . . 145 F2
Thorley Hill CM23 . . . . . 145 F5
Thorley Hill Prim Sch
CM23 . . . . 145 F4
THORLEY HOUSES 145 A5
Thorley La
Bishop's Stortford, Thorley
Houses CM23 . . . . 145 B5
Bishop's Stortford, Thorley
Park CM23 . . . . 145 D3
Bishop's Stortford, Thorley
Street CM23 . . . . 145 F3
Thorley Neighbourhood
Ctr CM23. . . . . 145 D4
THORLEY PARK 145 D4
Thorley Park Rd
CM23 . . . . 145 F4
THORLEY STREET 145 F3
Thornbera Cl CM23. . . . . 145 F3
Thornbera Gdns
CM23 . . . . 145 F3
Thornbera Rd CM23. . . . 145 F4
Thornberry Ave CO16. . . 140 F1
Thornbury Rd CO15 . . . . 188 F4
Thornbush La IP8 . . . . . . 16 A8
Thorncroft CB10 . . . . 22 F2
Thorndon Cl CO16 . . . . . 188 A4
Thorne Rd CO5 . . . . 158 B2
Thorney Rd IP9. . . . . 35 A1
Thornfield Ct CO2 . . . . . 136 D2
Thornfield Rd CM23. . . . 145 E8
Thorn Gr CM23 . . . . 146 B6
Thorn Grove Prim Sch
CM23 . . . . 146 B6
Thornhayes Cl IP2. . . . . . 17 A3
Thornhill CM3 . . . . 220 D1
Thornhill Cl CO13 . . . . . 170 F7
Thornley Dr IP4 . . . . 18 C8
Thorns Way CO14. . . . . . 171 A8
Thornton Dr CO4. . . . . . 109 F2
Thornton Rd CM6. . . . . . 148 F7
Thorn Way IP11 . . . . 221 C4
Thornwood CO4 . . . . . . 109 F4
Thornwood Cl CO5. . . . . 201 D6
Thoroughfare 🟫 IP1. . . . . 17 C6
Thoroughgood Rd
CO15 . . . . 188 B5
Thorpe Cross CO16 . . . . 169 D8
THORPE GREEN 141 E2
THORPE-LE-SOKEN 142 B1
Thorpe-le-Soken Sta
CO16. . . . . 168 F7
Thorpe Mews CM7 . . . . . 128 C3
Thorpe Park La CO16 . . . 169 E7
Thorpe Rd
Beaumont CO16. . . . . . . 142 B5
Clacton-on-S CO15. . . . . 188 F7
Kirby Cross CO13 . . . . . . 169 E7
Tendring CO16 . . . . 141 B5
Weeley CO16. . . . . 141 A2
Thorpe Wlk CO4 . . . . . . 136 F7
THORRINGTON 166 A5
Thorrington Cross
CO7 . . . . 165 F5
Thorrington Rd
Great Bentley CO7. . . . . . 166 C8
Little Clacton CO16. . . . . 168 C4
Thorrington Tide Mill★
CO7. . . . . 165 E3
Thracian Cl CO2 . . . . . . 135 A3
Threadneedle St
🟫 Chelmsford CM1 . . . . . 205 B3
Dedham CO7 . . . . 84 F7
Three Acres CO16. . . . . 187 A4
Three Crowns Rd CO4 . . 109 E2
Three Gates Cl CO9 . . . . 103 D8
Three Mile Hill CM4. . . . 215 D2
Tremhall Ave
Bishop's Stortford
CM23 . . . . 146 F8
Great Hallingbury CM22,
CM24 . . . . 147 C8
Takeley CM24 . . . . 121 A2
Threshelfords Bsns Pk
CO5. . . . . 158 E3
Thresher Cl CM23. . . . . . 145 C5

Thresher Rise CM77. . . . . 154 C8
Threshers End CO3 . . . . . 134 D5
Thrift Wood CM3 . . . . . . 218 F1
Thriftwood Sch CM2. . . . . 216 B3
Thrimley La CM23. . . . . . 118 C6
Thrushdale CO15 . . . . . . 188 F6
Thurlow Pl 🔟 CB9 . . . . 9 B8
Thurlston Cl CO4 . . . . . . 110 D1
Thurstable Cl CM9 . . . . . 199 E2
Thurstable Rd CM9 . . . . . 199 E2
Thurstable Sch CO5. . . . . 179 D6
Thurstable Way CM9. . . . 199 E2
Thurston Ct IP11 . . . . 221 A3
Thyme Mews CM8 . . . . . 176 E3
Thyme Rd CO5. . . . . 179 C5
Tiberius Cl
Colchester CO4 . . . . 110 B6
Haverhill CB9. . . . . 9 D7
Tiberius Gdns CM8. . . . . 194 E8
Tideswell Cl CM7 . . . . . . 128 D4
Tidings Hill CO9 . . . . 103 E8
Tiffin Dr CO5. . . . . 179 E5
TILBURY GREEN 29 D6
TILBURY JUXTA CLARE
. . . . 30 A5
Tilbury Rd
Great Yeldham CO9 . . . . . 30 A3
Ridgewell CO9. . . . . 29 C7
Tildesley Cl CO13 . . . . . . 170 A6
Tile Barn La CO11. . . . . . 85 C2
Tile House La CO6 . . . . . 109 B8
TILKEY 130 F3
Tilkey Rd CO6 . . . . 130 F3
Tillwicks Cl CO4 . . . . 105 A7
TILTY 96 D2
Timber Hill CO1. . . . . . . 136 C6
Timbers Cl CM77. . . . . . . 154 B7
Timber Yd CM7 . . . . 128 A2
Timsons La CM2 . . . . . . 205 E4
Tinabrook Cl IP2. . . . . . . 16 E1
Tindal Sq 🟫 CM1 . . . . . . 205 B2
Tindal St CM1 . . . . 205 B2
TINDON END 46 A1
Tindon End Rd CB10 . . . . 46 D2
Tinker Ave CM7. . . . . . . 73 C6
TINKERS GREEN 47 F5
Tinker St CO12 . . . . 116 D8
Tinnocks La CM0 . . . . . . 213 B1
Tintagel Way CM9 . . . . . 220 E8
Tintern Cl IP2 . . . . 17 A2
Tippett Cl CO4 . . . . 136 E6
TIPTREE 179 D5
Tiptree Hall La CO5 . . . . 179 B2
TIPTREE HEATH 179 A2
Tiptree Heath Prim Sch
CO5. . . . . 179 B3
Tiptree Mus★ CO5. . . . . 179 E4
Tiptree Rd
Great Braxted CM8,
CM9 . . . . 196 B8
Wickham Bishops CM8 . . . 195 F6
Titan Ct IP1 . . . . 16 D7
Titania Cl CO4 . . . . 136 F7
Titchwell Dr IP3 . . . . 38 C7
Tithe Cl CM8. . . . . 176 E3
Titus Way CO4 . . . . 110 B6
Tobruk Rd CM1 . . . . 204 F6
Tofts Chase CM3. . . . . . 207 E3
Tofts Wlk 🟫 CM7 . . . . . . 127 F3
Toga Cl CM2. . . . . 135 A2
Tog La
Great Horkesley CO6. . . . . 82 A3
Little Horkesley CO6. . . . . 81 F3
Tokely Rd CO7. . . . . 139 A3
Tokio Rd IP4 . . . . 18 A6
Toller Rd IP3 . . . . 17 E3
TOLLESBURY 199 D2
Tollesbury Rd CM9 . . . . . 198 F3
Tollesbury Sch CM9. . . . . 199 D1
TOLLESHUNT D'ARCY
. . . . 198 D4
Tolleshunt D'arcy Rd
CM9 . . . . 197 F3
Tolleshunt D'arcy St
Nicholas Prim Sch
CM9 . . . . 198 D4
TOLLESHUNT KNIGHTS
. . . . 180 A2
TOLLESHUNT MAJOR
. . . . 197 E4
Tollgate Ct CO3. . . . . . . 134 C6
Tollgate Dr CO3 . . . . 134 B6
Tollgate E CO3 . . . . 134 C6
Tollgate Rd CO3 . . . . . . 134 C5
Toll Gate Rd IP9. . . . . . . 35 A1
Tollgate Rdbt CO3 . . . . . 134 C6
Tollgate W CO3. . . . . . . 134 B5
Tolliday Cl CO7. . . . . . . 137 A2
Tolworth Rd IP4. . . . . . . 18 A6
Tom Davies Ho 🟫
. . . . 127 F2
Tomline Rd
Felixstowe IP11. . . . . . . 221 E4
Ipswich IP3. . . . . 18 A4
Tomlinson Rd CM6. . . . . 151 E6
Tom's La CM7 . . . . 72 A6
Tom Tit La CM8 . . . . 219 E2
Tony Webb Cl CO4 . . . . . 110 C4
Tooley's Ct (Almshouses)
🟫 IP4 . . . . 17 D5
TOPPESFIELD 50 C7
Toppesfield Rd CO9. . . . . 50 F8
Top Rd
Tolleshunt Knights
CM9 . . . . 180 A2
Wimbish CB10. . . . . 45 E3
Woodham Walter CM9. . . 208 D2
Torquay Rd CM1. . . . . . . 205 D5

Torrington Cl CM1. . . . . . 205 E5
Tortoiseshell Cl IP8. . . . . 36 E8
Tortoiseshell Way
CM7. . . . . 127 E1
Tortosa Cl CM2. . . . . . . 136 B4
Torver Cl CM77. . . . . 154 C6
TOTHAM HILL 196 E5
Totham Hill Gn CM9 . . . . 196 E6
Tot La CM3, CM24 . . . . . 119 D4
Totlands Dr CO15 . . . . . . 189 A2
Totnes Wlk CM1. . . . . . . 205 E6
Totteridge Cl CO16. . . . . 188 D5
Toucan Way CO15 . . . . . 188 F6
Toulmin Rd CM3. . . . . . . 194 A4
Tovell's Rd IP4 . . . . 17 E6
Tower Ave CM1. . . . . . . 204 F4
Tower Ct 🟫 CB9 . . . . 8 E7
Tower Cut CO7 . . . . 185 F6
Tower Cvn Pk CO15 . . . . 203 D6
Tower Est CO16 . . . . 185 E4
Tower Hill Redoubt Fort★
CO12. . . . . 91 E5
Tower Mill Rd IP1. . . . . . 16 F7
Tower Ramparts IP1. . . . 17 C6
Tower Ramparts Ctr 🟫
IP1 . . . . 17 C6
Tower Rd
Clacton-on-S CO15. . . . . 188 E1
Felixstowe IP11. . . . . . . 221 D3
Wivenhoe CO7. . . . . 137 B2
Towers Rd CM9 . . . . 210 C5
Tower St
Brightlingsea CO7 . . . . . . 185 F6
Ipswich IP1. . . . . 17 C6
Towers The CO15 . . . . . . 189 A2
Town Croft CM1. . . . . . . 205 A5
Town End Field CM8. . . . 194 F8
Townfield St CM1. . . . . . 205 B3
Townsend CM2 . . . . 206 B5
Townsend Rd CO5 . . . . . 179 C7
Town St CM6. . . . . 70 A2
Towse Cl CO16 . . . . 188 C5
Traddles Ct CM1. . . . . . . 204 F6
Trafalgar Cl IP4 . . . . 17 F6
Trafalgar Cotts CO12. . . . 90 F3
Trafalgar Ct
Braintree CM7. . . . . 128 B4
Brightlingsea CO7. . . . . . 185 F8
Trafalgar Ho 🟫 CM7 . . . . 127 F2
Trafalgar Rd
Clacton-on-S CO15. . . . . 188 C1
Colchester CO3 . . . . 134 C6
Trafalgar Way CM7 . . . . . 128 B4
Trajan Cl CO4 . . . . 110 B6
Tranter Dr CO4 . . . . 109 E4
Tredgetts CB10 . . . . 6 B1
Tree Cl CO15 . . . . 188 F7
Treetops
Colchester CO4 . . . . 110 B3
Felixstowe IP11. . . . . . . 221 C6
Treetops Ct CO4 . . . . . . 109 F5
Trefoil Cl IP2. . . . . 16 F4
Trefoil Ct 🟫 CB9. . . . . 8 F7
Trelawn CM3 . . . . 206 E8
Trelawny Ho IP11. . . . . . 221 B1
Trenchard Cres CM1. . . . 205 D8
Trenchard Lo CM1 . . . . . 205 D7
Trent Rd
Chelmsford CM1 . . . . . . 204 D5
Ipswich IP3. . . . . 17 F2
Witham CM8 . . . . 176 E2
Trevose IP11. . . . . 221 C4
Trews Gdns CO5. . . . . . . 158 C3
Triangle Garage CM8 . . . 210 B5
Triangle Sh Ctr CO14. . . . 170 F7
Trickett Ct CO7 . . . . 137 B1
Tricketts La CM7. . . . . . . 73 E4
Trimley Cl CO16 . . . . 188 B4
TRIMLEY ST MARY 221 B8
Trimley St Mary Prim Sch
IP11. . . . . 221 A7
Trimley Sta IP11. . . . . . . 221 A7
Trinity Ave IP11 . . . . 221 A4
Trinity Cl
Bishop's Stortford
CM23 . . . . 145 F6
Chelmsford CM2 . . . . . . 205 D3
Manningtree CO11. . . . . . 86 C3
Rushmere St A IP5 . . . . . 18 F7
West Mersea CO5 . . . . . . 201 C7
Wivenhoe CO7. . . . . 137 C1
Trinity Ct CO7 . . . . 76 E2
Trinity Farm Ct 🟫
CO11 . . . . 86 D4
Trinity Mews CO5. . . . . . 201 C7
Trinity Rd
Chelmsford CM2 . . . . . . 205 D2
Halstead CO9. . . . . 76 D1
Manningtree CO11. . . . . . 86 D3
Trinity Road Prim Sch
CM2 . . . . 205 D2
Trinity Sq 🟫 CO1. . . . . . . 135 F7
Trinity St
Bishop's Stortford
CM23 . . . . 145 F6
Colchester CO1 . . . . 135 F7
Halstead CO9. . . . . 76 D2
Ipswich IP3. . . . . 17 E4
Trinity Terr 🟫 CO9. . . . . . 76 D1
Trinity Way CM23 . . . . . . 145 F6
Trinovantian Way
CM7. . . . . 128 A2
Trippier Ho CO4 . . . . . . 136 E7
Triumph Ave CO15 . . . . . 203 E7
Triumph Cl CO4 . . . . 136 E5
Troon Gdns IP4. . . . . . . 18 B8
Trotters Field CM7 . . . . . 128 B3
Trotwood Cl CM1 . . . . . . 204 E7

Troys Chase CM3. . . . . . 175 C6
Trunette Rd CO15 . . . . . 188 C3
Trusses Rd CM0 . . . . 214 F3
Truswell Terr CO11 . . . . . 86 D7
Tryon Ct 🟫 CO9 . . . . 76 D1
Tucker Dr CM8 . . . . 176 F1
Tucker's Row 🟫
CM23 . . . . 145 F6
Tuddenham Ave IP4 . . . . 17 E7
Tuddenham Rd IP4 . . . . . 17 E7
Tudor CE Prim Sch
CO10. . . . . 15 F1
Tudor Cl
Brightlingsea CO7 . . . . . . 185 E8
Jaywick CO15 . . . . 188 A1
Sudbury CO10 . . . . 15 E1
Walton-on-t-N CO14 . . . . 144 D2
Witham CM8 . . . . 176 F1
Tudor Ct
🟫 Braintree CM7 . . . . . . 128 B2
West Mersea CO5 . . . . . . 201 C7
Tudor Gn
Clacton-on-S CO15. . . . . 203 F8
Jaywick CO15 . . . . 187 F1
Sudbury CO10 . . . . 15 E2
Tudor Par CO15. . . . . . . 203 G8
Tudor Pl 🟫 IP4. . . . . 17 D6
Tudor Rd CO10 . . . . 15 E1
Tudor Rose Cl CO15 . . . . 134 C7
Tudwick Rd CM9. . . . . . . 197 E6
Tufnell Way CO4. . . . . . . 109 D2
Tufted Cl CM77. . . . . 154 C6
Tugby Pl CM1 . . . . 204 E6
Tukes Way CB11. . . . . . . 43 F7
Tulip Cl CM1 . . . . 205 E2
Tulip Way CO15. . . . . . . 188 C4
Tulip Wlk CO4 . . . . 136 D7
TUMBLER'S GREEN 129 E8
Tumulus Way CO2 . . . . . 135 A3
Tunstall Cl CO16 . . . . . . 187 B5
Tupman Cl CM1. . . . . . . 204 D6
Turin St IP2 . . . . 17 C4
Turkentine Cl CO10 . . . . 34 D5
Turkey Cock La CO3,
CO6. . . . . 133 E2
Turkey Oaks CM1 . . . . . . 205 D3
Turner Ave CO11. . . . . . . 86 B5
Turner Cl
Black Notley CM77 . . . . . 155 B4
Wivenhoe CO7. . . . . 137 C5
Turner Rd
Colchester CO4 . . . . 109 F3
Ipswich IP3. . . . . 38 A8
Turners Cres CM23. . . . . 145 C4
Turnpike Cl CO7. . . . . . . 110 E8
Turnpike Pl CM7. . . . . . . 128 A3
Turnstone End 🟫
CO4. . . . . 136 F8
Turpins Ave CO15 . . . . . 189 C5
Turpins Cl CO15 . . . . 189 C5
Turpins Cl CO15 . . . . 189 C5
Turpins La
Kirby Cross CO13 . . . . . . 170 E7
Kirby-le-S CO13 . . . . 170 E8
Turret Green Ct 🟫 IP1. . . 17 C5
Turret Ho CO15 . . . . 189 A2
Turret La IP4 . . . . 17 C5
Turstan Rd CM8 . . . . 194 E8
Tusser Cl CM8 . . . . 177 B7
Tusset Ct CM2 . . . . 216 B2
Tusset Mews CO3 . . . . . 134 E7
Tweed Cl CO9 . . . . 103 D8
Twelve Acres CM7 . . . . . 128 D3
Twenty First St CM24 . . . 120 F3
Twining Rd CO3 . . . . 134 E4
Twin Oaks CM2 . . . . 206 A4
TWINSTEAD 54 C6
TWINSTEAD GREEN 54 A5
Twitten La CM2 . . . . 216 B2
Twitty Fee CM3. . . . . 219 A8
Two Acres IP9 . . . . 35 B2
Two Village CE Prim Sch
CO12. . . . . 90 B1
Twyford Bsns Ctr The
CM23 . . . . 146 A4
Twyford Bury La CM22,
CM23 . . . . 146 A4
Twyford Cl CM23. . . . . . . 146 A5
Twyford Gdns CM23 . . . . 145 F4
Twyford Ind Est
CM23 . . . . 146 A5
Twyford Mews CM22. . . . 146 A3
Twyford Mill CM22. . . . . 146 A3
Twyford Rd CM23 . . . . . . 146 A5
Tyburn Hill CO6. . . . . . . 106 A6
Tydeman Cl CO3 . . . . . . 134 C4
Tye Cnr CO10 . . . . 32 F2
Tyed Croft CO3 . . . . 134 C6
Tye Gn CO10. . . . . 2 B5
TYE GREEN
Braintree 155 E2
Elsenham 120 E6
Radwinter 45 C4
Tye Green Paddocks
CO10 . . . . 2 B5
Tye Green Rd CM22 . . . . 120 D6
Tye Hill CO11 . . . . 86 A3
Tyehurst Cres CO4 . . . . . 110 C2
Tye La CO7 . . . . 137 E3
Tye Rd
Elmstead Market CO7 . . . 137 E7
Ipswich IP3. . . . . 17 E4
Tye Rd The CO7. . . . . . . 167 B7
Tyler Ave
Clacton-on-S CO16. . . . . 188 B3
Little Dunmow CM6. . . . . 151 E5
Tylers CB10 . . . . 23 E1
Tylers Cl CM2. . . . . 216 B6

Tylers Gn IP11. . . . . 221 A7
Tyler St
Harwich CO12 . . . . 90 F5
Ipswich IP2. . . . . 17 D4
Tylneys Rd CO9. . . . . . . 77 C3
Tymperley Ct 🟫 CO1. . . . 136 A6
Tymperleys Clock Mus★
CO1. . . . . 135 F7
Tyndale Dr CO15. . . . . . . 188 A1
Tyndales La CM3. . . . . . . 219 B5
Tyndale Ct CO4 . . . . 110 B4
Tynedale Sq CO4 . . . . . . 110 B4
Tyne Way CM1. . . . . 204 D5
Tyrells Cl CM2. . . . . 205 E4
Tyrells Way CM2 . . . . . . 216 F7
Tyrrells Sch The CM1. . . . 205 E5
Tyssen Mead CM3 . . . . . 206 E8
Tythe Cl CM1 . . . . 205 E8
Tythings The
Halstead CO9. . . . . 103 D8
Howe Green CM2 . . . . . . 217 D2

U

Ufford Pl 🟫 CB9. . . . . 9 B8
UGLEY 93 E6
UGLEY GREEN 94 A3
Ullswater Cl CM77 . . . . . 154 C6
ULTING 208 C6
Ulting Hall Rd CM9. . . . . 208 E7
Ulting La CM9 . . . . 208 E6
Ulting Rd
Hatfield Peverel CM3 . . . 194 C2
Ulting CM9. . . . . 208 C8
Una Rd CO12 . . . . 90 F5
Undercliff Rd W IP11. . . . 221 D3
Union Rd CO15 . . . . 203 G8
Union St 🟫 IP4. . . . . 17 D6
Unity Cl CO2. . . . . 136 B4
Unity St IP3 . . . . 17 E4
Univ of Essex CO4 . . . . . 136 F4
Upland Cres CO5 . . . . . . 201 C7
Upland Dr CO4 . . . . 110 C2
Upland Rd
Ipswich IP4. . . . . 18 A6
West Mersea CO5 . . . . . . 201 C7
Uplands Com Mid Sch
CO10. . . . . 15 F1
Uplands Cres CO10 . . . . 15 F1
Uplands Cl CO15 . . . . . . 188 D1
Uplands Dr CM1 . . . . . . 205 D7
Uplands Rd
Clacton-on-S CO15. . . . . 188 D1
Sudbury CO10 . . . . 15 E1
Upleatham Ho CM1 . . . . . 204 E3
UPPEND 92 B1
Upper Acres CM8 . . . . . . 176 F5
Upper Barclay St 🟫
IP4 . . . . 17 D6
Upper Branston Rd
CO15 . . . . 188 D4
Upper Bridge Rd
CM2. . . . . 205 A1
Upper Brook St IP4 . . . . . 17 C5
Upper Cavendish St
IP3. . . . . 18 A5
Upper Chapel St CO9 . . . 76 E2
Upper Chase 🟫 CM2 . . . . 216 A8
Upper Cotts CO2. . . . . . . 162 A5
UPPER DOVERCOURT . . . 90 E3
Upper East St CO10 . . . . 33 F8
Upper Farm Rd CO10. . . . 29 D8
Upper Fenn Rd CO10 . . . 77 A2
Upperfield Dr IP11. . . . . . 221 F6
Upper Fourth Ave
CO13 . . . . 170 F5
Upper Gn
Alphamstone CO8 . . . . . . 54 F3
Stoke by C CO10 . . . . . . 11 C4
UPPER GREEN
Langley 40 D3
Radwinter 45 D4
Upper High St 🟫 IP1 . . . . 17 C6
Upper Holt St CO6 . . . . . 105 C6
Upper Houses CO10. . . . . 32 D3
Upper Mill Field CM6 . . . 150 E7
Upper Moors CM3 . . . . . 190 F7
Upper Orwell St IP4. . . . . 17 D5
Upper Park Rd
Brightlingsea CO7. . . . . . 185 E7
Clacton-on-S CO15. . . . . 188 D3
UPPER POND STREET
. . . . 40 F7
Upper Rd CO10 . . . . 55 E8
Upper Roman Rd
CM2. . . . . 205 B1
Upper Second Ave
CO13 . . . . 170 E5
Upper Sq CB10 . . . . 22 D2
Upper St
Stanstead CO10. . . . . . . 2 E8
Stratford St M CO7 . . . . . 58 D1
UPPER STREET 61 D2
Upper Third Ave
CO13 . . . . 170 E5
Upper Trinity Rd CO9 . . . 76 E1
Upsheres CB11. . . . . 43 F8
Upton Cl
Ipswich IP4. . . . . 17 E6
West Bergholt CO6 . . . . . 108 D4
Urban Hive CM77 . . . . . . 154 B8
Urban Rd CM23. . . . . 146 B7
Usterdale Rd CB10 . . . . . 22 E3
Uxbridge Cres IP3 . . . . . 18 C1

Valance Rd CB11........ **65** A7
Vale Cl CO4............ **110** E2
Vale End CM2.......... **216** C3
Vale La IP9............. **61** B4
Valens Cl CO4.......... **110** A5
Valentine Ct CM7....... **127** E4
Valentine Dr CO4....... **110** C3
Valentine Way CM8..... **156** D3
Valentinus Cres CO2.... **135** F3
Valfreda Way CO7....... **137** B2
Valkyrie Cl CM9........ **199** C2
Valletta Cl CM1........ **205** A3
Valletta Ct CM23....... **145** E5

Valley Bridge CM1...... **205** B6

Valley Cl
  Brantham CO11........... **60** D1
  Colchester CO3........ **134** E3
Valley Cres CO6........ **108** E3
Valley Ct CM23......... **145** E5
Valley Farm Holiday Pk
  CO15.................. **189** B5

Valley La
  Tattingstone IP9......... **36** F4
  Wherstead IP9........... **37** A3

Valley Rd
  Braintree CM7......... **128** A4
  Clacton-on-S CO15..... **189** A5
  Colchester CO4........ **136** F4
  Harwich CO12.......... **90** D2
  Ipswich IP1............ **17** B8
  Sudbury CO10.......... **34** F8
  Wivenhoe CO7......... **164** C8

Valley View
  Finchingfield CM7....... **72** D6
  Stanstead CO10.......... **2** F7
  West Bergholt CO6..... **108** E3
Valley View Cl CO4..... **110** A4
Valleyview Dr IP4....... **18** F4

Valley Wlk
  Felixstowe IP11....... **221** D5
  Walton-on-t-N CO14... **171** A4
Vallis Way CO5........ **179** E5
Valonia Dr CO7........ **164** B8
Vandenburg Circ CM7.... **73** D6
Van Diemans Ct CM2.... **216** C8
Van Dieman's La CM2... **216** C8

Van Dieman's Rd
  CM2.................. **216** C8
Vandyck Rd IP3......... **38** A8
Van Dyck Rd CO3...... **135** B5
Vane Ct CM8.......... **177** A5
Vane La CO6.......... **131** A2
Vanessa Dr CO7....... **137** B1
Vange Pl 7 CB9......... **9** B8
Vanguard Way CM7..... **128** B4
Vanners Rd CB9........ **9** A7
Vansittart St CO12...... **91** D5
Varden Cl CM1........ **204** F6
Vaughan Cl CM77....... **126** F2
Vaughan St 8 IP2...... **17** C4
Vaux Ave CO12.......... **90** F1
Vauxhall Ave CO15..... **203** E6
Vauxhall Dr CM7....... **127** D2
Vega Cl CO1.......... **136** C6
Vellacotts CM1....... **205** B7
Venmore Dr CM6...... **150** E8
Ventnor Dr CO15...... **189** A8
Ventris Cl IP2.......... **16** D5
Ventura Dr CO1....... **136** C6
Vermeer Ride CM1..... **205** F7
Vermont Cres IP4....... **17** D7
Vermont Cl CO15...... **189** A4
Vermont Rd IP4....... **17** D7
Vernon Ct CM23....... **145** E4
Vernon's Cl CM22...... **94** F4
Vernons Rd CO6...... **106** E5
Vernon St IP2.......... **17** C4
Vernon Way CM7...... **128** C5
Veronica Wlk CO4...... **136** E7
Vesta Cl CO1.......... **136** C6
Vesta Cl CO7.......... **130** F2
Veyses End CO7......... **58** D2
Viaduct Rd CM1....... **205** A2
Vica Cotts CM3....... **207** D5
Vicarage Ave CM8..... **155** F1

Vicarage Ct
  18 Bishop's Stortford
  CM23................. **145** F7
  Panfield CM7......... **126** B4
  Tolleshunt D'arcy CM9.. **198** D4
Vicarage Cres CM3..... **194** B4

Vicarage Ct
  Colchester CO3........ **135** A4
  Halstead CO9........... **76** D2
Vicarage Field CO10.... **34** B5
Vicarage Gdns CO15.... **188** E2
Vicarage La
  Berden CM23........... **92** B8
  Great Baddow CM2.... **216** F5
  Thaxted CM6........... **70** A3
  Thorpe-le-S CO16..... **141** F2
  Ugley CM22............ **93** E5
  2 Walton-on-t-N
  CO14................. **171** C8
  Wherstead IP9......... **37** B5
Vicarage Mdw CO9...... **76** E1
Vicarage Mead 1 CM6... **70** A3
Vicarage Mead Bglws 3
  CM6.................. **70** A3
Vicarage Mews CM2.... **216** F6
Vicarage Rd
  Belchamp St P CO10... **13** A1
  Chelmsford CM2...... **216** B8
  Felixstowe IP11....... **221** C4

Vicarage Rd continued
  Finchingfield CM7....... **72** D6
Vicars Orch CO10....... **32** E5
Vicerons Pl CM23...... **145** D4
Viceroy Cl CO2........ **136** B3
Victoria Ave
  Kirby-le-S CO13....... **170** D8
  Saffron Walden CB11.... **22** E1
Victoria Chase CO1..... **135** E8
Victoria Cl CO7....... **137** B2
Victoria Cotts CM9..... **210** A5
Victoria Cres
  Chelmsford CM1...... **205** A3
  Lawford CO11.......... **86** C4
Victoria Ct
  4 Braintree CM7...... **128** A2
  Chelmsford CM1...... **205** B3
  Clacton-on-S CO15.... **188** F3
  Colchester CO3....... **134** F7
  Harwich CO12.......... **91** C3
Victoria Espl CO5...... **201** E5
Victoria Gdns
  Colchester CO4....... **110** B3
  Saffron Walden CB11.... **22** E1
Victoria Ho
  Felixstowe IP11....... **221** E4
  Ipswich IP2........... **17** B4
Victoria Mews CO5..... **201** D6
Victoria Pl
  Brightlingsea CO7..... **185** F6
  Colchester CO1....... **136** B6
Victoria Rd
  Chelmsford CM1...... **205** B3
  Clacton-on-S CO15.... **189** A3
  Colchester CO3....... **135** C6
  Felixstowe IP11....... **221** D3
  Haverhill CB9........... **8** D7
  Maldon CM9.......... **210** A2
  Walton-on-t-N CO14... **171** C8
  Weeley Heath CO16... **168** B5
Victoria Rd S CM1..... **205** B2
Victoria St
  Braintree CM7........ **128** A2
  Felixstowe IP11....... **221** E4
  Harwich CO12.......... **91** D4
  Ipswich IP1........... **17** A6
Victor Rd CO1........ **136** B6
Victory Cl CO7........ **166** B4
Victory Ct
  Clacton-on-S CO15.... **188** E1
  Colchester CO3....... **134** E6
Victory Gdns CM7..... **128** B4
Victory Rd
  Clacton-on-S CO15.... **188** D3
  Ipswich IP4........... **18** A7
  West Mersea CO5..... **201** A6
Vienna Cl CO12......... **91** A1
Viking Rd CM9........ **209** E1
Viking Way CO15...... **189** F6
Villa Ct 4 CO1....... **136** C6
Village Cl
  Kirby Cross CO13..... **170** D7
  Little Clacton CO16... **168** D1
Village Gate CM2...... **206** A2
Village Sq CM2....... **206** A3
Village Way CO13..... **170** D6
Villa Ho CO3......... **134** C6
Villa Rd CO3......... **134** C5
Villiers Pl CM3....... **206** E8
Villiers-Sur-Marne Ave
  CM23................. **145** D4
Vince Cl CO5......... **201** C6
Vincent Cl IP1......... **16** E8
Vine Dr CO7......... **137** C3
Vine Farm Rd CO7..... **137** C3
Vine Par CO7......... **137** C3
Viner Cotts CM3...... **175** B3
Vine Rd CO5......... **179** C6
Vinesse Rd CO6........ **81** D3
Vine St CM7.......... **72** B2
Vineway The CO12...... **91** B4
Vine Wlk IP9.......... **35** A1
Vineyard Gate 4 CO2... **135** F6
Vineyard St CO2...... **135** F6
Vineyards The★ CM7.. **153** D6
Vineyards The CM2.... **216** F7
Vinnicombe Ct 3 IP2... **16** E1
Vint Cres CO3........ **135** C6
Viola Wlk CO4....... **136** E7
Violet Cl
  Chelmsford CM1...... **205** E7
  Ipswich IP2........... **16** F4
Virgil Rd CM8........ **176** F5
Virginia Cl CO15...... **188** A1
Virley Cl CM9........ **210** A2
Viscount Dr CO4....... **110** C5
**Visitor Ctr & Country
  Wlk**★ CB9............ **9** C6
Vista Ave CO13....... **143** D1
Vista Ct IP2.......... **17** B4
Vista Rd CO15....... **189** A3
Vitlus Cl CO4........ **110** B6
Vitoria Mews CO2..... **135** C2
Vivian Ct CO14....... **171** C8
Volwycke Ave CM9.... **220** F8
Vyntoner Ho CO16..... **187** A4

W

Waddesdon Rd CO12.... **91** D4
Wade Rd CO15....... **189** B8
Wade Reach CO14..... **171** B8
Wadgate Rd IP11..... **221** C4
Wadhurst Rd IP3....... **18** D3
Wadley Cl CO5....... **179** E5
Wagtail Dr CM9...... **210** C5
Wagtail Rd CO5...... **158** C2

Wainsfield Villas CM6.... **70** B2
Wainwright Ave
  CM77................ **154** D8
Wainwright St CM23.... **145** C5
Wakefield Cl
  Colchester CO1....... **136** A8
  Great Chesterford CB10... **3** D3
Wakelin Way CM8..... **177** B2
WAKES COLNE........ **106** C6
WAKES COLNE GREEN
  .... **79** C1
Wakes Hall Bsns Ctr
  CO6.................. **106** B6
Wakeshall La C10....... **30** C8
Wakes St CO6........ **106** C6
Waldeck Ct CB11....... **43** D7
Waldegrave Cl CO11.... **86** B3
Waldegrave Rd CO11.... **86** C3
**Waldegraves Farm Cvn
  Site** CO5............. **201** G6
Waldegraves La CO5.... **201** G7
Waldegraves The CO8.... **79** E4
Waldegrave Way CO11... **86** B3
Walden Ave CB10....... **44** E2
Walden Cl CM9....... **196** A4
Walden Ho CO13...... **170** F4
Walden House Rd CM8,
  CM9................. **196** A4
Walden Pl CB10........ **22** D2
Walden Rd
  Ashdon CB10.......... **23** E6
  Great Chesterford CB10.. **3** E3
  Hadstock CB1........... **5** B6
  Littlebury CB10........ **21** F4
  Radwinter CB10........ **45** D7
  Sewards End CB10..... **23** D1
  Thaxted CM6.......... **69** F5
  Wendens Ambo CB11... **42** F6
  Wendons Ambo CB11... **43** A6
Walden Way CO13..... **171** A6
Waldgrooms CM6...... **123** C1
Waldingfield Rd CO10.... **33** F8
WALES END............ **1** A7
Walford Cl CO6....... **131** A2
Walford Pl CM2....... **205** F2
Walford Way CO6..... **131** A2
Walker Cl IP3......... **18** C5
Walkers Cl CM1....... **205** D7
Walkfares CM3....... **206** F8
Walk The
  Eight Ash G CO6...... **134** A8
  Felixstowe IP11....... **221** C5
  10 Ipswich IP1......... **17** C6
Wallace Binder Cl
  CM9................. **209** F1
Wallace Cres CM2..... **216** D8
Wallace La CM3...... **172** B7
Wallace Rd
  1 Colchester CO4..... **109** E2
  Ipswich IP1........... **16** E8
Wallace's La CM3..... **192** F4
Wallasea Gdns CM1.... **205** F5
Wall Ct 6 CM7........ **127** F1
Waller's Gr IP2........ **16** F4
Wallflower Ct 11 CM1... **205** F6
Wallis Cl CO3........ **134** E3
Wall La CO11.......... **88** D4
Wall St CO16........ **202** D6
Walls The CO11........ **86** E4
Walmer Cl CO7....... **185** F7
Walnut Dr
  Bishop's Stortford
  CM23................ **145** D4
  Colchester CO4....... **109** D5
  Witham CM8.......... **177** A4
Walnut Gr CM7....... **127** E2
Walnut Tree Cotts
  CM3................. **190** E5
Walnut Tree Ho CO3.... **135** B4
Walnuttree Hospl
  CO10................. **33** D7
Walnut Tree La
  Harkstead IP9......... **63** B2
  Sudbury CO10.......... **33** D7
Walnut Tree Way
  Colchester CO2....... **135** B3
  Tiptree CO5......... **179** C7
Walnut Way
  Brightlingsea CO7..... **185** E7
  Clacton-on-S CO15.... **188** C2
Walnut Wlk CM6...... **123** B1
Walsingham Cl CO10.... **34** C5
Walsingham St E CM22... **37** A8
Walsingham Rd CO2.... **135** F6
Walter Porter Ct CO4... **110** D1
Walter Radcliffe Way
  CO7................. **164** C7
Walters Cl CM2....... **216** C3
Walters Yd 6 CO1..... **135** F7
Walter Way CM8...... **156** D4
Waltham Cl IP2........ **17** A2
Waltham Glen CM2.... **216** C7
Waltham Rd
  Boreham CM3......... **193** A3
  Terling CM3.......... **175** D4
Waltham Way CO13.... **171** A5
WALTON............ **221** D6
Walton Ave IP11...... **221** A2
Walton Ct
  Colchester CO4....... **136** F4
  Felixstowe IP11....... **221** D6
Walton Hall La CM3.... **220** B1
Walton Ho
  4 Ipswich IP1......... **17** A6
  Walton-on-t-N CO14... **171** B8
Walton Maritime Mus★
  CO14................. **144** D1

Walton-On-Naze Sta
  CO14................. **171** C7
WALTON-ON-THE-NAZE
  .... **171** D8
**Walton-on-the-Naze Prim
  Sch** CO14............ **144** D1
Walton Rd
  Clacton-on-S CO15.... **189** A3
  Frinton-on-S CO13.... **170** F6
  Kirby-le-S CO13...... **170** E8
  Thorpe-le-S CO13,
  CO16................. **142** D2
  Walton-on-t-N CO13,
  CO14................. **171** B7
Wantz Chase CM9..... **210** A2
Wantz Haven CM9..... **210** A2
Wantz Rd CM9....... **210** A2
Wapping La CO7...... **165** B2
Warburton Ave CO9..... **75** D8
Ward Cres CM23...... **145** E6
Warde Chase CO14.... **171** B8
Warder Cl CM6....... **123** E1
Wardle Way CM1..... **204** E2
Wardley Cl IP2......... **16** D1
Ward Path CM2...... **206** B4
Ward Rd IP8.......... **16** B2
Wards Croft CB11...... **43** D7
Wareham Ave IP3....... **18** D3
Warehouse Rd CM6.... **124** F4
Warehouse Villas 3
  CM6................. **125** A4
Ware View Terr 4
  CM9................. **209** F2
Wargrave Rd CO15.... **188** D4
Warham Rd CO12....... **90** F1
Warish Hall Farm
  CM24................ **121** D1
Warley Cl CM7....... **128** C4
Warley Way CO13..... **171** B6
Warner Cl CM7....... **126** F1
Warner Dr CM7....... **127** D4
Warners CM6........ **150** D8
Warners Mill 13 CM7... **127** F2
**Warner Textile Archive
  (Mus)**★ CM7......... **127** F2
Warner Way CO10...... **34** A8
Warnham Cl CO16..... **188** B6
Warren Cl
  Broomfield CM1...... **191** B3
  Takeley CM22......... **148** D7
Warren Ct 12 CB9........ **8** E7
WARREN HEATH....... **18** F1
Warren Heath Ave IP3... **18** E1
Warren Heath Rd IP3.... **18** E1
Warren La CO3....... **134** C2
Warren Lingley Way
  CO5................. **179** E6
Warren Rd
  Braintree CM7........ **128** C2
  Halstead CO9.......... **76** D1
Warrenside CM7...... **155** A8
Warrens The
  Kirby Cross CO13..... **170** E6
  Wickham Bishops CM8.. **195** F5
Warrington Rd IP1...... **17** B7
Warwick Bailey Cl
  CO4................. **109** D2
Warwick Cl
  Braintree CM7........ **128** B4
  Little Easton CM6..... **122** F5
  Maldon CM9.......... **210** A1
Warwick Cres
  Clacton-on-S CO15.... **188** E3
  Maldon CM9.......... **210** A1
Warwick Ct 2 CB9........ **8** E8
Warwick Dr CM9...... **210** A1
Warwick Rd
  Bishop's Stortford
  CM23................ **146** B6
  Clacton-on-S CO15.... **188** E3
  Ipswich IP4........... **17** E6
  Takeley CM6.......... **148** E7
Warwick Sq CM7...... **204** F4
Washall Dr CM77...... **154** D8
WASHBROOK.......... **35** E4
Wash Cnr
  Aldham CO6.......... **107** C3
  Ramsey CO12.......... **89** C1
Washford Gdns CO15... **188** D2
Washington Cl CM7.... **209** E1
Washington Ct CO3.... **134** E5
Washington Rd
  Harwich CO12.......... **91** A2
  Maldon CM9.......... **209** F1
Wash La
  Clacton-on-S CO15.... **188** D1
  Goldhanger CM9...... **211** B7
Wasses Cnr CO16..... **141** D5
WATCH HOUSE GREEN
  .... **152** E7
Watch House Rd CM6... **124** F5
Watch House Villas
  CM6................. **152** D7
Watchouse Rd CM2.... **216** C3
WATER END........... **24** B6
Waterfront Terr
  CO14................. **144** D1
Waterglade Ret Pk
  CO15................. **188** E2
Water Hall La CM7.... **100** F6
Waterhouse Bsns Pk
  CM1................. **204** F1
Waterhouse La
  Ardleigh CO7......... **112** B5
  Chelmsford CM1...... **204** F1
Waterhouse St CM1.... **204** F1

Water La
  Bishop's Stortford
  CM23................ **145** F8
  Bures CO8............. **55** E1
  Cavendish CO10......... **1** D2
  Colchester CO3....... **135** D8
  Debden CB11.......... **44** B1
  Great Easton CM6.... **122** C7
  Helions Bumpstead CB9.. **26** D7
  Little Horkesley CO6... **81** E6
  Newport CB11......... **43** A1
  Pebmarsh CO9......... **78** A7
  Radwinter CB10........ **45** E8
  Shalford CM7......... **100** F3
  Stansted Mountfitchet
  CM24................ **119** E6
  Steeple Bumpstead CB9.. **27** B6
  Stisted CM7.......... **129** C5
  Stoke-by-N CO6........ **56** E8
  Sturmer CB9............ **9** F5
Waterloo La CM1..... **205** C2
Waterloo Rd IP1....... **17** A7
Watermill La CM23,
  CM24................ **119** B5
Watermill Rd CO5..... **158** E4
Waterside
  Brightlingsea CO7..... **185** F5
  Stansted Mountfitchet
  CM24................ **119** E6
Waterside Bsns Pk
  CM8................. **177** B4
Waterside La CO2..... **136** D4
Waterside Rd CM0.... **214** F3
Waterson Vale CM2.... **216** C8
Waterville Mews CO2... **136** B3
Waterwick Hill CB11.... **40** B1
Waterworks Cl CO2.... **161** E3
Waterworks Cotts
  CO5................. **179** A6
Waterworks Dr CO16... **188** B5
Waterworks Rd CM9... **199** D2
Waterworks St 6 1P4... **17** D5
Watery La
  Coggeshall CO6....... **130** A1
  Great Dunmow CM6... **150** A2
  Manuden CM23......... **92** C1
Watling La CM6........ **69** F3
Watling St CM6........ **70** A3
Watsham Pl CO7...... **137** C2
Watson Rd CO15..... **188** E3
Watson's Cl CB10...... **47** B4
Watsons Yd 9 CM23... **145** F8
Watts Cl CM6........ **151** B4
Watts Ct 1P4.......... **17** D5
Watts Rd CO2........ **135** B2
Watts Yd CM23........ **93** A2
Wat Tyler Wlk 1 CO1... **135** F7
Wave Bridge Ct CM9... **210** B5
Wavell Ave CO2...... **135** C4
Wavell Cl CM1....... **205** D8
Waveney Dr CM1..... **205** C6
Waveney Rd
  Felixstowe IP11....... **221** C3
  Ipswich IP1........... **16** E4
Waveney Terr CB9....... **9** A7
Wavring Ave CO13.... **170** E7
Wayback The CB10..... **22** E2
Way Bank La CO10..... **10** E7
Waylands Dr CO16.... **140** E1
Wayletts Dr CM23.... **146** B7
Wayside CM3........ **218** E8
Waytemore Castle★
  CM23................ **146** A7
Waytemore Rd CM23... **145** E6
Wear Dr CM1........ **205** D6
Weathervane Cotts
  CM7.................. **72** B1
Weaver Cl IP1.......... **16** B8
Weaverhead Cl CM6.... **70** A3
Weaverhead La CM6.... **70** A3
Weavers Cl
  Braintree CM7........ **127** F3
  Colchester CO3....... **134** F5
Weavers Ct
  Halstead CO9.......... **76** E1
  Harwich CO12.......... **91** D4
  6 Sudbury CO10........ **33** E7
Weavers Dr CO10........ **2** B4
Weaversfield CM8..... **156** C5
Weavers Gn CO6..... **107** D6
Weavers La CO10....... **33** E7
Weavers Row CO9...... **76** F1
Weaver St CM23...... **145** C4
Weavers Terr 7 CO10... **33** E7
Webb Cl CM2........ **206** B3
Webb Rd CM6........ **151** E6
Webb St IP2.......... **17** C3
Webster Cl CO9........ **75** D8
Weddell Rd CB9......... **9** C6
Wedgewood Dr 4
  CO4................. **109** E2
Wedgewood End CM7... **72** B2
Wedow Rd CM6........ **70** A3
WEELEY............ **140** E1
Weeley By-Pass Rd
  CO16................ **140** E1
WEELEY HEATH..... **168** A5
Weeley Rd
  Great Bentley, Aingers
  Green CO7........... **166** F5
  Great Bentley CO7.... **166** F8
  Little Clacton CO16... **168** C4
Weeley Sta CO16...... **167** F8
Weetmans Dr CO4.... **110** A5
Weggs Willow CO4.... **136** C7

Weighbridge Ct CB11 . . . . 43 D8
Weight Rd CM2 . . . . 205 C2
Weir La CO2, CO5 . . . . 163 C7
Welbeck Cl IP11 . . . . 221 A7
Welhams Way CO11 . . . . 86 D8
Welland Ave CM1 . . . . 204 C5
Wellands CM8 . . . . 195 E5
Wellands Cl CM8 . . . . 195 D5
Weller Gr CM1 . . . . 204 E7
Wellesley Ho **7** CO3 . . . . . 135 E6
Wellesley Rd
  Clacton-on-S CO15 . . . . . 188 E4
  Colchester CO3 . . . . 135 E6
  Ipswich IP4 . . . . 17 F5
Wellfield CM1 . . . . 204 A1
Well Field CO9 . . . . 103 F8
Wellfield Way CO13 . . . . . . 170 D7
Well-Green Cl CB11 . . . . 43 E7
Wellhouse Ave CO5 . . . . . . 201 E7
Wellington Cl
  Braintree CM7 . . . . 128 C4
  Chelmsford CM1 . . . . . . 204 D5
Wellington Ct **5** IP1 . . . . 17 A7
Wellington Rd
  Harwich CO12 . . . . 91 E6
  Maldon CM9 . . . . 209 E2
Wellington St
  Brightlingsea CO7 . . . . . 185 F6
  4 Colchester CO2 . . . . 135 E6
  Ipswich IP1 . . . . 17 A7
Wellington Terr **7** CB9 . . . . 8 E7
Well La
  Clare CO10 . . . . 12 B7
  Danbury CM3 . . . . 218 C2
  Easthorpe CO5 . . . . 160 A6
  Galleywood CM2 . . . . . . 216 B2
Wellmeads CM2 . . . . 216 B8
Wells Cl **4** IP4 . . . . 17 E6
Wells Cres **7** CM1 . . . . . 205 A3
Wells Ct
  Chelmsford CM1 . . . . . . 205 D5
  Great Dunmow CM6 . . . . 123 C1
Wells Hall Com Prim Sch
  CO10 . . . . 34 B4
Wells Hall Rd CO10 . . . . 34 C4
Well Side CO6 . . . . 132 E3
Wells Mead CB11 . . . . 67 D4
Wells Rd CO1 . . . . 136 B8
Well's St **3** CM1 . . . . 205 A3
Well St CO7 . . . . 185 E7
Well Terr CM9 . . . . 210 B5
Wellum Cl **8** CB9 . . . . 8 E7
WELSHWOOD PARK 110 F2
Welshwood Park Rd
  CO4 . . . . 110 F2
Welwyn Ct CO15 . . . . 188 D1
Wenden Rd CB11 . . . . 43 B7
WENDENS AMBO 42 E5
Wendy Cl IP9 . . . . 63 F7
Wenham La CO7 . . . . 59 D6
Wenham Rd IP8 . . . . 35 C7
Wenlock Rd CO16 . . . . 167 F6
Wenlock Way CM9 . . . . 210 A4
Wentford Ct CB9 . . . . 8 C8
Wents Cl CO7 . . . . 139 E1
Wentworth Cl CM3 . . . . 194 B4
Wentworth Cres CM7 . . . . . 127 F5
Wentworth Dr
  Bishop's Stortford
  CM23 . . . . 145 D6
  Ipswich IP8 . . . . 16 C2
Wentworth Mdws
  CM9 . . . . 209 F2
Wentworth Prim Sch
  CM9 . . . . 209 F1
Wentworth Terr **5** CB9 . . . 8 E8
Wesel Ave IP11 . . . . 221 B3
Wesley Ave CO4 . . . . 136 C8
WESLEY END 28 E4
Wesley End Rd CO9 . . . . 28 D4
Wesley Way IP1 . . . . 16 F8
West Acre Ct CO3 . . . . 135 B7
West Area IP1 . . . . 16 C7
West Ave
  Chelmsford CM1 . . . . . . 204 F5
  Clacton-on-S CO15 . . . . . 188 E2
West Bank Ferry Terminal
  IP2 . . . . 17 C2
West Belvedere CM3 . . . . . 218 F7
WEST BERGHOLT 108 D4
WESTBOURNE 16 F7
Westbourne Ct **1** CB9 . . . 9 A8
Westbourne Gr CM2 . . . . . 216 D7
Westbourne Rd IP1 . . . . 16 F8
West Bowers Rd CM9 . . . . . 208 C4
Westbury Cl CO6 . . . . 133 D5
Westbury Ct CO13 . . . . 170 F4
Westbury Rd
  Great Holland CO13 . . . . 170 A5
  Ipswich IP4 . . . . 18 B8
West Chase CM9 . . . . 209 F3
Westcliff CO15 . . . . 188 E1
Westcott Cl CO16 . . . . 188 D6
West Dock Rd CO12 . . . . 90 E5
West Dr CM7 . . . . 73 C3
West End La CO12 . . . . 91 B1
West End Mews CO3 . . . . . 135 B7
West End Rd
  Ipswich IP1 . . . . 17 A5
  Tiptree CO5 . . . . 179 C4
Westerdale CM1 . . . . 205 D7
Westerfield Ct IP4 . . . . 17 D7
Westerfield Rd IP4 . . . . 17 D8
Westergreen Mdw
  CM7 . . . . 127 E1

Westerings
  Bicknacre CM3 . . . . 218 F2
  Purleigh CM3 . . . . 220 D1
Westerings The CM2 . . . . . 216 F5
Westerlings The
  CM77 . . . . 155 E6
Western Cl
  Rushmere St A IP4 . . . . . . 18 F4
  Silver End CM8 . . . . 156 E3
Western Ho CO5 . . . . 158 C2
Western La CM8 . . . . 156 E3
Western Prom
  Brightlingsea CO7 . . . . . 185 D5
  Point Clear B CO16 . . . . . 185 E4
Western Rd
  Brightlingsea CO7 . . . . . 185 E6
  Silver End CM8 . . . . 156 E3
Western's End CO11 . . . . . . 86 D8
Westfield CO10 . . . . 12 A6
Westfield Ave CM1 . . . . . . 205 A4
Westfield Cl CM23 . . . . 145 E8
Westfield Com Prim Sch
  CB9 . . . . 9 B7
Westfield Dr CO6 . . . . 131 A3
Westfield Rd CM23 . . . . . . 145 E8
West Fields CB11 . . . . 43 E8
Westgate St IP1 . . . . 17 C6
West Green Cotts
  CO11 . . . . 86 A7
West Hanningfield Rd
  CM2 . . . . 217 A3
Westholme Rd IP1 . . . . 17 A8
Westlake Cres CO7 . . . . . . 137 A2
Westlands Com Prim Sch
  CM1 . . . . 204 B7
West Lawn
  Galleywood CM2 . . . . . . 216 C2
  Ipswich IP4 . . . . 18 C8
Westleton Way IP11 . . . . . 221 B5
Westley La CB10 . . . . 22 D5
West Lo CO3 . . . . 135 C6
West Lodge Rd CO3 . . . . . . 135 D6
WEST MERSEA 201 C5
West Mill Gn IP9 . . . . 60 E6
Westminster Cl IP4 . . . . 18 B5
Westminster Ct
  Clacton-on-S CO15 . . . . . 189 B3
  Colchester CO2 . . . . 136 C4
Westminster Gdns
  CM7 . . . . 128 B4
Westmorland Cl CO11 . . . . . 87 B4
Weston Rd CO2 . . . . 136 B4
West Quay CO7 . . . . 164 B7
West Rd
  Bishop's Stortford
  CM23 . . . . 145 E6
  Clacton-on-S CO15 . . . . . 203 H8
  Halstead CO9 . . . . 76 E1
  Ipswich IP3 . . . . 38 E8
  Saffron Walden CB11 . . . . 43 D8
  Stansted Mountfitchet
  CM24 . . . . 119 E6
Westridge Way CO15 . . . . . 189 A6
Westropps CO10 . . . . 15 C5
Westside Ctr CO3 . . . . 134 A5
West Sq CM9 . . . . 209 F3
West St
  Coggeshall CO6 . . . . 130 E1
  Colchester CO2 . . . . 135 E6
  Harwich CO12 . . . . 91 D6
  Rowhedge CO5 . . . . 163 F8
  Tollesbury CM9 . . . . 199 C1
  Walton-on-t-N CO14 . . . . 171 C4
  Wivenhoe CO7 . . . . 164 B8
West Station Ind Est
  CM9 . . . . 209 E1
West Station Rd CM9 . . . . . 209 E1
West Station Yd CM9 . . . . . 220 E8
West Stockwell St
  CO1 . . . . 135 F7
West View CM22 . . . . 148 C8
West View Cl CO4 . . . . 110 B3
Westway
  Chelmsford CM1 . . . . . . 215 E8
  Colchester CO1, CO3 . . . . 135 E8
Westwood Ave IP1 . . . . 17 A4
Westwood Ct IP1 . . . . 17 A4
Westwood Dr CO5 . . . . 201 E6
West Wood Hill CO4 . . . . . . 109 B3
West Yd CO9 . . . . 103 E8
Wetherfield CM24 . . . . 119 D7
WETHERSFIELD 73 C3
Wethersfield CE Prim Sch
  CM7 . . . . 73 C3
Wethersfield Rd
  Blackheath CO2 . . . . 163 A8
  Shalford CM7 . . . . 100 E1
  Sible Hedingham CO9 . . . . 51 C1
Wet La CO4 . . . . 82 E5
Wetzlar Ct CO2 . . . . 136 B4
Weyland Dr CO3 . . . . 134 D4
Weymouth Cl CO15 . . . . . . 203 J8
Weymouth Rd
  Chelmsford CM1 . . . . . . 205 E6
  Ipswich IP4 . . . . 17 F6
Whalebone Cnr CO4 . . . . . . 83 F7
Whaley Rd CO4 . . . . 136 C7
Wharfe Cl CM8 . . . . 176 E2
Wharf La CO8 . . . . 79 F8
Wharf Pl CM23 . . . . 146 A6
Wharf Rd
  12 Bishop's Stortford
  CM23 . . . . 145 F6
  Chelmsford CM2 . . . . . . 205 C2
  Heybridge Basin CM9 . . . 210 F4
Wharton Dr CM1 . . . . 204 A7
Wheat Croft CM23 . . . . . . 145 E4
Wheater Ind Est CM8 . . . . . 177 B1

Wheatfield Rd CO3 . . . . . . 134 D5
Wheatfield Way CM1 . . . . . 204 F3
Wheatlands
  Ardleigh CO7 . . . . 111 E7
  Elmstead Market CO7 . . . 137 F6
Wheatley Ave CM7 . . . . . . 128 C3
Wheaton Rd CM8 . . . . 177 B2
Wheatsheaf Cl CO11 . . . . . . 88 D3
Wheatsheaf Ct **14**
  CO1 . . . . 136 A6
Wheatsheaf La CO11 . . . . . . 88 D3
Wheeler Cl CO4 . . . . 136 C7
Wheeler's Hill CM3 . . . . . . 191 D6
Wheelwrights Cl
  CM23 . . . . 145 C4
Wheelwrights The
  IP11 . . . . 221 A8
Wherry La **13** IP4 . . . . . . 17 D5
Wherry Quay IP4 . . . . 17 D5
Whinchat Cl IP2 . . . . 16 D3
Whinfield Ave CO12 . . . . . . 90 F1
Whitbreads Farm La
  CM3 . . . . 173 D4
Whitby Rd IP4 . . . . 17 F8
White Arch Pl CO4 . . . . 83 B6
WHITEASH GREEN 76 B2
White Barns CM3 . . . . 172 B6
Whitebeam Cl
  Chelmsford CM2 . . . . . . 215 F7
  Colchester CM6 . . . . 109 D5
White Bear CM24 . . . . 119 E8
White Caville CB9 . . . . 8 C8
WHITE COLNE 105 E6
White Cotts CM3 . . . . 174 E5
White Court Prim Sch
  CM77 . . . . 154 C6
White Cross CO11 . . . . 89 A2
Whiteditch La CB11 . . . . . . 42 F2
White Elm Rd CM3 . . . . . . 219 A2
White Elm St IP3 . . . . 17 E4
Whitefriars Way CO3 . . . . . 135 A5
Whitegate Rd CO7 . . . . . . 186 A6
Whitegates CM6 . . . . 97 F4
Whitegates Cl CM77 . . . . . 154 C6
Whitehall Cl CO2 . . . . 136 C4
Whitehall Ct CM8 . . . . 177 A2
Whitehall Ind Est
  CO2 . . . . 136 D4
Whitehall La
  Bishop's Stortford
  CM23 . . . . 118 F1
  Thorpe-le-S CO16 . . . . . 141 C3
Whitehall Rd
  Bishop's Stortford
  CM23 . . . . 118 E1
  Colchester CO2 . . . . 136 D4
White Hart Cotts
  CM2 . . . . 206 A6
Whitehart Ct CO12 . . . . 91 D6
White Hart La
  Chelmsford CM1 . . . . . . 205 F8
  West Bergholt CO6 . . . . . 108 E5
Whitehead Cl CM1 . . . . . . 215 B8
White Horse Ave CO9 . . . . 103 D8
White Horse Cotts IP9 . . . . . 36 D1
White Horse Hill IP9 . . . . . . 36 D1
White Horse La
  Maldon CM9 . . . . 209 F2
  Newport CB11 . . . . 43 A1
  Witham CM8 . . . . 176 F3
White Horse Rd
  Capel St M IP9 . . . . 35 B1
  East Bergholt CO7 . . . . . . 59 E1
Whitehouse Cres
  CM2 . . . . 216 D8
Whitehouse Hill CM9 . . . . . 199 A7
Whitehouse La
  Belchamp St P CO10 . . . . 13 B2
  West Bergholt CO6 . . . . . 108 D3
Whitehouse Rd CM6 . . . . . 124 F5
White Lodge Cres
  CO16 . . . . 142 C1
White Mead CM1 . . . . 191 B4
WHITE NOTLEY 155 E1
White Notley CE Prim Sch
  CM8 . . . . 155 E1
White Notley Sta CM8 . . . . 155 F2
Whitepost Ct CM23 . . . . . . 146 A5
White Post Field CM6 . . . . 150 E8
Whitesbridge La CM4 . . . . 215 D1
Whites Field CO7 . . . . 59 B3
Whiteshot Way CB10 . . . . . . 22 F2
Whites La CM3 . . . . 173 E6
White St CM6 . . . . 150 D8
Whitethorn Cl CO4 . . . . . . 136 D6
Whitethorn Gdns
  CM2 . . . . 216 C7
Whiteways IP3 . . . . 18 F1
Whiteways CB10 . . . . 3 C2
Whiteways Ct CM8 . . . . . . 176 E3
Whitewell Rd **10** CO2 . . . 135 F6
Whitfield Link CM2 . . . . . . 216 D7
Whitland Cl IP2 . . . . 37 A8
Whitlands CO10 . . . . 2 B6
Whitley's Chase CM7 . . . . . 48 D5
Whitmore Cres CM2 . . . . . 206 B4
Whittaker Way CO5 . . . . . . 201 B7
Whittington Way
  CM23 . . . . 145 F3
Whittle Rd IP2 . . . . 16 F6
Whitworth Cl IP2 . . . . 16 D2
Whybrews **4** CO4 . . . . . . 136 C8
Whytes Cotts CO6 . . . . . . 133 B8
Whyverne Cl CM1 . . . . 205 E6

WICKEN BONHUNT 66 C7
Wicken Rd
  Arkesden CB11 . . . . 41 F1
  Newport CB11 . . . . 66 F8
Wickfield Ash CM1 . . . . . . 204 D6
Wickham Bishop Rd
  CM3 . . . . 194 D4
WICKHAM BISHOPS 195 D5
Wickhambrook Ct
  IP11 . . . . 221 A4
Wickham Cres
  Braintree CM7 . . . . 128 A2
  Chelmsford CM1 . . . . . . 204 F6
Wickham Hall La
  CM8 . . . . 195 D3
Wickham Rd
  Colchester CO3 . . . . 135 D6
  Witham CM8 . . . . 194 F8
WICKHAM ST PAUL 53 C6
Wickham's Chase
  CM3 . . . . 219 C2
Wickhay Cotts CM3 . . . . . . 207 D5
Wick La
  Ardleigh CO7 . . . . 111 B8
  Fingringhoe CO5 . . . . . . 164 C3
  Harwich CO12 . . . . 91 B2
  St Osyth Heath CO7,
  CO16 . . . . 167 C3
Wicklow Ave CM1 . . . . 204 D6
Wick Rd
  Colchester CO2 . . . . 136 D2
  Great Bentley CO7 . . . . . 167 B5
  Langham CO4 . . . . 83 F3
  Thorington Street CO4,
  CO6 . . . . 57 C2
Wicks Cl CM7 . . . . 127 C4
Wicks Pl CM1 . . . . 205 A3
Wick Terr CO4 . . . . 83 F3
WIDDINGTON 67 E4
WIDFORD 215 E6
Widford Chase CM2 . . . . . . 215 F7
Widford Cl CM2 . . . . 215 F7
Widford Gr CM2 . . . . 215 F7
Widford Ind Est CM1 . . . . . 215 E8
Widford Lodge Prep Sch
  CM2 . . . . 215 F7
Widford Lodge Sch
  CM2 . . . . 215 F7
Widford Park Pl CM2 . . . . . 215 F7
Widford Rd CM2 . . . . 215 F7
Widgeon Cl IP2 . . . . 16 F3
Widgeon Pl CO5 . . . . 158 C2
Widleybrook La
  Blackmore End CM7 . . . . . 74 A2
  Wethersfield CM7 . . . . . . 73 F3
Wigborough Rd
  Layer de la H CO2 . . . . . . 161 E2
  Peldon CO5 . . . . 182 C5
Wigboro Wick La
  CO16 . . . . 186 F2
Wigeon Cl CM77 . . . . 154 C5
WIGGENS GREEN 8 E1
Wiggins View CM2 . . . . . . 206 B4
Wigmore Cl IP2 . . . . 16 F1
Wignall St CO11 . . . . 85 F3
Wilberforce St IP1 . . . . 17 A6
Wilbye Cl CO2 . . . . 135 B4
Wilbye Ho CO3 . . . . 135 A7
Wild Boar Field CM7 . . . . . 128 D3
Wilding Rd IP8 . . . . 16 B1
Wilkes Way CM6 . . . . 151 E6
Wilkin Cl CO3 . . . . 135 A4
Wilkin Dr CO5 . . . . 179 C5
Wilkinson Gr CM7 . . . . 155 B5
Wilkinson Pl CM3 . . . . 194 A3
Wilkinsons Mead
  CM2 . . . . 206 A4
Willets Pond CO7 . . . . 59 E1
Willett Rd CO2 . . . . 135 B3
Willetts Field CB10 . . . . 47 A3
William Booth Way
  IP11 . . . . 221 B5
William Boys Cl **1**
  CO4 . . . . 136 D8
William Cl CO7 . . . . 137 C4
William Dr CO15 . . . . 188 D2
William Groom Ave
  CO12 . . . . 91 A2
William Harris Way
  Beerchurch CO2 . . . . 162 F8
  Colchester CO2 . . . . 135 F1
William Ho **7** IP4 . . . . . . 17 D6
William Julien Courtauld
  Hosp CM7 . . . . 127 E2
William Paul Housing
  Trust **5** IP2 . . . . 17 C4
Williams Dr CM7 . . . . 127 F4
Williamson Ho **2**
  CO1 . . . . 136 A6
William Sparrow Ct
  CO7 . . . . 137 C2
Williams Rd CM1 . . . . 191 B1
William St **3** IP1 . . . . 17 C6
William's Wlk **8** CO1 . . . 135 F7
William Wood Ho **16**
  CO10 . . . . 33 E7
Willingale Rd CM7 . . . . 128 D4
Willingham Way CO4 . . . . . 136 E7
Willis Almshouses
  CM9 . . . . 196 B3
Willoughby Ave CO5 . . . . . 201 D6
Willoughby Dr CM2 . . . . . . 205 F2
Willoughby Rd IP2 . . . . 17 B4
Willoughby's La CM7 . . . . . 128 C8
Willow Ave
  Kirby Cross CO13 . . . . . . 170 D6
  Seawick CO16 . . . . 203 B6
Willowbank CM2 . . . . 216 B3

Willow Brook Prim Sch
  CO4 . . . . 110 C1
Willow Cl
  Ardleigh CO7 . . . . 110 D6
  Bishop's Stortford
  CM23 . . . . 145 E8
  Brightlingsea CO7 . . . . . 185 D6
  Broomfield CM1 . . . . 191 B1
  Sudbury CO10 . . . . 33 E6
Willow Cres CM3 . . . . 194 A3
Willow Dene CO9 . . . . 51 D2
Willow Hall La CO11 . . . . . 115 D8
Willow Mdws CO9 . . . . 75 E8
Willowmere Cvn Pk
  CO10 . . . . 34 B2
Willow Pk
  Copford CO6 . . . . 133 E5
  Weeley Heath CO16 . . . . 168 A6
Willow Rd CM6 . . . . 123 C1
Willow Rise CM8 . . . . 177 A5
WILLOWS GREEN 153 E4
Willows Prim Sch The
  IP2 . . . . 16 F2
Willows The
  Boreham CM3 . . . . 206 F8
  Chelmsford CM1 . . . . . . 205 A2
  Colchester CO2 . . . . 136 A3
  Frinton-on-S CO13 . . . . . 170 F5
  Great Chesterford CB10 . . . 3 D3
Willow Tree Ct **1**
  CO4 . . . . 136 E8
Willow Tree Way CO6 . . . . 105 B6
Willow Way
  Clacton-on-S CO15 . . . . . 203 G7
  Halstead CO9 . . . . 76 D1
  Harwich CO12 . . . . 90 F2
Willow Wlk
  Heybridge CM9 . . . . 210 C6
  Tiptree CO5 . . . . 179 C7
  Weeley CO16 . . . . 167 F8
Will's Ayley La CB10 . . . . . 23 F2
Wills Gn CO5 . . . . 158 F6
Willum Ho CB10 . . . . 22 D1
Wilmington Rd CO4 . . . . . . 110 C2
Wilmslow Dr IP2 . . . . 16 C2
Wilshire Ave CM2 . . . . 205 F3
Wilson Cl
  Bishop's Stortford
  CM23 . . . . 145 F5
  Wivenhoe CO7 . . . . 137 A2
Wilson Ct CO15 . . . . 189 B8
Wilson Marriage Rd
  CO4 . . . . 110 C1
Wilson Rd IP8 . . . . 16 B1
Wilson's Ct CM9 . . . . 210 B2
Wilson's La CO6 . . . . 132 E3
Wilton Cl CM23 . . . . 146 B7
Wilton Ho CO16 . . . . 188 C5
WIMBISH 45 C6
WIMBISH GREEN 45 E3
Wimbish Prim Sch
  CB10 . . . . 45 C4
Wimbish Wlk CB10 . . . . 44 E2
Wimborne Ave IP3 . . . . 18 E4
Wimbourne Gdns
  CO13 . . . . 170 F7
Wimbourne Ho CO12 . . . . . 91 D3
Wimpole Cl IP5 . . . . 18 F6
Wimpole Rd CO1 . . . . 136 B5
Wimsey Ct CM8 . . . . 177 A5
Wincelow Hall Rd
  CB10 . . . . 25 E2
Winchelsea Dr CM2 . . . . . . 216 E7
Winchelsea Pl CM7 . . . . . . 185 F8
Winchester Cl CM23 . . . . . 145 D4
Winchester Ct
  Chelmsford CM1 . . . . . . 205 A5
  Frinton-on-S CO13 . . . . . 171 A5
Winchester Rd
  Colchester CO2 . . . . 136 B5
  Frinton-on-S CO13 . . . . . 171 A5
Winchester Way IP2 . . . . . . 36 F8
Winckford Cl CM3 . . . . 191 B6
Windermere Cl IP3 . . . . 38 B8
Windermere Ct CO15 . . . . . 189 A3
Windermere Dr CM77 . . . . 154 C6
Windermere Rd
  Clacton-on-S CO15 . . . . . 189 C6
  Great Notley CM77 . . . . . 154 C7
  Sudbury CO10 . . . . 34 A8
Windham Rd CO10 . . . . 34 B8
Windhill CM23 . . . . 145 E7
Windhill Old Rd CM23 . . . . 145 E7
Windhill Prim Sch
  CM23 . . . . 145 E6
Winding Piece IP9 . . . . 35 A1
Windley Tye CM1 . . . . 204 B3
Windmill Cl
  Boxted CO4 . . . . 82 F4
  Great Dunmow CM6 . . . . 123 E1
  Ramsey CO12 . . . . 89 F1
  Stansted Mountfitchet
  CM24 . . . . 119 E7
Windmill Ct
  Clacton-on-S CO15 . . . . . 188 E5
  Colchester CO4 . . . . 109 E4
  Copford CO6 . . . . 133 D4
Windmill Fields CO6 . . . . . 130 F3
Windmill Gdns CM7 . . . . . 128 A8
Windmill Hill CB10,
  CB11 . . . . 22 B3
Windmill Pk CO15 . . . . 188 F5
Windmill Pl CO10 . . . . 2 E7
Windmill Rd
  Bradfield CO11 . . . . 87 C1
  Halstead CO9 . . . . 76 D1
Windmill Row CO10 . . . . . . 2 C5
Windmills CO6 . . . . 106 C1

Windmills The CM1 . . . . . 191 B3
Windmill The CM24 . . . . 119 D6
Windmill View C05 . . . . 179 C6
Windrush Dr CM1 . . . . 205 C6
Windsor Ave C015 . . . . 188 D3
Windsor Cl
 Colchester C02 . . . . . 136 A2
 Witham CM8 . . . . . . 194 F8
Windsor Ct
 1 Braintree CM7 . . . . 128 B2
 Brightlingsea C07 . . . . 185 F6
 6 Colchester C01 . . . 136 C6
Windsor Gdns
 Bishop's Stortford
 CM23 . . . . 145 C7
 Braintree CM7 . . . . . 128 B4
Windsor Ho C05 . . . . . 201 D7
Windsor Pl C010 . . . . . 34 A7
Windsor Rd
 Clacton-on-S C015 . . . 188 D3
 Felixstowe IP11 . . . . 221 C3
 Ipswich IP1 . . . . . . 16 F7
 West Mersea C05 . . . . 201 D7
Windsor Terr CB9 . . . . . 8 E8
Windsor View C09 . . . . 53 C6
Windsor Way CM1 . . . . 204 E1
Winfield Terr C014 . . . . 144 D2
Winfrith Rd IP3 . . . . . . 18 D4
Wingate Cl CM7 . . . . . 127 E5
Wingate Ho **6** IP1 . . . . 17 A7
Wingfield St 1P4 . . . . . 17 D5
Wingrove Ct CM1 . . . . . 205 A6
Winnocks **5** C01 . . . . 136 A6
Winnock's Almshouses **4**
 C01 . . . . 136 A6
Winsey Chase CM7 . . . . 72 C6
Winsford Way CM2 . . . . 206 C6
Winsgate Ho **6** IP1 . . . . 17 A7
Winsley Cl C01 . . . . . . 136 B6
Winsley Sq C01 . . . . . . 136 B4
Winstanley Rd CB11 . . . . 43 E7
Winston Ave
 Colchester C03 . . . . 135 B4
 Ipswich IP4 . . . . . . 18 C8
 Tiptree C05 . . . . . . 179 C6
Winston Cl
 Braintree CM7 . . . . . 127 E6
 Felixstowe IP11 . . . . 221 B5
Winston Ct C013 . . . . . 170 F4
Winston Way C09 . . . . . 77 A3
Winstree Cl C02 . . . . . 161 F5
Winstree Ct C03 . . . . . 134 C4
Winstree Rd C03 . . . . . 134 B4
Winterbournes C014 . . . . 171 A7
Winter's Hill C01 . . . . . 160 F1
Winter's Rd C05 . . . . . 160 E1
Wisdoms Gn C06 . . . . . 131 B3
WISSINGTON 81 D7
Wistaria Pl C016 . . . . . 188 C5
Wisteria Ct **3** C04 . . . . 136 C5
Wisteria Lo **7** CM1 . . . . 205 F6
Wiston Rd C06 . . . . . . 81 D8
Witch Elm C012 . . . . . . 90 F2
Witch La C06 . . . . 131 B8
Witchtree La CB10 . . . . . 25 F3
WITHAM 176 E4
Witham Lo CM8 . . . . . . 194 D7
Witham Rd
 Black Notley CM77,
 CM8 . . . . 155 B5
 Cressing CM77 . . . . . 156 B3
 Langford CM9 . . . . . 209 D7
 Terling CM3 . . . . . . 175 E2
 Tolleshunt Major CM9 . . 197 D5
 Wickham Bishops CM8 . . 195 E6
Witham Sta CM8 . . . . . 177 A3
WITHERMARSH GREEN
 . . . . 57 C7
Withersfield Rd CB9 . . . . 8 F8
Withipoll St 1P4 . . . . . . 17 D6
Withrick Wlk C016 . . . . . 187 A5
Witney Cl IP3 . . . . 38 D8
Witting Cl C016 . . . . . . 188 D5

Witton Wood Rd
 C013 . . . . 170 E5
WIVENHOE 137 C2
Wivenhoe Bsns Ctr
 C07 . . . . 164 C8
Wivenhoe Cross C07 . . . 137 C2
WIVENHOE PARK 137 A4
Wivenhoe Rd
 Alresford C07 . . . . . 165 B7
 Colchester C07 . . . . 111 C1
Wivenhoe Sta C07 . . . . 164 B8
WIX 115 C5
Wix By-Pass C011 . . . . 115 C6
WIX GREEN 115 D5
Wix Rd
 Beaumont C016 . . . . 141 E8
 Bradfield C011 . . . . . 87 E1
 Great Oakley C012 . . . 116 B3
 Ramsey C012 . . . . . . 89 F1
 Tendring C011 . . . . . 114 F8
 Wix C011 . . . . 115 C3
Wix & Wrabness Prim Sch
 C011 . . . . 115 B5
Woburn Ave
 Bishop's Stortford
 CM23 . . . . 145 C7
Woburn Ct CM2 . . . . . . 205 A1
Woden Ave C03 . . . . . . 134 D4
Wolfe Ave C01, C02 . . . 136 A5
Wolmers Hey CM3 . . . . 190 F7
Wolseley Ave C015 . . . . 203 E6
Wolseley Rd CM2 . . . . . 205 A1
Wolsey Art Gall* 1P4 . . . 17
 D6**Wolsey Ct** IP11 . . . . 221 E3
Wolsey Gdns IP11 . . . . 221 E3
Wolsey St **9** IP1 . . . . . 17 C5
Wolton Rd C02 . . . . . . 135 B2
Wolves Hall La C016 . . . 114 F1
Wood Barn La C011 . . . . 85 D1
Woodberry Way
 C014 . . . . 171 C7
Woodbridge Gr C016 . . . 188 A4
Woodbridge Rd
 Ipswich, California IP5 . . 18 B7
 Ipswich IP4 . . . . . . 17 E6
 Rushmere St A IP5 . . . 18 D7
Woodbridge Rd E IP4 . . . 18 D7
Wood Cnr
 Fordham Heath C06 . . . 107 F1
 Maldon CM9 . . . . . . 209 B2
Woodcock Cl
 Colchester C04 . . . . 136 E6
 Haverhill CB9 . . . . . . 9 C7
Woodcock Rd IP2 . . . . . 16 E2
Wood Dale CM2 . . . . . . 216 E6
Wood End CB11 . . . . . . 67 D3
WOODEND GREEN 95 A6
Woodfield Cl
 Stansted Mountfitchet
 CM24 . . . . 119 E6
 Walton-on-t-N C014 . . . 171 A7
Woodfield Cotts CM9 . . . 210 C6
Woodfield Dr C05 . . . . . 201 B7
Wood Field End C02 . . . 162 A5
Woodfield La IP9 . . . . . . 61 E3
Woodfield Rd CM7 . . . . 128 A3
Woodfields CM24 . . . . . 119 E6
Woodfield Terr CM24 . . . 119 E6
Woodfield Way CM3 . . . . 194 A4
Woodford Cl C015 . . . . 188 F8
Woodgates IP11 . . . . . 221 B6
WOODGATES END 121 D7
Woodgates Farm
 CM6 . . . . 121 E7
Wood Green Est C07 . . . 166 F5
WOOD HALL 65 D8
Woodhall Bsns Pk
 C010 . . . . 15 F2
Woodhall Cl C010 . . . . . 15 E1
Woodhall Com Prim Sch
 C010 . . . . 15 F2
Woodhall Gr CM23 . . . . 145 D6
Woodhall Hill CM1 . . . . 190 C2

Woodhall Par CM1 . . . . 205 A7
Woodhall Rd
 Chelmsford CM1 . . . . 205 A7
 Sudbury C010 . . . . . 15 E1
Woodham Dr CM3 . . . . 194 B4
WOODHAM MORTIMER
 . . . . 219 F6
Woodham Mortimer Rd
 CM9 . . . . 219 E8
WOODHAM WALTER 208 E2
Woodham Walter CE Prim
 Sch CM9 . . . . 208 D3
WOODHILL 218 B5
Woodhill Common Rd
 CM3 . . . . 218 B5
Woodhill Rd
 Chelmsford CM2 . . . . 217 E6
 Danbury CM3 . . . . . 218 B6
Woodhouse La
 Broomfield CM3 . . . . 191 A4
 Great Horkesley C06 . . . 109 A6
Woodhouse Sq **5** 1P4 . . . 17 D5
Wood La
 Birchanger CM23 . . . . 119 E2
 Brent Pelham SG9 . . . . 64 A6
 Clacton-on-S C015 . . . 169 C2
 Fordham Heath C03 . . . 107 F1
 Heybridge CM9 . . . . 210 A5
Woodland Chase C03 . . . 107 F1
Woodland Dr C03 . . . . . 134 F5
WOODLAND GREEN 9 E6
Woodland Rd CM1 . . . . 205 A4
Woodlands
 Bishop's Stortford
 CM23 . . . . 146 C8
 Braintree CM7 . . . . . 128 C3
 Broomfield CM1 . . . . 191 A4
 Chelmondiston IP9 . . . . 63 E7
 Colchester C04 . . . . 110 F2
 Great Oakley C012 . . . 116 B2
 Great Waltham CM1 . . . 190 F4
 Ipswich IP8 . . . . . . 16 C1
 Jaywick C016 . . . . . 188 A1
Woodlands Cl C015 . . . . 189 A8
Woodlands Park Dr
 CM6 . . . . 123 B1
Woodlands Rd IP9 . . . . . 62 D7
Woodlands Rise C016 . . . 140 F1
Woodlands The C07 . . . . 185 E8
Woodlands Way CM3 . . . 190 F4
Woodlands Wlk CM6 . . . 123 B1
Woodland Way
 Gosfield C09 . . . . . . 102 E8
 Wivenhoe C07 . . . . . 137 B1
Woodlark Cl CM1 . . . . . 16 C1
Woodlyn Ct C015 . . . . . 189 E6
Woodpecker Cl
 Bishop's Stortford
 CM23 . . . . 145 C6
 2 Colchester C04 . . . 136 F8
Woodpecker Rd IP2 . . . . 16 D3
Wood Rd CM9 . . . . 210 B6
Woodroffe Cl CM2 . . . . 206 A3
Woodrolfe Farm La
 CM9 . . . . 199 E1
Woodrolfe Pk CM9 199
 F2**Woodrolfe Rd** CM9 . . . 199 E2
Woodrose Lo **6** CM1 . . . 205 F6
Woodrows La C016 . . . . 188 B5
Woodrow Way C04 . . . . 136 E7
Woodrush End C03 . . . . 134 B6
Woodrush Rd IP3 . . . . . 18 E2
Woods Cl CB9 . . . . 9 E5
Woods Ct C04 . . . . 109 D2
Woodside
 Bishop's Stortford
 CM23 . . . . 146 D8
 Great Totham CM9 . . . 196 B3
 Little Baddow CM3 . . . 207 F1
 Walton-on-t-N C014 . . . 171 B7
Woodside Cl C04 . . . . . 110 E1
WOODSIDE GREEN 146 F1
Woodside Way CM6 . . . . 123 A1
Woodspring Cl **2** IP2 . . . 17 A2

Woods Rd CM3 . . . . . . 172 B6
Wood St CM2 . . . . 216 A7
Woodstock C05 . . . . . . 201 C7
Woodstock Pl CM2 . . . . 216 F5
Wooview Cl C04 . . . . . . 110 D4
Woodview Cotts C05 . . . 180 C8
Woodview Dr CM3 . . . . 174 A7
Woodview Rd CM6 . . . . 150 D8
Woodville Rd IP4 . . . . . 17 F5
Woodward Cl IP2 . . . . . 16 D5
Wood Way CM77 . . . . . 154 B6
Woodyards CM0 . . . . . 214 F3
Woollards Cl IP1 . . . . . . 17 A6
Woollards Gdns C010 . . . 15 C8
Woolner Rd C016 . . . . . 188 D6
Woolnough Ct CB9 . . . . 27 B6
Woolpack La CM7 . . . . . 127 C5
Woolpit Downs C08 . . . . 79 E8
Woolpit's Rd CM7 . . . . . 99 E1
Woolridge Pl CM8 . . . . 195 E5
WOOLVERSTONE 38 A1
Woolverstone Cl IP2 . . . 16 C1
Woolwich Rd C016 . . . . 188 C5
Wootton Dr IP1 . . . . . . 17 C8
Worcester Cl CM7 . . . . . 128 A1
Worcester Cres C07 . . . . 165 B8
Worcester Ct
 Clacton-on-S C015 . . . 188 E1
 Great Baddow CM2 . . . 217 A5
Worcester Ho CB9 . . . . . 9 B6
Worcester Rd
 Colchester C01 . . . . 136 A8
 Ipswich IP3 . . . . . . 38 B8
Wordsworth Ct CM1 . . . 205 A5
Wordsworth Rd
 Braintree CM7 . . . . . 127 F7
 Colchester C03 . . . . 134 F6
Wordsworths Way
 C016 . . . . 188 A5
Workhouse Cnr C012 . . . 116 C3
WORKHOUSE GREEN 55 E7
WORKHOUSE HILL 82 E4
Workhouse Hill C04 . . . . 82 E4
Workhouse Rd C06 . . . . 81 C2
Worlds End La C05 . . . . 158 D3
WORMINGFORD 80 E4
Worrin Rd CM6 . . . . . . 151 E6
Worsdell Way C04 . . . . 109 F2
Worsley Cl IP2 . . . . 16 D2
Worsnop Ho C02 . . . . . 136 B5
Wortham Pl CB9 . . . . . . 9 A8
Worthing Mews C015 . . . 203 I8
Worthington Way
 C03 . . . . 134 F4
WRABNESS 88 E4
Wrabness Local Nature
 Reserve* C011 . . . . . 88 C4
Wrabness Rd
 Ramsey C012 . . . . . . 90 A2
 Wrabness C012 . . . . . 89 D3
Wrabness Sta C011 . . . . 89 A4
Wraglins The CM23 . . . . 146 B5
Wratting Rd CB9 . . . . . . 9 A8
Wren Ave IP2 . . . . 16 D3
Wrenbrook Rd CM23 . . . 145 F6
Wren Cl
 Colchester C03 . . . . 134 C4
 Great Bentley C07 . . . 139 D1
Wrendale C015 . . . . . . 188 F6
Wren Ho C03 . . . . 134 F5
Wright Ct **2** CM7 . . . . 127 F3
Wright Mead CM2 . . . . 206 B4
Wright Rd IP3 . . . . 18 C2
Wright's Ave CM77 . . . . 155 E6
Wright's Piece CM22 . . . 95 A6
WRITTLE 204 A2
Writtle Cl C016 . . . . . . 188 B4
Writtle Coll CM1 . . . . . 204 B3
Writtle Jun & Inf Schs
 CM1 . . . . 215 A8
Writtle Rd CM1 . . . . . . 215 E8
Wroxham Cl C03 . . . . . 135 B6
Wroxham Rd IP3 . . . . . . 17 F3
Wryneck Cl C04 . . . . . . 109 F3
Wulvesford CM8 . . . . . 194 D8

Wyatts La C010 . . . . . . 55 D8
Wych Elm C02 . . . . . . 136 A3
Wycke Hill CM9 . . . . . . 220 D8
Wycke Hill Bsns Pk
 CM9 . . . . 220 E8
Wycke La CM9 . . . . . . 213 E8
Wycliffe Gr C01 . . . . . . 109 E1
Wycliffe Ho CM1 . . . . . 205 E5
Wyedale Dr C03 . . . . . 134 E5
Wye Rd IP3 . . . . 18 A3
Wykeham Rd CM1 . . . . 204 B1
Wykes Bishop St IP3 . . . 17 E4
Wyncolls Rd C04 . . . . . 110 D6
Wyndam Cl C02 . . . . . 163 B8
Wyndham Cres C015 . . . 189
 A5**Wynterton Cl** IP3 . . . 18 B1
Wynyard Rd CB10 . . . . . 22 E2
Wyseman Pl C011 . . . . 86 C7
Wyvern Ct C07 . . . . . . 137 B1
Wyverne CM6 . . . . 151 A5
Wyvern Rd IP3 . . . . . . 18 C1

Y

Yale Bsns Pk IP3 . . . . . 38 E8
Yale Mews C04 . . . . . . 110 B4
Yardley Hall La CM6 . . . . 69 D6
Yard The CM7 . . . . 128 A2
Yare Ave CM8 . . . . 176 D2
Yarmouth Cl C016 . . . . 188 E6
Yarmouth Pl CB9 . . . . . 9 A8
Yarmouth Rd IP1 . . . . . 17 A6
Yarwood Rd CM2 . . . . . 205 E2
Yeldham Lock CM2 . . . . 206 A2
Yeldham Pl CB9 . . . . . . 9 A8
Yeldham Rd C09 . . . . . 51 D3
Yeoman Cl IP2 . . . . 16 F6
Yeoman Lo CM2 . . . . . 205 F3
Yeoman Rd IP11 . . . . . 221 B3
Yeomans Cl CM23 . . . . 145 D6
Yerril Gdn CB9 . . . . 8 E7
Yetton Ward Ho IP11 . . . 221 C5
Yew Cl CM8 . . . . 177 B5
Yew Ct IP2 . . . . 17 B3
Yew Tree Cl
 Colchester C04 . . . . 136 E8
 Hatfield Peverel CM3 . . . 194 A5
Yewtree Gdns CM2 . . . . 216 C6
Yew Tree Pl CM23 . . . . 145 F8
Yewtree Gr IP5 . . . . . . 18 F7
Yewtree Rise IP8 . . . . . 16 C1
Yew Way C015 . . . . . . 203 F6
Yonge Cl CM3 . . . . 192 E1
Yorick Ave C05 . . . . . . 201 C6
Yorick Rd C05 . . . . 201 C6
York Cl C010 . . . . 33 E8
York Ct **4** CM7 . . . . . . 128 B2
York Gdns CM7 . . . . . . 128 B4
York Mans C015 . . . . . 189 E5
York Pl C01 . . . . 136 A8
York Rd
 Brightlingsea C07 . . . . 185 E6
 Chelmsford CM2 . . . . 216 A8
 Clacton-on-S C015 . . . 189 E5
 Earls Colne C06 . . . . 105 B6
 Felixstowe IP11 . . . . 221 E4
 Haverhill CB9 . . . . . . 8 E7
 Ipswich IP3 . . . . . . 18 A4
 Sudbury C010 . . . . . 33 E8
York St **7** C011 . . . . . . 86 D4
Young Cl C016 . . . . . . 188 C5
YOUNGS END 154 B3
Ypres Cotts C02 . . . . . 162 A4
Ypres Rd C02 . . . . 135 F4

Z

Zambesi Rd CM23 . . . . . 145 F5
Zinnia Mews C016 . . . . 188 C4

PHILIP'S MAPS

the Gold Standard for drivers

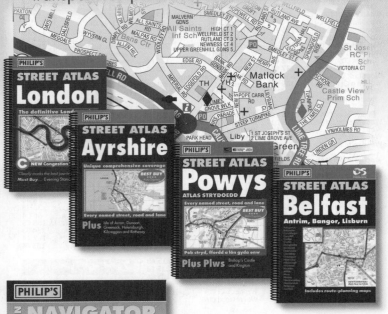